W9-AJR-630

seventh edition

Real Estate Law

ROBERT KRATOVIL

Professor of Law
John Marshall Law School (Chicago)

RAYMOND J. WERNER

Assistant General Counsel
Chicago Title Insurance Co.

PRENTICE-HALL, INC., Englewood Cliffs, New Jersey 07632

Library of Congress Cataloging in Publication Data

Kratovil, Robert, 1910–
Real estate law.

(Prentice-Hall series in real estate)
Includes index.
1. Real property—United States. I. Werner, Raymond J., joint author. II. Title.
KF570.K7 1979 346'.73'043 78-11512
ISBN 0-13-763268-1

PRENTICE-HALL SERIES IN REAL ESTATE

Editorial/production supervision
and interior design by Linda Stewart

Manufacturing buyer: Trudy Pisciotti

Printed in the United States of America

10 9 8 7 6 5 4 3 2 1

Prentice-Hall International, Inc., *London*
Prentice-Hall of Australia Pty. Limited, *Sydney*
Prentice-Hall of Canada, Ltd., *Toronto*
Prentice-Hall of India Private Limited, *New Delhi*
Prentice-Hall of Japan, Inc., *Tokyo*
Prentice-Hall of Southeast Asia Pte. Ltd., *Singapore*
Whitehall Books Limited, *Wellington, New Zealand*

TO
RUTH and TONY
AND
LENORE and BETH

Contents

Preface

The law continues to change at a rapid rate. Consumerism remains a strong force, and this, in turn, is transforming real estate law into a law where federal and state statutes and regulations supplant much of our decisional law. The cases lawyers looked to for "the law" are still important, but less dominant. Federal residential mortgage forms are rapidly replacing the wild diversity of forms of yesterday. FNMA and FHLMC regs tell us how a mortgage deal is to be handled. The energy crisis has sparked interest in solar easements. Couples living together without benefit of marriage have forced us to face new legal problems. The old rules of dower and curtesy no longer provide the answers. Franchising has made strong inroads into the real estate brokers' domain. Some broker's salespersons have become independent contractors. Uniform broker's commissions have disappeared, forced into oblivion by antitrust enforcement. The seller's broker now finds that he has important duties to the buyer. The merchant builder's implied warranties are recognized everywhere. Nondisclosure as misrepresentation by silence continues to displace caveat emptor. RESPA governs mortgage closings. The mortgagor-mortgagee relationship continues to change. The right to cure defaults expands. The due-on-sale clause breeds more litigation. The "impounds" for taxes and insurance attract more legislation. Zoning law changes constantly and tracks with land development regulation, as the expanding population places impossible burdens on sewer and water systems and schools or municipalities that have run out of funds needed for improvements. Forced dedication commands increased recognition. New Supreme Court decisions have turned over the entire field of land use and land regulation to the state courts. Zoning decisions proliferate at an astounding pace. Large shopping centers have been deprived of the "exclusive." Landlord and tenant law continues its development into pro-tenant law. Racial discrimination cases continue to multiply. If the nation's survival depends on protection of the wetlands that remain, the courts will be faced with one of the great controversies of the time. In short, change continues to be the rule.

Increasing emphasis is needed on the obvious proposition the judges are making law at a frantic pace to deal with today's novel problems. The old saw was that legislatures make law wholesale, the courts make it retail. It seems that the courts are going into the wholesale business.

Increasingly, also, one is forced to face the fact that the local character of real estate law is disappearing. Indeed, it has all but disappeared. Read any due-on-sale decision. Countless out-of-state decisions will be cited.

Legal periodicals also appear in great numbers as the law professors struggle to evolve rational patterns from the torrent of novel problems and decisions.

The reservation of sections at the end of each chapter requires explanation. In the year or more that it takes to process a completed treatise, law may change, and these sections allow room for inclusion of major changes.

Robert Kratovil and Raymond J. Werner

1

Sources of Real Estate Law

§ 1. **Lack of uniformity in laws governing real estate.** In each of the United States, two separate systems of law are in force: federal law and state law. With a few exceptions, federal laws operate uniformly throughout the country. Each state, however, has its own constitution, laws, and court decisions. Because of differences in local conditions, laws relating to real estate vary from state to state, and this variation is a factor that must be kept constantly in mind. However, the basic legal principles governing real estate transactions are much the same throughout the country, and our approach, in consequence, will be to describe these basic principles, mentioning, as space permits, the more important instances wherein the states do not agree.

§ 2. **Sources of and trends in real estate law.** The sources of real estate law include the Constitution of the United States, laws passed by Congress, regulations adopted by various federal boards and commissions, the state constitutions, laws passed by state legislatures, regulations adopted by various state and municipal boards, ordinances passed by cities and villages, and court decisions. The last is the most important source of real estate law.

EXPLANATION: Important decisions by lower courts are often appealed to higher courts. The higher courts, in announcing a decision, usually state the reasons for their decision and discuss the legal principles governing the particular case. Such a decision, with its accompanying discussion, is called an *opinion*. The opinions are bound in books called *reports* and serve as guides in the decision of similar cases in the future.

EXAMPLE: Roots from your adjoining poplar trees penetrate into my land and fill up my sewer and drain pipes. I cut off these roots, taking care to make the cut on my land. Your trees die and you sue me. The lower court holds I acted rightfully, and on appeal the supreme court of the state holds likewise, stating that a landowner may in this fashion protect himself against roots of adjoining trees. This is now the law of that state for all such cases that arise in the future. Lawyers will advise their clients accordingly, citing the case, *Michaelson* v. *Nutting*, 275 Mass. 232, 175 NE 490. This case may be found in Volume 275 of the Massachusetts Supreme Court Reports, page 232 and Volume 175 of the Northeastern Reporter, page 490.

Since our American real estate law stems in large part from the real estate law of England, it is not uncommon for courts today to base their decisions on similar cases that arose several hundred years ago in England. However, in dealing with present-day problems, the courts must often evolve new rules of law without much help from the past. Court decisions constitute the chief source of our real estate law.

Since law is manufactured from day to day by the judges, it follows that there will be variations from state to state, and from time to time in the same state, depending on the political, social, and economic views that dominate the court at the time a decision is made.

In textbooks, a statement of a rule of law is often followed by a reference to the case in which that particular point was decided. A well-reasoned case decided in any state often commands respect in other states. For example, the decision in *Michaelson* v. *Nutting* would be considered a correct statement of the law almost everywhere. This text endeavors to select such cases.

In recent times federal laws have assumed increasing importance in the field of real estate.

EXAMPLE: Federal Open Housing Law.

Also of greatly increasing importance in modern times is the "private law" that lawyers create in the preparation of real estate documentation.

EXAMPLE: Shopping center leases. In these documents the rights and duties of the parties in various existing and anticipated situations are set forth in some detail. One limitation on the rights of the parties to thus declare the "law" applicable to their situation is found in the tendency of courts today to refuse to enforce contract terms they regard as "unconscionable," meaning grossly unfair.

NEW DIRECTIONS: Seldom in history has the law moved so rapidly in new directions as at present. The Uniform Commercial Code, adopted in nearly all states, permits courts to strike down unconscionable contracts or unconscionable portions of a contract. An unconscionable contract is one that is grossly unfair to one of the parties. Although the Code applies mainly to personal property, modern courts choose to regard it as an expression of public policy applicable to all types of transactions. *Morse* v. *Consolidated Fisheries Co.*, 190 F2d 817, 822. Hence they feel free to apply the unconscionability test to transactions in real estate.

EXAMPLE: *L* leased a filling station to *T*. The lease gave *T* an option to purchase. *T* exercised the option. Due to awkward phrasing of the option, it appeared that it would take more than fifty years for full payment of the purchase price. The court said that *T* would have to accept reasonable terms of payment or pay all cash. *Rego* v. *Decker*, 482 P2d 834 (Alaska 1971).

NEW DIRECTIONS: We have moved into the age of *consumerism*. Ralph Nader has taught the lesson that even the largest corporations can be compelled to respect the needs of the consumer. This has launched a wave of tremendous force. The federal Truth-in-Lending Act compels disclosure of interest rates in terms that the ordinary consumer can understand.

Similar state laws have been passed. The Interstate Land Sales Act compels disclosures that enable the unwary prospective purchaser of vacant lots to avoid buying a pig in a poke. State laws of this type have also been enacted.

NEW DIRECTIONS: Where there is inequality of bargaining power and where the sophisticated party is pitted against an unsophisticated party the courts are intervening to protect the weaker party.

EXAMPLE: The trend toward reading implied warranties into sales of new homes and into apartment leases furnishes examples of this trend, as do the very recent cases limiting the mortgagee's right to declare an acceleration.

NEW DIRECTIONS: Consistent with all the foregoing is the strong trend in modern decisions toward rewriting *contracts of adhesion*. Wherever a relatively weak consumer is confronted with a contract full of fine print (lease, mortgage, sell-and-build contract, for example) modern courts will pull the teeth of any clause that bears oppressively on the weaker party.

NEW DIRECTIONS: Another development is the recent creation in many states of *home rule municipalities*. The theory is that with respect to its local affairs a municipality should be able to legislate without interference by the state legislature.

EXAMPLE: In earlier times each state adopted a zoning law and each municipality was required to tailor its zoning ordinances to the requirements of the state statute. Today home rule municipalities are free to adopt their own zoning ordinances without regard to the requirements of the state statute.

NEW DIRECTIONS: In the past much of real estate law consisted of rules created by court decisions. Today's trend toward protecting the consumer has resulted in the enactment of much state legislation giving the consumer protection greater than that afforded by the court decisions.

EXAMPLE: In many states laws have been enacted giving the mortgagor additional protection, for example, the right to cure defaults, set aside an acceleration of the mortgage debt, and causing a foreclosure suit to be dismissed. Matters of this character are found under the heading NEW LAWS.

NEW DIRECTIONS: The federal government is intervening in real estate transactions to a greater extent than in the past.

EXAMPLE: The Federal Trade Commission has greatly limited the use of exclusives in shopping center leases.

NEW DIRECTIONS: Quite a trend has developed in recent times for courts to look outside of their own state for guidance in evolving new rules of law.

EXAMPLE: In 1963 the Colorado Supreme Court decided that in every sale of a house erected by a merchant builder there was an implied warranty of habitability and freedom from defects. To arrive at this result, the Colorado court discarded numerous earlier Colorado decisions that held to the contrary. Over half of the states have since

followed Colorado's lead and probably all will do so. In brief, state courts do not hesitate today to create new law if that seems to produce a fair result.

Perhaps the most interesting aspect of the latter is that it does not qualify as a NEW DIRECTION. As far back as the year 1600 English courts decided that it was unconscionable to permit a mortgagor's default to end his rights in mortgaged land. Toward this end they invented the equitable right of redemption. And when mortgagees began to insert waiver of this right in the mortgage contract, the courts struck this down as unconscionable. Today the swing of the pendulum is away from enforcing contracts as written and toward resolving disputes in terms of what is fair.

RESERVED: **§§ 3 to 10.**

2

Land and its Elements

§ 11. **Land defined.** Land includes not only the ground, or soil, but everything that is attached to the earth, whether by course of nature, as are trees and herbage, or by the hand of man, as are houses and other buildings. It includes not only the surface of the earth, but everything under it and over it. Thus, in legal theory, a tract of land consists not only of the portion on the surface of the earth, but is an inverted pyramid having its tip, or apex, at the center of the earth, extending outward through the surface of the earth at the boundary lines of the tract, and continuing on upward to the heavens.

§ 12. **Minerals.** Since land extends to the center of the earth, it is clear that the owner of the land also ordinarily owns the minerals, which are a part of the land, and when the land is sold, the buyer ordinarily acquires such minerals, even though they are not expressly mentioned in his deed. However, a landowner may sell part or all of his land, as he chooses. Consequently, he may sell the minerals only, retaining title to the rest of the land; or he may sell the rest of the land and retain or reserve the minerals to himself.

EXAMPLE: *A*, a landowner, signs a deed conveying to *B* all the coal underlying *A*'s land. Now we have two layers of ownership. *A* continues to own the surface and may farm it or erect buildings on it. *B* owns the coal. *A* can sell or mortgage his layer of land, and *B* can do the same with his. *B* automatically has the right to sink shafts from the surface and build roads and tracks over the surface for the purpose of mining and transporting the coal. But he must not remove the coal in such a manner that the surface of the land will collapse.

Suppose that *A*, a farmer, sells and grants the coal under his farm to *B* Coal Company. The company tunnels beneath *A*'s farm and as it mines the coal uses the tunnels for transporting coal mined from adjoining areas. May the coal company do this? All courts agree that it may, although the explanations vary from state to state. In some states the interesting theory is advanced that a sale of coal and minerals includes not only the coal and minerals, but also the space they occupy, so that when the coal is mined out the coal company remains the owner of the space the coal formerly occupied. *Middleton* v. *Harlan-Wallins Coal Corp.*, 66 SW2d 30 (Ky. 1933); 83 ALR2d 665.

§ 13. **Oil and gas.** Contrary to popular opinion, oil does not occur in underground pools or reservoirs, but is tightly held in the tiny pores or openings of porous rocks. Natural gas is held in solution in this oil under great pressure. When a well is drilled into the rock that contains oil and gas, pressure is thereby released, and oil and gas gush forth just as a carbonated drink gushes from a warm pop bottle when the cap is removed. The oil will then flow to the low pressure area, namely, the well bore. Some states (Arkansas, Kansas, Misssissippi, Ohio, Pennsylvania, Texas, and West Virginia), impressed with the fact that oil in its natural state and before drilling occurs is immovably trapped in the rocks in which it is found, say that the landowner owns the oil beneath his land in much the same way that he owns coal or other minerals. These states are called *ownership states.* Other states (California, Louisiana, and Oklahoma), impressed with the fact that oil does move from one underground location to another when wells are drilled, hold that the landowner does not own the oil until he has pumped it and thereby taken possession of it. In all states, if the owner of the oil well pumps the oil and brings it to the surface, it then becomes his personal property.

In ownership states, a landowner may grant ownership of the oil beneath his land to another person. As a result, there will be two vertical layers of ownership, just as when a landowner sells and conveys to another all the coal and minerals beneath his land. Oddly enough, however, all oil states, including the ownership states, follow the rule of *capture,* which holds that if a man drills on his land, he will own all of the oil and gas produced, even though some of the oil or gas has migrated to his well from his neighbor's land. His neighbor, of course, can prevent such a result by drilling his own wells, *offset* wells, on his own land and pumping the oil that would otherwise move away from his land. All oil-producing states now have laws regulating and controlling the drilling of wells and the production of oil.

Landowners lack the skill, experience, capital, and gambling instinct necessary to drill for oil. Therefore, when the presence of oil is suspected, a landowner gives some oil company an oil lease. Many differing views are held as to the technical nature of the interest created by this lease. But the leases themselves tend to follow a pattern. As a rule, the landowner receives a bonus or cash payment for giving the lease. The lease then provides that if no well is drilled on or before a certain date, the lease shall automatically terminate, *unless* the lessee pays to the landowner a certain sum of money, called a *delay rental.* Such delay rental is a price the oil company pays for the privilege of keeping the lease in force without drilling. Delay rentals will continue to fall due as long as the oil company delays drilling. The lease will come to an end if no drilling takes place *unless* delay rentals are paid, this is known as an *unless lease.* Once wells are drilled and production begins. The usual lease gives the landowner as his compensation one-eighth of all the oil produced, payable either in oil or in cash, at the current market price, whichever the oil company chooses.

The lease provides that once oil production begins, the lease will continue as long as oil is produced in paying quantities.

the ownership of land. But there was need for a law of personal property to help men decide how cattle could be sold or who would succeed to ownership at the owner's death. And so the first crude rules of property law evolved, relating to cattle. The word *chattel* derives from cattle, the earliest subject of legal ownership. Later, when men learned to cultivate the soil, real estate law evolved to deal with questions regarding the ownership of land. Now lawyers are working through their associations to establish more uniformity, but differences still persist, as between the law relating to personal property and the law relating to real estate.

§ 17. **Trees and crops.** All trees, plants, and other things that grow are divided into classes:

1. Trees, perennial bushes, grasses, etc., which do not require annual cultivation, are called *fructus naturales* and are considered real estate or real property.

2. Annual crops produced by labor, such as wheat, corn, and potatoes are called *fructus industriales* and are considered personal property.

Since growing crops are personal property, they may be sold orally if the sale price is under the figure fixed by law for oral sales of personal property, *Stein* v. *Crawford,* 105 Atl. 780 (Md. 1919), or by bill of sale, as are other chattels.

RESERVED: §§ 18 to 28.

3

Fixtures

§ 29. **Fixtures defined.** A *fixture* is an article that was once personal property, but that has been installed in or attached to land or a building in some more or less permanent manner, so that such article is regarded in law as a part of the real estate.

EXAMPLE: A kitchen sink in a plumber's shop window is personal property. An article of personal property is called a *chattel*. After it has been installed in a house, it becomes a fixture and is part of the real estate.

Importance of the distinction. The distinction between real property and chattels is important.

EXAMPLE: *V* contracts to sell his house to *P*. All that is described in the contract is the land. *P* is entitled to receive the house as well as the land, because the house is a fixture and is legally part of the land. *P* is also entitled to receive the kitchen sink, furnace, toilets, and all other articles installed in the building with a view to remaining there permanently. However, *P* is not entitled to *V*'s furniture. Articles of furniture are chattels. They do not pass with a sale of land unless specifically mentioned in the contract. *V* can take his furniture with him when he moves. He cannot remove the sink, furnace, or toilets.

§ 30. **Tests to determine whether an article is a fixture.** It often becomes important to determine whether or not a particular article is a fixture.

In determining whether or not an article is a fixture, courts apply the following tests:

1. The manner in which the article is attached to the real estate.

EXPLANATION: If an article is attached to a building in such a permanent fashion that it could not be removed without substantial injury to the building, it is usually held to be a fixture. This test, in early times the only test of a fixture, has lost its pre-eminence in modern times. *Finley* v. *Ford*, 304 Ky. 136, 200 SW2d 138. However, conservative courts continue to attach importance to the test.

EXAMPLES: Water pipes, linoleum cemented to the floor.

2. The character of the article and its adaptation to the real estate.

EXPLANATION: If an article was specially constructed or fitted with a view to its location and use in a particular building, or if the article was installed in the building in order to carry out the purpose for which the building was erected, this tends to show that it was intended that the article should become a permanent part of the building. It is usually considered a fixture.

EXAMPLES: Pews in a church; a theater sign constructed for a particular theater; screens and storm windows specially fitted to the house; electronic computing equipment installed on a floor specially constructed for it. 5 ALR3d 497.

3. The intention of the parties.

EXPLANATION: There is a pronounced tendency today to emphasize the factor of intention. *Am. Tel. & Telegraph* Co. v. *Muller,* 299 F. Supp. 157 (1968). Was the article attached, the courts ask, with the intention of making it a permanent part of the building? Tests 1 and 2 are helpful in determining the intention of the parties, but once that intention is determined, it must govern. It is not the secret intention of the person installing the articles that governs. The test is an objective one, and intention is determined from the nature of the article, relation of the parties, adaptation, mode of annexation, and all the surrounding circumstances. Thus, the question boils down to this: Would the average person consider this article a permanent fixture?

EXAMPLES: Gas stoves are often installed in apartment buildings for the use of tenants. They are intended to remain there permanently, since they increase the rental value of the apartments. Therefore they are considered fixtures, even though they can be removed from the building with comparative ease. *Leisle* v. *Welfare B. and L. Ass.,* 232 Wis. 440, 287 NW 739. The same is true of electric refrigerators installed in apartment buildings. *Guardian Life Ins.* Co. v. *Swanson,* 286 Ill. App. 278, 3 NE2d 324, 7 ALR 1578. Air conditioners are necessities, not luxuries, in a modern apartment and are treated as fixtures when installed by the owner in a more or less permanent fashion. *State Mutual* v. *Trautwein* (Ky.) 414 SW2d 587; 43 ALR2d 1378. Again, it is important to remember that conservative courts are accustomed to stress Rule 1 above and would not consider a gas stove, electric range, or refrigerator installed in an apartment building a fixture. *Elliott* v. *Talmadge,* 207 Ore. 428, 297 P2d 310; 52 ALR2d 1103. There is substantial agreement on the point that a gas stove or refrigerator installed in a private house is not a fixture, since the owner usually intends to take it with him when he moves. The law of fixtures, however, is constantly developing, expanding, and changing. As customs have changed, articles once considered personal property have become fixtures. *Strain* v. *Green,* 25 Wash. 2d 692, 172 P2d 216. The luxuries of one generation become the necessities of the next. Since intention is the factor that determines whether or not an article is a fixture, the same type of article may be a fixture in one kind of building and a chattel in another. For example, an old-fashioned gas stove (one not built into the wall) is a chattel in a private home and would not go automatically to the buyer with a sale of the land. In an apartment building, exactly the same kind of stove would, in many states, be considered a fixture, passing automatically with a sale of the land. Articles of furniture (tables, chairs, and so forth), whether in a home, hotel, or furnished apartment, are universally considered chattels. *State* v. *Feves,* 228 Ore. 273, 365 P2d 97. The decisions on carpeting are in hopeless confusion. 55 ALR2d

1044. Obviously, the better rule is that wall-to-wall carpeting installed by the owner is a fixture, especially where installed on a concrete slab or rough plywood.

It will help you understand these fixture tests if you understand a little about the history of fixture law. Hundreds of years ago in agricultural England, where we find the beginnings of this law, buildings tended to be rather simple, and the annexation test worked well enough. In America some problems developed even in early times. A Virginia rail fence rests on the ground but is not attached to it. But the courts thought that, for obvious practical reasons, it ought to go with a sale of land, and they so decided. Later, when factories began to appear, it became evident that the annexation test was obsolete. If I buy a factory, obviously I am buying a going concern; yet under the old annexation test the seller would be allowed to remove the machinery, because this could be done without *injury to the building.* Thus, in response to this need, the courts invented the intention test, which enabled the buyer to claim the machinery. *Hopewell Mills* v. *Taunton Sav. Bank,* 150 Mass. 519, 23 NE 327 (1890); 109 ALR 1427. Still, later, when landlords began to put gas stoves and electric refrigerators in apartments, the courts faced the same problem, and some of them decided in favor of the intention test, but some did not. Those that did not were bothered by the flimsy connection between the appliance and the building, simply plugging a refrigerator in a wall socket, for example. The current problem takes this development one step further. A professional builder equips his homes with a variety of appliances that are attractive to the housewife, who, many builders will tell you, casts the deciding vote in the purchase of a home. The problem of this "package kitchen" has not, as yet, been fully litigated. It is best to ask the builder for a bill of sale as well as a deed, the bill of sale being used to transfer ownership of the appliances. In time, quite possibly, the courts will hold that the appliances pass with the deed as fixtures without the necessity of a bill of sale.

Probably most courts will treat package kitchen items as fixtures:

EXAMPLE: **Standard size dishwasher installed in well under formica counter top next to sink and attached to electric wiring of house by flexible metal conduit through junction box; standard model garbage disposal attached to underside of sink; and standard model range hood located over drop-in counter top range were permanent fixtures although removable without damage to the building. *Builders Appliance Supply* Co. v. *A. R. John Const. Co.,* 455 P2d 615 (Ore. 1969); *State Dept.* v. *Town & Country Inc.,* 256 Md. 584, 261 A2d 168.**

As you can see, in determining the intention of the party installing the fixture, the courts consider the nature of his interest in the property. It is unlikely that a tenant would wish to make permanent additions to the landlord's property. Hence the rules concerning tenant's fixtures were evolved, under which most of the tenant's installations are treated as removable chattels. But when the installations are made by the landlord, they are more likely to be thought of as true fixtures, which ought to go to a buyer landlord even though not mentioned in the deed.

§ 31. **Constructive annexation.** Certain objects, though in no way attached to the building, are regarded as so strongly connected with the building that they are fixtures under the doctrine of *constructive annexation.*

EXAMPLE: Ownership of the keys to a building passes when the deed is delivered to the buyer. *U. S. v. 967.905 Acres of Land,* 305 F. Supp. 83.

EXAMPLE: In the sale of a factory, spare or duplicate parts go with the land as fixtures because of their logical connection with the machinery. 109 ALR 1430.

EXAMPLE: A lathe in a factory is a fixture even though it simply rests on the floor and is not bolted thereto. 109 ALR 1431.

EXAMPLE: Car unit for an electric garage door opener.

§ 32. **Articles removable by tenants.** Special rules are applicable in the landlord and tenant situation. Articles that a tenant is allowed to remove are classified into the following three classes:

1. Trade fixtures.

EXPLANATION: In order to encourage a tenant to equip himself with the tools and implements of his trade, articles installed by a tenant for the purpose of his trade or business are classed as *trade fixtures* and may be removed by the tenant at the expiration of his lease. Intention is significant here also, for it is obvious that the tenant intends to take such articles with him when he moves.

EXAMPLES: Airplane hangars; bowling alleys; greenhouses; booths, bars, and other restaurant equipment; gasoline pumps and tanks in a filling station; barber chairs; soda fountains; oil derricks.

2. Agricultural fixtures.

EXPLANATION: Articles installed by a tenant farmer for the purpose of enabling him to farm the land are called *agricultural fixtures* and may be removed by the tenant when he quits the land.

EXAMPLES: Hen houses; tool sheds; maple-sugar houses.

3. Domestic fixtures.

EXPLANATION: Articles installed in a dwelling by a tenant in order to render it more comfortable and attractive are removable by the tenant.

EXAMPLES: Bookshelves; venetian blinds.

The three classes of articles that a tenant is allowed to remove are often referred to collectively as *tenant's fixtures. Fixtures,* as described in preceding sections, are real estate. *Tenant's fixtures* are personal property. Observe, also, that *the trade fixtures rule applies only to articles installed by tenants,* not to articles installed by *the landowner. Young Elec. Sign Co.* v. *Erwin Elec Co.,* 477 P2d 864 (Nev. 1970).

EXAMPLE: Gas pumps installed by a tenant in a rented service station are clearly trade fixtures. Pumps installed by a landowner would be true fixtures and would automatically go with a sale of the land. Machinery in a factory is a fixture if installed by the landowner. *Foote* v. *Gooch,* 96 N.C. 265, 1 SE 525.

It is important to remember that lease forms, invariably drafted for the landlord's benefit, often contain clauses forbidding removal of the tenant's installations. 30 ALR3d 998.

EXAMPLE: A lease of a filling station provided that at the termination of the lease all improvements on the premises would be the property of the landlord. The tenant was not permitted to remove gas pumps and tanks he had installed. 30 ALR3d 1034.

It is important also to remember that if the tenant moves out leaving his trade fixtures behind, they become the property of the landlord. 6 ALR2d 322. In the process they change from chattels to real estate, and ownership passes from tenant to landlord.

§ 33. **Fixtures attached after execution of real estate mortgage.** When only the landowner and the real estate mortgagee are involved, the rule is that fixtures bought, paid for, and installed by the landowner *after* the execution of a mortgage on the land become subject to the lien of the mortgage and cannot thereafter be removed by the landowner. In this situation, in other words, the mortgage lien attaches to *all* fixtures, even trade fixtures, thereafter installed by the mortgagor on the mortgaged premises. Such fixtures must not be removed without the mortgagee's consent. *Bowen* v. *Wood,* 35 Ind. 268. However, trade fixtures installed by a *tenant,* whether installed before or after the mortgage, are removable by the tenant. *Standard Oil Co.* v. *La Crosse Super Auto Service,* 217 Wis. 237, 258 NW 791, 99 ALR 60.

§ 34. **Conflicting claims of chattel security claimants under the Uniform Commercial Code where purchasers and mortgagees of real estate are involved.** The Uniform Commercial Code has been adopted in nearly all fifty states. Under the Code, a security interest in a chattel, including a chattel that has been or will be installed as a fixture, is created by means of a *security agreement,* which replaces the old *chattel mortgage* and *conditional sale contract.* This document, however, is not recorded. Instead, a brief notice of the existence of the security agreement is filed. This notice is called a *financing statement.* Where an article has become or is to become a fixture, the financing statement must be filed in the recorder's office where mortgages on real estate are filed. When thus filed, it gives notice to all that there exists a security interest in the article. Subsequent purchasers of the real estate and subsequent mortgagees of the land are bound by this filing, and if a default occurs under the security agreement, the articles can be repossessed and removed by the security holder without liability for any incidental damage to the building occasioned by the removal. If the financing statement is not filed as required by law, a subsequent purchaser or mortgagee of the land is protected against removal of the articles and need not pay the unpaid balance due on the articles. Where the article is purchased and installed on the land *after* the recording of a mortgage on real estate, the holder of the chattel security lien may remove the article from the real estate in case of default regardless of the incidental damage to the building. However, he must reimburse the real estate mortgagee for the cost of repairing any immediate physical injury in the building.

§ 35. **Severance.** If the landowner actually removes an article from the land or from the building to which it has been attached, with the intention that the removal shall be *permanent,* such article becomes personal property again and does not pass by a deed of the real estate. Thus, if a landowner tears down a fence and piles the material on the land, such material does not pass by a deed of the land. The fixture has again become personal property by *severance.* If the removal is for a *temporary purpose,* as the removal of a piece of machinery for repairs, the article remains a fixture, notwithstanding its removal from the soil, and passes by a deed of the real estate.

§ 36. **Building erected on wrong lot.** A perpetual source of legal controversy concerns the rights of one who through innocent mistake erects a building on the wrong lot, usually a lot adjoining the one he actually owns. Some states allow compensation to the builder in such cases. *Voss* v. *Forgue* (Fla.) 84 So2d 563; *Olin* v. *Reinecke,* 336 Ill. 530, 168 NE 676; *Hardy* v. *Burroughs,* 251 Mich. 578, 232 NW 200; but other states deny any compensation on the ground that if a man builds, it is his duty to see that he builds on the right lot. 5 *De Paul L. Rev.* 321; 104 ALR 577; 76 ALR 304.

The basis for the court decisions awarding compensation to the party making the innocent mistake is the law of *restitution,* which is designed to accomplish precisely that. The newer cases go strongly in this direction.

EXAMPLE: X, a landowner, hired Y, a builder to erect a house on X's lot. Y hired Z, a surveyor to place the survey stakes. Z, by mistake, placed the stakes on the lot next door. X was entitled to a lien on this lot (which was owned by a third party) for the value his building contributed to the lot. *Duncan* v. *Akers,* 262 NE2d 402 (Ind. 1970).

NEW DIRECTIONS: The courts are taking the view that the innocent improver is entitled to compensation unless he acquires *actual* knowledge of his mistake before he begins construction. *Johnson* v. *Stull,* 303 SW2d 110 (Mo. 1957). If the true owner, without protest, watches a stranger building on his land, he is sure to be subjected a lien for the value of the building. It is grossly unfair not to warn the stranger of his mistake. *Benedict* v. *Little,* 246 So.2d 491 (Ala.).

§ 37. **Mobile homes.** A mobile home has been held to be a fixture where owned and installed by a landowner.

EXAMPLE: X owned a five-acre plot on which he affixed a mobile home, which contained six rooms and weighed 7½ tons. The wheels were removed and the home placed on a concrete slab. It was a fixture. *George* v. *Commercial Credit Corp.,* 440 F2d 551; *State* v. *Work,* 449 P2d 806 (Wash. 1969).

RESERVED: §§ 38 to 48.

4

Easements

§ 49. **Easement defined.** An *easement* is a right acquired by the owner of one parcel of land to use the land of another for a special purpose.

EXAMPLE: *R* and *E* own adjoining tracts of land. By a written instrument, signed, sealed, and recorded in the proper office, *R* grants to *E* the right to cross *R*'s tract at a particular place for the purpose of ingress to *E*'s tract from a certain highway. The right thus created is called an *easement*. *R* remains the owner of the land over which *E* travels. *E* has only a special and particular right in that land.

§ 50. **Easement appurtenant runs with the land.** The easement described in the preceding section is an *easement appurtenant*. An easement appurtenant is created for the benefit of another tract of land. Consequently, for such an easement to exist, there must always be two tracts of land owned by different persons, one tract, called the *dominant tenement,* having the benefit of the easement, and another tract, called the *servient tenement,* over which the easement runs. In the example given in the preceding section, *E*'s tract was the one enjoying the benefit of the easement. It was therefore the dominant tenement. *R*'s tract was the servient tenement since it was the tract subject to the easement.

The dominant tenement need not adjoin the servient tenement. *Allendorf* v. *Dally,* 6 Ill. 2d 577, 129 NE2d 673 (1955). However, it usually does.

An easement appurtenant is regarded as being so closely connected to the dominant tenement that, upon a sale and deed of such tenement, the easement will pass to the grantee in the deed, even though the deed does not mention it. Such an easement is therefore said to *run with the land.* In the example, if *E* should sell his land to *X, X* would automatically acquire the right to cross *R*'s land. Whoever owns the dominant tenement owns the easement. A separate sale of the easement is not permitted.

Usually an easement is created by a landowner over his land and is in favor of another landowner. However, an easement can run in favor of any interest in land.

EXAMPLE: *R* leases a store to *E* and in the lease grants *E* an easement of ingress and egress over *R*'s adjoining land. This is valid. Easements in favor of tenants are common.

§ 51. **Easement and license distinguished.** It is often difficult to distinguish an easement from a *license.* Ordinarily an unauthorized entry on the land of another is called a trespass and makes the trespasser liable to pay damages to the landowner. The owner may, however, grant permission to enter for a particular purpose. This permission is called a license. An example is a theater ticket which authorizes the purchaser thereof to enter the theater for the purpose of viewing the performance.

An easement is usually created by a written instrument; a license is often created verbally. An easement is a more or less permanent right; a license is of temporary character. A license is a purely personal right and cannot be sold; the ownership of an easement changes with the ownership of the land to which it belongs. An easement cannot be revoked; a license is revocable.

EXAMPLE: *A* and *B* owned adjoining lots. They entered into a verbal agreement to establish a party driveway on the common boundary line between the lots. *B* thereafter built concrete walks and steps to the driveway. After this driveway had been in use for two years, *A* notified *B* that he intended to construct a driveway entirely upon his own lot and expected *B* likewise to provide for himself. When *A* sought to erect a fence along the common boundary, *B* filed a suit to prevent him from doing so. The court held that *A* was within his rights. Since the agreement was merely verbal, a license, not an easement, was created, and a license is revocable. *Baird* v. *Westberg,* 341 Ill. 616, 173 NE 820 (1930). With the present aversion to the unconscionable, it is doubtful the court would so hold today. *Monroe Bowling Lanes* v. *Woodfield Livestock Sales,* 244 NE2d 762 (Ohio, 1969).

Also courts today are likely to treat a license as an agreement for an easement where large sums of money are spent in reliance on it.

EXAMPLE: *X* owned Blackacre. *Y* wished to purchase the north half to erect a motel and restaurant. Contract of sale was entered into. *Y* explained that he would need to install drains over six inches of *X's* land. *X* orally agreed that he could do so. The deal was closed. *X* later demanded that *Y* remove the drain. The court held that this was an oral agreement for an easement that became irrevocable by *part performance* when *Y* erected his buildings. *Anastoplo* v. *Radford,* 14 Ill.2d 526, 152 NE2d 879 (1959); *Moe* v. *Cagle,* 385 P2d 56 (Wash. 1963); 11 Columb. L. Rev. 76 (1911).

EXAMPLE: In accordance with a verbal agreement, *A* and *B,* adjoining owners, erected buildings with a party wall and party stairway on the common boundary between their lots. The agreement was held irrevocable. *Binder* v. *Weinberg,* 94 Miss. 817, 48 So 1013 (1909).

§ 52. **Easement in gross.** An *easement in gross* resembles an easement appurtenant but there is no dominant tenement.

EXAMPLE: Right granted to a telephone and telegraph company to maintain poles and wires over grantor's land; right granted to a city to construct, maintain, and operate a canal through grantor's land; easements for railroads, street railways, pipelines and power lines.

Right of way easements acquired *by corporations* such as railroads and public utilities (*commercial easements in gross*) may be mortgaged and sold. *Northern Ill. Gas Co.* v. *Weincrank,* 66 Ill. App.2d 60, 214 NE2d 15 (1965), 12 U. of C. L. Rev. 276. Like an easement appurtenant, an easement in gross is irrevocable. The owner of an easement in gross need not, and usually does not, own any land adjoining that over which the easement exists.

§ 53. **Easements in gross—apportionment—CATV.** The question of the apportionability of an easement in gross has assumed new and special significance since the advent of CATV. Typically a utility company acquires from the landowner, by grant or condemnation, a broad easement in gross to install electric and telephone lines. Currently a CATV corporation approaches the utility and obtains a license or easement to attach its coaxial cables to the existing utility poles. Theoretically this adds a burden to the landowner's land and raises a further question as to whether an easement in gross can be conveyed to a third person or its use divided with a third person. There appear to be few decisions on the subject. Some hold that the easement in gross is legally apportionable. *Hoffman* v. *Capital Cablevision Systems, Inc.,* 383 N.Y.S.2d 674 (1976). Many states will so hold if the original easement grant refers to "assigns" or contains other language permitting assignment. 5 Restatement Property, 3053 Sec. 493b. But some courts hold that such an easement cannot be apportioned. *Jolliff* v. *Hardin Cable TV Co.,* 22 Ohio App.2d 49, 258 NE2d 244 (1970). This is poor law and creates problems.

EXAMPLE: X, a land developer, grants ABC *Utility* Co. an easement to install electric and telephone poles and wires in the development. CATV Co. seeks an easement to install cables. It must go to X for this easement but cannot use the ABC poles.

§ 54. **Creation of easement.** Easements may be created by *express grant, agreement, express reservation, implied grant, implied reservation, prescription, condemnation, sale of land by reference to a plat, and by estoppel.*

§ 55. **Express grant.** A landowner may create an easement over his land by express grant.

Since an easement is an interest in land, a grant of an easement should contain all the formal requisites of a deed. It should be in writing, should sufficiently describe the easement, the land subject thereto, the character of the easement (easement for ingress and egress, and so forth), and should be signed, sealed, witnessed, acknowledged, delivered to the grantee, and recorded in accordance with local rules governing deeds. But no particular words are necessary, and omission of the seal is not a fatal defect.

EXAMPLE: The first example given in this chapter is an illustration of the creation of an easement by grant.

Although an instrument granting an easement is technically known as a *grant,* this is no guarantee that an instrument granting an easement will be so labeled. Very often an instrument in the form of a deed will operate as a grant of an easement by reason of the insertion of language limiting the use of the land to a particular purpose.

EXAMPLE: *R,* a landowner, signed a warranty deed conveying to *E,* an adjoining landowner, a strip of land "to be used for road purposes." The quoted phrase appeared immediately following the property description in the deed. It was held that this deed did not make *E* the owner of the strip, but only gave him an easement thereover for road purposes. *Magnolia Petroleum* Co. v. *West,* 374 Ill. 516, 30 NE2d 24 (1940).

A grant of an easement may be incorporated in a deed that conveys land.

EXAMPLE: *R* owns Lots 1 and 2. He sells and conveys Lot 1 to *E.* After the property description in this deed, the following clause is inserted: "For the consideration aforesaid, the grantor grants to the grantee, his heirs and assigns, as an easement appurtenant to the premises hereby conveyed a perpetual easement for ingress and egress over and across the south ten feet of Lot 2 in the subdivision aforesaid." The deed accomplishes two objects: (1) It transfers ownership of Lot 1 to *E.* (2) It gives *E* an easement over the south ten feet of Lot 2.

§ 56. **Express reservation.** A landowner may, in selling and conveying part of his land, reserve in the deed an easment in favor of the tract retained by such landowner.

EXAMPLE: *R* owns Lots 1 and 2. He sells and conveys Lot 2 to *E* and, after the property description in the deed, inserts the following clause: "The grantor reserves to himself, his heirs and assigns, as an easement appurtenant to Lot 1 in the subdivision aforesaid, a perpetual easement for ingress and egress over and across the south ten feet of the premises hereby conveyed."

As in the case of grants of easements, reservations of easements, not labeled as such, are of frequent occurrence.

EXAMPLE: A, a landowner, sold and conveyed certain land to *E* by a deed containing the following clause: "Saving and excepting therefrom a strip of land forty feet wide along the bank of the east fork of Austin Creek all the way across said land, for a road to be built at some future time." The court held that, although the deed purported to except from its operation the forty-foot strip in question, nevertheless ownership of the forty-foot strip passed to the grantee in the deed, but the grantor had an easement thereover for road purposes. *Coon* v. *Sonoma Magnesite* Co., 182 Cal. 597, 189 Pac. 271 (1920).

§ 57. **Creation of easement by agreement.** Easements may be created by contract or agreement, such contract or agreement being, in effect, a grant of an easement. A familiar illustration is the party wall agreement.

Indeed, the law requires no technical formula of words to create an easement. The only essential is that the parties make clear their intention to establish an easement. *Scanlan* v. *Hopkins,* 270 A2d 352 (Vt. 1970).

§ 58. **Party walls.** Suppose you own Lot 1 and I own adjoining Lot 2. You plan to erect a building on your lot, and I purpose to erect an identical building on mine. If we can get together, we can effect an economy by means of a *party wall.* We will erect our buildings in such a way that on the common boundary line where our lots meet only one wall will be built, straddling the line, half on each side of it. Each of us will use that wall as a wall of his house. It will support my floors and roof and yours also. The economies of such an arrangement are obvious. The cost of the wall is shared. Land is conserved. Windows are eliminated, as is the expense of maintenance of one outside wall.

Legally I own the half of the wall that rests on my lot, and you own the half that rests on your lot. I have an easement of support in your half of the wall, and you have an easement of support in my half. Owners planning such an arrangement enter into a party wall agreement. Naturally a written agreement should be used, for an easement is an interest in land, and the law requires that interests in land be created in writing.

Suppose I plan to build at a time when you are not yet ready to go ahead. Here the party wall agreement gives me the right to put half of the wall on your lot and further provides that when you decide to build you will pay me half the cost of the wall.

The duty to repair a party wall falls equally on both owners. If either owner repairs the wall, he is entitled to collect from the other owner half the expenses thus incurred.

Unless the party wall agreement provides otherwise, either owner may increase the height of the wall without the consent of the other owner. However, the entire expense must be borne by the party who heightens the wall, unless the other owner decides to use the added wall.

Additional points on party walls. (1) Each owner has the right to extend the beams of his building into the party wall, but not beyond the centerline of the wall. (2) Use of the wall for flues and fireplaces is legal. (3) If an owner chooses not to erect a building on his side of the party wall, he may use that side of the wall for advertising signs. 2 ALR2d 1138, 69 CJS 154. (4) As a rule, if I wish to demolish my building on my side of the party wall, I may do so, but I must leave the wall intact for the support of your building. *Ceno Theater Co.* v. *B/G Sandwich Shops,* 24 F2d 31 (1928).

§ **59. Mortgages.** When *R* owns Lots 1 and 2 and mortgages Lot 1 to *E,* he may, at *E*'s insistence, include in the mortgage a grant of easement over part of Lot 2. Such a clause may run somewhat as follows:

> And as further security for payment of the debt above described, the mortgagor mortgages and grants to the mortgagee, his heirs and assigns, as an easement appurtenant to Lot 1 aforesaid, a perpetual easement for ingress and egress over and across the south ten feet of Lot 2 in the subdivision aforesaid.

Where *R* owns Lots 1 and 2 and is mortgaging Lot 1 to *E, R* may wish to reserve, for the benefit of Lot 2, an easement over part of Lot 1. In such case, an appropriate clause of reservation may be included in the mortgage.

The foregoing illustrations show how a *mortgage can create an easement.* When such a mortgage is foreclosed, ownership of the dominant and servient tenements passes into separate hands, and the real existence of the easement begins. Suppose, however, that *R* owns a lot that enjoys the benefit of a *previously created* easement. He mortgages the lot, and in the mortgage nothing is said concerning the easement. The mortgage is foreclosed. The purchaser at the foreclosure sale enjoys the benefit of the easement, for *an appurtenant easement runs with the land even though it is not mentioned in the mortgage or in the foreclosure proceedings.* 38 *Cal. L. Rev.* 426.

Also, an easement acquired by a mortgagor subsequent to the giving of a mortgage automatically comes under the lien of the mortgage and passes to the purchaser at any mortgage foreclosure sale. *First Nat. Bank* v. *Smith,* 284 Mich. 579, 280 NW 57, 116 ALR. 1078 (1938).

The effect of a mortgage on an easement and vice versa depends on which is *prior in time. Prior in time is prior in right.*

EXAMPLE: *R* mortgages Lot 1 to *E* in 1971. The mortgage is recorded and the mortgage funds are paid to *R,* thus creating a valid mortgage. In 1972 *R* gives *X,* his neighbor, an easement of access over Lot 1. In 1973 *E* forecloses his mortgage. The mortgage being *prior in time* to the easement was *prior in right.* The foreclosure destroys the easement. *Kling* v. *Ghilarducci,* 3 Ill.2d 455, 121 NE2d 752 (1954).

EXAMPLE: *R* gives *E* an easement of access over *R's* Lot 1 in 1971. It is recorded. In 1972 *R* mortgages the lot to *X.* Later the mortgage is foreclosed. The easement being *prior in time* is *prior in right* and is not affected by foreclosure of the mortgage. 46 ALR2d 1197.

§ 60. Implied grant or reservation. Often when the owner of two tracts of land sells or mortgages one of them, there is no mention at all of easements, and yet as a result of the transaction an easement is created. In such cases, the situation of the land is such that the courts feel the parties intended to create an easement even though they did not actually say so. Such easements are called *implied easements.* They are created by *implied grant* and *implied reservation.* Where a landowner uses one part of his land for the benefit of another part, and this use is such that, if the parts were owned by different persons, the right to make such a use would constitute an easement, then upon a sale of either of such parts an implied easement is created. *Cheney* v. *Miller,* 485 P2d 1218 (Ore. 1971).

EXAMPLE: *R* owned two adjoining lots, on each of which there was a two-story building. The buildings were separated by a partition wall. The stairway to the second floor was located entirely on one lot, and there were doors through the partition wall by which occupants of the second floor on the other lot reached their apartments. *R* sold and conveyed the lot on which the stairway was located to *E.* There was an implied reservation of an easement for the use of the stairway, and *R* could continue to use such stairway even though the deed made no mention whatever of any easement. If *R* had instead sold *E* the lot that had no stairway and had retained the lot on which the stairway was located, there would have been an implied grant of an easement to *E* to use such stairway. *Powers* v. *Heffernan,* 233 Ill. 597, 84 NE 661 (1908).

§ 61. Requirements for creation of implied easement. The following are the requirements for the creation of an implied easement:

1. The prior use of one part of the land for the benefit of the other part must have been apparent and obvious. That is, the use must have been such that it would have been disclosed on a reasonable inspection of the premises. The theory is that the parties intended to continue the obvious arrangements existing when the sale took place. *Burns Mfg. Co.* v. *Boehm,* 356 A2d 763 (Pa. 1975).

EXAMPLE: Suppose a man owns Lots 1 and 2, and sewage from his house on Lot 1 drains through an underground pipe running across Lot 2. There is a catch basin on Lot 2. If *A* buys Lot 2, the presence of the catch basin with a visible cover on the surface of the ground will give *A* notice and thereby create an implied easement for drainage over Lot 2. 58 ALR 824.

2. The prior use must have been continuous.

EXAMPLE: A visible and necessary drain is thought to be continuous in its operation. Usually a permanent and clearly defined way is thought of as continuous. Thus, where *A* owned the two adjoining lots and constructed a driveway on the common boundary line between the lots and thereafter sold one of the lots to *B,* an implied easement was created for use of the driveway as a common or party driveway. *Walters* v. *Gadde,* 390 Ill. 518, 62 NE2d 439 (1945); *Gorman* v. *Overmyer,* 199 Okla. 451, 190 P2d 447 (1947). Another example would be a party wall, and still another would be a well on the boundary line serving two adjoining properties. *Frantz* v. *Collins,* 21 Ill.2d 446, 173 NE2d 437 (1961).

3. The easement must be necessary. That is, the easement must be highly convenient and beneficial to the property. The test of whether or not an easement is necessary is this: Can a substitute for this easement be obtained without unreasonable expense and trouble? If it cannot, the easement is necessary.

4. The ownership of the two tracts of land must be in one person when the use commences and become separated thereafter, so that one person owns the benefited tract and someone else owns the burdened tract. This is obvious, for as long as one man owns both tracts there can be no easement. By definition, an easement is a right in another's property. The manner in which the separation of ownership takes place is immaterial. Usually it takes place when the original owner sells either the benefited or the burdened tract to another person, but any other manner of separating the ownership will do. For example, if the owner of two such tracts places a mortgage on one of them, and such mortgage is later foreclosed, the ownership of the two tracts passes into different hands and an implied easement is created. *Liberty Bank* v. *Lux,* 378 Ill. 329, 38 NE2d 6 (1941). Or if the owner of two such tracts dies, leaving a will by which he gives one tract to *A* and the other to *B,* an implied easement will be created. *Hoepker* v. *Hoepker,* 309 Ill. 407, 141 NE 159 (1923). Or if a tract of land is divided up by a partition suit, an implied easement may be created. *Deisenroth* v. *Dabe,* 7 Ill.2d 340, 131 NE2d 17 (1955).

Suppose *A* rents *B* an apartment, office, or store. Naturally *B* will have implied easements to use the stairways, elevators, fire escapes, porches, bathrooms, etc., that are used in common by the tenants. 24 ALR2d 123. It is true that the lease does not create a separation of ownership, but, rather, it puts lawful possession into two or more different persons, and that answers the purpose of the rule.

As is evident, all implied easements are appurtenant easements.

§ 62. An easement can be implied from the circumstances.

EXAMPLE: *R* owns a lot having lake frontage and a lot landward of the beach lot. He sells the landward lot to *E* with an easement for use of the beach. An easement will be implied to cross the beach lot to reach the beach. *Ames* v. *Prodon,* 60 Cal. Reptr 183 (1967).

§ 63. Implied easements—common scheme or plan. It has been pointed out that where two adjoining owners erect buildings with a party wall straddling the boundary line an easement is created even though no written document exists. This idea can be carried a step further. Where two adjoining landowners engage in a scheme of common development that cannot exist without easements, easements exist. 152 ALR 543.

EXAMPLE: *A* owns lot 1 and *B* owns lot 2 adjoining. By verbal agreement they erect buildings with an arcade of shops straddling the boundary line between the lots. Easements for the arcade now exist even though there is no written document. *Blakeney* v. *State,* 163 NE2d 69 (N.C. 1968).

EXAMPLE: *R* owns a large lot on which he erects row houses or town houses at right angles to the street. He sells off the town houses. Implied easements come into being for ingress, egress, sewer, water, electricity, etc. *Gilbert* v. *CT&T Co.,* 7 Ill.2d 492, 131 NE2d 1 (1956).

§ 64. Easement of necessity. When the owner of land sells a part thereof that has no outlet to a highway except over his remaining land or over the land of strangers, a right of way by necessity is created by implied grant over the remaining land of the seller.

§ 65. Prescription. *Prescription* is the acquiring of a right by lapse of time. An easement may be acquired by prescription. Usually the period of time required for the acquisition of an easement by prescription is the same period as that required for the acquisition of ownership of land by adverse possession. This period, called the *prescriptive period,* varies from state to state. Periods of ten, fifteen, and twenty years are common.

EXAMPLE: *A* owned a private alley and an apartment building adjoining thereto. *B* owned a neighboring apartment building. Without any permission from *A, B*'s tenants constantly used *A*'s private alley in order to enter their apartments from the rear. Whenever *A*'s tenants parked their cars in the alley, *B* would call the police and have them put out. This continued for more than twenty years. Then *A* attempted to stop this use of the alley by *B*'s tenants. It was held that he could not do so, since *B* had acquired an easement by prescription. *Rush* v. *Collins,* 366 Ill. 307, 8 NE2d 659 (1937).

EXAMPLE: *A* owned a house and lot. He constructed a garage in the rear of the lot. Because the space adjoining his house was inadequate for a driveway, he constructed one that ran partly across *B*'s adjoining land. This was done without seeking *B*'s permission. *A* used this driveway for over twenty years. He has a prescriptive easement to continue to use it. *Nocera* v. *De Feo,* 340 Mass. 783, 164 NE2d 136 (1959).

The following are the requirements for the creation of an easement by prescription:

1. The use must be *adverse*. If it is under permission or consent of the owner, the use is not adverse. There must be such an invasion of the landowner's rights as would entitle him to maintain a suit against the intruder. If the use by me of my neighbor's land is, on its face, permitted by my neighbor as a matter of neighborly accommodation, the use is not adverse or hostile.

EXAMPLE: A had a driveway running to his garage in the rear of his house, *B,* his neighbor, often used this driveway to get his car into his backyard. He never sought *A*'s permission, although they were good friends. This use will not ripen into a prescriptive easement. It is, on its face, a matter of neighborly accommodation. *Stevenson* v. *Williams,* 188 Pa. Super. 49, 145 A2d 734 (1958).

2. The use must be *under claim of right,* in that there must be no recognition of the right of the landowner to stop the use.

3. The use must be *visible, open,* and *notorious,* so that the landowner is bound to learn of it if he keeps himself well informed about his property.

EXAMPLE: The secret placing of a drainpipe in a wooded gully would not be considered notorious.

4. The use *must not be merely as a member of the public.* The use by the claimant of the easement must be sufficiently exclusive to give notice of his *individual* claim of right.

5. The use must be *continuous* and *uninterrupted* for the required period of time. That is, the easement must be exercised whenever there is any necessity therefor, and the use must be of such frequency as to apprise the landowner of the right being claimed against him.

EXAMPLE: Occasional entries upon a neighbor's land, for example, to put up screens or storm windows, to paint a wall, to trim a hedge, or to clean gutters, are not such continuous use as will ever ripen into a prescriptive easement. *Romans* v. *Nadler,* 217 Minn. 174, 14 NW2d 482 (1944).

It is not necessary that the adverse use be that of one person only.

EXAMPLE: In Illinois the prescriptive period is twenty years. Suppose that *A* and *B* are neighbors. *A* builds a driveway over *B*'s land without *B*'s permission. He uses it for five years. *A* sells his land to *C*, who also uses the driveway for five years. *C* sells to *D,* who uses the driveway for ten years. Now *D* has a prescriptive easement. The prescriptive uses that *A, C,* and *D* made can be *tacked,* that is, added together to make up the required twenty years. 171 ALR 1279. Also, since the easement was used for the benefit of a tract of land, it is an easement appurtenant and will thereafter run with the land so benefited. 171 ALR 1279.

Nearly all prescriptive easements are appurtenant easements.

Party driveways. Suppose you and I own adjoining lots, each with a house on it, and pursuant to a verbal agreement we build a party driveway, straddling the boundary line between our lots and serving our garages in the rear of our lots. Each of us uses this driveway continuously for the required period of time. Most courts hold that a party driveway easement has been created by prescription. 98 ALR 1096. This is quite a legal oddity, for obviously such common use is permissive, not adverse. Yet to prevent injustice courts allow prescriptive easements to be created by such use. *Peterson* v. *Corrubia,* 21 Ill.2d 525, 173 NE2d 499 (1975); 27 ALR2d 332.

State laws. State laws have been enacted, as in Illinois, that prevent the creation of an easement by prescription if the landowner posts signs forbidding use of his land. This relieves the landowner of making periodic inspections of his vacant land to see if strangers are using it.

§ 66. **Prescription for public highways.** When the public has used a privately owned strip of land for the purpose of passage for the required period of time, courts often hold that an easement for a public highway has been created by prescription.

§ 67. **Creation of easement by condemnation.** Although in some states laws provide that complete ownership of the land may be acquired by condemnation, the general rule is that where land is taken by condemnation for a street, highway, railroad right of way, or telephone or electric power line the taker acquires only an easement. All such easements are easements in gross.

EXAMPLE: The city of X wishes to open a street across A's land, but A is unwilling to sell. The city files a condemnation suit against A, and a judgment is entered fixing the full market value of the strip to be taken for the opening of the street. The city pays this amount into court. Although the city pays the full market value of the strip, it acquires only an easement thereover, and A remains the owner subject to the easement. Thus A may construct subvaults beneath the street without any liability to the city for payment of rent.

§ 68. **Scenic easements.** As the population continues to explode, concern grows for the preservation of open spaces, especially for scenic treasures that remain in private ownership and offer tempting sites to land developers. Under recent legislation and court decisions the state may condemn or purchase a scenic easement that, in effect, forbids the landowner to build upon his land. The Federal Highway Beautification Act offers incentives to the State to create such easements. *Markham Advertising Co.* v. *State,* 439 P2d 248 (Wash. 1968).

EXAMPLE: A owns a stretch of rolling farm land through which a lovely river winds, abutting a highway that commands an excellent view of the scene. The state condemns A's right to build upon his farm and pays him compensation for depriving him of this right. (See § 131.) He may continue to occupy and farm the land, but it will never be built upon. This right acquired by the state is called a *scenic easement. Kamrowski* v. *State,* 31 Wisc.2d 256, 142 NW2d 793 (1966). The state has acquired the farmer's *"development rights."*

§ 69. **Sale by reference to plat.** Where a landowner subdivides his land into lots, blocks, streets, and alleys and thereafter sells lots in the subdivision, each purchaser of a lot automatically acquires an easement of passage over the streets and alleys shown on the plat or map of the subdivision, even though the deed to the lot makes no mention whatever of such right. Such a private easement becomes important where the subdivider attempts to close up a street or alley before the public has acquired the right to insist that such street or alley remain open. The lot owners are in a position to keep the street open by virtue of their easement rights, even though the street never becomes a public street. 7 ALR2d 607.

The plat also gives the city rights in the dedicated streets and public rights. In some instances the city acquires full ownership of the dedicated streets. In other cases it acquires only an easement. 11 ALR2d 549.

§ **70. Solar easements.** England has a doctrine called *ancient lights.*

EXAMPLE: *A* owns lot 1 on which he has a house, which has been there for many years. *B* owns a vacant lot next door. In England *B* would not be permitted to erect a high building on his lot that would cut off *A*'s light.

In America the situation is treated quite differently:

EXAMPLE: Take the facts of the previous case. In America *B* can build any building that is permitted by local law even if it cuts off *A*'s sunlight.

EXAMPLE: The Fountainbleu Hotel in Miami Beach added 14 stories to its structure. This cast a shadow on the swimming pool of Eden Roc Hotel nearby. The court held that the Eden Roc was without any legal remedy. *Fontainbleau H. Corp.* v. *Forty-Five Twenty-Five, Inc.,* 114 So.2d 357 (Fla. 1959). *See also Blumberg* v. *Weiss,* 17 A2d 823 (N.J. 1941): 1 Am.Jur.2d 753.

Of course, if an action is prompted by pure spite, the law will provide a remedy.

EXAMPLE: *A* owns a house, and *B* owns an adjoining vacant lot. They quarrel. *B* attempts to erect a wall for the sole purpose of blocking light and air from *A*'s windows. The courts will stop this.

And purchase of a solar easement is perfectly legal.

EXAMPLE: *A* owns a lot on which he proposes to build a solar home. He approaches *B,* his neighbor. For a money consideration *B* grants *A* an easement that limits the height of any building *B* may build so that *A*'s solar energy will not be obstructed. The easement is recorded. It is binding on *B* and all subsequent owners of his lot.

Also height restrictions ordinances are valid in proper cases.

EXAMPLE: The *Village* of *X* zones an area for single-family dwellings and imposes reasonable height, side-line, and front-line restrictions, such that any lot owner can safely build a house utilizing solar energy. The ordinance is valid.

New laws. Oregon and Colorado have enacted laws giving added protection to solar heating. Probably every state will do the same. Probably, also, the laws will vary. Where energy is plentiful and office buildings are encouraged (in Texas, for example), the laws will be lenient. However, federal legislation is almost certain to give increasing tax benefits to energy-efficient buildings.

§ 71. **Easements—streets.** Easements vary, of course, as to their scope.

EXAMPLE: *R* grants *E* an easement for ingress and egress. This easement cannot be used for installation of water pipes or electric conduits.

However, whenever a city has an easement for street purposes, the courts give this a very broad interpretation. The adjoining owners own the land constituting the street. But the city's easement permits the use of the street for transportation of all kinds, including transportation of electricity (electric poles) or transportation of messages (telegraph poles). Kratovil, Easement Draftmanship and Conveyancing, 38 *Calif. L. Rev.* 426. The city usually grants to utility companies the right to install these poles. This right is called a *franchise*. So far as cable television is concerned, the CATV company would have to obtain a franchise from the city. But if it intends to fasten its cable to existing telegraph poles, it must also obtain a written agreement from the telegraph company.

In most, but not all, states, if a deed of land refers to an adjoining street or other way, it automatically creates an easement of access over the street or way if the grantor owns the land comprising the street or way. 46 ALR2d 461.

EXAMPLE: *R* owns Lot 1 in Block 1 in Chicago Heights and a strip of land east and adjoining known in the neighborhood as Holden Court. Holden Court is not a public street. He makes a deed to *E* of part of Lot 1 described as "bounded on the east by Holden Court." This gives *E* an easement right in Holden Court. This is sometimes called an *easement by estoppel*. 25 Am.Jur.2d 431. Obviously this is a poor substitute for a properly planned easement grant.

§ 72. **Easement by estoppel.** There are other instances of the creation of an easement by *estoppel*.

EXAMPLE: *R* owns sewer and water pipe in a street running past his house and other vacant land he owns. *R* makes a deed of a vacant lot to *E* but nothing is said about the sewer and water pipes. *E* builds a house and *R* without objection watches *E* tie into the sewer and water pipes. An easement to use the sewer and water service has been created by estoppel. *Monroe Bowling Lanes* v. *Woodfield Livestock Sales,* 244 NE2d 762 (Ohio 1969).

EXAMPLE: *R Corporation* leased a co-op apartment in its apartment building to *E*. The corporation had a plat in its office, showing a recreation area with swimming pool adjoining the building, and its agent always referred to this recreation area when making his sales pitch on apartments. An easement by *estoppel* has been created. *E* can use the recreation area. *Hirlinger* v. *Stelzer,* 222 So2d 237 (Fla. 1969).

§ 73. **Unlocated easements and relocation.** If *R* owns a large tract of land and grants to *E* an easement thereover, manifestly it is not *R*'s entire tract that comprises the servient tenement, for it is not intended that *E* shall wander aimlessly over the premises. It is, rather, the intention of the parties that some small part of the tract shall become the easement tract. The parties have simply failed to specify the precise location of the easement. In such cases, the owner of the servient tenement has, in the first instance, the right to designate the location of the easement, provided he exercises such right in a reasonable manner, having regard to the suitability and convenience of the way to the rights and interests of the owner of the dominant tenement. If the owner of the servient tenement fails or refuses to locate the way, the owner of the dominant tenement acquires the right to make his own selection of a location, having due regard to the interests, rights, and conveniences of the other party. 110 ALR 174. Court action may be necessary if the parties cannot agree. Disputes and litigation can be avoided through the simple device of employing a surveyor to locate and monument the easement tract on the ground, whereupon a legal description can be prepared and included in the easement grant.

§ 74. **Pipeline easements.** Most unlocated easements are pipeline easements. Pipelines extend over many miles of ground. The pipeline companies send out *right of way* crews to acquire the easements. Once a member of such a crew has determined the ownership of a farm, he whips out a simple form which the farmer and his wife sign. It gives the pipeline company an easement over the entire farm. This is perfectly valid. *Collins* v. *Slocum,* 284 So.2d 98 (La. 1973).

A land developer who buys a farm for development cannot live with an unlocated easement.

SUGGESTION: The developer should contact the pipeline company and purchase a release of the easement over all of the farm except the land through which the pipeline runs. Homebuyers cannot have pipe lines running under homes. Record the release of the easement. Usually no problem is presented. The pipeline company keeps the pipeline near the highway to facilitate repair. If there is a mortgage on the pipeline, that is also released except as to the line of the pipe.

Once a pipeline has been installed in a pipeline easement, some courts hold that additional pipes or a larger pipe cannot be installed. *Winslow* v. *City of Vallejo,* 148 Cal. 723, 84 P 191 (1906). The far better rule is precisely to the contrary. *Standard Oil Co.* v. *Buchi,* 72 N.J.Eg. 492, 66 A 427 (1907), 17 *Yale L.J.* 200, *Weaver* v. *Natural Gas Pipeline Co.,* 27 Ill.2d 48, 188 NE2d 18 (1963). This problem should be covered in the grant.

Once an easement has been placed in location or its location fixed by the easement grant, its location cannot be changed without the consent of the easement owner.

EXAMPLE: *R* owns two lots. Lot 1 abuts on a highway. *R* sells Lot 2 to *E*, simultaneously granting an easement of ingress and egress to the highway. The easement runs through the middle of Lot 1, rendering it unusable. *R* has no right to change the location of the easement. *Sedillo Title Gty. Inc.* v. *Wagner*, 457 P2d 361 (N.M. 1969).

But the easement can be relocated if both parties acquiesce, even without a written document.

EXAMPLE: In the last example, suppose *R* and *E* verbally agree on relocation. *R* blacktops a new driveway along the edge of Lot 1 and the old drive is torn up. The easemen has been relocated by acquiescence. 80 ALR2d 743.

§ 75. **Declaration of easements.** Easements are used so extensively in the town house, condominium, and planned unit development that they are physically separated from the deeds and mortgages and incorporated in a separate document. As a matter of convenience, this document also includes building restrictions, liens and covenants and is called a Declaration of Restrictions, Easements, Liens and Covenants.

§ 76. **Complex easements.** Today complex easements are employed in a number of situations.

NEW DIRECTIONS: It is almost commonplace today to find a single multistory building divided into two ownerships. The lower portion, devoted, let us say, to office building use is owned by A. The upper portion, devoted to apartment purposes, is owned by *B*. *B* may even choose to divide his apartment area into condominium ownership so that each apartment is separately owned. Such, indeed, is the situation in the case of the John Hancock Building in Chicago. The structural members of the bottom building support the upper building. Elevator shafts serving the upper building travel through the lower building. Heating, ventilating, and air-conditioning ducts, as well as water and utilities, travel through both buildings. A very lengthy Easement and Operating Agreement is prepared. There are problems, to be sure, but they are all capable of solution.

§ 77. **Structure easement—easement through structure.** Where an easement is created in a *structure* without creating any interest in the land, ordinarily destruction of the structure destroys the easement.

EXAMPLE: X owned lot 1 on which he erected a two flat residence. When the city passed an ordinance requiring second-story apartments to have two exits, X acquired from Y, his neighbor, the right to make an opening into Y's building, which was flush against X's building, and to use Y's stairway as the second exit. Y's building was destroyed by fire. The easement is extinguished. 154 ALR 82.

§ 78. **Easement in favor of structure.** If an easement is created *in favor of* a structure only, destruction of the structure terminates the easement.

EXAMPLE: X and Y were neighbors. Intending to build a stable for his riding horse, X purchased from Y *driveway rights* over Y's land to and from the *stable* to be erected on the rear of *X's* land. Ultimately the stable was destroyed by fire. The easement is gone. 2 Thompson, Real Property 764, 766 (perm. ed.).

§ 79. **Right to profits of the soil.** An easement does not confer on the owner thereof any right to the profits of the soil, such as oil, hay, coal, or minerals.

EXAMPLE: The County of *X* acquired a highway over *A's* land by condemnation. The county has no right to drill oil wells on the land thus acquired, for it has only an easement for road purposes.

It is the landowner whose land is subject to the easement who has the right to oil, minerals, and other profits of the soil.

EXAMPLE: A landowner whose land is subject to an easement for railroad right of way purposes may tunnel under the railroad right of way and mine the coal thereunder.

§ 80. **Use of easement premises—dominant and servient tenements.** An easement appurtenant can be used only for the benefit of the dominant tenement. It may not be used for the benefit of any other tract of land. *Land acquired by the owner of the dominant tenement after the creation of the easement has no right to the use of easement. It is non-dominant land.*

EXAMPLE: A owned Lot 1. There was an easement appurtenant in favor of Lot 1 to use a spur or switch track over land adjoining Lot 1 to the west. A thereafter bought Lot 2, which adjoined Lot 1 to the east, and erected a powerhouse on Lot 2. It was held that the switch track could not be used to service the powerhouse since the switch track easement was appurtenant only to Lot 1. *Goodwillie Co.* v. *Commonwealth Co.*, 241 Ill. 42, 89 NE 272 (1909); *Ogle* v. *Trotter*, 495 SW2d 558 (Tenn. 1973). *College Inns.* v. *Cully*, 460 P2d 360 (Ore. 1969).

Particularly in the case of industrial easements it is well to keep in mind at the time easement is created that the dominant owner may later wish to acquire other neighboring land for plant expansion. The easement grant should provide that such subsequently acquired property shall enjoy the benefit of the easement. For example, suppose that the dominant tenement happens to fall in Government Section 34, then let the easement grant provide as follows:

SUGGESTED FORM: Said easement is also appurtenant to any land in said Section 34 that may subsequently come into common ownership with said dominant tenement.

If the dominant tenement is divided, the easement runs in favor of each part into which it is divided. 10 ALR3d 960.

EXAMPLE: *R*, owning the bed of a lake and the land surrounding the lake, sells *E* a lot that does not have lake frontage. The deed includes an easement of access to the lake and a right to use the lake for recreation. *E* sells half his lot to his brother, both parts abutting on the easement of access. Both *E* and his brother can use the easements. There is some limit, not very clearly defined, on how far you can go with this. 10 ALR 3d 968. Suppose *E* were to divide his lot into fifty lots. The courts might not permit use of the easements. This is an excessive *increase of burden. Crocker* v. *Advanced Science,* 268 A2d 844 (N.H. 1970).

Where an easement of ingress and egress is created by grant, it may be used by the easement owner for all reasonable purposes, and use is not restricted to such purposes as were reasonable at the date of the grant.

EXAMPLE: Use of the easement by automobiles will be permitted even though an easement was created when horse-drawn vehicles were in use. 3 ALR3d 1287.

And with changing conditions more intensive use may be made of the easement than was contemplated at the time the easement was created.

EXAMPLE: At the time an easement of ingress and egress was created, the dominant tenement was occupied by a private dwelling. Later this dwelling was replaced by a hotel. It was held that the hotel could continue to use the easement. *White* v. *Grand Hotel* (1913) 1 Ch. 113.

However, where an easement is acquired by *prescription,* use of the easement after the prescriptive period has expired must remain pretty much the same as the use that took place during the prescriptive period.

If the width of an easement is fixed at the time of its creation, it will not grow wider even though conditions change.

EXAMPLE: In 1918 *A* grants *B* a ten-foot easement for ingress and egress. The fact that today's big trucks cannot use so narrow a way does not increase the size of the easement. *Feldstein* v. *Segall,* 198 Md. 285, 81 A2d 610 (1951).

On the other hand, if I grant you a ten-foot passage easment, I have no right to diminish it by placing pillars or other structures in the passageway. You have the right to use the full ten feet for passage. *Wurlitzer Co.* v. *State Bank,* 290 Ill. 72, 124 N.E. 844 (1919).

If you have a driveway easement over my land, you can park to load and unload but cannot park overnight. 37 ALR2d 944. This does not mean, however, that the owner of an easement for ingress and egress has the *exclusive* right to use the surface of the land for that purpose. The landowner, since he remains the owner of the easement premises subject only to the prescribed rights of the easement owner, has the right to make any use of the easement tract that does not interfere with the easement.

EXAMPLE: In the case of an easement of ingress and egress, the landowner may travel over the easement tract as long as he does not interfere with the easement owner's right of travel. The landowner, indeed, may even erect structures or run power lines above the easement, so long as he leaves space at the surface adequate for travel by the easement owner. *Sakansky* v. *Wein,* 86 N.H. 337, 169 Atl. 1 (1933); *Cleveland Railway* Co. v.

Public Service Co., 380 Ill. 130, 43 NE2d 993 (1942). Or a landowner may tunnel and mine minerals beneath an easement for ingress and egress or build over a water pipe easement.

Since an easement is a right to use another's land for a special purpose only, the easement owner must use the easement premises only for that purpose for which the easement exists.

EXAMPLE: A grants *B*, his neighbor, an easement for ingress and egress over a part of *A*'s land. *B* has no right to lay gas pipes in the easement premises. 3 ALR3d 1278.

§ **81. Maintenance and repair easement facilities.** The fact that *A* gives *B* an easement over *A*'s property imposes no duty on *A* to pave the easement tract, keep it in repair, or do anything at all for *B*'s benefit. 169 ALR 1152.

EXAMPLE: A gave *B* an easement to take water from a well on *A*'s land. It was held that *A* was not obliged to operate the pump to furnish *B* water even though that was the physical situation at the time the easement was created. *Gowing* v. *Lehmann*, 98 N.H. 414, 101 A2d 463 (1953).

Therefore if the parties agree that the owner of the burdened land is to have some affirmative duties, they must be spelled out in the easement grant.

Of course the easement owner has the right to take all steps necessary to make this easement usable. For example, in an easement of ingress and egress the easement owner would have the right to repair or improve an existing road, to lay down a new road, to build bridges across streams, to trim encroaching trees and shrubs, to blast rocks, and otherwise to remove impediments, and so forth. 169 ALR 1153.

Also, where a private road is used by *both the* landowner and the easement owner, they must divide the cost of repairs in proportion to their use of the road, even though the easement agreement is silent on this score. *Stevens* v. *Bird-Jex Co.*, 81 Utah 355, 18 P2d 292 (1933).

If the easement tract is used only by the easement owner and falls into disrepair as a result of his neglect, he has no right to deviate from the prescribed way and travel over other land belonging to the landowner. *Dudgeon* v. *Bronson*, 159 Ind. 562, 64 NE 910 (1902). On the other hand, if the landowner obstructs the easement, the easement owner has the right to travel around the obstruction over other land belonging to the landowner.

§ **82. Termination of easement.** Easements may be terminated in the following ways:

1. When an easement has been created for a particular purpose, it ceases when the purpose ceases.

EXAMPLE: A party wall agreement ceases when both buildings are destroyed by fire, unless the party wall agreement provides otherwise. An easement for railroad purposes ends when the railroad tears up its tracks and discontinues service. 95 ALR2d 482.

MODEL EASEMENT GRANT*

This EASEMENT GRANT is made between__________ ______________________________(hereinafter referred to as "the grantor") and______________________________ (hereinafter referred to as "the grantee").

The following recitals of fact are a material part of this instrument:

A. The grantor is the owner of a tract of land described as follows and hereafter referred to as "Parcel 1":

(Here insert legal description)

B. The grantee is the owner of a tract of land described as follows and hereafter referred to as "Parcel 2":[1]

(Here insert legal description)

C. The grantor wishes to grant and the grantee wishes to receive an easement over, under and across that part of Parcel 1 described as follows and hereafter referred to as "The easement premises:"[2]

(Here describe the land to be subject to easement)

D. Parcel 1 is presently improved with a building used for__________________and Parcel 2 is improved with a building used for__________________.

Now, therefore, in consideration of________________ and other valuable consideration, the receipt and sufficiency of which are hereby acknowledged,[3] the following grants, agreements, and covenants and restrictions are made:

1. GRANT OF EASEMENT. The grantor hereby grants[4] to the grantee, his heirs and assigns,[5] as an easement appurtenant to Parcel 2,[6] a perpetual[7] easement for ingress and egress[8] over, under and across thc easement premises.

2. USE OF EASEMENT PREMISES. Use of the easement premises is not confined to present uses of Parcel 2, the present buildings thereon, or present means of transportation.[9] The installation or maintenance by the grantee of pipes, conduits, or wires, under, upon or over the easement premises is forbidden.[10] Exclusive use of the easement premises is not hereby granted.[11] The right to use the easement premises, likewise for ingress or egress, is expressly reserved by the grantor. In addition, the grantor reserves the right to make the following uses of the easement premises:

a. The right to erect a building over the easement premises, provided all of such structure shall be located at a height of not less than______feet above the surface of the easement premises, but construction of the improvement shall be so conducted as not to unreasonably interfere with grantee's use of the easement premises during construction.[12]

b. Any subsurface use that does not unreasonably interfere with grantee's use of the easement premises.[13]

3. USE OF PARCELS 1 AND 2. As long as this easement grant remains in effect Parcel 2 shall not be used for other than commercial or residential purposes and no building other than one suited only for commercial or residence purposes shall be constructed thereon.[14]

4. ADDITIONS TO DOMINANT TENEMENT. Said easement is also appurtenant to any land that may hereafter come into common ownership with Parcel 2 aforesaid and that is contiguous to Parcel 2.[15] An area physically separated from Parcel 2 but having access thereto by means of public ways or private easements, rights or licenses is deemed to be contiguous to Parcel 2.

5. DIVISION OF DOMINANT TENEMENT. If Parcel 2 is hereafter divided into two parts by separation of ownership or by lease, both parts shall enjoy the benefit of the easement hereby created.[16] Division of the dominant tenement into more than two parts shall be deemed an unlawful increase of burden and use of the easement may be enjoined.

6. PARKING. Both parties covenant that vehicles shall not be parked on the easement premises except so long as may be reasonably necessary to load and unload.[17]

7. PAVING OF EASEMENT. Grantee covenants to promptly improve the easement premises with a concrete surface at least______feet in width suitable for use by delivery trucks and[18] will at all times maintain same in good repair.[19]

8. WARRANTIES OF TITLE. Grantor warrants that he has good and indefeasible fee simple title to the easement premises, subject only to the following permitted title objections:[20]

(here list encumbrances)

9. TITLE INSURANCE AND ESCROW. Should grantee so desire, he may apply forthwith for a title insurance policy insuring the easement hereby granted and grantor will make available for inspection by the title company any evidence of title in his possession.[21]

10. RELOCATION OF EASEMENT. Grantor reserves the right to relocate the easement premises as follows.[22]

1. He shall first notify the grantee of the proposed relocation by mailing notice to the grantee at his last address furnished pursuant hereto showing the proposed relocation, probable commencement and completion dates, all by mailing same, postage prepaid, at least 30 days prior to commencement of relocation.

2. The easement premises shall be moved not more than______feet from their present location.

3. Grantor shall improve the new easement premises with a concrete driveway similar to the one replaced, to be suitable for use by delivery trucks, with connections at the termini of the driveway to be replaced, and reasonably convenient for the uses then existing on Parcel 2.

4. At the completion of the work, grantor shall record an easement grant in recordable form granting the new easement to the grantee, shall cause the same to be delivered to the grantee, and shall furnish the grantee evidence of title satisfactory to the grantee showing an unemcumbered easement in such grantee, whereupon the change in location of the easement

2. When the owner of an easement becomes the owner of the land that is subject to the easement, the easement is extinguished by *merger*.

3. The owner of an easement may release his right to the owner of the land that is subject to the easement.

4. The owner of an easement may terminate it by abandonment. There must be an intention to abandon the easement and acts manifesting such intention.

premises shall become effective, and appropriate releases of the prior location shall be executed in recordable form and exchanged between the parties hereto, their successors or assigns.

11. RUNNING OF BENEFITS AND BURDENS. All provisions of this instrument, including the benefits and burdens, run with the land and are binding upon and enure to the heirs, assigns, successors, tenants and personal representatives of the parties hereto.[23]

12. TERMINATION OF COVENANT LIABILITY. Whenever a transfer of ownership of either parcel takes place, liability of the transferor for breach of covenant occurring thereafter automatically terminates, except that the grantor herein remains liable for breaches of covenants of title set forth in Paragraph 8.[24]

13. ATTORNEY'S FEES. Either party may enforce this instrument by appropriate action and should he prevail in such litigation, he shall recover as part of his costs a reasonable attorney's fee.[25]

14. CONSTRUCTION. The rule of strict construction does not apply to this grant. This grant shall be given a reasonable construction so that the intention of the parties to confer a commercially usable right of enjoyment on the grantee is carried out.

15. NOTICE. Grantor's address is_______________ _________and grantee's address is_______________ __________. Either party may lodge written notice of change of address with the other. All notices shall be sent by U.S. mail to the addresses provided for in this paragraph and shall be deemed given when placed in the mail. The affidavit of the person depositing the notice in the U. S. Post Office receptable shall be evidence of such mailing.

16. RELEASE OF EASEMENT. The grantee herein may terminate this instrument by recording a release in recordable form with directions for delivery of same or to grantor at his last address given pursuant hereto whereupon all rights duties, and liabilities hereby created shall terminate. For convenience such instrument may run to "the owner or owners and parties interested" in Parcel 1.[26]

17. JOINDER OF SPOUSE.____________________ spouse of grantor joins herein for the purpose of releasing dower, homestead and all other marital rights, all of which are waived with respect to this easement.[27]

In witness whereof the grantor, his spouse and the grantee[28] have hereunto set their hands and seals this __________day of________________A.D. 19_______.

____________________________________(Seal)

____________________________________(Seal)

____________________________________(Seal)

FOOTNOTES

1. It is not necessary to describe the dominant tenement in the easement grant. The area intended to be served can be gathered from the attendant circumstances. However, as appears from the General Observations, questions often arise. Hence it is good draftsmanship to describe the dominant tenement.

2. Often enough *R* owning Blackacre, grants to *E* an easement of ingress and egress over "Blackacre." Obviously it was never the intention of the parties that *E* would roam over all of Blackacre. The courts have devised a means of pinning down the easement area. 110 ALR 174. But to fail to pinpoint the easement premises is wretched draftsmanship.

3. Since easements existed long before the doctrine of consideration was invented, no recital of consideration is necessary. Occasional decisions nevertheless mention the presence of consideration. It seems best to recite consideration.

4. Words of grant are necessary according to a few decisions. This corresponds to the requirement of words of conveyance in a deed. The numerous decisions holding that easements can be created by contract are obvious proof that the requirement is less formal in easement drafting.

5. There are many statutes to the effect that words of heirship are not necessary to create a few simple by deed. Easements are rarely mentioned, but by analogy the word "heirs" is not needed to create a permanent easement. But there are some court decisions saying that an easement endures only for the life of the grantor unless words of heirship are included. *Elwell v. Miner*, 174 NE2d 43.

6. An easement appurtenent need not be so characterized. Normally the courts will strain to find the easement is appurtenant rather than in gross. Good draftsmanship requires that the proper label be affixed.

7. The same estates exist in easements as exist in corporeal hereditaments. Thus, you can have an easement in fee simple, for life, for years, etc. *Texas Co. v. O' Meara*, 377 Ill. 144, 36 NE2nd 256; 154 ALR5. It is not the practice to use the estates terminology. Instead of talking of an easement *in fee simple*, we talk of a *perpetual easement*.

8. There is no such thing as a plain "easement." It must be for ingress and egress, for light and air, or for some other specific purpose.

9. The opening sentence of paragraph 2 is a statement of existing law. 3 ALR3d 1287. However, it forces the parties to think about changes that will take place in the future. If the dominant owner tears down his store and erects an industrial plant, will the servient owner be unhappy with this turn of events? If he will be, he must provide against this.

10. This is also a statement of existing law. 3 ALR3d 1278. Again the existence of litigation indicates the need for covering this point.

11. An easement that excludes the servient owner from use of the easement premises is extremely rare. *Etz v. Morrow*, 72 Ariz. 228, 233 P2d 442. An exception is the railroad easement, which is exclusive by its very nature. But dominant owners always seem surprised when they hear the rule stated. Hence it belongs in the grant.

12. This is also a statement of existing law. *Sakansky v. Wein*, 86 N.H. 337, 169A 1; *Minneapolis Athletic Club v. Cohler*, 177 NW2d 786 (Minn. 1970). The presence of litigation indicates it is not generally understood. Of course, there are easements one cannot build over, such as a pipeline easement. *Tide Water Pipe Co. v. Blair Holding Co.*, 42 N.J. 591, 202 A2d 405; 28 ALR2d 626. This would block the dominant owner's efforts to repair a break. For similar reasons the servient owner cannot put a lake over a pipeline easement. *Sumrall v. United Gas Pipeline Co.*, 97 So2d 914.

13. Also a statement of existing law. *E.M. & S. W. R.R. v. Sims*, 228 Ill. 9, 81 NE 782.

14. The dominant owner can change the nature of the use unless the easement grant restricts this right.

15. The dominant tenement is determined at the time the easement is created. Land acquired by the dominant owner thereafter is non-dominant land. It cannot use the easement. Weathers v. Icoa Life Ins. Co., 460 P2d 361 (Ore. 1969). This is the most common error in easement drafting and the most costly. Of course, one can easily draft around the problem. You can make the additions to the *dominant tenement clause* much broader, if you wish. For example:

"Said easement is appurtenant to any land in the Northwest quarter of Section 34 that may subsequently come into common ownership with said dominant tenement."

In passing, attention is drawn to the fact that by the modern rule contiguity of the dominant tenement to the easement premises is not required. *Allendorf v. Daly*, 6 Ill. 2d 577, 129 NE2d 673.

16. The easement runs in favor of all parts, where the dominant tenement is later divided. 10 ALR3d 960. There are some limits, however, which the courts have not clearly defined. 10 ALR3d 968. This grant sharply limits the right to divide.

17. This again is a statement of existing law. 37 ALR2d 944. Litigation over parking suggests the need to spell this out.

18. In the absence of such a clause there is no duty on the dominant owner to pave the way.

19. The dominant owner has the right, though not the duty, to repair. Kratovil, *Real Estate Law* (5th ed 1969) §37. *But see Lynch v. Keck*, 263 NE2d 176 (Ind. 1970).

21. Where beneficial use of his land by the dominant owner depends on dependable access via the easement, he needs title insurance on the easement as much as he needs title insurance on the land.

22. The servient owner has no right to relocate the easement unless the easement grant confers this right. An awkwardly located easement can virtually destroy the value of industrial or commercial property.

23. Covenants running with the land can be included in the easement grant. An easement grant creates the requisite privity of estate.

24. The original covenantor remains liable even after he has disposed of his land. This clause reverses the rule.

25. A litigant pays his own attorney unless the contract provides otherwise.

26. The dominant owner may wish to get rid of his covenant liability by terminating the easement when other means of ingress have been acquired. This form of clause eliminates the need for a title search of the servient tenement to get the names of the parties to whom the release is to run.

27. The authorities are divided as to the need for a spouse to join. *See*, e. g. Arkansas *State Highway Comm. v. Marlar*, 447 SW2d 329 (Ark. 1969).

28. Since covenants by the grantee are included it is appropriate for all parties to sign and acknowledge this document. Of course, it should also be recorded.

§ 83. **Tax sale.** In some states a tax sale of the servient tenement extinguishes the easement. In others, it does not. 26 ALR2d 873. In many states, as in Illinois, the matter is governed by statutes that preserve the easement.

§ 84. **The authors have enjoyed much success by suggesting the use of the Model Easement Grant that appears on these pages.**

RESERVED: §§ 85 to 95.

5

Land Descriptions

§ 96. **Legal descriptions.** Every deed, mortgage, or lease contains a description of the land involved. The purpose of such a description, obviously, is to fix the boundaries of the land intended to be sold, mortgaged, or leased. The description delineates a specific piece of land and cannot apply to any other. A street address is adequate for the purpose of guiding guests to your home or for mail delivery, but greater precision is needed to fix the exact point where your land ends and where your neighbor's begins. Hence, we have the legal description. Whenever you read a legal description, keep in mind that before the description had been written, some person, probably a land surveyor, went out and located on the land the boundaries of the tract of land involved. He then put into words written directions for locating the lines he had traced on the land. These written directions are called a legal description of the land. Various methods have been devised for describing tracts of land.

§ 97. **Metes and bounds descriptions.** *Metes* are measures of length, such as inches, feet, yards, and rods. *Bounds* are boundaries, both natural and artificial, such as streams or streets. In a *metes and bounds description,* the surveyor takes you by the hand, as it were, and leads you over the land. He starts at a well-marked point of beginning and follows the boundaries of the land until he returns once more to the starting point. Landmarks called *monuments* often mark the several corners of the tract. A monument may be a natural monument, such as tree or river, or an artificial monument, such as a fence, stake, wall, road, or railroad.

EXAMPLE: A tract of land in Chicago, Cook County, Illinois, is described as follows, to wit: Beginning at a point in the east line of Mason Street one hundred feet north of the north line of Washington Street; running thence east on a line parallel to the north line of Washington Street 125 feet to the west line of an alley; thence north along the west line of said alley, twenty-five feet; thence west on a line parallel to the north line of Washington Street, 125 feet to the east line of Mason Street; thence south along the east line of Mason Street, twenty-five feet to the place of beginning.

The earliest descriptions in history were metes and bounds descriptions. All property in the thirteen original colonies of the United States was originally described by metes and bounds, the descriptions usually running from the mouth of a stream, or from a tree or a stump.

§ **98. The Government Survey.** By the treaty with England at the end of the Revolutionary War, the United States became the owner of the vast Northwest Territory, consisting of the present States of Illinois, Indiana, Ohio, Michigan, and Wisconsin. The end of the war found the United States heavily burdened with debts incurred during the war. It was decided that the new land should be sold and the proceeds used to retire the national debt. However, in selling the land to settlers, metes and bounds descriptions could not be used, for the new land was an untrodden wilderness. Hence some new system of describing land was needed. The system so devised was the rectangular system of land surveys, known as the Government Survey. Under this system, whenever a district, such as part of a state, was ready for private ownership, the government arranged for a survey of the land to be made. To begin a survey of this character, it is necessary to have some substantial landmark from which a start may be made. A place that can readily be referred to, such as the mouth of a river, is usually selected. From such a point, a line is run due north to the margin of the district to be surveyed. This first north and south line is called a *prime meridian,* or *principal meridian.* Some principal meridians have been numbered, such as the First Principal Meridian, which runs north from the mouth of the Great Miami River on the boundary between Ohio and Indiana and which governs the surveys of public lands in Ohio. Others have been named, as the Tallahassee Meridian, the Mt. Diablo Meridian, the Humboldt Meridian, and the San Bernardino Meridian.

An east and west line is run intersecting the principal meridians at some prominent point. This line is called the *base line.* Both north and south of the base line, additional east and west lines are run at intervals of twenty-four miles.

Since it is the object of the survey to create a huge checkerboard of identical squares covering the entire tract to be surveyed, it is plain that many north and south lines are needed. Owing to the curvature of the earth's surface, however, all true north and south lines converge as they approach the North Pole. This is obvious, since no matter how far apart two north and south lines are at the equator, they must meet at the North Pole. Hence if continuous north and south lines were to be used in the survey, it is clear that because of the convergence of the north and south lines the squares thus formed would grow narrower and narrower as the surveyors worked north. Now this is an imperfection that cannot be altogether eliminated. However, it can be minimized in the following manner: Along the base line, both east and west of the principal meridian, and at intervals of twenty-four miles, lines running due north are run. These are called *guide meridians.* But they are run only as far north as the next *correction line,* i.e., a distance of twenty-four miles. Then new intervals of twenty-four miles are measured off along this correction line, and a new series of guide meridians based on these new intervals is run for another twenty-four miles. This process is repeated until the boundaries of the tract are reached. Similar guide meridians are run based on the correction lines lying south of the base line.

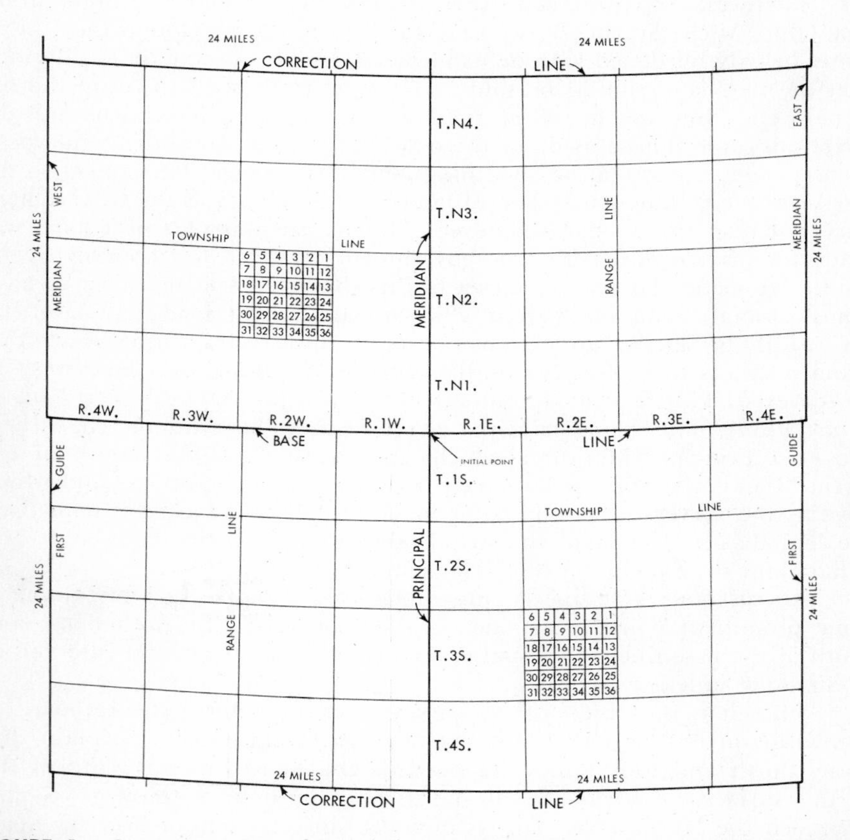

FIGURE 1. Correction Lines and Guide Meridians with Division of Townships into Sections.

Thus the district surveyed is divided into tracts approximately twenty-four miles square. These tracts are further divided into parts six miles on each side. These smaller parts are called *townships*.

Each row, or tier, of townships running north and south is called a *range*. The first row east of the principal meridian is referred to as *Range 1 East* of that meridian. Thus, the first row of townships east of the Third Principal Meridian is referred to as *Range 1 East of the Third Principal Meridian*. The row of townships next adjoining to the east is called *Range*

2 *East of the Third Principal Meridian,* and so on. Each row or tier of townships running east and west is identified by the number of townships intervening between it and the base line. Thus, a township in the first row north of the base line is called *Township 1 North.* The township next adjoining to the north is called *Township 2 North,* and so on. To identify a

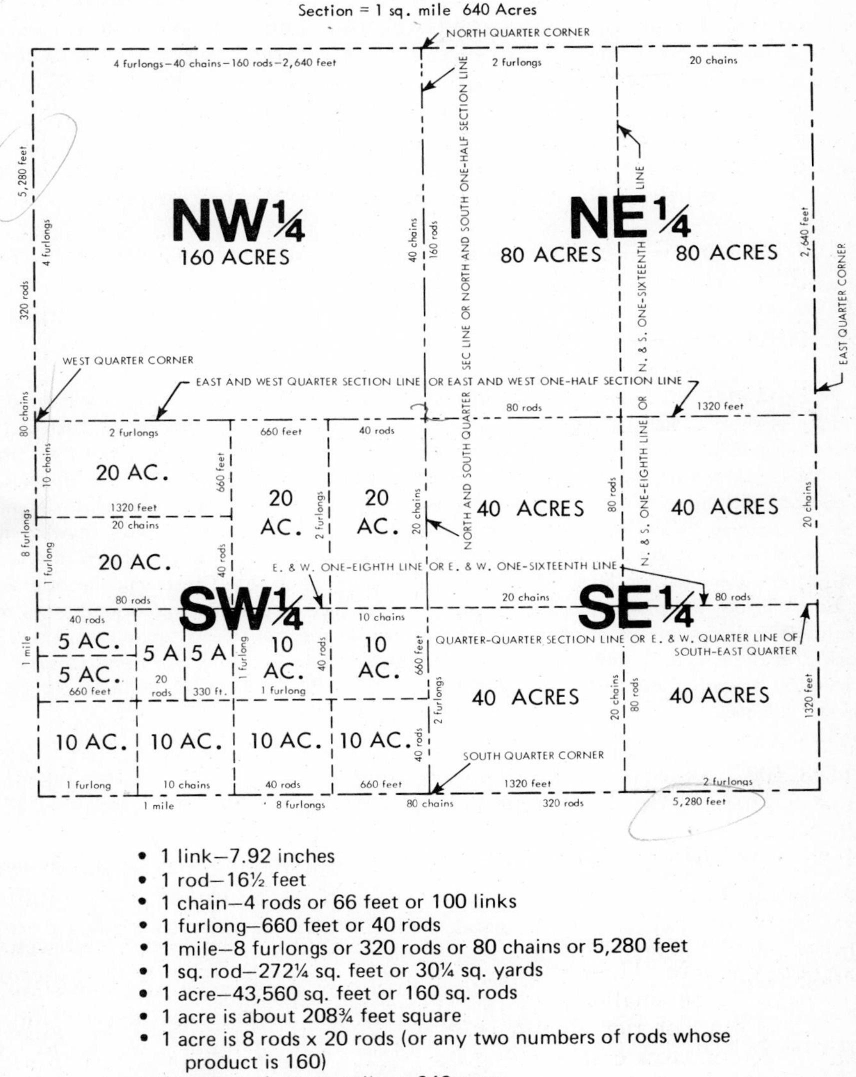

- 1 link—7.92 inches
- 1 rod—16½ feet
- 1 chain—4 rods or 66 feet or 100 links
- 1 furlong—660 feet or 40 rods
- 1 mile—8 furlongs or 320 rods or 80 chains or 5,280 feet
- 1 sq. rod—272¼ sq. feet or 30¼ sq. yards
- 1 acre—43,560 sq. feet or 160 sq. rods
- 1 acre is about 208¾ feet square
- 1 acre is 8 rods x 20 rods (or any two numbers of rods whose product is 160)
- 1 section—1 square mile or 640 acres

FIGURE 2. Section of Land Divided into Quarters and Showing Acreage and Distances

township completely, both the range number and the township number must be given, as *Township 40 North, Range 13, East of the Third Principal Meridian.* The township thus identified is in the fortieth row north of the base line and in the thirteenth row east of the Third Principal Meridian. Such a description is often abbreviated, and becomes *T. 40 N., R. 13 E. of the 3rd P.M.*

Each township is divided into thirty-six tracts, each approximately one mile square. These tracts are called *sections.* The sections in a township are numbered from one to thirty-six, always commencing with the section in the northeast corner of the township. Sections are often divided into quarters, and these quarters are also often divided into quarters.

The government system of rectangular surveys has been employed in surveying the lands of the states of Alabama, Florida, Mississipppi, and all of the states north of the Ohio and west of the Mississippi Rivers, except Texas.

Local surveys, which in some respects resemble the Government Survey, will occasionally be encountered in the other states.

§ **99. Plats.** Large tracts of land are often subdivided into building lots. Thereafter each building lot is conveyed by its lot number.

EXAMPLE: A, believing that the tract is ripe for subdivision, buys the Northeast Quarter of the Northeast Quarter of Section 7, Township 40 North, Range 13 East of the Third Principal Meridian, in Cook County, Illinois. He hires a surveyor, who divides the tract into *blocks,* separated by streets. Each block is divided into *lots.* The lots and blocks are numbered, and the streets and the subdivision are named. For this particular subdivision, A selects the name "Highwood." The surveyor prepares a map, called a *plat,* showing the lots and blocks, their dimensions and numbers, the width and names of the streets, the location of the quarter-section lines, and other similar information. After receiving the approval of local officials, the plat is filed or recorded in the office where deeds and mortgages are recorded. A description of a lot in this subdivision will read somewhat as follows: Lot 2 in Block 5 in Highwood, a subdivision of the Northeast Quarter of the Northeast Quarter of Section 7, Township 40 North, Range 13 East of the Third Principal Meridian in Cook County, Illinois.

§ **100. Description by popular name.** Descriptions by the popular name of the tract have been held sufficient, as where a deed conveys "The Old Merchant Farm." *Hayes* v. *O'Brien,* 37 NE 73 (Ill. 1894).

§ **101. General description.** A deed sometimes contains no definite description, but merely purports to convey all land owned by the grantor in a certain district, as "all the land owned by the grantor in Cook County, Illinois." Such descriptions are held to be sufficient.

§ **102. Street address.** A description by street address alone should never be used in a deed or mortgage. Since the proper legal description is not always available when a contract for the sale of land is being drafted, descriptions by street address will be found in contracts.

A danger sometimes present in street address descriptions is revealed by the following illustration.

EXAMPLE: *R* leased to *E* "certain premises known as 10 East Chicago Avenue, Chicago, Illinois." The building in question bore this address. It was a restaurant. *R* also owned a vacant lot adjoining, which patrons of the restaurant sometimes used as a parking area, although it was not a regular parking lot. It was held that a lease by street number includes only the lot on which the building is situated. *Killian* v. *Welfare Engineering Co.,* 66 NE2d 305 (Ill. 1946).

§ 103. Area. Land may be described by its area, as the "North one acre of the Southeast Quarter of Section 1, Township 44 North, Range 2 East of the Third Principal Meridian, Lake County, Illinois."

§ 104. Adjoining owners. Lands are also described by reference to adjoining lands.

EXAMPLE: A deed described the land as follows: "Bounded on the east by a fifty-acre tract of land owned by G. B. Turner purchased by him from N. W. Rodden; bounded on the north by the right of way of the Texas and Pacific R. R.; and on the west by a fifty-acre tract owned by the said G. B. Turner and known as the J. F. Neal tract of land; bounded on the south by the Katie Moore Boham tract of land." Cox v. *Campbell,* 143 SW2d 361 (Tex. 1940).

§ 105. Foreign grant. Portions of this country were once owned by France, Holland, Mexico, and Spain. In fact, the titles to some of the most valuable lands on Manhattan Island are based upon Dutch grants. Hence descriptions employing foreign units of land measure, such as the *vara* and the *arpent,* are often encountered.

§ 106. Indefinite description. A deed, mortgage, or other document must describe the land conveyed. The land must be so described that it can be located and identified.

EXAMPLE: A deed was made of the "southeast half" of a certain section. This deed was held void for uncertainty in the description. *Pry* v. *Pry,* 109 Ill. 466 (1884).

It is often difficult to determine whether a description is good or bad.

EXAMPLE: A deed was made to "one acre of land in the northwest corner of Block 20" in a certain subdivision. This deed was held good, because a surveyer could go to the northwest corner of the block and measure out a sufficient distance west and south to include one acre of land. *Richey* v. *Sinclair,* 47 NE 364 (Ill. 1897).

A deed of "my house and lot" is not considered indefinite. Oral evidence can be introduced in court to show what tract of land was intended. *Brenneman* v. *Dillon,* 129 NE 564 (Ill. 1920).

When a deed description is too indefinite to identify the land, but the grantee, by consent of the grantor, takes possession of premises that are within the general terms of the description and erects permanent improvements on them, the defect in the description is thereby cured.

EXAMPLE: *R* made a deed to a railroad of "a strip of land one hundred feet in width over the Northeast Quarter of Section 12, Township 14 North, Range 2 East of the Third Principal Meridian." The railroad, with *R*'s consent, actually occupied a strip of land one hundred feet in width and erected railroad tracks thereon. The description, though originally too indefinite, became sufficient by occupation.

The rule that possession cures an indefinite description is also applicable to leases and to contracts of sale.

§ **107. Description containing omissions.** A deed, mortgage, or other document is valid, even though part of the description is omitted, if enough remains to identify the land conveyed.

EXAMPLE: A deed to land described as being in Santa Cruz County, California, failed to name the meridian from which the township and range were numbered. This did not invalidate the deed, since all descriptions of land in that county are numbered from the Mt. Diablo Meridian. *Harrington* v. *Goldsmith,* 68 Pac. 594 (Cal. 1902).

§ **108. Correction of deed description by court order.** When an error occurs in the land description in a deed and the seller refuses to give a new deed to correct the error, a court order can usually be obtained correcting the erroneous description. This is known as *reformation* of an instrument. And if in the meantime the grantee has been in possession of the land, probably no great harm will result from the error. If, however, the grantee has not gone into possession, as where the land is vacant, third persons, such as judgment creditors of the grantor, may acquire rights in the land superior to those of the grantee.

§ **109. Streets or highways as boundaries.** As previously pointed out a city often does not own the land comprising its roads, streets, or alleys, but only has an easement thereover for street purposes. When a deed or mortgage is made of land abutting on such a road, street, the land sold or mortgaged generally runs to the center of such road, street, or alley. 49 ALR2d 982.

EXAMPLE: *R* gives *E* a deed selling and conveying that part of a certain section of land "lying south of Dundee Road." By this deed, *E* acquires all land in that particular section lying south of the *center* of Dundee Road.

The reason for this rule is obvious. The seller, having parted with ownership of his land, would have no use for the strip of road adjoining thereto. Hence it is presumed that he intended half of the adjoining road to pass to the buyer with the land sold.

When a street is used as a boundary, keep in mind that legally the street usually includes much more than the paved roadway over which cars travel. It includes the sidewalk, the planted area known as the *parkway* and may even include a narrow strip of land on the house side of the sidewalk. Check the recorded subdivision plat to locate the true street line.

§ **110. Waters as boundaries.** If *R* owns land through which a stream flows and his ownership includes the stream bed, a deed, mortgage, or lease of land "lying south of Plum Creek" will, under a rule analogous to the highway rule, include the south half of the creek.

§ **111. Parts of lots.** Care should be exercised in drafting descriptions of parts of lots.

EXAMPLE: A subdivision plat indicates that Lot 2 in Block 3 is eighty feet wide. *R*, the owner, gives *E* a deed to the "east forty feet of Lot 2." When *R* sells the remainder of the lot, his description thereof should be "Lot 2, except the east forty feet thereof," and not "the west forty feet of Lot 2." The reason is obvious. Suppose Lot 2 is actually slightly more than eighty feet in width, as it well may be, for land measurements are not perfectly accurate. Deeds of the east forty feet and the west forty feet of the lot would leave a small strip of land in the middle of the lot still owned by the seller.

When the lot is not a perfect square or rectangle, use of descriptions such as the "east half" or "north half" of the lot should be avoided, since the word "half" usually is considered to mean half by area, and the boundary line will be located with an equal number of square feet on either side thereof. This may result in an unequal division of the frontage of the lot.

A deed of a part of a lot that abuts on a diagnoal street should use descriptions like the "northwesterly thirty feet" rather than the "north thirty feet," since, if the diagonal street runs in a true northwesterly or northeasterly direction, it is difficult to determine which side of the lot is the "north" side. Cases will be found where two of the boundary lines may lay equal claim to being the "north" line of the lot.

§ **112. Buildings.** Since buildings are usually fixtures and, as such, are part of the land, a deed of the land will automatically give the buyer the buildings thereon. They need not be mentioned in the deed.

§ **113. Tax bills.** Tax bills contain abbreviated, vague, and unsatisfactory descriptions of the land. They should never be used in drafting a deed, contract, or lease.

RESERVED: §§ 114 to 124.

6

Land Titles and Interests in Land

§ 125. **Estates in land.** Just as land may be divided into layers by a sale of "air rights" thereover or minerals thereunder, so the ownership of land may be divided into various types of interests. The highest type of interest, of course, is complete ownership.

EXAMPLE: A owns a tract of land. No one else has any interest whatever in the land. He is said to be the owner *in fee simple*. This is merely a technical phrase connoting ownership of the land. When one hears it said that "A has title" to a particular tract of land, it is understood that A is the *fee owner,* he owns the land *in fee,* or *in fee simple,* or *in fee simple absolute*. All these are different ways of expressing the idea that A owns the land, that his ownership is of unlimited duration, and that so long as he obeys the law, he may do as he chooses with the land, and, on his death, it will go to his heirs, or, if he leaves a will, to the persons named in his will.

Suppose, however, that *A,* being the owner in fee simple of a tract of land, executes a ten-year lease thereof to *B*. Now *A* has parted with a portion of his rights. He has given up for ten years his right to occupy the land and, in return, has received *B*'s promise to pay rent for those ten years. *B* has acquired the right to occupy the land in accordance with the provisions of his lease, but has not, of course, become the owner in fee simple. He has merely acquired a *leasehold estate* or *term for years* in the land. A leasehold estate, even where the lease is for many years, is, for most purposes, legally considered to be personal property. *Chicago* v. *University of Chicago,* 134 NE 723 (Ill. 1922) (lease for 1,000 years).

EXAMPLE: R makes a lease to E. E assigns the lease to A. E's wife need not join in the assignment because dower rights do not exist in personal property.

But for some purposes a lease is said to be a *chattel real*. That is, it has some of the attributes of real property. Thus, a lease is entitled to be recorded in the real estate records, like a deed or mortgage of land. *Lincoln National Bank. & Tr. Co.* v. *Nathan,* 19 NE2d 243 (Ind. 1939). The same would be true of a mortgage of the leasehold estate. A leasehold estate can be partitioned in the same manner as real estate. *Pierce* v. *Pierce,* 123 NE2d 511 (Ill. 1954).

The word *estate* is used to express the degree, quantity, nature, duration, or extent of an interest in land. Complete ownership is an *estate in fee simple,* but there are many other estates, such as *life estates* and *leasehold estates.* Each differs from the others with respect to the rights and duties of the owner of the estate in question.

§ **126. Life estates.** The owner of a life estate can use and enjoy the land only during his lifetime.

EXAMPLE: A, a landowner, dies leaving a will giving land to his widow, B, for her life, and, at her death, to their children, C and D. B thus acquires a *life estate* in the land and becomes a life tenant. She is entitled to the reasonable and necessary use of the land for her lifetime, but she must not do anything that will in any way injure the permanent value of the property. She may collect and use the rents of the land, but must keep the property in repair and must pay the real estate taxes and the interest on the mortgage. She must not drill any new oil wells or open new mines, but may take oil or minerals from existing wells and mines. On her death, all her rights in the land will cease.

Life estates may be created by will or deed. Often, to save the expense of probating his will after his death, a father while still living will give a deed of his land to his son or daughter, and in the deed will reserve to himself a life estate.

Certain special kinds of life estates are created by law, rather than by will or deed, such as dower, curtesy, and homestead.

§ **127. Trusts.** A *trust* is an equitable obligation, binding a person (who is called a *trustee*) to deal with property over which he has control (which is called the *trust property* or *trust estate*) for the benefit of persons (who are called the *beneficiaries*), any of whom may enforce the obligation. Trusts are of various kinds.

EXAMPLE: A, a landowner, dies leaving a will by which he gives all his property to B, in trust, with power to sell the property and make investments, the income of the trust to be payable to A's widow, C, during her lifetime, and on her death the trust property to be distributed among A's children then living. Since this trust was created by A's last will and testament, it is known as a *testamentary trust.*

EXAMPLE: A, a landowner, signs a deed conveying his land to B, in trust, with power to sell the property and make investments, the income of the trust to be payable to A during his lifetime, and after A's death to his widow, C, during her lifetime, and on her death the property to be distributed among A's children then living. Since this trust becomes effective during A's lifetime, it is known as a *living trust.*

EXAMPLE: A plans to acquire a tract of land. However, he wishes to conceal his ownership of the property. He also wishes to prevent his wife and his judgment creditors from acquiring any interest in the land. On purchasing the land, A directs the seller to convey the land to B, as trustee. The deed gives B full power to sell and mortgage the land, but does not mention A's name. The deed is filed for record. The deed to B and also a separate unrecorded agreement signed by A and B recite that all title to the land is vested in *B* and that the beneficiary's (that is, *A*'s) interest is only personal property. However, in the unrecorded agreement *B* agrees that he will deal with the land only when directed so to do by *A*. *A* has accomplished his purpose. The public records do not disclose his ownership of the land. Since the trust specifically provides that *A*'s interest is only personal property, no dower rights attach, and judgments against *A* are not liens on the land. *C.T. & T. Co.* v. *Mercantile Tr. and Sav. Bank,* 20 NE2d 992 (Ill. 1939). This is called a land trust.

The land trust is recognized as valid in Florida, Illinois, Indiana, North Dakota, and Virginia.

REFERENCES: Kenoe, Land Trust Practice (1974); Garret, Land Trusts, 1955 *Law Forum* 655; Land Trust Act, 18 *U. Miami L. Rev.* 699 (1964); Comment, 14 *Kan. L. Rev.* 97 (1965): Note, 45 *N.D.L. Rev.* 77 (1968).

§ 128. **Cemetery lots.** When a cemetery corporation sells a lot, or burial site, the purchaser does not become the absolute owner of the lot. The deed gives him merely an easement right of burial. *Steele* v. *Rosehill Cemetery Co.,* 19 NE2d 189 (Ill. 1939); Note 109 *U. of Pa. L. Rev.* 378 (1961). He also has the right to enter the cemetery to care for the graves, subject to the reasonable regulations adopted by the cemetery company as to visiting hours, monuments, grave decorations, and so on. Like any other easement, the easement of the burial may be lost by abandonment. *Trustees of First Presbyterian Church* v. *Alling,* 54 N.J.S. 141, 148 A2d 510 (N.J. 1959).

§ 129. **Modes of acquiring title to or ownership of land.** While title to or ownership of land is most often acquired by deed, by will, or by descent, there are other modes of acquiring title to land, among them, condemnation and adverse possession.

§ 130. **Condemnation.** When land is needed for some public use, it can be acquired by the exercise of the power of eminent domain. The power of eminent domain is exercised: (1) by the United States, the state in which the land lies, cities, villages, school boards, and other public bodies; (2) by quasi-public corporations, such as railroads and public utility corporations; (3) in some states, private individuals have the right of eminent domain in limited instances as, for example, when they are landlocked. The power is subject to two conditions: The use to which the property is to be devoted must be a public one, and just compensation must be paid.

Exercise of the power of eminent domain involves a condemnation proceeding, which is usually a court proceeding initiated by the city or other public body desiring to acquire title. The just compensation to which the landowner is entitled is the fair, market value of the land at the time of the taking of the land. This value is often determined by a jury.

By condemnation, the condemnor acquires either an easement or fee simple title, although federal legislation now permits the United States to acquire by condemnation the right to occupy the land for a term of years only if that is what is desired. If an easement will serve the purpose for which the land is to be acquired, the condemnor, under many laws, acquires only an easement.

EXAMPLE: As a rule, an easement only is acquired by a railroad condemning for a right of way, a city condemning for a street, a telephone company condemning for a telephone line, or a drainage district condemning for a drainage ditch. In such cases, even though the landowner receives the full market value of the land condemned, he retains the ownership of the land so condemned. The point is of importance, since if an easement for street or right of way purposes acquired by condemnation is later abandoned, the original landowner still retains his ownership free and clear of the easement. *Bell* v. *Mattoon Water-Works & Res. Co.*, 92 NE 352 (Ill. 1910).

In many cases, however, it is necessary that fee simple title be acquired, as when land is condemned for a courthouse site. Many states, therefore—Illinois, Kansas, Kentucky, Massachusetts, Michigan, Minnesota, Ohio, Pennsylvania, Texas, Virginia, and Wyoming, for example—permit the condemnor to acquire fee simple title by condemnation.

§ 131. Adverse possession. Often the public records will show a complete and perfect succession of perfect deeds from the government down to John Smith. This is known as the *record title* or *paper title*. Yet the true ownership of the land may be outstanding in someone who holds possession of the land without a single document to show his ownership. The ownership here referred to is that acquired by taking possession of the land and staying in possession for a certain number of years fixed by law. At the end of that period, which varies from state to state, the party in possession has ownership to the land. He need not have any deed to the land. He may have entered on the land without any right whatever to do so. He need not place any instrument on the public records showing his title. Yet he owns the land.

The law providing for the acquiring of title to land by going into possession was passed for two reasons: (1) It encourages the use of the land. If persons living in other states or other parts of the state own land in our vicinity and make no attempt to use the land for very long periods of time, it is better for the community to have the title placed in someone who is more interested in using it. (2) Ownership of real estate often depends on transactions that occurred so long ago that the witnesses who were familiar with the transaction are dead or have forgotten the facts. Therefore it is better to discourage any attempt to evict a person who has been in possession for a long period of time, since he might find it very difficult to find the witnesses who could prove that his claim is rightful.

Not every possession of land will ripen into ownership. Possession, in order to ripen into ownership must be adverse possession. For possession to be adverse it must be *hostile, actual, notorious, exclusive, continuous, and under claim of right.*

For possession to be adverse, it must be actual. As the judges put it, the occupant must unfurl his flag on the land and keep it flying so that the owner may see, if he wishes, that an enemy has invaded his domain and planted the standard of conquest. In other words, the occupant must do something that will make the owner notice that a stranger has occupied his land. This does not mean, however, that the occupant must live or reside on the land.

EXAMPLE: A fences and farms some vacant land adjoining his farm in Illinois. This continues for twenty years. He now owns this adjoining land by reason of his adverse possession.

This rule is of importance in boundary disputes, since if a landowner erects a fence on what he claims is the boundary of his land and claims all the land to the fence, his possession will eventually ripen into ownership even though the fence is actually over on his neighbor's land. The same is true when a building encroaches over and upon adjoining land.

Usually possession is not *hostile* when the person in possession occupies a relation of trust and confidence toward the holder of the paper title.

EXAMPLE: A father's possession is not hostile to the child, the possession of a husband is not hostile to the wife, and the possession of an agent is not hostile to his employer.

The requirement that possession be *notorious* merely means that the possession of the occupant must be such that the real owner would be likely to notice it.

Adverse possession, in order to ripen into title, must be continuous. However, seasonal possession is often sufficient, for the possession need only be such as is usual with respect to land of similar character. For example, it is sufficient if farmland is farmed in the farming season, timberland logged in the logging season, and so on.

EXAMPLE: A occupied *B*'s hunting shack each year during the hunting season. Ultimately, *A* acquired good title by adverse possession. *Kraus* v. *Mueller,* 12 Wis.2d 430, 107 NW2d 467.

For a person to acquire title by adverse possession he must claim that he is the owner of the land, but it is enough if his acts and conduct indicate that he claims to be the owner of the land.

EXAMPLE: A and *B* owned adjoining lots, *A* owning Lot 9 and *B* owning Lot 8. *A* built a frame cottage on Lot 9, but the same extended two feet over on Lot 8. He thought the house was entirely on his own lot and never made any oral claim to this two-foot strip. He paid taxes on Lot 9 and *B* the taxes on Lot 8. After twenty years, a survey was made which disclosed the encroachment. Although *A* had made no oral claim to the two-foot strip, his acts, namely, erecting a building on this strip, showed that he claimed title to the strip. He therefore had acquired title by adverse possession. *Cassidy* v. *Lenahan,* 128 NE 544 (Ill. 1920).

RESERVED: §§ 132 to 142.

7

Deeds

§ **143. Defined.** A deed is a written instrument by which a landowner transfers the ownership of his land.

§ **144. Types of deeds.** The deeds commonly used in the United States are *quitclaim deeds, warranty deeds,* and *deeds of bargain and sale.*

§ **145. Quitclaim deed.** A quitclaim deed purports to convey only the grantor's *present interest in the land,* if any, rather than the land itself. Since such a deed purports to convey whatever interest the grantor has at the time, its use excludes any implication that he has good title, or any title at all. Such a deed in no way obligates the grantor. If he has no interest, none will be conveyed. If he acquires an interest after executing the deed, he retains such interest. If, however, the grantor in such deed has complete ownership at the time of executing the deed, the deed is sufficient to pass such ownership.

A seller who knows that his title is bad or who does not know whether his title is good or bad usually uses a quitclaim deed in conveying.

§ **146. Warranty deed.** A warranty deed contains covenants of title.

§ **147. Deed of bargain and sale.** There are deeds that convey the land, and not merely the grantor's *interest* therein. Therefore they are not quitclaim deeds. They do not include warranties of title. Therefore they are not warranty deeds. Such a deed is a deed of *bargain and sale,* or *deed without covenants.*

§ **148. Requirements of a valid deed.** The essential elements of a deed are a competent grantor, a grantee, recital of consideration, words of conveyance, adequate description of the land, signature of grantor and his spouse, and delivery of the completed instrument to the grantee. In addition, a deed may (though it need not) contain warranties of title, recitals showing mortgages and other encumbrances, a date, witnesses, an acknowledgment, and documentary stamps. Delivery is followed by filing or recording of the deed in the proper public office.

§ **149. Grantor.** Every deed must have a grantor. The grantor is he who conveys the property. The fact that the name used by the grantor differs from his true name does not invalidate the deed.

The name of the grantor must appear in the body of the deed.

EXAMPLE: *A, B,* and C own certain land. A deed is made, and the names of A and *B* appear in the body thereof, but all three owners sign the deed. C's interest does not pass under the deed. *Harrison* v. *Simons,* 55 Ala. 510 (1896).

However, a deed beginning "In consideration of ten dollars, I do hereby convey" is sufficient if signed by the landowner, even though his name does not appear in the body of the deed. *Bowles* v. *Lowery,* 62 So 107 (Ala. 1913). The same is true where the deed begins with the phrase "The undersigned." *Frederick* v. *Wilcox,* 24 So 582 (Ala. 1898).

A mistake in the spelling of the grantor's name or a variance between the spelling of the name in the body of the deed and the spelling in the signature will not invalidate the deed where the identity of the person intended to be designated is obvious.

EXAMPLE: A deed is good though it names "Emmonds" as grantor, but is signed "Emmens." And a deed is good though it names "Abraham B. Kain" as grantor but is signed "A. Boudoin Kain." *Lyon* v. *Kain,* 36 Ill. 362 (1865).

The grantor and his spouse must be of legal age and of sound mind. In many states, a deed by a person who has been declared insane by a court is void. Even if the grantor has not been declared insane, his deed may later be set aside if, as a matter of fact, he lacked the mental capacity to understand in a reasonable manner the nature of the transaction in which he was engaged and its consequences and effects on his rights and interest.

EXAMPLE: *W,* a widower, has three children, *A, B,* and C. When *W* becomes too feeble to take care of himself, *A,* a married but childless daughter, moves into *W*'s home with her husband. As time passes *W* becomes senile and requires constant care. *A,* feeling she should be rewarded for her care of her father, prepares a deed of the home running to herself as grantee and has *W* sign it. After *W*'s death *B* and C learn of the deed. They file a suit to set it aside. If they can show that *W* was too senile to understand that he was parting with ownership of his home when he signed the deed, the court will set it aside. Cases of this sort occur by the thousands.

In most states, an individual achieves majority, comes of age, at the age of eighteen. Ages of majority, however, vary from state to state. A person who is not of age is an *infant* and, after achieving majority, may sue to set aside any deed executed by him while an infant. If it is necessary that the land of an infant or an insane person be sold for his support or for some other proper purpose, court proceedings may be instituted for that purpose.

A favorable vote of the directors or trustees of a corporation is usually necessary to authorize the sale of corporate real estate. Laws will often be encountered requiring a vote of the holders of two-thirds of the corporate stock to authorize any sale of substantially *all* the corporate assets. A vote of the majority of the members of a church corporation or a nonprofit corporation may be necessary for a sale of the property.

§ 150. **Grantor's spouse.** Whether or not the grantor's spouse must join in the deed depends, of course, upon the local law. Generally speaking, however, it is necessary for the grantor's spouse to join in the deed for one or more of the following reasons:

1. In most states, land occupied by a husband and wife as their home is known as their homestead. Any deed or mortgage of the homestead must be signed by both husband and wife, the theory being that the home should not be disposed of unless a new home satisfactory to both parties has been furnished.

2. In most states, a wife has certain rights in her husband's land, and her rights in any particular parcel of land are not defeated by any deed made by her husband unless she has joined therein.

3. Depending on the local law, a husband may have *curtesy, dower,* or other rights in the land owned by his wife, and his signature on his wife's deed is required in order to relinquish these rights.

4. Some of the western states have the community property system, and in most of these states it is required that deeds of community property be signed by both husband and wife.

5. In some states (Illinois, for example) laws have been passed that seem to give some property interest in the land that is awarded to the other spouse in a divorce. This appears to make it prudent to have both spouses join in any deed of the real estate that is owned by either spouse.

It is obvious from the foregoing that the marital status of the grantor should be clearly stated in the deed, as *bachelor, widow, spinster, or divorced and not remarried.*

§ 151. **Grantee.** Every deed must have a grantee. If it does not, it is void.

EXAMPLE: A makes out a deed to *B*, who, unknown to A, is dead at the time. The deed is void. A dead grantee is no grantee at all. 148 ALR 252.

The grantee need not be named in the deed if he is sufficiently described therein. Thus a deed to "John Smith and wife" vests good title in John Smith and his wife. *Ballard* v. *Farley,* 226 SW 544 (Tenn. 1920).

A deed running directly to an unincorporated association is void for want of a grantee.

EXAMPLE: A number of persons attended a particular church that was known as the "First Avenue Baptist Church." The church, however, was not incorporated. One of the members of the congregation made a deed of gift of his real estate to "First Avenue Baptist Church." The deed was void. *Heiligenstein* v. *Schlotterbeck,* 133 NE 188 (Ill. 1921).

The fact that the name inserted in the deed is not the grantee's true name does not invalidate the deed. In other words, for the purpose of any particular real estate transaction I may assume any name I wish. If I should buy land and direct the seller to insert the name "Robert Cook" as grantee in the deed, intending to hold ownership of the land by that name, the deed is perfectly valid. *Chapman* v. *Tyson,* 81 Pac. 1066 (Wash. 1905).

This situation frequently occurs with respect to persons who pass as husband and wife although they are not legally married.

EXAMPLE: A deed designated as grantees Fabrio Casini and Lucy Casini, his wife. Actually, Lucy was not the wife of Fabrio, although they passed as husband and wife. The deed was a valid deed, and the grantees became co-owners of the property. *Casini* v. *Lupone,* 72 A2d 907 (N.J. 1950); *Michael* v. *Lucas,* 137 Atl. 287 (Md. 1927).

A misspelling of the grantee's name will not invalidate the deed where the identity of the person intended to be designated is obvious. This is also true of deeds to corporations.

EXAMPLE: I attend a church whose proper corporate name is First Avenue Methodist Church, and, intending to convey land to this church, I make out a deed to The Methodist Church of First Avenue. The deed is valid. *Church of Christ* v. *Christian Church,* 61 NE 1119 (Ill. 1901). This defect is technically termed a *misnomer.* Misnomer does not invalidate a deed.

In a few states, a husband cannot convey directly to his wife, or vice versa, since according to the ancient view, the husband and wife together are but one person, and it takes two persons to make a deed. However, both husband and wife may join in a deed to a third person, who may thereupon convey to the wife.

A deed to a minor or an insane person is valid.

In many states it is required that the deed show the address of the grantee, and a deed will not be accepted for recording unless this appears in the deed. However, failure to show the address does not invalidate the deed.

§ 152. **Deeds in blank.** The problem of whether a deed is void for want of a grantee often arises in connection with deeds where the name of the grantee is left blank at the time the deed is signed by the grantor. Of course if the blank space for the grantee's name is never filled in, the deed cannot be a good deed, for a deed must convey the land to someone. Where the name of the grantee is inserted by an agent of the grantor after the grantor has signed the deed, the deed is usually valid.

EXAMPLE: O, a landowner, signs a deed complete in all respects, except that the name of the grantee is left blank. He delivers this deed to a trusted agent, *A,* with directions to sell the property for not less than a certain sum. *A* interests *P* in the purchase of the property. *P* is willing to pay the stipulated price. *A* fills in *P*'s name as grantee and delivers the deed to *P. P* pays the purchase price, not knowing that his name was filled in after the deed was signed. Such a deed is generally held valid, even though *A*'s authority was merely verbal. *West* v. *Witschner,* 428 SW2d 538 (Mo. 1968); 75 ALR 1294. But a deed delivered with the land description left blank is held void in many states. *West* v. *Witschner,* 428 SW2d 538 (Mo. 1968).

§ 153. **Consideration.** The *consideration* is the price paid for the land. Every deed should contain a recital showing that a consideration was given for the deed. Except in Nebraska, the actual price paid, however, need not be stated. It is customary, in many states, for the deed to recite a consideration of $1.00 or $10, "and other good and valuable consideration."

If the deed recites a consideration, the fact that the deed represents a gift of the land and that actually no money changed hands will not invalidate the deed. An individual may give away his land if he wishes. However, a man must be just before he is generous. If the grantor is indebted at the time of the making of the gift, his creditors may thereafter have the deed set aside as in fraud of their rights. The payment of a nominal consideration, such as $10, will not suffice to sustain the deed in such a case. A valuable consideration is needed to sustain a deed against existing creditors of the grantor.

§ 154. **Support deeds.** Parents often convey their land to a son or daughter on the understanding that such son or daughter will support the parents for the rest of their lives. Or an elderly person without close relatives may convey his land to a stranger or to a rest home in return for a promise of support. While ordinarily a deed cannot be set aside for *failure of consideration,* that is, for the reason that the grantee failed to receive what he bargained for, support deeds form an exception to the rule. *Bruno* v. *Bruno,* 172 A2d 863 (Pa. 1961). Where the grantee fails to keep his promise to support, the deed can usually be set aside.

EXAMPLE: A father and mother conveyed land to their son. The mother had owned the land, and it had been the home of the parents. The deed recited a consideration of $2500. The actual consideration, however, was the son's agreement to support the parents and give them a home for the rest of their lives. Several years later, the son stopped supporting them and became so abusive that they moved out and went to live with another son. The deed was set aside. *Worrell* v. *West,* 296 P2d 1092 (Kan. 1956). The grantee is not living up to his promise unless he furnishes kindness and attention, as well as physical necessaries. *Zarembski* v. *Zarembski,* 48 NE2d 394 (Ill. 1943).

§ 155. **Words of conveyance.** Every deed must contain words of conveyance. These differ from state to state. In warranty deeds, *convey and warrant or grant, bargain, and sell are often used.* In quitclaim deeds the words usually are *convey and quitclaim* or *remise, release, and forever quitclaim.*

§ 156. **Description of land.** A deed must describe the land conveyed.

§ 157. **Warranties of title.** A warranty deed (sometimes called a *general warranty deed*) contains certain assurances or guarantees by the grantor that the deed conveys a good and unencumbered title. Such guarantees are called *covenants of title.* These covenants differ somewhat in their scope, depending on the local practice, but those usually encountered warrant or guarantee in substance:

1. That the grantor has good title to the land conveyed. This is called the *covenant of seizin.*

2. That there are no encumbrances on the land except as stated in the deed. This is called the *covenant against encumbrances.*

3. That the grantee, or his grantees, will not be evicted or disturbed by a person having a better title or lien. This is called the *covenant for quiet enjoyment.*

If the grantee suffers a loss because the title is not good as covenanted, he may sue the grantor for damages.

If any encumbrances exist that are not mentioned in the deed, the covenant against encumbrances is violated. An encumbrance, within the meaning of this covenant, includes any lien, such as a mortgage, tax lien, or judgment lien, also an easement, a restriction on the use of the land, or an outstanding dower right. The grantor's liability on this covenant is not affected by the fact that the grantee knew of the encumbrance. 64 ALR 1479. If the grantor wishes to escape liability on this covenant, he must insert some qualifying language in the deed, such as *subject to a certain mortgage* (describing the mortgage), or *subject to restrictions of record.* This is called the *subject clause.*

It is still customary in many localities to set out in full in the warranty deed the various covenants of title. However, in many states, laws exist under which the usual covenants of title are implied from the use of certain specified words. When these particular words are used, the deed must be read as though the usual covenants of title were set out in full therein. In Alaska, Illinois, Kansas, Michigan, Minnesota, and Wisconsin, the words *convey and warrant* make a deed a general warranty deed. The same result is achieved in Pennsylvania, Vermont, Virginia, and West Virginia by use of the words *warrant generally,* and in Arkansas, Florida, Idaho, Missouri, and Nevada by the words *grant, bargain, and sell.*

The fact that the seller is willing to give a general warranty deed is little or no assurance that he has good, clear title to the land. Suppose that I were to sit down this instant and write out a warranty deed conveying the Empire State Building to you. Clearly this warranty deed would give you no title to that valuable property for the simple reason that I don't own it. You would, of course, have the right to sue me for breach of my covenants of warranty.

A *special warranty deed* is one in which the grantor covenants only against the lawful claims of all persons claiming by, through, or under him. The grantor is liable in such case if his grantee is disturbed by some claim arising through an act of the grantor himself. For example, if, prior to the execution of the deed, the grantor has himself placed a mortgage on the land that the deed fails to mention, and thereafter the grantee is compelled to pay off the mortgage, the grantor is liable for the damages thus sustained by the grantee. But if the grantor has in no way encumbered the title, but later an outstanding title is asserted by some third person, the grantor is not liable. In some states, Mississippi, Pennsylvania, Vermont, Virginia, and West Virginia, for example, use of the words *warrant specially* is sufficient to create a covenant of special warranty. In California, Idaho, and North Dakota, use of the word *grant* achieves the same purpose.

§ 158. **Waiver of dower and homestead.** In some states, a deed must contain a clause releasing and relinquishing all homestead, dower, and curtesy rights in the premises.

§ 159. **Date.** A date is not essential to the validity of a deed, though it is the universal custom to date all deeds.

§ 160. **Signature.** The signature of the grantor is essential to the validity of the deed. A *forgery* (a deed to which some unauthorized third person has affixed the grantor's signature) is a nullity and conveys no title whatever.

The fact that the grantor's signature is misspelled will not invalidate the deed.

If the grantor is unable to write, he may sign by mark, in which case the signature line appears as follows:

His
"John × Smith (Seal)"
Mark

Everything but the "×" may be typed. The "×" must be affixed by the grantor.

Occasionally a deed is signed not by the grantor himself, but by an *attorney in fact*. An attorney in fact is simply an agent authorized by the landowner to sell and convey his real estate. In order for such deed to be valid, the following requirements exist:

1. The landowner must first sign and deliver to his attorney in fact a written instrument, called a *power of attorney*, authorizing such attorney to sell and convey the land in question. Such an instrument must be as formal as the deed itself. In states that require a deed to be sealed, the power of attorney must be sealed. In states that require a deed to be witnessed, the power of attorney must be witnessed. All the other requirements relating to deeds should be observed, including acknowledgment and recording.

2. The deed must name the landowner, not the attorney in fact, as the grantor.

3. The name signed to the deed should be that of the landowner. Under the usual method, the attorney signs the grantor's name and then places his name beneath that of the grantor, as follows:

"John Smith (Seal)"
"By Henry Brown, his Attorney in Fact."

4. The grantor must be alive on the date of the delivery of the deed, since death of the grantor automatically terminates the power of attorney. Insanity of the grantor may have the same result.

5. Since the landowner ordinarily has the power to terminate the agency at any time and thus take away the attorney's power to execute deeds on his behalf, it should be established that the agency actually had not been terminated or revoked at the date of the delivery of the deed.

NEW DIRECTIONS: Some states have enacted so-called "durable power of attorney" laws. These statutes provide that the power continues notwithstanding the incompetency of the grantors. Mich. Stat. Ann. §§ 26. 1225 (1).

The technical mode of executing the deed of a corporation is for the proper officer to sign the corporate name, adding his own signature and official title beneath the name of the corporation. Usually the corporate bylaws provide that deeds shall be signed by a president or vice-president and attested to by a secretary or assistant secretary.

§ 161. **Seal.** In some states, principally eastern states, a seal is essential to the validity of a deed. In most states, however, a seal is unnecessary, though the custom of using a seal persists. But even in those states where a deed by an individual need not bear a seal, a deed executed by a corporation should have the official corporate seal affixed.

§ 162. **Witnesses.** In many states a deed must be witnessed, two witnesses being the number commonly required. Most states require witnessing where the deed is signed by mark.

§ 163. **State tax.** State laws imposing a tax on deeds will be encountered in many states. It is usually required that such tax be paid or the land sale be noted on the tax records before recording of the deed will be permitted. Cities and villages also enact such laws.

§ 164. **Delivery of deeds.** Delivery is essential to the validity of a deed. The word *delivery* is somewhat misleading, since it would lead one to believe that it is necessary that the deed be actually handed by the grantor to the grantee. This is not the case. Delivery is simply the final act by which the grantor, who has previously signed the deed, signifies his intention that the deed shall take effect. Whether or not a deed has been delivered depends primarily on the *intention* of the grantor. The test is: Did the grantor *do* or *say* anything to show his intention to pass ownership of the land to the grantee? A deed may be delivered by acts without words or by words without acts, though ordinarily there are both words and acts in the making of a delivery.

EXAMPLE: At the closing of a deal, the buyer, *B*, hands, *S*, the seller, a check. *S* signs the deed and, without saying a word hands it to *B*. There is a delivery.

EXAMPLE: At the closing of a deal all the papers, including *S*'s signed deed, are on the closing table. Having received his check *S* tells *B* (the grantee) to take his deed. There is a delivery.

EXAMPLE: *S* signs a deed conveying real estate to *B* and hands it to *B*, not with the intention of passing title, but with the understanding that *B* will check the legal description to see if it is sufficient. There is no delivery.

EXAMPLE: *S* signs a deed conveying real estate to *B* but leaves it in his office while he is still thinking over the deal. *B* steals the deed from *S*'s office and shows it to *T*, who purchases from *B*, relying on *B*'s possession of the deed. *T* acquires no title. There is no delivery of the deed.

§ 165. **Delivery problems where there are several grantors.** Suppose *A* and *B* own certain land, and both of them sign a deed running to *C* as grantee. *A* hands the deed to *B* for the sole purpose of having the deed checked by their lawyer. Without *A*'s permission, *B* hands the deed to *C* and collects the sale price from him. This is not a good deed so far as *A* is concerned. He still owns his half interest. One joint grantor, who is not authorized by his co-tenant, cannot make a valid delivery of the deed that will be binding on the latter. 162 ALR 892.

When land is owned by several persons, all of them named as grantors in one deed, and one of the grantors signs the deed and hands it to the grantee with the statement that his consent to the sale of the land is conditioned on the other grantors also signing the deed, such deed is inoperative unless all grantors sign. *Logue* v. *Von Almen,* 40 NE2d 73 (Ill. 1941); Note, 14 *Columb. L. Rev.* 389 (1914).

§ 166. Delivery during lifetime of the grantor. Delivery of a deed must be made in the lifetime of the grantor.

EXAMPLE: On *S*'s death, an envelope with *S*'s name on it is found in *S*'s safety deposit box. The envelope is opened and found to contain a deed from *S* to *B*. The deed is void for want of delivery.

A deed is the proper instrument for transferring ownership of land from one living person to another, and, in general, this means that the deed, to be effective, must operate while both parties are alive.

However, I may legally deliver a deed to you here and now with a clause therein stating that the deed is to take effect only at my death. The deed gives you the right *now* to enjoy the property at my death. 31 ALR2d 532.

§ 167. Delivery to third persons. Where the grantor hands the deed not to the grantee, but to some third person, a wholly new set of rules comes into play. A number of different situations present themselves.

EXAMPLE: *S* signs a deed running to *B* as grantee and hands the deed to *B*'s lawyer, *L*, with the intention of giving *B* ownership of the land here and now. This is delivery to an *agent of the grantee* and is good delivery.

EXAMPLE: *S* signs a deed running to *B* as grantee and hands the deed to his own lawyer to check its form. There is no intention to transfer ownership and no delivery. Here the deed has been handed to the *agent of the grantor*.

EXAMPLE: *S* enters into a contract to sell land to *B* and pursuant thereto signs a deed to *B*. However, he hands the deed to *XYZ* Bank with directions to deliver the deed to *B* when certain moneys are paid by *B* to the bank. This is an *escrow*. (See Chapter 13.)

EXAMPLE: *S* signs a deed running to his son, *B*, as grantee, hands the deed to C, and directs C to hand the deed to *B* after *S*'s death. This brings up the subject of *death escrows*. This is a good delivery as long as it is clear that *S* intended to part with all control over the land once he handed the deed to C. Oddly enough, the courts allow *S*, in such cases, to use the land during his lifetime. They do not regard this as inconsistent with the passing of ownership to *B*. It is as though *S* had conveyed outright to *B*, but had reserved a life estate in the property. *Bury* v. *Young,* 33 Pac. 338 (Cal. 1893).

§ 167a. Delivery—family transactions. If a father executes a deed to a minor child, which deed is beneficial to the child, and the father indicates by his words and conduct that he intends the deed to operate at once, actual delivery is unnecessary. Indeed, the courts are most reluctant to upset a deed that is made as a gift by a parent to a child.

§ **168. Acceptance.** For a deed to transfer ownership of land, it is necessary that the grantor intend to transfer ownership to the grantee and that the grantee intend to accept ownership of the land. *Blankenship* v. *Meyers,* 544 P2d 314 (Id. 1975). That is to say, delivery by the grantor must be accompanied by acceptance of the deed by the grantee. 74 ALR2d 992. Only rarely will disputes arise regarding acceptance, and the courts are not disposed to be technical about it. Indeed, the courts have gone so far as to hold that if the grantor makes and records a deed without the knowledge of the grantee, ownership will nevertheless pass if the grantee, on being informed of the deed, assents to it, even though this takes place after the death of the grantor. *Mann* v. *Jummel,* 56 NE 161 (Ill. 1891). Also, if the grantee dies before learning of the deed, his acceptance will be presumed and the deed held good. *Lessee of Mitchell* v. *Ryan,* 3 Ohio St. 377 (1854). A parent may accept for an infant. *Whitworth* v. *Whitworth,* 210 SE2d 9 (Ga. 1974).

§ **169. Acknowledgment.** A deed is usually acknowledged by the grantors before a notary public or some other official.

§ **170. Recording.** Virtually all deeds are filed for record in some public office.

§ **171. Official conveyances.** Deeds by executors, administrators, guardians of minors, conservators or guardians of insane persons, sheriffs, masters in chancery, receivers, trustees in bankruptcy, and other similar conveyances usually depend for their validity on prior court proceedings. In addition, numerous technical requirements exist that frequently expose such deeds to attack. A discussion of such requirements is not within the scope of this book.

§ **172. Fraud, coercion and mistake.** A deed obtained by fraud, misrepresentation, or coercion may be set aside by proper court proceedings. This is particularly true when through old age, mental weakness, ignorance, illness, or some other cause, the grantor was incapabable of coping with the grantee, and due to such incapacity of the grantor the grantee has obtained the property for substantially less than its value.

Mutual mistake occurs where both parties are under some misapprehension.

EXAMPLE: *S* owns tracts one and two. Believing he is buying one, *B* receives and pays for a deed conveying tract two, while *S* believes *B* wishes to buy tract two. The deed will be set aside and the money refunded to *B.*

§ **173. After acquired title.** If the grantor in a warranty deed does not have title, or does not have complete title, at the time of executing the deed, but thereafter acquires title, such title will automatically pass to his grantee without any additional conveyance.

EXAMPLE: *X,* a landowner dies without a will, leaving three sons, *A, B,* and *C,* as his only heirs. Each thus becomes an owner of a one-third interest in *X's* land. *A* and *B,* believing C to have died long ago, after a mysterious disappearance, make a warranty deed of the land to *D.* After that, C who was living in a different town under an assumed name, dies, leaving his brothers *A* and *B* as his sole heirs. The title, thus acquired by *A* and *B* from C immediately passes to *D,* giving him complete title to the land. The result would be opposite if *A* and *B* had conveyed to *D* by quitclaim deed. 44 ALR 1276; 162 ALR 566.

§ 174. **Title conveyed by deed.** If the grantor owns the land in fee simple, and the deed contains no qualifying language, the deed gives the grantee good fee simple title to the land. However, deeds often contain qualifying language, which results in the grantee's acquiring something less than the fee simple title.

EXAMPLE: *A* makes a deed conveying land to *B* "and the heirs of his body." In some states, *B* acquires only a life estate by such deed, and his children acquire the remainder. In other states, such a deed will give *B* the full fee simple title to the land.

EXAMPLE: *A* conveys land to *B* by a deed that contains the following clause: "to have and to hold for and during the grantee's life." *B* acquires only a life estate by this deed.

The law on this subject is so complex and contains so many refinements of reasoning that no one but an experienced attorney should attempt to interpret a deed containing any qualifying language whatever. In particular, words such as *heirs, heirs of the body, issue, and death without issue* are danger signals. Indiscriminate use of such language is an invitation to a lawsuit.

§ 175. **Title conveyed by deed—fee or easement.** If language is added to the deed indicating the purpose for which the land is to be used, this may result in giving the grantee something less than full ownership of the land.

EXAMPLE: By warranty deed *S* deeded to *E* "a right of way one rod wide" over certain land. This deed gave *E* only an easement of travel. A deed that conveys a right, especially a right of way, rather than land, gives the grantee only an easement. 136 ALR 390.

EXAMPLE: *S* makes a deed to *E Railroad* of a "right of way over" certain land. The railroad acquires only an easement. 6 ALR3d 973.

But if the deed conveys the land, with the words of purpose following the property description, the courts are not in agreement.

EXAMPLE: *S* made a deed to *E* of a strip of land "to be used for road purposes." The court held that *E* acquired only an easement for road purposes. *Magnolia Petroleum* Co. v. *West,* 30 NE2d 24 (Ill. 1940). But in other states exactly the same kind of deed will be held to give *E* full ownership of the strip. *Biggs* v. *Wolfe,* 178 A2d 482 (Del. 1962);

136 ALR 379. The same split in the decisions occurs where land is deeded to a railroad "for right of way purposes" or "for railroad purposes," some cases saying the railroad gets only an easement for railroad purposes and others saying it gets good, saleable ownership of the land. 6 ALR3d 973.

Where a deed runs to a charitable corporation, frequently some reference is made in the deed to the use of the land for the charitable purposes of the corporation. Normally this nevertheless leaves the corporation with a saleable ownership title to the land. Bogert, The Law of Trusts and Trustees, § 324 (2nd. ed. 1964); 4 Scott, The Law of Trusts § 348.1 (3rd ed. 1967).

EXAMPLE: *S* deeds his vacant land to *E Hospital* "for hospital purposes." The hospital finds the land not well adapted to hospital purposes. It sells the land to X. This is a valid transaction. *X* gets good title to the land.

Where a deed runs to a city, village, park district, or other public body and contains language descriptive of the use to which the land is to be put, questions may arise as to the nature of the ownership thus acquired, particularly when such use is abandoned, though in most cases the courts struggle to find that the public body acquired a good, saleable title to the land. 28 AmJur2d *Estates* § 149; 10 McQuillin, *Municipal Corporations,* § 28:19 (3rd ed. 1966).

EXAMPLE: *S* sold and deeded his land to *E City* "to be used for the use and benefit of the citizens of *E City,*" this language appearing in the deed. *E City* found the land unusable for city purposes and sold it to *X*. This can be done. *X* acquires good ownership of the land. *City* v. *Jones,* 122 NW2d 503 (Neb. 1963).

The fact that the deed was made because of the threat of condemnation by the public body does not alter this rule. *Mattion* v. *Trustees,* 279 NE2d 66 (Ill. 1971). *Contra: Kendrick* v. *City of St. Paul,* 6 NW2d 449 (Minn. 1942).

There is an exception to this rule in some states:

EXAMPLE: *S* deeded his land to the *City of Milwaukee* "for highway purposes." By this deed the city acquired only an easement to use the land for highway purposes and could not sell the land. 136 ALR 399. This exception is confined to deeds for street, alley, and highway purposes, and even then, in some states the city gets good, saleable ownership of the land. 136 ALR 394.

Where a deed runs to some public body "for park purposes" there is no agreement whatever as to what such a deed conveys. 15 ALR2d 975.

§ **176. Exceptions and reservations.** In conveying land, the grantor often wishes to retain some part of the land described or to reserve some right therein. This is accomplished by inserting in the deed the proper clauses of *exception* and *reservation.* An exception withholds from the operation of the deed title to a part of the land described in the deed. Thus, a deed of Lot 1 *excepting the north twenty feet thereof* does not pass ownership of the north twenty feet of the lot. That portion was *excepted* from the conveyance. A *reservation* is the creation by the deed of a new right in favor of the grantor, usually an easement or life estate. Thus, in a deed of Lot 1 *reserving to the grantor an easement for ingress and egress over and across the north twenty feet of Lot 1,* ownership of the north twenty feet passes to the grantee, but an easement is reserved in favor of the grantor. Sometimes the terms *excepting* and *reserving* are used inaccurately, and the courts will hold that a true reservation was created by use of the word *excepting* or that a true exception was created by the use of the word *reserving.*

EXAMPLE: *S* conveys certain land to *E* "except the north ten feet for a right of way." Ownership of the entire tract, including the north ten feet, passes to *E,* but the quoted clause reserves an easement for *S* over the north ten feet. 139 ALR 1348.

It is possible for the grantor in a deed to reserve a life estate in the property conveyed. Often to save the expense of probating a will after his death, a father, while still living, will give a deed of his land to his son or daughter, and in the deed will reserve to himself a life estate. The grantee becomes the owner of the land, and the grantor retains the use thereof for his lifetime.

WARNING: Once such a deed is signed, the grantor cannot recall it. The psychological effect of this change in circumstances often brings about friction between the parent and child. Hence such transactions should be avoided, if possible.

§ 177. Suggestions.

1. Form of deed. If there is a contract for the sale of land, find out if the contract specifies the form of deed to be given. If the contract specifies that the seller is to give a warranty deed, then, of course, a warranty deed form must be used. If the contract does not specify the form of the deed, in most states a quitclaim deed will suffice. The seller will prefer to use this form, since it subjects him to no personal liability for defects in title. If there is no written contract for the sale of the land, the sellers will again prefer to give a quitclaim deed.

2. Grantor. Check the deed by which the grantor acquired ownership and see that his name is spelled the same way in the deed by which he is conveying the land. Any difference in spelling may lead to an objection when the title is examined. If a woman acquires title by her maiden name and subsequently marries, the deed should show both names: *Mary Jones, formerly Mary Smith.* Any examiner of the title will thus find a connected chain of title to the land. The grantor's marital status should be given: *bachelor, spinster, widow, widower, divorced and not remarried.* If the grantor is married, his spouse should also be named as grantor, and their marital status given: *John Smith and Mary Smith, his wife.* A married woman or widow should never be described as "Mrs. John Jones." Her legal name is "Mary Jones." Don't describe yourself as "R. John Smith." Legally your middle name or middle initial is no part of your name. Hence you should at least describe yourself as "Robert John Smith," for it is poor practice to use initials only in legal documents. If the state law requires, give the street address of the grantor and grantee. Special forms of deeds are used where the grantor is a corporation, trustee, executor, and so on. Of course all the landowners must convey if the buyer is to get good title, but different landowners may use different deeds. As a rule it is best for a husband and wife to join in the same deed.

3. Grantee. Have the proposed grantee write out his name on a slip of paper—

first name, middle initial, if any, and last name—and copy the name in this identical form in the proper place in the deed form. His or her marital status may, but need not, be given. State grantee's place of residence. If two or more persons are acquiring title, the names of all must be shown in the deed. If they are taking title as joint tenants, use a joint tenancy form deed. Legal stationers usually print a special form for joint tenancy transactions. Following the names of the grantees in this form is a phrase reading somewhat like this: *as joint tenants with the right of survivorship and not as tenants in common nor as tenants by the entireties.* When husband and wife are taking title, their marital relation should be shown, as *John Smith and Mary Smith,* his wife. If a corporation is taking title, its charter should be checked and the name copied exactly and without the slightest deviation. For example, if the charter describes a corporation as The Elite Hat Shop, Inc., do not omit the *The* and do not spell out the *Inc.* A deed to a trustee should clearly identify the trust. Never draft a deed running simply to *John Smith, as trustee.* Have the deed run to *John Smith, as trustee under Trust Agreement dated June 15, 1946, and known as the Pinecrest Liquidation Trust,* or other proper designation. Have before you the trust instrument creating the trust and describe it accurately in the deed. If the deed to the trustee also creates the trust, it is serving a double purpose. (1) It is operating as a deed of the land and must contain all the necessary elements of a deed. (2) It is creating a trust and must contain all the requisite elements for the creation of a trust. Such a document should be drafted only by one thoroughly conversant with the law of trusts.

The deed should conform to the contract of sale with respect to the grantees. For example, if A contracts to sell to *B* and *C*, A should not, even though *B* requests it, make a deed running to *B* only. That would violate C's rights and make A liable for damages if C suffers a loss.

If you are creating a corporation that is to acquire real estate, be sure that the corporation's charter has been issued and that all other formalities for corporate existence are complied with *before* the deed to the corporation is made out. In other words, be sure you have an existing, legal grantee to whom to convey.

4. Consideration. Let the deed recite a monetary consideration, as *in consideration of the sum of $10 and other good and valuable consideration.* In a few states, it is customary or necessary to recite the true sale price of the land. In deeds by corporations, trustees, executors, and so forth, the deed should recite the true sale price.

5. Words of grant. Every printed form of deed contains words of grant. It is not necessary to tamper with these, since the warranty deed form will have words appropriate for a warranty deed and the quitclaim deed form will also have appropriate words.

6. Description. Do not attempt to draft a description unless you are sure you know what you are doing. If a title policy, abstract, or Torrens certificate has been previously issued on the land that is being sold, and the land sold is identical with the tract mentioned in the title policy, abstract, or Torrens certificate (that is, there have been no subsequent conveyances of portions of the tract, and so forth), then the description may be copied from title policy, abstract caption, or Torrens certificate, since such documents usually contain accurate descriptions. After the description has been copied into the deed form, have someone read it aloud to you while you follow the description in the title policy, abstract, or Torrens certificate, since even a microscopic error in typing may throw the whole description off.

7. Subject clause. If the grantor in a warranty deed wishes to avoid personal liability, he should include in the subject clause all defects in title, such as mortgages, unpaid taxes, existing leases, restrictions, and so forth. However, the contract of sale usually specifies to what objections the title will be subject when conveyed to the buyer; the seller, in preparing the deed, has no right to add items to this list. For example, if the seller agrees, by his contract, to convey the land to the buyer subject only to a certain mortgage, he cannot include in the deed *subject to mortgage recorded as document No. 10356789 and also to restrictions of record.* The buyer has the right to object to the inclusion of the portion relating to the restrictions, since restrictions were not mentioned in the contract. In a quitclaim deed, a subject clause is unnecessary and inappropriate.

8. *Mortgages.* If the land is being sold subject to a mortgage that the grantee is to assume and agree to pay, let the deed so state.

SUGGESTED FORM: "Subject to a mortgage recorded in Book 100, Page 101, as Document No. 999, which the grantee herein assumes and agrees to pay."

Where the buyer is paying part cash and giving back to the seller either a mortgage or mortgage trust deed for part of the purchase money, it is better that the deed contain a recital somewhat as follows: "As part of the consideration for this transaction, the grantee herein has this day executed to __________, as trustee, a trust deed, of even date herewith, securing a promissory note in the sum of $__________, which represents part of the purchase price for said premises." This is particularly desirable where a mortgage deed of trust is involved, since if *A* sells and conveys land to *B*, and *B* simultaneously executes a mortgage trust deed to *C*, as trustee, the public records do not clearly show that the trust deed was given as part of the purchase price unless the deed contains the suggested recital. Of course the trust deed or mortgage should also contain a recital that "this trust deed is given to secure payment of part of the purchase price of said premises."

9. *Statement of purpose of deed.* Inexperienced conveyancers tend to put in deeds various legal-sounding phrases without having any clear idea of what purpose such phrases were intended to serve. This is a very dangerous practice. Do not insert a single syllable in a deed unless you are certain what the legal effect of that insertion will be. Remember that if you add in your deed phrases like "to be used for road purposes," the result may be to create a grant of an easement out of what started to be a deed of the land. It is neither necessary nor desirable to state in the deed the purpose for which the land is to be used.

10. *Restrictions and conditions.* Restrictions and conditions must be drafted with care. Because of the drastic consequences attendant upon the enforcement of a reverter clause, the grantee should view with suspicion any attempt to insert a reverter clause in the deed. If there is a written contract for the sale of the land, the grantor has no right to insert in the deed any restrictions or conditions not provided for in the contract. If the contract provides for a building restriction, but says nothing about a condition or reverter clause, the grantor has no right to provide in the deed for a reverter of title in the event of a breach of condition. Be sure you understand the words you use in drafting restrictions, as, for example, residence purposes, dwellings purposes, business purposes. Certain words have a well-known technical meaning, and if you use such words in a deed, courts will give them their usual meaning, regardless of what special, individual meaning they may have in your own mind. You will not even be allowed to testify that such a word has a special meaning for you. On the other hand, inexperienced draftsmen often use words that have no meaning at all, such as the provision that "only houses of standard construction shall be erected on said premises." It would be difficult to get two people to agree on the definition of "standard construction." Such a phrase is so devoid of meaning that courts cannot enforce it.

11. *Easements.* A deed may contain a grant to the grantee of an easement over other lands of the seller. If there is a written contract of sale, and it makes no mention of such an easement, the seller is under no obligation to include it in the deed. A deed may reserve to the grantor an easement over the land conveyed. If there is a written contract of sale, and it makes no mention of such an easement, the grantor has no right to insert such a clause in the deed.

12. *Waiver of dower and homestead.* Almost without exception, deed forms prepared by your local stationers include the necessary waivers of dower and homestead rights. For this and other reasons, it is dangerous to use a deed form printed in your state in conveying land lying in some other state. Obtain a form printed in the state where the land lies.

13. *Date.* It is the custom to date all deeds.

14. *Signature.* Before permitting the grantor to sign, have him write his name on a piece of paper. Check the spelling with the spelling of his name in the body of the deed. Be sure that the two correspond, since even trivial variations are frequently objected to by title examiners. Type the name of the grantor beneath the signature line and direct him to sign exactly as his name is typed.

15. *Seal.* If a seal is needed on deeds of land in your state, deed forms printed in your state will show a seal on the signature line. If there are more signatures on the deed than there are printed signature lines, be sure the word *Seal* appears after each signature. The corporate seal is always necessary on deeds made by corporations.

16. *Tax stamps.* The necessary tax stamps should be attached where the state law requires.

17. *Witnesses.* Always have two or more witnesses sign the deed if any grantor has signed by mark. If all grantors are able to write, their signatures need not be witnessed unless the state law requires witnesses. Some states require that all deeds be witnessed.

18. *Acknowledgment.*

19. *Recording.* File your deed in the proper public office immediately after it has been acknowledged. Delay may prove disastrous.

20. *Statutory requirements.* Make sure to comply with all applicable state laws relating to various recitations that are required to appear on the face of the deed, *i.e.*, compliance with local subdivision ordinances and plat acts, mailing address of the grantee, name and address of the person preparing the deed. Readiness avoids recording problems and delay.

21. *Take care in preparing the deed.* Erasures and alterations raise danger signals which proper draftsmanship and transcription should avoid. 1 *Merrill on Notice* 106.

RESERVED: §§ 178 to 186.

8

Acknowledgments

§ **187. Defined.** An acknowledgment is a formal declaration made before some public officer, usually a notary public, by a person who has signed a deed, mortgage, or other instrument, that the instrument is his voluntary act and deed. *In re McCauley's Adoption* 131 NW2d 174 (Neb. 1964). This ceremony is the act of acknowledgment.

§ **188. Certificate of acknowledgment.** The officer before whom this declaration is made attaches his certificate to the instrument or fills in the printed form of certificate that appears on virtually all deed and mortgage forms. This is known as the certificate of acknowledgment. It usually recites that the grantor appeared before the officer and acknowledged that he executed the instrument as his free and voluntary act and deed. However, the form of the certificate of acknowledgment varies considerably from state to state, and from situation to situation, *i.e.,* an acknowledgment taken from an individual differs from an acknowledgment taken from a corporate officer. It is important that the proper form be followed. *In re Viking Co., Inc.,* 389 F.Supp. 1230 (1974).

An acknowledgment must not be confused with an affidavit. An affidavit is a statement made under oath and put in writing. At the conclusion of the affidavit the officer, usually a notary, recites that it was subscribed and sworn to. An affidavit is not acceptable as a substitue for an acknowledgment. The two serve different purposes. *Hatcher* v. *Hall,* 292 SW2d 619 (Mo. 1956). The acknowledgment merely makes the *prima facie* showing that the instrument was duly executed. The affidavit or verification goes to the truth of the matters therein set forth. *D. J. Fair Lumber Co.,* v. *Karlin,* 430 P.2d 222 (Kan. 1967).

§ **189. Waiver of dower and homestead rights.** In some states the certificate of acknowledgment must specifically state that dower and homestead rights were understandingly relinquished.

§ **190. Necessity of acknowledgment.** In a few states, Arizona and Ohio, for example, an unacknowledged deed is not valid. In a number of states, certain types of instruments, such as deeds of married women or deeds or mortgages of homestead land, must be acknowledged. Other deeds, however, are legally valid though not acknowledged. This statement is without significance, since, as a practical matter, every deed or mortgage should be acknowledged. In the great majority of the states an unacknowledged instrument is not entitled to be recorded (59 ALR2d 1302), and an unrecorded title is a precarious one indeed. Lack of an acknowledgment on a deed may render title unmarketable. Other technical reasons make an acknowledgment a practical necessity.

§ 191. **Who may take an acknowledgment.** A deed or mortgage may be acknowledged before a notary public or some other officer designated by the local law. Such a person, it is said, *takes* the acknowledgment of the grantor. Generally, a notary who is an attorney is competent to take the acknowledgment of his client. 21 ALR3d 523. However, if the officer has any financial interest in the transaction, he is disqualified. For example, a grantee in a deed would be clearly disqualified from taking the grantor's acknowledgment. Other disqualified parties include the grantor in a deed, mortgagor and mortgagee in a mortgage, and the trustee in a trust deed. In some states, a stockholder of a corporation that is a party to the instrument is disqualified from taking the acknowledgment of the corporation. In other states the rule is the reverse.

§ 192. **Venue.** The venue of the certificate of acknowledgment is the caption, which is usually shown as follows:

STATE OF ILLINOIS }
                                } SS
COUNTY OF COOK }

The venue shows the place where the acknowldgment took place, that is, the place where the grantor appeared before the notary and made his formal declaration that the deed was his voluntary act.

§ 193. **Effect of invalidity of acknowledgment.** It is important to keep in mind the fact that invalidity of the *acknowledgment* does not make the *deed* void. However, in most states, a valid acknowledgment is essential for proper recording; that is, if the acknowledgment is void, the deed, though recorded, is treated as an unrecorded deed.

§ 194. **Foreign acknowledgments.** One who owns land located in a state other than that in which he resides, may sign and acknowledge a deed in the state of his residence. The acknowledgment will be valid if it conforms either to the law of the state of his residence or to the law of the state where the land lies. An acknowledgment taken outside of the state where the land lies is known as a *foreign acknowledgment*. In some states, it is required, either by custom or by law, that every acknowledgment taken outside of the state have attached thereto a certificate by a court clerk to the effect that the officer taking the acknowledgment was authorized by law to do so. This is known as a *certificate of authenticity*, or a *certificate of magistracy*. If the certificate goes on to recite that the acknowledgment is in due form, it is known as a *certificate of authenticity and conformity*, or *certificate of magistracy and conformity*.

§ **195. Date of certificate of acknowledgment.** The date of the certificate of acknowledgment is unimportant. Hence omission of the date of the certificate or insertion of an incorrect date will not invalidate the acknowledgment.

§ **196. Signature of officer taking acknowledgment.** The certificate of acknowledgment must be signed by the officer taking the acknowledgment. Otherwise it is not valid. The certificate should also show the official character of the person taking the acknowledgment, as Notary Public, Justice of the Peace, and so forth.

§ **197. Seal.** An acknowledgment taken by a notary public is usually invalid unless his official seal is placed on the certificate. The requirements as to seals of officers other than notaries vary from state to state.

§ **198. Date of expiration of commission.** Failure of the notary public to show the date his commission expires does not invalidate the certificate.

§ **199. False acknowledgment.** Both the notary public and the surety on his official bond will be liable for damages caused by the notary's willful misconduct, as where the notary falsely certifies to a forged mortgage and the mortgage is sold to an innocent purchaser. 44 ALR3d 555. The notary and his surety will also be liable when the notary's negligence causes damage, as when the notary acknowledges the signatures on a forged mortgage without knowing the parties who appear before him and without procuring any evidence or information as to their identity. 44 ALR3d 555.

REFERENCE ON CERTIFICATE OF ACKNOWLEDGMENT: 25 ALR2d 1124.

RESERVED: §§ 200 to 210.

9

Recording and Constructive Notice

§ 211. **Necessity of recording.** Every state has a recording law. These laws provide, in substance, that, until recorded, a deed, mortgage or other instrument is ineffective and void so far as subsequent purchasers or mortgagees of the same land are concerned. The policy behind these laws is that the ownership of real estate should be disclosed by the public records, and that purchasers of land should be able to rely on these records and should be protected against secret, unrecorded deeds and mortgages. Under these laws, although an unrecorded deed or mortgage is good and valid *as between the parties to the instrument,* the grantee or mortgagee is in great danger of losing his rights, because persons who deal with the real estate in ignorance of the unrecorded deed or mortgage will be protected against such unrecorded deed or mortgage.

EXAMPLE: A, the owner of certain vacant land, sells the same to *B* and gives *B* a deed, which *B* fails to record. Later A dies, and his heirs, not knowing that he had previously sold the land, deed the land to C, who records his deed. C purchases in ignorance of the earlier deed to *B*. C gets good title to the real estate. He is an *innocent purchaser* or *bona fide purchaser.*

§ 212. **Constructive notice from the records.** The recording laws have a double operation or effect. While they protect a purchaser or mortgagee who acts in ignorance of an earlier unrecorded deed or mortgage, they also provide that if a deed or mortgage is, in fact, recorded, it will be taken for granted that all persons who thereafter have occasion to deal with the tract of land do so with full knowledge of such recorded deed or mortgage. The courts will not permit a man to say that he acted in ignorance of a recorded deed or mortgage. Every purchaser or mortgagee of land, it is said, is *charged with notice* of prior recorded deeds and mortgages. The courts say that the public records impart to all subsequent purchasers and mortgages *constructive notice* of all prior recorded deeds and mortgages.

EXAMPLE: A conveys land to *B,* who records his deed. Thereafter A persuades C to buy the same land, telling C that he still owns the land. C fails to examine the public records relating to this tract of land. *C* acquires nothing. He has constructive notice of the deed to *B*.

§ 213. **Office where deeds are recorded.** The name of the officer charged with the duty of keeping the public records of deeds and mortgages varies from state to state. He is known variously as a recorder of deeds, county recorder, register of deeds, and registrar of deeds. For convenience, the officer in charge is hereinafter referred to as the *recorder,* and the public office where deeds are filed or recorded is referred to as the *recorder's office.*

§ 214. **What constitutes recording.** A person wishing to record a deed or mortgage simply deposits it with the recorder. Such a deed or mortgage is said to be filed for record. It is thereupon deemed to be recorded, and all the world must take notice of its existence. The recorder copies the document in his record books, indexes it, and returns the original to the person who left it for recording. He does not pass on the validity of the document.

§ 215. **Persons protected by recording laws.** The recording laws are designed primarily to protect subsequent *bona fide purchasers* of the land. A bona fide purchaser is one who has paid the purchase price in good faith and without knowledge of the prior unrecorded deed or mortgage. A mortgagee who loans money in reliance on the public records is also considered a bona fide purchaser and is entitled to the protection of the recording laws.

EXAMPLE: *A* mortgages his land to *B*, which mortgage is not recorded. Thereafter, *A* puts a mortgage on the same land to *C*, and *C* records his mortgage. *C* does not know of the earlier mortgage to *B*. *C* has a first mortgage on the land.

A number of states add the requirement that to be entitled to protection the subsequent purchaser or mortgagee must file his deed or mortgage for record before the recording of the earlier deed or mortgage. Under this rule, for example, it will not suffice that *A* has purchased a tract of land in good faith and in ignorance of an earlier unrecorded mortgage. He must also record his deed before the prior mortgage is recorded. But if he records his deed in apt time, *A* is protected even if the mortgagee later discovers his oversight and proceeds to record his mortgage.

In some states, a judgment creditor is also protected against prior unrecorded deeds and mortgages.

EXAMPLE: *R* makes a mortgage to *E* on November 15. The mortgage is recorded on November 20. On November 17, *X* obtains a judgment against *R*. The judgment enjoys priority of lien over the mortgage, since it was rendered prior to the recording of the mortgage.

A substantial number of states, however, do not extend such protection to judgment creditors.

A person who has acquired land by gift is not protected by the recording laws.

EXAMPLE: *R* mortgages his land to *E*. *E* fails to record the mortgage. *R* thereafter gives his daughter, *X*, a deed to the land as a gift, and *X* records her deed. *E* can nevertheless enforce the mortgage against her. But if, prior to the recording of the mortgage, *X* should sell the land to *Y*, *Y*, being a purchaser, would get good title free and clear of the prior, unrecorded mortgage.

A person who acquires title by will or as an heir of the landowner is not protected.

EXAMPLE: A makes a mortgage to *B*, which *B* fails to record. Thereafter A dies leaving a will whereby he gives this land to his son, C. *B* may enforce this mortgage against C.

§ **216. Instruments entitled to recording.** Deeds, mortgages, release deeds, satisfactions of mortgages, assignments of mortgages, and other instruments affecting the title to land should be recorded. However, it is only the original instrument that is entitled to be recorded. The recording of an unsigned carbon copy of an instrument is without legal effect. *Herzer* v. *Dembosz,* 167 NE2d 210 (Ill. 1960).

§ **217. Foreign language.** A deed or mortgage written in a foreign language, though valid as between the parties thereto, does not impart constructive notice and must be treated as an unrecorded document. *Moroz* v. *Ransom,* 285 N.Y.S. 846 (1936).

§ **218. Prerequisites to valid recording—defective instruments.** In a great majority of the states, an instrument must be properly acknowledged by the grantor or mortgagor in order to be entitled to recording. In a number of states, proper witnessing is accepted as a substitute for an acknowledgment. But, if the instrument is neither witnessed nor acknowledged, or the witnessing or acknowledgment is fatally defective, the instrument is not considered as a recorded instrument even though the recorder accepts it and copies it on the public records. 59 ALR2d 1299.

Since a purchaser or mortgagee is under no obligation to examine the records affecting lands other than those that he is buying or upon which he is loaning money, the record of an instrument that was intended to convey or affect the same but which has such an erroneous description that it does not appear to affect the land in question does not bind any subsequent purchaser, mortgagee, or judgment creditor.

EXAMPLE: A owns the West Half of the Northwest Quarter of Section 14, Township 38 North, Range 13 East of the Third Principal Meridian. A executes a mortgage to *B* that is intended as a mortgage on this same land but which, through inadvertence, describes the land as falling in Section 24 instead of Section 14. The mortgage is recorded. A person searching the records as to *A's* title has no way of knowing that this mortgage was intended for the particular land in question. Therefore this mortgage does not impart constructive notice, and subsequent purchasers, mortgagees, and judgment creditors will be protected against this mortgage. *Landis* v. *Miles Homes, Inc.,* 273 NE2d 153 (Ill. 1971).

§ **219. Chain of title.** Except in a few states a title searcher tracing title by means of the public records employs an official index of names, called the Grantor-Grantee Index. Suppose, for example, that the United States Government records show that the United States sold a particular tract of land to John Jones on March 15, 1840. The title searcher will turn to the Grantor Index, which is arranged alphabetically, and, beginning with the date March 15, 1840, he will look under the letter "J" for any deeds or mortgages made since March 15, 1840, by John Jones. Naturally he would not expect to find any deeds or mortgages of that land made by Jones prior to March 15, 1840, because Jones did not become the owner until that date. Therefore the law does not require him to look for any such deeds or mortgages prior to that date. Suppose he finds that John Jones conveyed the land to Joseph Smith by deed dated September 10, 1860, and recorded November 1, 1860. He will now look under the letter "S" for any deeds or mortgages made by Smith on or after September 10, 1860, the date when Smith acquired title. This process is repeated until he has brought the title down to the present. This process is called *running the chain of title.*

To be considered properly recorded, a deed or mortgage must be in the *chain of title,* that is, it must be dated in the proper chronological order.

EXAMPLES: At a time when his negotiations for the purchase were virtually concluded, Joseph Smith made a mortgage on the land dated September 5, 1860, and recorded September 6, 1860. Both of these dates were prior to the date of the deed by which Smith later acquired ownership, namely, September 10, 1860. A title searcher would not find this mortgage, since he would not look under the name "Smith" for any deed or mortgage prior to September 10, 1860. Such a mortgage is not in the line of title. It is also said that the mortgage is not in the *chain of title. The legal result is the same as though the mortgage had not been recorded at all.* A person buying the land not knowing of the existence of this mortgage would get good title free and clear of the mortgage.

In other words, the records show the ownership of land passing from one person to another, and the name of each successive owner as that name appears on the public records must be searched only during the period of his ownership as such period is revealed by the public records to see what recorded deeds and mortgages he has signed.

Because of the *chain of title theory,* it is important that names be spelled correctly in deeds and mortgages.

EXAMPLE: A deed runs to *John O. Malley* and a mortgage is thereafter made by *John O'Malley.* The mortgage is not in the chain of title and is treated as an unrecorded mortgage. The deed is indexed under *M,* the mortgage under O.

The chain of title theory is a two-edged sword. One, constructive notice is given of those instruments that are in the chain of title. Two, instruments outside of the chain of title do not impart constructive notice. *Pease* v. *Frank,* 105 NE 299 (Ill. 1914).

§ **220. Tract indexes.** In a few states (Iowa, Louisiana, Nebraska, North Dakota, Oklahoma, South Dakota, Utah, Wisconsin, and Wyoming, for example), the name index (Grantor-Grantee Index) has been supplemented by a Tract Index. This index allocates a separate page in the index to each piece of property in the county, and if you are interested in a particular piece of property, you simply locate the proper page in the index, where you will find listed all recorded deeds and other documents relating to this piece of property.

§ 221. **Record as notice of contents of deed or mortgage.** An instrument duly recorded is notice to subsequent purchasers and mortgagees not only of the instrument itself, but also of all of its contents.

EXAMPLE: A warranty deed contained a covenant that the premises were free and clear of all encumbrances "except a certain mortgage for $900." This mortgage had not been recorded. This was notice to the grantee and to all other persons of the existence of the mortgage.

§ 222. **Effect of actual knowledge.** Of course one who actually knows of a prior unrecorded deed or mortgage is not protected against it.

EXAMPLE: *A* makes a mortgage to *B*, which *B* fails to record. Thereafter, *A* mortgages the land to *C*, who knows of the existence of the earlier mortgage. *C* takes subject to the earlier unrecorded mortgage.

Similarly, where a subsequent purchaser takes with *actual knowledge* of an instrument which was recorded, but because of some defect, does not impart *constructive notice,* no bona fide purchaser protection attaches. 3 ALR2d 589.

EXAMPLE: *P*, a purchaser, obtained a title report which raised a defectively recorded deed to *X*. This deed, though taken by the recorder did not legally give constructive notice because it bore no acknowledgment. *P* will not be a bona fide purchaser and will take subject to *X*'s right. 59 ALR2d 1318.

§ 223. **Possession as notice.** The law requires every prospective purchaser or mortgagee to examine into the possession of the real estate and to ascertain what rights are claimed by the parties in possession. Whether or not he actually does make this inspection, such purchaser or mortgagee is deemed to know the facts that such an investigation would have disclosed. In other words, possession imparts constructive notice in much the same way as the recording of a deed.

EXAMPLE: *R* sells and conveys his home to *E*. *E* fails to record the deed but moves into the house. *R* offers to sell the land to *X*. *X* examines the records in the recorder's office and finds title in *R*, but he fails to examine into the possession of the premises. He takes a deed from *R*. This deed passes no title. *E*'s possession gave *X* constructive notice of this deed.

It is obvious that failure to record or a defective recording of a deed is usually less dangerous than the failure to record or the defective recording of a mortgage. This follows, since the purchaser usually goes into possession of the land after receiving his deed, and this possession gives all the world notice of his rights, whereas a mortgagee rarely goes into possession before a default has been made and is therefore entirely dependent on the public records to give other persons notice of his rights.

In a few states, South Carolina and Virginia, for example, possession does not impart constructive notice.

§ 224. **Liens that need not be recorded.** There are certain liens, such as real estate tax liens, inheritance tax liens, and franchise tax liens, that are binding on all persons though not recorded.

RESERVED: §§ 225–235.

10

Brokers and Managers

§ **236. Defined.** A broker is an agent employed in negotiating the sale, purchase, or exchange of land. Compensation is usually in the form of a commission payable only if a deal is successfully signed up.

§ **237. License.** In many states, a person is not authorized to act as a real estate broker unless he first produces a broker's license. Real estate brokerage is a profession requiring knowledge, experience, and honesty, and in order to obtain a license, a candidate must have the qualifications that are specified by the local law. In order for a real estate broker to recover commissions, he must have his license at the time he is hired to perform the services for which he claims a commission. *Schoene* v. *Hickham,* 397 SW2d 596 (1966). The rule that unlicensed brokers cannot recover a commission is applied quite strictly. Thus, if it can be shown that the broker has agreed to divide his commission with some unlicensed person, the broker will be unable to collect a commission. *Freeman* v. *Greaves,* 80 Ohio App. 341, 74 NE2d 860 (1947). But to make the deal possible, the broker can share his commission with the buyer. 63 ALR3d 1211. This is unobjectionable.

§ **238. Salesmen.** Virtually every brokerage office maintains a staff of salesmen, who do the actual leg work of showing houses and filling in sales contract forms. A salesman is required to have a state license and pass a state exam, but the exam is less comprehensive than the broker's exam. In recent times the broker makes a determined effort to establish the relation between himself and a salesman as that of *independent contractor.* There is a distinction between an *employee,* who must take orders from his employer, and an independent contractor, who is hired to do a job, *but does it pretty much his own way.* The objective is to avoid the employer-employee relationship, so that the broker need not withhold income taxes, and so forth. There seem to be no decided cases on this new idea. Problems may arise. Salesmen often go to the "boss" on complex deals, and as soon as he starts giving directions he may become an *employer.* But the whole idea is untested. 41 Am.J.2d 735. No doubt many real estate offices prefer the employer-employee relationship. This, of course, gets the employer involved in income tax withholdings, and so forth. In any event, whatever the legal relationship is, courts are bound to hold the broker liable for fraudulent representations made by his salesmen.

§ 239. **Necessity for contract of employment.** A real estate broker acts as an *agent*. The person who hires him is known as the *principal*. Usually the broker is hired by the landowner for the purpose of procuring a buyer. In return for finding a buyer willing to buy on the landowner's terms, the broker receives a commission from the landowner. Occasionally the broker is hired by a person wishing to buy real estate. In either case, in order to recover a commission, the broker must be able to show that he was hired by the person from whom he claims a commission. If he claims a commission from the seller, he must show that the seller hired him. And if he was hired by the buyer only, he cannot claim a commission from the seller. Otherwise stated, a broker must show that the person from whom he claims a commission employed him to make the sale. However, an employment contract of agency may be *implied* from the conduct of the parties.

EXAMPLE: *A*, a landowner, gave *B*, a broker, a description of his property and requested that *B* sell it at a designated price. This is a contract of employment as agent, and *B* is entitled to a commission if he finds a buyer. The fact that compensation was not discussed is immaterial. *A* must have understood that *B* would expect to be paid if he produced a buyer. *Long* v. *Herr,* 10 Colo. 380, 15 Pac. 802 (1887).

EXAMPLE: *A*, a real estate broker, without any prior request from *B*, the landowner, submitted to *B* an offer of $3000 for the purchase of the land. *B* declined, stating that his price for the land was $4000. *A* thereupon procured a buyer who was willing to buy for $4000. *B* refused to sell. *B* is not liable for a commission. The mere statement by a landowner that he will take a certain sum for his land is not sufficient to authorize the person to whom the statement is made to act as agent for its sale. *B* is entitled to assume that *A* is acting for the buyer and will look to the buyer for his compensation. *O'Donnell* v. *Carr,* 189 N.C. 77, 126 SE 112 (1925).

As is evident from the foregoing illustrations, a broker usually tries to collect from the seller. This is due to the obvious fact that it is financially easier to collect money from the seller, who after all is being paid the purchase price of the property, than from the buyer, who may be stretching his finances in order to buy the property. Legally, the fact remains that the broker cannot collect from the seller unless he can show that the seller hired him. If there is no formal listing contract, at the very least the seller must say or do things that make the broker believe he has been hired by the seller. *Reeve* v. *Shoemaker,* 200 Ia. 938, 205 NW 742 (1925). Or the broker must so conduct himself that it is clear to the seller that he expects to be paid a commission. *Korzendorfer Realty Inc.* v. *Hawkes,* 178 SE2d 524 (Va. 1971).

EXAMPLE: Suppose in the EXAMPLE last given, the broker had asked, "When will my commission be paid?" Suppose the owner had replied, "At closing." This is enough to show a contract of employment.

§ 240. **Persons who may employ a broker.** A person other than the property owner may list the property for sale and become liable for a commission. 12 Am Jur.2d *Brokers* § 163, p. 902.

EXAMPLE: *W* owned certain real estate. *H,* her husband, listed the property for sale with *B,* a broker, who knew that *W* owned the property. *B* found a buyer for the property, but *W* refused to sell. *H* was held liable to *B* for a full commission. *B* was entitled to assume that at the proper time *H* would procure *W*'s consent to the sale. *Aler* v. *Plowman,* 190 Md. 631, 59 A2d 196 (1948); *Rose* v. *Knoblock,* 194 SW2d 943 (Mo. 1946).

EXAMPLE: The land was held in community property but the husband alone signed the listing. He is liable for the full commission. *C. Forsman Real Estate* Co. v. *Hatch,* 547 P2d 1116 (Idaho).

EXAMPLE: Property was owned by *H* and *W,* husband and wife, in joint tenancy. *H* alone without *W*'s permission, listed the property for sale with *X,* a real estate broker. *X* found a buyer for the property, but *W* refused to sign the contract of sale and the deal fell through. *H* was held liable to *X* for a full commission. 10 ALR3d 665.

§ 241. **Necessity for written contract.** Because of the endless litigation that has arisen concerning the existence of an employment contract, in many states the contract of employment must be in writing in order for the broker to be entitled to a commission and must state the amount of commission agreed on. 9 ALR2d 747.

§ 242. **Form of contract.** Often the hiring of a broker is an informal, oral affair. However, written contracts, called *listing contracts,* are also used. These are usually brief documents, often in the form of printed cards. When such a form is filled in, it contains the following: (1) names of seller and broker; (2) description of property, usually by street address. 30 ALR3d 935; (3) terms of sale, including sale price, whether sale is for cash or on terms, and so forth; (4) duration of broker's employment; (5) commission to be paid; (6) special agreements, such as the provision for an exclusive agency.

§ 243. **Statutes and regulations.** In a number of states (Illinois and Oklahoma, for example) there are statutes or regulations requiring the listing to state a specific ending date.

§ 244. **Unconscionability.** The new law requires the broker to use a listing form that is fair to the party employing him. Unconscionability and the Real Estate Broker's Employment Contract, 5 *Memphis S.U.L.Rev.* 59.

§ 245. **Real estate board forms.** Each of the countless real estate boards is likely to have its own listing form.

§ 246. **Flat fee sales.** A new type of brokerage contract has made its appearance.

NEW DIRECTIONS: The flat-fee broker competes with the regular commission broker. He charges a flat fee to the seller, which is much smaller than the regular broker's commission. He gives the seller an appraisal of his house and a FOR SALE sign, and displays a photo of the house and a fact sheet in his office. The homeowner must show and sell the house himself. There is no multiple listing service. The disadvantages are that home-

owners do not know how to sell their homes or get financing for the buyer. It is workable when there is a great scarcity of houses. If a sharp speculator shows up as a buyer, the seller is likely to lose.

§ 247. **Contract provisions.** Quite commonly a *contract of sale* will contain a provision that a commission will be paid by the seller to the broker at closing. Even if there is no proof of a *contract of employment,* this contract clause suffices to make the seller liable to the broker. *Moran* v. *Audette,* § 217 A2d 663 (D.C. 1966); *B. Woodworth* v. *Vranizen,* 539 P2d 1055 (Ore. 1975). The broker is what the lawyers call a "third party beneficiary." Of course, the broker's rights rest on the terms of the contract.

EXAMPLE: **The contract of sale provided that the seller would pay the broker a commission at closing. This contract, however, was contingent on the buyer's ability to obtain financing. The buyer was unable to obtain financing. The broker collects no commission. *Shumaker* v. *Lear,* 235 Pa. Super. 509.**

§ 248. **Code of Ethics.** Many controversies involving brokers, especially those involving conflicts between two brokers, are settled by resort to the Code of Ethics established by the National Association of Realtors or by some local real estate board. Punishments are given according to the nature of the offense—the most severe being expulsion from the board. This cuts the broker from the multiple listing service maintained by the board, and is an effective punishment indeed.

EXAMPLE: **A broker was punished for failure to observe a sign indicating that a rezoning of the land was imminent. As a result, the lot was sold for one-eighth of its market value.**

§ 249. **Open listing.** There are several different types of listing contracts. The *open listing* contains no provision forbidding the landowner to sell the land himself or to hire other brokers, and ordinarily an owner may hire two or more brokers unless he specifically agrees not to do so. *Kelly* v. *Beaudoin,* 298 A2d 831 (Vt. 1972). Virtually all informal, verbal listing arrangements are open listings. The disadvantage of this type of contract is that it is likely to produce quarrels over the commission where several brokers produce buyers.

EXAMPLE: **A, a landowner, employed a broker to obtain a purchaser. The broker obtained a purchaser on the specified terms, but A refused to pay a commission on the ground that he had already concluded an agreement to sell to a purchaser obtained by another broker. The broker sued A. The court held for A. The primary object to be attained in the employment of agents to sell real estate, the court said, is the production of a single purchaser for such real estate, and that object is attained where one of several agents produces to the owner a purchaser who is ready, able, and willing to buy the real estate on the owner's terms. Where several agents are employed, the sale of the property either by the owner in person, or by any of the brokers, operates at once to terminate the authority of all the brokers, although they had no actual notice of the sale. This is a provision the court "reads into" every open listing.**

When different brokers have the property for sale, and no one of them has the exclusive right to make the sale, the broker who first finds a buyer ready, able, and willing to buy is the procuring cause of the sale and is the one entitled to the commission.

§ 250. **Exclusive agency.** Unless there is an agreement to the contrary, the landowner may hire two or more brokers to sell the same property and will be liable only to the broker who first finds a buyer. Fear that time and money spent in locating a buyer may be wasted if another broker is working on the deal has led brokers to favor a listing contract which assures the broker that as long as his employment continues no other broker will be hired. Such a listing is called an *exclusive agency.* The giving of an exclusive agency does not bar the landowner from selling the property through his own efforts, without the assistance of other brokers. If the property owner sells the property through his own efforts, the exclusive agency automatically comes to an end, without any liability on the landowner's part for a commission and regardless of the employment period specified in the listing contract. *Martin Realty Co.* v. *Fletcher,* 103 N.J.L. 294, 136 Atl. 498 (1927); *Des Rivieres* v. *Sullivan,* 247 Mass. 443, 142 NE 111, 88 ALR2d 936. This is a provision the court "reads into" the listing.

The mere fact that the listing contract refers to the broker as an *exclusive agent* is enough to create an exclusive agency. *Harris and White* v. *Stone,* 137 Ark. 23, 207 SW 443 (1918).

§ 251. **Exclusive right to sell.** The *exclusive right to sell* goes one step further than the exclusive agency. It not only makes the broker the sole agent of the landowner for the sale of the property, but also provides that the named broker will receive a commission in the event the property is sold by the named broker, by the owner, *or by anyone else.* Thus, even if the owner makes a sale through his own efforts, he must pay the broker, *Bourgoin* v. *Fortier,* 310 A2d 618 (Me. 1973); *Flynn* v. *La Salle Nat. Bank,* 9 Ill.2d 129, 137 NE2d 71; 88 ALR2d 941.

A broker who desires an exclusive right to sell should draft his listing contract with great care. Thus it has been held that a listing contract giving the broker the *exclusive sale* of a parcel of land creates an exclusive agency, not an exclusive right to sell. *Roberts* v. *Harrington,* 168 Wis. 217, 169 NW 603 (1918). Other courts have held that such language creates an exclusive right to sell. *Harris* v. *McPherson,* 97 Conn. 164, 115 Atl. 723 (1922). Again, it has even been held that a contract that gives the broker the *exclusive right to sell* merely creates an exclusive agency. *Sunnyside Land & Inv. Co.* v. *Bermier,* 119 Wash. 386, 205 Pac. 1041 (1922); *Hedges Co.* v. *Shanahan,* 195 Ia. 1302, 190 NW 957 (1922). These courts feel that, to create a true exclusive right to sell, the contract must in unequivocal terms negate the right of the landowner to sell the property himself. 88 ALR2d 948. However, other courts feel that a contract granting the broker an exclusive right to sell means just what it says. *Torrey & Dean, Inc.* v. *Coyle,* 138 Ore. 509, 7 P2d 561 (1932); *Piatt & Heath Co.* v. *Wilmer,* 87 Mont. 382, 288 Pac. 1021 (1930). The better reasoning appears to lie with the courts that require unequivocal language. Mere use of the phrase *ex-*

clusive right to sell does not convey to the average person's mind the notion that it involves a surrender by the landowner of the right to make a sale through his own efforts.

SUGGESTION TO BROKER: Let the listing read that commission is payable to broker if the land is sold during the life of the listing by the broker, the landowner, or any other person whatever.

Occasionally the landowner cannot resist the temptation to negotiate secretly with his own property during the existence of the listing, often with the broker's prospect. He then signs the contract of sale the day after the listing expires. The broker collects no commission. *Simank Realty Inc.* v. *De Marco,* 6 Cal. App.3rd 610, 46 *L. A. Bar Bull.* 67. (But see §§ 256 and 258.)

SUGGESTION TO BROKER: Let the listing read that the broker is entitled to a commission on a sale to any person with whom negotiations took place during the term of the listing.

§ 252. **Multiple listing.** Multiple listing is simply a means by which brokers in a given area pool their efforts to sell properties listed with any member of the pool. 45 ALR3d 190. The original, or *listing broker* obtains from the property owner an exclusive right to sell. He then furnishes a copy thereof to all members of this pool, or this is done through a central office. If any member other than the original broker sells the property, the commission is divided between the original broker and the *selling broker* who effects the sale. In some systems the central registration office shares in the commission also. Only the original broker has the right to sue the property owner for a commission. The property owner has no contract of employment with members of the pool other than the original broker. Therefore he can neither be sued by them, *Goodwin* v. *Gleck,* 139 Cal. App. 2d 936, 294 P2d 192 (1956), nor is he liable for misrepresentations made by them. 58 ALR2d 41. However, the members of the pool working on the sale, owe the landowner the usual duties of a broker such as loyalty. *Frisell* v. *Newman,* 429 P2d 64 (Wash. 1967).

Since multiple listing systems may either fix a commission rate or specify a recommended rate, they have come under fire as violations of the antitrust laws. 70 *Columb. L. Rev.* 1325; 60 Ill. B.J. 856. Court decrees have been entered prohibiting fixing of commission rates.

A real estate board that has operated a multiple listing system, limiting the persons who could be admitted to membership, has been held to violate the antitrust laws. *Grillo* v. *Board of Realtors,* 219 A2d 635 (1966).

§ 253. **Performance required of broker.** Suppose that *A* contracts with *B* to perform some act for *A,* such as building a house. *A* will pay *B* a stated sum for such performance of the contract. *B* has earned the contract price when he has completed performance of the contract. The same is true of a broker. He has earned his commission only when he has completed performance of a task he has undertaken. Thus, generally a broker has earned his commission when he produces a buyer who is ready, able, and willing to buy on either the terms specified by the seller in the listing contract, or on other terms acceptable to the seller. *Bonanza Real Estate Inc.* v. *Crouch,* 517 P2d 1371 (Wash. 1974).

EXAMPLE: A the landowner, hires *B* a broker, to find a buyer. *B* finds a prospect *C*, who signs a contract at less than the price asked by the seller. A and C negotiate until they agree on a price. *B* helps in the negotiations, and therefore earns his commission.

At times, the broker may submit a contract signed by the buyer for the full contract price requested by the seller. Such a contract is a mere *offer to buy.* Until the seller signs it also, he is not bound to the contract. The broker has performed what he was hired to do, and therefore has earned a commission even if the seller changes his mind and refuses to sign the contract.

Likewise, if the seller and buyer reconsider after a contract of sale has been signed, causing the deal to be cancelled, the seller remains liable to the broker. 74 ALR2d 459. Also, if the buyer has signed a contract which the seller has also signed, and thereafter refuses to complete the deal, the broker has nevertheless earned his commission. 74 ALR2d 443.

The word *able* in the phrase "ready, able, and willing to buy" refers to financial ability. The buyer must be able to command the necessary funds to close the deal within the time required. *Pellaton* v. *Brunski,* 69 Cal. App. 301, 231 Pac. 583 (1924). He must have the sum of money necessary to meet any cash payment required, and be financially able to meet any further payments. *Raynor* v. *Mackrill,* 196 Ia. 1298, 164 NW 335 (1917). Otherwise stated, he must have the present ability to pay. *Boutelle* v. *Chrislaw,* 35 Wis. 2d 665, 150 NW2d 486 (1967). Thus, a newly organized corporation having limited funds might be considered not *able* to buy. However, it is not necessary to show that the buyer is standing outside the office door with all cash in hand. It is sufficient if the buyer is *able* to command the necessary funds on reasonable notice. *Perper* v. *Edell,* 160 Fla. 447, 35 So2d 387 (1948). Thus, a buyer is *able* to buy if he has already arranged with some mortgage house to loan him the funds necessary to pay for the property. *Schaaf* v. *Iba,* 73 Ohio L.Abs. 46, 136 NE2d 727 (1955). To *produce* a willing buyer requires that the broker must reveal his identity to the seller. 2 ALR3d 1128.

A *willing* buyer is one who is willing to enter into an unconditional cash sale contract enforceable against the buyer at the time it is signed by the parties. Or, if the contract is *conditional* the buyer becomes a *willing* buyer (willing to be personally liable to the seller) only when the condition is performed.

This point is of great importance because most residential contracts contain the condition that the contract is contingent on the buyer's ability to obtain financing. It is normal and expected that the broker will tender a contract signed by the buyer that differs from the contract called for by the listing contract. Once this takes place, the broker's rights rest on the terms of the contract he tendered, and was accepted by the seller. If the contingency inserted by the buyer is his ability to obtain financing, the broker's right to a commission depends on the buyer's ability to obtain financing. *Schumaker* v. *Lear,* 235 Pa. Super 509. However, since every contract by implication requires a good faith effort on each party to perform, the buyer must make a good faith effort to obtain financing. If he fails to do so, this condition drops out of the contract and the buyer is unconditionally liable to the seller. Hence the broker has earned his commission.

EXAMPLE: If the buyer needs a large loan in order to complete the sale, he may insist that the sale contract allow him to cancel the contract if within a specified period of time he is unable to procure the required loan. Since such a contract does not impose unqualified liability on the buyer, the broker is entitled to a commission only if the buyer gets the necessary loan. *Cooper* v. *Liberty Nat. Bank,* 332 Ill. App. 459, 75 NE2d 769 (1947); *Slonim, Ltd.* v. *Bankers Mortgage & Realty Co.,* 133 N.J.L. 45, 42 A2d 396 (1945).

There are numerous other examples that illuminate the matter of the *willing* buyer.

EXAMPLE: The broker procured a purchaser who signed a contract with seller contingent on obtaining plat approval by the buyer. The city refused to approve the buyer's plat. The broker had earned no commission. *Larkins* v. *Richardson,* 502 P2d 1156 (Ore. 1972).

EXAMPLE: No commission is payable if the buyer is willing to sign only an installment contract. 8 ALR2d 382. But, if the *seller* also is willing to sign the installment contract with the buyer, the broker earns his commission when the first installment is paid unless the contract provides otherwise. 8 ALR2d 382. The seller must act in good faith.

EXAMPLE: Seller's broker procured a buyer who signed a contract contingent on buyer's ability to procure financing within a set time. Before the time expired, the seller sold the land to third party. The broker recovers his commission because the seller acted in bad faith. *Wuadrant Corp.* v. *Spake,* 504 P2d 1162 (Wash. 1973).

But when the broker procures a purchaser ready, willing, and able to purchase on the authorized terms, and through the fault of the *owner* the sale is not consummated, the broker is entitled to a commission. Thus, the broker is entitled to a commission:

1. When the deal falls through because the owner changes his mind and refuses to sign the deed to the purchaser or a contract to sell. The rule is the same where the land has increased in value and the owner rejects the broker's buyer for this reason. If the seller refuses to sign, giving as his only reason the fact that he has changed his mind, he cannot thereafter shift his ground and claim that the buyer's offer was not in compliance with the listing. *Russell* v. *Ramm,* 200 Cal. 348, 254 Pac. 532 (1927).

2. When the deal falls through because the owner's wife refuses to sign the contract or deed. 10 ALR3d 665. This assumes state law requires her signature.

3. When the deal falls through because of defects in the owner's title. *Triplett* v. *Feasal,* 105 Kan. 179, 182 Pac. 551 (1919).

4. When the deal falls through because of the owner's fraud. *Hathaway* v. *Smith,* 187 Ill. App. 128.

5. When the deal falls through because the owner is unable to deliver possession within a reasonable time.

6. When the deal falls through because the seller insists on terms and provisions not mentioned in the listing contract, as where the seller insists on the right to remain in possession after the deal has been closed. *Brown* v. *Ogle,* 75 Ind. App. 90, 130 NE 147 (1927).

7. When after the contract of sale has been signed the seller and buyer get together and cancel the contract. *Steward* v. *Brock,* 60 N.M. 216, 290 P2d 682 (1955).

8. When the deal falls through because the buyer cannot procure financing and the contract is not contingent on ability to procure financing.

However, if the seller signs a contract with the broker's buyer, the fact that the terms differ from those set forth in the listing is unimportant. *Adelman* v. *Caputi,* 181 SE2d 608 (Va. 1971).

If a binding contract is entered into, the broker is entitled to his commission even though the buyer refuses to pay the purchase price. The owner is not required to accept a buyer produced by a broker without opportunity for investigation as to his ability to comply with the terms of the contract, but where he does accept such purchaser, it is a determination by him of the purchaser's ability to perform the contract, and if the purchaser fails to perform the contract, the owner cannot defeat the broker's commission on the ground that the purchaser was not able to buy the property. 74 ALR2d 454.

§ 254. Ellsworth Dobbs:

There is some thinking very recently that since the broker is so much better informed as to the buyer's financial ability to consummate the deal, if the deal falls through because the buyer cannot command the necessary financial resources, the seller should not be liable for a commission. *Ellsworth Dobbs Inc.* v. *Johnson,* 50 N.J. 528, 236 A2d 843 (1967).

REFERENCES: On *Ellsworth Dobbs Inc.* v. *Johnson:* 9 *Ariz. L.Rev.* 519; 17 *Catholic U. L.Rev.* 487; 72 *Dick. L.Rev.* 522; 19 *Mercer L.Rev.* 460; 30 *Ohio St. L.J.* 600; 23 *Rutgers L.Rev.* 83; 13 *Vill. L.Rev.* 681; 10 *W.&M. L.Rev.* 240.

NEW CASES: Cases following *Ellsworth Dobbs* are *Tristram's Landing Inc.* v. *Wait,* 327 NE2d 727 (Mass. 1975) and *Shumaker* v. *Lear,* 345 A2d 249 (Pa. 1975). Predictably, this case will become law throughout the country because it squares with the normal expectation of the parties.

In addition to the cases that directly follow *Ellsworth Dobbs,* one can count Rhode Island (*Gartner* v. *Higgins,* 100 R.I. 285, 288, 214 A2d 849, 851 [1965]), the District of Columbia (*Moore* v. *Burke,* 45 A2d 285 [1946]) and Alabama (*Taylor Real Estate & Ins. Co.* v. *Greene,* 274 Ala. 694, 151 So. 2d 397 [1963]) as basically following *Ellsworth Dobbs* thinking. Colorado has the rule by statute. Idaho, Connecticut, Vermont and New York have indicated they will follow *Ellsworth Dobbs. 5 Memphis State U.L. Rev. 59, 71.*

Performance continued. The broker is entitled to no compensation or reimbursement whatever for unsuccessful efforts to sell unless the listing contract expressly so provides.

Often after a seller has listed property with a broker, and after the broker has found a buyer who is ready, able, and willing to buy at the listed price, the seller changes his mind and looks for some way to turn down the buyer without being liable to the broker for a commission. Such a seller seeks to take refuge behind the rule that if the terms offered by the broker's prospect differ from the terms specified by the seller, the broker is not entitled to a commission. 18 ALR2d 376. This is obvious where the broker's prospect offers less than the seller's listing price, or offers to buy on an installment contract where the seller's listing contemplates a cash deal. But in addition, keep in mind that if the broker's listing contract is silent on other terms of the transaction, the law will read various implications into it. And if the terms of sale as set forth in the contract of sale do no harmonize with the terms of sale set forth *or implied* in the listing contract, the seller may reject the broker's prospect without incurring any liability for commission.

EXAMPLE: If the broker's listing is silent, the seller is required to convey only the land, building, and articles that are technically fixtures. If the contract of sale tendered by the broker requires the seller to convey furniture or other personal property, the seller may reject the contract without any liability for commission. *Sharkey* v. *Snow,* 300 NE2d 279 (Ill. 1973).

However, customary contract provisions, like those requiring a seller to have good title, are unobjectionable. *Adelman* v. *Caputi,* 181 SE2d 608 (Va. 1971).

§ 255. **"No deal, no commission" provision.** While ordinarily the broker has earned his commission as soon as he has found a buyer who is ready, able, and willing to buy, the parties may validly contract, by means of the so-called *no deal, no commission clause* inserted in the listing contract, that payment of the commission is contingent upon the closing of the deal and full payment of the purchase price to the seller. Thus, if the seller cannot clear his title, or if the buyer refuses to go through with the deal, the seller need not pay a commission. 74 ALR2d 437. However, if the seller's refusal to complete the sale is arbitrary and without reasonable cause or in bad faith, the broker is entitled to his commission. *Huntley* v. *Smith,* 153 Minn. 297, 190 NW 341 (1922); *Goldstein* v. *Rosenberg,* 331 Ill. App. 374, 73 NE2d 171 (1947).

In effect, the *Ellsworth Dobbs* case makes every broker's listing contingent on the procuring of financing by the buyer. Also, it is a rule of some real estate boards that no commission is to be collected unless the deal closes.

§ 256. **Procuring cause of sale.** A broker who has been hired by the landowner has earned his commission when his efforts were the primary and procuring cause of the sale. When the owner or several brokers have been active and a sale is concluded, a broker, to justify his claim to a commission, must show that he was the efficient cause of the sale. The following are typical situations in which the problem arises:

1. The broker finds a prospect and introduces him to the owner. Thereupon the owner and the prospect, without the broker's intervention, negotiate and conclude a sale. The broker is the procuring cause of the sale and is entitled to a commission. *Ranney* v. *Rock,* 135 Conn. 479, 66 A2d 111 (1949).

2. When several brokers are involved, the rule appears to be substantially this: If

the first broker's efforts result in a disagreement or if negotiations are abandoned, and thereafter a second broker steps in and brings the parties together, the second broker is the procuring cause of the sale. 46 ALR2d 865. But if the first broker brings about a substantial agreement, and the second broker merely works out details of the transaction, the first broker is the procuring cause of the sale. In other words, the broker whose efforts predominate in bringing about the sale gets the commission.

There are cases where the broker is entitled to damages or compensation even though he has not been the procuring cause of the sale: (1) For example, in the case of an exclusive agency, the broker will be entitled to compensation from his employer if the employer hires another broker, who succeeds in selling the property, because the employer breached his contract, which obligated him to refrain from hiring other brokers. This exposes the seller to payment of two commissions. 29 ALR3d 1229. (2) Also, in the case of an exclusive right to sell, the broker may be entitled to compensation even if his employer sells the building through his own efforts. Here the employer has breached his contract not to try to sell the building through his own efforts. *Bell* v. *Demmerling,* 149 Ohio St. 165, 78 NE2d 49 (1948). (3) Or the listing contract may provide that the broker will be entitled to compensation if the property is sold to a person with whom the broker *has negotiated,* or *whose name has been furnished the seller* by the broker. Here a broker who engages in negotiations with a prospect collects even though the deal is ultimately clinched by the landowner himself or another broker. *Delbon* v. *Brazil,* 134 Cal. App.2d 461, 285 P2d 710 (1955).

SUGGESTION TO BROKER: Let the listing contract provide that broker will be entitled to a commission if within the specified time the property is sold to a person with whom the broker negotiated. 51 ALR3d 1149.

§ 257. Effect of seller's ignorance that buyer was procured by broker. When a seller hires a broker to sell his property, and thereafter sells the property to a buyer procured by the broker, in most states the broker is entitled to a commission despite the fact that the seller is ignorant that the buyer was procured through the broker. *Ranney* v. *Rock,* 135 Conn. 479, 66 A2d 111 (1949); 142 ALR 275. Having hired a broker, the seller should know that the appearance of a buyer may have been caused by the broker. The seller should check with his *broker* whenever a prospective buyer comes in. Inquiring of the *buyer* is rather pointless, for obviously many buyers, hoping to get a reduced price, will conceal the fact that a broker interested them in the property. Suppose, however, that *A,* a landowner, hires *B,* a broker, and *B* interests *C* in the purchase of the property. *C* procures a dummy or strawman, *D,* to make an offer for the property. *A* inquires of *B* if *B* had interested *D* in the purchase of the property. Not knowing that *D* is only a nominee for *C, B* says no, and *A* cuts his price by the amount of the commission he would have paid to *B. B* gets no commission. *A* has done all he could to protect his broker. *Zetlin* v. *Scher,* 217 A2d 266 (Md. 1966).

If the seller reduces his price to a prospect in ignorance of the fact that the prospect was procured by the seller's broker, some states, as above stated, allow the broker to collect his commission. The seller is at fault because he failed to check with the broker. Other states refuse the broker a commission. 46 ALR2d 872, 877. These latter states feel that the broker should notify the seller of each prospect he procures.

SUGGESTION TO BROKER: As soon as you find a prospect, send a postcard to the seller notifying him of the name and address of the prospect you have found.

The broker can collect damages from a buyer who attempts to cheat him out of a commission.

EXAMPLE: *V* hired *B*, a broker, and *B* interested *P* in the purchase of the property. *P* then contacted *V* directly and got *V* to cut his price. He did this by representing to *V* that no broker was involved. *V*, feeling he would not be paying a commission, cut his price. *B* discovers this. He can sue *P* for damages. 29 ALR3d 1251. *P* was guilty of a wrongful interference with a business relationship.

Quite often in cases like the example last given, the buyer is aware of the broker's rights. He meets with the seller. They arrange with another broker to pretend to procure a dummy buyer, at a higher price, of course. This deprives the first broker of his commission. If the first broker learns of this conspiracy, as he will when he sees his prospect take possession, he can sue the buyer for interfering with his contractual relations with his seller. 29 ALR3d 1246. For similar reasons, he can sue the seller and the second broker. 97 ALR 1275, 146 ALR 1419. Such liability is called *tort liability*. A "*tort*" is a wrongful act.

EXAMPLE: The seller's broker found a buyer, and a contract of sale was signed. The seller and buyer contrived a phony termination of the contract in order to swindle the broker. Both are liable to the broker. *Seno* v. *Franke*, 16 Ill. App. 2d 39, 147 NE2d 469 (1957); *Allen* v. *Powell*, 248 Cal. App. 2d 502, 29 ALR3d 1218 (1967).

§ 258. Duration and termination of employment. Many controversies arise as to the duration and termination of the broker's employment.

When no time limit is specified. If the listing contract specifies no duration, the broker's authority automatically lapses after expiration of a reasonable time. 27 ALR2d 1346, 1390. If after a reasonable time has expired the broker continues to work on the deal without encouragement from the landowner and succeeds in finding a willing buyer, the seller may, without any liability to the broker, refuse to sell. But even before a reasonable time has expired, if no duration is specified, the landowner has the right to revoke the listing at any time before the broker has found a buyer ready, able, and willing to buy—an even while the broker is negotiating with a prospect, so long as the negotiations are not virtually completed. 49 LRANS 985. Such revocation must be in good faith, of course; for example, the landowner has decided in good faith to withdraw the property from sale. The fact that the broker has expended time and money on the deal does not prevent revocation, for the ordinary broker's listing contemplates that such expenditures will be made and that the landowner will nevertheless enjoy freedom of action. 49 LRANS 994. A special rule applies, however, where the listing contemplates extraordinary expenditures by the broker.

EXAMPLE: A landowner listed a large tract of land with a broker under an agreement that the broker was to grade, survey, and subdivide the land, put in streets, etc., at his own expense. His compensation was to come from commission on lot sales. No duration was fixed. After the broker had completed the subdivision, the owner revoked the broker's employment. The owner must pay damages to the broker. *McMillan* v. *Quincey*, 137 Ga. 63, 72 SE 506 (1911); 49 LRANS 999. The owner cannot revoke until a reasonable time has elapsed.

What is a reasonable time for a broker to sell the property depends on the circumstances. Some properties are harder to sell than others; for example, a one-purpose building, such as a church. A longer period will be allowed in such case than would be true in the case of a quick-selling item, such as a modern single-family dwelling.

Where the listing contract fixes the period of employment. Listing contracts, often provide that they are to continue for a specified time. In such case, the broker is not entitled to a commission unless within the time limit he procures a customer who is ready, able, and willing to buy.

EXAMPLE: A a landowner, gave the broker an exclusive right to sell, with a time limit of six months. During this period the broker showed the property to *B*. *B* thought the price too high. The day after the listing expired, *A* called the broker and asked if he would have to pay the commission if he sold the property to someone who had been shown the house during the period of the listing. The broker said that *A* would be liable. Nevertheless *A* advertised the property for sale. *B* appeared in response to the ad. A contract of sale was entered into at a price of $45,000. The listing price had been $53,000. The court held that the broker was not entitled to a commission. *Brenner & Co.* v. *Perl*, 72 N.J.S. 160, 178 A2d 19 (1962), 27 ALR2d 1348.

However, in the following cases the broker will recover a commission even if he fails to find a purchaser within the period of the listing.

1. When the expiration of the listing time is attributable to the bad faith of the owner, as when the owner deliberately postpones agreement with the broker's buyer, hoping thereby to defeat the broker's claim for compensation. 27 ALR2d 1346, 1357.

2. If negotiations are begun within the time specified in the listing contract, continue without interruption, and are completed after the time has expired, the broker is entitled to his commission, particularly where the delay is due to the fault of the owner, as where it is occasioned by a defect in title. The seller is considered to have waived or extended the time limit.

3. When the listing contract contains some clause protecting the broker. For example, some listing forms, in large type, purport to run for a fixed period of time, such as thirty days, but following this will be a fine-print provision continuing the listing until a termination notice has been served on the broker. Other listing forms provide that the owner will protect the broker on sales made within ninety days of the expiration of the listing to pros-

pects with whom the broker had *negotiated* or who had been *introduced* to the seller by the broker before expiration of the listing period. 27 ALR2d 1346, 1408.

CAUTION: Courts are unfriendly to these provisions for automatic extension of the listing period. Even if the listing contract is an exclusive agency or exclusive right to sell, it will be considered an *open listing during the extended period* if it is at all ambiguous. When a listing stated it was to be "sole and exclusive for three months and thereafter until sixty days written notice had been given," it was exclusive only for the initial three-month period. Thereafter it was only an open listing. *Boggess Realty* Co. v. *Miller,* 227 Ky. 813, 14 SW2d 140, 27 ALR2d 1420 (1929); *Wilson* v. *Franklin,* 282 Pa. 189, 127 Atl. 609 (1925). Some states require a specified time limit.

Revocation where listing fixes a specified time and broker has begun performance. Where the listing contract fixes a period of employment, such as thirty days, the owner may terminate the employment before the agent has expended money or effort, but not afterward. The technical reason for this rule is that the typical listing contract is a *unilateral contract* in which the landowner makes a promise to pay commission when the broker has performed an act, that is, found a buyer ready, able, and willing to buy, and such a contract is revocable by the promisor only up to the time the other party begins performance. *McMenamin* v. *Bishop,* 493 P2d 1016; *Stort* v. *Reinhard,* 183 SE2d 601 (1971); *Hutchison* v. *Dobson-Bainbridge Realty Co.,* 31 Tenn. App. 490, 217 SW2d 6 (1946); *Patton* v. *Wilson* (Tex. Civ. App.), 220 SW2d 184 (1949); 1 Corbin, Contracts 154; 37 *Ia. L. Rev.* 370; 12 AmJur2d 796; 64 ALR 404.

In these cases, any revocation after the broker has begun performance is wrongful and makes the owner liable to the broker for damages.

EXPLANATION: There are many classes and classifications of contracts. One classification divides contracts into *unilateral* and *bilateral.*

EXAMPLE: A hires *B,* a broker, to sell A's house for $30,000. Note that *B* does not promise to do anything. He simply does an act i.e. he finds C, who is willing to buy the house for $30,000. Most broker's listings are of this character. Older decisions allowed A to revoke *B*'s authority any time before he *completed* his performance. Starting work did not prevent revocation. Some courts still follow this rule. *Bartlett* v. *Keith,* 325 Mass. 265, 90 NE2d 308 (1950).

On the other hand, one or two states hold that an exclusive listing is irrevocable from the date it is signed, even though the broker has not begun performance. This is on the theory that by accepting employment the broker *impliedly agrees* to use reasonable efforts to find a buyer, and this makes the contract *bilateral* and irrevocable until the specified time has expired. *Hayes* v. *Clark,* 95 Conn. 510, 111 Atl. 781 (1920). This implied agreement makes the contract *bilateral.*

In a bilateral contract *A* makes a promise to *B,* and *B* in return makes a promise to *A.* The contract is enforceable when made. Either party may sue the other if that other fails to keep his promise.

We are beginning to see listing contracts that are technically *bilateral contracts.* This means that in return for the owner's promise to pay a specified commission for a buyer, the broker promises to perform certain specified acts, such as advertising the property in a specified paper at least once a week. Here the broker has a legal obligation to do as he has promised. Any revocation by the owner before the listing period has expired will be wrongful, so long as the broker is keeping his part of the bargain.

SUGGESTION TO BROKER: Let the listing contract call for some acts by the broker, for example, provide that "broker agrees to publish an advertisement of the property at least once in a newspaper of general circulation in the county." The listing should be signed by the broker. This listing is irrevocable from the date it is signed, assuming, of course, that the broker advertises the property as agreed.

Revocation after broker has performed. Of course the landowner has no right to revoke the broker's employment after the broker has brought in a buyer ready, able, and willing to buy.

Revocation in bad faith. In all types of listings the owner will be liable to the broker for damages if he acts in bad faith in revoking the broker's employment. 27 ALR2d 1346, 1395. Even when no time of employment is specified, when the broker is concluding negotiations with a prospective purchaser the owner cannot revoke the agency *in bad faith for the purpose of avoiding payment of commission.* In other words, when the broker has found a prospect and is concluding negotiations with him, so that the commission is virtually earned and the broker is approaching success, the owner cannot discharge the broker and thereupon step in and consummate the transaction, thus defeating the broker's right to his compensation. Restatement, Agency § 446.

EXAMPLE: *A*, a landowner, hired *B*, a broker, to sell his land. While *B* was negotiating with a prospect, *A* sold the land to his wife and discharged *B*. Thereupon *A* and his wife sold to *B*'s prospect. They were liable for *B*'s commission. *Alexander* v. *Smith*, 180 Ala. 541, 61 So. 68 (1912); 36 *Boston U. L. Rev.* 302.

Revocation by sale. A wrongful revocation of the broker's exclusive right to sell takes place if the owner contracts to sell the land to a purchaser not procured by the broker or even if he gives the purchaser only an option to purchase. The option removes the property from the market. *Hunt* v. *Smallidge*, 321 NYS2d 825; *Coleman* v. *Mora*, 263 Cal. App.2d 137, 69 Cal.Reptr. 166.

Notice of revocation of employment. When a landowner decides to withdraw his land from sale, he must give the broker notice of the revocation of his employment before the broker has finished the job. If the broker brings in a buyer ready, able, and willing to buy, obviously no judge will allow the owner to say, "I fired you mentally five days ago." 12 CJS. 152; 12 AmJur2d 817.

Revocation by sale by a person other than broker. A different situation is presented when the revocation of employment takes place by virtue of the fact that the land has been sold by someone else. As previously explained, in an open listing the employment of all brokers hired by the owner *automatically ends when a ready, able, and willing buyer is found either by the owner or by one of the brokers;* and in an exclusive agency the broker's employment automatically ends if the owner, through his own efforts, finds a willing buyer. No duty to notify brokers rests on the owner in most states, because all brokers understand that in these situations their employment is subject to such automatic termination. *Des Rivieres* v. *Sullivan,* 247 Mass. 443, 142 NE 111; 12 AmJur2d 817. These termination provisions are "read into" the listing contract by the courts. A few cases hold, however, that after the land has been sold the owner ought, within a reasonable time, to notify all his brokers of the sale. If he fails to do so, and if one of his brokers also finds a willing buyer, the owner may be compelled to pay him a commission. *Lane* v. *Albright,* 49 Ind. 275; 49 LRANS. 1003.

SUGGESTION TO OWNER: Notify all your brokers promptly as soon as the land is sold.

Suppose that in an open listing a broker finds a willing buyer. However, he fails to notify the owner of this fact, and thereafter the owner signs a contract with some other buyer, procured, let us say, through another broker, the owner being still ignorant of the first broker's successful efforts. The first broker loses his commission. It is his duty to notify the owner promptly on finding a buyer. *Wilson* v. *Franklin,* 282 Pa. 189, 127 Atl. 609.

SUGGESTION TO BROKER: Notify the owner as soon as you have found a willing buyer.

Damages for wrongful revocation of employment. Suppose that under one of the rules discussed in this section the owner's revocation of the broker's employment is legally wrongful. How much should the courts award the broker? Some courts give the broker only the expenses incurred by him for advertising and so forth and a sum that will compensate him for the reasonable value of his services. *Ferguson* v. *Bovee,* 239 Ia. 775, 32 NW2d 924 (1948); *Nicholson* v. *Alderson,* 347 Ill. App. 496, 107 NE2d 39 (1952); 12 AmJur2d 819. Most courts, however, on one theory or another award the broker a full commission. 37 *Ia. L. Rev.* 367; 69 ALR3d 1269.

The broker will have a better chance of collecting a full commission if the listing contract has a clause covering the possibility of the sellers' withdrawing the property from sale.

SUGGESTED FORM: Let the listing provide that the broker will receive a full commission "if, within the time above specified, the premises are sold by the broker, owner, or anyone else, or if, within said period, the owner withdraws the property from sale or terminates the broker's employment." *Baumgartner* v. *Meek,* 126 Cal. App.2d 505, 272 P2d 552 (1954); *McMenamin* v. *Bishop,* 493 P2d 1016 (Wash. 1972).

§ 259. **Sale for less than price fixed.** Where an agent is employed to sell real estate for the owner, and the owner fixes a sale price, the broker is entitled to a commission if he finds a purchaser and the owner sells to the purchaser for less than the price fixed. The owner has the right to insist on the terms quoted to the broker and may reject a buyer who will not meet his terms. But if he voluntarily reduces his price in order to make the sale to a buyer produced by the broker, the broker is entitled to a commission on the sale price.

§ 260. **Amount of compensation.** In a case where the broker has found a buyer, he is entitled to the commission agreed upon, and if no commission has been fixed by the parties, he is entitled to the usual and customary commission for such services. He is usually not entitled to extra compensation for incidental services.

The compensation is computed on the gross sale price.

EXAMPLE: A owns land on which there is a $12,000 mortgage. He lists the building with a broker at $15,000, and the broker finds a buyer. Although A will obtain a net of only $3,000 ($15,000 less the $12,000 required to pay the mortgage) he must pay a commission based on a price of $15,000.

§ 261. **Lien for commission.** A broker hired by the seller has no lien on the seller's land for the payment of his commission unless the listing contract so provides. 125 ALR 921. In other words, even though the broker has earned his commission, his only remedy, if the seller fails to pay, is to sue the seller and obtain a judgment against him. The broker cannot do anything to block sale of the land by the seller to the broker's customer or anyone else.

§ 262. **Earnest money.** The seller's broker ordinarily has no authority to accept an earnest money deposit. 30 ALR2d 805, 810. Quite commonly however, the broker is permitted to hold the earnest money with no written agreement regarding disposition of such money. If the sale is completed, the money must be returned to the seller. *Mader* v. *James,* 546 P2d 196 (Wyo. 1976). If the sale is not completed, and the buyer is not at fault, the broker must return the money to the buyer. *Mader* v. *James,* 546 P2d 190 (Wyo. 1976); 12 Am. Jur. 2d 852; 38 ALR2d 1382. But if the seller is not at fault, the broker is liable to the seller if he returns the earnest money to the buyer. *Lake Co.* v. *Molan,* 131 NW2d 734 (Minn. 1965). A seller's broker, who returns the earnest money to a defaulting purchaser, also loses his commission. 69 ALR2d 1244. Most cases hold that where the seller's title proves defective, or the deal falls through for some other fault of the seller, the broker must return the earnest money to the buyer. 38 ALR2d 1382. But the better rule it seems, is that when a deal falls through, the broker should return the earnest money to his seller-employer, leaving it to the buyer to collect from the seller. *Schultz* v. *Clements,* 7 Ill. App. 2d 510, 130 NE2d 1 (1955); 12 Am. Jur. 2d 852. The broker should not be asked to assume the role of judge and thus determine, as between seller and buyer, who is entitled to return of the deposit. Of course, either the listing contract or the contract of sale can give the broker specific directions on this score, and he should follow them.

Many states require the broker to keep earnest money deposits in a neutral bank account.

§ 263. **Risk of loss caused by broker's embezzlement.** Where the earnest money is in the hands of the seller's broker, the rule is a simple one. If the broker is not authorized *by the seller* to accept a deposit, the money is the buyer's money entrusted to the broker, and he must bear the loss resulting from the embezzlement. 30 ALR2d 808. If the listing contract authorizes the broker to accept a deposit, risk of loss is on the seller.

Even when a seller accepts a *down payment* taken by the broker from the buyer, it does not constitute authority by the seller to the broker to accept the balance of the purchase price. The seller is entitled to assume that the broker was acting as the *buyer's agent* in transmitting the down payment. Suppose that the listing contract authorizes the broker to sign a contract of sale on behalf of the seller. Here the broker necessarily has implied authority to accept the down payment, for a down payment is made when the contract is signed. 30 ALR2d 816. The broker holds the money as agent of the seller, and if the broker embezzles the money, the loss falls on the seller. If the listing contract authorizes the broker to *sell and convey* the property, or if the seller entrusts the deed to the broker for delivery to the buyer, then the broker has implied authority to receive all of the purchase price. This must be so, for the seller's agent, not the seller, will be present at the closing of the deal, and the buyer must pay someone.

§ 264. **Two-broker deals.** A broker may become liable to another broker for wrongful deprival of a commission.

EXAMPLE: *V* listed land for sale with *B-1*, a broker. *B-2*, a broker, contacted *V* and was told to obtain *V*'s terms from *B-1*, which *B-2* did. *B-2* found *P-1*, a buyer ready, able, and willing to buy, and *V* accepted him. *B-1* and *B-2* agreed that they would share the commission equally. Then *B-1* persuaded *V* to sell the land to *P-2* in a deal with *B-1* obtaining all of the commission. *B-1* is liable to *B-2* for the commission of which *B-2* was deprived by *B-1*'s wrongful conduct. It is wrongful to interfere with a contract right. 34 ALR 3d 730.

And if the broker hired by the seller asks a second broker to help him sell it and the second broker finds a buyer and collects a commission, he must divide the commission with the first broker. *Wheeler* v. *Waller,* 197 NW2d 585 (Ia. 1972). The brokers have engaged in a joint venture, and each party in a joint venture owes a duty of good faith to the other.

§ 265. **Duties of the broker: loyalty and double agency.** In general, the duties of a broker are the same as those of any other agent. They arise because the broker is an agent. They need not be spelled out in the listing contract. An agent must be loyal to his principal. If, without the knowledge and consent of his principal, he is also acting for the other party to the transaction, the principal may, when he discovers this fact, declare the contract void. This is true even though the transaction is a good one for the principal and the other party acts in good faith and was unaware of the double agency. *Gordon* v. *Beck,* 196 Cal. 768, 239 Pac. 309 (1925). It is to the interest of the seller to obtain the highest possible price and of the buyer to pay the least. Clearly, no one agent can serve both these interests. *Duffy* v. *Setchell,* 38 Ill. App. 3d 146, 347 NE2d 218 (1976). Such a broker also loses his commission.

EXAMPLE: A hired *B*, a broker, to sell his land, and C hired *D*, a broker, to find land of this character for C to purchase. *B* and *D* conferred and agreed to split their commissions down the middle. Neither broker can collect any commission. 63 ALR3d 1211, 1219.

Suppose a broker is hired by the buyer to find land or a building in a certain area, the buyer to pay a commission. Suppose that thereafter a property owner lists land of this description for sale with this broker. The broker reveals this fact *to the buyer only,* and a deal is closed between the seller and buyer, without, however, any knowledge on the seller's part that the broker was originally hired by the buyer. The broker collects his commission from the seller and now sues the buyer. To the broker's surprise, the buyer claims that the broker cannot collect any commission whatever in a double agency situation. This is correct. The fact that the buyer knew of the double agency makes no difference. A fraud was perpetrated on the *seller,* and the law will not help a party to the fraud, the broker, to collect from the other party to the fraud, the buyer. *McConnell* v. *Cowan,* 44 Cal.2d 805, 285 P2d 261 (1955); 80 ALR 1077, 1087. The fact that the broker felt he was acting for the best interests of both parties is immaterial.

A *middleman,* who merely brings the parties together, leaving them to negotiate, may serve both parties. Here the double agency rule does not apply. 14 ALR 472; 58 ALR2d 42, 58. But if the broker assists either party or in some degree influences the parties, he is not a middleman. It is obvious that very few agencies fall in the middleman category.

§ 266. **Duties of the broker: conflict of interest problems.** An agent must not have any individual interest in the transaction without the knowledge and consent of his principal.

EXAMPLE: *X* placed his property with *A* and *B*, brokers. Negotiations resulted in a sale by *X* to *Y* for $3200, the brokers receiving a commission of $160. After the deed was given, *X* discovered that the real purchaser was *B*, *Y* being one of *B*'s employees. *X* was entitled to have the conveyance set aside. *Johnson* v. *Bernard,* 323 Ill. 527, 154 NE 444 (1926). *X* also gets the commission back.

The rule even precludes a sale by the broker to his wife unless the seller is informed of the relation. If, however, the broker fully discloses the facts to the landowner, he may buy for himself, for a relative, or for himself and others.

§ 267. **Duties of the broker: disclosure and nondisclosure.** An agent must make full disclosure to his principal of all matters that may come to his knowledge pertaining to the subject of the agency. 2 ALR3d 1123.

EXAMPLE: A placed his property with *B*, a broker. *B* wrote *A*, stating that he *(B)* and several other parties would buy the land at $400 per acre. The contract was signed, and *B* received a commission. Later A discovered that, prior to making this offer, *B* had received an offer for this property of $600 per acre. A was entitled to have the contract canceled. *Rieger* v. *Brandt,* 329 Ill. 21, 160 NE 130 (1928); 7 ALR3d 693.

EXAMPLE: The broker is liable if he transmits an offer to the principal but conceals a more favorable offer. 7 ALR3d 696.

EXAMPLE: While the property is listed with the broker, it increases in value. The owner is ignorant of this fact, but the broker knows of it. He fails to disclose this circumstance to the owner. He has violated his duty of full disclosure. *Eastburn* v. *Jos. Espalla, Jr. & Co.,* 112 So 232 (Ala. 1927); 53 ALR 134.

EXAMPLE: The buyer procured by the broker has a poor financial status. The broker knows this, but fails to reveal it to the seller. A contract is signed, but the deal fails to go through because the buyer cannot raise the necessary funds. The broker has violated his duty of full disclosure. *McGarry* v. *McCrone,* 97 Ohio App. 543, 118 NE2d 195 (1954); *Nugent* v. *Scharff,* 476 SW2d 414 (1972); *Mason* v. *Bulleri,* 543 P2d 478 (Ariz. 1975).

EXAMPLE: The buyer procured by the broker is a distant relative of the broker. He must reveal this fact to the seller. 26 ALR2d 1308. The broker must dislose the true identity of the purchaser. 2 ALR3d 1119.

In other words, the broker's duty is not discharged simply by his handing a contract to the seller for signing. He must notify the seller of all facts that might influence the seller in accepting or rejecting the offer. He must give his opinion as to the price that can be obtained, the likelihood of a higher price being offered in the future, the possibility of making a favorable trade or other use of the property, etc. *Moehling* v. *O'Neil Construction Co.,* 20 Ill.2d 255, 170 NE2d 100 (1960).

The converse of the broker's duty of disclosure is his duty not to reveal secret information to prospective buyers. Thus the seller's broker violates his duties if he reveals to a prospective buyer that the seller will take less than the listed price for the property, for obviously no buyer will pay the listed price if he knows that the seller will take less. *Haynes* v. *Rogers,* 70 Ariz. 257, 219 P2d 339 (1950).

§ 268. Duties of the broker: misrepresentations. A broker hired by the seller will be held liable to the buyer in damages if the broker, acting on his own, makes a willful misrepresentation that induces the buyer to enter into the contract of sale. 58 ALR2d 10, 27; 8 ALR3d 553.

EXAMPLE: The broker falsely represented that the house was stucco-covered brick, whereas it was not brick. *Perkins* v. *Green,* 26 Ariz. 219, 224 P 620 (1924). He was liable to the buyer.

The broker can also become liable to the seller for making fraudulent misrepresentations.

EXAMPLE: *V* hired *B,* a broker, and *B* found *P* a purchaser. *B* made fraudulent misrepresentations to *P* that induced *P* to enter into and consummate the transaction. When *P* learned of the fraud, he sued *V* for damages, and *V* paid *P*. He was obliged to do so because he was liable for the fraudulent acts of his agent, *B*. *V* can now sue *B*. 61 ALR2d 1237.

§ 269. **Duties of the broker: skill and care.** Like other agents, a broker must exercise skill and care in the service of his employer.

EXAMPLE: A broker hired to sell land found a buyer and drew a contract of sale, which the parties signed. Thereafter the buyer refused to go through with the deal. The court held that the contract was so poorly drawn that the buyer was not legally bound. The broker thereby forfeited his commission. *Dingman* v. *Boyle,* 285 Ill. 144, 120 NE 487 (1918). Moreover, he is liable to the seller for any damages the seller has suffered. *Mattieliegh* v. *Poe,* 356 P2d 328 (Wash. 1960).

EXAMPLE: A broker hired to buy or trade has a duty to determine the value of the real estate he acquires for his employer. If he fails in this respect and the property turns out to be a poor buy, he is liable and forfeits his commission. *Smith* v. *Carroll Realty Co.,* 8 Utah2d 356, 335 P2d 67 (1959).

EXAMPLE: A broker employed to find a property for a buyer must exercise skill and care if he undertakes to close the deal for the buyer without an attorney. Thus if the broker fails to procure a clear title for the buyer, he is liable to buyer for damages. *Lester* v. *Marshall,* 143 Colo. 189, 352 P2d 786 (1960).

EXAMPLE: A broker held liable for loss caused by his ignorance of zoning. *Burien Motors Inc.* v. *Balch,* 513 P2d 582 (Wash. 1973).

EXAMPLE: A broker held liable for careless title search. *Mayflower Mtg.* Co. v. *Brown,* 530 P2d 1298 (Colo. 1975).

§ 270. **Duties of the broker: liabilities and penalties for breach of duty.** Where the broker breaches his duties toward his employer, one or more of several penalties may follow.

1. In almost every case the broker will lose his commission. If he has already been paid, he must refund it. 2 ALR3d 1126.
2. If he has made a profit, as where the broker has bought the property from his employer through a nominee and resold it at a profit, he must pay such profit over to his employer.
3. If his employer has suffered any damages as a consequence of the broker's breach of duty, the broker will be liable for such damages.
4. Where the broker's misconduct is deliberate, as where he secretly buys the property from his employer, the court may see fit to punish the broker by compelling him to pay exemplary damages, that is, damages greater than the damage the employer has actually suffered. *Ward* v. *Taggart,* 51 Cal.2d 736, 336 P2d 534 (1959).
5. For a serious offense, such as secretly buying his employer's property, failing to disclose material facts to his employer, embezzling his employer's funds, etc., the broker may have his license suspended or revoked altogether. 56 ALR2d 573. Fraud in his own land transactions will also result in the loss of his license. *Holland Realty Inv.* Co. v. *State,* 436 P2d 422 (Nev. 1968).

As is true with respect to lawyers, doctors, architects, and others, the courts are holding brokers to higher and higher standards of professional ethics and competence. This is a desirable trend and is likely to continue.

In those states that require the broker to post an official bond, the surety on the bond will be liable for the broker's misconduct, as where the broker misappropriates a down payment that has been entrusted to him by the buyer. 17 ALR2d 1021.

§ 271. **Duties to purchaser.** A seller's broker has certain duties to the buyer and will be liable if he fails to attend to them.

EXAMPLE: A seller's broker failed to communicate to seller an offer made by a prospective buyer. As a result, the latter lost the deal. The broker is liable to this prospective buyer. *Amato* v. *Lattor & Blum,* 79 So.2d 873 (La. 1955).

EXAMPLE: A seller's broker undertook to procure a mortgage for a buyer, and by lack of care, procured a short-term mortgage which buyer signed. He is liable to buyer.

EXAMPLE: A seller's broker will be liable to the buyer if he misrepresents the age of the building, identity of the school servicing the area, and so forth. 8 ALR3d 550.

EXAMPLE: A broker was suspended for misrepresenting the condition of the heating plant.

§ 272. **Unauthorized practice of law.** The law appears to differ from state to state with respect to the propriety of a broker's filling in a form contract of sale where this is merely incidental to the earning of his commission for procuring a buyer. 53 ALR2d 796. However, if the broker makes a separate charge for filling in a form, he is guilty of unauthorized practice of law. 53 ALR2d 804. Likewise, if a broker prepares a will or deeds to put land in joint tenancy, he is guilty of the unauthorized practice of law. 53 ALR2d 807.

§ 273. **Authority of broker to sign contract.** Ordinarily a broker does not have authority to sign a contract on behalf of his employer. 43 ALR2d 1014.

§ 274. **Racial discrimination.** The law places a heavy burden on the broker and salesman with respect to racial discrimination.

§ 275. **Franchising.** A new development in brokerage law is the advent of franchising. The real estate broker retains his independent status. However, the franchiser furnishes advertising, procedure manuals, forms, and so forth. Each franchiser is furnished a list of other franchisees, which enables each franchiser to furnish a national referral service, for example, in employee-transfer situations. This is a promising new development, but the courts have not yet tested it. If the franchising agreement gives the franchiser the right to allocate territory, that portion of the agreement is likely to draw fire from the federal government. The laws against monopolies forbid territory allocation. Dowling & Hines, *Here Comes the Real Estate Franchise,* 7 *Real Estate Rev.* 48 (summer 1977).

§ 276. **Managers.** A building manager is the agent of the property owner. An agent owes to his employer the duty of loyalty. This precludes the taking of secret commissions from suppliers with whom the manager deals and also precludes the taking of secret bonuses from tenants. A manager must not enter into any deal to procure a lease through a dummy or nominee unless his interest is revealed to his employer. An agent also is bound to exercise care, diligence, and skill. This means that the manager must procure proper insurance, appropriate to the situation, which may include fidelity bonds, plate glass insurance, elevator liability insurance, workmen's compensation insurance, and other types that a careful manager would be expected to procure. The manager must make periodic inspections, arrange for necessary repairs, rerent vacant space promptly, see that ordinances are complied with, and do all the other things that a careful owner would do with respect to his property. An agent must keep his employer informed. This means that the manager must promptly forward to his employer all legal notices served by tenants and must notify his employer of any rent delinquency, "lease-jumping" by a tenant, offers of purchase, notices of ordinance violations, and the like. An agent must keep proper records and accounts and must not mingle his funds with those of his employer. A management contract is personal. It is not binding on a purchaser of the property.

RESERVED: §§ 277 to 286.

11

Contracts for the Sale of Land

§ 287. **Why a contract for sale of land is needed.** Where *A,* a landowner, agrees to sell his land to *B* for $10,000 in cash, one may ask why it is necessary that a contract be signed. Why does not *A* then and there give a deed to *B,* and *B* pay *A* the agreed price? The chief reason is that at the time the agreement is reached, *B* has no assurance, other than *A*'s statement, that *A* is in fact the owner of the land and that there are no defects in his title. Ordinarily, therefore, *B* will insist that a contract be signed and that it provide for an examination of *A*'s title, such examination to show that *A* has good title, before *B* pays the purchase price. In other words, the prudent purchaser is unwilling to buy a pig in a poke. The cash sale contract defines the type of title the seller will deliver, how, when, and where proof is to be made that title is good, and what is to be done if defects in title are revealed. In the meantime, the parties are bound to their bargain by the contract. The seller cannot sell to someone else who offers a higher price, and the buyer is bound to go through with the deal on the agreed terms set forth in the contract. Also, a land sale involves matters other than the sale of the land itself. There are insurance policies to be transferred, leases to be assigned, mortgages to be paid, and many other matters to be attended to. The rights and duties of seller and buyer with respect to these matters should be set forth in the contract.

The cash sale contract contemplates that the deal will be closed as soon as the seller's title is examined and found to be good. There is also a type of contract called the *installment contract, contract for deed* or *land contract.* An installment contract provides for a down payment, with balance of purchase price payable in monthly installments. The buyer receives his deed when all the installments have been paid or when the unpaid balance of the purchase price has been reduced to a certain agreed figure, whereupon the buyer is to receive a deed and give the seller a purchase money mortgage for the balance of the purchase price.

§ 288. **Necessity for written contract.** It is necessary that the fundamentals of a contract for the sale of land be in writing. Oral contracts cannot be enforced. The law that so provides is known as the *Statute of Frauds.*

To satisfy the Statute of Frauds the *memorandum* of the contract must contain the names of seller and buyer, a sufficient description of the land, the contract price, the terms of sale if other than cash, and the signature of "the party to be charged," that is, the signature of the party against whom suit is brought on the contract. A few states require both parties to sign the contract, and there appears to be a trend in this direction. As a rule, oral testimony cannot be introduced in court for the purpose of supplying omissions in the written document. *Kris* v. *Patterson,* 159 Minn. 219, 198 NW 541 (1924). The fact that a sale is intended should also appear in the writing.

Suppose that I enter an oral contract with you to buy your land, and I give you a down payment. Thereafter, I change my mind. Although you cannot sue me for the balance of the contract price, neither can I get my down payment back from you as long as you are willing to go through with the deal. 169 A.L.R. 187.

No particular form is required, so that a binding contract may be in the form of one or more letters, escrow instructions, receipt, a check, a promissory note, and so on.

EXAMPLE: *P,* the buyer, gave *V,* the seller, his check payable to *V*. On the face of this check was written the following: "Deposit for land on Galvin Road, Watertown, price thirty-two cents a foot." This was the only land that *V* owned. It was held that this was a sufficient contract. 153 ALR 1108. (The letter *V* is used herein to designate the seller or vendor and the letter *P* to designate the buyer or purchaser.)

EXAMPLE: A contract was as follows:

Chicago, January 8, 1904

Received of Anton Ullsperger $100 on said purchase of property No. 1031 Milwaukee Avenue, Chicago, Illinois at a price of $14,000. C. Meyer

Meyer refused to perform, and Ullsperger sued him. The court compelled Meyer to give Ullsperger a deed. *Ullsperger* v. *Meyer,* 217 Ill. 262, 75 NE 482 (1905).

It will be observed in the last example that Ullsperger, who had *not* signed the contract, was allowed to enforce the contract against Meyer, who *had* signed it. However, Meyer could not have enforced the contract against Ullsperger. This is in accord with the general rule that in a land contract a seller may legally compel performance if he can produce a contract signed by the buyer, and the buyer can demand performance if he can produce a contract signed by the seller. Signature by both parties is not necessary.

Such a contract, although it meets the minimum requirements of the law, is altogether unsatisfactory, as will become apparent from the subsequent discussion. Obviously, it is best to have both seller and buyer sign the contract, and this is the usual practice.

Many documents that are legally sufficient as contracts for the sale of land are quite short, as the foregoing discussion reveals. Moreover, such documents are often given misleading names, such as *sales deposit receipt* or *offer to purchase.* People sign such documents without realizing that they have obligated themselves to buy or sell real estate. Sometimes such brief documents state that the parties will later sign a "regular" real estate contract. The court decisions are conflicting as to the effect of the inclusion of this phrase. As long as the main terms of the sale are stated in the document, most courts hold that the failure to sign a formal, detailed contract is unimportant, especially where the parties proceed with the details of the transaction as though a binding contract existed. *Phillips* v. *Johnson,* 514 P2d 1337 (Ore. 1973); *Sewel* v. *Dalby,* 171 Kan. 640, 237 P2d 366 (1951); 122 ALR 1217; 165 ALR 765. Other states feel that the parties did not intend to be bound until a formal, detailed contract was executed, as called for in the short form, and therefore hold that the short document is not binding. *Scott* v. *Fowler,* 227 Ill. 104, 81 NE 34 (1907); *Brunette* v. *Vulcan Materials Co.,* 119 Ill. App.2d 390, 256 NE2d 44 (1970); *Lippman* v. *Featherston,* 247 Mich. 153, 225 NW 489 (1929).

§ 289. Questions the parties intending to enter into a contract should ask. Before listing his property with a broker for sale, the *seller* should ask himself:

1. Do I really want to sell?

COMMENT: If I list my property and the broker finds a buyer ready, able, and willing to buy at my price, I must pay a commission even if I then decide that I really don't want to sell.

2. Does my wife want to sell?

COMMENT: If the broker finds a buyer and I am willing to sign the contract of sale, but my wife refuses to do so, in most states the buyer will refuse to go through with the deal because, unless she signs the contract, she is not legally obligated to sign the deed, and this will leave her dower or other legal rights outstanding. The deal fails, but the broker gets his commission.

3. Am I really in a position to sell?

COMMENT: Suppose my broker finds a willing buyer, but it develops that my title is defective, or I cannot pay off the existing mortgage, or my new house will not be ready for occupancy for a long time. Again the deal falls through, but I must nevertheless pay a commission.

Before signing a contract of sale the *buyer* should ask himself these questions and attend to the following matters:

1. If I am buying vacant land, are there any zoning or environmental ordinances that forbid or hamper the use I wish to make of the land?

COMMENT: Suppose I sign a contract to buy a vacant lot and intend to erect a filling station thereon, and thereafter I discover that the lot is zoned for residences only. I must nevertheless go through with the deal. Suppose my *building* complies with the ordinance. Do my plans provide adequate off-street parking to comply with the ordinance? Or does an environmental ordinance forbid any building on wetlands?

2. Under local ordinances, how far from the front, side, and rear lines must buildings be erected? Does this leave room for the type of building that I have in mind?

3. If I plan to use septic tank construction, is the lot big enough to qualify for septic tank construction under local ordinances?

4. If there is an airport in the vicinity, are there any regulations prohibiting the erection of electric poles or other structures that might prove a hazard to aircraft?

5. If there is a building on the land but I expect to remodel it, are there any ordinances that prohibit such remodeling?

6. Does the building on the property violate existing zoning or building ordinances?

COMMENT: If it does, I may be compelled to remodel the building to conform to the ordinances, or even to tear it down.

7. Is the building a nonconforming use?

COMMENT: If it is, I cannot enlarge or alter it or rebuild it if it is substantially damaged by fire. If it was legally abandoned, the city can forbid its use.

8. Especially if the building is new, has a certificate of occupancy been issued?

9. Does the seller have a permit for any structure that requires a city permit, such as a swimming pool, a water tank on a roof, or a sign that extends over a sidewalk? Where a cocktail lounge is involved, am I, as the buyer, certain that I can procure an assignment of the liquor license?

10. If the contract of sale states that title will be subject to building restrictions, easements, mineral rights, and so on, how will these affect my building plans?

11. Are there sewers and water pipes in adjoining streets, and if there are, will I have the legal right to connect my proposed building to them?

12. Are there any utility lines, including underground lines, drainage ditches, draintiles, and so on, that will interfere with my building program?

13. Are existing streets, walks, sewers, or water pipes fully paid for and if not, will they be paid for by the seller, buyer, or by future special assessments? What does the contract say regarding this matter?

14. Will my building program interfere with my neighbor's drainage?

15. Keeping in mind that the law often says, "let the buyer beware," are there any defects in the building, for example, termites, defective heating plant, basement that floods, inadequate well or septic tank?

16. Is the soil adequate for my building program, and should soil tests be made?

17. Is the building I'm buying so close to adjoining vacant land that, if my neighbor excavates, there is danger that my building will fall into the excavation?

18. Is my neighbor's building so close to the boundary line that, if I build on the vacant land I'm buying, my excavation will involve possible collapse of his building and possible litigation?

19. Keeping in mind that I will become personally liable for personal injuries as soon

as the deal is closed, are the elevators, boilers, gas, water, and sewer in the building in safe condition?

20. Since risk of loss in many states falls on the buyer as soon as the contract is signed, is the existing insurance policy for an adequate amount? Suppose, for example, that the building burns to the ground before the deal is closed.

21. Is the property being used for a purpose that invalidates existing insurance policies?

SUGGESTION: Have the insurance policies checked by a reliable insurance broker. Have a rider (*contract of sale clause*) attached immediately to the policies so that you, as well as the seller, are covered. Only the seller is covered until this is done.

22. Are any public projects scheduled for this area that may result in the taking of this property by the public?

COMMENT: It is discouraging for a businessman to build up neighborhood goodwill over a period of time and then find his property taken for a superhighway.

23. Are any zoning or building code changes likely to take place that will interfere with my building program?

24. Are there any judgments against me?

COMMENT: Once I sign a contract to buy land, the seller will be obligated to deed the land to me, and then my creditors may take it away from me.

25. Where the contract calls for the buyer to accept the property subject to "existing leases," what do the leases provide?

COMMENT: If the leases contain clauses that are very burdensome to the landlord, the buyer may wish to reconsider the desirability of entering into the deal.

26. If the contract requires the buyer to accept the property subject to the existing mortgage, the contract should require the seller to furnish, at closing, a statement signed by the mortgagee showing the balance due on the mortgage. The buyer should check the mortgage to make sure it does not give the mortgagee the right to declare the mortgage debt due in case the mortgagor sells the property without the mortgagee's permission.

27. Has the building been designated as a landmark or historical site? Is it in a flood plain?

28. Inquire about proposed new construction in the area which might make the neighborhood undesirable.

29. Confirm operating costs and taxes and determine whether special property assessments are planned. They could impose a financial burden on the buyer.

§ 290. Questions the *seller* should ask before signing the contract.

1. Is my title to the property a good, clear title?

COMMENT: If not, I may be liable for damages if I cannot clear the title.

2. What problems will I have with my existing mortgage in the property?

COMMENT: If I, as seller, must get my existing mortgage released, I should check to see that it has a prepayment clause, and, if not, determine that the mortgagee is willing to accept prepayment. I should also get the mortgagee to agree either to accept payment at the closing of the deal or to deposit his mortgage papers and release or satisfaction thereof in escrow since I will have no funds to pay the mortgage debt before then.

3. Can I accept the buyer's word that I will not have to pay my broker a commission?

COMMENT: The buyer may be seeking a reduction in the seller's asking price on the ground that no broker's commission is involved. Check with the *broker* as to the truth of the buyer's claim that the broker was not instrumental in interesting this buyer in the property.

§ 291. Informal contracts. On occasion a contract of sale is entered into informally.

EXAMPLE: *P* sends *V* a letter offering to purchase certain land for $100,000. *V* writes back accepting the offer. A contract exists.

One problem here relates to the fact that the "acceptance" may seek to add terms to the offer or change it in some way. Any such change, if material, is treated as a "counteroffer." It is tantamount to a rejection of the offer.

EXAMPLE: *V* sends *P* a letter offering to sell *P* certain land for $100,000. Nothing is said concerning the type of deed to be given. *P* writes back stating, "I accept your offer but will insist on a warranty deed." In almost all states the deal is dead. *P* rejected the offer. 16 ALR3d 1430. Ordinarily, the purchaser is not entitled to a warranty deed unless the contract calls for it. (See § 302.) However, the rigor of the older decisions is likely to be tempered in modern times. Uniform Commercial Code § 2-207 states that additional terms in the acceptance do not prevent formation of a contract unless the acceptance is expressly made conditional on assent to the additional or different terms. This provision was intended to get rid of the technical "ribbon matching" or "mirror" rules of the decisions requiring the acceptance to conform literally and in every respect with the offer. *Dorton* v. *Collins Aikman Corp.*, 435 F2d 1161. The U.C.C. thinking is finding its way into the area of real estate law.

§ 292. Unconscionable contracts or terms. Section 2-302 of the Uniform Commercial Code provides that the court may refuse to enforce an unconscionable contract, or strike an unconscionable clause, or so tailor enforcement as to prevent an unconscionable result. This section crystallizes a trend that was already present in the progressive court decisions. 18 ALR3rd 1309. But it will serve to push the courts faster and harder in this direction. The literature on the subject is extensive.

EXAMPLE: *V* gave *P* an option to purchase the land. *P* exercised option. If the literal terms of the option were enforced, *P* would have more than fifty years to pay the purchase price and would have no security meanwhile. The court ordered that *P* must either pay cash or accept reasonable terms. *Rego* v. *Decker*, 482 P2d 834 (Alaska, 1971). This tendency will be accelerated as a result of the Uniform Commercial Code § 2-302.

§ **293. The seller.** Just as a deed must have a grantor, a contract must have a seller.

EXAMPLE: A hotel known as the Glen House, together with its furniture, was sold at auction to Joseph Grafton for $90,000. He refused to go through with the deal. The only document signed by Grafton was the following:

"I, the subscriber, do hereby acknowledge myself to be the purchaser of the estate known as the Glen House, with furniture belonging to it, in Green's Grant, New Hampshire, and sold at auction, Tuesday, May 16, 1871, at 11 o'clock a.m., and for the sum of $90,000, the said property being more particularly described in the advertisement hereunto affixed; and I hereby bind myself, my heirs, and assigns to comply with the terms and conditions of the sale, as declared by the auctioneer at the time and place of sale. Joseph Grafton."

The court held that this was not an enforceable contract of sale, since the seller was not named therein. *Grafton* v. *Cummings*, 99 U.S. 100 (1878).

The following are the chief requirements as to the seller: (1) If the title is held by coowners, all should be named as seller. (2) The seller should be an adult of sound mind. (3) If the seller is a corporation, the sale must be authorized by its directors and sometimes by its stockholders. (4) Where the seller is a trustee or executor, a check should be made to determine that he had the power to sell the land, since neither an executor nor trustee has power to sell land unless the will or trust instrument expressly gives him that power.

A contract by a shareholder in a corporation to cause the corporation to sell and convey corporate land is valid. *Borg* v. *Warner*, 16 Ill.2d 234, 156 NE2d 513 (1958).

Subpurchase. Not uncommonly a seller in a contract is himself merely the buyer under another contract relating to the same land. This is unobjectionable.

EXAMPLE: *A* contracts to sell to *B* and *B* contracts to sell to C. They can hold a double closing, preferably in escrow, and *A* and *B* will get their money, and C will get ownership of the land. *Waggoner* v. *Saether*, 207 Ill. 32, 107 NE 859 (1915).

§ **294. Signature of seller's spouse.** In some states, the spouse of a landowner has certain rights, dower, and curtesy in the land and these rights cannot be extinguished without the spouse's signature. When the seller's spouse, in such a state, has not signed the contract of sale and refuses to sign a deed to the property, courts differ as to the courses open to the buyer. In general, the buyer may decline to go through with the deal and may obtain return of his down payment on the ground that the seller is unable to deliver clear title.

In those community property states that require the wife's consent to a disposition of the community property, the wife's consent is needed for a valid contract to convey community real estate.

Where land is occupied by a family as their home, then regardless of whether the land is owned by the husband or the wife, both must join in any deed of the land. Laws relating to homestead require the double signature. Both must join in the contract to sell.

In states that have abolished dower and curtesy, and that also permit either spouse to convey his or her own land without the signature of the other spouse, the spouse's signature is not necessary either on the contract of sale or on the deed, unless, of course, the land to be sold is a homestead.

In states that have abolished dower, but have substituted some statutory interest that the wife retains if she fails to sign the husband's deed, the courts show the same conflict of opinion as prevails in the states that still have dower. Some allow a deduction from the purchase price to compensate the buyer when the seller's spouse refuses to sign the deed and some do not. *Free* v. *Little,* 31 Utah 449, 88 Pac. 407 (1907).

The failure of the spouse to join in the contract is a harmless mistake if she is willing to join in the deed. *Davis* v. *Dean Vincent Inc.,* 465 P2d 702 (Ore. 1970).

§ **295. The buyer.** Just as a deed must have a grantee, so a contract must have a buyer. The buyer should be named in the contract. If there are two or more buyers and they wish to acquire title as joint tenants, it is necessary that they be so described in the contract. Otherwise serious difficulties may develop if one of the buyers dies before the deed is executed. The buyer should be an adult of sound mind.

§ **296. Sale price—payment provisions.** The contract of sale must state the sale price. A common fault in contracts is the failure to state precisely how the purchase price will be paid.

§ **297. Property sold.** Disputes over a deficiency in the quantity of land sold are common, especially in the case of farmland. The usual rule is that a deficiency in quantity is immaterial if the sale is *in gross.* A sale in gross is a sale of a specific tract of land by name or description. 1 ALR2d 18.

EXAMPLE: *V* contracts to sell to *P* "the Evergreen Ranch in Coles County, Colorado containing 640 acres, more or less, at a price of $500,000." A survey shows the ranch contains only 620 acres. No deduction will be allowed from the sale price. The sale was of the ranch, not of 640 acres. The fact that the price was a gross price, not a *per acre* price helps establish this. 1 ALR2d 28. This rule will be applied unless the deficiency is very great. *Maxwell* v. *Reid,* 496 P2d 1320 (Kan. 1972). Deficiencies as high as 20 percent have been disregarded.

Where the sale is on a price per acre basis the buyer is sometimes given some sort of relief if there is a deficiency in quantity.

EXAMPLE: *V* contracted to sell to *P* "the North seven acres of the Hawkins Tract at a price of $5,000 per acre." The deal was closed and $35,000 paid to *V*. Thereafter, it was discovered the tract conveyed was short three-fourths of an acre. *P* can sue *V* for the deficiency. 153 ALR 37.

In an acreage sale it is best to insert a *usable acreage* clause.

CLAUSE: At a price of $__________ per usable acre, but if survey reveals acreage of less than __________ usable acres, buyer shall have the right to rescind within __________ days after delivery of copy of survey to seller. Areas falling in (1) open or dedicated public streets or ways, (2) recorded private easements of ingress, or (3) areas fenced by adjoiners are not deemed usable acres. All other acres are deemed usable.

The land sold necessarily includes all fixtures comprising part of the land. However, in the case of apartment buildings, hotels, and so on, there may be items of personal property used in connection with the land sold that might not be considered fixtures, such as furniture. If these items are also to go to the buyer, the contract should contain a provision to the effect that such personal property shall be transferred to the buyer at the time of the signing of the deed. In the absence of such provision, the buyer is not entitled to any items that are not fixtures.

§ **298. Description of the land sold.** The contract must contain a reasonably certain description of the land sold. While the description need not be as formal as that contained in a deed, it must be sufficiently definite to identify the land sold with reasonable certainty. 23 ALR2d 6.

There are two views as to the sufficiency of a contract that contains some description of the property but that requires resort to oral testimony to identify the particular property intended to be sold. In states that take a strict view, such contracts are not enforceable.

EXAMPLE: A contract described the land as "real estate situated in the County of Cook and State of Illinois, to wit: One five-room flat and two six-room flats at 3517 Palmer Street." The city in which the land was located was not mentioned. It was held that this description was too indefinite. *Herous* v. *Romanowski,* 336 Ill. 297, 168 NE 305 (1929). Since verbal evidence would be needed to establish the city and state in which the land is located, the contract is not sufficient. This is the rule followed in most states.

On the other hand, liberal courts enforce such contracts.

EXAMPLE: A contract identified land as "305 S. Negley Ave." Oral testimony was admitted to prove that the seller owned property of this addess in Pittsburgh, Pennsylvania. *Sawert* v. *Lunt,* 360 Pa. 521, 62 A2d 34 (1948).

If the city and state are given, a description by street address is sufficient. 23 ALR2d 39. But it is preferable, of course, to use a correct legal description of the land sold.

Where a contract contains a defective street address description but also states that the legal description may be inserted later, the court decisions are conflicting. One line of cases states that the buyer can insert the proper legal description. *Schmalzer* v. *Jamnik,* 407 Ill. 236, 95 NE2d 347

(1950). Other courts hold the contract void. *Murphy* v. *Morse,* 96 Ga.App. 623, 100 SE2d 623 (1957).

Where *V* owns a house and vacant lot adjoining great care must be exercised in preparing the description. Likewise, care should be taken where the building has several addresses. *Goebel* v. *Benefit Tr. Life Insurance Co.,* 88 Ill.App.2d 19, 232 NE2d 211 (1967).

§ 299. **Completeness.** In order to be enforceable, a contract must be complete in all its parts. All the terms of the contract must be settled, and none must be left to be determined by future negotiation. 68 ALR2d 1222.

EXAMPLE: A contract called for a sale price of $75,000, $5000 cash, "time of possession and balance of payment to be arranged at a later date." This contract is not enforceable even if the buyer wishes to pay cash. *Murphy* v. *Koll Grocery Co.,* 311 Ky. 771, 225 SW2d 466. Note that if the contract had simply stated a price of $75,000 and had said nothing regarding terms, the contract would have been good. The court would have read into the contract that a cash deal was intended, deal to be closed in a reasonable time. But since the parties intended something other than a cash deal, but left the exact terms unsettled, the contract was incomplete. A similar holding followed where a contract stated that balance of price was payable "by future agreement on or before January 1, 19—." *Bentzen* v. *H. N. Ranch,* 78 Wyo. 158, 320 P2d 440 (1958); 68 ALR2d 1221 (1958). The court held likewise where the contract stated that a price of $85,000 was payable "as per terms agreed on." *Roberts* v. *Adams,* 164 Cal. App.2d 312, 330 P2d 900 (1958). The same was held where the contract stated "balance in monthly payments." *Cefalu* v. *Breznik,* 15 Ill.2d 168, 154 NE2d 237 (1958). The court also held likewise where the contract said that the balance of $50,000 was payable "as lots are released at purchaser's convenience." *Edward H. Snow Co.* v. *Oxsheer,* 62 N.M. 113, 305 P2d 727 (1957).

In other words, where the written memorandum indicates on its face that the parties intended additional terms that were to be negotiated at some future time, the contract is incomplete. The courts explain that they can enforce a contract that the parties have made but cannot make or complete a contract that the parties have failed to complete, by leaving some provisions for future bargaining. Quite commonly this rule is applied when it appears that some sort of credit sale was contemplated, but the terms were not agreed upon. Today's courts will supply minor terms that the parties have omitted. Corbin, Contracts § 1137; 11 Willison Contracts (Jaeger ed.) § 1424.

If the contract calls for a purchase money mortgage but fails to specify the due date thereof, it is incomplete and cannot be enforced. *Sweeting* v. *Campbell,* 8 Ill.2d 54, 132 NE2d 523 (1956); 60 ALR2d 251. And where a contract provided that the seller would give the buyer a deed that would reserve a vendor's lien for the balance of the purchase price, and the contract further provided that "the rate [of interest] will be agreed upon later," it was too incomplete and indefinite to be enforced. *Hume* v. *Boyle,* 204 SW 673 (Tex. Civ. App. 1918).

§ 300. **Certainty.** In addition to being complete, the contract must be definite and certain. If the court cannot tell what the parties agreed upon, it cannot force them to carry out their agreement.

EXAMPLE: *A* agreed to sell certain land to *B* for $5000, "one-half cash, balance one to four years, with interest at 7 per cent." This contract is too vague and indefinite to be enforced. No one can be certain what the quoted portion means. *Crawford* v. *Williford,* 145 Ga. 550, 89 SE 488.

§ 301. **Type of title, deed, and evidence of title.** There are three separate ideas that are sometimes confused.

EXAMPLE: A contract of sale is silent as to the *type of title* the buyer is to receive. In such case the buyer is entitled to a marketable title, free of all encumbrances. This will be explained later.

EXAMPLE: The contract is silent as to the *type of deed* the buyer is to receive. In most states the buyer must be content with a quitclaim deed.

EXAMPLE: The contract is silent as to the *type of evidence of title* (abstract, title policy) the buyer is to receive. In such case the buyer must procure his own evidence of title at his own expense.

§ 302. **Type of deed.** A contract is enforceable even though it does not specify the type of deed to be given. Nevertheless, since there is a vast difference between a quitclaim deed and a warranty deed, the contract should specify the type agreed upon.

If the contract is silent regarding the type of deed to be given, in most states the seller need only give a quitclaim deed or a deed of bargain and sale without covenants. *Morris* v. *Goldthorp,* 390 Ill. 186, 60 NE2d 857 (1945); *Boekelheide* v. *Snyder,* 71 S.D. 470, 26 NW2d 74 (1947); *Vitra Seal Co.* v. *Jaycox,* 1 N.J.S. 560, 62 A2d 431 (1948); *Tymon* v. *Linoki,* 16 N.Y.2d 293, 213 NE2d 661 (1965); 16 ALR3d 1430. This does not excuse the seller from giving a marketable title. It simply means that once the title has been shown to be marketable, the seller may deliver a quitclaim deed and be rid of any possibility of future worry regarding presently unknown title defects.

It is best for the buyer to insist on a warranty deed. In a number of states, the mere fact that the buyer is content to take a quitclaim deed is enough to keep him from being a bona fide purchaser, and he will take the land subject to unrecorded deeds, mortgages, liens, and so forth.

EXAMPLE: Pursuant to a contract of sale *V* gave *P* a quitclaim deed. *P* then discovered that *V* had placed an unrecorded mortgage on the property. In some states a grantee in a quitclaim deed is not considered a bona fide purchaser and the unrecorded mortgage would be good against *P*.

The deed should comply with the contract in all respects.

EXAMPLE: *V* contracts to sell to *H* and *W* in joint tenancy. He made the deed to *H* only. *W* is entitled to have the deed reformed to run to *H* and *W* as joint tenants. *Wahl* v. *Fairbanks,* 405 Ill. 290, 90 NE2d 735 (1950).

EXAMPLE: *V* contracts to sell to *E*. The deed calls for a warranty deed. Nothing is said about encroachments. A survey shows the building encroaches 3 inches into the street. *R* wants to make his warranty deed subject to the encroachment. He cannot do so. The deed must follow the contract.

EXAMPLE: *V* contracts to sell to *E* and to give *P* a warranty deed. Actually *V* has the property in the name of *N*, a nominee, and offers *P* a warranty deed signed by *N*. *P* need not accept it. 57 ALR 1507.

WARNING: One must not attach too much importance to the giving of a warranty deed. After all, I could sit down at this moment, write out, sign, and deliver to you a warranty deed purporting to convey to you the Merchandise Mart, the Tower of London, Westminster Abbey, and all the motels in the Holiday Inn chain. As a result of this activity you would own absolutely nothing. I cannot convey what I do not own. A warranty deed is like the frosting on a cake. It's nice to have if the grantor really owns the land. But, if you really want to know that I own what I am trying to convey, you must insist on receiving evidence of title, written proof that I really own the land I am attempting to convey. If the land is really owned by the grantor in the warranty deed, but the title search fails to show some unpaid real estate tax, unpaid mechanic's lien, and so forth, the warranty deed might help the grantee collect from the grantor the tax he is compelled to pay to protect his title. This however, is about all the warranty deed is useful for.

§ 303. **Marketable title.** Unless the contract provides otherwise, the seller must convey a marketable title. Such a title is also described as a *merchantable title*. This means that the seller must have a good title, free from liens, encumbrances, or defects other than those specified in the contract. As a general rule, every buyer of land has a right to demand a title that shall put him in all reasonable security against loss or annoyance by litigation. He should have a title that is free from doubt, one that will enable him not only to hold his land, but to hold it in peace and free from the hazard of litigation. If he wishes to sell the land, he should be reasonably sure that no flaw will come up to disturb its market value. *Firebaugh* v. *Wittenberg*, 309 Ill. 536, 141 NE 379 (1923).

SUGGESTION: The contract should contain a *subject clause* specifying the *permitted objections*. These are the objections the seller knows are against his title, usually those that were in existence when he bought the land, and usually of a character such that they cannot be removed, like building restrictions, and usually such that the buyer finds unobjectionable. As long as they are listed in the subject clause, they do not render title unmarketable.

The question of marketability of title must be disposed of before the deal is closed. In other words, if the buyer wishes to avail himself of his right to insist upon a marketable title, he must point out such defects as he discovers and must do this before he pays his money and receives his deed. Once the deal is closed, the money paid, and the deed delivered, the buyer cannot demand his money back if the title proves defective. 57 ALR 1261; 84 ALR 1025, 1027, 1032; 92 CJS 15; 92 CJS 559. However, if the buyer has received a warranty deed from the seller, he may sue the seller for damages, should the title prove defective.

§ 304. **Marketable title—mortgages and other liens.** Unless the contract provides otherwise, the buyer has the right to demand a title free and clear of all mortgages, tax liens, judgment liens, mechanics' liens, and all other liens. It is not sufficient for the seller to offer to deduct the amount of such liens from the purchase price. The buyer may reject the title unless it is actually cleared of such liens. Suppose, however, that there is a mortgage or other lien on the property, and the seller can arrange to have the mortgagee present at the closing of the deal, so that, at the closing of the deal, the mortgage will be paid in full out of the purchase money due the seller and the mortgagee will deliver a release of the mortgage to the buyer. Must the buyer go through with the deal in this manner if the contract does not require him to do so? In quite a number of states, the answer is in the affirmative. The seller's title is not considered unmarketable if he can arrange to have the owner of the mortgage, judgment, or other lien present at the closing of the deal, ready to turn over proper releases to the buyer on receiving payment of the amount due from the buyer. *Gibson* v. *Brown,* 214 Ill. 330, 73 NE 578 (1905); *Joslyn* v. *Irvin Dick Co.,* 168 Minn. 279, 209 NW 889 (1926); *Robeson-Marion Develop. Co.* v. *Powers Co.,* 183 SE2d 455 (S.C. 1971); *Sparks* v. *Helmer,* 142 Okla. 219, 286 Pac. 306 (1930). In other states, a contrary rule is followed. Any mortgage or other lien not mentioned in the contract must be cleared before the deal is closed. *Johnson* v. *Malone,* 252 Ala. 609, 42 So2d 505 (1949); *Carey* v. *Minor C. Keith Inc.,* 250 N.Y. 216, 164 NE 912 (1929).

Many lawyers feel that where the contract requires good title to be established by title insurance, by inference this requires the seller to produce to the buyer a title company policy or commitment free and clear of any existing mortgage. Inferentially, the contract obviously contemplates that the *title company* must, before the deal is closed, be satisfied with documents produced to discharge the mortgage.

CLAUSE FOR SELLER'S BENEFIT: If at the date of closing there is any mortgage encumbrance which the vendor is obligated to pay and discharge, the vendor may use any portion of the balance of the purchase price to satisfy the same, provided the vendor shall at closing of deal either (1) deliver to the purchaser an instrument in recordable form sufficient, in the judgment of purchaser's title company, to satisfy such encumbrance of record, or (2) deposit with the purchaser's title insurance company sufficient money required by it to insure the recording of such satisfaction and the issuance of title insurance to the purchaser free of any such encumbrance, together with the mortgagee's letter indicating its willingness to accept such payment.

§ 305. **Marketable title—easements.** Easements render the title unmarketable, unless, of course, the contract requires the buyer to take title subject to easements.

NEW DIRECTIONS: In recent decisions the title is not rendered unmarketable by the existence of *visible* and *beneficial* easement.

EXAMPLE: The contract is silent regarding easements. A utility company has an easement over the rear five feet of the land for an electric power line, and such a power line is, in fact, located on the rear five feet. The power line services the property in question. In many states, the title would be considered marketable. 57 ALR 1426.

SUGGESTION TO SELLER: Check your title insurance policy or other evidence of title. If it shows your title to be subject to an easement, state in contract that title will be subject "to easement recorded as Document No. 1234567."

SUGGESTION TO BUYER: Do not sign a contract stating that seller will deliver title subject "to easements of record." This would obligate you to take title subject to a recorded easement for a one hundred-foot highway running right through the middle of the house. Insist that the contract specifically describe the easements to which the title is subject and read them over before you sign the contract.

§ 306. Marketable title—building restrictions. Often the use to which a tract of land may be devoted is restricted by building restrictions contained in recorded deeds or subdivision plats. Unless the contract provides otherwise, the buyer is not required to accept a title encumbered with restrictions as to the character of the buildings that may be erected, the use to which the property may be put, and so on, even though such restrictions actually enhance the value of the property.

EXAMPLE: *V* contracts to sell *P* a vacant lot in a high-class residential subdivision. The contract does not mention restrictions. In the recorded plat of the subdivision, there is a restriction providing that only single-family dwellings may be erected in the subdivision. *P* may reject the title. 57 ALR 1414.

Suppose the contract requires the buyer to accept title subject to "building line and building restrictions," but it appears that the building on the property violates existing restrictions. The buyer may decline to go through with the deal, for a *violation of a restriction* is a defect or encumbrance separate and distinct from the restriction itself.

EXAMPLE: A contract required the buyer to accept title subject to building and use restrictions. There was a building restriction prohibiting the erection of buildings within five feet of any side line. The buildings actually extended into the prohibited area. It was held that the buyer could refuse to go through with the deal. *Herb* v. *Severson,* 32 Wash.2d 159, 201 P2d 156 (1948); *Lohmeyer* v. *Bower,* 170 Kan. 442, 227 P2d 102 (1951).

SUGGESTION TO BUYER: Never sign a contract which states that title will be subject to "restrictions of record." This obligates you to take title subject to any restriction, no matter how absurd, even a restriction that the only building permitted on the land is a chicken coop. If the seller's title insurance policy is available, look at it. If it shows a restriction, go to the title company or the recorder's office and read the restriction. If you have no objection to it, let the contract read that title will be "subject to restriction recorded as Document No. 123456." Where the contract must be signed at a time when information as to existing building restrictions is not available, and the land is improved with a building that is the principal subject matter of the sale, you might employ the following clause: "Subject to covenants and restrictions of record, provided same are not violated by the existing improvements and the use thereof." When you are buying *vacant* land you *must* insist on reading the restrictions in full before signing the contract.

§ 307. **Marketable title—zoning and building code violations.** Building restrictions imposed by deeds or plats must be distinguished from zoning and building ordinances. Such ordinances, though they may greatly restrict the use that may be made of the land, do not render title unmarketable. Generally the attitude of the courts is that zoning and building ordinances are part of the law of the land, and all persons are supposed to take notice of them. 39 ALR3d 370. Ignorance of the law excuses no one. Suppose that the premises contain actual, existing *violations* of zoning or building ordinances. Here the rule is different. In most of the recent decisions, courts have held that substantial existing violations of *zoning ordinances* render title unmarketable. 5 *American Law of Property* § 11.49; *Lohmeyer* v. *Bower,* 170 Kan. 442, 227 P2d 102 (1951); *Mayer* v. *De Vincentis,* 107 Pa. Super. 588, 164 Atl. 111 (1933); *Hartman* v. *Rizzuto,* 123 Cal. App.2d 186, 266 P2d 539 (1954); 39 ALR3d 375.

EXAMPLE: A building containing three apartments was erected in an area where the ordinance prohibited construction of a building containing more than two apartments. The court held that the buyer could terminate the contract and obtain return of his down payment. *Oates* v. *Delcuze,* 226 La. 751, 77 So2d 28 (1954).

In many cities, violations of building ordinances (like those forbidding basement apartments, requiring certain minimum sanitary arrangements, requiring separate exits for each apartment, requiring fireproof material, etc.) now entail drastic punishment, for cities have come to recognize that the fight against the slum is a fight for survival. Building ordinance violations, like zoning ordinance violations, are being recognized as flaws in the marketability of title, for they impose on a purchaser the same hazards of litigation that the rule of marketability of title was designed to avoid. *Brunko* v. *Pharo,* 3 Wis.2d 628, 89 NW2d 221 (1958) noted, 1958 *Wis. L. Rev.* 641; *Bronen* v. *Marmer,* 206 N.Y.S.2d 909 (1960). *Contra: Stone* v. *Sexsmith,* 28 Wash.2d 947, 184 P2d 567 (1947); *Ableman* v. *Slader,* 80 Ill. App.2d 94, 224 NE2d 569 (1967).

The prudent buyer will insist that the contract of sale provide that the seller will deliver the property "free from all violations of zoning and building ordinances," and a check with city officials for such violations should be made before the deal is closed. The seller will not be allowed to avoid by trickery or subterfuge his responsibility for ordinance violations.

EXAMPLE: The sale involved a house with an illegal basement apartment. The seller could not bring the building into compliance by tearing out the illegal apartment, for what the contract really contemplates is that the seller will get a permit from the city legalizing the condition as it was when the contract was signed. As it stands, the title is unmarketable. *Hammer* v. *Michael,* 243 N.Y. 445, 154 NE 305 (1926).

Advertising for sale a building that contains ordinance violations may constitute a fraud upon the buyer.

§ 308. **Marketable title—leases and tenancies.** Unless the contract so provides, the buyer need not accept a title subject to existing leases, or even to existing tenancies without leases. *Haiss* v. *Schmukler,* 201 N.Y.S. 332. If such leases or tenancies exist, the contract should provide that the title is subject to such leases or tenancies.

SUGGESTION TO BUYER: Do not sign a contract to accept title subject to *existing leases and tenancies.* The existing leases may be very favorable to the tenant and disadvantageous to the property owner. The seller should therefore be required to include a schedule, either in the contract or in a separate document, listing the expiration date, tenants, and rentals on all existing leases and tenancies, together with a statement as to whether the leases include an option to renew or to purchase the property.

§ 309. Marketable title—encroachments. Encroachments are of three kinds: (1) The building on the land sold encroaches on neighboring land. (2) The building on the land sold encroaches on adjoining streets or alleys. (3) Buildings on adjoining land encroach upon the land sold. 47 ALR2d 331.

When the seller's buildings extend over and upon neighboring land, the factor that renders title unmarketable is the danger that the neighbor may obtain a court order directing removal of the offending portion of the structure, a task that may involve great expense; or the neighbor may institute litigation in an effort to obtain such an order, and the buyer will be put to the expense of defending the litigation. This is in harmony with the principle that a title is not marketable if there is an appreciable risk of litigation. *Very slight* encroachments will not render the title unmarketable, as where a wall of the building on the premises sold extends three-fourths of an inch on neighboring land. *Traxler* v. *McLeran,* 116 Cal. App. 226, 2 P2d 553 (1931). The reason such property remains marketable is that, when (a) the encroachment of my building on your land is slight, (b) the cost of removal is great, and (c) the benefit to you from removal of the building is slight, courts will not compel removal of the encroachment. *Nitterauer* v. *Pulley,* 401 Ill. 494, 82 NE2d 643 (1948). Also, when the building that encroaches on neighboring land is old or dilapidated, or a temporary structure of small value, or a structure that is removable at only slight effort or expense, the title is deemed marketable. With respect to permanent structures, it is hard to draw the line between objectionable and unobjectionable encroachments. The encroachment of a house one and one-half inches on neighboring land has been held to render title unmarketable. *Stokes* v. *Johnson,* 57 N.Y. 673.

When buildings on neighboring land encroach on the premises being sold, courts are more liberal. At the worst, the buyer will be deprived of some portion of the land that the seller has agreed to sell. If the area occupied by the encroaching building is insignificant when compared with the total area of the land being sold, the title is marketable. *Merges* v. *Ringler,* 54 N.Y.S. 280.

When buildings on the land sold extend over adjoining streets or alleys, as in the case of buildings extending over and upon neighboring privately owned land, there is danger that a suit will be instituted to compel removal of the encroachment. Title is unmarketable. Still, if the encroachment is trivial, so that action by the city authorities is highly improbable and it is unlikely that a court would order the encroachment removed, the title is marketable.

EXAMPLE: A building encroached two inches on an adjoining street. The title was held to be marketable. *Mertens* v. *Berendsen,* 213 Cal. 111, 1 P2d 440 (1931).

Suppose the contract provides that the seller agree to deliver a title "subject to questions of survey" or "subject to such a state of facts as an accurate survey would show." Such clauses are inserted to relieve the seller of all responsibility with respect to encroachments. If the existence of encroachments is revealed, the buyer must nevertheless go through with the deal. *McCarter* v. *Crawford,* 245 N.Y. 43, 156 NE 90 (1927).

Suppose the contract requires the seller to deliver title "free from all encumbrances and encroachments." Here the existence of trivial encroachments, such as would ordinarily not render title unmarketable, will nevertheless justify the buyer's rejection of the title.

§ 310. Marketable title—chattels. Many sales of land specifically include valuable chattels, as where a hotel is being sold. The buyer is entitled to marketable title to the chattels. *Peters* v. *Spielvozel,* 163 So.2d 59 (Fla. 1964).

§ 311. Marketable title—miscellaneous defects. There are many other defects or encumbrances that may render a title unmarketable. For example, a deed signed by some prior landowner may be defective in that the property is not properly described therein, or a signature may be lacking, or the grantor's wife may have failed to sign the deed. Court proceedings on which the title depends, such as mortgage foreclosures, sales by guardians, and the like, may have been defectively conducted. Estates of deceased landowners may have been improperly probated. It is impossible to enumerate within the allotted space the many defects that may render a title unmarketable. Marketability of title plays an important part in those situations where the buyer, after having signed a contract to purchase the land, regrets his bargain and wishes to get out of the deal. His attorney will then subject the title to a minute scrutiny, hoping to find some defect that renders the title unmarketable, so that his client may declare the contract at an end and obtain a return of his down payment.

§ 312. Marketable title—title insurance. The fact that a title company is willing to insure the seller's title does not make it marketable.

EXAMPLE: *V* entered into a contract to sell real estate to *P*. The contract required *V* to furnish a clear policy of title insurance. The title search revealed a recorded easement. The title company was willing to issue a clear policy. *P* was permitted to back out of the deal. *P* is entitled to a marketable title *and* title insurance. *New York Investors, Inc.* v. *Manhattan Beach Bathing Parks Corp.,* 243 N.Y.S. 548, 30 *Columb. L. Rev.* 1215.

SUGGESTION TO SELLER: Let the contract provide that the title policy is conclusive evidence that the title is good as therein stated but it shall not be evidence of any matters not insured by said policy.

§ 313. **Marketable title laws.** With each passing year it has grown increasingly difficult to prove that any given title to land is marketable. Year by year the chain of deeds, mortgages, wills, and other recorded matters relating to the title, beginning with the original grant from the government, grows longer and more complex. In consequence, abstracts of title and title searches grow longer, more difficult, and more complex. Many more opportunities present themselves for technical errors that impair the marketability of title. For these difficulties a solution had to be found. It has, indeed, been found in a number of states. In these states (Illinois, Indiana, Iowa, Massachusetts, Michigan, Minnesota, Nebraska, North Dakota, Ohio, South Dakota, and Wisconsin, for example) new laws have been passed to promote the marketability of title. In general, laws such as this select a particular period of time. In Illinois, for example, the period is forty years. If an examination of the public records shows that for the last forty years title to a particular tract of land has passed from one person to another in a connected fashion, that this connected chain of title culminates in a deed to *X*, and that *X* is in peaceable possession of the land in question, *X* will be deemed to have good and marketable title to that tract of land free and clear from any adverse claims to the title that antedate the forty-year period. This does not mean that all claims that are forty years old or more are automatically wiped out. Each of these marketability laws provides a period of time during which a person claiming an interest that is more than forty years old (or whatever the statutory period may be) may record an affidavit or other claim stating the nature of his interest in a particular piece of land. In this fashion, any claim to the title of land must appear on the records within the last forty years or it is automatically outlawed. Consequently, a person searching the title to the land need only search the title during the past forty years, and if he finds a connected chain, he need not concern himself with recorded matters that antedate the forty-year period. Each of these marketability laws lists certain interests that are not affected or outlawed by the legislation.

EXAMPLE: A common provision is to the effect that a person claiming an easement need not record his claim of easement if the existence of such an easement is revealed by a physical examination of the land itself. Thus if a neighbor claims party wall rights or an easement for a driveway extending over the premises, it is fairly clear that a mere glance at the property will reveal the existence of such easement claims. Therefore they need not be rerecorded.

Another common exception relates to claims of the United States Government. No state has the power or right to pass laws that extinguish the rights of the United States Government. But whatever the claim may be, if it does not fall within the list of claims not affected by the legislation, it is outlawed unless a document in proper form showing the existence of such claim is recorded within the forty-year period. As to these laws see 71 ALR2d 846; Basye, Clearing Land Titles (2d ed., 1970) §§ 171–189.

§ 314. **Time of existence of good title.** Ordinarily the seller need not have good title on the date of the contract. It is sufficient if he has good title at the time fixed for delivery of the deed, or even later, for example, at the time the court, in a specific performance suit, orders the contract to be enforced. *Gibson* v. *Brown,* 214 Ill. 330, 73 NE 578 (1905).

If the contract provides that time is of the essence and also provides that the seller will furnish the buyer an abstract of title or other evidence of title within a specified period of time, the seller must meet this deadline, or the buyer will have the right to declare the contract at an end.

§ 315. **Evidence of title.** It is important to distinguish between the seller's duty to deliver good title and his duty to furnish evidence that his title is good. As above stated, unless the contract provides otherwise, the seller must furnish the buyer a *marketable title.* But if the contract does not require him to do so, the seller is under no obligation to furnish the buyer *any evidence that the title is good.* The buyer makes his own title search unless the contract specifies otherwise.

§ 316. **Time for furnishing evidence of title and curing defects in title.** If the contract requires the seller to furnish evidence of title, but does not fix a time limit for the furnishing and examination of the abstract or other evidence of title, it is assumed that a reasonable time was intended. In such case:

1. The seller has a reasonable time to furnish the buyer the abstract or other evidence of title.
2. The buyer has a reasonable time to examine the abstract and point out defects in title.
3. The seller has a reasonable time to eliminate or cure defects in title disclosed by the abstract or other evidence of title.

To eliminate uncertainties and speculation by either party on the rise or fall of the value of the property before choosing to perform his part of the contract, the contract should:

1. Fix the time allowed the seller to furnish the buyer evidence of title.

EXPLANATION: When the contract requires the seller to furnish evidence of title by a day named and provides that time is of the essence, and the title evidence is not furnished by the day named, the buyer may rescind, i.e., declare the contract terminated, and may recover his deposit. *Johnson* v. *Riedler,* 395 Ill. 412, 70 NE2d 570 (1941). Most forms of contracts fix a specific time for furnishing the evidence of title and provide that time is of the essence.

2. Fix the time allowed the buyer to examine the abstract and require him to point out any defects in title within the time limited, failure to do so to constitute an acceptance of the title as good.
3. Fix the time allowed the seller to cure defects in title.
4. Fix a time within which the buyer must choose to accept or reject a defective title that the seller cannot cure within the time allowed him.

§ 317. **Earnest money.** Earnest money is a deposit or down payment made by the buyer as a guaranty that the contract will be performed on his part. If he does perform, it applies as a part payment of the purchase price. If he defaults, it is retained by the seller. Usually, the contract specifically permits the seller to retain the earnest money where the buyer defaults. But even in the absence of such a provision, a buyer who is in default cannot recover his earnest money from the seller. *Zersky* v. *Sheehan,* 413 F2d 481 (1969); *Bruce Builders Inc.* v. *Goodwin,* 317 So.2d 868 (Fla. 1975); 31 ALR2d 8. Courts have allowed the seller to retain rather substantial down payments; for example, $300,000 on a sale price of $3,000,000, and $35,000 on a sale price of $140,000. Corbin, The Right of a Defaulting Vendee to the Restitution of Installment Unpaid, 40 *Yale L.J.* 1013 (1931). But retention of an earnest money deposit of $30,000 on a sale for $95,000 is unconscionable. *Hook* v. *Lomar,* 320 F2d 536 (5th Circ. 1968).

SUGGESTION TO SELLER: The seller should for his protection, require a deposit large enough to cover the broker's commission, the expense of the title search, and the compensation to the seller for the loss of his bargain should the buyer default.

SUGGESTION TO BUYER: Provide that the earnest money shall be held in escrow by some third person pending the closing of the deal to insure that the buyer will experience no difficulty in obtaining a return of his deposit should it prove impossible for the seller to deliver clear title. *Gauss* v. *Kirk,* 77 A2d 323 (D.C. 1950).

SUGGESTION TO BUYER: If you put up a check as earnest money, be sure there is money in your bank account to cover it. If the seller attempts to have the check certified, and the bank refuses because funds are lacking, the seller then has an excuse that gives him the right to refuse to carry out the deal. *Gallinero* v. *Fitzpatrick,* 267 NE2d 649 (Mass. 1971).

SUGGESTION TO BUYER: If the seller insists that his broker hold the earnest money, let the contract provide that if the broker fails to return the money to the buyer when the buyer is entitled to it, the seller will pay the amount of the earnest money to the buyer. This will force the seller to think twice about entrusting a large amount of money to an individual. Banks, title companies, and trust companies charge a very small fee for holding earnest money deposits.

§ 318. Mortgages and financing in real estate sales—contacts contingent on procuring financing. In the financing of real estate sales several possibilities are present:

1. The land may have no mortgage on it, and the buyer may be ready to pay cash. No mortgage figures in the sale of the land.

2. The land may have no mortgage on it, but the seller may be willing to accept part cash and to take back a purchase money mortgage for the balance of the purchase price. For example, an insurance company owns a building that it has acquired by foreclosure of a mortgage. It will wish to sell the land, since it is not in the real estate business, but since it also wishes to keep its money in good investments, a purchase money mortgage may be the ideal solution for both seller and buyer.

3. The land is clear of mortgages, but the buyer will need to mortgage the property in order to raise the full purchase price.

4. The land is subject to an existing mortgage, and the buyer is willing to buy the property subject to such existing mortgage.

5. The land is subject to an existing mortgage, but it is too small, or the payments are not convenient for the buyer, so that it will be necessary for the buyer to put a new mortgage on the property for an amount and payable on such terms as will meet his needs. This means that the sale involves paying the existing mortgage and simultaneously placing a new mortgage on the property.

6. The sale may be by an installment contract with clause reserving right to seller to mortgage the land, buyer to take title subject to the mortgage.

7. The sale may be by an installment contract with provision that buyer will receive deed when specified amount is paid in, buyer then to give seller mortgage for balance of purchase price.

8. The sale may be by an installment contract with no mortgage provisions.

Special laws. In Maryland, a law provides that when the purchaser in an installment contract has paid 40 per cent of the purchase price he is entitled to demand a deed upon executing a purchase money mortgage to the seller for the balance. 13 *Rutgers L. Rev.* 625.

Unless the contract provides otherwise, the buyer need not accept title subject to a mortgage. If there is a mortgage on the land and the buyer is to accept the land with the mortgage remaining unpaid, the contract should specify: (1) that the land is being sold subject to such mortgage; (2) the amount remaining unpaid thereon; (3) whether or not the buyer *assumes and agrees* to pay the mortgage, since if he does, he becomes personally liable to the mortgagee for the mortgage debt. If he does not *assume and agree* to pay the mortgage, he may lose the land by foreclosure should he default in his mortgage payments, but no personal judgment can be rendered against him. If the contract calls for the buyer to take the land subject to a mortgage but misdescribes the mortgage, the buyer can back out of the deal. *Crooke* v. *Nelson,* 195 Ia. 681, 191 NW 122 (1922).

§ **319. Contingent contracts.** Often a clause will be inserted in a contract making it subject to some contingency, so that if the specified event does not occur, the deal is off and the buyer gets back his down payment. Usually such clauses are inserted at the buyer's request. One example would be a clause making the contract contingent on the buyer's ability to procure a mortgage loan of a specified sum. Or the contract may be contingent on the buyer's ability to procure a transfer to himself of the seller's liquor license. Or the contract may be contingent on the rezoning of the premises within a specified time. 39 ALR3d 385. For example, if a buyer needs the property for an industrial plant but it is presently zoned for residential purposes, he will insist that the contract have a provision rendering it void unless rezoning is obtained within a certain number of days.

At times these contingency clauses tend to be rather vague. Nevertheless some courts will enforce them.

EXAMPLE: Where the contract called for a soil compaction report satisfactory to the buyer, the court held that this meant a report satisfactory to a reasonable person. *Collins* v. *Vickter Manor,* 47 Cal.2d 875, 306 P2d 783 (1957).

Some, but not all, modern decisions seem to sanction a good bit of indefiniteness in the contingent clause.

EXAMPLE: The contract stated it was contingent on the buyer's procuring a mortgage loan of a stated sum "with interest at current prevailing rate." This was held to be sufficiently definite. *Barto* v. *Hacks,* 184 SE2d 188.

EXAMPLE: A contract of sale for $28,000 stated it was contingent on the buyer obtaining a mortgage of $__________. The court held that a mortgage for a "reasonable amount" was intended, and where the buyer tried to get a mortgage of $21,000 and failed, the contract was at an end. *Grayson* v. *LaBranche,* 225 A2d 922 (1967).

The buyer must make a reasonable effort to procure financing. *Fry* v. *George Elkins Co.,* 327 P2d 905 (Cal. 1958). What defines a reasonable effort is not always clear.

If the contract is contingent upon the buyer's procuring a mortgage of a specified amount, and he makes *no effort* to procure one (as is likely to occur when the buyer has changed his mind about buying the property), the clause is waived, and the seller is entitled to forfeit the buyer's earnest money. *Huckleberry* v. *Wilson,* 284 SW2d 205 (Tex. 1955). The buyer must act in good faith.

It is best that the contract give details of the mortgage such as interest rate, time of payment, and so forth. Often the contract gives the buyer ten days to procure financing, and if he fails the seller is then given ten additional days to procure financing for the buyer. A seller may procure a mortgage loan of the desired amount for the buyer and the buyer reject it in horror because the interest rate is too high. Obviously, all such details should be covered in the clause. If, however, the details are omitted, the courts are likely to insist that the terms of the offered mortgage be "reasonable" otherwise the buyer is not required to accept it. *Lach* v. *Cahill,* 138 Conn. 418, 85 A2d 481 (1951). *Chambers* v. *Jordan,* 262 A2d 505 (Md. 1970). Minds differ so much as to what is reasonable that controversy and litigation easily develop in such a situation.

SUGGESTION TO SELLER: Also tie the contingent clause into the printed clause of the contract form. The contract may give the buyer *thirty* days in which to procure a mortgage of a specified amount. Yet the printed portion of the contract may state that the seller must deliver to the buyer evidence of seller's good title within *twenty* days of the date of the contract. Why should the seller have his title examined when he does not even know that he has a deal with the buyer?

If the contract is contingent on the buyer's obtaining a mortgage, describing it adequately, and if the buyer acting in good faith cannot procure the mortgage, he is entitled to a return of his earnest money deposit. *Levicki* v. *Chrachol,* 56 Ill.App.2d 54, 205 NE2d 491 (1965).

§ 320. **Possession and rents.** The general rule of law is that the right to possession of land follows the legal title. Since the purchaser does not acquire the legal title to the land until he receives his deed, as a rule he is not entitled to possession until that time. 56 ALR2d 1272. The contract, however, may expressly authorize the buyer to take possession before he receives his deed. Such a provision should normally be included in an installment contract, for in such a contract, a purchaser usually expects to take possession long before he is ready to receive his deed. Also, the contract may by implication confer the right of possession on the buyer, as where it contains a provision requiring the buyer to keep the buildings in repair or to give up possession in case of default.

The party who is entitled to possession is entitled to the rents of the land. Ordinarily, therefore, rents falling due before the seller gives the buyer a deed belong to the seller, and rents due after the delivery of the deed are payable to the buyer.

§ 321. **Taxes.** Unless the contract provides otherwise, the seller must give the buyer good title free and clear of taxes that were a lien at the time the contract was made. In fact, if the seller remains in possession after the contract is made, and taxes become a lien while the seller is in possession, the seller must pay these taxes. However, if the buyer goes into possession and taxes thereafter become a lien, the buyer must pay these taxes. To eliminate questions, the contract usually specifies the taxes to which the land will be subject when the deed is made.

§ 322. **Insurance and risk of loss.** It sometimes happens that before the deal is closed the building is destroyed or damaged by fire or other casualty. In most states, the loss so caused falls on the buyer. In other words, the buyer must go through with the deal and pay the full contract price, even though the building has been destroyed. 27 ALR2d 466. This risk is not limited to fire. It includes damage from flood, windstorm, vandalism, boiler destruction, hurricane, erosion, subsidence, collapse of retaining wall, and freezing of an orange grove. Friedman, Contracts and Conveyances of Real Prop. § 4.11 (3d ed. 1975). But most states give the buyer the benefit of the seller's insurance. *Id.* But in an increasing number of states, including California, Connecticut, Illinois, Kentucky, Maine, Massachusetts, Michigan, New Hampshire, New York, Oregon, Rhode Island, South Carolina, South Dakota, and Wisconsin, laws or court decisions put the risk of loss on the seller, so that if a substantial loss by fire or other casualty occurs before the buyer has been given a deed to the property, the buyer may cancel the deal and obtain return of his down payment. However, an important factor in some of these states is the fact of possession. The one in possession is in a better position to prevent fires. Hence in these states, if the buyer is put in possession before the deal is closed, you will find the courts or the laws assigning this as a reason for putting the risk of loss back on the buyer.

In all states the risk of loss falls on the seller where: (1) The contract specifically provides that risk of loss pending closing of the deal rests on the seller. (2) The seller does not have a good marketable title at the time of the loss, the reason being that it is unfair to put the risk of loss on a buyer when the seller is in no position to perform his obligations under the contract. *Eppstein* v. *Kuhn,* 225 Ill. 115, 80 NE 80 (1906). (3) The seller is at fault in causing the delay in closing the deal, and during this delayed period a loss occurs. (4) The loss is due to the carelessness of the seller, as when he leaves the house during a cold spell without draining the heating system and all the radiators are cracked by ice formation. 3 Corbin, *Contracts* 661.

§ 323. **Prorating or apportionment.** Provision is frequently made for prorating, adjustment, or apportionment of rents, taxes, insurance, premiums, water taxes, interest accrued on mortgage indebtedness, personal property taxes on personal property transferred to the buyer, gas and electric bills, janitor's salary, management fees on current rent collections, and charges on service contracts, such as exterminator or scavenger service. It is also customary to provide that fuel on hand shall be purchased by the buyer at current prices as of the proration date. Although it is usual to prorate certain items not mentioned in the contract, it must be remembered that, in the event of controversy, the party contending that an item should be prorated will be unable legally to compel proration in the absence of provision in the contract therefor. *Lathers* v. *Keogh,* 109 N.Y. 583, 17 NE 131 (1888); *Antietam-Sharpsburg Mus.* v. *William H. Marsh, Inc.,* 249 A2d 221 (Md. 1969); *Wilson* v. *Campbell,* 425 SW2d 518 (Ark. 1968). A special prorating clause is needed where there are percentage leases, since the actual rental will not be known until after the deal is closed. See § 379.

§ 324. **Date.** The contract need not be, but usually is, dated.

§ 325. **Signature.** As heretofore pointed out, the contract must be signed by the party against whom enforcement of the contract is sought. Of course in practice the contract is almost invariably signed by both seller and buyer.

Suppose land is owned jointly by *A* and *B*. *C* negotiates with *A* for the purchase of the property and agrees with *A* that the land will be sold for the sum of $10,000. A contract is prepared, designating *A* and *B* as sellers and *C* as buyer. *A* and *C* sign the contract; *B* refuses to sign. Is the contract binding on *A*? No, for the contract shows on its face that a sale was intended only if both landowners agreed. *Madia* v. *Collins,* 408 Ill. 358, 97 NE2d 313 (1951); 154 ALR 778; 92 CJS 547.

§ 326. **Contracts signed by agents.** A person may authorize an agent to enter into contracts on his behalf for the purchase or sale of real estate. In many states, this authorization must be in writing, and in all states it is customary to employ a written authorization. Such an agent is called an *attorney in fact,* and the document granting this authority is called a *power of attorney.*

§ 327. **Seal.** A seal is not necessary to the validity of a contract.

§ 328. **Delivery.** Suppose you list your land with a broker for sale and he finds a buyer interested in its purchase but who does not wish to pay the price you are asking. The buyer prepares and signs a contract of sale stipulating a lower price. This is an *offer.* He hands the contract to the broker, who hands it to you. You sign the contract and return it to the buyer. This is an *acceptance.* The contract is now in force. Suppose, however, that you simply hold on to the contract, hoping that a higher offer will appear, and refuse to answer the buyer's telephone calls. This last situation poses the questions: (1) Must the buyer be *notified* that his offer has been accepted? In other words, can he legally withdraw his offer at any time before he is *notified* that the offer has been accepted? (2) Is delivery necessary to the validity of a contract? The buyer, you will notice, is in an awkward spot. He cannot risk signing a contract to buy some other house, for if he does, he may find himself obligated to buy two houses. Some courts protect the buyer and allow him to revoke his offer in this last situation, stating either that the acceptance is ineffective until the buyer is notified thereof or that delivery is necessary for a written contract to be binding. *Hollingshead* v. *Morris,* 172 Mich. 126, 137 NW 527 (1912). However, there are also contrary decisions. 1 Corbin, Contracts 93, 208.

SUGGESTION TO BUYER: Let the contract be prepared in duplicate. The buyer signs both duplicates. Each duplicate contains a provision that the buyer's liability, if any, is terminated and his down payment returned, unless a duplicate signed by the seller is delivered to the buyer within three days after the date of the contract. The buyer hands both duplicates to the seller but retains a carbon copy, so that he can always prove his nonliability if he fails to receive a signed duplicate within the specified time.

§ **329. Acknowledgments.** An acknowledgment is not necessary, although it is desirable since it simplifies proof of the contract in any suit brought thereon. If the contract is to be recorded, acknowledgment is necessary in nearly all states.

§ **330. Witnesses.** If the contract is not acknowledged, it should, as a practical matter, be witnessed, although this is not necessary as a matter of law. The fact that the signatures are witnessed simplifies use of the contract in any litigation that may develop.

§ **331. Recording.** Some contracts will go so far as to include a clause providing that the contract is void if the buyer records it. A buyer who is hopelessly in default will sometimes record the contract, hoping thereby to cloud the seller's title and to obtain a return of part of the purchase price paid. In view of the public policy behind recording law, such provisions are of doubtful validity, but their use may well dissuade the buyer from recording. 12 *Wayne L. Rev.* 402.

§ **332. Effect of contract—interest of purchaser.** The signing of a contract for the sale of land does not give the buyer legal title to the land. Ownership can be transferred to the buyer only by a deed. However, the buyer does acquire an interest in the land. This interest is known as equitable title.

The equitable title of the buyer results from the doctrine of equitable conversion. *Shay* v. *Penrose,* 25 Ill.2d 447, 185 NE2d 218 (1962); 91 CJS *Vendor and Purchaser* § 106. In most states this equitable title arises the moment the contract is entered into.

EXAMPLE: *V* enters into an installment contract with *P. P* dies without a will, leaving *H* as his only heir. *A* is appointed administrator of *P's* estate. The equitable interest of

P passes to his heir, *H*, as real estate. 33 C.J.S. *Executors and Administrators*, § 112. Suppose *V* dies and *ABC Company* is appointed his administrator. ABC Company will be entitled to collect the contract payments. 33 C.J.S. *Executors and Administrators* § 112. Since *P* was the equitable owner of the land, the courts will, for most purposes, treat *V*'s interest under the contract as personal property, going to his administrator.

As a result of this rule, a contract purchaser can mortgage his contract interest by means of a real estate mortgage. 73 ALR2d 1400.

§ 333. **Effect of deed.** When the deal is closed and the seller's deed delivered to the buyer, the deal is regarded as consummated. The contract of sale has served its purpose. It is *merged* in the deed. 38 ALR2d 1310. The contract no longer exists. For this reason, if matters remain to be attended to after closing of the deal, it is best that they be set forth in the deed. This is particularly important as to title matters, for the buyer waives his right to cancel the contract because of defects in title if he accepts and pays for a deed while the title is defective or encumbered. 84 ALR 1001, 1031. However, there are some exceptions to the merger rule. In particular, when the contract calls for something to be done after the deal is closed, delivery of the deed does not extinguish that aspect of the contract.

EXAMPLE: The contract required the seller to lay water mains and sewers after closing of the deal. The deal was closed, and the deed delivered to buyer. Thereafter, the seller failed to lay the water mains and sewers. The buyer filed a damage suit against the seller, and the seller was held liable. *McMillan* v. *American Suburban Corp.*, 136 Tenn. 53, 188 SW 615. The same would be true where the contract requires the seller to build a house on the land sold. 84 ALR 1023. If the contract warrants that the building is in sound condition, this warranty survives the closing of the deal, for that obviously was what the parties intended. *Levin* v. *Cook*, 186 Md. 535, 47 A2d 505 (1946). Contract provisions as to the date on which possession will be turned over to the buyer are not merged in the deed. In all these cases the buyer's only remedy, if the seller fails to perform, is to sue the seller for damages. He cannot sue to get his money back. *De Bisschop* v. *Crump*, 24 F2d 807 (1928).

Also when the deal is closed and the deed accepted by the buyer-grantee, all questions of *marketability of title* are at an end. 66 C.J. 847, 1480; 84 ALR 1025, 1027, 1032; 57 ALR 1261. Of course, a grantee who receives a warranty deed can sue the grantor for damages if a title defect shows up; but he cannot get his money back. The buyer's right to sue the seller for the seller's misrepresentations is not affected by the closing of the deal. Normally the buyer does not discover these misrepresentations until after he has taken possession.

RECAPITULATION: Thus, it can be said with respect to merger:

(1) that the obligations of the seller to furnish a title of a particular character, or evidence of such title, ends with the closing of the deal

(2) that the obligations of the seller to perform acts *after closing* (such as landscaping) do not end with closing

(3) that the buyer's rights with respect to the seller's misrepresentations or nondis-

closure do not end with closing, since normally they are not discovered until after the buyer takes possession.

§ 334. **Assignment of the contract.** The buyer may assign his interest in the contract. By virtue of the contract, the buyer has the right to demand a deed to the property on performing his part of the contract. He may sell and transfer this right to a third party, which is accomplished by means of a brief instrument called an *assignment.* Such third party is called the *assignee.* The assignee has the right to make the payments required by the contract and to demand a deed from the seller. In other words, the assignee steps into the shoes of the buyer and may compel the seller to perform his part of the contract.

However, the assignee does not become personally liable to the seller for payment of the purchase price, unless the assignment provides that the assignee *assumes and agrees to pay* the purchase price. *Lisenby* v. *Newton,* 120 Cal. 571, 52 Pac. 813 (1898).

Of course, the buyer cannot escape personal liability for payment of the purchase price by assigning the contract. He remains liable to the seller notwithstanding the assignment. If the rule were otherwise, a buyer could always rid himself of a burdensome contract by assigning it to a pauper.

Installment contracts quite commonly provide that there can be no assignment without the written consent of the seller.

§ 335. **Deed by seller to stranger.** When the seller, after entering into the contract, sells and conveys the land to some third party, the question arises as to whether the buyer under the contract can compel such third party to give him a deed to the land on payment of the contract price. The buyer can compel such third party to give him a deed on payment of the contract price in the following cases:

1. When the contract was recorded prior to the making of the deed to the third party.
2. When, though the contract was not recorded, the buyer took possession of the land prior to the making of the deed to the third party.
3. When, even though the contract was not recorded and the buyer did not take possession of the land, the third party actually knew of the earlier contract at the time he received his deed.

If the case does not fall within these three rules, the buyer cannot compel the third party to give him a deed. In other words, he has lost all his rights in the land. However, the buyer may then sue his seller and recover from him any amounts paid on the purchase price.

If the contract requires the seller to give a warranty deed, the buyer need not accept a warranty deed signed only by the seller's grantee. The seller must also join in the deed. *Crabtree* v. *Levings,* 53 Ill. 526 (1870).

§ 336. **Time for performance.** The contract should specify the date on which the deal is to be closed. If the contract does not specifically fix the time when it is to be performed, it will be implied that it is to be performed within a reasonable time, and the purchase price must be paid at that time. Most contracts fix a specific time for the performance of all acts thereunder. If the contract provides that *time is of the essence,* each act required by the contract must be done promptly at the time specified. In a cash sale, where time is of the essence, if either party fails to perform promptly he will be unable to obtain specific performance.

EXAMPLE: Contract called for earnest money down payment, balance to be paid within five days after seller's title was shown to be good, and time to be of the essence. Seller delivered evidence of good title on August 5. Buyer did nothing. On August 19, seller served notice on buyer to close deal within five days. Buyer again did nothing. On September 10, buyer tendered balance of purchase price. Seller refused to accept. Buyer now filed suit for specific performance and the court refused to grant it. Buyer was in default and time was of the essence. *Johnson* v. *Riedler,* 395 Ill. 412, 70 NE2d 570 (1946).

§ 337. **Installment contracts.** The installment contract has already been mentioned. It presents a number of problems.

The sellers. Of course, all persons owning the land, if there are two or more owners, should execute the contract as sellers, and their spouses should join to release dower or other marital rights.

Payment of purchase price to sellers. Since the contract may take several years to complete, there is the possibility that one of the sellers may die during this period. Therefore the contract should make provision for this contingency.

EXAMPLE: *H* and *W,* joint tenants, enter into an installment contract to sell land to *E.* Let the contract read that purchase price is payable to *H* and *W, as joint tenants with the right of survivorship and not as tenants by the entireties or as tenants in common.*

Seller's title. It is sufficient in installment contracts if the seller has good title on the date fixed for the delivery of the deed. Thus if the buyer contracts to pay the purchase price in installments, the seller is entitled to the entire life of the contract in which to clear up his title. The buyer may thus find himself making payment after payment to a seller whose title later proves defective. 66 C.J. 847, 1480; 57 ALR 1261; 84 ALR 1025, 1027, 1032; 109 ALR 242. This danger is aggravated where the seller is a corporation having little or no financial responsibility. If, however, during the life of the contract it develops that the defects in the seller's title are hopelessly incurable, the buyer may declare the contract at an end even though the time for conveyance has not yet arrived. 109 ALR 242.

EXAMPLE: While the purchaser was paying on an installment contract, he learned that a recorded public utility easement ran through the middle of the property. He may declare the contract at an end.

EXAMPLE: The purchaser discovered that the seller held title to the land in tenancy by the entireties with his wife. She had not signed the contract. The purchaser could terminate the contract and get a refund of the money he had paid. *Waskey* v. *Thomas,* 235 SE2d 346 (Va. 1977).

At times the courts have bent the law a bit to protect the installment buyer.

EXAMPLE: *V* enters into an installment contract with *P*. *P* defaults in his payments. *V* sues *P* for the delinquent installments. The court renders judgment for *V* but orders that the judgment cannot be enforced until *V* deposits his deed to *P* with the court. *Noyes* v. *Brown*, 142 Minn. 211, 171 NW 803 (1919); 34 *Mich. L. Rev.* 545.

Seller's evidence of title—preliminary contract. Since the seller in an installment contract need not have title until the time for giving the deed arrives, he need not furnish evidence of title until that time arrives even where the contract requires the seller to furnish evidence of title. *Tolbird* v. *Howard*, 101 Ill.App.2d 236, 242 NE2d 468 (1968). However, in larger transactions this situation is covered specifically.

EXAMPLE: *V* agrees to sell his land to *P* for $500,000, purchase price payable in installments. A preliminary contract is entered into calling for an earnest money deposit of $20,000. *V* is thereupon to have his title examined and furnish *P* evidence that his title is good. He does so. *P* then deposits an additional down payment of $80,000 and an installment contract is entered into.

Where a preliminary contract of sale is entered into, looking toward the subsequent signing of an installment contract of sale, the usual rules requiring completeness and certainty are applicable.

EXAMPLE: A preliminary contract between *V* and *P* states that after *V*'s title has been shown to be marketable and free from all liens and encumbrances, "an installment contract will be signed by the parties." This is too indefinite to be enforced. The details of the installment contract and preferably the form of contract should be set forth.

Also the rule of *merger* is applicable. Once the installment contract has been signed, the provisions of the preliminary contract cease to have any legal force. *Peters* v. *Fenner*, 199 NW2d 795 (Minn. 1972).

The buyer. Again, since one of the buyers may die during the life of the contract, let the contract make provision for this.

EXAMPLE: Let the contract provide that *V* agrees to sell to *H* and *W* *as joint tenants with the right of survivorship and not as tenants by the entireties or as tenants in common.*

Of course if a tenancy by the entireties is preferred, that can be stated.

Acceleration clause. From the seller's point of view it is desirable that an installment contract authorize the seller to declare the entire purchase price due in case of default. Otherwise a chronically delinquent buyer can drive a seller to distraction by curing his defaults each time the seller serves notice on him of the seller's intent to declare a forfeiture.

EXAMPLE: *V* contracts to sell real estate to *P*, purchase price of $20,000 payable in monthly installments. *P* is constantly late in making payments. The contract contains an acceleration clause. *V* sends *P* notice to cure all his defaults within 30 days, otherwise *V* will declare the entire purchase price due. This is permitted under the acceleration clause. After acceleration has taken place, *V* is in a position to forfeit unless *P* can come up with the entire purchase price. This is helpful in getting rid of the chronic delinquent. But as in the case of mortgage law today, the seller must not exercise his rights unfairly.

The acceleration clause is commonly regarded as valid. *Benincash* v. *Mihailovich,* 188 NW2d 136 (Mich. 1971). However, it is probably necessary for the seller to give the purchaser notice to cure his defaults and a reasonable time to do so. *Brannock* v. *Fletcher,* 155 SE2d 532 (N.C. 1967). And if the seller accelerates unfairly, courts will set the acceleration aside.

EXAMPLE: The seller cannot declare an acceleration where there is an honest dispute as to the amount due. *Moore* v. *Bunch,* 185 NW2d 565 (Mich. 1971).

Prepayment privilege. The buyer should insist that the contract give him the right to prepay the purchase price. He does not have this right unless the contract gives it to him. *Burns* v. *Epstein,* 413 Ill. 476, 109 NE2d 774 (1952).

Truth in Lending. The federal Truth in Lending Act applies to installment sales of land. Kratovil, Truth in Lending, 48 *Title News* 18 (May 1969). If the required disclosures are not made, the purchaser may rescind, that is, cancel the deal and get his money back. The purchaser is required to tender the property back to the seller, but if the seller does not take possession of the property within ten days after the tender the purchaser may keep the land without any obligation to pay for it. 15 *USCA* Sec. 1635(b), Reg. Sec. 226.9 (d).

Prorations. Normally the contract gives the buyer the right of possession as soon as both parties sign it. Thereafter, the contract requires the buyer to pay taxes, insurance, and so forth. Hence the contract should require that all such items be prorated as of the date of the contract.

Remedies of the parties. The matter of the remedies of the parties, including forfeiture, foreclosure and rescission is discussed elsewhere.

§ 338. **Remedies and rights.** The law of real estate deals with both rights and remedies.

EXAMPLE: *V* enters into a contract to sell certain land to *P*. Each of the parties now has a *right* to have the other party perform his obligations under the contract.

Often however, you have to go to court to enforce your rights. At that time you have a choice of *remedies,* namely:

1. *Court-made remedies.* In the above example, if *P* arbitrarily refuses to close the deal, *V* can sue for damages. Alternatively, he can sue *P* for *specific performance,* which will be discussed later. If *V* refuses arbitrarily to go through with the deal, *P* has his choice of the same two remedies. There are other court-made remedies also.

2. *Agreed remedies.* The parties are at liberty to agree on remedies other than those invented by the courts. For example, in an installment contract, it is a common practice to insert a forfeiture clause under which, if the buyer defaults, the seller can declare the con-

tract forfeited and retain all payments the buyer has made. There are, of course, limits imposed by the courts on agreed remedies. The courts will not allow the parties to agree to let the seller forfeit an installment contract and then collect damages also. Nor will they allow either party to collect $50,000 in damages if he has suffered only damages of $10,-000.

3. *Statutory remedies.* There are a number of remedies that exist by virtue of the laws passed by the legislature. In Illinois for example, where the seller forfeits out the buyer, he can oust the buyer from the property by a forcible detainer suit.

Because of the tendency today for the parties to agree upon remedies and set them forth in the contract, there is less tendency on the part of the courts to set forth hard and fast rules. Rather they read the contract to see what remedies the parties had in mind. *Hooper* v. *Reynolds,* 81 N.M. 255, 466 P2d 101 (1970).

§ 339. Remedies of seller—retention of defaulting buyer's payment. In this area of seller's remedies there are various situations:

1. The deal is a cash deal and the buyer has made a reasonable earnest money deposit, say about 10 percent. Since this is a reasonable amount, it seldom provokes litigation. Thus, so far as *cash sales* are concerned, the problem is usually relatively simple. The seller must, within the time allowed by the contract, do the things he is required to do. For example, if the contract requires the seller to furnish the buyer, within thirty days of the date of the contract, an abstract showing good title in the seller, this must be done. Then, at the time and place fixed for closing, the seller should be present and should offer or tender his deed to the buyer and demand payment for the balance of the purchase price. *Frink* v. *Thomas,* 20 Ore. 265, 25 Pac. 717 (1891). If the buyer fails to pay the balance of the purchase price, the seller may declare the contract terminated and retain the earnest money, and the buyer's rights are at an end. *Boston* v. *Clifford,* 68 Ill. 67 (1873). The seller need not make a formal tender where the buyer clearly has shown an intention not to perform, so that tender would be a useless act. Since in a cash sale the buyer is rarely permitted to take possession before the deal is closed, possession offers no problem. As long as the seller has done the things that the contract requires of him (for example, furnishing evidence of marketable title within the time allowed by the contract) the seller will have the right to declare a forfeiture of the buyer's earnest money and contract rights *even though the contract does not spell this out.* 31 ALR2d 96. After all, earnest money is given to prove that the buyer is earnest. If he is not, he deserves to lose his deposit. However, it is better to have a clause in the contract spelling out this right of forfeiture, although it is not necessary. 31 ALR2d 20, 34, 36. A seller who has done all that the contract requires of him need not give the buyer notice and warning of his intention to forfeit the earnest money. He may simply send the buyer a notice declaring the contract forfeited when the buyer defaults.

2. Some courts look at the earnest money to see that it is reasonable in amount, and may permit the buyer to recover any excess. Friedman, Contracts and Conveyances of Real Property (3d ed. 1975) p. 779. Indeed, it is quite likely that any court would take this view if the earnest money deposit is extraordinarily large. Initially earnest money is not a part payment of the purchase price. It must be held as security by the seller until the deal closes. Then it is applied on the sale price. The seller cannot use it for his own purposes. Corbin, The Right of a Defaulting Vendee to the Restitution of Installments Paid, 40 *Yale L. J.* 1013, 1039 (1931). Viewed from this angle, the seller should have the right to only a reasonable security.

3. *Providing the seller keeps his part of the bargain and holds himself available to*

give the buyer specific performance of the contract, the defaulting buyer cannot recover any money he has paid to the seller. *Glenn* v. *Price,* 337 Ill. App. 637, 86 NE2d 542 (1942); Corbin, The Right of a Defaulting Vendee to the Restitution of Installments Paid, 40 *Yale L. J.* 1013 (1931). One who has defaulted cannot make his default an occasion for suing the party not in default.

4. In most states if the seller instead of holding himself available to grant specific performance, resells the land to a third party, the buyer is nevertheless powerless to recover money he has paid to the seller. This again is based on the theory that *the buyer cannot make his default an occasion for suing the seller. Lawrence* v. *Miller,* 86 N.Y. 131 (1888); Friedman, Contracts and Conveyances of Real Property (3rd ed. 1975) p. 778; 31 ALR2d 96; 92 CJS 572.

It must be remembered that a seller is rarely compensated fully for his loss by retaining the earnest money. He has held his property off the market while the first contract was in force, and may have lost a profitable new sale. He is often forced to pay two broker's commissions. He may have purchased another home, which he is forced to resell at a loss. His children may have changed schools in reliance on the first sale. The seller may have sustained expenses commuting between his old home and his new home.

5. A few states take the view that if buyer defaults and seller conveys to a third party, the seller can retain only that part of the money paid him as will make him whole. This is on the theory that such an act is tantamount to a rescission by mutual agreement. *Smith* v. *Treat,* 234 Ill. 552, 85 NE 289 (1908); Dobbs, Remedies (1974) p. 864. In the eyes of these courts the actions of both parties indicate that they agreed to terminate the contract. When this occurs, the courts like to restore the parties as close to the situation that existed before the contract was made as possible. Ordinarily this rule finds its chief application in cash deals, so that one need not worry about rents, since the purchaser has not yet taken possession.

§ 340. Remedies—forfeiture of an installment contract. Every installment contract contains a forfeiture clause. In this respect it differs from a cash sale, which usually calls for an earnest money deposit. The situation differs from the cash sale situation in several respects. First, the buyer has usually occupied the property and thinks of it as his home, his store, or the like. Second, the buyer usually has been making payments over a period of years, and when he stops making payments it is often because he has suffered some personal disaster, such as illness or loss of employment. For these reasons the courts are far more sympathetic toward the buyer than in the case of cash sales.

As against this is the fact that, in installment contracts, the buyer's down payment is usually small. If I want to buy a house for $15,000 and have saved $3000 for a down payment, I can get a mortgage for $12,000. If I default in my payments, I will have all the protection of redemption laws, public auction sale laws, and the other protective measures that the law accords a mortgagor. But if I am buying an old, single-family dwelling for $10,000 and can make a down payment of only $200, no one in his right mind is going to give me a mortgage. I must buy this house on an installment contract. To ask the seller to go through the expense of a costly foreclosure suit, with redemption rights in many states, is unrealistic. The only sensible solution is to allow the seller to declare a forfeiture if I should default and to evict me in the same way a landlord evicts a tenant who does not pay his rent. Forfeiture is an agreed remedy.

In order to create an enforcible right of forfeiture, *it is indispensable that an installment contract contain a provision giving the seller the right to declare a forfeiture in the event of the buyer's default.* This is what distinguishes *forfeiture from rescission.* If there is no provision in the contract regarding forfeiture, then in the event the buyer defaults, the seller has the right to terminate the contract. But such termination is called *rescission.* The seller who rescinds must refund to the buyer the payments he has made, less a fair rent for the time the buyer has been in possession. *Hillman* v. *Busselle,* 66 Ariz. 139, 185 P2d 311 (1947). *Forfeiture* is a right expressly given in the contract itself. *Realty Securities Corp.* v. *Johnson,* 93 Fla. 46, 111 So 532 (1927). By declaring a forfeiture the seller terminates the contract and *retains all payments previously made by the buyer.* 77 Am. Jur.2d *Vendor & Purchaser* § 500.

Just as we so often find that tenants do not pay their monthly rent exactly on the day it is due, so we often find that purchasers under installment contracts do not pay their payments exactly on the day they are due, or they may from time to time make payments of less than the amount due. The overwhelming majority of installment sellers go along with the buyer, hoping that he will ultimately be able to straighten out his finances. Ultimately the seller may decide that he can no longer be indulgent. Then he faces a problem that his own indulgence has created.

EXAMPLE: An installment contract provided that time was of the essence, but the seller often accepted payments after the dates fixed for payment. This constituted a waiver of the provision that time was of the essence. The reason is that the seller, by accepting payments after the dates fixed, had led the buyer to believe that he would not insist on the provision that payments must be made strictly on the specified dates. It would therefore be highly unjust to permit the seller suddenly to declare a forfeiture of the contract for the buyer's failure to pay one of the installments promptly. *Fox* v. *Grange,* 261 Ill. 116, 103 NE 576 (1913); 31 ALR2d 55, 85.

The seller may *revive* the provision that time is of the essence. He may serve a *warning notice* on the buyer that in the future he will insist on strict performance of the contract according to its terms, and thereafter the buyer must make his payments promptly or the seller may declare a forfeiture. This warning notice must be followed by a declaration of forfeiture if the buyer fails to cure his defaults within the allotted time. Such a warning notice must not be a mere dun. It must state unequivocally that the contract will be forfeited if the defaults are not cured within the specified time. *Monson* v. *Bragdon,* 159 Ill. 61, 42 NE 383 (1895). Many printed contract forms contain a provision that acceptance of late payments shall not constitute a waiver of the provision that time is of the essence. Some courts refuse to give this provision effect. *Morrey* v. *Bartlett,* 288 Ill. App. 620; *Scott* v. *Cal. Farming Co.,* 4 Cal. App. 2d 232, 40 P2d 850 (1940). In many states, a warning notice must always be given before an installment contract is forfeited. *County of Lincoln* v. *Fischer,* 216 Ore. 421, 339 P2d 1084 (1954); 31 ALR2d 14.

Even where a forfeiture has been declared, it is possible that the buyer's rights may be revived. This occurs where the seller waives the forfeiture by conduct indicating that he considers the contract still in force, as by negotiating with the buyer concerning the title of the property, possible repurchase by the seller, extension of time of payment, and the like. 107 ALR 345. All owners of the land must join in the notice of forfeiture. 66 C.J. *Vendor & Purchaser* § 62 p. 762.

Where a recorded contract has been properly forfeited, the seller can obtain a court decree declaring the buyer's rights terminated.

Where the buyer is in military service, the contract cannot be forfeited without a court order. The court may either postpone the forfeiture or order the repayment of prior installments before permitting forfeiture of the contract.

In California, Georgia, Montana, South Dakota, Wisconsin, and Utah, a purchaser whose contract has been forfeited is allowed to get back the amount he has paid, less a reasonable compensation to the seller for the use of his land. Illinois, Iowa, and Minnesota allow the purchaser to cure his defaults within a specified grace period and thus preserve this contract. Arizona also provides a grace period that increases in proportion to the amount paid on the contract. 13 *Rutgers L. Rev.* 624; 24 *Mo. L. Rev.* 244. In Florida, Indiana, and Maryland, the contract must be foreclosed like a mortgage. *Mid-State Inv. Corp.* v. *O'Steen* (Fla.) 133 So2d 455; *Stendzel* v. *Marshall,* 301 NE2d 641 (Ind. 1973). However, in most states, the forfeiture provisions in the contract will be enforced. *Coe* v. *Bennett,* 46 Ida. 62, 266 Pac. 413 (1928); 31 ALR2d 38, 71.

Perhaps the most important clause in an installment contract, from the seller's point of view, is the forfeiture clause.

§ **341. Remedies of seller—forfeiture—relief against forfeiture—forfeiture and damages.** Courts will on occasion set aside a forfeiture of an installment contract. 55 ALR3d 10; Restatement, Contracts, §§ 275, 276. The more money the buyer has paid in, the more likely the court is to do this. Where the buyer has made substantial improvements, he is quite likely to obtain this sort of relief. *Krentz* v. *Johnson,* 36 Ill. App. 3d 142, 343 NE2d 165 (1976). The more lenient the seller has been in accepting short payments or delayed payments, the greater the likelihood that the forfeiture will be set aside. *Krentz* v. *Johnson, supra.* Where the buyer's breach consists of failing to make repairs, the seller's notice must give him a reasonable time to make repairs. Otherwise the forfeiture cannot stand. *Reeploeg* v. *Jensen,* 490 P2d 445 (Wash. 1971). Where the forfeiture notices were sent to the wrong address, the forfeiture cannot stand. *Kingsley* v. *Roeder,* 2 Ill. 2d 131, 117 NE2d 82 (1954). Whenever it would be unreasonable to let the seller keep the buyer's payments and oust him from the land, the forfeiture is set aside. *McWilliams* v. *Urban Land Co.,* 194 NW2d 920 (Mich.). In such cases the court may order foreclosure by sale, which gives the buyer a right to redeem. *Ruhl* v. *Johnson,* 159 Neb. 810, 49 NW2d 687 (1951). Where the buyer's payments amount to little more than the rental value of the land he has occupied, his case for relief is poor. But where the seller is himself in default, any forfeiture he declares will be set aside. And if the seller has been guilty of making fraudulent representations, the fact that he has forfeited out the buyer does not deprive the buyer of his right to sue the seller for damages. *Garrett* v. *Perry,* 340 P2d 315 (Cal. 1959).

§ 342. **Remedies of seller—foreclosure.** A seller may file a foreclosure suit if the buyer defaults. The foreclosure may be a *strict foreclosure. Walker* v. *Runnenkamp,* 373 P2d 559 (Ida. 1962); 77 ALR 282. In such a foreclosure, the purchaser will be given a period of time to pay up, and if he fails to do so, his rights are extinguished. Or the court may order a foreclosure sale of the land. 77 ALR 276. If foreclosure is by sale, some states allow some sort of redemption period. 51 ALR2d 672. Other states allow no redemption period.

As in the case of forfeitures, the court may hold in foreclosure cases that the seller has waived the contract provision that time is of the essence.

EXAMPLE: *V* entered into an installment contract with *P*. It contained an acceleration clause. From time to time *P* was delinquent in his payments and *V* wrote him dunning letters. Finally, *V,* in exasperation, declared all the contract price due and filed a suit to foreclose. *P* tendered all his back payments into court. The court dismissed the foreclosure. *Stinemeyer* v. *Wesco,* 487 P2d 65 (Ore. 1971).

NEW DIRECTIONS: This last example is new law but is likely to become the law in many states. In this age of consumerism, the courts, in their desire to ameliorate hardships, are quite likely to set aside accelerations.

§ 343. **Remedies of the seller—remedies other than forfeiture or foreclosure.** If the buyer fails or refuses to perform, the seller, in lieu of declaring a forfeiture, may pursue one of the following courses:

1. He may rescind the contract. Rescission is not the same as forfeiture. Coe v. *Bennett,* 46 Ida. 62, 266 Pac. 413 (1928). By rescinding, the seller declares the contract at an end and surrenders all rights thereunder. Both seller and buyer must be restored, as far as possible, to the situation existing before the contract was made. The seller, on rescinding, must give back to the buyer the payments he has made, less a fair rent for the time the buyer has been in possession. *Hillman* v. *Busselle,* 66 Ariz. 139, 185 P2d 311 (1947). The right to rescind does not depend upon any provision in the contract. However, most contracts give the seller the right to declare the contract forfeited if the buyer defaults. Forfeiture is a right expressly reserved in the contract itself. *Realty Securities Corp.* v. *Johnson,* 93 Fla. 46, 111 So 532 (1927). By declaring a forfeiture, the seller terminates the contract but retains all payments previously made by the buyer, since this right is expressly conferred by the contract. The seller may thereupon file a suit to clear his title of the cloud created by the forfeited contract. *Ibid.*

   Some states allow the seller to rescind, apply the earnest money in reduction of his damages, and sue the buyer for any other damages he has sustained. Dobbs, Remedies (1974) p. 855. This is a sensible rule. *Anderson* v. *Long Grove Country Club Estates,* 111 Ill.App.2d 127, 249 NE2d 343 (1969).

2. In some states, he may tender a deed to the buyer and then sue the buyer for the purchase price.
3. He may sue the buyer for damages.
4. He may sue the buyer for specific performance of the contract.
5. He may simply retain the earnest money.

§ 344. **Remedies of the buyer.** In case of the seller's refusal or failure to perform, the buyer may pursue one of the following courses:

1. He may *rescind,* that is, declare the contract terminated, and recover his deposit. To rescind is the buyer's normal remedy when the land has decreased in value. One difficulty here is that the seller usually is reluctant to give back the buyer's deposit. The buyer, of course, has the right to file a suit against the seller and obtain a judgment, which can be enforced in the usual ways, by levy on property, by garnishment, and so forth. However, while the suit is pending, the seller may very well decide to sell the particular land to someone else and then spend or secrete the money.

2. The buyer has a lien on the land as security for repayment of purchase money paid in and may enforce such lien if the seller is unable or unwilling to convey good title. 33 ALR2d 1384. A buyer who wishes to obtain return of his down payment from a defaulting seller would be well advised to file a suit to enforce his purchaser's lien, for this ties up the seller's property and prevents him from selling the land to others. This is not true if the buyer merely sues the seller for a money judgment.

3. The buyer may sue the seller to compel *specific performance* of the contract, that is, to compel the seller to give him a deed on receiving payment of the purchase price. The buyer will resort to this remedy when he wants the land for some particular purpose, for example, to keep out a competitor, or when he anticipates that the land will appreciate in value. In general, specific performance is a more effective remedy than a suit for money damages, since damages are always hard to prove and judgments for money are hard to collect.

4. The seller, of course, cannot compel the buyer to accept a bad title. But sometimes the buyer wants to go through with the contract and the seller refuses. The seller's title may be clouded with some unpaid tax, unpaid mortgage, or easement. To make things more difficult for the buyer, the seller refuses to make any effort to eliminate these defects. Here the buyer may wish to file a suit for specific performance and ask the court to make deduction from the purchase price because of the defects in title.

EXAMPLE: The contract price is $10,000. An examination of title reveals the existence of $1000 in unpaid taxes. The court will order specific performance on the buyer's depositing $9000 in court for the seller if the seller refuses to pay the taxes. This remedy of the buyer is called *specific performance with an abatement from the purchase price.*

5. Where the seller will not or cannot go through with the deal, the buyer may sue the seller for *damages.* In such an action, the buyer ultimately will receive a judgment for money damages. In the meantime, however, while the suit is pending, the seller is at liberty to sell the land to others, and any buyer who gets a deed before the buyer obtains his judgment takes the land free of the buyer's claims.

§ 345. **Remedies—restitutionary damages—promissory estoppel.** On occasion, *even where a contract has not been signed,* there will be a liability for damages.

EXAMPLE: Hoffman and his wife owned a small store. Red Owl, a national franchiser, advised Hoffman to sell his store, promising to find a party to buy some land, build a bigger building and lease it to the Hoffmans with an option to purchase. The Hoffmans would receive a Red Owl franchise. All this was arranged orally. The Hoffmans sold their store in reliance on Red Owl's promises. Red Owl refused to go through with the deal.

Red Owl was held liable for all the damages the Hoffmans suffered. Red Owl made a promise knowing the Hoffmans would rely on it. Under modern ethical concepts of the law (promissory estoppel) the promisor is liable for the damages his promisee incurs. Although the promises were made to Hoffman only, Red Owl could foresee that his wife would also rely on Red Owl's promise. Hence they are liable to her as well. *Hoffman* v. *Red Owl Stores Inc.,* 26 Wis.2d 683, 133 NW 267 (1965). Lawyers often speak of this as *detrimental reliance.*

§ 346. **Remedies—election of remedies.** Some remedies are so inherently inconsistent that if a party chooses one he cannot resort to remedies he would otherwise have:

EXAMPLE: A seller in an installment contract elects to exercise his forfeiture clause. He cannot thereafter sue the buyer for payment of the purchase price. 66 C.J. 1210.

EXAMPLE: In some states an installment seller has a *statutory right* to cancel the contract by giving the buyer notice of his default and forfeiture. Thereafter he cannot sue the buyer for damages. *Zirinsky* v. *Sheehan,* 413 F2d 481 (1969).

§ 347. **Remedies of the seller and buyer—exclusiveness of the remedies spelled out in contract—choice of inconsistent remedies.** In the case of a cash sale, even though the contract is silent on the point, the seller may, in the event of default by the buyer, retain the buyer's earnest money deposit. This is a form of forfeiture that is universally permitted. Often the contract specifically provides that in the case of the buyer's default the seller may declare the contract ended and keep the earnest money. This is not an *exclusive remedy.* 81 CJS 531; 32 ALR 584, 98 ALR 887. In other words, the seller, *in lieu of retaining the earnest money, has the right to sue the buyer for specific performance or for damages.*

But, the contract often provides that, in the event the seller's title proves defective, the buyer must either take the title *as is* or be content with a return of his earnest money deposit. This is then the buyer's exclusive remedy if the seller is *in good faith unable* to clear his title. *Old Colony Trust Co.* v. *Chauncey,* 214 Mass. 271, 101 NE 423 (1913); *Nostdal* v. *Morehart,* 132 Minn. 351, 157 NW 584 (1916). If the buyer wishes to accept title *as is,* he must notify the seller of his decision within the time allowed by the contract. *Miller* v. *Shea,* 300 Ill. 180, 133 NE 183 (1921). However, if the seller's title examination reveals defects that the seller could easily clear, but he refuses to do so because of his reluctance to go through with the transaction or if the seller knew his title was defective when he signed the contract of sale, then the clause is not deemed to provide an exclusive remedy, and the buyer may file for specific performance with an abatement from the purchase price or for damages. *Mokar Properties Corp.* v. *Hall,* 179 NYS2d 814 (1958). This clause protects the seller only where he is truly unable to deliver a clear title and was unaware of the defects in his title. *Blau* v. *Friedman,* 140 A2d 193 (N.J. 1958).

If a seller has a right to declare a *forfeiture* of the contract because of the buyer's default, and he does so, he cannot thereafter sue the buyer for damages or for the balance due on the purchase price. *Morey* v. *Huston,* 85 Ill. App.2d 195, 28 NE2d 44 (1967). 92 CJS 311. He must choose to forfeit *or* sue for damages or recovery of the purchase price. And if the seller files a suit to foreclose the contract, this automatically sets aside any forfeiture that the seller has previously declared because of the buyer's defaults. *Zumstein* v. *Stockton,* 199 Ore. 633, 264 P2d 455 (1953).

§ 348. **Abandonment.** Through abandonment, either buyer or seller may lose his rights under the contract. If either party clearly shows by his acts that he does not intend to go through with the contract, the other party may assume that he has abandoned the contract. 68 ALR2d 581.

EXAMPLE: The buyer, under an installment contract, took possession of the premises. Later he fell far behind in his payments and eventually accepted a lease from the seller. When oil was discovered, he attempted to enforce the contract. The court held that his rights had been lost by abandonment. *Dundas* v. *Foster,* 281 Mich. 117, 274 NW 731.

§ 349. **Warranties of the building.** In the sale of a completed building, whether the sale is by one who has constructed the building or by some later owner, it is possible for the seller to give the buyer a written warranty that the building is structurally sound, and, if this proves false, the buyer may sue the seller for damages or may even rescind the contract and get his money back. Indeed, where a builder sells an FHA-insured home, the FHA regulations require that a written warranty be given. It is good for one year.

But if there is no written warranty and the sale is of a completed building, the courts will not read into the contract any implied warranty that the building is sound. 78 ALR2d 440; 8 ALR2d 221. However, where the house is partly completed or has not yet been begun when the contract of sale is entered into, the situation is governed by the rules of the builder liability. And if the seller knows of a serious defect that cannot be discovered by the buyer on an ordinary inspection, then even in the case of the sale of a completed building the situation is governed by the rules relating to fraud and nondisclosure.

NEW DIRECTIONS: As stated in an earlier edition of this book, there is a trend toward creating an implied warranty of the building in a sale of a new building. Kratovil, *Real Estate Law* (5th ed.), § 443. A flood of recent decisions have established this as an overwhelming trend. There is a warranty of quality and habitability in the sale of a new dwelling by its builder. *Smith* v. *Old Warson Develop. Co.,* 479 SW2d 795 (1972); 25 ALR3d 413. Thus, the doctrine of *caveat emptor* has all but disappeared in the sale of *new houses. Theis* v. *Heuer,* 280 NE2d 300 (Ind. 1972).

Among the newer decisions following this view are: *Hartley* v. *Ballon,* 209 SE2d 776, 286 N.C. 51 (1974); *Balkum* v. *Staab,* 346 A2d 210 (Vt. 1975); *Casavant* v. *Campiano,* 327 A2d 831 (R.I. 1979); *Hanavan* v. *Dye,* 4 Ill. App. 3d 576, 281 NE2d 398 (1972); *Tucker* v. *Crawford,* 315 A2d 737 (Del. 1974); *Frasher* v. *Coper,* 160 SE2d 560 (S.C. 1968); *Lyon* v. *Ward,* 221 SE2d 727 (N.C. 1976); *Elderkin* v. *Caster,* 288 A2d 771, 447 Pa. 118 (1972); *Smith* v. *Old Warson Development Co.,* 479 SW2d 795 (Mo. 1972) (citing many legal periodicals); *Weeks* v. *Slavick Builders, Inc.,* 180 NW2d 503 (Mich. 1970); *Gay* v. *Cornwall,* 494 P2d 1371 (Wash. 1972). This is but a partial list of the many decisions that have adopted this rule since 1964. Obviously, it will be adopted with virtually unanimous acceptance. *Wawak* v. *Stewart,* 449 SW2d 922 (Ark. 1970); *Cochran* v. *Keeton,* 252 So2d 307 (Ala. 1971), 25 ALR3d 383. Unsophisticated buyers are ill-equipped to detect defects in jerry-built housing.

EXAMPLE: Among the defects the courts have held the seller-builder liable for are: Leaking roof. Defective heating or air conditioning. Water seepage through foundation. Well water polluted. Abnormal settling of foundation. Sewer pipe not connected with city sewer. No mortar in chimney flue of fireplace. Faulty drainage of septic system. Radiant heating system failed.

CAUTION: The doctrine of implied warranty has not been applied as yet to sale of anything but *new houses* including condominiums. *Gable* v. *Silver,* 258 So.2d 11 (Fla. 1972). It has not been applied to sales of commercial or industrial property or vacant land. It has not been applied to used houses.

Thus, it is now the rule that a builder-seller of a residence, completed or in the process of construction, impliedly warrants to his *first purchaser* that the house was, in its major structural features, constructed in a good and workmanlike manner. That is, the structure is of reasonable quality, is reasonably fit for its intended purpose, and is free of building code violations. Bixby, Implied Warranty of Habitability: New Rights for Home Buyer, 6 *Clearinghouse Rev.* 468. The theories behind this rule are that the buyer of a new house relies on the skill of a seller-builder, that the buyer is incapable of detecting defects in construction, and that most defects in construction are hidden from view.

Also it has been said that this rule would tend to discourage much of the sloppy work and jerry-building that has become perceptible over the years. *Cochran* v. *Keeton,* 252 So2d 307 (Ala. 1971) (citing 7 Williston, Contracts, 3rd ed. 1963 § 926).

It has also been said that the idea of caveat emptor ("let the buyer beware") is out of harmony with modern home buying practices. *Humber* v. *Morton,* 426 SW2d 554, 562 (Tex. 1968).

One court, in applying the rule, stated that it found indefensible the difference in protection accorded the purchaser of a kitchen mop (money back if defective) and a $50,000 home (no remedy under the old law if building collapsed). *Wawak* v. *Stewart,* 449 SW2d 922 (Ark. 1970), noted 24 *Ark. L. Rev.* 245.

§ 350. Liability of contractors for merchant builders. A contractor who constructed a new house for the merchant-seller is liable to third parties for an inherently dangerous defect.

EXAMPLE: The contractor constructed a foldaway attic stairway using sixpenny nails instead of twelvepenny nails to anchor it. The wife of the purchaser fell on this collapsing stairway. The contractor was negligent, and the situation was inherently dangerous. *Lambert* v. *R. & R. Const. Co.,* 266 So.2d 560 (1972) aff'd 268 So.2d 260.

§ 351. Liability of seller-builder—remedies. Among the remedies available against a seller-builder who has breached his implied warranty are the following:

1. The buyer may rescind (terminate the transaction) and obtain *restitution of the money he paid the seller-builder. Bethamy* v. *Bechtel,* 91 Ida. 55, 415 P2d 698 (1966); *Tavaris* v. *Horstman,* 542 P2d 1275 (Wyo. 1975). This is a risky business. To back out of the deal, the buyer must move out. There is danger of vandalism and then the ultimate danger, the possibility that he will not win his lawsuit.

2. The buyer may sue the builder-seller for *damages for personal injuries* suffered as a result of the defective condition. *Tavaris* v. *Horstman,* 542 P2d 1275 (Wyo. 1975); *Calvera* v. *Green Springs Inc.,* 220 So2d 414 (Fla. 1960).

3. The buyer may sue the seller-builder for damages *equal to the difference between the sale price and the actual value of the defective building.* This is the normal recourse of the buyer. *Hanavan* v. *Dye,* 4 Ill.App.3d 576, 281 NE2d 398 (1972); *Crowley* v. *Terhune,* 437 SW2d 743 (Ky. 1969).

§ 352. **Fairness and inadequacy of consideration.** A contract for the sale of land will be enforced, regardless of whether the price is too high or too low. Although a person has made a very bad bargain, the courts will force him to carry out his contract.

EXAMPLE: The holder of a tax title to a tract of land went to the owner of the land and told him that his, the owner's, title was worthless, since the land had been sold for taxes. However, the tax title holder said he was willing to give the owner $125 for a deed to the land. The owner accepted the $125 and gave the tax title holder a deed. The land was worth about $3200, and the tax title was really worthless. It was held that the deed would not be set aside. *Grant* v. *Fellows,* 58 Ill. 242 (1871).

However, if the price is far below the real value of the land, and the parties are not on equal terms, as when the buyer is an experienced businessman and the seller is ignorant, mentally feeble, or inexperienced, the court will refuse to compel the seller to give a deed.

EXAMPLE: Shortly after the Chicago Fire, the owner of certain lots in Chicago, a weak-minded man who was ignorant of the value of the land and of business generally and who was unable to understand English well, was persuaded by a shrewd man to sell the lots for $21,000. The lots were worth much more, and their value was rapidly rising. Owners of adjoining lots had just made arrangements to build on these adjoining lots. These facts were known to the buyer but not to the seller. The court refused to compel the seller to give a deed. *Fish* v. *Leser,* 69 Ill. 394 (1873).

§ 353. **Mistake.** The very word *contract* implies that there must be a meeting of the minds. Occasionally both parties to the contract are mistaken as to some matter. This is called a *mutual mistake.* When there is a mutual mistake, either party may cancel or rescind the contract.

EXAMPLE: The owner of certain land verbally offered to sell the land for $6000. The buyer misunderstood the price to be $3000 and agreed. Under such misunderstanding the deed was executed and delivered. There was no meeting of the minds here, and the owner was entitled to a reconveyance. *Neel* v. *Lang,* 236 Mass. 61, 127 NE 512 (1920).

§ 354. **Misrepresentation and fraud.** So many statements are made by each party in the course of a sale of land that almost always some untrue statement, called a *misrepresentation,* is made. If the misrepresentation is of some unimportant or trivial matter, generally speaking, it will not affect the contract. Such a misrepresentation is said to be immaterial. Suppose, however, that a misrepresentation is made as to some important matter. It is clear, first of all, that such a misrepresentation does not make the contract null and void. After the misrepresentation has been discovered, the party who was deceived may nevertheless wish to enforce the contract. He may do so. If the contract has not yet been performed—that is, the seller has not yet given a deed, and the buyer has not yet paid the purchase price—and the fraud is discovered, and the party who was guilty of the fraud files a suit to enforce the contract, the other party may use the fraud as a defense to such a suit. He will bring to the court's attention the fact that the party who is bringing the suit made a misrepresentation as to an important matter, and the court will refuse to enforce the contract.

If the contract *has* been performed—that is, the seller has given the deed and the buyer paid the purchase price—and one party then discovers that an important misrepresentation has been made, he may file a suit to get his land back, if he was the seller, or get his money, if he was the buyer.

Remember that the buyer is seldom in a position to discover the seller's misrepresentations until he has taken possession of the property. And the buyer may rescind (get his money back) even if the misrepresentation was not intentional, which is rare.

Some matters with respect to which misrepresentation are common follow:

1. rents, profits, volume of business, or income of the property
2. location of boundaries of the property
3. area or frontage of the property
4. age of buildings on the property
5. drainage conditions
6. buildings erected on filled ground
7. true identity of purchaser
8. existence or nonexistence of encumbrances, such as tax liens, mortgages

A misrepresentation by the seller's broker is tantamount to a misrepresentation by the seller if the seller insists on trying to hold the buyer to the deal. 58 ALR2d 10; 61 ALR2d 1237. Likewise the broker who makes a misrepresentation becomes liable to the purchaser for damages. *Sawyer* v. *Tildahl,* 148 NW2d 131 (1967).

§ 355. **Misrepresentation—opinion, value, and puffing.** Misrepresentations of matters of *opinion* will not justify cancellation of the contract.

It is often difficult to distinguish an expression of opinion from a representation of a fact. For example, a misrepresentation by the seller's broker that *he now has a commitment from a mortgage house to make a loan of a certain sum on the property* allows the buyer to cancel the deal, but a statement by the broker that a loan of a certain amount *can be obtained* is simply his opinion and does not allow the buyer to back out if such a loan cannot be obtained. *Owen* v. *Schwartz,* 177 F2d 641 (1949). 14 ALR2d 1337.

A representation made by a *builder* will sometimes be held to be a representation of fact even though such a representation made by someone else would be a matter of opinion. *Pacesetter Homes Inc.* v. *Brodkin,* 85 Cal. Reptr. 39.

EXAMPLE: A builder who owned the house he had constructed stated to a buyer that it was "well constructed in a good and substantial manner." This was untrue. The builder was liable for fraud. *Tate* v. *Jackson,* 22 Ill. App.2d 471, 161 NE2d 156 (1959). Likewise where the builder said "there will be no water in the cellar," he was liable for fraud. *Pietrazak* v. *McDermott,* 341 Mass. 107, 167 NE2d 166 (1960).

Value is usually a matter of opinion. Representations as to the value of the property, though greatly exaggerated, do not ordinarily justify a cancellation of the contract when the other party had an opportunity to learn the truth or falsity of the representations. If the buyer has an opportunity to examine the land, it is his duty to make use of this opportunity. He can then form an opinion as correct as the seller's as to the worth of the land.

Puffing is praise of the property by the seller couched in more or less general terms. Generally the law requires the buyer to be wary of such puffing talk. Unwarranted praise that does not include concrete misrepresentations of specific facts does not entitle the buyer to back out of the deal.

EXAMPLE: The seller told the buyer that he "could not go wrong" in buying the house and that he "would never regret" the purchase. This is mere puffing. *Fegeas* v. *Sherrill,* 218 Md. 472, 147 A2d 223 (1958).

§ 356. **Misrepresentation as to zoning or building ordinances.** When a seller makes a misrepresentation as to zoning or building ordinances affecting the property—for example, when the seller states that the land is in a district zoned for manufacturing, whereas it is in fact in a district zoned for stores—the buyer, upon discovering the facts, may sue the seller for damages. *Bobak* v. *Mackey,* 107 Cal. App.2d 55, 236 P2d 626 (1951); 175 ALR 1055.

In an effort to give greater protection to buyers against imposition, courts have evolved the idea of *tacit misrepresentation.* Under this doctrine, it is not necessary that the seller be guilty of a direct falsehood for a misrepresentation to exist. What he says and does may amount to a misrepresentation.

EXAMPLE: The seller showed the property to the buyer as a multiple-family dwelling and commented on the rents he collected. This was a *tacit representation* that the premises were legally usable as an apartment building, which was false, for such use violated the city ordinances. It was held that the buyer could rescind (declare contract void) on discovering the imposition. *Gamble* v. *Beahm,* 198 Ore. 537, 257 P2d 882 (1953).

This would be true also if there is any statement in the contract or advertisment for sale that can be construed as representing that the existing use of the building is a *legal one,* as when the contract describes the building as a "store and dwelling" but such use is actually illegal. 27 *Rocky Mt. L. Rev.* 258; 1958 *Wis. L. Rev.* 641.

The fact that the zoning ordinance is a public document, available to all the public, is immaterial. The building may have been constructed before the ordinance was passed, for example. It would then be a legal nonconforming use. The buyer has a right to rely on the seller's representations as to zoning. Also, having told part of the story, for example, that there is a basement apartment, the seller must tell the rest, namely, that the apartment is illegal. The presence of zoning or building ordinance violations may render title unmarketable. Or it may give the buyer a right to sue the seller for damages.

§ **357. Right to rely upon a representation.** Even a misrepresentation of a material fact will not always entitle the other party to cancel the contract. For example, some courts say that a buyer has no right to rely on a representation when the sources of information are equally available to both parties.

EXAMPLE: Seller represented to buyer that the tax assessor had valued the property at a certain figure. Actually, the assessor's figure was a good deal lower. The court held that the buyer was not entitled to rely on this information since the tax assessor's valuation was a public record equally available to both parties. *Morel* v. *Masalski,* 333 Ill. 41, 164 NE 205 (1928).

Again, some courts say that the buyer is not entitled to rely on the seller's representation as to matters that would be disclosed by the buyer's inspection of the property.

EXAMPLE: The seller made a false representation as to the volume of water and the daily flow in the well on the property. It was held that the buyer had no right to rely on this representation, for it was a matter that an inspection would reveal. *Hays* v. *McGinness,* 208 Ga. 547, 67 SE2d 720 (1951).

Along the same lines is the rule that the buyer cannot rely on the seller's representations as to the condition of the building when the buyer has actually made a careful inspection of the building, for in such case he is relying on his own observation, not on the seller's representation. 70 ALR 942. But if the buyer makes only a cursory or casual inspection, the rule does not apply, for in such case he is really relying on the seller's representations. 70 ALR 924. For example, where a buyer inspects the land but makes no attempt to check the seller's representations as to area, the buyer may rescind the contract if there is a misrepresentation in this respect. 54 ALR2d 690. But a buyer who learns of a defect, such as decay or crumbling of the foundation, has no right to make a merely casual inspection. He must make a careful inspection. *Carpenter* v. *Hamilton,* 18 Cal. App.2d 69, 62 P2d 1397 (1937).

NEW DIRECTIONS: The rule forbidding a buyer to rely on certain representations made by the seller is a bad one. In effect, it legalizes fraud in many situations. Many courts have discarded this barbarous rule, and no doubt it will disappear in time. *Yorke* v *Taylor,* 332 Mass. 368, 124 NE2d 912 (1955). No rogue should enjoy his ill-gotten plunder for the simple reason that his victim is by chance a fool.

When the parties are not dealing on equal terms, the party to whom a representation is made is usually justified in relying thereon.

EXAMPLE: The seller was a real estate dealer, familiar with the locality, and the buyer was a laborer from the city, unacquainted with farming. The seller misrepresented the number and condition of fruit trees on the land. The buyer was entitled to rescind (cancel the contract), even though he had inspected the land. The seller had superior means of knowledge. *Mitchell* v. *Coleman,* 127 Ark. 373, 192 SW 231 (1917).

EXAMPLE: A farm broker misrepresented to the buyer, who was a city rooming house operator, the amount of acreage in the farm. It was held that the buyer could rescind. Owen v. *Schwartz,* 177 F2d 641 (1949).

§ 358. Misrepresentation—buyer's fraud. Fraud and misrepresentation on the buyer's part are uncommon. When they occur, the result is the same as where the seller is the guilty party. When the buyer has been guilty of fraud, the seller may either rescind the contract or sue the buyer for damages. 52 ALR 1153.

EXAMPLE: Where the parties were negotiating for the sale of timber land, the buyer sent in a timber cruiser, who determined that there were in excess of 2,300,000 feet of timber in the tract. The buyer represented to the seller that the cruise disclosed the presence of 1,537,500 feet of timber. Later the seller discovered the misrepresentation. He may sue the buyer for fraud. *Heise* v. *Pilot Rock Lumber* Co., 222 Ore. 78, 352 P2d 1072.

EXAMPLE: A buyer's misrepresentation of his intended use of the land gives the seller a right to rescind. 35 ALR3d 369.

§ 359. Nondisclosure—caveat emptor or caveat vendor. The old law was *caveat emptor,* "let the buyer beware." The buyer had to investigate before buying. If he failed to discover defects in the building, that was his bad luck. Nowadays the courts are getting away from this primitive rule.

NEW DIRECTIONS: Many modern courts say that when the seller knows certain material facts relating to defects in the property being sold, and knows them not to be within the reach of reasonable inspection by the buyer, the seller is bound to disclose such facts to the buyer, and failure to do so renders the seller liable to damages. *Theis* v. *Heuer,* 280 NE2d 300 (Ind. 1972); *Sorrell* v. *Young,* 491 P2d 1312 (Wash.); *Jenkins* v. *McCormick,* 184 Kan. 842, 339 P2d 8; Prosser, Torts (4th ed. 1971) 697. Under the modern view, nondisclosure is often regarded as *misrepresentation by silence.* Cooper v. *Cordova Sand & Gravel Co.,* 485 SW2d 261 (Tenn. 1972); 80 ALR2d 1453.

EXAMPLES: The seller knew that the house being sold was inadequately based on filled earth. When the buyer discovered this, he was entitled to a return of his money on deeding the property back to the seller. *Rothstein* v. *Janss Inv. Corp.,* 45 Cal.App.2d 64, 113 P2d 465 (1941); *Wolford* v. *Freeman,* 150 Neb. 537, 35 NW2d 98 (1948); 80 ALR2d 1453; Prosser, Torts (4th ed. 1971) 698. The seller knew that the driveway of the premises was partly on adjoining property and failed to disclose this fact. Again, on discovering this, the buyer was entitled to a return of his money. *Dugan* v. *Bosco* (Del.), 108 A2d 586 (1954). Seller failed to disclose that the adjoining owner claimed two feet of the sixty-foot lot being sold. Buyer could rescind. *Hall* v. *Carter* (Ky.), 324 SW2d 410 (1959).

OTHER EXAMPLES: Seller failed to disclose the following defects and the court held it was fraud: (1) the house was built over a ditch covered with decayed timber; (2) a drain-tile ran beneath the house and caused water to accumulate; (3) the basement was subject to flooding; (4) rents charged were in excess of those allowed by law; (5) the house was in a slide area, dangerous to life; (6) there was a defective sewer installation potentially dangerous to health; 8 *West. Res. L. Rev.* 5; *Kaze* v. *Compton* (Ky.), 283 SW2d 204 (1954); *Lawson* v. *Citizens Bank,* 180 SE2d 206 (S.C. 1971). (Seller held liable for damages.)

EXAMPLES: A developer-builder failed to disclose installation of an underground water conduit or irrigation ditch beneath the house. *Bethlahmy* v. *Bechtel,* 91 Ida. 55, 415 P2d 698 (1966), approved in *Tobin* v. *Paparone Constr. Co.,* 349 A2d 574 (N.J. 1975). A developer-builder failed to disclose to buyer that massive cracks in the foundation were concealed by plasterboard. *Haberman* v. *Greenaman,* 82 Misc.2d 263 (N.Y.). A broker and his seller knew that sewer backed up, inundating basement. They were under a duty to disclose this fact to buyer. *Shane* v. *Hoffman,* 324 A2d 532 (Pa.). A drain tile beneath the house caused water to accumulate. The seller was under duty to disclose. *Kaze* v. *Compton,* 283 SW2d 204 (Ky.). A seller failed to disclose termite infestation and was held liable. *Lorio* v. *Kaiser,* 277 So2d 633 (La. 1973). Foundation constructed with untreated concrete blocks below soil level and subsidence occurred. The seller held liable. *Jackson* v. *Goad,* 385 P2d 279 (N.M. 1963). A building was constructed by developer on filled land and there was no disclosure to the purchaser. The buyer could *rescind,* that is, terminate the deal and obtain the return of his money. *Sorrell* v. *Young,* 491 P2d 1312 (Wash. 1971). A house was in a slide area dangerous to life. No disclosure. The buyer could rescind and obtain the return of his money. *Henderson* v. *Johnson,* 403 P2d 669 (Wash. 1965). A developer filled in a gully with stumps and other rubble to a depth of 25 feet and concealed the fill. The house began to sink. Buyer could recover damages. *Lawson* v. *Citizens & Southern Nat'l. Bank,* 180 SE2d 206 (S.C. 1971). Lot on fill, soil saturated with oil, which precluded building of footings except at unreasonable cost. Seller liable. *Nolt* v. *Palumbo,* 383 P2d 1015 (Ore. 1963). A house was built over a dangerous and defective sewer. No disclosure. The buyer could rescind for fraud. *Lilley* v. *Copeland,* 399 SW2d 496 (Ark. 1966). Percolation tests revealed cellar could not be built. No disclosure. The seller was held liable. *Lodigiani* v. *Potter,* 170 NE2d 359 (1960). The seller encouraged a buyer in the belief that a fence marked the boundary of land although the boundary was 4 feet 3 inches short of fence. The court held that the buyer was entitled to claim up to fence, since seller owned that land. *Webb* v. *Culver,* 509 P2d 1173 (Ore. 1973). Seller and broker held liable for failure to disclose that easement existed over property. *Gilbey* v. *Cooper,* 310 NE2d 268 (Ohio). The buyer of a homesite discovered that the presence of salt water made growing of lawn impossible. Seller liable for damages. *Griffith* v. *Byers Const. Co.,* 510 P2d 198 (Kan. 1973). Seller failed to disclose that his garage was located partly on adjoining premises. Buyer could rescind. *Webb* v. *Culver,* 509 P2d 1173 (Ore. 1973). Seller failed to disclose neighbor was planning to build tennis court. Held, fraud. *Tobin* v. *Paparone Const. Co.,* 349 A2d 574 (1975).

Some courts still cling to the old, primitive notions.

EXAMPLE: The buyer, after purchasing the house found it was infested with termites, a matter not readily disclosed by inspection. The court held that the seller had no duty to disclose this fact to the buyer. *Swinton* v. *Whittinsville Savings Bank,* 311 Mass. 677, 42 NE2d 808 (1942). Most courts today would allow the buyer to get his money back in these circumstances. *Fraser* v. *Amling,* 277 So2d 633 (La. 1973); *Phoenix* v. *Stevens,* 127 NW2d 640 (Ia. 1964); *Obde* v. *Schlemeyer,* 56 Wash.2d 449, 353 P2d 672 (1960); 22 ALR3d 972. Alternatively he can sue the seller for damages.

Consider the case of a house infested with termites. Either the seller or the buyer must take the loss. The law cannot protect both. The seller knows what he is doing. He is unloading a defective product on an unsuspecting buyer. Most buyers lack the sophistication to get a termite inspection. The law is beginning to force the seller to disclose. If he does not, he can be sued for damages. *Hughes* v. *Stusser,* 415 P2d 89 (Wash. 1956); *Obde* v. *Schlemeyer,* 56 Wash.2d 449, 353 P2d 672 (1960); *Fraser* v. *Amling,* 277 So.2d 633 (La. 1973); 22 ALR3d 972; Prosser, Torts (4th ed. 1974) 696. The decisions that protect the seller are surely singularly unappetizing cases.

Naturally the seller is guilty of fraud if he deliberately hides a defect.

EXAMPLE: The basement of a house flooded from time to time. Before showing the house to the buyer, the seller washed and painted away the water marks. This is fraud. *Russow* v. *Bobola,* 2 Ill.App.3d 837. This is an example of the rule that fraud or misrepresentation can take place by acts as well as by words. *Batey* v. *Stone,* 192 SE2d 528 (Ga. 1972).

The buyer is ordinarily under no duty to disclose to the seller facts in his possession that increase the value of the property, such as the fact that oil has been discovered in the vicinity. 56 ALR 429. But the result is different where the seller is related to the buyer or is in a position of trust and confidence, as where the buyer is the seller's attorney, partner, and so forth. *Ibid.*

Of course the seller must disclose to the buyer all matters covered by the Interstate Land Sales Act. 15 U.S.C.A. § 1701.

NEW DIRECTIONS: The rule of seller liability for nondisclosure is applicable to sales of both new and used houses. The termite cases all involve *used homes.* A totally different situation is presented where a *developer-builder* is saddled with the *implied warranty* that began its existence when the courts began to hold that in every sale of a newly built residence by a builder-seller there is an *implied warranty* that the home was built in a workmanlike manner and is fit for habitation. Here the seller is held liable to the first purchaser without any requirement of proof *that he knew of the defect.* Obviously, since he built the house *it is almost certain that he knew of the defect. But that is not an element the buyer is required to prove and indeed it can be difficult to prove.* And in this latter situation the liability extends only to the *first purchaser.*

§ 360. Nondisclosure—violations of zoning and building ordinances. When a seller knows that the building sold violates a zoning or building ordinance, it is his duty, according to recent court decisions, to disclose that fact to the buyer, and if he fails to do so, he is liable for damages. *Barder* v. *McClurg,* 93 Cal.App.2d 476, 252 P2d 378 (1953); *Heckrotte* v. *Riddle,* 224 Md. 491, 168 A2d 879 (1961); 3 *Okla. L. Rev.* 435.

EXAMPLE: A builder violated the building code in that the wall studs of the building were spaced too far apart and plaster had been applied on an unauthorized base. The builder was under a duty to disclose these ordinance violations to the buyer, and, where he failed to do so, the buyer had the right to revoke the deal and obtain a return of his down payment. The fact that the buyer inspected the property was immaterial, for these are matters that no ordinary inspection is likely to reveal. Moreover, the seller has superior means of knowledge. *Milmoe* v. *Dixon,* 101 Cal. App.2d 257, 225 P2d 273 (1951). (Seller liable for damages.)

NEW DIRECTIONS: The modern view is that concealment is tantamount to actual fraud when the seller knows of facts that materially affect the desirability of the property and that he knows are unknown to the buyer.

Again, you will find more conservative courts following the old "let the buyer beware" line.

EXAMPLE: Seller failed to disclose that a septic tank did not comply with the building code. He was held not liable. *Egan* v. *Hudson Nut Products Inc.,* 142 Conn. 344, 114 A2d 213 (1955).

§ 361. **Nondisclosure—half-truths.** To tell part of the truth is often the same as telling a lie. If a man states a fact that by itself is true, he must tell all the other facts that qualify or modify the fact stated. Otherwise he will be liable for damages. *Franchey* v. *Hannes,* 207 A2d 268 (Conn. 1965). Prosser, Torts (4th ed. 1974) p. 696.

EXAMPLE: The seller told the buyer that he personally constructed the building and that it was well built. He now has a duty to go on and state, if that is the case, that he built it without a building permit, for even a well-built structure may violate an ordinance, and costly alterations may be needed to bring the building into compliance with the law. *Milmoe* v. *Dixon,* 101 Cal. App.2d 257, 225 P2d 273 (1951). (Seller liable for damages.)

EXAMPLE: The seller stated that the buyer could use all the water he wanted at a flat rate of $2 per month. It was held that the buyer could set the deal aside when he discovered that the water was never supplied by the water company between 7 P.M. and 7 A.M., *Simmons* v. *Evans,* 185 Tenn. 282, 206 SW2d 295 (1947).

EXAMPLE: The seller of a hotel disclosed the amount of its income accurately but failed to reveal that the source of the income was largely through the operation of a brothel. The seller is liable for fraud. *Ikeda* v. *Curtia,* 43 Wash. 449, 261 P2d 684 (1953).

EXAMPLE: The seller had two engineers make a report on the property but disclosed only the favorable report to the buyer. Seller is guilty of fraud. *Gilbert* v. *Corlett,* 171 Cal. App.2d 116, 339 P2d 960 (1959).

§ 362. **Returning benefits received under the contract.** If a party wishes to cancel a contract for fraud, he must offer to return whatever he has received under the contract.

EXAMPLE: The buyer went into possession of the farm he had purchased and, after discovering a fraud, sold all the livestock on the farm. He could not rescind, since he could not return what he had received under the contract.

§ 363. **Ratification.** If a misrepresentation is made, and the other party, after discovering the fraud, fails to take prompt action to call the deal off, he is said to ratify or approve the contract and thereafter cannot have it set aside.

EXAMPLE: The seller of a saloon property told the buyer that the tenant in possession of the property was making money, when in fact the tenant was losing money and had lost over $4000 in the business in the last four years. The seller also said that there was sufficient stock on hand in the saloon to run for thirty to sixty days, when the supply was in fact good for only three or four days. The buyer paid the purchase price and went into possession. He discovered the misrepresentation almost immediately, but remained in possession over seven months, trying to make the business pay. It was held that this constituted a ratification of the contract, and the buyer was not entitled to get his money back.

§ 364. **Hardship.** At times, if circumstances change after the contract is signed, and as a result it would be a substantial hardship to compel performance of the contract, the courts have refused to enforce it. 11 ALR2d 390.

EXAMPLE: After the contract was signed the city rezoned the land for residence purposes. The buyer, as was known to seller, planned to erect a factory. The court refused to enforce the contract.

§ 365. **Options.** A valid contract of sale is binding on both seller and buyer. Each can be compelled to do the things he has promised to do. An option is simply a contract by which a landowner gives to another person, called the optionee, the right to buy the land at a fixed price within a specified time. The owner does not then sell his land or any interest in it. The optionee gets, not lands or an interest therein or an agreement that he shall have lands, but the right to call for and receive lands if he so chooses. *Keogh* v. *Peck,* 316 Ill. 318, 147 NE 266 (1925). If, within the time specified in the opinion, the optionee gives the owner notice that he elects to exercise the option, the option then ripens into a contract of sale. If the optionee lets the specified time go by without taking any action, he has no further rights in the land, nor can he recover from the landowner the money paid for the option.

§ 366. **Options—use of.** There are really two kinds of options. An *option in gross* is one used to acquire vacant land, principally in land assemblies.

EXAMPLE: A needs to acquire Lots one to four in a subdivision on which he plans to erect an apartment. Each lot is owned by a different owner. *A* hires *XYZ Realty Inc.* to acquire these lots. He does not want to own any lot unless he can acquire them all. *XYZ* goes out and contacts each lot owner. It offers $2000 for an option to acquire the lot for $10,000 within one year. The option runs to *XYZ* to hide *A*'s identity. If *XYZ* gets an option on each of the lots, it exercises the option, acquires a deed to each lot, and deeds the four lots to *A*. The advantage to *A* is that he has no personal liability to any of the lot owners. If any of the lot owners refuses to sell on *A*'s terms, *A* forfeits the option price. The advantage to the lot owner is that he gets to keep the $2000 if no contract is signed. When the option is exercised, often the option agreement provides that the option price is applied on the sale price. Not necessarily, however. The lot owner may insist that he get to keep the $2000 or some percentage thereof, typically 50%, as compensation for keeping his lot off the market. Options are always recorded. There is no set period for options to run except it must not exceed twenty-one years. It can be for two days or two years. If the buyer is planning to acquire acreage for a big development, the option price is usually a per acre price. If the buyer needs to get rezoning, the contract will give him a time figure for procuring the zoning change. In some ordinances the lot owner is required to join in the zoning application. In that event the option will require this but will also provide that all costs and expenses will be borne by the optioner.

EXAMPLE: *L* leases an industrial plant to *T* for 20 years. Under the lease *T* is authorized to remodel and renovate the existing building at considerable expense. *T* will want to protect his investment. Hence the lease will give *T* an option to purchase the property during the life of the lease. The option price may be stated under an escalating formula, for example, going up 5 percent at the end of each year. This protects *L*, the theory being that the escalation covers the rising value of the land as time goes on. Obviously options *in leases* run for longer periods than an *option in gross.*

As to drafting options, *see,* Kratovil, Modern Real Estate Documentation, Chapter 20.

§ 367. Suggestions on contract draftsmanship.

Preliminary observations. The goal to be achieved in drafting a contract of sale is twofold: (1) to draft a contract that the courts will enforce, since many contracts are so poorly drafted that courts cannot and will not enforce them; (2) after the seller and buyer have explored all aspects of the deal and reached an agreement as to all their rights and duties, to specify all the terms that the parties have agreed on, and to state them so clearly that there can be no controversy as to their meaning.

Parties. In general the suggestions made regarding parties to deeds are applicable to contracts to parties.

Purchase price. State the purchase price and terms of payment, including prepayment privilege, if any, and acceleration clause, in complete detail and with utmost clarity. If sellers are joint tenants, state that price is payable to them "as joint tenants with right of survivorship and not as tenants in common or by the entireties."

Earnest money. For the seller's protection, the deposit should be adequate. Insist on a certified or cashier's check. Buyer should insist that money be held in escrow by a bank or trust company.

Purpose for which buyer is purchasing the property. Careful thought must be given to the purpose for which the buyer is purchasing the property. For example, it may be that the buyer intends to use the property for a purpose forbidden by the zoning ordinance. If so, the contract must contain a clause for the buyer's protection requiring an amendment to the zoning ordinance to be procured within a limited time, and in default thereof, the buyer to be entitled to cancel the contract and obtain a return of his money. If the contract is prepared and signed at a time when information concerning the provisions of recorded building restrictions or applicable zoning and building ordinances is unavailable, but the seller feels that neither restrictions nor ordinances will prevent use for the buyer's intended purpose, a clause may be added giving the buyer the right to terminate the contract within a specified time if it shall appear from recorded covenants, conditions, or restrictions or from zoning or building ordinances, official maps or plans, or applicable statutes that the premises cannot legally be used for the intended purposes.

Description of the land. In considering the adequacy of the land description of the contract, the parties should consult also the specific suggestions hereinafter set forth.

Streets and alleys. The seller will usually have some right, title, or interest in and to the streets or alleys adjoining the premises sold, including private streets and vacated streets, and it is desirable that the contract of sale call for the seller to convey, without warranty, all such right, title, and interest.

Items to be conveyed to buyer or retained by seller. A contract for the sale of land obligates the seller to deliver title to the land and all fixtures, including the building, for it, of course, is a fixture, and fixtures are part of the land. *Chattels,* however, such as furniture, are not included, unless the contract expressly so provides. Any items that are clearly personal property or might give rise to controversy.

Chattel clause. Together with the following chattels for which a bill of sale will be given at closing:

Air conditioning equipment, awnings, bar and bar stools, bookcases, cabinets, carpets (particularly stair carpets), chandeliers and lighting fixtures, clothes washer and dryer, crops, curtains, curtain rods, draperies and other interior decorations, dryers, electric fans, electrical equipment, fireplace grates and andirons, dishwasher, doorbells and chimes, fuel, furniture, garage door openers and car units, garbage cans, garbage disposal, garden statuary, gas logs, high fidelity or stereo equipment that has been built in, ironing boards, lamps, lawn mowers, and garden equipment, linoleum, mirrors, perennial plants, refrigerators, rugs, screen doors, security systems, shelves, space heaters sprinkling equipment, stokers, storm doors and windows, shrubbery, stoves, supplies, TV antennas and masts, tools and equipment (particularly janitor's tools), water softener, trade fixtures, venetian blinds, ventilators, wash tubs, water heaters, towel racks and bars, water meter, window shades, and window screens.

Easements. Does the buyer need an easement over adjoining land to provide access to the land purchased? If he does, let the contract provide for execution of an easement grant, and since the buyer will want an abstract or title insurance policy to evidence the seller's good title to the land sold, consider whether a similar precaution is not advisable as to the land over which the easement passes. Only the man who really owns the land can grant an easement over it. As a minimum, the contract should require the seller to warrant his title to the easement premises. Are there leases to tenants or fire insurance policies? Let the contract call for the assignment and delivery thereof to the purchaser. The contract should also require seller to assign to buyer any other items that buyer wishes to receive, e.g., service contracts (contracts with exterminators, scavengers, and so on) roof guaranties, or tenant's deposits.

Fixtures. What does the seller expect to retain after the deal is closed? Once the contract is signed, the seller is obligated to deliver to the buyer all fixtures, for they are legally part of the land. If the seller expects to retain attached machinery or other items that might be considered fixtures, provision to this effect should be included in the contract. If the seller needs to reserve an easement over the land sold, a provision to that effect should be included in the contract.

Encumbrances to which the title is to be subject and to which the buyer agrees. The seller should see that he has listed in the contract all the encumbrances or other defects in title that he does not propose to clear before the deal is closed. Most contract forms contain a printed list of common encumbrances, such as leases or building restrictions, but it is intended that the seller will add to this list as necessary. Suppose, for example, that the seller's title is subject to an easement. Is it mentioned in the contract? If not, and the buyer changes his mind and decides to back out of the deal, he may be able to do so because the title, as finally examined before the deal is closed, must reveal no encumbrances other than those listed either in general or in specific language in the contract.

The buyer should carefully analyze every encumbrance listed by the seller. For example, if in the contract he agrees to take subject to "existing leases," he must accept the property subject to any lease, no matter how ridiculously low the rent may be. If the contract says that the buyer will accept title subject to "building and other restrictions of record," "easements of record," and "mineral rights," as many printed forms provide, will any of these restrictions, easements, or mineral rights interfere with his building program, assuming that he is buying land to build on? Moreover, will some easement documents to which the land is subject obligate the buyer in some way as owner of this land? For example, an easement for road purposes may obligate me to keep my neighbor's road in repair. Similar personal liability provisions may be contained in restriction documents.

Mortgage provisions. These should be detailed and complete. For example, if the contract calls for a purchase money mortgage, are the amount, interest rate, maturity date, and form of mortgage clearly set forth? Similar details should be included in a clause giving the buyer the right to cancel if he cannot procure a mortgage of a specified amount, and in this clause also specify the time allowed to procure the mortgage. If land is being sold subject to a mortgage, specify the amount and whether or not the buyer assumes personal liability. If the seller has a mortgage on his land that must be released, the contract should provide that the seller will have the right to pay it off at the closing of the deal, using the buyer's sale price for this purpose, the seller to have the mortgagee present prepared to release the mortgage and surrender the canceled papers. Occasionally a seller in an installment contract wants to reserve the right to mortgage the land. In these cases the contract should: (1) give details of the loan, maximum amount, maximum interest rate, and so forth; (2) specify that the mortgage will be prior and superior to the rights of the contract buyer; (3) give the buyer the right to make the mortgage payments if the seller fails to do so and to deduct payments so made from his contract payments.

Evidence of title. The contract should provide: (1) What type of title evidence is to be furnished, title insurance, abstract, and so forth. (2) Who is to furnish and pay for same. (3) Time allowed: (a) for furnishing evidence of title, (b) for buyer to point out defects in title not permitted by the contract, (c) for seller's clearance of objections, and (d) for buyer to decide whether to accept title *as is* if objections cannot be cured. (4) If abstract of title is specified, for the seller's protection a clause should be included giving the seller the right to cure any of the buyer's objections to the title by delivery of a clear policy of title insurance. This may save the seller the time and expense of a quiet title suit when the buyer's attorney raises numerous unimportant objections to the title. (5) The seller should not sign a form of contract that calls for title insurance if his land is registered under the Torrens system, for this will subject him to a double expense if the buyer insists on his contract rights.

Clearing title by escrow deposits. For the protection of the seller, the contract should contain a provision allowing the seller to leave money in escrow with some bank or title company if his title is not clear on the day that he must deliver clear title. Otherwise a deal may fall through simply because a seller is not in a position to remove some trivial defect, such as a small mechanic's lien, within the time allowed for clearing title.

Chattel lien search. Specify if the seller is to furnish search for financing statements or other liens on personal property being sold, and if so, time allowed for same.

Building ordinance violations. If the seller is to furnish a formal, official report as to building code violations, cover this, including time allowed for this purpose. The buyer should endeavor to have the contract provide that the seller "warrants the building on said premises is now and at the date of closing will be free and clear of all violations of laws and ordinances, and for breach of this warranty buyer may rescind this contract, before or after closing, or, at his election, may sue for damages."

Survey. If the seller is to furnish a survey, specify the time allowed for this and that it is to be satisfactory to the buyer's attorney. The time allowed for the buyer to raise objections based on the survey should tie into the time allowed the buyer for raising objections to the title. If the seller objects to paying for a survey, the buyer may decide to get one at his own expense. Is a survey necessary? Business judgment should be used in answering this question. For example, if A is buying a forty-year-old dwelling where the fences have also been up for that length of time, it is unlikely that any encroachment trouble will develop. Age has set the matter at rest. If, on the other hand, A is buying a recently erected commercial building that apparently extends to the property lines, a survey is definitely advisable, for the building may actually extend over property lines. Again, how can the buyer be sure that the legal description in the contract covers the property that the buyer has inspected and wants to buy? The only really satisfactory proof of this is a land survey. A survey is always advisable if new construction is contemplated, so that the building is set within the lot lines and within lines established by ordinances and private restrictions.

Building and other restrictions. If the seller wishes to place building restrictions on the land sold, he must make provision for this in the contract.

Risk of loss. Suppose the building is destroyed or damaged by fire or other casualty before the deal is closed. The right of the buyer to cancel the deal and his right to insurance money if he does not back out, should be covered.

Warranties of building. The buyer should try to get a clause in the contract stating that basement does not flood, building is free of termite infestation, roof does not leak, and heating plant and electrical system are now and at closing will be in good working order.

Miscellaneous documents to be furnished to the buyer. If a new building requires a certificate of occupancy or an approval by the underwriters of electrical installations, or if it is customary to obtain similar certificates with respect to plumbing and the like, the contract should provide that the seller will deliver these at the closing. In case of a new building, guaranties by the subcontractors are customary. There is usually a roof guaranty and a guaranty of the plumbing and heating equipment and electrical installations. The contract should provide that the seller will transfer and deliver these to the purchaser at the closing.

Installment contracts. The forfeiture clause is of the greatest importance here. Also cover the buyer's duty to pay taxes, carry insurance, and keep buildings in repair and free of mechanic's liens, restrictions on assignment of contract, and so forth. The seller should be given the right to declare the entire purchase price due if the buyer defaults. For the seller's protection provide that the buyer shall not assign the contract without the seller's consent. Also provide that the buyer is to pay taxes and furnish insurance with seller named in the policy. Buyer should agree to keep the premises in repair and in compliance with ordinances and laws, not to remodel without the seller's consent, and to keep the premises free from mechanic's liens.

Possession. Cover the date on which possession is to be given.

Leases. Provide for assignment to buyer of all seller's leases, including leases for advertising signs.

Concessionaire contracts. Provide for assignment of all such contracts.

Tenant's security deposits. Assignment of tenant's security deposits to buyer must be covered specifically.

Advance payments of rent. The contract should allow the buyer a credit against the purchase price where a tenant has already paid the seller the rent for the last several months of the term.

Prorated items. These should be covered in great detail to avoid arguments at closing over who pays for janitor's vacation pay, water bills, and so forth.

Income tax. The seller should consider whether an income tax savings will result if the property is sold under an installment contract rather than for cash.

Building construction. If the contract calls for construction of a building, many additional matters must be considered.

Documents. All miscellaneous documents that the buyer will need should be provided for in the contract. The seller is under no legal obligation to furnish any document that the contract does not call for.

Signatures, acknowledgment, witnessing. All the parties must sign, being careful to sign as their names appear on the contract. Witnessing and acknowledgment are desirable, so that the buyer may record the contract, for without witnessing or acknowledgment, the contract is not recordable in many states.

RESERVED: §§ 368 to 371.

12

The Closing

§ 372. **Sale closing defined.** After the contract of sale has been signed, there are a number of details that must be attended to. For example, the title must be examined to determine if the seller really owns the property and what mortgages, liens and restrictions exist. A survey must be ordered. The premises must be inspected to ascertain the presence of unrecorded easements and the unrecorded rights of parties in possession. At the end, the seller gives the buyer the deed, and the buyer is paid the balance of the purchase price. All this is the process of "closing the deal." Often, much the same process is taking place with respect to the buyer's mortgage. So there will be a contemporaneous "mortgage closing" also.

While the two closings, sale and mortgage, involve a process that occurs simultaneously and may culminate in a single meeting when both transactions are finalized, the processes will be dealt with separately here. This is in recognition of the two distinct sets of relationships, which, although they involve the same subject matter, give rise to different rights and obligations.

§ 373. **The lawyer's role.** The need for counsel in the real estate transaction can best be demonstrated by example.

EXAMPLE: *P* signed a contract to buy a corner vacant lot intending to erect a filling station thereon. He had no lawyer. The deal was closed. After closing, he discovered that the lot was zoned for single-family dwellings. Lawyers are taught to inquire into zoning.

EXAMPLE: *P*, without consulting a lawyer, put down a payment of $15,000 on the purchase of a vacant tract. The contract was a preprinted form reciting that buyer would accept title subject to "recorded building restrictions." *P* intended to erect a dog hospital. When the title search came out, it showed recorded building restrictions that permitted only residential use. *P* lost his $15,000. He had no use for a residence. Lawyers are taught to be wary of building restrictions.

Obviously examples like these take place each year. They need not occur. The attorney is needed from the precontract stage through the closing. Many people fail to recognize this need until it is too late. Particularly in residential transaction, which, to most, is the largest transaction of their lives. They eagerly execute a document and rely upon sheer luck to pull them through. Inflation has caused many "average" homes to have selling prices of six figures, but these buyers and sellers only rarely have representation when the blueprint for this transaction, the real estate sales contract, is executed. What is more incredible is the number of people who carry the transaction through to closing without counsel only to find to their chagrin that they were penny wise and dollar foolish.

§ 374. **Conflict of interest.** It has long been a rule of legal ethics that a lawyer is forbidden from representing conflicting interests in a transaction without full disclosure and consent by all of the parties. This disclosure must not only be of the multiple representation, but also of the effect of this representation upon the exercise of the lawyer's professional judgment on behalf of each party. Disciplinary Rule 5-105. The real estate sales transaction is a somewhat frequent scene for this practice, as where a developer's attorney is automatically denominated as buyer's counsel as a form of repayment for services rendered to the developer. *See: In re Kamp,* 194 A2d 236 (N.J. 1963). This activity may lead to professional sanctions being taken against the lawyer. *The Florida Bar* v. *Tietelman,* 261 So2d 140 (Fla. 1972). It may also have repercussions for the clients.

EXAMPLE: A purchaser was entitled to rescind a real estate sales contract when he was represented by seller's counsel who failed to disclose to the purchasers the existence of a lien on the property. The court found this to be a material fraud on the part of the seller. *Holley* v. *Jackson,* 158 A.2d 803 (Del. 1959).

REFERENCE: 68 ALR3d 697.

§ 375. **Matters to be considered before closing.**

Evidence of title. If the contract requires the seller to furnish an abstract or other evidence of title, he should do so *within the time allowed by the contract,* for if he fails to do so, a reluctant buyer may seize the opportunity to cancel the deal. If the seller is furnishing a title commitment, be sure it is a signed, original commitment. The buyer, in turn, should *within the time allowed by the contract,* draw attention to any defects in title not permitted by the contract. Otherwise he will be regarded as waiving such defects. The seller should then, *within the permitted time,* cure any defects pointed out by the buyer. When the contract specifies that the seller shall furnish an abstract of title showing clear title, the buyer has a right to insist that quitclaim deeds needed to clear the buyer's title objections be recorded in the recorder's office and included in the abstract of title. *Kincaid* v. *Dobrinsky,* 225 Ill. App. 85 (1922). When the contract calls for a title insurance policy showing clear title in the seller, the buyer has the right to insist that all unauthorized objections be cleared from the title policy by the seller.

Since closings are apt to be fairly hectic, it is a good idea for the parties to submit to each other, in advance of closing, all the documents that will then be exchanged, such as the deed, mortgage note, survey, leases, assignments. The documents are then checked in the quietude of one's office and pencil initials are placed in a corner of the document. Further scrutiny of the form at the time of closing is then omitted through a check of signatures will still be needed at that time.

Checking the survey. Check the date on the survey. A survey made ten years ago, for example, obviously will not cover buildings erected since then. Does the survey locate the property with reference to known monuments, such as government section corners? Does it show the location of all out buildings? All neighboring buildings? Our walks, drives, fences, and those of our neighbors? Are all buildings, walks, and so on well within the lines of the lot on which they belong? Do any structures extend over the setback lines established by city ordinances or building restrictions? Does the survey show whether upper portions of the building (bay windows or eaves) extend over the lot lines? Are there possible subsurface encroachments, such as footings on the building, extending into adjoining land?

The certificate of the survey should also be checked for an express declaration that it is intended to be relied upon, and, if erroneous, can be sued upon by the buyer, his mortgagee, and their title companies. *Rozny* v. *Marnul,* 250 NE2d 656 (Ill. 1969); Note, 64 *N.W.U.L. Rev.* 903 (1961). See Kratovil, Modern Real Estate & Documentation, Chapter 7 (1975).

Chattel lien search. If valuable chattels are included in the sale, a search of the Uniform Commercial Code records should be made for financing statements affecting such chattels. This search requires care. Code filings relating to fixtures, crops, and consumer goods (stoves, refrigerators, and other appliances found in the ordinary home) are found in some local office, often the recorder's office, but in some states in a department separate from the department where ordinary deeds are filed. Filings covering furniture and other chattels in a hotel or furnished apartment, or raw materials in an industrial plant, are likely to be found in some central office, usually that of the Secretary of State in the state capitol.

Ordinance violations search. If in the particular community it is possible to procure a title company or other search of city records as to building ordinance violations, this should be done. In lieu thereof, an architect or engineer should check the building carefully for violations.

Inspection of the property by the buyer. Before closing the deal the buyer should make a careful physical check of the property. Possession imparts constructive notice. The buyer will take subject to the rights of the grantee in an unrecorded contract, or to other rights disclosed by occupancy. Tenants' leases should be checked for options to renew or to purchase. If the premises are occupied by tenants, their occupancy is notice of their rights. The buyer must not accept the seller's assurance that tenants are month-to-month tenants. He should check with the tenants. This check with the tenants will also determine what furniture, appliances, etc., the tenants claim belong to them.

EXAMPLE: **A is selling a furnished apartment building to *B*. The entire building is under lease to C. The lease has only one month to run, and *B* plans to operate the building**

himself. *B* inquires of C and finds that C owns all the furniture. *B* must plan to acquire new furniture or plan to buy the old furniture from C.

As the buyer, during the inspection, check for the existence of unrecorded easements that inspection would reveal, for the buyer takes subject to unrecorded easements if their existence would be revealed by an inspection of the premises. Check to see whether this particular sale will result in the creation of any implied easements. Check to see whether rear or side exits run over adjoining property, thus making an easement necessary, and whether shutters open over adjoining premises. Check to see if heat is furnished by an adjoining building, thus making a written agreement necessary. Check for vaults, marquees, and so forth extending into public streets, which would make permits necessary. If you defer inspection until after the abstract or other evidence of title has been furnished, you can check to see whether the building violates any recorded building restrictions. It should be remembered that, even if the contract requires the buyer to take subject to "building restrictions," he is not required to take subject to violations of restrictions. Such violations constitute a separate and distinct defect in title. Check also for violations of zoning or building ordinances and for recent repairs or construction that might ripen into a mechanic's lien. If valuable chattels are included in the sale, inquire of the tenants whether they claim ownership of such chattels.

It is also customary to have an inspection shortly prior to the closing so that mechanical systems (heating, air conditioning, and so forth) can be checked to determine whether they are in operating condition and how they function. Sometimes the buyer may want an inspection by a qualified home inspection company. An appropriate contingency clause is often inserted in the contract, stating that the sale will close only if the inspection shows all systems in working order. Where other than single family property is involved, it is customary for the buyer's engineer to make an inspection of the building. This is also a good time for the seller to set out the drawings, blueprints, plans and specifications, warranties, instruction manuals, and so forth for the buyer and his staff. If there is a reluctance on the seller's part actually to surrender these items until the sale actually closes, at least the buyer will know where to find these things when possession is obtained.

Prior approvals. All will admit that it is better to take care, before closing, of questions of form and substance of the transaction documents. The questions, if they erupt at closing, can cause arguments and even failure to close. If the parties exchange unexecuted forms of these documents, problems can be ironed out in advance and approved documents can be initiated by the attorneys. Closing can then be devoted to ministerial acts and exchanges. If the documents are other than standard form, it is also good to have a title company officer check and initial them.

Closing agent. Closing practices vary from locality to locality, and even within the same county or city. In various areas, closings are conducted by lending institutions, title insurance companies, escrow companies, real estate brokers, and attorneys for the buyer or seller.

Maintenance of property from date of contract to date of closing. It is the seller's responsibility to maintain the property in a reasonable manner between the date of contract and the date of closing. If he permits it to deteriorate, the buyer may sue him for damages even after the deal is closed. Goldberg, Sales of Real Property 442; 92 CJS *Vendor & Purchaser* § 286a.

§ 376. **Bulk sales affidavits and notices.** A sale of real estate may incidentally involve the sale of the entire stock of goods, wares, or merchandise of some retail establishment operated by the seller on the premises. It is necessary that such a sale comply with the local Bulk Sales Act, which usually involves giving notice of the pending sale to the creditors of the business so that they can protect their rights. 37 CJS 1325.

§ 377. **Closing date.** The contract of sale should fix a closing date, the time the deed is to be delivered and the balance of the purchase price paid. If no closing date is fixed in the contract, it is presumed that the deal is to be closed within a reasonable time, and either buyer or seller may select a reasonable date and notify the other that he will be prepared to close at such time. Often one of the parties is not prepared to close on the date specified in the contract and requests an adjournment of closing. In such case, the other party, in granting the request for adjournment, specifies that the prorating or apportionment will be computed as of the original date or the adjourned date, whichever is more favorable to him. For example, if the adjournment is made at the request of the seller and the income of the building is greater than the carrying charges, the buyer will insist that the apportionment or prorating be computed as of the original date. The buyer will receive the rents from the date originally fixed for closing, and the seller will be entitled to interest on the unpaid balance of the purchase price and the purchase money mortgage from the original closing date. Of course if the contract fixes a closing date and provides that time is of the essence, the party who is ready to close on the date fixed need not grant a request for an adjournment.

Some contracts fix a date that is to govern the prorating of apportionment, regardless of the date of the delivery of the deed. Other contracts provide that prorating or apportionment shall be computed as of the date of the delivery of the deed.

The buyer should not rely on any extension of time granted by the seller's lawyer or broker. Normally, neither of them has the power to grant extensions.

§ 378. **Matters to be attended to at closing.**

Title. The buyer should make a final check to see that the title is clear and subject only to the encumbrances permitted by the contract of sale. If the deal is not closed in escrow, an informal check should be made of the records to cover the period between the date of the abstract or title search and the date of the closing of the deal. Judgments or other liens may attach during the interval, and will, of course, be good against the buyer. The buyer should at least insist that the seller's attorney give him a written statement that he will not turn the buyer's check over to the seller until after the deed to the buyer has been recorded and the title searched to cover that date. Of course if the deal is closed in escrow, all danger from this source is obviated. If, by agreement, the seller is to clear certain objections after closing, the buyer should retain part of the purchase price, usually double the amount of the lien involved, to insure performance on the part of the seller.

Form and contents of documents involved. The documents should all be checked to see if they are in proper form and comply with the contract. For example, if the deed to be given is a warranty deed, the subject clause of the deed should be checked to make certain that it does not include any items that were not included in the subject clause of the contract. The deed should also be checked to see if the recorder of deeds will accept it for recording. For example, in many states, laws forbid "metes and bounds" subdivisions, that is, the division of a tract of land into plots for sale without the formality of recording a subdivision plat. The recorder will often reject such a deed, and the buyer is left with a deed that he has paid for but cannot record.

If, as is so often the case, the major portion of the purchase price is being furnished by the buyer's mortgage lender, the attorneys will make a final check of the mortgage and note to see that the principal amount, interest rate, and monthly payments are in accordance with the loan commitment. If this has not previously been attended to, a similar check should be made of the other loan documents, such as the assignment of rents or waiver of defenses.

Water and other utility bills. The buyer should call for the production of paid water and other utility bills. If these bills have not been paid, service to the building may be cut off.

Insurance premiums. The buyer should see that the seller's insurance premiums have been paid, since the seller will receive credit for insurance in the prorating.

Production of seller's deed. The buyer should require the seller to produce the deed by which he acquired title. This affords some measure of protection against forgery and impersonation.

Prorations or adjustments. Prorations or adjustments should be computed and a closing statement prepared.

Payment of purchase price and delivery of documents. The balance due according to the closing statement should be paid and the documents to which each party is entitled delivered to him.

§ 379. Apportionment or prorating—the closing statement. The contract of sale usually provides that various items shall be adjusted or prorated. Items not mentioned in the contract are nevertheless often prorated because of the prevailing local custom. *O'Donnell* v. *Lutter,* 156 P2d 958 (Cal. 1945); *Valley Garage, Inc.* v. *Nyseth,* 481 P2d 17 (Wash. 1971). This prorating, or adjustment, results in credits and debits against each party. These are usually shown on a closing statement, which is also called a settlement sheet. Forms of closing statements vary and may be imposed by a regulatory agency, i.e. HUD's RESPA mortgage closing statement. A form commonly used lists in one column all credits due the seller and in a separate column all credits due the buyer. The completed statement is approved by buyer and seller.

Number of years, months and days	RENTS One Month		TAXES & INS.		INSURANCE						Number of years, months and days
	Days to Month		One Year		Three Years			Five Years			
	30	31	Months	Days	Years	Months	Days	Years	Months	Days	
1	.0333	.0323	.0833	.0028	.3333	.0278	.0009	.2000	.0167	.0006	1
2	.0667	.0645	.1667	.0056	.6667	.0556	.0019	.4000	.0333	.0011	2
3	.1000	.0968	.2500	.0083	1.0000	.0833	.0028	.6000	.0500	.0017	3
4	.1333	.1290	.3333	.0111		.1111	.0037	.8000	.0667	.0022	4
5	.1667	.1613	.4167	.0139		.1389	.0046	1.0000	.0833	.0028	5
6	.2000	.1935	.5000	.0167		.1667	.0056		.1000	.0033	6
7	.2333	.2258	.5833	.0194		.1944	.0065		.1167	.0039	7
8	.2667	.2581	.6667	.0222		.2222	.0074		.1333	.0044	8
9	.3000	.2903	.7500	.0250		.2500	.0083		.1500	.0050	9
10	.3333	.3226	.8333	.0278		.2778	.0093		.1667	.0056	10
11	.3667	.3548	.9167	.0306		.3056	.0102		.1833	.0061	11
12	.4000	.3871	1.0000	.0333		.3333	.0111		.2000	.0067	12
13	.4333	.4194		.0361			.0120			.0072	13
14	.4667	.4516		.0389			.0130			.0078	14
15	.5000	.4839		.0417			.0139			.0083	15
16	.5333	.5161		.0444			.0148			.0089	16
17	.5667	.5484		.0472			.0157			.0094	17
18	.6000	.5806		.0500			.0167			.0100	18
19	.6333	.6129		.0528			.0176			.0106	19
20	.6667	.6452		.0556			.0185			.0111	20
21	.7000	.6774		.0583			.0194			.0117	21
22	.7333	.7097		.0611			.0204			.0122	22
23	.7667	.7419		.0639			.0213			.0128	23
24	.8000	.7742		.0667			.0222			.0133	24
25	.8333	.8065		.0694			.0231			.0139	25
26	.8667	.8387		.0722			.0241			.0144	26
27	.9000	.8710		.0750			.0250			.0150	27
28	.9333	.9032		.0778			.0259			.0156	28
29	.9667	.9355		.0806			.0269			.0161	29
30	1.0000	.9677		.0833			.0278			.0167	30
31		1.0000									31

Example:

Rent $135.00 per mo.
To find value of 23 days of a 31 day mo.
From Table:—
23 days = .7419
.7419 × 135.00 = $100.16

Example:

Taxes = 1215.12.
To find value of 7 mos. and 19 days
From Table:—
7 mos. = .5833
19 days = .0528
7 mos. 19 days = .6361
.6361 × 1215.12 = 772.95

Example:

3 Year Policy Premium = 58.75
To find the value of 1 yr. 3 mos. 11 days
From Table:—
1 yr. = .3333
3 mos. = .0833
11 days = .0102
1 yr. 3 mo. 11 days = .4268
.4268 × 58.75 = 25.07

Example:

5 Yr. Policy Premium 312.82
To find value of 3 yrs. 4 mos. 13 days
From Table:—
3 yrs. = .6000
4 mos. = .0667
13 days = .0072
3 yrs. 4 mos. 13 days = .6739
.6739 × 312.82 = 210.81

Pro-rating Table for Rents, Taxes and Insurance

Prorations can be computed by reference to the prorating table on the preceding page.

§ 380. Credits due seller. The following are the usual credits due the seller:

1. Full purchase price.
2. Unearned insurance premiums.
3. Fuel on hand.
4. Any items paid by seller in advance, as water tax (if same has been so paid), prepayments on exterminator or other service contracts, prepayments on taxes and insurance made by seller to mortgagee under the terms of the mortgage, when such mortgage is to be assumed by buyer.

§ 381. Credits due buyer. The following are some of the credits due the buyer:

1. Earnest money.
2. Existing mortgages if the sale is for part cash and balance by assumption of existing mortgages.
3. Interest accrued and unpaid on existing mortgages that are to be assumed by the buyer.
4. Amount of purchase money mortgage if seller has agreed to receive such mortgage as part of the purchase price.
5. Unearned rents that have already been collected, since rents are usually collected on the first of the month. If the deal is closed after the first of the month, the buyer is, under most contracts, entitled to his proportionate part of the current month's rent collections. This includes unearned rent on leases of advertising space or advertising signs.
6. Deposits by tenants made as security for payment of rent for the last month of the lease.
7. Taxes. Since the seller has had possession of the rents of the property for prior years and for part of the current year, it is only fair that he pay all taxes for prior years and his proportionate part of the taxes for the current year, if these have not already been paid, and contracts usually so provide. In some localities, however, it is not customary to apportion current taxes. In periods of rising taxes, a clause in the contract may call for proration of taxes at a base in excess of the latest bill, for example, "107 percent of the latest available tax bill." As an alternative the contract may call for reproration of taxes if the actual bill, when finally received, exceeds the latest available bill substantially, say by 10 percent or more. Without such provision, neither buyer nor seller can seek adjustment if the variation is costly. *3700 S. Kedzie Bldg. Corp.* v. *Chicago Steel Foundry Co.*, 156 NE2d 618 (Ill. 1959). Do not confuse taxes with special assessments. While the former may be proratable, the latter are not unless the contract expressly so provides. *Alder* v. *R. W. Lotto, Inc.*, 517 P2d 227 (Wash. 1973).
8. Items based on meter readings, such as water tax, electricity, and gas, if same are not paid in advance.
9. Wages and other charges accrued and unpaid, such as janitor's salary or scavenger service.
10. Release fee and recording charge, when buyer will record or obtain release of mortgage that seller should have removed from his title.

§ 382. **Other items.** The buyer pays for recording of the deed, unless the contract provides otherwise. Since the seller would otherwise bear this expense, the contract usually requires the buyer to pay for the recording of any purchase money mortgage and for the abstract or other evidence of title to cover the said mortgage. The escrow agreement specifies who pays for the escrow. These items may or may not be included in the closing statement.

§ 383. **Documents to be obtained by buyer.** The following are some of the items and documents to be obtained by the buyer at closing:

1. Deed.
2. Abstract, title policy, or other evidence of title.
3. Bill of sale of personal property.
4. Receipt for purchase price paid.
5. Survey.
6. All paid notes on existing mortgages, which buyer assumes, since these notes will be needed in obtaining a release deed; also any mortgage and mortgage notes that have been paid in full and the release or satisfaction of the mortgage, if such release has not yet been recorded.
7. Statement by mortgagee showing amount due on existing mortgage, so that mortgagee cannot thereafter assert that any greater amount remains due. This applies where buyer is taking land subject to an existing mortgage or where buyer is to pay off the mortgage.
8. Insurance policies and assignments thereof.
9. Leases and assignments thereof, including leases of advertising space or advertising signs.
10. Letter by seller to tenants advising them to pay future rent to buyer.
11. Letter by seller to seller's building manager or rental agent advising him of sale of building and of termination of his authority.
12. Statement by seller as to names of tenants, rents paid and unpaid, and due date of rents, and that no rents have been paid in advance except for current month.
13. Rent control registration.
14. Service contracts (for example, elevator maintenance contract, scavenger service contract, exterminator contract), roof guaranties, and so forth, if they are to be assigned to buyer, with assignment thereof.
15. Last receipts for taxes, special assessments, gas, electricity, and water.
16. Seller's affidavit of title, which states, among other things, that there are no judgments, bankruptcies, or divorces against him, no unrecorded deeds or contracts, no repairs or improvements that have not been paid for, that the seller knows of no defects in his title, and that he has been in undisputed possession of the premises. The affidavit of title has several functions: (1) In many cases, the abstract or title search covers only the date of the contract, and the deal is closed at some later date. The affidavit covers the period between the date of title search and the date of closing. (2) Some defects in title are not revealed by a title search, for example, a divorce obtained in some other state. Indeed, the only way in which one can be assured of the seller's marital status is by procuring an affidavit relative thereto. Other defects, such as mechanics' liens for work or material furnished in the building, may also not be revealed by the title examination. (3) The warranty deed gives the buyer the right to sue for *damages* if a defect in title is

later revealed. But the affidavit may give the buyer the right to have the seller prosecuted *criminally* for obtaining money through false pretenses. The threat of a criminal prosecution is often more effective than the threat of a suit for damages.

17. Securities deposited by tenants as security for payment of rent and money deposits by tenants made as security for payment of rent for last month of lease. But if lease does not provide that on any sale of property the deposit shall go to buyer, tenants' consent should be obtained to a transfer of the deposit.

18. If the property being sold has employees, seller should furnish employment records, social security data, Fair Wages and Hours Law records, income tax withholding records, union agreements, if any, and agreements with janitor.

19. Affidavit by seller that: (1) all chattels included in the sale are fully paid for; (2) seller knows of no building or zoning ordinance violations affecting the property; (3) rents are being collected according to the leases, that is, no rents have been collected in advance and no concessions have been granted tenants, such as one month's free rent each year; (4) seller has no knowledge of any contemplated acquisition of the property for public purposes.

20. If the seller is selling only part of his land, he should sign and deliver to the buyer all documents necessary to have future real estate taxes apportioned as between the land sold and the land retained by the buyer.

21. The keys to the building.

§ 384. **Documents to be obtained by seller.** At closing, the seller should obtain the balance of the purchase price. If a purchase money mortgage is given, the seller should receive the purchase money mortgage and notes, chattel mortgage on personal property sold, fire insurance policies, and abstract of title.

§ 385. **Matters to attend to after closing.** After closing, the buyer should immediately record his deed and any release of mortgage obtained at the closing and have his evidence of title brought down to cover the same. The seller should do likewise with any purchase money mortgage. The buyer's title insurance policy and the title policy covering the mortgage the buyer put on at closing should be issued as soon as possible. If this has not already been attended to, the seller should notify the janitor, building manager, scavenger, exterminator, and so forth of the termination of their employment and that he will no longer be responsible for their compensation. The buyer should: (1) have water, gas, and electric bills, and real estate tax books changed to his name; (2) arrange for janitor, scavenger, building manager, and other services; (3) obtain consent of insurance company to assignment of policy; (4) have mortgage loss clause attached to existing insurance policies if mortgage has been executed; (5) obtain workmen's compensation and employer's liability insurance, if necessary.

The closing letter. After the deal has been closed, the buyer's lawyer writes the buyer a closing letter. The letter encloses the documents the buyer is receiving and describes them briefly and describes the documents that the mortgagee retains (fire insurance policy, abstract, etc.) and the documents that are still to come. For example, it takes the recorder of deeds a while to complete recording of the deed, and this is normally mailed to the buyer by the recorder.

The letter should suggest to the buyer what he is to do in the future, for example, giving the date on which tax bills become delinquent.

§ 386. **Mortgage closing defined.** Just as a sale is closed by delivery of the deed to the buyer and delivery of the balance of the purchase price to the seller after examination of the title and disposition of other details, for the protection of buyer and seller, a mortgage transaction is closed by delivery of the mortgage and note to the lender and disbursement of the mortgage funds to the mortgagor after attending to the details that insure the mortgagee that he has a good first lien on the property.

§ 387. **Borrower's concerns.** In shopping for a lender, the borrower should have numerous areas of concerns beyond the obvious questions of rate of interest, term of loan, points, and equity required. The borrower should also ask the lender the following questions:

1. Is the borrower required to carry life or disability insurance? Must he obtain it from a particular company? He may prefer no insurance or may wish to obtain it at a better premium rate elsewhere.

2. Is there a late payment charge? How much? How late may the payment be before the charge is imposed? The Borrower should be aware that late payments may harm his credit rating.

3. If the Borrower wishes to pay off the loan in advance of maturity (for example, if he moves and sells the house), must he pay a prepayment penalty? How much? If so, for how long a period will it apply?

4. Will the lender release the Borrower from personal liability if the loan is assumed by someone else when the house is sold?

5. If the Borrower sells the house and the buyer assumes the loan, will the lender have the right to charge an assumption fee, raise the rate of interest, or require payment in full of the mortgage?

6. If the Borrower has a financial emergency, will the terms of the loan include a future advances clause, permitting him to borrow additional money on the mortgage after he has paid off part of the original loan?

7. Will the Borrower be required to pay monies into a special reserve (escrow or impound) account to cover taxes or insurance? If so, how large a deposit will be required at the closing of the sale? May a savings account be posted in lieu of monthly impound payments? How large an account is needed? How long must it remain posted?

8. In looking for the best mortgage to fit the Borrower's particular financial needs, the Borrower may wish to check the terms and requirements of a private conventional loan versus a loan insured through the Federal Housing Administration or Farmers Home Administration or guaranteed by the Veterans Administration. The FHA, VA, and Farmers Home Administration loans involve Federal ceilings on permissible charges for some settlement services, which may be of interest to the Borrower. Ask lenders about these programs.

9. If the Borrower is dealing with the lender who holds the existing mortgage, he might be able to take over the prior loan, in a transaction called "assumption." Assumption usually saves money in settlement costs if the interest rate on the prior loan is lower than that being asked in the market. In times of inflation in the housing market, a higher down payment might be required than if you had obtained a new loan. The Borrower may want to ask the seller whether he would be willing to "take back" a second mortgage to finance part of the difference between the assumed loan and the sales price.

§ 388. **RESPA.** The Real Estate Settlement Procedures Act, 12 USC

§ 2601, has caused a great deal of consternation among lenders, brokers and real estate attorneys.

In its present form, the act's primary impact upon the closing process is directed toward lenders of "federally related mortgage loans." These are loans that are both secured by a first lien on residential (one to four family) real properties and meet any one of the following four criteria: (1) the loan is made by a lender which has its deposits insured by or which is regulated by the Federal government; or (2) the loan is insured, guaranteed, supplemented, or assisted under a Federal housing or urban development program; or (3) the loan is intended to be sold to FNMA, GNMA or FHLMC; or (4) the loan is made by any creditor who makes or invests in residential loans aggregating more than $1,000,000 per year. 12 USC § 2602. As you can see, the coverage of the act is very broad, with most lenders being made subject to its strictures.

At the time of application for a loan, the mortgage lender must give the borrower a copy of the HUD booklet, "Settlement Costs and You," together with a good faith estimate of the amount or range of charges for specific closing services that the borrower is likely to incur. 12 USC § 2604. The lender or his closing agent must make the settlement form or closing statement available to the borrower at or before the closing. The statement must then contain all information relating to settlement charges within the lender's knowledge. The lender must provide the borrower with the settlement statement at the closing or as soon as practicable thereafter. No charge can be imposed for the preparation of RESPA or Truth-In-Lending forms.

REFERENCE: Field, RESPA in a Nutshell, 11 R.P.P&T.J. 447 (1976).

§ **389. Title defects.** It is, of course, important to the mortgagee to be sure that his mortgage is a first lien on the land and that no title defects exist. Among the precautions he would take in this regard are the following:

1. Check mortgage for errors in filling blanks, signatures, witnesses, acknowledgment, etc. Have mortgage filed or recorded and bring abstract or other evidence of title down to cover the date of the recording of the mortgage before paying out. This will disclose any other liens that have appeared of record prior to the recording of the mortgage. Any such liens should be paid and released or subordinated to the mortgage. The prudent lender will weigh the true worth of the various means of evidencing title. Sophisticated lenders tend to insist on the ALTA mortgage title insurance policy. Among other advantages, it insures that the mortgage is valid and enforceable. It also insures against unfiled mechanics' liens, unrecorded leases, unrecorded easements, encroachments and other questions of survey, and lack of legal access to the mortgage property. If the lender is forwarding funds to a title company's agent or its approved attorney, the lender should insist on receiving its *insured closing letter,* which insures the mortgagee against embezzlement of loan funds or the agent's failure to follow the mortgagee's directions. This, incidentally, insures the lender that all prior liens shown on the title search will be paid off, for all mortgagee's directions require this, and the insured closing letter insures that this will be done. If the mortgage is being assigned to your company, require the title company to issue its endorsement to the mortgage title policy insuring the validity of the assignment and substituting the name of your company as the party assured.

2. Analyze all objections to the mortgagor's title disclosed by the examination of title. All defects in title should be cleared. If the title search reveals building restrictions or conditions, ascertain whether existing buildings violate such restrictions. Of course, copies of the instruments creating restrictions, easements, and so forth should be obtained and analyzed.

3. The mortgagee should inquire into the rights of parties in possession for the purpose of discovering unrecorded leases with options to purchase, unrecorded deeds and contracts, unrecorded easements, and so on. He must keep in mind the fact that the mortgagee, in nearly all states, takes his mortgage subject to the interests of all parties in possession of the premises.

4. The mortgagee should: (a) inspect the building carefully for signs of recent work, and if any appears, demand to see paid bills and demand mechanic's lien waivers for any substantial work, as in construction loans; (b) get affidavit from mortgagor that all work or materials furnished to permises have been paid in full, which, if false, will subject him to criminal prosecution; (c) if the building is occupied by persons other than the mortgagor (tenant, contract purchaser, and so on), see that notice of nonliability for mechanics' liens is posted on the property in the states where such notice is effective.

5. A survey should be obtained to determine whether any encroachments or other survey defects exist.

6. The mortgagee should obtain the usual mortgagor's affidavit to the effect that there are no judgments, bankruptcies, and so on against such mortgagor.

7. Within the time limits specified by the law and regulations, the lender must disclose to the borrower all matters required by the Federal Truth-in-Lending Act (15 USCA §§ 1601–1665).

§ 390. Suggestions as to the loan closing statement.

Seldom does the borrower receive the full amount of the mortgage loan. Various deductions are made for title searches, surveys, recording fees, and other items. Therefore, on disbursement of the loan, the mortgagee will prepare a loan settlement statement similar to that prepared in sales of land. This form should be used for three reasons: (1) it furnishes the borrower with a complete record of all disbursements made by the mortgagee from the proceeds of the loan; (2) it provides the mortgagee signed authorization by the borrower for all such disbursements and thus eliminates all possibility of any legal action that might be taken if the mortgagor claims improper charges were made against his loan; and (3) in those cases where there is no binding loan commitment, it fixes the date on which the mortgage becomes a lien on the land, since where there is no binding commitment, the mortgage does not become a lien on the land in some states until the date on which the loan is paid out to the mortgagor. In general, this settlement statement shows the full amount of the loan, and all deductions from it and their amount. It also shows the net amount available to the mortgagor and contains an acknowledgment by him that he has received that amount. The statement should be dated and signed by both mortgagor and mortgagee. The loan settlement statement is signed when the loan is closed.

§ 391. Zoning and building code violations. A check should be made for violations of local zoning and building ordinances which the mortgagee might be compelled to remedy at his own expense were he to to acquire title by foreclosure.

§ 392. Insurance. Existing fire insurance policies should be checked to determine that the amounts thereof are adequate and that the policies are properly written with mortgagee clause attached.

§ 393. Documents of the loan file.

The mortgagee's loan file should include the following papers:

1. Application for the loan, signed by borrower, and copy of mortgagee's letter of commitment.

2. Plat of survey.

3. If the loan is made to finance the purchase of property, the mortgagee should have a copy of the contract of sale in his files. This will prove helpful in making an appraisal of property.

4. Appraisal.

5. Mortgage, mortgage note, chattel lien on personal property in building, and assignment of rents and leases.

6. Assignment of mortgage and waiver of defenses if loan was purchased from original lender.

7. Credit reports on the borrower.

8. Insurance policies, with mortgagee loss clauses attached.

9. Abstract and opinion, mortgage title policy, Torrens certificate, or other evidence of title.

10. Mortgagor's affidavit as to judgments, divorces, recent improvements, and other pertinent facts.

11. Copy of escrow agreement, if loan was closed in escrow.

12. Loan closing statement, including receipt for loan proceeds signed by borrowers.

13. If loan was a refinancing loan, the canceled mortgage and note that was taken up by the new loan.

14. Waiver or encroachments by FHA, and all other FHA documents, which, of course, applies only when loan is FHA-insured.

15. Loan guaranty certificate and other documents needed in case of loans insured under the G.I. bill, or copies of such documents. If the loan is a G.I. loan, the form of application, loan closing statment, and appraisal report must be as specified by the regulations. The appraiser and credit agency should be required to submit two copies of their reports, so that mortgagee can retain copies for his files.

16. Subordination of reverter if one was obtained. If any other prior mortgage or other lien was subordinated to the current mortgage, the subordination agreement, of course, should also be in the loan files.

17. Certified copy of corporate resolutions if mortgage was made by corporation. If property mortgage is all, or substantially all, of the assets of the corporation, resolutions by both directors and stockholders may be necessary.

18. Will, trust indenture, or other trust instrument, or copy of these, if mortgagor is a trustee.

19. Full copy of building restrictions affecting the mortgaged premises, particularly if loan is a construction loan.

20. Leases to key tenants and assignments thereof to mortgagee.

21. Necessary statements, waivers, and so forth necessary to document compliance with federal and state disclosure laws, the Real Estate Settlement Procedures Act (12 USCA § 2601 *et seq*) and similar local laws. A discussion of these disclosure laws may be found in Barron, Federal Regulation of Real Estate (1975 with 1976 supp.).

RESERVED: §§ 394 to 404.

13

Escrows

§ 405. **Nature of escrow.** A deed is delivered *in escrow* when it is deposited with a third person with directions to deliver the deed to the grantee only upon the performance of some condition set forth in the escrow instructions but not in the deed. The third person, to whom the deed is delivered, is called the *escrow holder, escrow agent,* or *escrowee.* The instructions defining the conditions to be performed prior to delivery of the deed to the grantee are called the *escrow agreement* or *escrow instructions.*

§ 406. **Operation and purpose of escrows.** A contract for the sale of land usually requires the seller to furnish an abstract or other evidence of title showing the condition of his title *on the date of the contract.* Suppose that on May 10, *R* agrees to sell certain land to *E* for $5000. The contract is not recorded, and the seller remains in possession of the land. *R* orders an abstract or other evidence of title. This abstract is received by *R* on May 20. It does not, however, show the condition of the title on May 20, but on some earlier date, probably May 10. *E*'s lawyer completes his examination of the abstract on May 25 and finds title clear in *R* as of May 10. On May 26 *E* pays the money to *R,* and receives his deed. Then it develops that on May 11 the United States had filed an income tax lien of $1,000 against *R.* This is a lien on the land, like a mortgage. Other objections to the title may also arise during this interval between the date of the contract and the recording of the deed, such as judgment liens or suits attacking the title. The seller might even mortgage the land in the interval. Or he might die during the interval, leaving minor heirs, who obviously would be incapable of signing any deed.

In order to avoid these and other similar risks, sales may be closed in escrow. Escrows usually operate somewhat as follows: Both the deed and the purchase price are delivered to some disinterested third party, often a title insurance company, with written instructions to record the deed, to order an examination of title, and, if the title shows clear *in the buyer,* to pay over the purchase price to the seller. The escrow agreement also provides that, if it shall appear that the seller's title is defective and the defects are not cured within a certain specified time, the buyer shall be entitled to the return of his money upon reconveying the title to the seller. In those cases where the seller has not had his title examined as of some recent date in the past, the procedure is often divided into two steps. First, before the deed is recorded, the escrow holder is instructed to cause the seller's title to be examined down to the date of the contract. This first step may even be taken before the escrow agreement is signed. Then if title shows clear in the seller, the instructions provide that the deed be recorded and the examination of title brought down to cover the recording of the deed.

When the transaction follows the procedure above outlined, it is common for the grantee to deposit with the escrowee a quitclaim deed conveying the land back to the grantor. Then if the title proves defective, the quitclaim deed can be recorded by the escrowee so that the records will once more show title in the grantor.

In counties where it is possible to examine titles very quickly, the procedure may follow these lines: The seller will have his title examined down to the date of the contract of sale. If title shows clear, the seller deposits his deed with a title company as escrowee. The escrowee orders a second examination of title to cover the period intervening between the date of the last examination and the close of recording hours on the day the deed is deposited. This examination can be made quickly, for it covers a period of only a few days. If title shows clear, the seller's deed is recorded the next morning the moment the recorder's office opens.

Under either system, the buyer's money is not paid to the seller until the buyer is assured of receiving clear title.

Escrow practices and the frequency of their use differ quite a bit from state to state. In many communities, escrows are virtually unknown. This is particularly true of small communities where seller and buyer know and trust each other. The danger here that the seller will make a deed or mortgage to some third person in order to get out of the deal is not so great as in larger communities, where relationships are apt to be more impersonal. When a deal is closed without benefit of escrow, the buyer often requires the seller, at the time the deal is closed, to give an affidavit that he has not signed any deeds, mortgages, or contracts since the date of the contract of sale, and that since that date no judgments have been rendered against him.

Another benefit of the escrow is that if objections to the title that can be removed by use of the purchase money appear, such as judgments against the seller or unpaid taxes, the buyer may with absolute safety, after title is recorded in his name, allow the escrow holder to use part of the purchase money for the purpose of removing such objections. An escrow also protects the buyer against the seller's changing his mind and conveying the property to some third person in order to escape performance of the agreement. On the other hand, it assures the seller that the purchase price will be paid to him if the title is clear and enables a seller who has liens against his title to use the buyer's money to pay off such liens.

§ 407. **Requirements of valid escrow.** The following are the requirements for a valid escrow for the sale of land:

1. There must be a valid and enforceable contract for the sale of the land. *Johnson*

v. *Wallden,* 173 NE 790 (Ill. 1930). The escrow agreement may in itself contain all the essential requirements of a contract of sale. *Wood Bldg. Corp.* v. *Griffitts,* 330 P2d 847 (Cal. 1958). The existence of a valid contract of sale, either in the escrow instructions or in a separate instrument, is, however, indispensable for a binding escrow. If this were not true, it would be possible to have what is in effect a contract for the sale of land without the written agreement that the law requires for land sales. *Campbell* v. *Thomas,* 42 Wis. 437.

EXAMPLE: Two landowners executed deeds to each other pursuant to an oral exchange agreement and delivered such deeds to an attorney with verbal directions to deliver each deed to the grantee named therein when each landowner had presented a receipt showing payment of back interest on existing mortgages. Before these receipts were delivered, one of the landowners demanded return of his deed. The court held that he was entitled to return of his deed. The contract of exchange was only oral and therefore unenforceable. *Jozefowicz* v. *Leickem,* 182 NW 729 (Wisc. 1921).

2. The escrow agreement must contain a *condition,* something that must be done before the buyer's money is paid to the seller. The usual condition, of course, is the showing of clear title of record in the buyer, subject only to those objections listed in the contract of sale and escrow instructions.

3. The deed must be a good and valid deed.

4. The escrow holder must be some third person. Neither buyer nor seller may act as escrow holder.

§ **408. Contents of escrow agreement.** The escrow agreement usually covers the following matters:

1. Names and signatures of buyer and seller and name of escrow holder.

2. Documents to be deposited by seller, such as deed, insurance policies, separate assignments of insurance policies, leases, assignments of leases, abstracts or other evidence of title, tax bills, canceled mortgage notes, notice to tenants to pay rent to buyer, and service contracts.

3. Deposits to be made by buyer, such as purchase price and purchase money mortgage, if any.

4. When deed is to be recorded, whether immediately, after buyer's check clears, or after seller furnishes evidence of good title at date of contract.

5. Objections to which buyer agrees to take subject.

6. Type of evidence of title to be furnished.

7. Time allowed seller to clear defects in title.

8. How and when purchase price is to be disbursed, with directions as to what items are to be prorated or apportioned if escrow holder is to do the prorating.

9. Directions to deliver deeds, leases, insurance policies, assignments of policy, and service contracts to buyer when title shows clear.

10. Return of deposits to the respective parties where title cannot be cleared.

11. Reconveyance by buyer to seller if deed to buyer has been recorded immediately on signing of escrow agreement and examination of title thereafter discloses seller's title was defective and cannot be cured.

12. Payment of escrow, title and recording charges, broker's commission, and attorney's fees.

While an escrow often takes the form of *instructions* by the buyer and seller to the escrowee, the legal fact remains that it is an agreement or contract, and is so referred to herein.

§ **409. Escrow is irrevocable.** When a valid escrow agreement has been executed and the instruments therein provided for are delivered to the escrow holder, neither party can revoke the escrow and obtain return of his deposit. At times one party to a sale of land changes his mind and makes a demand on the escrowee for return of his deposit. The escrowee is justified in refusing to comply with an unwarranted demand. If the situation is legally doubtful he may insist on a court adjudication of the rights of the parties. *Franks* v. *North Shore Farms, Inc.*, 253 NE2d 45 (Ill. 1969); *Cocke* v. *Transamerica Title Ins. Co.*, 494 P2d 756 (Ariz. 1972).

§ **410. Conflict between contract of sale and escrow agreement.** Since the escrow is a means of carrying out the terms of the contract of sale, there should be no conflict between the two agreements. In the event of conflict, however, disposition of the deed and money deposited in escrow must be governed by the escrow instructions. *Widess* v. *Doane,* 112 Cal. App. 343, 296 Pac. 899 (1931).

§ **411. When title passes.** Prior to the performance of the condition specified in the escrow, title to the land remains in the seller even though his deed to the buyer is recorded. Even an innocent purchaser or mortgagee from the grantee is not protected in such cases. *Osby* v. *Reynolds,* 103 NE 556 (Ill. 1913); *Clevenger* v. *Moore,* 259 Pac. 219 (Okla. 1927).

EXAMPLE: An escrow agreement required the buyer to deposit the purchase price in escrow. Before this was done, the buyer persuaded the escrow holder to give him the deed, which the buyer thereupon recorded. He thereafter placed a mortgage on the property. When the seller discovered this mortgage, he filed suit, and the court canceled the mortgage as a cloud on his title, even though the mortgagee had acted in entire good faith. *Blakeney* v. *Home Owners' Loan Corp.,* 135 P2d 339 (Okla. 1943).

However, if the grantor allows his deed to be recorded, an innocent purchaser from the grantee will usually be protected if the grantor has also allowed the grantee to take possession of the land, for in such case *both the records and the possession show the grantee as the apparent owner,* and an innocent purchaser from such grantee should be protected, for there is nothing to apprise him of the grantor's rights. *Mays* v. *Shields,* 45 SE 68 (Ga. 1903).

Immediately upon the performance of the conditions specified in the escrow agreement, ownership of the land passes to the buyer and ownership of the purchase price passes to the seller. Thereupon the escrow holder becomes the agent of the buyer as to the deed and of the seller as to the money. *Shreeves* v. *Pearson,* 230 Pac. 448 (Cal. 1924). Since at that moment the escrow holder holds the deed for the grantee, this is as though the grantee himself held the deed. Thus delivery of the deed has been completed, and actual manual delivery of the deed by the escrow holder to the grantee adds nothing to the grantee's title. *Shirley* v. *Ayers,* 14 Ohio 307. However, it is the practice to provide for a delivery of the deed by the escrow holder to the grantee. This is the so-called *second delivery*. Since ownership of the land remains in the seller until the conditions specified in the escrow instructions have been met and performed, then, even though a deed from seller to buyer has been recorded, the seller remains in possession, collects the rents, and pays taxes, until the escrow conditions have been performed.

Likewise if the building is destroyed or damaged by fire or other calamity before the terms of the escrow have been met and performed, the risk of loss falls on the seller, for he is still the owner of the land. The seller's insurance company is liable to him even though he has signed a deed to the buyer because the deed has not as yet taken effect. However, escrow companies carry blanket insurance to cover the situation where the seller's insurance company denies liability.

§ 412. **Relation back.** Where the grantor delivers a deed in escrow, then dies, and therafter the condition of the escrow is performed, the deed is considered as passing title as of the date of the delivery of the deed to the escrow holder. It is said that the title *relates back* to such time.

EXAMPLE: *R* enters into a written contract to sell land to *E*. *R* signs a deed to *E* and delivers this deed to *X* as escrowee. *E* also deposits the purchase price with *X*. *X* records the deed under escrow instructions, which provide that the purchase price is to be paid to *R* when an examination of title shows the title clear of all objections. Before the examination is completed, *R* dies, leaving minor children as his heirs. Thereafter the title examination is completed and shows clear title in *E*. The deed is good, since the transfer of title to *E* relates back to the time when *R* was alive.

The same is true when the seller marries or becomes insane after delivering a deed in escrow.

If the *grantee* dies after the deed has been delivered in escrow, and the condition of the escrow is thereafter performed, the deed will be treated as relating back to the delivery in escrow and may be delivered to the grantee's heirs. *Prewitt* v. *Ashford,* 7 So 831 (Ala. 1890).

The rule that title relates back to the time of the original delivery of the deed to the escrowee is confined to the examples given above. In other situations, *transfer of ownership of the land takes place as of the time when the terms and conditions of the escrow are performed,* illustrated by the defalcation cases. For example, if the escrowee absconds with the buyer's purchase money before the terms and conditions of the escrow have been performed, the loss must fall on the buyer, because *at the time of the defalcation the purchase money still belongs to the buyer. Hildebrand* v. *Beck,* 236 Pac. 301 (Cal. 1925); 39 ALR 1080. On the other hand, if the terms of the escrow have been performed and thereafter the escrowee absconds with the money, the loss falls on the seller, because *after the escrow terms have been met and performed, the money on deposit belongs to the seller. Lechner* v. *Halling,* 216 P2d 179 (Wash. 1950); *Lawyers Title Ins. Co.* v. *Edmar Const. Co.,* 294 A2d 865 (D.C. 1972).

Thus, if a lender is a party to an escrow and the escrowee embezzles the mortgage money before the title has been cleared as required by the escrow instructions, the mortgage funds still belong to the mortgagee, and therefore he must suffer the loss of his funds and cannot collect from the mortgagor even though he holds the mortgagor's promissory note. *Ward Cook, Inc.* v. *Davenport,* 413 P2d 387 (Ore. 1966).

§ **413. Mortgages.** Since a mortgage does not become a lien until a debt which the mortgage secures exists, mere recording of a mortgage does not create a lien. Liens attaching to the land *prior to the time that the mortgage money is disbursed to the mortgagor may obtain priority of lien* over the mortgage. But if the mortgagee deposits his mortgage money in escrow, with directions to pay the money over to the mortgagor if an examination of title shows the mortgage as a first lien on the date of its recording, then immediately upon the recording of the mortgage its position as a first lien is established. Payment into escrow is treated as payment by the mortgagee to or for the benefit of the mortgagor. Thus there are mortgage escrows as well as sale escrows.

Again, there are cases where a buyer is borrowing money to complete his purchase. The mortgagee does not want his money paid out until title shows clear in the buyer, who is the mortgagor. The seller will not want to give a deed until and unless he is assured of receiving the purchase price. This difficult situation is easily taken care of through an escrow. The deed, mortgage, and mortgage money are deposited with an escrowee under written instructions to record the deed and mortgage and pay the mortgage money to the seller if the title examination shows the mortgage as a first lien. The interests of all parties are protected.

EXAMPLE: The contention has been advanced by the creditors of the mortgagor that they can garnishee such funds. The courts have rejected this contention. Kratovil, Modern Mortgage Law and Practice, § 225. The same result occurs where creditors attempt to garnishee construction money held by the mortgagee. *Ibid.* § 225. The funds cannot be garnisheed.

§ **414. Long-term escrows.** In the West and Southwest, the long-term escrow is used in the financing of real estate. This operates somewhat as follows: *A,* a land owner, enters into a contract to sell the land to *B*. *B* is unable to pay the full price at once. *A* desires to retain control of the land so as to insure the payment of the price in full or the restoration of the land to him. *A* therefore executes a deed of the land to *B* and places the deed in the hands of *C,* as escrowee, to be delivered to *B* on full payment of the price by *B* to *C*. If *B* makes timely payment of the price to *C,* the latter will hand the deed to *B*. *C* will also pay the money to *A*. If *B* fails to make such payment, *C* will be under a duty to return the deed to *A*. Bogert, Trusts and Escrows in Credit Conveyancing, 21 *Ill. L. Rev.* 655 (1927). The disadvantages of this arrangement are as follows:

1. Until completion of the payments, the public records show title in A, and this gives A the opportunity to defraud B by making a deed or mortgage to some third person who is unaware of the contract's existence. *Waldock* v. *Frisco Lumber Co.,* 176 Pac. 218 (Okla. 1918). This would not be true if the contract were recorded or if the buyer went into possession of the land.

2. The depositary may deliver the deed to the buyer notwithstanding the fact that he has not completed his payments, and recording of this deed will cloud the seller's title.

3. Default on the buyer's part after he has made substantial payments may result in a lawsuit against the depositary. *Phoenix Title & Trust* Co. v. *Horwath,* 19 P2d 82 (Ariz. 1933).

4. In some states a buyer in an escrow deal takes subject to judgments rendered against the seller while the deal is in escrow but before the purchase price is fully paid and the deed recorded. *May* v. *Emerson,* 96 Pac. 454 (Ore. 1908); 117 ALR 69, 85–88. The danger from this risk is increased when the escrow extends over a long period of time. In addition to the danger of judgments, there is the danger that, while the escrow is running, federal income tax liens may be filed against the seller or the seller may go into bankruptcy. These matters would cloud the buyer's title.

RESERVED: §§ 415 to 425.

14

Evidence of Title

§ 426. **In general.** Every prudent purchaser insists upon production of satisfactory evidence that the seller has good title to the land in question. The fact that the seller is willing to sign a deed to a tract of land is by no means satisfactory proof that he has good title to the land. He may have title to all, part, or none of the land. And if he has title, it may be a good title or it may be so heavily encumbered as to be worthless. And since a lender demands a mortgage precisely because he is unwilling to rely on the mortgagor's unsecured promise, it is clear that proof of good title is as important to a mortgagee as it is to a purchaser.

There are four kinds of evidence of title: *abstract and opinion, certificate of title, title insurance, and Torrens certificate.* The certificate of title is used extensively in the Eastern states and in some Southern states. In urban centers in a great many sections of the country, title insurance occupies a dominant position in real estate transactions. In farm areas the abstract and opinion method is common. To a great extent, the acceptability of a particular kind of evidence of title depends on the local custom.

§ 427. **Abstract.** An abstract is a history of the title to a particular tract of land. It consists of a summary of the material parts of every recorded instrument affecting the title. It begins with a description of the land covered by the abstract, which description is called the *caption,* or *head,* of the abstract, and then proceeds to show, usually in chronological order, the original governmental grant and all subsequent deeds, mortgages, release deeds, wills, judgments, mechanics' liens, foreclosure proceedings, tax sales, and other matters affecting the title.

Of course all these items are shown in a highly abbreviated form. In fact, usually a bare outline of the deed, mortgage, or other instrument is shown. "Fine print" provisions are omitted altogether or summarized in a few words. The manner in which the instrument was signed is not shown unless there is some irregularity in this respect. If the acknowledgment is in due form, the abstracter merely indicates that the instrument was acknowledged. A purchaser or mortgagee may rely on the abstracter to draw attention to these irregularities, since where an abstract purports to state the substance of a deed, mortgage, or other instrument, and there is nothing on the face of the abstract to indicate an error, the customer is justified in assuming that no irregularity exists in those portions of the document that the abstracter has omitted from his abstract. *Equitable B. & L. Assn.* v. *Bank of Commerce & Trust Co.*, 102 SW 901 (Tenn. 1907).

The abstract concludes with the *abstracter's certificate.* This discloses what records the abstracter has examined and, what is more important, what records he has *not examined.* For example, some abstractors will not examine records located outside of the county seat, and their certificates reflect that fact. In such case, it is necessary to supplement the abstract by obtaining the necessary searches. If an abstractor certifies that he has made no search of federal court proceedings affecting the property, it will be necessary to write to the clerk of the district court, who will supply the search for a small charge. The certificate also shows the date covered by the abstracter's search of the records. Because of the unavoidable delay intervening between the filing in the recorder's office of a particular day's deeds and mortgages and the entry of the same on the abstracter's books, the abstracter is not in a position to certify on any particular day as to the status of the record title on that day. His certificate will certify today as to the status of the record title on some previous day.

§ **428. The abstracter.** Abstracts are prepared by public officials, lawyers, and abstract companies. In some states, an abstracter is required to post a bond to protect all those who rely on his abstracts against any loss resulting from a lack of care or skill on his part. Many abstracters keep their own books. They take great pride in their "abstract plant," and, in many communities, the abstracter's records are more accurate than the public records. Other abstracters prepare their abstracts from the public records.

Since abstracting is a profession requiring much legal knowledge and careful research, a prudent purchaser or mortgagee will rely only on abstracts furnished by abstracters possessing the requisite skill, care, and experience. The financial responsibility of the abstracter and the existence and limits of his *errors and omissions insurance* are likewise important, since if an error is made in preparing the abstract of the title to a valuable tract of land, there should be no doubt as to the ability of the abstracter to respond in damages.

§ **429. Abstracter's liability.** The abstracter is in no sense a guarantor of title. He merely undertakes to exercise due care in the preparation of his abstract. He renders no opinion as to the title. If he includes in his abstract all recorded instruments affecting the title, and, as a consequence, the abstract discloses a fatally defective title, the abstracter has fully discharged his responsibilities. But, if an intending purchaser orders an abstract prepared and the abstracter negligently omits therefrom a mortgage, judgment, or other lien that the purchaser is thereafter compelled to pay, the purchaser can obtain reimbursement from the abstracter. 28 ALR2d 891. The abstracter's liability may also extend to third persons not parties to the contract for abstracting services. 34 ALR3d 1122.

EXAMPLE: Purchasers relied upon an abstract prepared for sellers by abstract company. The court held that the purchasers could recover even though the abstract was prepared before the contract of purchase. *Williams* v. *Polgar,* 204 NW2d 57 (Mich. 1972).

To be safe it is best for anyone who relies upon the abstract to have it certified to that person, and to the purchaser's mortgagee.

§ 430. Examination of title. The mere fact that a purchaser or mortgagee has received an abstract of title affords him no protection. In fact, examination of the abstract may disclose that the title is hopelessly clouded. Hence, after an abstract has been prepared by a reliable abstracter and certified so that the buyer or mortgagee can rely thereon, it should be delivered to a competent attorney for examination. This attorney will thereupon examine the abstract and prepare his *opinion* as to the title, which will show the name of the titleholder and all defects and encumbrances disclosed by the abstract.

§ 431. Certificate of title. In some localities the making of an abstract is dispensed with. The attorney merely examines the public records and issues his certificate, which is his opinion of title based on the public records that he has examined. Like an abstracter, such an attorney is liable only for damages occasioned by his negligence. 59 ALR3d 1176. The same is true when a certificate of title is issued by a title company. *Lattin* v. *Gillette,* 30 P. 545 (Cal. 1892); *Bridgeport Airport Inc.* v. *Title Guaranty & Trust Co.,* 150 A. 509 (Conn. 1930).

§ 432. Risks involved in relying on record title. There are certain defects in title that even a perfect abstract or certificate of title will not disclose because these hidden defects cannot be discovered by an examination of the public records. Among these defects are:

1. *Forgery.* A deed in the chain of title may seem entirely regular but may nevertheless be a forgery. Such a deed is totally void and a purchaser or mortgagee of such title is not protected. Likewise, a forged release of mortgage does not discharge the mortgage lien.

EXAMPLE: Suppose that you own some land and someone forges your signature on a deed purporting to deed the land to him or even to some innocent person to whom the forger represents that he is the real owner. Obviously, you would expect the law to protect you, even as against an innocent purchaser. It does. Or suppose that you owned a mortgage of $100,000 on an apartment building, and the apartment owner signed your name to a release purporting to discharge this mortgage. Even if the land were sold to an innocent purchaser, you would expect the law to permit you to foreclose your mortgage. It does.

2. *Insanity and minority.* A deed or release of mortgage executed by a minor or insane person may be subject to cancellation by subsequent court proceedings.

3. *Marital status incorrectly given.* A deed or mortgage may recite that the grantor or mortgagor is single, whereas in fact he may be married. This may later result in a dower or other claim by his spouse.

EXAMPLE: *H* owns an apartment building and is married to *W*, but is separated from her. *H* has an opportunity to sell the building to you at a good price, and does so. *H* signs *W*'s name to the deed. Her dower remains outstanding, and if *W* survives *H*, she will be able to force a sale of the building and her dower rights will be paid her out of the sale price.

4. *Defective deeds.* A recorded deed may never have been properly delivered. For example, it may have been found by the grantee among the grantor's effects after the grantor's death and then placed on record. Such deeds, of course, pass no title.

EXAMPLE: *A* owns an apartment building. He is a bachelor. He shares a safety deposit box with his nephew, *X*. *A* dies. *X* opens the box and finds a deed from *A* to *X* of the apartment building, with a note pinned to it, stating that *A* wants *X* to have the building. *X* records the deed. The deed is void. The mere fact that the deed was recorded after *A*'s death discloses that there is something wrong with the deed.

There are many other defects in title that the public records do not disclose.

There are also certain other risks not of a legal character that are encountered when a deal is closed in reliance on a certificate of title or abstract and opinion. One of these risks is the risk of unwarranted litigation attacking the title. A landowner's title may be good as a matter of law, but if some other person entertains the notion that he has some title to, or interest in, the land, he may institute litigation asserting his supposed rights, and such litigation, even though successfully defended, may prove costly. Again, a competent attorney examining an abstract for a purchaser may reach an entirely correct opinion that the title is good. But when the purchaser, in turn, is selling or mortgaging the land, the attorney for the subsequent buyer or mortgagee may arrive at a different conclusion. This may necessitate the institution of litigation to clear the title. It is this fear of objections to the title by some subsequent examiner that prompts attorneys to scrutinize abstracts closely and raise every technical objection apparent therefrom. This practice is known as *fly-specking*.

§ 433. **Nature of title insurance.** It is the function of title insurance to shift or transfer to a responsible insurer risks such as those mentioned in the preceding section. Title insurance is a contract to make good a loss arising through defects in title to real estate or liens or encumbrances thereon. *Beaullieu* v. *Atlanta Title & Trust Co.,* 4 SE2d 78 (Ga. 1939). As a rule, a title company will not insure a bad title any more than a fire insurance company would issue a policy on a burning building. However, title companies disregard many of the technical objections that would be raised by an attorney examining an abstract. If an examination of the title discloses that good title is vested in a particular person, the company will issue its policy whereby it agrees, subject to the terms of its policy, to indemnify such person against any loss he may sustain by reason of any defects in title not enumerated in the policy and to defend at its own expense any lawsuit attacking the title where such lawsuit is based on a defect in title against which the policy insured.

§ 434. **The title insurance policy.** Title companies issue both *owner's policies* and *mortgage policies,* the latter being known also as *loan policies.* The owner's policy is usually issued to the landowner himself. Mortgage policies, of course, are issued to mortgagees. Unlike other types of insurance policies, which insure for limited periods of time and are kept in force by periodic payment of renewal premiums, an owner's title insurance policy is bought and paid for only once, and then continues in force without any further payment until a sale of the property is made. At that time, the title is examined to cover the period of time since the issuance of the policy, and a new policy is issued to the purchaser. A charge is usually then made for the issuance of this new policy. The mortgage policy terminates when the mortgage debt is paid. However, if the mortgage is foreclosed, then the protection of the mortgage policy continues in force, protecting against any defects of title that existed on, or prior to, the date of the policy. In both policies, the company usually undertakes, subject to the terms of its policy, to defend at its own expense any lawsuit attacking the title where such lawsuit is based on a defect in title against which the policy insures. This is one of the attractive features of title insurance to property owners, since "nuisance" litigation affecting real estate is quite common and is expensive to defend, even though not well founded. A policy of title insurance usually shows the name of the party insured and the character of his title, which is usually fee simple title, although title policies are also issued on other interests, such as leaseholds or easements. It also contains a description of the land and, if the policy is a mortgage policy, a description of the mortgage. The policy lists those matters which affect that particular tract of land, such as any mortgage, easement, lien, or restriction thereon. Like other insurance policies, it contains printed conditions and stipulations.

Common printed exceptions found in owner's policies relate to the rights of parties in possession and questions of survey. Often real property is in the possession of those whose rights are not disclosed by the records. Common instances are tenancies under oral or unrecorded leases and rights of those in possession under unrecorded contracts of purchase. When no survey has been furnished the company, it has no means of knowing what encroachments exist, if any. The policy will therefore be subject to encroachments and other matters that a survey would reveal, also the rights of persons in possession claiming under some unrecorded document.

Title insurance policies are largely standardized throughout the country in that the American Land Title Association (ALTA) forms have become far and away the most popular.

§ 435. **Endorsements.** Where the evidence of title reveals defects not permitted by the sale contract (or permitted by the contract only where title insurance thereover is available), the parties may choose to avail themselves of title insurance coverage afforded against the potential loss or damage which could be incurred by the existence of such defects. Also, the insured may desire greater coverage than that given by the standard form of policy. Title companies offer a variety of endorsements to the title policy which extend such coverage. By way of illustration, the following are some of the endorsements issued by one title insurance company in such situations.

1. *Encroachment Endorsement 1.* This form of endorsement is issued to protect the buyer against any loss resulting from a mandatory injunction compelling removal of an encroachment of the insured building on adjoining land. Normally, the company will issue the endorsement where the encroachment is so trivial that it is highly improbable that a successful action to obtain the injunction could be maintained or where the encroachment is protected against removal by reason of over twenty years of adverse possession.

2. *Encroachment Endorsement 2.* This endorsement is issued to protect the buyer against any loss resulting from a mandatory injunction to remove encroachment of an improvement on the land over a private easement crossing the insured land. As in the case of Encroachment Endorsement 1, it is issued by the company where the triviality of the encroachment or adverse possession would defeat any action to remove the encroachment.

3. *Restriction Endorsement 1.* This endorsement can be used to provide protection where a deed in the chain of title contains a restriction with a reverter clause and the insured building violates the restriction but the violation is barred by the Reverters Act.

4. *Restriction Endorsement 4.* This is used where a restriction exists and is violated by the insured building but the violations are trivial or the restriction has become unenforceable because of other nearby violations or changes in neighborhood.

5. *Restriction Endorsement 4A.* This is used where the insured building violates a building line.

6. *Restrictions Endorsement 5.* This form of endorsement furnishes assurance to the buyer of vacant land that a contemplated improvement in violation of one or more restrictions affecting the land will not furnish a basis for injunctive relief against the construction or maintenance of the improvement. It is normally issued where the restrictions being violated have become unenforceable by reason of changes in the neighborhood or abandonment.

7. *Special Endorsement 1.* This form of endorsement extends assurance to a buyer of a condominium apartment that the condominium was created in conformity with the Condominium Property Act.

8. *Location Endorsement 1.* This form of endorsement informs a buyer as to the location of the land by a reference to its distance from an identified street or alley and, if available, to its street address. It extends assurance to the buyer that the contract describes the land he intends to purchase and such land is covered by the title policy. Similar forms of endorsements are available for the condominium and townhouse situation.

9. *Location Endorsement 4.* This form of endorsement assures the buyer that two or more parcels of land described in his contract of sale and in the title policy are contiguous.

§ 436. **Leasehold policies.** Suppose a tenant is about to take a lease on a store, theater, restaurant, or other commercial location in which he plans to make a substantial investment for remodeling. Just as a buyer of land needs to know that his seller has a good, clear title, this tenant needs to know that his landlord has a good, clear title to the leased premises and that the tenant will not be dispossessed in the middle of his lease by foreclosures or mortgages or other liens on the landlord's title. Contracts for such leases are drawn along the lines of a contract for the sale of land. They require the landlord to have his title examined and to furnish the tenant a *leasehold policy* issued by a title company insuring the validity of the tenant's lease free from mortgages or other encumbrances. Also, when the leasehold is the security for a mortgage, the lender will require a leasehold loan policy.

In 1975, ALTA promulgated standard forms of leasehold owners and loan policies. Prior to that time various title companies insured leaseholds by "doctoring up" regular owner's and loan policies. The new policies define the insured leasehold estate to include the right of possession for the terms of the lease subject to the conditions of the lease. The policies also describe a method of evaluating the leasehold estate and lists the items of incidental damages which will be paid if the insured is forced to surrender occupancy of the premises due to matters insured against.

§ 437. **Easement policies.** Suppose you are selling me a tract of industrial property that has access to a railroad by means of an easement for a spur track over adjoining land. The validity of the easement is just as important to me as the fact that you have good title to the land I am buying. I will therefore insist that the policy you furnish me insures the validity of the easement.

§ 438. **Title commitments.** Suppose that *A* had purchased some land in 1940 and had received a title policy at that time. He is now selling this same land to *B*. Naturally, *B* would not want to rely on such an outdated document. Therefore, the contract of sale will call upon *A* to have the title company bring its title search down to the present date, which they will do. The title company will issue a *commitment* obligating the company to issue its policy to *B* subject only to the matters shown in the commitment. If any defects appear on the commitment that the seller must clear up—unpaid back taxes, for example—the seller pays off the item, receives paid tax bills or other documents and exhibits them to the title company, which thereupon stamps the item "waived." When the title is clear, the land is conveyed by the seller to the buyer, the deed recorded and a title policy issued in the name of the buyer.

§ 439. **The Torrens system.** In a few counties in the United States, there is, in addition to the system of transferring title under the Recording Acts, a system known as the *Torrens system.* Under the Recording Acts, when a deed is made conveying land, the grantee in the deed usually takes it to the recorder's office and leaves it there for recording. The recorder makes a copy of the deed, places this copy in record books, which are available to the public, and returns the original deed to the grantee. The recorder does not pass upon the validity of the deed. If the grantee wishes to satisfy himself that he has received a good title, he may obtain title insurance, an abstract and opinion of title, or a title certificate.

The Torrens system operates quite differently. A landowner who wishes to register his land under the Torrens system first obtains a complete abstract of title to the land. He then files in the proper public office an application for the registration of title. This application lists the names of all persons who appear to have any interest in the land. These names are obtained from the abstract and from an investigation of the possession of the premises. The application constitutes the filing of a lawsuit against all persons named therein, and any person wishing to contest the applicant's claim of title may do so on receiving notice of the filing of the application. If the applicant is successful in proving that he is the owner of the land, the court enters an order so finding and also stating the mortgages, liens, restrictions, and so on to which said title is subject. The court also orders an official known as the *Registrar of Titles* to *register* such title. The registrar then makes out a *certificate of title,* showing the title as found by the court. These certificates are bound up in books and are public records. At the same time that the registrar makes out the original certificate, he makes out a *duplicate certificate of title,* which he delivers to the owner.

When a tract of land has been registered under the Torrens system, no subsequent transaction binds the land until such transaction has also been registered. When the land is sold, the deed itself does not pass ownership of the land. The deed must be taken to the registrar's office, and if the registrar is satisfied that the deed is valid, he cancels the old certificate of title and issues a new one to the grantee. It is this *registration* that puts ownership in the grantee. The deed is not returned to the grantee but remains in the registrar's office. In other words, the registrar of titles, unlike the recorder of deeds, investigates to determine the validity of the transfer, and only after he is satisfied that the transfer of title is valid will he issue a new certificate in the grantee's name. Thus, as to Torrens land it is said that "title passes by registration, not by deed." Likewise, a mortgage is not effective against the property until the registrar has checked it as to form and signature and entered it on the certificate of title. However, the registrar does not check on or guarantee the essential validity of the mortgage, for example, to see whether or not the mortgage money has been paid out or whether the interest is usurious. No judgment or other lien is valid against Torrens property until a copy has been filed in the registrar's office and the lien noted on the certificate of title.

Use of the Torrens system is largely confined to a few metropolitan areas, Boston, Chicago, Duluth, Minneapolis-St. Paul, and New York City.

The Torrens certificate purports to be conclusive proof that the title is as therein stated. As in the case of other evidences of title, there are exceptions and objections that the Torrens certificate does not cover. These vary somewhat from state to state. Unlike a policy of title insurance, the Torrens certificate does not require the registrar to assume the defense of litigation attacking the title of the registered owner. The property owner must defend the litigation at his own expense, and if he is successful, he cannot obtain reimbursements from the registrar for the expenses of the litigation.

RESERVED: §§ 440 to 450.

15

Insurance

§ 451. **Development of standard fire policy.** The need for fire insurance first became apparent after the Great Fire of London in 1666. However, the policies that came into use in England following that catastrophe contained numerous and varied fine-print exceptions that led to much litigation and disappointment on the part of the policyholders. These conditions also prevailed in America, and, in 1873, agitation for a standard policy led to the adoption of a standard policy form in Massachusetts. In 1886, New York adopted a standard policy form, which was revised by a law effective in 1918. This policy still strongly favored the insurer, and in 1943 New York adopted a revised form more favorable to the insured. This form has been widely adopted in this country, and the discussion on this chapter is largely keyed to this form of policy.

§ 452. **Hazards covered—fire loss.** The policy covers direct loss and damage *caused by fire*. Loss and damage caused by hazards *other than fire* must be covered by riders attached to the policy, for which an additional premium is charged, or by separate insurance. Among the hazards *not* covered are:

1. Explosion damage. If an explosion not caused by fire occurs on the premises and no fire results, none of the damage is covered. If a fire starts *first* and the fire causes an explosion, all loss is covered whether due to fire or explosion, for the fire is the cause of the loss. 82 ALR2d 1128. If an explosion occurs first and fire results, the policy covers the damage caused by the fire but not the damage caused by the explosion.
2. Water damage not resulting from a fire, as damage from water seepage in a basement or from a leaking sprinkler system.
3. Windstorm damage. As in the case of explosions, if a fire results from windstorm damage, the fire loss is covered by the policy.
4. Loss from hail, riot, civil commotion, aircraft, and many other hazards.

Breakage, water damage, and damage from chemicals caused through efforts to extinguish the fire are considered to be caused by fire and are therefore covered by the policy.

§ 453. **Extended coverage endorsement.** A rider attached to the fire policy on payment of an extra premium is known as an *extended coverage endorsement.* Its content varies according to locality, but it often covers loss from windstorm, hail, explosion, riot, civil commotion, aircraft, vehicles, and smoke from friendly fires, except those in fireplaces. The windstorm damage coverage of the extended coverage endorsement does not cover rain, snow, or other water damage as such, except where caused by or resulting from windstorm or another peril specified in the extended coverage endorsement.

EXAMPLE: In a heavy rain, the sewer backs up and floods the basement of your house. The damage is not covered by the extended coverage endorsement.

EXAMPLE: A tornado tears off a roof and the debris breaks water pipes. The water rushes out of the pipes, causing damage. All the damage is covered by the insurance, for the basic cause of the entire loss is the windstorm.

EXAMPLE: A hailstorm breaks windows, and the rain and wind sweep in, causing damage. All the damage is covered, because the original cause is a hailstorm, which is a peril specified in the extended coverage endorsement.

Damage caused by explosion of a steam boiler on the premises is not covered. Damage caused by vehicles driven *by the landowner* is not covered, but if, for example, a delivery truck entering a side drive runs into the house this damage is covered.

§ 454. **Homeowners policies.** As insurance became more sophisticated, it became obvious that the basic fire policy was not sufficient for the great bulk of home owners. Thus developed the homeowner's policy, which is a direct descendent of the first standardized fire policy instituted in New York. These policies are available in most prime markets and a second generation homeowner's policy has been introduced. This latter policy does away with fine print, long sentences and lawyer's language. Rather, it opts for a booklet type of presentation with readable type, simple sentences, and the absence of hypertechnical language.

Homeowner's policies are designated HO-1, HO-2, HO-3 and HO-5. The HO-4 policy is for renters and HO-6 is for condominium owners. Protection generally increases the higher the number, with HO-3 and HO-5 being all risks policies, which cover all fortuitous losses not resulting from misconduct or fraud unless the policy contains a specific provision expressly excluding the loss from coverage. *Phoenix Ins. Co.* v. *Branch,* 234 So.2d 396 (Fla. 1970).

REFERENCE: Gorman, All Risks of Loss v. All Loss: An Examination of Broad Form Insurance Coverages, 34 *Notre Dame Lawyer* 349 (1959); 88 ALR2d 112.

With the exception of the renters' and condominium owners' policies, coverage generally extends to the dwelling, with its additions, appurtenant structures, equipment and fixtures, together with unscheduled personal property. Coverage also extends in some policies to additional living expenses incurred by the insured as a result of a covered peril rendering the property untenantable. These coverages are generally based upon a percentage of the dollar amount of coverage of the insured dwelling. Depending upon the extent of coverage selected, the policies insure against loss to the property covered by the following perils: fire or lightning; windstorm and hail; explosion; riot or civil commotion; vehicles or aircraft; smoke; vandalism; theft; falling objects; the weight of ice, snow or sleet; collapse; the sudden and accidental breaking of a steam or hot water heating system or of an appliance for heating water; the accidental discharge of water or steam; the freezing of plumbing, heating, air conditioning and domestic appliances; and the sudden and accidental injury from electrical currents artificially generated to electrical appliances.

These policies do not insure against loss occasioned by the enforcement of ordinances or laws regulating the construction, repair or demolition of buildings, earth movement, flood, sewer backup, ground water pressure, power heating or cooling failure, and wear and tear.

Consistent with the concept of providing the homeowners with a package of insurance, the policies generally provide coverage for liability because of bodily injury or property damage. The policies are not so rigidly standardized as to permit no special coverage and, indeed, it is quite typical that homeowners schedule or list their inventory of valuables in a rider to the policy. This scheduling will remove the restrictions caused by the formula coverage for personal property.

EXAMPLE: Typically, unscheduled personal property is covered to the extent of 50 percent of the coverage on the building. The face of the policy so states. A policy with $50,000 in coverage would provide $25,000 in coverage for *unscheduled* personalty.

Scheduling also helps to eliminate questions of valuation in the event of loss.

EXAMPLE: If the family jewelry is scheduled together with an appraisal, the insurer is hard pressed to say the property was not worth the appraised value when loss occurs.

Special endorsements may also be obtained.

EXAMPLE: A debris removal endorsement may be obtained to provide coverage for the removal of tree limbs knocked down in a storm but which do not damage any of the structures in falling.

The popularity of certain forms of coverage varies from region to region. For example, in the Midwest, earthquake coverage is cheap but practically never purchased. In California, it is popular, and its price varies depending upon the type of structure and locale.

In making the decision as to which coverage is appropriate, it is good to note that the disparity in price between the premiums for the least comprehensive and most comprehensive homeowner policies is relatively minor. The extra coverage is well worth the few dollars spent.

§ 455. **Hazards covered—hostile and friendly fires.** The fire policy does not cover damage caused by smoke from a fire that is confined to the place where it is intended to be. Such a fire is called a *friendly fire.* Damage caused by smoke and soot issuing from a defective furnace is not covered. Damage caused by steam escaping from heat pipes is not fire damage, since the fire is a friendly one. But if the fire, though originally kindled in a stove, furnace, or fireplace, escapes therefrom, it becomes a hostile fire, and loss caused is covered by the policy. Nor is it necessary that the hostile fire be on the premises covered by the policy. For example, if my neighbor's house catches fire and the heat destroys the paint on the wall of my house, this is fire damage, covered by my policy, even though my building does not catch fire. Damage from smoke or soot is covered if it is caused by a hostile fire.

§ 456. **Hazards covered—rent loss and business interruption.** Since the policy covers fire damage to the *building,* it does not cover loss of rents when a rental building is rendered untenantable by fire, nor does it cover loss of *profits* when operation of a business is interrupted by fire. Both items can be covered by riders attached to the policy or by separate insurance such as rent insurance and business interruption insurance.

§ 457. **When protection attaches.** It often takes some time for a formal policy of insurance to be prepared and forwarded to the insurer. Hence oral coverage is perfectly valid, pending the issuance of the policy. This gives the insured the coverage of the standard policy subject to its terms and conditions. *Bersani* v. *General Accident, Fire & Life Assur. Corp.,* 330 NE2d 68 (N.Y. 1975).

§ 458. **Description of the property insured** The property insured should be accurately described in the policy, and all policies applying to the same property should contain identical descriptions.

The street address of the property is often used in insurance policies. There has been a tendency in recent times, however, to insist on the insertion of a full legal description so that there will be no dispute as to the property covered. This is particularly true with respect to houses recently constructed which often do not have a street address at the time the policy is written.

§ 459. **Insurable interest.** The insured must have some insurable interest in the property. Otherwise the policy is void. Persons having an insurable interest include both buyer and seller in a contract for the sale of land, mortgagor, mortgagee, part owner, trustee, receiver, and life tenant.

§ 460. **Interest covered by policy.** The present form of policy is an *interest policy. It protects only the party insured and covers only the financial loss suffered by the insured, which can never be more than the value of his interest in the property and which may be less than the actual damage to the building.*

This aspect of the policy is of importance in co-ownership situations. Suppose, for example, that *H* and *W* (husband and wife) own property in joint tenancy, but the policy is issued in the name of *H* only. If a fire loss occurs while both are alive, it is doubtful that the company is legally liable to *H* for the full amount of the loss, for he is the owner of only a one-half interest in the property, although, of course, companies often make voluntary payment of the full amount of the loss in such cases. Suppose further that a loss occurs after *H*'s death. Here his entire interest in the property has passed to *W*, but *W* has no insurance whatever, for the insurance does not pass with the property. It insures the *person,* not the *property.*

This aspect of insurance is frequently overlooked. Suppose *A* owns property, takes out insurance, and thereafter has title to the property placed in joint tenancy or tenancy by the entireties. Often the parties neglect to change the fire insurance to cover the new situation. Where land is owned by co-owners, insurance taken out by one does not benefit the other.

EXAMPLE: *H* and *W*, husband and wife, owned their home in joint tenancy. They became estranged. *H* took out a policy in his name only for the full value of the property. Then he died. *W* has no right to collect on this insurance. *Russell* v. *Williams,* 374 P2d 827 (Cal. 1962).

It is obvious that when property is owned by several people and the insurance is intended to cover all of them, the names of all co-owners should appear in the policy.

Since insurance does not cover the building, but only the interest of the insured in the building, and persons other than the insured cannot collect on the policy, persons having liens on insured property are not covered by the insurance.

EXAMPLE: A city has no right to have insurance money applied to payment of delinquent real estate taxes, which are a lien on the insured property. *Shelton* v. *Providence Washington Ins. Co.,* 131 SW2d 330 (Tex. 1939). Nor can a mechanic's lien claimant become entitled to fire insurance proceeds. 9 ALR2d 307.

Insurance taken out by a tenant does not benefit the landlord, nor does the landlord's insurance benefit the tenant. Insurance taken out by a builder does not benefit the landowner. *Russell* v. *Williams,* 374 P2d 827 (Cal. 1962).

§ 461. Amount recoverable. The insurer is not liable for damage in excess of the face amount of the policy, and any insurance paid reduces the amount of coverage. For example, if I take out a policy for $5000 and the company pays me $1000 for a loss, its maximum liability thereafter is $4000. Some policies have riders containing an automatic reinstatement clause under which small losses do not reduce the amount of insurance, and the homeowner's policy expressly provides that loss will not reduce the limit of liability.

If only part of the building is destroyed, but rebuilding the structure is prohibited by law (as where the building is a nonconforming use under the zoning ordinance), the loss is treated as total and the insured is allowed to collect the full face amount of the policy up to, but not exceeding, the full value of the building before the fire loss occurred. *Metropolitan Mutual*

Fire Ins. Co. v. *Carmen Holding Co.,* 220 A2d 778 (Del. 1966). However, it is customary to add a rider extending the policy to cover such loss.

Replacement cost insurance can be procured by adding a rider to the fire policy and it is part of the homeowner's policy. Instead of getting paid the actual cash value of the destroyed building, the insured is paid the actual cost of replacing or restoring the building. This eliminates the guesswork and argument involved in agreeing on the value of a destroyed building, but it does have disadvantages. For example, you recover the cost of replacing an identical building, but this will create problems when the building destroyed is old and of a type that one would not build today. If the insured spends more in replacing the building than was actually necessary, he will probably not recover the full amount spent. The new building may be on a different site, if the insured prefers. He also has the option of settling on the old "actual cash value" basis.

The homeowner form of policy provides recovery for the full cost of repair or replacement, without deduction for depreciation, if the building is insured for eighty percent or more of the replacement cost.

§ 462. **Acts of the assured.** Naturally, where the party insured causes the loss, as where he sets the building on fire in order to collect the insurance, the insurance company is not liable.

§ 463. **Unoccupancy clause.** The policy provides that the insurer shall not be liable while the building is vacant or unoccupied beyond a period of thirty consecutive days. The words *vacant* and *unoccupied* are not synonymous. *Vacant* means without inanimate objects; *unoccupied* means without animate occupants. A dwelling is unoccupied when it has ceased to be a customary place of habitation or abode and no one is living in it. Thus, if furniture remains in the building, it is not vacant, but if the owner has left the dwelling with the intention of permanently residing elsewhere, the building is unoccupied, and the insurance may become void. *Vandalism coverage* usually ceases if the building is unoccupied for thirty days.

Because the danger of vandalism has greatly increased in recent times, insurance companies are enforcing this clause. This requires that the owner obtain an endorsement waiving the clause or provide an occupant if a lengthy absence is planned.

§ 464. **Increase of hazard.** The policy provides that the company shall not be liable for any loss occurring while the hazard is increased by any means within the control or knowledge of the insured. The operation of this clause is restricted to physical changes in the building or in the use or occupancy of the premises. Any alteration or change in the building or in the use of the property that will increase the risk violates this clause if it is of a more or less permanent nature. 28 ALR2d 762.

EXAMPLE: The following operations increase the hazard and invalidate the insurance: (1) Tenant began operating a still. (2) Owner turned off a sprinkler system. (3) Owner brought fireworks on the premises. (4) Owner began use of a room as a tinshop.

But doing something that involves risk, that is a more or less normal and expected routine operation, is not considered an increase of hazard that invalidates the policy, for example, using a torch to burn off old paint preparatory to repainting. 28 ALR2d 771. Also, the increase of the hazard must contribute to or cause the loss. *Northern Assurance Co.* v. *Spencer,* 246 F.Supp. 730 (1965).

§ **465. Double insurance.** The policy provides only that other insurance may be prohibited by endorsement attached to the policy. Unless such endorsement is attached, the insured may procure additional insurance. However, the liability of each company is limited to the proportion of the loss that its insurance bears to the whole insurance covering the property. Thus if the same property is insured in two companies through two policies of $5000 each, and if a loss of $2000 occurs, the maximum liability of each company would be $1000.

The insured should check to see that all portions of all policies covering the same property read exactly alike.

§ **466. Co-insurance clause.** Very few fires cause a total destruction of the property. Property owners are aware of this fact. If it were not for the co-insurance clause, many property owners would save themselves premiums by taking out insurance for half the value of the property, or even less. To prevent this, the policy generally requires the property owner to take out insurance equal to at least 80 per cent of the value of the property. When he does so, the property owner collects the *full amount* of any loss. But if he insures for less than 80 per cent of value, a co-insurance clause is added. Suppose a building is worth $10,000. The company requires insurance up to 80 per cent of value, or $8000. The insured takes out only a policy of $4000. Under the co-insurance clause, the company will pay only $4000/$8000, or one-half of the loss.

Customary use of this 80 per cent in co-insurance clauses stems from the fact that generally only 80 per cent of the building's value is destructible by fire. A certain portion of the masonry and concrete work will remain standing.

§ **467. Mortgage interests.** Both the mortgagor and the mortgagee have an insurable interest. Both interests may be, and usually are, covered in one policy. But each may take out a separate policy. This right is of value to the mortgagee when the mortgagor has defaulted in his mortgage payments and declines to take out insurance since he feels that he will lose the property anyway. If the mortgagee obtains his own insurance with his own money and a loss occurs, the mortgagor is not entitled to the insurance money. If the insurer pays off the mortgage in such case, he is entitled to an assignment thereof and may foreclose. Of course the mortgagee's recovery is limited to the balance due on the debt, for that is the measure of his interest in the property.

On the other hand, in the absence of any clause in the mortgage requiring the mortgagor to insure for the mortgagee's benefit, the mortgagee is not entitled to insurance money paid under a policy obtained by the mortgagor in his own name and at his own expense. 9 ALR2d 299. However, most mortgage forms require the mortgagor to keep the buildings insured for the benefit of the mortgagee, and if a loss occurs in such case, the mortgagee is entitled to have insurance money applied in reduction or payment of the mortgage debt. *Sureck* v. *U.S. Fidelity & Guaranty Co.,* 353 F.Supp. 807 (1973). Where a mortgage containing a covenant to insure is assigned, a right to the insurance proceeds is created in the assignee. *Kintzel* v. *Wheatland Mutual Ins. Assn.,* 203 NW2d 799 (Iowa, 1973).

§ 468. **The mortgage clause.** Formerly it was customary for the mortgagor to take out insurance in his own name and, with the insurer's consent, to assign the policy to the mortgagee. This did not adequately protect the mortgagee. He simply stood in the mortgagor's shoes, and if the mortgagor violated the conditions of the policy so that it became void, the mortgagee was unable to collect the insurance. For example, if the mortgagor committed arson, the policy became void. The same result followed where the *open mortgage clause* was used. This clause simply stated that loss, if any, was payable to the mortgagee *as his interest shall appear,* which still left the mortgagee's insurance subject to be destroyed by the ignorance, carelessness, or fraud of the mortgagor. *Central National Insurance Co.* v. *Manufacturer's Acceptance Corp.,* 544 SW2d 362 (Tenn. 1976). Hence the *mortgagee loss clause,* also known as the *New York, standard, or union loss clause,* was developed. *Syndicate Ins. Co.* v. *Bohn,* 65 Fed. 165 (1894). This clause, now in general use, provides that the insurance shall not be invalidated by acts of the mortgagor. Under this clause, if the mortgagor does any act that would ordinarily make the policy void, for example, commits arson or brings dynamite on the premises, *such act merely makes the policy void as to the mortgagor, but the insurance remains in force for the benefit of the mortgagee. City-Wide Knitwear* v. *Safeco Ins. Co.,* 366 NYS2d 81 (1973). When such a clause is used, there are really two separate contracts, one between the insurer and the mortgagor and the other between the insurer and the mortgagee, and most matters that would invalidate the first of these contracts leave the second intact and in full force.

Under the standard mortgage clause, the following are some matters that will not render the mortgagee's insurance void:

1. Cancellation without the mortgagee's consent. *Mutual Creamery Ins. Co.* v. *Iowa Nat. Mutual Ins. Co.,* 294 F.Supp. 337 (1969).
2. Misrepresentation or concealment by mortgagor.
3. Increase of hazard of which the mortgagee remains ignorant.
4. Any act or neglect of mortgagor, including arson by the mortgagor.
5. Foreclosure of the mortgage. *Northwestern Nat. Ins. Co.* v. *Mildenberg,* 359 SW2d 380 (Mo. 1962). *But see* 5A Appleman, Insurance Law and Practice, § 3403 (1970). But it is safer to procure new insurance as soon as the foreclosure sale is held.
6. Deed by mortgagor to mortgagee given in satisfaction of the mortgage debt and in lieu of foreclosure. *Union Central Life Ins. Co.* v. *Franklin County Farmers Mutual Ins. Assn.,* 270 NW 398 (Ia. 1936). *But see Insurance Co.* v. *State Savings & Loan Assn.,* 425 F.2d 1180 (1970).
7. Failure of mortgagee to notify insurer that it has acquired a deed from the mortgagor. *Guardian S. & L. Assn.* v. *Reserve Ins. Co.,* 276 NE2d 109 (Ill. 1971).
8. Attempted cancellation of the policy by the mortgagor. *Mutual Creamery Ins.*

Co. v. *Iowa Nat. Mutual Ins. Co.*, 294 F. Supp. 337 (1969). Do not confuse cancellation with expiration. In the latter situation the insurer is not even required to give the mortgagee notice. 60 ALR3d 164.

9. The fact that the mortgage is a forgery. *Great Am. Ins. Co. v. Southwestern Finance Co.*, 297 P2d 403 (Okla. 1956).

10. Agreement between mortgagor and insurance company as to the amount of loss. *Beaver Falls B. & L. Assn. v. Allemania Fire Ins. Co.*, 157 A 616 (Pa. 1931).

There are limits on the protection afforded by the mortgagee loss clause, namely:

1. When the mortgagee clause requires the mortgagee to notify the company of commencement of foreclosure proceedings, failure to do so will make the policy void. But a provision in the mortgage clause requiring the mortgagee to notify the company "of foreclosure" means foreclosure of the mortgagee's own mortgage and does not require him to give notice of the filing of a foreclosure suit on any second mortgage. *National Mutual S. & L. Assn. v. Hanover Fire Ins. Co.*, 53 P2d 641 (N.M. 1936).

2. The mortgage clause requires the mortgagee to notify the company of any change of ownership or occupancy or any increase of hazard that shall come to his knowledge, and failure to comply with this requirement renders the mortgagee's insurance void. *Wright v. Firemen's Ins. Co.*, 291 NYS 508 (1936). Purchase by a stranger at the foreclosure sale may violate this clause if the company is not notified. *Royal Ins. Co. v. Drury*, 132 A 635 (Md. 1926). But the change of ownership occurring when a mortgagee acquires title by foreclosure is not a change of which the company must be notified. *Washburn Mill Co. v. Fire Assn.*, 61 NW 828 (Minn. 1895). Obviously, the prudent mortgagee will procure an endorsement as any important event occurs.

3. The mortgagee must submit proof of loss in the event of the mortgagor's failure to do so.

4. The one-year limitation for bringing suit on the policy applies to the mortgagee. *Greater Providence Trust Co. v. Nationwide Ins.*, 355 A.2d 718 (R.I. 1976).

5. Under a standard mortgage clause the mortgagee is bound by the insurer's option under the policy to repair or rebuild instead of paying for the loss. *Abbottsford B. & L. Assn. v. William Penn Fire Ins. Co.*, 197 A 504 (Pa. 1938).

6. So far as the company's liability to the mortgagor is concerned, the mortgagor is not bound by any settlement of the amount of loss arranged between the company and the mortgagee. *Montello v. Manhattan F. & M. Ins. Co.*, 294 NYS 1015 (1937). Some mortgage forms expressly authorize the mortgagee to settle the loss.

7. The mortgagee is bound by the co-insurance clause.

8. The mortgagee clause may or may not include a contribution clause. If more than one policy is written on the property, the contribution clause provides that the company shall be liable only for that proportion of the loss that the face amount of the particular policy bears to the aggregate face amount of all policies on the property. The mortgagee should insist on the *no contribution* type of mortgagee clause.

9. Since the mortgage clause is a separate and independent contract of insurance, the name of the mortgagee as party insured must be stated in the mortgage clause. *Pacific Ins. Co. v. R. L. Kirmsey Cotton Co.*, 151 SE2d 541 (Ga. 1966). And if the mortgage is released and a new mortgage placed on the property, then a new mortgagee clause must be issued even though the mortgage runs to the same mortgagee who was covered by the previous mortgage clause. *Attleborough Sav. Bank v. Security Ins. Co.*, 46 NE 390 (Mass.

1897). The homeowner's policy provides for the opposite result. Coverage runs to the named mortgagee under "present or future mortgages."

A serious problem exists as to the rights of the mortgagee after the foreclosure sale. In most cases the mortgagee is the highest bidder at the foreclosure sale, and he usually bids an amount close to the amount of his mortgage debt. In a number of cases the courts have stated that this amounts to a satisfaction or payment of the mortgage debt in the amount of the sale price. The thinking here is that if a third party had been the successful bidder, his cash money would have gone to the mortgagee in reduction of the mortgage debt, and the result should be the same where the mortgagee "bids his mortgage" at the foreclosure sale. The consequence is that if a fire occurs after the foreclosure sale, the mortgagee recovers at a maximum the difference between the foreclosure sale price and the amount due on the mortgage debt, which difference is usually a trifling amount. *Northwestern Nat. Ins. Co.* v. *Mildenberger,* 359 SW2d 380 (Mo. 1962). *Whitestone S. & L. Assn.* v. *Allstate Ins. Co.,* 270 NE2d 694 (N.Y. 1971). Other courts say that the mortgagee should be allowed full recovery. *Trustees of Schools* v. *St. Paul Fire & Marine Ins. Co.,* 129 NE 567 (Ill. 1921); *City* v. *Magnur,* 329 NE2d 312 (Ill. 1975). The obvious moral is that the mortgagee should procure a new fire policy or a rider to the existing policy the moment he has made his successful bid at the foreclosure sale.

§ **469. Contracts for the sale of land.** When a landowner takes out insurance and thereafter contracts to sell the land to a purchaser, the sensible course is to have the insurance endorsed to cover both parties as their interests may appear. Then, in case of serious loss, the company will pay the seller the balance due on the contract, and the balance will be paid to the buyer.

When the buyer takes out the insurance in his own name, with a loss payable clause for the benefit of the seller, and the fire is caused by the buyer, the company is not liable to either seller or buyer. *Langhorne* v. *Capitol Fire Ins. Co.,* 44 F.Supp. 739 (1942).

When a policy taken out by the buyer is payable to the seller, and a fire occurs and the company pays the unpaid balance of the purchase price to the seller in satisfaction of the insurance claim, all rights of the seller in the property are extinguished, and the company is not entitled to any assignment of the contract. *Fields* v. *Western Millers Mutual Fire Ins. Co.,* 37 NYS2d 757 (1942). The buyer is entitled to a deed to the land since the insurance money has paid the purchase price. *Dysart* v. *Colonial Fire Underwriters,* 254 Pac. 240 (Wash. 1927).

When the buyer takes out a policy with loss payable to the buyer and seller as their interests may appear, and thereafter the seller declares the contract forfeited because of the buyer's default in his payments, the seller is still covered by such insurance. *Aetna Ins. Co.* v. *Robinson,* 10 NE2d 601 (Ind. 1937). And mere default in his payments does not terminate the buyer's insurance. He remains covered until the seller declares a forfeiture of the contract.

Suppose the contract of sale (as is customary in installment contracts) requires the buyer to take out insurance for the benefit of seller and buyer, but the buyer takes out insurance in his own name only. If a loss occurs, the courts will require the buyer to carry out his contract by forcing him to apply his insurance money in payment of the contract price due to the seller. *American Equitable Assurance Co.* v. *Newman,* 313 P2d 1023 (Mont. 1957); 64 ALR2d 1416.

It now seems clear that where a landowner has entered into a contract of sale and a fire occurs after the buyer has substantially reduced the balance due, the seller may nevertheless collect for the full amount of the loss.

EXAMPLE: A took out a fire insurance policy and thereafter contracted to sell the land to *B*. When the contract had been paid down to $16,000, a fire loss occurred. A was allowed to collect $46,750 in fire insurance. *First National Bank* v. *Boston Ins. Co.,* 160 NE2d 802 (Ill. 1959); *Edlin* v. *Security Ins. Co.,* 269 F2d 159 (1959).

§ 470. Assignment. Assignment of the policy does not render the policy void, but the assignment itself is not valid except with the written consent of the company. For this reason, when the policy is assigned in connection with a sale and deed by the seller of all his title to the property, the seller could not collect on the policy for a subsequent loss since after sale he has no insurable interest in the property. Nor could the buyer collect if the assignment had not been consented to by the company. In other words, hazard insurance does not "run with the land." It must be assigned to the buyer for the buyer's protection. *Eastway Const.* v. *New York Property Underwriting Assn.,* 382 NYS2d 949 (1976). The prudent buyer will procure oral coverage and/or a binder giving protection until the assignment is consented to.

The right to the insurance proceeds is assignable *after loss. Travelers Indemnity Co.* v. *Isseal,* 354 F2d 488 (1965).

As a practical matter the problem of assignment has become less significant in recent years. Frequently, the seller's policy, because of its schedule of personalty, is appropriate only for the seller and is cancelled upon closing. Similarly, the buyer must tailor his protection and seek his own coverage possibly written by the family insurance man. Always oral coverage and/or a binder should be obtained to procure coverage until the new policy is issued.

§ 471. Business interruption insurance. This type of insurance protects from loss of income and continuing expenses when a business property is destroyed or damaged. There are two kinds of business interruption insurance. The "gross earnings" form pays you an amount roughly equal to the gross earnings lost while business was interrupted. Proving the amount of loss under this form is fairly complicated, as is obvious. Another form is the "valued business interruption insurance" form. At the time the policy is written you agree with the insurance company as to the duration and amount of coverage.

EXAMPLE: You take out a policy that pays you $1000 per week for a period of not more than six months while your plant is shut down by fire damage. There is a fair amount of guesswork in this type of coverage.

By writing to the INA Corporation, 1600 Arch Street, Philadelphia, Pa., 19101, you can get the booklet, "Business Interruption Insurance." The bigger your operation, the more desirable it is to consult an insurance counselor before making a decision. His services are especially valuable in helping you determine the type and amount of insurance to purchase.

REFERENCE: Miller, Business Interruption Insurance: A Legal Primer, 24 *Drake L. Rev.* 799 (1975).

§ 472. **Liability insurance for contractors.** A liability policy issued to a general contractor is likely to contain exclusions colloquially referred to as "x," "c," and "u." The "x" exclusion excludes liability for blasting. An endorsement can be obtained deleting this exclusion. The "c" exclusion excludes liability for collapse of building, and coverage for this liability should be purchased. The "u" exclusion excludes liability for damage to underground facilities such as conduits and sewers. Coverage should be obtained.

Completed operations insurance covers liability for a completed job.

EXAMPLE: A contractor completes a bridge and later it collapses, causing bodily injury and property damage.

In general a mortgage lender wants to see that all proper insurance is obtained.

EXAMPLE: *E* is lending money on a large construction loan, with C acting as general contractor. A bridge built by C in another state collapses. With no insurance coverage, C goes broke. A new contractor must be found and costs go up astronomically.

RESERVED: §§ 473 to 481.

16

Co-Ownership

§ 482. **In general.** A person can be the sole owner of a tract of land. However, a tract of land may also be owned by two or more persons. Such co-owners are known as *co-tenants.* There are different kinds of co-ownerships, or co-tenancies, as they are called. Persons may own the land as *joint tenants,* as *tenants by the entireties,* or *as tenants in common.*

§ 483. **Joint tenancy and tenancy in common distinguished.** When a deed is made to two or more persons who are not husband and wife and nothing is said in the deed concerning the character of the tenancy created by the deed, the grantees acquire title as tenants in common. That is, on the death of either party, his interest in the real estate will go to his heirs if he dies without leaving a will, or, if he leaves a will, to the persons named therein.

EXAMPLE: *X* conveys land to *A* and *B,* who are brothers. Since the deed is not in joint tenancy form, *A* and *B* are tenants in common. *A,* a widower, dies without a will, leaving *C* and *D* as his only children. *B, C,* and *D* own the land as tenants in common, *B* owning a half and *C* and *D* each a fourth.

If, however, the deed runs to two or more persons as joint tenants, a different rule applies. While both joint tenants are alive, they are co-owners of the land, but as soon as one dies, his title passes automatically to the surviving joint tenant.

EXAMPLE: *X* makes a deed of his land to *A* and *B* as joint tenants. *A* dies. Without the need of any will or probate, *B* succeeds to *A*'s interest and becomes the sole owner of the property. This is the chief advantage of a joint tenancy. It renders probate of an estate unnecessary.

Any number of persons may hold real estate in joint tenancy.

EXAMPLE: *X* makes a deed to *A, B, C,* and *D,* as joint tenants. *D* dies. *A, B,* and *C* now own the land as joint tenants. *A* dies. *B* and *C* own the land as joint tenants. *B* dies. *C* is now the sole owner.

§ 484. **Creation of joint tenancy.** To create a joint tenancy, a deed must state that the grantees are acquiring title as joint tenants. The actual language used varies somewhat from state to state, but it is best to use comprehensive language in creating a joint tenancy. 46 ALR2d 523.

SUGGESTED FORM: *To A and B as joint tenants with the right of survivorship, and not as tenants in common nor as tenants by the entirety, nor as community property.*

A deed to persons who are husband and wife poses special problems. It may create a tenancy by the entireties. 32 ALR3d 570. It may create community property. But if it does neither of these things and is not a joint tenancy deed, the husband and wife are tenants in common.

EXCEPTION: In Wisconsin, a deed to husband and wife creates a joint tenancy unless the deed states otherwise.

A joint tenancy may also be created when the parties have ineffectively attempted to create a tenancy by the entireties.

Rather frequently today we find a husband and wife helping a newly married son or daughter to procure housing. Often the two couples buy a two-apartment dwelling for their joint occupancy, each couple acquiring a one-half interest in the property. The old couple wants their half interest held in joint tenancy, but does not want the young couple to have any interest in the old couple's half. The young people feel the same about their half. Each couple wants its half to be in joint tenancy, so that when one dies the surviving wife or husband will own the entire half interest, but they want a tenancy in common as between the two half interests.

SUGGESTION: John and Mary Smith, his wife, wish to buy a two-flat with William, their son, and his wife, Helen. Use two separate joint tenancy form deeds, one going to the John Smiths, the other to the William Smiths. Before the land description in each deed, insert: "An undivided half interest in." Thus, each couple will have its own deed.

EXAMPLE: In the SUGGESTION above, if one of the Smiths dies, his or her spouse will own their half interest as surviving joint tenant. The others continue to own their half as joint tenants. The two halves are as separate for this purpose as if they were separate tracts of land.

§ 485. **Abolition of survivorship.** Some states, Alabama, Arizona, Florida, Georgia, Kansas, Kentucky, Maine, North Carolina, Ohio, Oregon, Pennsylvania, South Carolina, Tennessee, Texas, Virginia, Washington, West Virginia, and perhaps others, have laws that purport to abolish the joint tenant's right of survivorship, so that on the death of a joint tenant, his share goes to his heirs or to the persons named in this will, just as if a tenancy in common had been created. However, in these states, if the deed expressly states that the property shall go to the surviving grantee, the right of survivorship is thereby created. *Chandler* v. *Kountze,* 130 SW2d 327 (Tex. 1939).

EXAMPLE: In a state where the law states that the right of survivorship in joint tenancies is abolished, *R* makes a deed to *H* and *W* "as joint tenants with the right of survivorship and not as tenants in common." *H* dies. *W* takes all as the survivor. However, the cases are not in agreement as to the nature of the interest created by the deed. One line of cases says that a joint tenancy was created by agreement of the parties. It becomes an ordinary joint tenancy. In other states it creates an estate for lives with the right of survivorship. Neither party can sever it by deed as can be done in an ordinary joint tenancy. It is an indestructible right of survivorship. *Anson* v. *Murphy,* 32 NW2d 271 (Neb. 1948); *Bernhard* v. *Bernhard,* 177 So2d 565 (Ala. 1965); statutes of the type discussed will likely disappear in time. They cause difficulties with common, necessary joint tenancies, such as those in bank accounts.

§ 486. The four unities. Not every deed that describes the grantees as joint tenants is sufficient to create a joint tenancy. In the creation of a joint tenancy, there must be present the four unities of time, title, interest, and possession. That is, the joint tenants must have one and the same interest, acquired by one and the same deed, commencing at one and the same time; and they must hold by one and the same undivided possession.

EXAMPLE: A owned a tract of land. Thereafter, he married and executed a deed to himself and his wife "as joint tenants." No joint tenancy was created by this deed. A and his wife did not acquire title at the same time or by the same conveyance, since A had owned the land long prior to the making of the deed. The unities of time and title were not present. The deed actually created a tenancy in common. A and his wife should have conveyed title to a third person, and this third person should have thereupon reconveyed the title to A and his wife as joint tenants. *Deslauriers* v. *Senesac,* 163 NE 327 (Ill. 1928).

Pointless technicalities like these are going out of fashion. Hence in many states—Alabama, Arizona, California, Colorado, Illinois, Iowa, Kansas, Kentucky, Maryland, Maine, Massachusetts, Michigan, Missouri, Nebraska, Nevada, New Hampshire, New Jersey, New Mexico, New York, North Dakota, Ohio, Oklahoma, Pennsylvania, Rhode Island, Tennessee, Virginia, Wisconsin, and perhaps others—laws have been passed under which a deed by a landowner to himself and another in joint tenancy creates a good joint tenancy. For reasons relating to community property, dower, and homestead, the landowner's spouse should join in the deed. One often sees a landowner and his wife conveying to themselves as joint tenants, and the whole thing, though odd, is quite legal in most states. 44 ALR2d 605.

When a deed reveals an intention to create a joint tenancy, but fails to for some technical reason, some modern courts tend to show little patience with the old technicalities and give the property to the survivor, even though a true joint tenancy has not been created.

EXAMPLE: A husband who owned some land in his own individual name signed a deed conveying a half interest in this land to his wife, the deed stating that they were to hold the land as joint tenants. Obviously this is no way to create a joint tenancy, for the four unities are lacking. Nevertheless, on the death of the husband the court awarded the entire property to the surviving wife. *Runions* v. *Runions,* 207 SW2d 1016 (Tenn. 1948). There can be a right of survivorship even though the land is not owned in joint tenancy, which is something of a subtle distinction but has the happy result of achieving what the parties wanted.

It is impossible to make a deed to *A* of a one-fourth interest in the land and to *B* of a three-fourths interest to hold as joint tenants. A deed creating joint tenancies must give the joint tenants equal shares as to the property conveyed in joint tenancy. This does not prevent a joint tenant from owning a different and distinct interest in the land.

EXAMPLE: *X* conveys a half interest to *A* and a half interest to *A* and *B* as joint tenants. This is perfectly valid. *In re Galletto's Estate,* 171 P2d 152 (Cal. 1946).

§ 487. Severance of joint tenancy. There is nothing sacred about a joint tenancy. Either joint tenant has the right to break the joint tenancy as he wishes. 64 ALR2d 918. Certain actions will break the joint tenancy and convert it into a tenancy in common even against the wishes or without the knowledge of the other parties.

1. A conveyance by a joint tenant to a third party destroys the joint tenancy.

EXAMPLE: A conveys to *B* and C in joint tenancy. C conveys his half of title to *D*. *D* thereafter conveys this interest back to C. C dies. His title passes to his heirs, not to *B*. The conveyance from C to *D* severed or terminated the joint tenancy. The joint tenancy was not revived by the reconveyance. At C's death, *B* and C were holding title as tenants in common. *Szymczak* v. *Szymczak,* 138 NE 218 (Ill. 1923). It is not necessary that *B* be informed of the fact that C is breaking the joint tenancy. *Burke* v. *Stevens,* 70 Cal. Reptr. 87 (1968).

Where there are three or more joint tenants, and only one makes a deed to a third party or to one of the other joint tenants, some highly technical problems are encountered.

EXAMPLE: A, *B,* and C own land as joint tenants. C conveys his third to *D*. A and *B* continue to hold their two thirds as joint tenants. *Morgan* v. *Catherwood,* 167 NE 618 (Ind. 1929); *Hammond* v. *McArthur,* 183 P2d 1 (Cal. 1947).

EXAMPLE: A, *B* and C own land in joint tenancy. A conveys to *B* by quitclaim deed. *B* and C continue to own a two-thirds interest in the land in joint tenancy, and *B* owns a one-third interest as tenant in common. *Shelton* v. *Vance,* 234 P2d 1012 (Cal. 1951); *Jackson* v. *O'Connell,* 177 NE2d 194 (Ill. 1961).

EXAMPLE: A, *B* and C own land in joint tenancy. C conveys one-twentieth of his interest to X. A and *B* continue to own their two thirds in joint tenancy. C and X are tenants in common. *Giles* v. *Sheridan,* 137 NW2d 828 (Neb. 1968); Swenson & Degnan, Severance of Joint Tenancies, 38 *Minn. L. Rev.* 466, 472 (1954).

This severance occurs notwithstanding the fact that the deed was not recorded. *Carmack* v. *Place,* 535 P2d 197 (Colo. 1975).

2. An involuntary transfer of title will sever a joint tenancy.

EXAMPLE: *A* and *B* hold title as joint tenants. *A* goes into bankruptcy. Under the Bankruptcy Act, title to all of *A*'s property is automatically transferred to his trustee in bankruptcy. This transfer severs the joint tenancy. *In re Victor,* 218 F.Supp. 218 (1963).

EXAMPLE: *A* and *B* hold title as joint tenants. C obtains a judgment against *A,* and a sheriff's sale is held to obtain money to pay the judgment. *D* purchases the property at the sheriff's sale and obtains a sheriff's deed. This sever the joint tenancy. *D* and *B* now hold as tenants in common. However, the rendition of a judgment against one joint tenant and the making of a levy on his interest will not sever a joint tenancy. *Van Antwerp* v. *Horan,* 61 NE2d 358 (Ill. 1945); *Hammond* v. *McArthur,* 183 P2d 1 (Cal. 1947); *Eder* v. *Rothamel,* 85 A2d 860 (Md. 1953). It has even been held that a sheriff's sale under such a judgment does not sever the joint tenancy and that the joint tenancy is not severed until a sheriff's deed issues. If the joint tenant against whom the judgment was rendered dies before the sheriff's deed issues, the other joint tenant takes all the property free and clear of the judgment creditor's rights. *Jackson* v. *Lacey,* 97 NE2d 839 (Ill. 1951).

3. In title and intermediate states, a mortgage executed by one of the joint tenants severs the joint tenancy notwithstanding the fact that the mortgage is subsequently paid and released by the mortgagee. 64 ALR2d 918.

EXAMPLE: *A* and *B* hold title as joint tenants. *A* executes a mortgage on his half of the title and thereafter pays off the mortgage, which is released. Thereafter, *B* dies. *B*'s half of the title passes to his heirs, not to *A*. *A*'s mortgage severed the joint tenancy.

But a mortgage executed by *both* joint tenants does not sever the joint tenancy.

EXAMPLE: *A* and *B* hold title as joint tenants. They both join in a mortgage. Thereafter, *A* dies. *B* takes title as the surviving joint tenant.

The cases do not agree as to the effect of a mortgage by one joint tenant in a lien state. *People* v. *Nogarr,* 330 P2d 858 (Cal. 1958); Comment 11 *Stan. L. Rev.* 574 (1959).

EXAMPLE: *H* and *W* owned land in joint tenancy. *H* gave a mortgage on his interest to *E* without the knowledge of *W*. *H* died. The mortgage was thereby terminated. It attached only to an interest that would itself terminate unless the mortgagor survived his joint tenant. *D.A.D. Inc.* v. *Moring,* 218 So2d 451 (Fla. 1969). This is the better rule in lien states, but not all will follow it.

4. A contract by one joint tenant to sell or convey his interest in the land to a third person will operate as a severance of the joint tenancy. *Naiburg* v. *Hendriksen,* 19 NE2d 348 (Ill. 1939).

EXAMPLE: *A* and *B* own land in joint tenancy. *A* enters into a contract to sell his half interest to C. The joint tenancy is severed. Suppose *B* dies, for example. His half goes to his heirs.

5. One joint tenant files a partition suit against the other, and a partition decree is entered. The joint tenancy is now severed. *Schuck* v. *Schuck,* 108 NE2d 905 (Ill. 1952); *Hammond* v. *McArthur,* 183 P2d 1 (Cal. 1947).

6. A husband and wife own land in joint tenancy. One files a **divorce suit against**

the other. A divorce decree is entered. It orders the land sold and the proceeds of sale divided between them. The joint tenancy is now severed. *Baade* v. *Ratner,* 359 P2d 877 (Kan. 1961). Indeed, if a husband and wife own land in joint tenancy and they enter into a separation agreement providing that the land will be sold when the divorce decree is entered and the proceeds of sale divided between them, this agreement will sever the joint tenancy. *Carson* v. *Ellis,* 348 P2d 807 (Kan. 1960).

7. A simple, written, signed, and recorded declaration by one joint tenant that the tenancy has been severed has been held sufficient to terminate the joint tenancy, thereby converting it into a tenancy in common. *Hendrickson* v. *Minneapolis Fed. S. & L. Assn.,* 161 NW2d 688 (Minn. 1968). This is a pretty liberal decision and has been criticized. It is safer to have the party deed out to a dummy and have the dummy deed back.

8. Any agreement between the joint tenants that shows an intention to treat the land as a tenancy in common will cause a severance. 64 ALR2d 941.

9. In one or two states the making of a lease by one joint tenant severs the joint tenancy. *Alexander* v. *Boyer,* 253 A2d 359 (Md. 1969).

There are other events that do not break the joint tenancy:

1. A will by the deceased joint tenants.

EXAMPLE: A and *B* own land as joint tenants. A makes a will giving all his property to C. *A* dies. *B* takes all the joint tenancy property, and C gets no part of it. A's will does not break a joint tenancy. *Eckardt* v. *Osborne,* 170 NE 774 (Ill. 1930).

2. A lien created against one of the joint tenants.

EXAMPLE: A and *B* own land as joint tenants. A judgment lien, internal revenue lien, or other lien is filed against *A* only. *A* dies before he has lost his title through enforcement of the lien. *B* takes the entire title free and clear of the lien. In other words, if *A* is a joint tenant, a lien against him attaches not to the land *but to A's interest in the land,* which is an interest that will be totally extinguished if *A* dies before *B* does, so long as the parties are joint tenants when *A* dies. One who has a lien on *A*'s interest ordinarily can have no greater rights than A has, and if *A*'s rights will be extinguished by his breach, so will the lien. 134 ALR 957.

3. An easement created by one joint tenant only.

EXAMPLE: A and *B* own land as joint tenants. *A* alone signs an easement grant to C, and *A* dies before *B* does. *B* then owns the entire title free and clear of the easement.

4. Dower and curtesy of a spouse of a deceased joint tenant.

EXAMPLE: If *A* and *B,* both married men, own land as joint tenants, and *A* dies first, his wife has no dower in the land because at *A*'s death all his title to the land is extinguished, leaving nothing to which dower can attach.

5. Divorce. State laws differ on the subject of divorce.

EXAMPLE: In some states, a divorce does not break a joint tenancy. Where no specific law exists, if *H* and *W* own land as joint tenants are divorced, and if nothing is said in the divorce decree about the property, the joint tenancy is unbroken. Suppose that *H* thereafter marries another person, *X*. *H* dies before *W* does. *W*, the former wife of *H*, takes the entire property, and *X* takes nothing. *H* could have prevented this by breaking the joint tenancy by deed. On the other hand, in some states the entry of a divorce decree automatically converts the joint tenancy into a tenancy in common. This is by virtue of special laws.

6. The making of a lease by one of two joint tenants does not sever the joint tenancy. *Tindall* v. *Yeats*, 64 NE2d 903 (Ill. 1946); *Hammond* v. *McArthur*, 183 P2d 1 (Cal. 1947); *Tennet* v. *Boswell*, 18 Cal. 3d 150, 554 P2d 330 (1976). *Contra: Alexander* v. *Boyer*, 253 A2d 359 (Md. 1969). See Note 7 *Baylor L. Rev.* 97 (1955); Comment 25 *Calif. L. Rev.* 203 (1937). The court decisions holding that a lease severs a joint tenancy are absurd.

EXAMPLE: *H* and *W*, husband and wife, own an apartment building in joint tenancy. *H* manages the building and signs the leases to the tenants. It is absurd to hold that the joint tenancy is broken.

7. One joint tenant files a partition suit against the other, but one of them dies *before* a partition decree is entered. The survivor takes all as surviving joint tenant. 129 ALR 813.

8. A deed by one joint tenant to himself does not sever the joint tenancy because it is nothing but an empty ceremony. *Clark* v. *Carter*, 70 Cal.Rptr. 923 (1968).

9. Where one of two joint tenants grants a life estate to another this does not sever the joint tenancy. *Hammond* v. *McArthur*, 182 P2d 1 (Cal. 1947).

10. The mere granting of an option to purchase by one joint tenant does not sever the joint tenancy. *Alexander* v. *Boyer*, 253 A2d 359 (Md. 1969).

§ 488. Disadvantages of a joint tenancy. Rather frequently, when title is held in joint tenancy by a husband and wife and one of them dies, the survivor, impressed with the simplicity of transfer of ownership on the death of a joint tenant, ponders the advisability of creating a new joint tenancy in which the surviving spouse will be joint tenant with one of the spouse's children. This has certain disadvantages. Once such a deed is made it cannot be unmade without the consent of both parties. Suppose that the surviving spouse and the child named as joint tenant quarrel, which is not uncommon. Indeed, the mere fact that the parties share ownership of the real estate seems to trigger quarrels. The child may file a partition suit and put property up for sale. Thus, the surviving spouse may find himself or herself without a place to live. Perhaps judgments may be rendered against the child, and creditors will force the property to a sale. Many lawyers counsel the surviving joint tenant to avoid setting up a joint tenancy such as this. Where a will is made, it can always be changed. It gives no one any right in the property until the landowner dies. Perhaps this may strike a cynical note, but the fact remains that when there is a will rather than a deed, there is much less likelihood of family quarrels.

§ 489. Tenancy by the entireties—in general. In Arkansas, Delaware, District of Columbia, Florida, Indiana, Kentucky, Maryland Massachusetts, Michigan, Mississippi, Missouri, New Jersey, New York, North Carolina, Oklahoma, Oregon, Pennsylvania, Rhode Island, Tennessee, Utah,

Vermont, Virginia, and Wyoming, a form of joint tenancy, known as tenancy by the entireties, exists. This is a tenancy that exists only where the co-owners are husband and wife, and it is based upon the common law notion that they are one person, and each are holders of the entire estate. Unlike a joint tenancy, no words are necessary to create such a tenancy.

EXAMPLE: In a tenancy by the entireties state, *X* makes a deed to *H* and *W*, husband and wife. Nothing is said as to the character of their co-ownership. They are tenants by the entireties.

EXCEPTION: In Kansas, Kentucky, Massachusetts, Mississippi, Montana, Oklahoma, Rhode Island, Utah and Virginia, laws have been passed stating that the deed must expressly show an intention to create a tenancy by the entireties. 52 *Mich. L. Rev.* 804.

Tenancy by the entireties resembles joint tenancy in that upon the death of either husband or wife the survivor automatically acquires title to the share of the deceased spouse.

Tenancy by the entireties differs from joint tenancy in that neither spouse has the power to defeat or sever the tenancy by any deed or mortgage to a stranger made without the signature of the other spouse. *Hoffman* v. *Newell,* 60 SW2d 607 (Ky. 1932).

EXAMPLE: A deed is made to a husband and wife, nothing being said as to the character of their tenancy. Thereafter, the husband makes a deed that purports to convey his interest in the land to *X*. The wife does not join in this deed. Thereafter, the husband dies. The wife now has full title to all the land. *X* has nothing.

However, a deed by both husband and wife will, of course, give the grantee good title.

As long as the marriage exists neither spouse may have a partition of the estate by the entireties. *Lawrence* v. *Lawrence,* 190 A2d 206 (N.J. 1963).

EXAMPLE: *A* and *B* hold property as *tenants in common*. If they disagree upon the disposition of the property, they can ask the court either to physically divide the property between them (this is called partition in kind) or sell the property and divide the proceeds. This relief is not available to *tenants by the entireties.*

EXAMPLE: Where *H* and *W* hold property as tenants by the entireties and *W* sues *H* for divorce, *H* can ask that the court, if a divorce is allowed, divide the property or sell it and divide the proceeds. *Bastians* v. *Bastians,* 321 NYS 2d 480 (1971).

In community property states, tenancy by the entireties is not recognized.

§ 490. **Creation of tenancy by the entireties.** In the states where tenancies by the entireties are recognized, there is much difference of opinion as to the legal effect of a deed to a husband and wife that describes the grantees as joint tenants. In some states, Indiana, Maryland, New Jersey, New York, and Wyoming, for example, such a deed creates a joint tenancy rather than a tenancy by the entireties. *Witzel* v. *Witzel,* 386 P2d 103 (Wyo. 1963). But in most of the states that recognize tenancies, such deeds are held to create a tenancy by the entireties. *Hoag* v. *Hoag,* 99 NE 521 (Mass. 1912); 161 ALR 470. If a joint tenancy is desired, the deed should always state that the grantees are "joint tenants and not tenants in common or by the entireties." In this way, litigation can be avoided.

However, when a deed to a husband and wife describes them "as tenants in common," such a deed is almost universally regarded as creating a good tenancy in common rather than a tenancy by the entireties.

For the creation of a tenancy by the entireties, it is necessary that the grantees be husband and wife. If they are not husband and wife, even express language in the deed declaring an intention to creat a tenancy by the entireties will not create such a tenancy.

§ 491. Defective tenancy by entireties as creating a joint tenancy. Tenancy by the entireties exists only as between husband and wife. A deed to parties who are not husband and wife creates some other kind of tenancy even though a tenancy by the entireties is specified.

EXAMPLE: A deed to *A* and *B,* who claimed to be, but were not, husband and wife, recited that it was made to them as tenants by the entireties and not as tenants in common. Since this revealed a general intention to create survivorship rights, but could not create a tenancy by the entireties, the parties not being husband and wife, the court held that a joint tenancy was crected. *Morris* v. *McCarthy,* 32 NE 938 (Mass. 1893); *Coleman* v. *Jackson,* 286 F2d 98 (1960); *Righter* v. *Righter,* 275 A2d 4 (Pa. 1971); Kepner, The Effect of an Attempted Creation of An Estate by the Entirety in Unmarried Persons, 6 *Rutgers L. Rev.* 550 (1952); Note 37 *Notre D. Law* 441 (1962); Note 37 *Cornell L. Q.* 316 (1952).

EXAMPLE: In New Hampshire and Wisconsin, which do not recognize tenancy by the entireties, a deed to husband and wife "as tenants by the entireties" creates a joint tenancy. *In re Ray's Will,* 205 NW 917 (Wisc. 1925); 1 ALR2d 247.

EXAMPLE: A deed to two sisters "as tenants by the entireties" has been held to create a joint tenancy. *In re Richardson's Estate,* 282 NW 585 (Wisc. 1938). Likewise this was true where the deed was to two brothers. *Penn. Bank & Tr. Co.* v. *Thompson,* 247 A2d 771 (Pa. 1968).

However, in most states a deed to *H* and *W,* describing them as tenants by the entireties or as husband and wife creates only a tenancy in common if they are in fact not married. *Pierce* v. *Hall,* 355 P2d 259 (Ore. 1960); 83 ALR2d 1051.

EXAMPLE: A deed was made to Charles Smith and Julia Smith, *husband and wife.* Actually they were not married. Julia died. Charles, describing himself as a "surviving spouse," made a deed to a purchaser. Then three sisters of Julia appeared and claimed her half of the property as her heirs. They succeeded. Only a tenancy in common existed and Charles was not even an heir. *Thurmond* v. *McGrath,* 334 NYS2d 917 (1972).

§ 492. Tenancy by the entireties—deeds between spouses. Suppose a husband or wife owns land in his or her own name, or they own land as tenants in common. They wish to put the land in their names as tenants by entireties. The traditional way of accomplishing this is to have the husband and wife join in a deed to a straw man, or nominee, and such nominee then deeds the land back to the husband and wife as tenants by the entireties. Just as in the case of joint tenancies, the old rule is: in order to have a good tenancy by the entireties, the husband and wife must acquire title by the same deed, and the dummy conveyance satisfies this requirement.

Just as in the case of joint tenancies, recent laws and court decisions allow a husband or wife to create a tenancy by the entireties without deeding out to a dummy. In these states, among which are Arkansas, Florida, Massachusetts, Michigan, Missouri, New Jersey, New York, Oklahoma, Oregon, Pennsylvania, Rhode Island, Tennessee, and Utah, if the husband owns land and wishes to create a tenancy by the entireties with his wife, he makes out a deed running to himself and his wife "as tenants by the entireties, and not as joint tenants or as tenants in common." Phipps, Tenancy by Entireties, 25 *Temple L. Q.* 24, 43 (1952); 44 ALR2d 598. For reasons relating to dower and homestead, the wife should join in this deed as co-grantor.

However, in a few other states it has been held that it is still necessary, if a good tenancy by the entireties is to be created, that the husband landowner and his wife join in a deed to a third person, who thereupon conveys to the husband and wife. This practice should be followed unless it is clear that your state has abolished the need for a third party conveyance.

When land is held in tenancy by the entireties, a deed by the husband to the wife gives her good title even though she does not join in the deed to herself. The same is true of a deed by the wife to the husband. 8 ALR2d 634.

§ 493. **Tenancy by the entireties—deeds, mortgages, leases, rents, and brokers' listings.** As a rule, a deed or mortgage of property owned in tenancy by the entireties must be signed by both husband and wife.

In most states, when a tenancy by the entirety exists, a deed to a stranger signed by the husband or wife alone is void. Phipps, Tenancy by Entireties, 25 *Temple L. Q.* 24, 46 (1952). In a few states, the deed is given some effect, but the effect, varies from state to state. It may grant a share of the rents or may be operative if the grantor survives the other spouse. In any event, in all states the deed becomes void if the spouse who did not join in the deed survives the spouse who conveyed.

Both parties should sign any lease. In many tenancy by the entirety states, husband and wife have equal rights to rents and possession, and any lease must be signed by both. Phipps, Tenancy by Entireties, 25 *Temple L. Q.* 26, 46 (1952); 141 ALR 202.

Certainly this is the impact of new laws designed to equalize the rights of the wife with those of the husband. Mich. Stat. Ann. § 26.210(1).

If the husband alone lists property with a real estate broker for sale, he will be liable for a commission if the broker finds a buyer. It is no defense that the wife failed to sign. *Taub* v. *Shampanier,* 112 Atl 322 (N.J. 1921).

§ **493A. Tenancy by the entireties—creditor's rights.** In most tenancy by the entireties states, a judgment creditor of either husband or wife alone can acquire no rights by a sheriff's sale of the land. Since neither husband nor wife alone can make a voluntary sale of his or her interest in the land, an involuntary or forced sale of the interest of either husband or wife alone cannot be valid. 75 ALR2d 1175. In a few states, Arkansas, New Jersey, New York, and Oregon, for example, a husband's interest can be sold by the sheriff under a judgment against the husband alone, but the sheriff's deed will automatically become void if the wife survives the husband. The wife then remains the sole owner, free of the judgment. Phipps, Tenancy by Entireties, 25 *Temple L. Q*. 24, 39 (1952); 75 ALR2d 1183.

Of course if the judgment is against both husband and wife, the land may be sold by the sheriff, provided it is not their homestead.

As above stated, in most of the tenancy by entirety states, the rents of the land belong to the husband and wife jointly. Therefore a creditor of either the husband or wife alone cannot reach the rents, income, or crops of the land.

EXCEPTIONS: In Arkansas, New Jersey, New York, and Oregon, creditors of either the husband or wife are allowed to reach the debtor's share of the rents, income, or crops of the land. In Massachusetts and North Carolina, creditors of the husband, but not those of the wife, may reach all the income of the land held in tenancy by the entireties while the tenancy continues. Phipps, Tenancy by Entireties, 25 *Temple L.* Q. 24, 39 (1952).

§ **494. Tenancy by the entireties—divorce.** A divorce converts a tenancy by the entireties into a tenancy in common. Some states, however, have an opposite rule which holds that divorce changes a tenancy by the entireties to a joint tenancy with the right of survivorship. *Shepherd* v. *Shepherd,* 336 So2d 497 (Miss. 1976).

§ **495. Joint tenancies and tenancies by the entireties—murder.** When one joint tenant or tenant by the entireties murders his cotenant and later is convicted of such murder in a court trial, one of three results is possible.

1. The murderer will, despite his crime, take the entire property by virtue of his right of survivorship. This is a bad rule that is certainly doomed to disappear in time.

2. The murderer, because of his crime, loses all his interest in the property, and the heirs of the murdered co-owner take the entire property, which rule is followed in Minnesota and Wisconsin. *Vesey* v. *Vesey,* 54 NW2d 385 (Minn. 1952); *In re King's Estate,* 52 NW2d 885 (Wisc. 1952).

3. The murder is regarded, in legal effect, as converting the tenancy into a tenancy in common, so that the murderer retains his half interest, and the heirs of the murdered cotenant take the other half. This rule is followed in most states. *Abbey* v. *Lord,* 336 P2d 226 (Cal. 1959); *Bradley* v. *Fox,* 129 NE2d 699 (Ill. 1955); Note, 5 *DePaul L. Rev.* 316 (1956).

Of course if in the murder trial the killer is acquitted—on the ground of self-defense, for example—the killing is not murder but justifiable homicide, and the survivor will take the entire property even though he caused the death of his cotenant.

§ 496. Joint tenancies and tenancies by the entireties—contracts of sale. A contract to sell property owned in tenancy by the entireties obviously should be signed by both husband and wife. If it is not, the buyer will be unable to obtain specific performance, though the seller who signed might be liable for damages. *Cartwright* v. *Giacosa,* 390 SW2d 204 (Tenn. 1965).

In tenancy by the entireties states, when a landowner signs a contract to sell his land to a husband and wife, the buyers hold the contract interest as tenants by the entireties, so that if either dies before the deal is closed, the seller's deed should be made to the survivor. *Comfort* v. *Robinson,* 118 NW 943 (Mich. 1908).

If the state does not recognize tenancy by the entireties or community property, a contract to sell land to *H* and *W,* who are husband and wife, creates a tenancy in common in the contract interest. If *H* dies, his contract interest passes to his heirs or devisees, and the seller must not make the deed to *W* alone. Obviously when an installment contract is involved, it may take years to pay up, and the death of one of the buyers is a distinct possibility.

SUGGESTED FORM: To avoid the endless complications of tenancy in common or necessity of probate, suggest to the buyers that they agree to buy the land "as joint tenants with the right of survivorship, and not as tenants in common nor by the entireties nor as community property."

Of course if land is owned in joint tenancy, all owners must join as sellers in any contract to sell the land.

Where a husband and wife enter into a contract to sell their land, and one of them dies before the purchase price is fully paid, questions arise as to who gets the balance of the purchase price, the surviving spouse or the estate of the decedent. Where the sellers held the land in joint tenancy or tenancy by the entireties some courts hold that the right to the money goes to the survivor just as though there were a right of survivorship as to the contract price. *Watson* v. *Watson,* 126 NE2d 220 (Ill. 1955); *Hewitt* v. *Biege,* 327 P2d 872 (Kan. 1958); *DeYoung* v. *Mesler,* 130 NW2d 38 (Mich. 1964). *In re Maguire's Estate,* 296 NYS 528 (1937).

EXAMPLE: *H* and *W*, joint tenants, enter into a contract to sell their land to *X*. After a few payments are made on the contract, *H* dies leaving a will giving all his property to children by a former marriage. *W* will get the entire remainder of the purchase price.

There are cases taking a contrary view.

EXAMPLE: *H* and *W*, joint tenants, entered into a contract to sell land. *H* dies.

His heirs got his share of the sale price. In a few states sale proceeds are treated as though held in tenancy in common. *Register of Wills* v. *Madine,* 219 A2d 245 (Md. 1966). *In re Baker's Estate,* 78 NW2d 863 (Iowa 1956); *Buford* v. *Dahlke,* 62 NW2d 252 (Neb. 1954). These cases are poor law.

EXAMPLE: *H* and *W,* tenants by the entireties, entered into a contract to sell land. *H* died. His heirs got his share of the purchase price. *Panushka* v. *Panushka,* 349 P2d 450 (Ore. 1960); Note, 14 *Vand L. Rev.* 687 (1961). This result is dictated by the rule in some tenancy by the entireties states which do not recognize this type of tenancy in money or *personal property.*

Of course once the money has been paid by the buyer to the sellers, the cash money, even if held intact by the sellers in a joint safety deposit box, is owned by them in tenancy in common. *Ill. Public Aid Commission* v. *Stille,* 153 NE2d 59 (Ill. 1958).

Suppose that the sellers are tenants by the entireties. They give a deed to the buyer and take back a purchase money mortgage. Some states hold that the mortgage is owned as tenants by the entireties. *Ciconte* v. *Barba,* 161 Atl. 925 (Del. 1932). Others hold that the mortgage is owned in tenancy in common. *Webb* v. *Woodcock,* 290 Pac. 751 (Ore. 1930); 64 ALR2d 8.

The problem extends even to condemnation awards.

EXAMPLE: *H* and *W* owned land in tenancy by the entireties. The city condemned the land and deposited $100,000 as a condemnation award. *H* died. *W* takes the entire award as the surviving tenant by the entireties. *H*'s other heirs take nothing. *Smith* v. *Tipping,* 211 NE2d 231 (Mass. 1965); *In re Idlewild Airport,* 85 NYS2d 617 (1948).

Community property states present special problems.

EXAMPLE: In a community property state, *H* and *W,* joint tenants, entered into a contract to sell land. The proceeds of sale are community property. *Smith* v. *Tang,* 412 P2d 697 (Ariz. 1966).

The problem also exists with respect to the proceeds of fire insurance policies.

The better rule is that the money goes to the survivor. Had the parties been asked about this when they received their deed, virtually all would have been astonished to hear any question raised as to the right of the survivor to get the money. This intention ought to be controlling.

SUGGESTION: Let the contract read that the price is payable to the sellers *as joint tenants with the right of survivorship and not as tenants in common nor as tenants by the entireties nor as community property.*

It seems rather odd that the courts seldom mention a rule of contract law that on the death of one of several promisees (sellers) the survivor or survivors have the right to collect from the promisor (buyer). The estate of the deceased promisee collects from the surviving promisees unless the contract shows that the parties had some contrary intention. Murray, Contracts (*2d ed* of Grismore on Contracts, 1974) § 274. In other words, the situation lends itself to contract law rather than property law.

§ 497. Joint tenancy and tenancy by the entireties—inheritance and estate tax. The automatic transfer of title to a surviving joint tenant or tenant by the entireties when his co-owner dies is subject to state inheritance tax and federal estate tax if the deceased owner's estate is in excess of the exemptions allowed by law. It follows that the lien of such tax attaches to the land of the survivor.

§ 498. Tenancy in common—in general. Co-owners who are not joint tenants, tenants by the entireties, or owners of community property are tenants in common. Their shares need not be equal. For example, one co-owner may have an undivided one-tenth interest and the other the remaining undivided nine-tenths interest. They need not have acquired their titles at the same time or by the same instrument.

Tenancies in common often occur when title is acquired by descent or will.

EXAMPLE: X, a widower, dies without a will, leaving his children, *A, B,* and *C,* as his only heirs. The children own *X's* real estate as tenants in common.

EXAMPLE: X, a widower, dies leaving a will, by which he gives his land to his children, *A, B,* and C in equal shares. They own the land as tenants in common.

Tenants in common are entitled to share the possession and rents of the property according to their shares in the property. Except for their sharing of possession and rents, however, the situation is almost as if each tenant in common owned a separate piece of real estate. Each tenant in common may convey or mortgage his share, and the share of each tenant in common is subject to the lien of judgments against him.

§ 499. Partition. If tenants in common, or joint tenants, for that matter, wish to terminate their joint possession of the land, any of the co-tenants may file a suit to partition the real estate. The court will appoint commissioners to divide the land into separate tracts according to the shares of the co-tenants, so that each will become the sole owner of the tract set aside for him. If the land cannot be divided in this manner, the court will order the land sold and will divide the proceeds of the sale among the co-tenants according to their respective interest.

EXAMPLE: A dies owning a tract of land improved with a single family dwelling and leaving no widow and no will, but leaving as his heirs a son, *B,* and two grandchildren, C and *D,* who are children of a deceased son, *E. B* owns one half of the title, and C and *D* own one fourth each. *B* files a partition suit against C and *D.* The courts finds, as it obviously must, that the land cannot be divided among the three tenants in common. It orders the land sold at public auction, whereupon the same is sold to *F,* the highest bidder, for $6000. *B* receives *$3000* from the proceeds of the sale, and C and *D* each receive $1500.

Partition can, of course, be accomplished by the voluntary action of all co-owners without the necessity of court proceedings. Frequently this action is impossible, since many co-ownerships involve minor heirs, who cannot participate in voluntary partition.

As a rule, community property and land held in tenancy by the entireties are not subject to partition during the continuance of the marriage. *Stanley* v. *Mueller,* 350 P2d 880 (Ore. 1960); *Lawrence* v. *Lawrence,* 190 A2d 206 (N.J. 1963).

§ **500. Rights and obligations of co-owners.** Co-owners must, as a rule, contribute ratably toward payment of taxes, special assessments, mortgages, and repairs of the property. 48 ALR2d 1305. If one co-owner, through refusal of the other co-owners to contribute, is compelled to pay more than his share of the necessary expenses, he thereby acquires a lien analogous to a mortgage lien on the shares of the other co-owners, and he may foreclose such lien if they persist in their refusal to contribute. *Calcagni* v. *Cirino,* 14 A2d 803 (R.I. 1940). But one co-owner cannot purchase the property at a mortgage foreclosure sale or tax sale of the land and thus acquire a title that would enable him to oust the other co-owners. The title thus acquired is acquired for the benefit of all co-owners if they seasonably contribute their respective proportions of the expense incurred by the tenant who purchased the outstanding title. *Laura* v. *Christian,* 537 P2d 1389 (N.M. 1976).

If one co-owner collects all the rents but does not himself occupy the land, he must account to the other co-owners for their share of the rents. *Thompson* v. *Flynn,* 58 P2d 769 (Mont. 1936). A few states have laws making a co-owner liable to the other co-owners for rent where he alone occupies the land, collecting no rent therefrom. *Hazard* v. *Albro,* 20 Atl. 834 (R.I. 1890). But in many states, a co-owner who personally occupies the premises and does not rent them out is not liable to the other co-owners for the rental value of the premises unless he has agreed to pay them rent or has forcibly kept them out of possession. *Burk* v. *Burk,* 22 So2d 609 (Ala. 1945). But, a co-owner who exclusively possesses the premises must bear the entire burden of taxes, repairs, and mortgage interest payments. *Clute* v. *Clute,* 90 NE 988 (N.Y. 1910).

§ **501. Grants by one cotenant.** Obviously a mortgage signed by only one of the co-owners does not bind the others. It creates a lien only on the interest of the one who signs. *Rostan* v. *Huggins,* 5 SE2d 162 (N.C. 1939). Likewise, a judgment, federal lien, or other lien against one of the co-owners creates no lien on the shares of the others. The lessee of one cotenant becomes, for the term of the lease, a cotenant of the nonjoining owners, *Garland* v. *Holston Oil Co.,* 386 SW2d 914 (Tenn. 1965). The actions of the nonjoining cotenants may amount to a ratification thereby estopping them from denying the validity of the lease even as against their interest.

EXAMPLE: *H* and *W* owned recreational property. *H* leased the property to *T*. *W* knew of lease renewals and received some rent payments. The court held that *W* acquiesced in *H*'s leasing of the property and was estopped from denying the validity of the lease. *Gleason* v. *Tompkins,* 375 NYS2d 247 (1976).

REFERENCES ON TAX ASPECTS OF COTENANCIES: 11 *RPP&TJ* 405.

RESERVED: §§ 502 to 512.

17

Rights of Spouses and Unmarried Cohabitants

§ **513. Dower—in general.** Dower is the interest in the real estate of the husband which the law in many states gives to the widow to provide her with a means of support after her husband's death. It is a life estate in one-third of the lands that the husband owned during the continuance of the marriage relation. The requirements for dower are: (1) a valid marriage; (2) that the husband own the land during the continuance of the marriage relation; and (3) that the husband die prior to the death of the wife.

The right of dower originated in early times when a man's wealth consisted largely of real estate. Nowadays it is necessary for the widow's protection to give her rights in her husband's stocks, bonds, and other personal property as well as his realty, and many states have passed laws giving the widow a portion of the personal property left by her husband.

The widow's dower rights are seldom the same in any two states.

In all states laws have been enacted that alter the old rules concerning the rights of one spouse in land owned by the other. These laws must be consulted.

§ **514. Inchoate and consummate dower.** During her husband's lifetime, the wife's rights consist merely of the possibility that she may become entitled to her dower. Until his death, the wife's dower is said to be *inchoate*. It is not such an interest that the wife can convey to a stranger, nor can it be sold at a forced sale to pay the wife's debts. It can be released to a purchaser by joining in her husband's deed. Should she predecease her husband, even this incipient right is automatically extinguished. Thus, if her husband has previously conveyed his land without obtaining her signature on the deed, the grantee's title thereupon becomes perfect. It is as though her dower had never existed.

On the husband's death, her dower becomes *consummate*. It has ripened into something that she is certain to enjoy.

If the husband conveys his land without his wife joining in the deed, and the wife survives her husband, she then becomes entitled to her dower. The fact that the purchaser from the husband acted innocently does not protect him.

EXAMPLE: *H,* a married man, buys Lot 1. He becomes estranged from his wife, *W. H* sells and conveys Lot 1 to *E,* describing himself as "a bachelor." *E* believes this representation. Later *H* dies and *W* survives him. She can now go into court and obtain her dower rights.

EXCEPTION: In some states, Massachusetts, for example, dower exists, but if the husband conveys the land in his lifetime without his wife's signature, her dower in that land is wiped out.

§ 515. **Assignment of dower.** On the husband's death, one-third of the land that the husband owned during the marriage and in which the wife did not release her dower (which includes the land owned by him at the time of his death and also the land that he conveyed during the marriage without obtaining her signature) is set apart for the widow, usually by court order. This is called *assignment of dower.* In this third, the widow has an ordinary life estate. She may occupy the land herself or rent it to a tenant. On her death, all her rights therein are terminated.

If the land cannot be divided, the widow may be given one-third of the rents for her lifetime as her dower. Or, in many states, the land will be sold and a portion of the proceeds allotted to her.

In any case, if the husband is indebted at the time of his death, the widow's dower rights are superior to any claims of his creditors in and to the land. This is one of the important characteristics of dower.

§ 516. **Joint tenancy and dower.** Although a widow has dower in lands owned by her husband in tenancy in common with others, there is no dower in a joint tenancy.

EXAMPLE: Two men, *A* and *B,* hold title in joint tenancy. *A* is married to *C,* and *B* is married to *D. A* conveys to *X. A's* wife, *C,* does not join in the deed. Ordinarily when a wife does not join in her husband's deed, her dower remains outstanding, but here no dower remains outstanding in *C* because *A* held title as a joint tenant. However, *B* and *X* now hold title as tenants in common, and their wives have dower in the real estate. *Johnston* v. *Muntz,* 4 NE2d 826 (Ill. 1936).

EXAMPLE: *H* and *W,* husband and wife, own land in joint tenancy. *H* conveys his half interest to *X. X* takes this interest free of any dower rights of *W,* because when *H* signed the deed, he was a joint tenant and there is no dower in a joint tenancy. *Laterza* v. *Murray,* 117 NE2d 779 (Ill. 1954). However, *H* now has dower in *W's* half interest.

§ 517. **Mortgages and other liens.** When a wife fails to join with her husband in the execution of a mortgage on the husband's land, any title acquired through foreclosure of such mortgage will be subject to the wife's dower in states where dower is recognized. *Thomas* v. *Thomas,* 18 S2d 544 (Ala. 1944). An opposite result occurs where the mortgage provides the purchase money for the property mortgaged. *Frederick* v. *Emig,* 57 NE 883 (Ill. 1900). The same result follows in some states that have substituted some ownership share for dower but require the wife to join in any deed in order to release her ownership share. And the same result follows in many states where the husband has curtesy, dower, or an ownership share in the wife's real estate and fails to join in her mortgage. Obviously where land is owned by either husband or wife, it will usually be necessary for the spouse to join in any mortgage on the land.

Dower is subject to any liens or encumbrances to which the land was subject at the time of the marriage or at the time the husband acquired title.

EXAMPLE: A buys a tract of land on which there is a mortgage. On foreclosure of this mortgage, the dower of A's wife will be extinguished.

EXAMPLE: *H* places a mortgage on his land and thereafter marries *W*. *W*'s rights again are subject to those of the mortgagee, and foreclosure will extinguish her rights.

EXAMPLE: *X* obtains a judgment against *H*, a landowner. Thereafter, *H* marries *W*. *W*'s dower is subject to the lien of *X*'s judgment. But if a judgment is rendered against a married man, as a rule any sheriff's sale under such a judgment will be subject to the wife's dower. *Seibert* v. *Todd*, 9 SE 822 (S.C. 1889).

§ 518. **Leaseholds.** The leasehold interest of a tenant under his lease is personal property, and since dower is a right that attaches to real estate only, a tenant's wife has no dower in the leasehold. Ordinarily a tenant may assign his leasehold without the wife's signature when no homestead rights are involved.

§ 519. **Contract for sale of land.** If I sign a contract for the sale of my land, but my wife does not join, she cannot be compelled to give a deed to the buyer. If she does not join in a deed to the buyer, her dower remains outstanding. Obviously any prudent buyer will insist that the wife sign. Dower acquired by a landowner's spouse after he has signed a contract of sale, however, does not affect the rights of the contract purchaser.

EXAMPLE: *H*, a bachelor, signs a contract to sell land to *B*. Thereafter, *H* marries *W*. When the last of the purchase price is paid, *W* refuses to sign the deed to *B*. Nevertheless, *H*'s deed to *B* gives *B* good title to the land, free of the wife's dower. Her dower was subject to the contract. *J. J. Newberry Co.* v. *Shannon*, 167 NE 292 (Mass. 1929); 63 ALR 136.

§ 520. **Release of dower.** The widow is entitled to have dower assigned out of any land conveyed, mortgaged, or leased by her husband during the marriage without her signature. Hence, it is important that the landowner's wife release her dower by joining with him in any deed, mortgage, or lease of his land.

Even if a grantor or mortgagor describes himself in the deed or mortgage as a bachelor or widower, and the grantee or mortgagee honestly believes that the grantor's marital status is as he describes it to be, the wife, should the grantor or mortgagor actually have one, is entitled to dower in the land if she survives the grantor or mortgagor. However, in a number of states, the widow's dower is limited to the land owned by the husband *at the time of his death*, so that any deed made by him in his lifetime defeats her dower even though she did not sign the deed. And in some states, a woman who is residing outside of the state at the time her husband makes a deed to land within the state has no right of dower even though she does not sign the deed.

§ 521. **Dower—election.** Many states where dower exists give the widow, at her husband's death, a right to elect between her dower or some ownership (fee simple) share of the land.

§ 522. **Dower—fee title given in lieu of dower.** In a number of states, a widow is given a share in fee simple of her deceased husband's land in lieu of dower. Instead of acquiring merely a life estate, she may become the owner of one third, or some other fraction, outright of her husband's land on his death. Remember that dower is only a life estate.

The law of some of these states gives the widow's share only in lands that the husband owned *at his death*. Thus, the widow has no claim whatever upon land conveyed by the husband during his lifetime and without the wife's signature. In other states that give the widow an ownership share in lieu of dower, the widow is entitled to her share in any land conveyed by the husband in his lifetime without her signature. Obviously in these last states, the wife's signature is necessary on any deed, mortgage, or contract of sale given by the husband.

§ 523. **Curtesy.** In some states, a widower has a life estate known as *curtesy,* in the lands owned by his wife during their marriage. It is somewhat analogous to the widow's dower, but there are these points of difference:

1. In some curtesy states, a child must be born to the couple for this interest in land to arise. Most laws have abolished this requirement.

2. The widower's curtesy, according to the old English law, was a life estate in all the land owned by the wife during the marriage, as contrasted with the one third allowed the widow as her dower. In most of the curtesy states, however, the husband's share has been reduced by modern laws to some fraction, such as one third.

In a number of states the husband is given dower instead of curtesy.

Whenever a husband has dower or curtesy, obviously he should join in the wife's deed, mortgage, or contract of sale of her property. However, in some states, a deed given by the wife conveying her own land bars the husband's curtesy even if he does not join in the deed.

In a number of states, a surviving husband is given a share in fee simple of the wife's lands in lieu of curtesy. In some of these states, for example, the widower's share is limited to the land that the wife owned at her death. He has no claim whatever upon land conveyed by her in her lifetime without his signature.

In still other states that give the widower an ownership share in lieu of curtesy, the widower is entitled to his ownership share in any land conveyed by the wife in her lifetime without his signature.

Many states that give a widower curtesy or dower allow him, at the wife's death, to choose an ownership share instead.

§ 524. **Divorce.** Divorce terminates dower, curtesy, and their statutory substitutes. Some state laws provide however that a divorce bars only the dower or curtesy of the spouse for whose fault the divorce was obtained.

§ 525. **Community property—in general.** The community property system is of Spanish origin and obtains in states that were subject to Spanish influence, namely, Arizona, California, Idaho, Louisiana, Nevada, New Mexico, Texas, and Washington. The law of these states recognizes two kinds of property that may belong to the spouses in case of marriage—the *separate property* and the *community property*. The separate property of either husband or wife is what he or she owned at the time of marriage and what he or she acquired during marriage by inheritance, will, or gift. The separate property of each spouse is wholly free from all interest or claim on the part of the other and is entirely under the management and control, whether by deed, mortgage, will, or otherwise of the spouse to whom it belongs. All other property is community property.

§ 526. **Theory of community property.** It is the theory in these states that the husband and wife should share equally property acquired by their joint efforts during marriage. Thus, the husband is as much entitled to share equally in acquisitions by the wife through her industry as she is entitled to share equally in acquisitions by the husband, and each spouse owns one-half of all that is earned or gained, even though one earned or gained more than the other or actually earned or gained nothing. See Calif. Civ. Code § 5105.

§ 527. **Property acquired during the marriage.** Property *purchased* with separate funds is the separate property of the purchaser, whereas property purchased with community funds is community property.

Property acquired by *purchase* during the marriage is ordinarily presumed to vest in the husband and wife as community property, regardless of whether the deed is made to the husband, wife, or both. Under the community property system, the ownership of property does not depend upon the question of who happens to be named as grantee in the deed.

In California prior to January 1, 1975 and in New Mexico prior to July 1, 1973, it was provided that real estate conveyed to a married woman in her own separate name was presumed to be her separate property. So far as the husband and wife are concerned, this presumption can be destroyed by proof that the property was purchased with community funds and that the placing of title in the wife's name was not made with the intention of making a gift to her. Such property is community property. But the presumption that the property is the separate property of the wife and can be sold or mortgaged without the husband's signature is conclusive in favor of purchasers and mortgagees dealing with the wife in good faith and for a valuable consideration. *Fulkerson* v. *Stiles,* 105 Pac. 966 (Cal. 1909).

Except possibly in Louisiana and Texas, a husband and wife may by agreement change the status of property from separate to community property or from community to separate property. Income tax returns are often received as evidence of such agreements.

A deed by the husband to the wife raises a presumption that this was intended to convert the land into her separate property. But this presumption can be rebutted. 41 CJS. *Husband & Wife* § 491(c).

In Arizona, California, and Nevada, a deed to husband and wife as joint tenants makes the property the separate property of each, which property they hold in ordinary joint tenancy. *Collier* v. *Collier,* 242 P2d 537 (Ariz. 1952); *Siberell* v. *Siberell,* 7 P2d 1003 (Cal. 1932). However, oral evidence can be admitted in court to show that the husband and wife really intended this to be community property, and such intention will prevail. *Gudelj* v. *Gudelj,* 259 P2d 656 (Cal. 1953). In New Mexico, the opposite is true. A deed to a husband and wife in joint tenancy gives them the land as community property, unless evidence can be found that the parties did not intend the land to become community property. *In re Trimble's Estate,* 253 P2d 805 (N.M. 1953). In Idaho, Louisiana, and Texas, the rents of separate property are community property. In other states, rents of separate property are separate property.

A gift made to both spouses is community property.

§ **528. Deeds and mortgages of community property.** In Nevada and Texas, the husband may convey community property without the wife's signature, except that both must sign if the property constitutes their home. In other states, the wife must join in the deed.

Either spouse may convey or mortgage his or her separate property without the consent of the other, except in Texas, which requires the wife to obtain her husband's signature on deeds or mortgages of her separate property.

In any event, it is desirable and customary in most states for the husband and wife to join in any deed of land. And in most states, their joining is legally necessary where the land conveyed is occupied by the parties as their home. In most community property states that require the wife's consent to a deed of community property, the wife's signature is also needed for a valid contract to convey community property. *Rundle* v. *Winters,* 298 Pac. 929 (Ariz. 1931); *Chapman* v. *Hill,* 137 Pac. 1041 (Wash. 1914); *Elliott* v. *Craig,* 260 Pac. 433 (Id. 1927); *Adams* v. *Blumenshine,* 204 P 66 (N.M. 1922). The wife should also join in all but short-term leases of community property. *Bowman* v. *Hardgrove,* 93 P2d 303 (Wash. 1939).

NEW DIRECTIONS: The aspects of the community property system that give control to the husband are under attack on constitutional grounds. The battle is being fought both in the state legislature and the court house.

EXAMPLE: In *Kirchberg* v. *Feenstra,* 430 F.Supp. 642 (1977) *H* secured his debt by mortgaging the family home held in the name of *H* and *W*. *W* challenged the power of *H* to mortgage the home. While she lost the lawsuit the statute was amended now to require in all instances *W*'s written authority for *H*'s lease, mortgage, or sale of realty held in the name of *H* and *W*. La. Civ. Code. Art 2334.

§ **529. Wills and descent of community property.** The descent of community property when there is no will varies from state to state. It must be remembered in this connection that, regardless of the legal title, each spouse owns one-half of the community property.

In California, Idaho, New Mexico, Washington, and Nevada the surviving spouse succeeds to the decedent's share of community property in the absence of a will. In Arizona, Louisiana, and Texas the decedent's share goes in whole or in part to his or her descendants. All community property states recognize the right to make a will by the first spouse to die.

§ 530. **Dower and curtesy.** Neither dower nor curtesy exists in community property states.

§ 531. **Divorce and separation.** On entry of a divorce decree, the court usually divides up the community property between the spouses. And even without a divorce, the spouses may in most states enter into an agreement dissolving the community and dividing their property.

§ 532. **Homestead.** When a family owns and occupies a tract of land as its home, in many states that portion of the tract which does not exceed in area or value the limit fixed by law for homesteads is the family homestead, and certain rights, called homestead rights, are created therein. These homestead rights may, of course, extend to the entire tract if it is within the area and value limits fixed by law.

There are three principal motives behind the various state homestead laws. One is the protection of the family against being evicted from their home by enforcement of the claims of creditors. The homestead portion of the tract of land is protected against sheriff's sales on a judgment against the landowner.

The second object of the homestead laws is to protect the wife against the husband. The lawmakers thought it would be a good idea if the husband were not allowed to sell his own home if the wife was opposed to the idea. Evidently the theory was that the old home should not be disposed of until a new home suitable for the famly had been provided. To accomplish this result, the lawmakers provided that the husband could not convey good title to his own home unless his wife signed the deed. It is therefore necessary that both husband and wife join in any deed or mortgage of homestead property, except, of course, a purchase money mortgage.

As a final protection of the wife against the husband and his creditors, the homestead laws provided some protection for the widow after the death of her husband. This was necessary because dower did not afford the widow adequate protection. Dower does not give the widow any right to the occupation of any real estate until a particular tract of land has been set apart or assigned to her as dower. Immediately upon the husband's death, the widow might be subject to eviction from the home. Protection was afforded by the laws providing for the widow's homestead. Even a husband who has quarreled bitterly with his wife cannot legally deprive her of this protection. A final development in this direction was the *probate homestead,* which created a home for the widow in land that the husband had never occupied as his home. In this regard, the widow's rights are superior to the rights of any creditor of the deceased husband. Land so occupied by the widow cannot be sold to pay the deceased husband's debts.

The homestead here discussed exists only under state laws and has nothing to do with the Federal Homestead Law.

For a valid deed or mortgage of the homestead, it is necessary that both husband and wife join in the same deed or mortgage. The wife is thus protected against the improvidence of the husband. In some states, it is necessary that the deed or mortgage of the homestead contain a clause expressly releasing or waiving all homestead rights, and in many states a deed or mortgage of the homestead land must be acknowledged in order to be valid.

§ 533. **Unmarried cohabitants.** Recent years have seen an increase in the number of instances where, for whatever reason, individuals have established housekeeping units without the benefit of formal marriage. This may cause problems.

EXAMPLE: A a bachelor and *B*, a spinster, buy a house. The deed simply runs to them as *A* and *B*. Both sign the mortgage required for part of the purchase price. Both contribute to the cash payment, since both have jobs. There is no contract between them. *A* dies. *B* is a stranger and inherits nothing from *A*. Still *B* must continue making payments on the mortgage to prevent foreclosure.

Of course, they can solve the problem simply.

EXAMPLE: In states where joint tenancy is recognized, *A* and *B* can have the deed run to them as joint tenants.

And in states that recognize tenancy by the entireties and joint tenancy, some courts come to the rescue.

EXAMPLE: *A* and *B*, unmarried persons, buy a home and the deed runs to them "as tenants by the entireties." Some states will treat this as a joint tenancy.

Dower, curtesy, spouse's rights statutes, and the law relating to distribution of property upon divorce are inapplicable to unmarried cohabitants except in those jurisdictions which still recognize common law marriage.

Various reasons have been given by courts in the various states in refusing to recognize property rights in unmarrieds. The most extreme of these is the courts' refusal to enforce contracts relating to property rights of unmarried persons who live together. Courts in other states will honor the contract if it is properly drawn.

Some courts make a distinction between cases involving parties who honestly thought they were married and those who know full well that they were not married. Evans, *Property Interests Arising from Quasi-Marital Relations*, 9 Cornell L. Q. 246 (1924).

EXAMPLE: *M*, thinking his divorce from *F* is final, engages in a marriage ceremony with *W*. Both *M* and *W* intend to marry and have otherwise complied with all form requirements. The failure of *M* to be finally divorced from *F*, however, rendered the marriage of *M* to *W* a nullity. This is a *putative* marriage and *M* and *W* are *putative husband and wife*. The courts will treat their property as if they were husband and wife.

EXAMPLE: *M* and *W* decide to live together and engage in sexual relations without the benefit of any formal marriage. The older decisions refer to this as *concubinage*. Some courts refuse to recognize property rights by either in the property of the other.

There are various grounds for awarding property rights to the parties of a nonmarital relationship. Primary among them is the *express agreement*. The parties may expressly agree to pool their assets and share in their accumulations, enter into a partnership or joint venture agreement, or exchange property for services. An express agreement is certainly the preferable course of action, since they are almost always enforced by the courts if sexual conduct is not mentioned in the contract. Unfortunately, most cohabitants do not have the foresight to enter into such agreements. This is folly especially where substantial assets are involved.

It is also preferable that these agreements be in writing. The intent of the parties and the terms of the agreement are more easily proved. Oral agreements are nonetheless enforceable. *Marvin* v. *Marvin,* 557 P2d 106 (Cal. 1976). While these agreements are sometimes subject to the defense of illegality as encouraging immorality, they will only be declared invalid where sexual services are the principal consideration. Courts frequently hold, however, that if the woman makes a financial contribution, she will be protected.

EXAMPLE: *M* and *W* lived together for seven years. All property acquired during this period was taken in *M*'s name. At the outset of the relationship, *M* and *W* orally agreed that while the parties lived together they would combine their efforts and earnings and would share equally in all accumulations as a result of their individual or combined efforts. *W* also agreed to render services as companion and homemaker. *M* agreed to provide for *W*'s financial support and needs for the rest of her life. *W* gave up a lucrative singing career to devote her time to her household responsibilities. During the period of cohabitation, and as a result of their efforts and earnings, *M* and *W* acquired substantial property in *M*'s name. The relationship then came to an end. The court allowed the enforcement of this oral contract even though sexual relations may have been involved. *Marvin* v. *Marvin,* 557 P2d 106 (Cal. 1976).

There are other grounds for awarding property to parties of a nonmarital relationship. The courts may struggle to find some sort of partnership, trust, or gift.

Modern courts allow the bargain to be enforced rather than allow one of the parties to retain assets accumulated during the relationship and the other to be deprived of what was jointly accumulated. *Latham* v. *Latham,* 547 P2d 144 (Ore. 1976). The decisions go so far as to order specific performance of an oral promise to convey real estate. *Tyranski* v. *Piggins,* 205 NW2d 595 (Mich. 1973).

Older decisions that deny protection to the unmarried woman no longer appear to be valid. The courts should be free to inquire into the conduct of the parties to determine whether their conduct demonstrates an implied contract or implied agreement of partnership or some sort of trust. Also, the older barrier against recovery for the reasonable value of services rendered may well be removed. *Marvin* v. *Marvin,* 557 P2d 106 (1976).

REFERENCES: Bruch, Property Rights of De Facto Spouses Including Thoughts on the Value of Homemaker's Services, 10 *Fam. L. Q.* 101 (1976); Evans, Property Interests Arising from Quasi-Marital Relations, 9 *Cornell L. Q.* 246 (1924). Note, 50 *Ind. L. J.* 389 (1975).

RESERVED: §§ 534 to 544.

18

Liens

§ 545. **In general.** A *lien* is a right conferred on certain classes of creditors to have their debts paid out of the debtor's property, usually by means of a sale thereof. The opposite of a *lien creditor* or a *secured creditor* is the *unsecured creditor* who has no lien on the debtor's property. In that instance, the debtor may sell or mortgage his property and the purchasers or mortgagees will be unaffected in any way by the creditor's rights.

EXAMPLE: On January 5, 1968, *D* borrows $5,000 from C. *D* signs a promissory note for this amount, but he does not give C any mortgage on his land to secure repayment of the debt. C is therefore an *unsecured creditor.* On January 26, 1969, *D* borrows $500 from *M* and gives *M* a mortgage on his land. The giving of the mortgage creates a lien. The lien attaches to *D*'s land at that time. *M* immediately records the mortgage. The recording of the mortgage perfects the lien. *M* is a *secured creditor.* If *M* forecloses his mortgage and becomes the owner of the mortgaged land by means of the foreclosure, C will have no rights whatever in the land so acquired by *M.* All persons acquiring any interest in the land after January 26, take subject to *M*'s lien, i.e. enforcement of the lien will extinguish their interest.

Often a lien creditor is required to take some steps to perfect his lien, that is, to make it effective as to any person but the debtor.

EXAMPLE: On January 30, 1968 the United States discovers that *A,* a taxpayer, has failed to pay $50,000 of his income tax and it therefore assesses a tax against him. On February 1, 1968 *A* sells and conveys his land in Chicago to *B.* On February 28, 1968 the United States files a notice of lien in the Recorder's office in Chicago. *B* is unaffected by this lien, since he purchased before the lien was *perfected* by filing.

A time limit is placed on the enforcement of virtually all liens. If the lien creditor fails to enforce his lien by appropriate action prior to the expiration of the specified period, his lien cannot thereafter be enforced.

EXAMPLE: *A,* a landowner, hires *B* to put a new roof on his house. *A* fails to pay for the roof, and *B* files a mechanic's lien against the land. In Illinois, where the land is located, such a lien has a duration of two years. *B* takes no action to foreclose his lien, and after two years have elapsed, *A* sells the land to *C*. *C* has good title to the land unencumbered by any lien of *B*'s.

To determine a particular creditor's rights in the land in question, then, it is necessary to inquire: (1) Does he have a lien? (2) If he has a lien, when was it created, that is, when did it *attach* to the land? (3) Was the lien properly *perfected?* (4) What is the *duration* of the lien? (5) Has the lien been voluntarily released or waived by the lien creditor? (6) Has the debtor paid the lien creditor? What evidence of payment is there?

§ 546. **Types of liens.** So far as real estate is concerned, the main classes of liens are *contractual liens, equitable liens,* and *statutory liens.*

EXAMPLE: *A* mortgages his land to *B* and *B* records the mortgage. *B* has a *contractual lien* on *A*'s land.

EXAMPLE: *X* dies leaving certain vacant land to his sons, *A* and *B*. *A* fails to pay the real estate taxes, and *B* is therefore forced to pay all the real estate taxes. He has an *equitable lien* on *A*'s share of the land as security for reimbursement for *A*'s share of the taxes.

Equitable liens arise where there is an intent to charge a particular property with a debt or obligation.

EXAMPLE: A building contract provides that the builder will have a lien on the structure until the cost of construction is paid in full. *Pincus* v. *Collins,* 22 So2d 361 (Miss. 1945).

The principal statutory liens are *mechanics' liens, judgment liens, tax liens, attachment liens,* and *execution liens.*

§ 547. **Subordinations.** It is always possible that the parties may want to reorder the priorities as they are established. This is typically done by a subordination agreement.

EXAMPLE: *M* has a mortgage on *O*'s land. *J* has a judgment lien. *O* wants to improve the land, and *M* will give additional funds secured by a second mortgage only if he will have priority for these additional funds over *J*. Since the improvements will make the land more valuable, *J* may be willing to subordinate his position to *M*'s new position after the additional funds are advanced. He does this by signing a document stating that his lien is subordinate to *M*'s mortgages.

§ 548. **Mechanics' liens.** Mechanics and materialmen are persons who furnish labor or materials in the construction of improvements on land. A mechanic or materialman who has furnished such labor or material on the landowner's order can, by complying with certain formalities, acquire a lien on the land and improvements in question if the landowner fails to pay him. The lien is called a *mechanic's lien,* and the person furnishing the work or material is the *mechanic's lien claimant.* These liens resemble mortgages and in many states are foreclosed in the same manner as mortgages.

Certain kinds of labor and materials are not *lienable*. For example, if labor or materials are furnished to a tenant and the articles thereby produced are, in legal contemplation, *trade fixtures* and thus removable by him at the termination of his tenancy, a lien will not attach to the landlord's title.

EXAMPLE: A leases a store to *B* as a barber shop. C installs barber chairs at *B's* order. C has no lien on the land for any unpaid balance due on the chairs. The chairs are trade fixtures.

Generally, lienable work and materials must be such as become a permanent part of the building structure. Thus, medical care furnished an employee of the contractor, even if the injury was suffered on the building site, is not lienable. Printing, stationery, and telephone service furnished the contractor are not lienable. Nor is the furnishing of tools, machinery, cranes, hoists, and so forth, lienable, for these do not become a permanent part of the building. 57 CJS 536; 36 AmJur 57. In a number of states the law has been amended recently to give a mechanic's lien for the rental of machinery needed in construction.

§ 549. Contract or consent of owner. Mechanics' lien laws differ from state to state in dealing with the problem of work ordered by one other than the landowner. In some states, a lien claimant must show that he was hired by the landowner *or his agent* to furnish the labor or materials for which a lien is claimed. Laws of this kind are known as *contract statutes*. In other states, it is sufficient if the lien claimant can show that the owner had knowledge of and consented to the doing of the work, even though the work was ordered by some person other than the owner, such as the tenant. These laws are known as *consent statutes*.

Consent usually involves more than a mere failure to object to the doing of the work. Often the landowner is powerless to prevent the third person, such as a tenant, from ordering the construction or improvements. Some *affirmative consent* by the landowner is required, as when a lease requires the tenant to erect a building. At times, however, the same result is reached regardless of which statute is applied.

EXAMPLE: A, a landowner, leases an obsolete movie theatre to *B*, the lease providing that *B* will use the premises only as a savings and loan association and that *B* will make the necessary alterations at his own expense. Here, if *B* fails to pay for the work and materials, those furnishing the same will have mechanics liens on A's land. In a consent state, the lease is treated as giving consent for the doing of the work, and in a contract state the lease is regarded as making *B* the agent of A for the ordering of the work. Thus the result is at times the same whether the state is a contract or a consent state. 79 ALR 962.

Knowledge and consent also figure in the situation where the landowner has entered into an installment contract to sell the land to a purchaser and the purchaser has ordered work done on the building. If the seller has no knowledge of the work and it is not provided for in the installment contract, the seller's title does not become subject to the mechanic's lien, and the lien attaches only to the buyer's equity. As in the case of leases, however, where the contract of sale expressly requires the doing of certain specific work, the resulting mechanic's lien claim is binding on the seller. 57 CJS 573.

Whether work ordered by one spouse will ripen into a lien binding on the other spouse is a subject on which the laws differ from state to state. 57 CJS 552, 592.

A number of states, including California, Colorado, Minnesota, Nevada, New Mexico, Oregon, South Dakota and Washington, have a special type of consent statute. In these states, the landowner is deemed to have authorized and consented to improvements ordered by others (tenants, contract purchasers, and so on) unless within a specified time of learning of the work (usually three to ten days) the landowner posts a notice of nonresponsibility in some conspicuous place on the premises. 123 ALR 7, 85 ALR2d 949. In Nevada, the notice of nonresponsibility must also be recorded.

As far as co-owners are concerned, no lien will attach to the interests of those co-owners who do not consent to the work.

EXAMPLE: A father and his minor children owned the property as tenants in common. The father ordered certain labor and materials. The mechanic's lien attached only to the father's interest in the property. *Patrick* v. *Bonthius,* 124 P2d 550 (Wash. 1942). One co-owner cannot put a lien on the shares of his nonconsenting co-owners.

§ **550. Contractors and subcontractors.** Mechanics' lien laws distinguish between contractors and subcontractors. A *contractor* is one who was hired by the landowner to construct the improvement. A *subcontractor* has not dealt directly with the landowner, but has a contract with, or was hired by, the contractor.

EXAMPLE: O, a landowner, hires GC, a general contractor, to build a house. GC hires *SC* to do the electrical work. *SC* buys his electrical supplies from *MM*. *GC* is a contractor. *SC* is a subcontractor. *MM* is called a subsubcontractor, treated differently from a subcontractor in some states.

Since the legal rights of general contractors differ from those of subcontractors, and since the procedures that they must follow to establish their liens are also quite different, the distinction between general contractors and subcontractors is important. Laymen may sometimes mistake a general contractor for a subcontractor.

EXAMPLE: *A,* a landowner, retains *B* as his architect to supervise construction and to let the various contracts for plumbing, electrical work, and so on. All the individual contractors are *general contractors,* for they are dealing with the landowner through his agent.

In some states the law places on the landowner and on the construction lender the burden of seeing to it that the subcontractors are paid for their work and materials. This is something of an oddity. If I hire you to build a building for me, very likely the construction contract will call for me to pay the contract price to you. Nevertheless, the law steps in and says that, despite the contract, my mortgage lender and I must hold back part of the contract price and pay it to the subcontractors. In order that the landowner may know those whom it is his duty to protect and also to enable him to hold back adequate funds to pay them, the law usually requires subcontractors to give the landowner personal notice of their liens within a set time, and failure to do so invalidates their liens. *Gray* v. *McKinley*, 43 So2d 421 (Ala. 1949). This notice must be given to all landowners.

EXAMPLE: *A* and *B* own land in joint tenancy. They hire *GC* to erect a building. *GC* hires *SC* to do the plumbing. *SC* is a subcontractor. If he serves notice of his subcontractor's lien only on *A*, *SC* has a lien only on *A*'s half interest in the land. He has no lien on *B*'s share. *Liese* v. *Hentze*, 158 NE 428 (Ill. 1927).

§ **551. Performance by contractor.** In general, where the general contractor seeks to assert a lien, he must show that the contract was *substantially performed* by him. 57 CJS 605. Likewise, any subcontractor seeking to assert a lien would have to show that his job was substantially performed by him. Where the contract specifies that no payment will be made without production of an architect's certificate, a general contractor claiming a lien must be able to produce the certificate. 57 CJS 606.

§ **552. Inception and priority of lien.** The law as to the particular time when a mechanic's lien attaches to the land varies from state to state. There are definite groupings or classifications of states in this regard:

1. In a few states (Washington, for example), the lien of any particular mechanic attaches when he commences *his* particular work. In such states, the mechanic's lien is not prior to any mortgage that was recorded prior to the commencement of the very work for which the lien is filed.

EXAMPLE: *A* and *B* commence work on a building, and afterward the owner mortgages the land to *M*. Thereafter, *D* and *E* begin work on the same construction job. *A* and *B* have priority over *M*, and *M* has priority over *D* and *E*.

2. In many states (Arkansas, California, District of Columbia, Georgia, Louisiana, Michigan, Minnesota, Nevada, New Mexico, Ohio, Oklahoma, Tennessee, Utah, and Wisconsin, for example), all mechanics' liens growing out of a particular construction job date back to the beginning of the job.

EXAMPLE: O, a landowner, hires GC to erect a building, and GC hires SC to dig the foundation. SC begins work in January, 1968. In February, 1968, O records a mortgage to *M* which mortgage is intended to provide funds for construction. The carpenter, mason, electrician, and so on, come on the job in March, 1968. All mechanics' liens date back to January, and all liens therefore have priority over *M*'s mortgage.

3. In a few states (Illinois and Maine, for example), a mechanic's lien attaches to

the land as of the date of the contract for the improvement; that is, as of the date on which the owner ordered the work done.

EXAMPLE: O, a landowner, hires GC on January 8, 1968, to build a building in Chicago. As is true of most contracts for construction, the contract is not recorded. On January 10, 1968, O records a mortgage to *M*, which mortgage is intended to provide funds for construction. Work on the construction site begins on January 17, 1968. GC's mechanics' lien dates back to January 8, 1968, and therefore enjoys priority over M's mortgage.

4. In a few states (New York and South Carolina, for example), a mechanics' lien does not arise *as against the mortgagee* until notice thereof is filed in the proper public office.

EXAMPLE: O, a landowner, on January 8, 1968, hires GC to erect a building. GC commences work on January 12. On January 19, 1968, O records a construction mortgage to *M*, and *M* disburses funds under this mortgage for such construction until February 28, when a mechanics' lien claim is filed by a subcontractor. *M* discontinues disbursement and files a foreclosure suit. *M* has complete priority over the mechanics' liens, because all his disbursements were made prior to the filing of any mechanics' liens.

5. In some states (Colorado, Illinois, Missouri, North Dakota, Oregon, South Dakota, Virginia, and Wyoming, for example), the law declares that a mechanic's lien for work or materials furnished after a mortgage lien has attached to the land shall have priority over the mortgage *as to the building but not as to the land*. In a number of these states the matter of priority of lien as between the construction mortgage and the mechanic's lien claimants is decided in a way that is quite disadvantageous to the mortgagee.

EXAMPLE: O, an owner of vacant land, procures a construction loan mortgage from *M* which is recorded on January 10, 1968. On January 17, O hires GC to build the building. Construction begins on January 24. Mechanics' liens were filed. Both *M* and the mechanic's lien claimants file suits to foreclose. The court will hold that the mechanic's liens are a prior and superior lien as to the buildings, so that, in practical effect, the mechanics' liens will be a prior lien as to most of the value of the property, and the mortgagee will have no choice but to pay off the mechanic's lien claimants. 107 ALR 1012.

6. In Indiana the mechanics' liens enjoy equality of lien with the construction mortgage. *Ward* v. *Yarnelle*, 91 NE 7 (Ind. 1910); 80 ALR2d 187.

7. In Missouri a curious rule is followed. The construction lender is considered, from the very fact that he has made a construction loan, to have subordinated his mortgage to the mechanics' liens. *H. B. Deal Const. Co.* v. *Labour Discount Center*, 418 SW2d 940 (Mo. 1967).

Of course, no great harm comes to the mortgagee if the landowner remains solvent and is able to pay off all mechanic's lien claimants. Unfortunately for mortgage lenders, many construction projects do not get completed and sold as planned, so that the construction mortgage and the mechanic's lien claimants are plunged into a contest as to their respective rights in the land and buildings.

§ 553. **Notice of lien.** In many states, laws require a mechanic's lien claimant to file a notice of his lien in some public office within some specified time, usually within some period after completion of the work. Usually it is required that this notice state the amount claimed to be due, the name and address of the claimant, the type of improvement, a description of the land, and the name of the landowner or landowners. 57 CJS 693; 52 ALR2d 12; 27 ALR2d 1169. The requirement that lien claims be filed within a specified time of the completion of the work often leads to controversies.

EXAMPLE: In Illinois, the law provides that lien claims must be filed within four months after completion of the work. X completes his work satisfactorily, but more than four months elapses before X realizes that he has failed to file his lien claim. X sends a workman back to perform some trifling task, like repairing a defective lock. This does no good. The job was really finished more than four months ago, and X cannot prolong this period by subterfuge. 57 CJS 661.

§ 554. **Waiver and release of lien.** As construction or repair work goes forward, liens of the general contractor and subcontractors attach to the land. Both the landowner and any mortgagee involved naturally want to get rid of these liens, which can be accomplished by procuring waivers of their liens from the parties furnishing labor or material. There are *partial waivers* and *final waivers*. Suppose that a subcontractor, such as a plumbing, electrical, or plastering subcontractor, has finished half his job and wants to be paid for that half. When the homebuilder pays him, he demands from the subcontractor a waiver of his lien for the work and materials furnished. This waiver recites that it waives all liens for *work and materials furnished*. This means of course, for work and materials furnished *up to the date of the waiver*. No lien is waived as to the work still to be done. When final payment is made to that particular party, the homebuilder demands from him a final waiver, which waives all lien *for work and materials furnished or to be furnished* meaning that he has no lien at all on the land or buildings. Even if he must come back to repair or replace defective work or material, he can claim no lien on the property, which is important, because the objective is always to get the building built at the price and at the bids submitted by the various mechanics. There is trouble ahead if any of the mechanics is legally able to assert a lien for a sum greater than the amount he agreed to work for.

When a mechanic has filed a lien claim in some public office as required by law, it becomes necessary, when his claim has been paid or settled, to release his lien from the public records. As a rule, the waiver form is not appropriate for this purpose. Instead, a form called *release of mechanic's lien* is used. It is very similar to a release of mortgage and is filed in the same office where the lien claim has been filed.

§ 555. **Time limit on enforcement of lien.** It is usually provided that a mechanic's lien ceases to exist unless steps are taken to enforce or foreclose it within a specified time, usually one or two years, after the filing of the lien claim.

§ 556. **Judgments.** When *A* brings to a successful conclusion a lawsuit filed against *B* on some personal liability, such as that arising on *B*'s promissory note or because of personal injuries inflicted by *B,* the court enters an order directing that *B* pay *A* the amount found due. This order is a judgment. *A* is the judgment creditor; *B,* judgment debtor. In some states judgments create a lien on land.

EXAMPLE: A obtains a judgment against *B*. The following year, *B* acquires title to a tract of land. The lien of *A*'s judgment immediately attaches to this land.

A judgment concludes with a direction that *execution* issue. An execution is an order, signed by the clerk of the court that rendered the judgment, directing the sheriff or some other public officer to sell the property of the judgment debtor in order to pay off, or satisfy, the judgment. The execution does not issue automatically. It is necessary for the judgment creditor to go to the court clerk and request its issuance.

The first step in the enforcement of the judgment lien is the issuance of the execution and its delivery to the sheriff. In some states, the sheriff then delivers a copy of this execution to the judgment debtor and demands payment of the judgment. The next step is a purely formal and technical one. It is known as a *levy* and consists of those acts by which a sheriff sets apart and appropriates a particular part of the judgment debtor's property for the purpose of satisfying the command of the execution. A levy on real estate often consists of nothing more than the sheriff's statement on the execution that he has levied on certain real estate, followed by a description of the real estate. Next, the sheriff publishes notice of the coming sale and posts copies thereof in certain public places. At the date fixed for sale, the sheriff auctions off the real estate to the highest bidder, who is usually the judgment creditor, since he can bid up to the amount of his judgment without producing any cash other than the sheriff's costs. In many states, there is a redemption period, just as in the case of mortgage foreclosure sales, one year being the period most frequently encountered. About one-quarter of the states, however, have no redemption period whatever. Ultimately, if no redemption is made a sheriff's deed issues to the purchaser.

A title acquired by such an execution sale, although not as precarious as a tax title, is nevertheless vulnerable to numerous objections and should be viewed with great suspicion.

The duration of a judgment lien varies from state to state. Ten years is the period most frequently encountered. This period is of great importance to prospective purchasers and mortgagees of real estate.

EXAMPLE: In Indiana, a judgment is a lien for ten years. *A*, who is about to purchase certain Indiana land from *B*, makes a check of the public records, which discloses that *B* has owned the land for fifteen years. *A* need only search for judgments against *B*, since all judgments against prior landowners will be more than ten years old. And *A* need not search for any judgments against *B* rendered prior to this ten-year period.

When a judgment is paid, the judgment creditor files a formal discharge of the judgment, known as satisfaction.

§ 557. **Attachments.** A judgment, obviously, cannot create any lien on the judgment debtor's land until judgment has been rendered. Nor can execution issue before there has been a judgment. In the meantime, the lawsuit may drag on and on, and an opportunity is afforded the defendant to dispose of his property and thus leave no real estate that can be sold to satisfy the judgment, when rendered. To prevent such a result, many states provide that on commencement of the suit, the plaintiff, that is, the person who has filed the suit, may, under conditions specified by the local law, have an attachment issued. As a rule, it is required that the plaintiff file a bond to indemnify the defendant for any injury that the latter may sustain by reason of a wrongful attachment. On filing of the bond and on compliance with the other conditions specified by the local law, a writ of attachment is issued, and the sheriff endorses on the writ a statement that he has levied on the defendant's real estate, which he thereupon describes. In addition, some states require that the sheriff issue and file in the register's or recorder's office a certificate describing the real estate attached and stating that the same has been levied on. A valid attachment creates a lien on the defendant's interest in real estate, which can be enforced by issuance of execution after judgment has been rendered in favor of the plaintiff. It effectively prevents the defendant from disposing of his real estate while the suit is pending, as any purchaser takes subject to the attachment. *Crocker Nat. Bank* v. *Trical Manufacturing Co.,* 373 F.Supp. 461 (1973).

§ 558. **Miscellaneous liens.** Among the many other liens that may attach to land are federal estate tax liens; federal gift tax liens; federal internal revenue liens (usually for income tax); liens for state inheritance or estate tax, gift tax, income tax, corporation tax, sales tax, and so forth; and old-age assistance liens.

19

Mortgages

§ 559. **Mortgage defined.** A mortgage may be defined as a conveyance of land given with the intention of being security for the payment of a debt. On analysis, this definition discloses the existence of two elements: (1) Like a deed, a mortgage is a conveyance of land. (2) However, the intention is not, as in the case of a deed, to effect a sale of land, but to provide security for the payment of a debt.

§ 560. **History of mortgage law.** The history of mortgage law is the history of hundreds of years of ceaseless struggle for advantage between borrowers and lenders. The lawbooks reflect the constantly shifting fortunes of this war. Occasionally, the battle has gone in favor of the lenders. More recently, however, the consumerism wave has resulted in the passage of many laws favorable to the borrowers. The tide of battle, as it has many times in the past, has shifted in their favor. To understand how the modern mortgage developed out of these centuries of struggle is to take a long step forward toward understanding modern mortgage law. Much of our mortgage law comes to us from England. In that country, mortgage arrangements of various kinds existed even in the Anglo-Saxon times before the conquest of England by William the Conqueror in 1066. However, it will suffice for our purposes to begin with the mortgage of the fourteenth century. This document was a simple deed of the land, running from the borrower (mortgagor) to the lender (mortgagee). All the ceremonies needed for a full transfer of ownership took place when the mortgage was made. The mortgagee became the owner of the land just as if a sale had taken place. However, this ownership was subject to two qualifications:

1. The mortgagee, as owner, could oust the mortgagor, take immediate possession of the property, and collect the rents. However, the rents so collected had to be applied on the mortgage debt. For this reason, the mortgagee often permitted the mortgagor to remain in possession.

2. The mortgage described the debt it secured and stated a date of payment, known as the *law day*. The mortgage gave the mortgagor the right to pay the debt on the law day. If he did so, the mortgage provided that it was thereby to become void. This provision was known as the *defeasance clause*, for payment of the debt on the law day defeated the mortgage and put ownership back in the mortgagor.

In early times, the courts enforced the mortgage as it was written. Foreclosure proceedings did not exist. Failure to pay the mortgage debt when due, termed a *default,* automatically extinguished all the mortgagor's interest in the land.

§ 561. **The equity of redemption.** For many years no one dreamed of questioning this scheme of things. Then, slowly at first, and later in greater numbers, borrowers who had lost their property through default began to seek the assistance of the king. A typical petition by such a borrower would set forth the borrowing of the money, the making of the mortgage, the default in payment, and the resulting loss of the land. The petition would continue with the statement that the borrower now had funds and offered to pay the mortgage debt in full, with interest. The petition would then ask that the king order the mortgagee, who now owned the land, to accept the proffered money and to convey the land back to the borrower. The king had little time or inclination to tend to these petitions personally, and so he habitually referred them to a high official, the Lord Chancellor. Since the king was the fountain of all justice, it was the Chancellor's duty to dispose of these petitions justly and equitably, according to good conscience. This he did. In cases of hardship or accident, for example, where the mortgagor had been robbed while on his way to pay the debt, the Chancellor would order the mortgagee to accept payment of the debt from the borrower and to convey the land back to the borrower. A mortgagee who refused to do as he was told was sent to jail. In time, by about the year 1625, what had begun as a matter of grace on the part of the king had developed into the purest routine. Borrowers filed their petitions directly with the Chancellor, who was now functioning as the judge of a court, and with routine regularity his order was issued commanding the mortgagee to reconvey. Thus, a new and very important right was born, the right of the mortgagor to pay his debt even after default and in this manner to recover his property. This right came to be known as the *equitable right of redemption,* or the *equity of redemption.* Later the courts held that the mortgagor could sell this equitable right of redemption, that he could dispose of it by his will, and that if he died leaving no will the right could be exercised by his heirs. You will perceive that as a result of these developments, the mortgagor, even after default, retained very important rights in the land. Technically the mortgagee became full owner of the land upon default, but practically the mortgagor could now be regarded as the owner even after default, since he could reacquire ownership by exercising his equitable right of redemption.

§ 562. **Waiver of right of redemption.** The mortgagees reacted to the development of the equitable right of redemption by inserting clauses reciting that the mortgagor waived and surrenderd all of his equitable rights of redemption. The courts, however, nipped this idea in the bud by holding that all such clauses were void. This result was based upon the courts' feeling that it was their duty to protect the needy borrower who would sign anything. This rule flourished and exists in full vigor today. Any provision in the mortgage purporting to terminate the mortgagor's ownership in case of failure to make payments when due is against public policy and is void. *Once a mortgage, always a mortgage.* It cannot be converted into an outright deed by the mere default of the mortgagor. No matter how the mortgage seeks to disguise an attempted waiver of the equitable right of redemption, the courts will strike it down.

EXAMPLE: At the time the mortgage was made, the mortgagor signed a deed conveying the property to the mortgagee. He then delivered the deed to a third person in escrow with directions to deliver the deed to the mortgagee in case of default in the mortgage payments. This deed and escrow were held invalid as an attempted waiver of the equitable right of redemption. *Plummer* v. *Ilse,* 82 P.1009 (Wash. 1905); *Hamud* v. *Hawthorne,* 338 P2d 387 (Cal. 1959).

§ **563. Clogging the equity.** Other means were invented to in some way hamper the exercise of the equitable right of redemption. Rather than waiving the right, mortgagors executed documents which limited the manner of exercise of right of redemption. Courts would not allow arrangements where the right of redemption could only be exercised for a certain period after law day or only by the mortgagor himself. Osborne, Handbook on the Law of Mortgages, §§ 96 and 97 (2nd ed. 1970). The courts will also use their powers to invalidate any agreement whereby the mortgagee oppresses or takes unconscionable advantage of the mortgagor.

EXAMPLE: *R* mortgaged his lot 1 to *E*. *E* demanded and received from *R* an option to buy *R*'s lot 2. When *E* sought to exercise this option, *R* resisted and litigation ensued. The court held the option void. *Humble Oil & Refining Co.* v. *Doerr,* 303 A2d 898 (N.J. 1973). A mortgagee is entitled to payment of the mortgage debt. He cannot take advantage of the mortgagor by compelling him to grant "collateral advantages."

§ **564. Development of foreclosure.** The efforts of the courts to rescue the mortgagor in turn placed the mortgagee at a disadvantage. The mortgagee, it is true, became the owner of the land when the mortgagor defaulted, but he could not be certain he would remain the owner, for the mortgagor might choose to redeem. To remedy this situation a new practice sprang up. Immediately upon default in payment of the mortgage debt, the mortgagee would file a petition in court, and the judge would enter an order, called a decree, allowing the mortgagor additional time to pay the debt. If he failed to pay within this time, usually six months or a year, the decree provided that his equitable right of redemption was thereby barred and foreclosed. Thereafter he could not redeem his property. Thus developed the *foreclosure suit,* a suit to bar or terminate the equitable right of redemption.

The method of foreclosure just described is known today as *strict foreclosure.* It is still used in Connecticut and Vermont and occasionally elsewhere.

The next development was foreclosure through public sale. The idea emerged that in mortgage foreclosures, justice would best be served by offering the land for sale at public auction, for if at such sale the property sold for more than the mortgage debt, the mortgagee would be paid his debt in full and the surplus proceeds of the sale would be salvaged for the mortgagor. This method of *foreclosure by sale* is the most common method of foreclosure in America today. This development constituted another major victory for the mortgagor. More important still, it led to another and even greater victory for the borrowers. As the practice of foreclosure by sale grew more common, the view began to emerge that *the mortgage, despite its superficial similarity to a deed, was really not a deed of conveyance but only a lien on the land—that is, merely a means of bringing about a public sale to raise money for the payment of the mortgage debt.*

§ 565. **Title and lien theories.** The relatively recent view that the mortgage is not really a conveyance of land but only a lien, has reached its fullest development in the agricultural and western states. Certain states, called *title theory states,* still take the older view that a mortgage gives the mortgagee some sort of legal title to the land. In other states, called *lien theory states,* the view that the mortgagee has the legal title is entirely superseded by the view that he has merely a lien to secure his debt. Some states take a position midway between these two views. These are called *intermediate states.*

It is not possible, however, to draw any hard and fast line between these groups of states, since vestiges of title theory will be found in lien theory states, and many title theory states have adopted rules developed by lien theory courts. The differences in point of view are of importance in determining the mortgagee's rights with respect to possession and rents of the mortgaged property.

§ 566. **Statutory redemption.** When a mortgage foreclosure sale is held, the equitable right of redemption ends. Indeed, the whole object of the foreclosure suit is to put an end to the mortgagor's equitable right of redemption. In the last hundred years, however, laws have been enacted giving the mortgagor an additional concession. Under these laws, the mortgagor is given one more chance to get his property back.

EXPLANATION: Suppose that a farmer whose farm is mortgaged has a bad crop year. He cannot meet his mortgage payments, and the mortgage is foreclosed. Perhaps next year the weather and crops will be good, and he will have enough to pay all of his debts. To afford farmers and other mortgagors one last opportunity to salvage their properties, many legislatures have passed laws allowing additional time, often one year, after the foreclosure sale during which the mortgagor can, by paying the amount of the foreclosure sale price, get his property back from the mortgagee. This right is called the statutory right of redemption. Thus, the equitable right of redemption ends, and the statutory right of redemption begins with the holding of the foreclosure sale.

§ 567. **Types of mortgages.** There are several different types of mortgage instruments. Those commonly encountered are regular mortgages, deeds of trust, equitable mortgages, and deeds absolute given as security for debts.

§ 568. **Regular mortgages.** The ordinary printed form of mortgage encountered in most states today is referred to herein as the regular mortgage. It is, in form, a deed or conveyance of the land by the borrower to the lender followed or preceded by a description of the debt and including a provision to the effect that such mortgage shall be void on full payment of such debt. The content of the additional paragraphs of "fine print" varies considerably.

§ 569. **Deeds of trust.** The regular mortgage involves only two parties, the borrower and the lender. In the trust deed, also known as the deed of trust, the borrower conveys the land, not to the lender, but to a third party, a *trustee,* in trust for the benefit of the holder of the note or notes that represent the mortgage debt.

The deed of trust form of mortgage has certain advantages: the chief one is that in a number of states it can be foreclosed by trustee's sale under the power of sale clause without any court proceedings. The power of sale trust deed is used in Alabama, Alaska, California, Colorado, District of Columbia, Mississippi, Missouri, Montana, Nebraska, Nevada, New Mexico, North Carolina, Oregon, South Carolina, Tennessee, Texas, Virginia, Washington, and West Virginia.

§ 570. **Equitable mortgages.** As a general rule, any instrument in writing by which the parties show their intention that real estate be held as security for the payment of a debt will constitute an equitable mortgage, capable of being foreclosed in a court of equity.

EXAMPLE: A landowner borrowed money from a mortgagee giving a promissory note to evidence the debt. On this note the borrower placed the following recital: "This note is secured by a real estate mortgage on. . . ." (here followed a description of the land). Actually no separate mortgage was executed. The court held that the note itself, with the quoted endorsement, constituted an equitable mortgage on the land, for it clearly expressed an intention that the land should stand as security for the debt. *Trustees of Zion Methodist Church* v. *Smith,* 81 NE2d 649 (Ill. 1948).

An instrument intended as a regular mortgage, but which contains some defect, may also operate as an equitable mortgage.

EXAMPLE: When through inadvertence, a trust deed altogether omitted the name of a trustee, it was obviously ineffective to transfer title or create a power of sale in any one since it lacked a grantee. However, it was sustained as an equitable mortgage, which could be foreclosed by means of a foreclosure suit. *Dulany* v. *Willis,* 29 SE 324 (Va. 1898).

§ 571. **Deeds absolute given as a security.** Often when a landowner borrows money he gives as security an absolute deed to the land. By "absolute deed" is meant a quitclaim or warranty deed such as is used in an ordinary land sale. On its face, the transaction looks like a sale of the land. Nevertheless, the courts treat such a deed as a mortgage where the evidence shows that the deed was really *intended* only as *security for a debt.* If such proof is available, the borrower is entitled to pay the debt and to demand a reconveyance from the lender, just as in the case of an ordinary mortgage; whereas if the debt is not paid, the grantee must foreclose just as if a regular mortgage had been made.

EXAMPLE: *R* owns a home, which is already mortgaged to a bank. He needs money for medical expenses and goes to his brother, *E*, for a loan of $1000. *E* loans *R* the money but insists that *R* sign a simple promissory note and give a quitclaim deed to his home. It is agreed orally that if the debt is paid when due, *E* will quitclaim the property back to *R*. *R* fails to pay the debt. *E* is not the owner of the land. He merely holds a mortgage on it, which he must foreclose. And remember that all the world has notice of the true nature of his deed, for undoubtedly *R* will remain in possession, and possession imparts constructive notice.

A deed such as that described in the above example is regarded by the courts as an attempt to "waive the equitable right of redemption." The courts often use the maxim, "Once a mortgage, always a mortgage." It cannot be converted into a conveyance of absolute ownership by mere default. Hence it becomes necessary for the courts to go back to the very beginning of the transaction. The task is a simple one. Either the deed was *then intended* as an absolute *transfer of ownership* (as in a land sale), or it was *then* intended merely to provide *security to a lender*. So the court listens to all the testimony regarding the beginnings of the transaction. Oral testimony is received as to what was said and done. And the court hears testimony as to what occurred thereafter. Usually it is child's play to distinguish between a deed intended to transfer absolute ownership and one that was merely intended to provide a lender with security.

The following circumstances are usually considered:

1. Adequacy of consideration. If *R* conveys land worth $10,000 and receives only $5,000, the indication is that the transaction is a mortgage. Normally land will sell for its full value.

2. Prior negotiations between the parties. When *R* applies to *E* for a loan and the transaction is consummated by *R* giving *E* a deed to the land, this tends to show that the transaction is a mortgage. It is as if *E* had said: "I will loan you the money, but give me a deed as security." Of course, if it appears that *E* rejected the application for a loan, this tends to show that the transaction is a sale. It is as if *E* had said: "I will not loan you any money, but I am willing to buy your land."

3. Subsequent conduct of the parties. If *R* receives money from *E* and gives *E* a deed to *R*'s land, but *R* thereafter remains in possession, paying taxes, insurance premiums, and so on, this tends to show that the transaction is a mortgage, for in a normal land sale the buyer takes possession.

4. Possession. If the transaction is merely a security transaction, almost invariably the borrower retains possession of the land, and his possession gives the whole world notice of the fact that the deed was merely a security deed and that foreclosure must take place.

REFERENCE: Cunningham & Tischler, Disguised Real Estate Security Transactions as Mortgages in Substance, 26 *Rutgers L. Rev.* 1 (1972).

Note, there is a second type of *deed absolute* problem. It is described in § 611.

§ 572. Sale and leaseback—conditional sale. A deed absolute given to secure a debt, which the law treats as a mortgage, must be distinguished from a *conditional sale of land*. In the latter transaction, a landowner sells his land for its full value and the buyer contemporaneously grants the seller an option to repurchase the land, which the seller may or may not exercise, as he pleases. Often the buyer also leases the land back to the seller for a term of years. This type of transaction is valid. Its advantage to the landowner lies in the fact that he gets the full value of the property instead of the smaller amount that he could obtain on a mortgage, and he is under no obligation to repay this amount if he is willing to forego his repurchase of the land. In other words, he is not saddled with a debt, as he would be if he had made a mortgage on his land. The advantage to the buyer is that foreclosure is not necessary if default is made in the rent payments, since the transaction is a sale and lease, not a mortgage.

Use of this device in a modified form is common today. An industrial corporation wants money to use in its business. It sells its plant to an investor, receiving the full cash value. The investor then leases the land back to the industrial corporation. Hence the term *sale and leaseback.* The lease is usually for a term ranging between twenty and thirty years, and the tenant is given an option to renew the lease for an additional period. The rental on the original terms pays back to the buyer an amount equal to the purchase price plus a return much higher than could be obtained on a conventional mortgage loan. The lease is a *net lease,* that is, the lessee is required to pay all real estate taxes, fire insurance, repairs, and so forth, so that all rental paid is "net" to the landlord.

Among the advantages to the lessee of such an arrangement are the following:

1. A tax advantage. In computing its income for income tax purposes, the lessee deducts its rent payments under the lease. Were the transaction a mortgage, the only permitted deductions would be interest and depreciation. Also, if the building is not newly constructed, it may be that the current value and sale price are substantially less than the price paid when the seller-lessee bought the building, and the sale to the investor represents an income tax loss to the seller-lessee.

2. By selling the property for its full value to the lessor, the lessee obtains much more cash money than it could raise on a mortgage, for no mortgagee will loan up to 100 per cent of the value of the property.

3. Existing mortgages, corporate charters, debenture agreements, or other documents binding on the lessee may place restrictions on its right to borrow money. Since a lease is not a loan, the leaseback arrangement provides a method of getting around these restrictions.

4. A mortgage note would appear as a liability on the mortgagor's financial statements. Liability for rent under a lease is a fixed and certain legal liability. Yet under accounting practice, it is not shown as a liability. It appears on the financial statement, if at all, only as a footnote. This facilitates borrowing, sale of stock, and so forth.

The chief disadvantages to the lessee are:

1. If the building goes up in value, the investor, not the lessee will reap the benefit of this increase once the lease expires.

2. The lessee has all the burdens of ownership, for the lease requires the lessee to

pay taxes, insurance, and so on. But the lessee lacks the freedom of action that an owner enjoys. Under the terms of the lease, the lessee cannot sell the leasehold without the consent of the investor. Even if the investor consents, there are many prospective purchasers who are reluctant to buy leaseholds. Moreover, the lessee cannot tear down or remodel buildings as business needs dictate unless the investor consents. Likewise, to erect new buildings would be foolish, for they would belong to the landlord at the end of the lease period.

§ 573. Sale and leaseback—usury problems. Occasionally you will encounter a sale and leaseback that presents a usury problem.

EXAMPLE: *A Corp.* conveys its plant to *X*, investor, who leases the plant back to *A Corp.* for 40 years. The lease contains a provision that on *X's* demand, *A Corp.* will repurchase the property from *X*. The total returns to *X* from rent and the repurchase price would exceed the usury rate. Courts would probably regard this as a disguised mortgage. 24 *U. of Miami L. Rev.* 642; 175 ALR 1384. The repurchase obligation looks exactly like a mortgage obligation.

§ 573a. Vendor's lien reserved by deed. In some states, a seller, in lieu of taking back a mortgage from the buyer, expressly reserves in his deed to the buyer a lien on the land to secure payment of the balance of the purchase price. Such a lien is called a *vendor's lien*. It is really a mortgage.

EXAMPLE: *A*, a landowner, conveyed to *B* by a warranty deed that warranted that title was free from all encumbrances excepting three certain notes executed by *B*, for which a vendor's lien was retained until said notes and the interest thereon should be fully paid. The court held that this clause created a lien on the land. Such a lien is regarded as partaking of the nature of an equitable mortgage. This device is governed by the same rules as a mortgage and must be foreclosed as such. *Crabtree* v. *Davis*, 186 So 734 (Ala. 1939).

Such a lien enjoys priority over subsequent liens and encumbrances and, like a purchase money mortgage, has priority over prior judgments against the purchaser. The grantee under such deed does not become personally liable for the purchase money unless he has signed a promissory note, as in the above example, or otherwise obligated himself personally to pay the debt. And a purchaser from such grantee does not become personally liable to the holder of the vendor's lien unless by his deed he assumes and agrees to pay the unpaid balance of the debt. The debt may be assigned, and the assignee will have the right to foreclose the lien.

§ 573b. Purchase money mortgages. Purchase money mortgages taken back by sellers provide a major form of home financing in periods of tight credit. They also can be useful to retired couples looking for stable earnings.

EXAMPLE: *H* and *W* are ready for retirement. They have purchased a condominium in Florida. They plan to sell their existing home. Amortization payments and inflation have given them a substantial equity in the home. Knowing that the home is solidly built and is in a stable community, *H* and *W* decide to finance the sale themselves by taking back a purchase money mortgage from the homebuyer thereby earning slightly more than is available through thrift institutions.

§ 574. **Application and commitment.** A mortgage transaction usually begins with an application for a loan. The application serves a double purpose: (1) it is a source of information on which the lender will base his decision as to making the loan; and (2) it defines the terms of the loan contract. The application is usually made on the mortgagee's preprinted form and signed by the prospective borrower. After investigating the prospective borrower's financial circumstances and appraising the real estate, the lender may write the applicant a letter stating that the loan application has been accepted. This letter is sometimes referred to as a *commitment*. This will usually result in a contract for the making of a mortgage loan.

Technically, the application is an *offer* by the mortgagor to give a mortgage and note on the terms specified in the application. The commitment is an *acceptance* of the offer, *Burns* v. *Washington Savings,* 171 So2d 322 (Miss. 1965), which, under basic contract law, creates a contract. If the letter of commitment makes any changes in the terms, it is technically a *counter-offer*. There is no contract in this instance unless the applicant agrees to the new terms, which he may do by writing the word "accepted" and his signature on the mortgagee's letter of commitment. To the lawyer this is the typical "offer and acceptance" problem.

Since the application and commitment define the terms on which the loan is to be made and constitute a contract that neither party can change or add to without the other's consent, the application should state the terms in detail. Indeed, a failure to include essential terms, will lead a court to hold that no binding contract came into existence. *Calosso* v. *First National Bank,* 143 So2d 343 (Fla. 1962). All contracts must be complete and certain. The mortgagee will of course want to see to it that the offer and acceptance contain various other clauses which may or may not be essential to the formation of a contract. Included among these other terms is the agreement of the borrower to sign a note and mortgage in a certain specified form; the borrower's agreement to furnish evidence of title and survey at his expense; the borrower's agreement to sign chattel security documents and to sign an assignment of leases and rents; provisions for deducting title and other charges from the proceeds of the loan; provisions that the lender shall have possession of the fire insurance policies and shall have the power to determine the quality and quantity of coverage afforded by those policies.

Commitment fees. Quite commonly, in larger loans, the borrower pays a commitment fee which is refundable only if he performs his part of the bargain.

EXAMPLE: *R* procured a commitment from *E* for a mortgage loan on a shopping center. The commitment was contingent upon *R's* procuring eight leases with major tenants. *R* paid *E* a commitment fee. *R* was able to procure only six leases. *E* could keep the fee. *Boston Road Shopping Center* v. *Teachers Ins. & Annuity Assn.,* 11 NYS2d 831 (1962). *Accord, White Lakes Shopping Center Inc.* v. *Jefferson Standard Life Ins. Co.,* 490 P2d 609 (Kan. 1971).

Damages. For failure to live up to his commitment, the lender is liable for damages. *St. Paul at Chase Corp.* v. *Manufacturer's Life Ins. Co.*, 278 A2d 12 (Md. 1971); *Liben* v. *Nassau S. & L. Assn.*, 337 NY2d 310 (1972); 36 ALR 1408 (1925).

EXAMPLE: *E* commits to give *R* a mortgage loan in the amount of $1,000,000 at 7 percent interest. *E* refuses to perform and *R* gets a similar loan from *E-1* at 8 percent interest. *E* is liable for the difference between 7 percent and 8 percent.

Although it is generally held that specific performance will not be granted for a contract to loan money, an argument can be made for the opposite result. Draper, The Broken Commitment: A Modern View of the Mortgage Lender's Remedy, 59 *Cornell L. Rev.* 418 (1974). In fact, there have been some cases with rather unusual circumstances that have resulted in specific performance being granted against the lender. *Vandeventer* v. *Dale Construction Co.*, 534 P2d 183 (Ore. 1975).

EXAMPLE: *R* gives *E* a mortgage which is a construction loan to build an office building. *E* makes the loan in reliance on *X*'s commitment to make a new mortgage when the building is completed, the funds to be used to pay *E*'s mortgage. When the building is completed, the mortgage market and office building market are dead. Funds are simply unobtainable elsewhere. Specific performance can be used to force X to go through with his commitment.

Flood insurance. Mortgages must not only be concerned with the creditworthiness of the applicant and the value of the security, they must also consider the impact of the Flood Disaster Protection Act. 42 USCS §§ 4001 *et. seq*. The act requires that the lender determine whether the property is in a flood-prone area, notify the purchaser of such hazard and require flood insurance, if it is available.

A problem exists in that flood insurance is not automatically available to all applicants, but rather it is only obtainable in those communities which qualify and participate.

REFERENCES: Deason, Mandatory Federal Flood Insurance and Land Use Control, *49 Fla. B.J.* 302 (1975); Haines, The Flood Insurance Imperative, 3 #4 *ABA Probate and Property* (Winter 1975).

Discrimination in the application process. By enacting the Equal Credit Opportunity Act, 15 USCS §§ 1691 *et. seq.*, Congress has acted to make credit available with fairness, impartiality, and without discrimination on the basis of race, color, religion, national origin, sex, marital status, or age. While marital status inquiries are not absolutely prohibited to the mortgage lender, 12 CFR § 202.4(c)(1), only the terms "married," "unmarried," or "separated" may be used. 12 CFR § 202.4(c)(2). The thought is that other inquiry is not directed toward an applicant's credit worthiness. The creditor cannot discount the income of an applicant or an applicant's spouse solely because it is derived from part-time employment, but the probable continuity of such income may be considered. 12 CFR § 202.5(e). Inquiries into the birth control practices and child-bearing intentions of the applicant are forbidden. 12 CFR § 202.4(h).

Redlining. Both the states and the federal government have reacted to the practice of some lenders whereby applications for loans on property located in certain metropolitan areas have been automatically rejected. Basically, these laws take the form of requiring disclosure or reporting of various types of application and commitment data by census tract or some other defined geographical area. 12 USCS §§ 2801 *et. seq;* Ill. Rev. Stat. 1975 ch. 95, § 201. At least one state, New Jersey, has, however, enacted a law prohibiting redlining and fining those guilty of violations. Aside from the reporting aspects, redlining has been held to constitute discrimination under the Fair Housing Act. *Laufman* v. *Oakley Bldg. & Loan Assn.,* 44 L.W. 2381 (USDC S. Ohio 1976).

REFERENCE: Duncan, Red Lining Practices, Racial Resegregation and Urban Decay: Neighborhood Housing Services as a Viable Alternative, 7 *Urban Lawyer* 510 (1975).

§ 575. **The mortgage note.** After the mortgagee has given his commitment to make the loan, the mortgagor signs a promissory note and mortgage. The mortgage stands as security for payment of the note. *The chief function of the note is to make the mortgagor personally liable for payment of the mortgage debt.* If the mortgagor signs such a note and then decides that he does not want the building, he cannot simply abandon the property and move elsewhere. Wherever he goes he takes his personal liability with him, and if the mortgage is foreclosed, the mortgagee can obtain a personal judgment against him for any deficiency between the foreclosure sale price and the amount of the mortgage debt. Armed with such a judgment, the mortgagee can garnishee the mortgagor's wages or have his other property sold to pay the balance due.

§ 576. **Parties to the mortgage.** The borrower, who corresponds to the grantor in a deed, is known as the *mortgagor.* The lender, who corresponds to the grantee in a deed, is known as the *mortgagee.* It is important that the names of the parties be given accurately and fully in the mortgage. The marital status of the mortgagor, as *bachelor, spinster,* or *widower,* should be recited. The same considerations that require the grantor's spouse to join in his deed require the mortgagor's spouse to join in his mortgage. A mortgage by a minor or an insane person is subject to the same objections that exist in the case of deeds. A mortgage by a corporation must be authorized by proper corporate resolutions, which should show that the money is being borrowed for proper corporate purposes. In general, the requirements relative to the grantor and grantee in a deed are applicable to the mortgagor and mortgagee in a mortgage.

§ 577. **Foreclosure provisions and power of sale.** Provisions are usually included in the mortgage for the foreclosure thereof, and, in states permitting foreclosure by exercise of power of sale, the power of sale is fully set forth in the mortgage.

§ 578. **Waiver of homestead and dower.** In some states, a mortgage on homestead land must include a clause releasing and waiving homestead rights. Again, in some states, a mortgage signed by the spouse of the mortgagor should contain a clause stating that such spouse thereby waives all dower as against the mortgagee.

§ 579. **Execution.** The mortgagor and his spouse should sign the mortgage. Some states require that the word "SEAL" appear after their signatures. A corporation should always affix its corporate seal. In some states witnesses are required. The mortgage should also be acknowledged and delivered to the mortgagee.

§ 580. **Recording.** As a practical matter, a mortgage must be recorded, since an unrecorded mortgage is void as to subsequent purchaser, mortgagees, or, in some states, judgment creditors who are ignorant of the existence of such mortgage. It is important that the mortgage be filed or recorded as soon after its execution as possible.

As a general rule, the priority of successive liens often is determined by priority of recording, the first mortgage recorded being a first lien on the land, the second mortgage recorded being a second lien, and so on. The importance of early recording thus becomes obvious, since foreclosure of a first mortgage will wipe out and extinguish all junior liens, such as second mortgages.

In states that have mortgage taxes, the recorder will want proof that the tax was paid.

§ 581. **Master mortgage.** To save recording expenses, mortgagees are turning to the *master mortgage*. A mortgage lender records his usual mortgage form with none of the blanks filled in. This is the *master mortgage*. Thereafter each mortgage recorded by the mortgage company simply refers to the book and page of the master mortgage for the fine print provisions, enabling the mortgagee to get all the necessary recordable data of each mortgage in a one-page document. Laws permitting this have been enacted in many states.

§ 582. **Debt—in general.** In order for a mortgage to exist there must be a debt for the mortgage to secure. Without the debt there is nothing to secure, and the mortgage has no effect. Ordinarily the debt takes the form of an obligation to pay money such as a promissory note or a bond which may or may not be negotiable. This is not necessarily so, however, and the debt may be in the form of any contractual relation.

The requirement of a debt is not a requirement that there be *personal liability* for the payment of the debt. It is competent for the parties to make any bargain on this subject as they please. They may agree that the mortgagee will look only to the real estate as security for repayment of the loan. *Gagne* v. *Hoban,* 159 NW2d 896 (Minn. 1968). In such case, the mortgagee cannot obtain a personal judgment or deficiency decree against the mortgagor should the mortgaged land prove insufficient to satisfy the mortgage debt.

The mortgage lien is measured by the amount of the mortgage debt. Thus if a mortgage recites a debt of $10,000, but actually only $5000 is loaned, the mortgage stands as security for only $5000. Likewise, the mortgage lien diminishes as the mortgage debt is reduced by payment. Thus if a mortgage of $10,000 is paid down to $5000, the mortgage lien is reduced accordingly, and if the mortgagee thereafter loans the mortgagor additional funds, these additional funds are not secured by the mortgage unless the mortgage contains a clause covering *future advances.*

§ 583. **Debt—priority of lien.** Any discussion of mortgage debt inevitably involves questions of priority of lien. Often there will be two or more liens against the same property.

EXAMPLE: *B* mortgages his property to *A* in 1971 and then mortgages the same property to *C* in 1972. If both mortgages are valid and both are properly recorded, *A's* mortgage is a first lien, and if he is compelled to enforce it by foreclosure, he will extinguish *C's* mortgage, which is a subordinate or inferior lien. Of course, *C* has the right to pay *A's* mortgage to prevent this extinguishment and to foreclose for the amounts due on both mortgages. It is said, in such circumstances, that *A* enjoys priority of lien. *C's* lien is subject to *A's*.

The same situation exists when the liens are of different kinds.

EXAMPLE: *A* acquires a mortgage lien on the property in 1978. *B* acquires a judgment lien on the same property in 1979. *C* acquires a mechanic's lien on the property in 1980. Normally, these liens have priority according to the time they attach to the land. First in time is first in right. There are, however, many exceptions to the rule.

§ 584. **Debt—description of debt.** A mortgage must in some way describe and identify the debt that it is intended to secure. 145 ALR 369. The character and amount of the debt must be defined with reasonable certainty in order to preclude the parties from substituting debts other than those described. *Bowen* v. *Ratcliff,* 39 NE 860 (Ind. 1895). Otherwise, in some states, subsequent mortgagees, purchasers, or judgment creditors will acquire rights superior to those of the mortgage. 2 Merrill on Notice, § 1090 (1952); 5 Tiffany on Real Property, § 1407 (1939).

EXAMPLE: *A* borrows $10,000 from *B* and gives *B* his note therefor. To secure the loan, *A* gives *B* a mortgage, but the mortgage does not recite the amount of the loan. The mortgage is recorded. Thereafter, *X* obtains a judgment against *A*. *X's* judgment is a prior lien, coming in ahead of *B's* mortgage. *Bullock* v. *Battenhousen,* 108 Ill. 28 (Ill. 1883). *See also Flexter* v. *Woomer,* 197 NE2d 161 (Ill. 1964).

The mortgage need not state the maturity date of the debt. 1 *Jones on Mortgages,* 549, 559 (8th ed. 1928). *Contra: Sullivan* v. *Ladden,* 125 A.250 (Conn. 1924). However, it is advisable that it do so. Similarly, the mortgage need not state the interest rate. *Metropolitan Life Ins. Co.* v. *Kobbeman,* 260 Ill. App. 508 (1931).

§ 585. **Debt—future advances—in general—obligatory advances.** A mortgage debt is rarely created at the same instant that the mortgage is signed. Normally the mortgagor will receive his money sometime after the signing and recording of the mortgage. The question that arises is whether the mortgage has priority over junior mortgages, judgments, and other liens that may attach to the land before the money is paid out. The problem usually arises in three situations:

EXAMPLE: An ordinary mortgage loan is applied for. The mortgage is executed and recorded. Payment of the mortgage money to the mortgagor is delayed pending the completion of a title search. A judgment or other lien attaches to the land after the recording of the mortgage. Thereafter the mortgagee's title search is completed, but since the search covers only the date of the recording of the mortgage, the mortgagee is unaware of the judgment. Thereafter the mortgagee pays out the mortgage money to the mortgagor. Discussion follows.

EXAMPLE: An ordinary mortgage loan is made and the mortgage money is properly paid out to the mortgagor. The mortgage contains a provision to the effect that it also secures future advances to the mortgagor not in excess of $2000, or some other sum. This is called an *open-end mortgage*. A year or so after the mortgage has been made, the mortgagor applies to the mortgagee for additional funds and receives an additional loan of $2000. Before he receives his money, a judgment or other lien attaches to the land. The mortgagee pays out the $2000 in ignorance of the existence of the judgment lien. Discussion follows.

EXAMPLE: A construction loan is involved. The mortgagee doles out the mortgage money as the building goes up, and before construction is completed other liens attach to the land. Discussion follows.

Where a mortgagee is obligated, by contract with the mortgagor, to advance funds to be secured by the mortgage, such mortgage will be a valid lien from the time of its recording, as against all subsequent encumbrances, even though the mortgage money is paid to the mortgagor after such subsequent encumbrances have attached to the mortgaged land. This holds true even though the mortgagee is actually aware of the existence of the subsequent encumbrances at the time he pays out the mortgage money. 80 ALR2d 199, 191, 196, 217, 219. Such advances are called obligatory advances. Because of the mortgagee's obligation to pay out the money, the mortgage debt is regarded as being in existence from the very beginning. The obligation is usually created in one of two ways: (1) where the mortgagor has made written application for a mortgage loan and the mortgagee has given his commitment to make the loan, the mortgagee is contractually obligated to go through with the transaction; (2) where a construction loan is involved, the obligation is usually created by a construction loan agreement, which is an agreement entered into between mortgagor and mortgagee when the purpose of the loan is to provide funds for the construction of a building. This agreement authorizes the mortgagee to disburse the mortgage funds as the building goes up and seems to obligate disbursement. *See* Kratovil & Werner, Mortgages for Construction and the Lien Priorities Problem—The "Unobligatory" Advance, 41 *Tenn. L. Rev.* 311 (1974). It also binds the mortgagor to complete the erection of the building and to turn over to the mortgagee for disbursement such money as the mortgagor is furnishing from his own funds toward the erection of the building. The agreement also authorizes the mortgagee to act as the mortgagor's agent in dealing with the contractor and subcontractors. This agreement should dovetail into the construction contract between the mortgagor and his builder, so that the builder will not be clamoring for money at a time when the mortgagee is not yet required to pay out funds.

Let us return to consideration of the application and commitment. It is not always easy for mortgage men to think of these documents as creating a contract for a loan so that the money subsequently advanced is an obligatory advance, and yet a simple illustration will prove that is the case.

EXAMPLE: *A* applies to *ABC Corporation* for a $1,000,000 mortgage loan at 5 percent interest on his hotel building. The corporation gives a commitment to make this loan. Thereafter, *ABC Corporation* refuses to honor its commitment. *A* goes to *XYZ Corporation,* which gives him a loan on the same property at 6 percent interest. Without the slightest doubt, *ABC Corporation* is liable to *A* for the difference between 5 percent and 6 percent interest over the life of the loan. This is so because *ABC Corporation* broke its obligation to loan the funds to *A* at 5 percent.

Of course, in all states expenditures made by the mortgagee to preserve the lien of his mortgage, such as payments made by the mortgagee on delinquent real estate taxes that the mortgagor has failed to pay, are considered obligatory expenses, and the mortgagee has the same lien for such advances as he has for his original debt.

§ 586. **Debt—future advances—optional advances.** Suppose that the mortgage does not absolutely bind the mortgagee to fund the mortgage debt. Advances under such a mortgage are called *optional advances.* Despite the fact that such mortgage is duly recorded, it is by no means certain that it will operate as a lien from the date of its recording as against all other liens attaching after that date. The argument that can be made against the mortgage is that a mortgage is a conveyance to secure a debt and that without a debt there is no mortgage. It must therefore follow that *until* the money has actually been advanced to the mortgagor no legal mortgage exists, for until that time the mortgagor owes no money to the mortgagee, and therefore no debt exists. In the case of obligatory advances, the courts dispose of the argument by saying that since the mortgagee must at all events loan the money, as he has contracted to do, for all practical purposes the debt exists as soon as the obligation to make the loan is created. Since this obligation is normally created, either by application and commitment or by a construction loan agreement, an obligatory advance mortgage is good against the whole world, including subsequent lienors, from the date the mortgage is recorded. As to mortgages where the mortgagee has not entered into a binding contract to advance the funds, the problem is far more complex, as the ensuing discussion of the open-end mortgage reveals.

Note that the same debtor and creditor may have both secured and unsecured relationships.

EXAMPLE: *L* gave *B* a loan secured by a mortgage. This defines the extent of the secured relationship between *L* and *B*. *L* may later extend other credit to *B* that is completely unrelated to the mortgage. Unless the mortgage has an anaconda or dragnet clause the other advance would be unsecured.

§ 587. **Debt—future advances—open-end mortgages.** The open-end mortgage provides that the mortgage secures not only the original note and debt, but also any additional advance that the mortgagee may choose to make to the mortgagor in the future. This means that if in the future, the mortgagor wishes to borrow additional funds for the addition of a room or garage or for some other purpose, he can borrow this money from the mortgagee if the latter sees fit to lend it. The advantages are obvious. The expense of executing a new mortgage is obviated. The mortgagee's security is enhanced by the additions or repairs. Recourse to short-term high-rate consumer financing is eliminated.

Clearly, the open-end mortgage is an optional advance mortgage. That is, the mortgagee is under no legal obligation to loan the additional funds. The problem here is one of intervening liens.

EXAMPLE: A borrows $10,000 from *B* on January 31 and gives *B* a future advance type (open-end) mortgage. The mortgage is duly recorded. On July 1, A borrows $1000 from C and gives him a junior mortgage on the land, which he records. On December 1, *A* comes to *B* and borrows an additional $1000 under the future advance clause of the mortgage. Will this new advance, with the original first mortgcge amount enjoy priority over the junior mortgage of July 1, or will the July 1 mortgage enjoy priority over the new advance so that it is in effect, a third mortgage on the property? In a majority of the states, the additional advance will enjoy priority over the intervening lien, the junior mortgage of July 1, unless *B* has cctual knowledge of the second mortgage when he gave A the advance. In Illinois, Michigan, Ohio, and Pennsylvania, a mortgagee must before making an optional future advance, search the records for intervening liens. Record notice of intervening liens is enough to give the intervening lien priority over the additional advance. 138 ALR 566. In these states title companies make special, inexpensive title searches to cover mortgages who propose making additional advances.

A mortgage secures only the debt described therein. Hence, a mortgage designed to secure optional future advances should draw attention to that fact. The older decisions are somewhat liberal in this regard. Comment, 5 *DePaul L. Rev.* 76, 80 (1955); 81 ALR 631. However, since the open-end mortgage has become popular, the notion that such mortgages should describe such future advances seems to be winning acceptance. At a minimum today, for safety's sake, the mortgage should specify the upper limit of the future advances to be made.

NEW LAWS: A great many states have enacted laws governing open-end mortgages.

EXAMPLE: In Rhode Island an open-end advance that does not exceed $3000 has the same priority as the original mortgage.

It is necessary also, that the future advances fall within the description thereof given in the mortgage.

EXAMPLE: If the mortgage, by its terms, secures future advances made to the mortgagors, an advance made to one of the mortgagors probably is not secured by the mortgage. *Capocasa* v. *First Nat. Bank,* 154 NW2d 271 (Wisc. 1967). Likewise, an advance made to a grantee of the mortgagors might not be secured by the mortgage unless the mortgage so provides. *Walker* v. *Whitemore,* 262 SW 678 (Ark. 1924).

Finally, the documents evidencing the future advance should refer to the mortgage, so that it is evident that such advances were meant to be advances secured by the mortgage.

WARNING: If the mortgage makes no reference to future advances, any later document evidencing future advances must be executed and acknowledged like an original mortgage, recorded, and the title searches brought down to cover recording, for it is, in legal effect, a new mortgage on the property.

HUD MORTGAGES: Additional FHA insurance is available to cover additional advances for improvement or repair of property subject to FHA insured mortgages which contain open-end advance provisions. The advance must, however, be made for improvements or repairs which substantially protect or improve the basic livability or utility of the property, and the additional advances, when added to the unpaid balance of the original principal obligation, cannot exceed the amount of the original principal obligation unless the mortgagor certifies that the advance will be used to finance the construction of additional rooms. 12 USC Sec. 1715p. 24 CFR Sec. 203.44.

NEW LAWS: Some states, Florida, for example, require that a mortgage given to secure future advances so state. Fla. Stat. Ann. § 697.04(1). Other states provide that the mortgage lien shall not exceed at any one time the maximum amount stated in the mortgage. Kan. Stat. Ann. § 9–1101(4). Some states expressly allow revolving credit type future advances clauses if the statute is complied with. Fla. Stat. Ann. § 697.04(1).

EXAMPLE: *M* lends money to *B* under a revolving-credit-future-advance type of mortgage which states that no more than $15,000,000 may be outstanding at any one time. The initial advance is $5,000,000 and interim advances bring the total to the $15,000,000 mark. *B* repays $5,000,000. Under the common law, this payment extinguishes the lien to the extent of $5,000,000. If the lender wanted to advance additional funds he would have to put on a new mortgage and be subject to intervening interest holders to the extent of any subsequent advances. Under this statutory scheme, however, *M* may advance more money, not exceeding $15,000,000 total and rely upon the security and priority of the original mortgage.

§ 588. Debt—anaconda clause. One type of future advance clause is called the anaconda clause.

EXAMPLE: A mortgage from *R* to *E* secures a promissory note of *R* for $10,000 and all other obligations of *R* owned by *E*. Here *E* can buy up *R*'s other obligations, perhaps at ten cents on the dollar, and enforce the mortgage for the face amount of all such debts in addition to the $10,000. 172 ALR 1079. The clause is also called a *dragnet clause*.

The courts are hostile to these mortgages and construe them strictly.

EXAMPLE: *H* and *W* give *E* a mortgage securing a note and all other obligations of *H* and *W* acquired by *E*. *E* bought a note signed by *H* only. The court held that this note was not secured by the mortgage. It was not an obligation of *H* and *W*. 172 ALR 1101.

In order for this type of clause to include other indebtedness, the second indebtedness must have been reasonably within the contemplation of the mortgagor and mortgagee at the time of the mortgage transaction. *Airline Commerce Bank* v. *Commercial Credit Corp.*, 531 SW2d 171 (Tex. 1975).

EXAMPLE: This clause in a normal mortgage transaction will not be allowed to embrace a claim for damages for breach of contract.

§ 589. Participations. The mortgagee may sell a share of his mortgage to a third party. This is called a participation.

EXAMPLE: *R* gives a mortgage to *E* for $100,000. *E*, the *lead*, sells a 50 percent interest in the mortgage to *E-1*, the *participant*. Nothing is recorded as to this participation and no notice is given to *R*. There is a participation agreement between *E* and *E-1*, outlining *E*'s rights and duties. But as to the rest of the world, it is as if *E* remained the full owner of the mortgage.

EXAMPLE: In the foregoing example, *R* and *E* conspire to defraud *E-1*. *E* records a release of the mortgage, and *R* sells the land to *X*, a bona fide purchaser. The mortgage is extinguished. All *E-1* can do is sue *R* and *E*.

REFERENCE: Armstrong, The Developing Law of Participation Agreements, 23 *Bus. Lawyer* 689 (1968).

§ 590. Description of the mortgaged property. An accurate description of the mortgaged land is of great importance. Even greater care must be exercised in this regard than is necessary in the case of deeds, since a purchaser usually goes into possession of the land under his deed and thereby gives all the world notice of his rights, whereas a mortgagee rarely goes into possession and therefore depends entirely on the recording of his mortgage to give subsequent purchasers and mortgagees notice of his rights.

When a mortgage is foreclosed, the mortgagee should be in a position to take over the mortgaged building as a functioning and operating unit. This is something to be considered at the time the mortgage is made. For example, if the building contains personal property necessary for its proper functioning, such as furniture in a furnished apartment building, some arrangement must be made to enable the mortgagee to take over these items in the event the mortgage is foreclosed. To accomplish this, it may be necessary to have the mortgagor sign a financing statement and security agreement under the Uniform Commercial Code on such personal property; for a real estate mortgage, although it covers fixtures, does not cover personal property.

In the *package mortgage* method of financing, the home loan also finances the purchase of equipment such as stoves, refrigerators, dishwashers, or washing machines which are essential to the livability of the property. Following the legal description in the mortgage is a clause containing a general catchall enumeration of the common items and a provision reciting that all such items are fixtures and therefore part of the real estate. The package mortgage attempts to make specific articles fixtures by means of an agreement between the mortgagor and mortgagee, even though in the absence of such agreement, the articles would be chattels. The practical advantages of this course are obvious. Installation of such equipment by the builder makes the house more salable. Moreover, it enables the prospective home buyer to finance the initial purchase of such equipment at a lower interest rate and over a longer term than if the purchase were made separately from a department store. The legal objection to the use of the real estate mortgage to cover these articles has yet to be fully tested in the court. Kratovil, Fixtures and the Real Estate Mortgage, 97 *U. Penn. L. Rev.* 180, 210 (1948); Comment, 6 *Kan. L. Rev.* 66 (1957).

When the article is actually removed from the mortgaged premises and then sold to a bona fide purchaser, it is then to all appearances a chattel, and in some states such a purchaser will acquire good title to the article. If this were not the law, any purchaser of chattels would incur the risk of losing them if it should later develop that they were wrongfully removed from mortgaged land. In other states, the real estate mortgagee is permitted to reclaim such articles, even when he finds them in the possession of an innocent purchaser. And generally a purchaser of such articles who buys them while they are still installed on the mortgaged land will not be protected. *First Mortgage Bond Co.* v. *London,* 244 NW 203 (Mich. 1932); *Dorr* v. *Dudderar,* 88 Ill. 107 (1878). To prevent such articles from passing into the hands of a bona fide purchaser, mortgagees have initiated the practice of pasting a notice directly on the equipment stating that the article is covered by the real estate mortgage. Purchasers of articles so marked would not be protected if they saw the notice, since they would not be bona fide purchasers.

Since it is by no means certain that, even with elaborate fine-print clauses, the real estate mortgage alone will afford the mortgagee protection against the removal of readily removable articles, many mortgagees insist upon a separate security agreement and financing statement under the Uniform Commercial Code. In other words, where chattels form a substantial part of the mortgage security, the mortgagor will give the mortgagee a security agreement, and both will sign a financing statement which will be filed with the appropriate chattel filings under the Uniform Commercial Code.

§ **591. Interest—usury.** The mortgage should state the rate and time of payment of interest, though failure to do so will not invalidate the mortgage.

Most states have laws limiting the rate of interest that may be charged. Charging a rate of interest in excess of that permitted is *usury*. The penalty for usury varies from state to state. Thus, in some states, the entire mortgage is void if usury is present; in others, the lender forfeits all interest; in other states, the lender only forfeits all interest in excess of the highest rate chargeable; and in still other states the mortgagor can sue the mortgagee for some statutory penalty, like double the interest paid.

In a number of states a corporate borrower may validly agree to pay more than the normal permitted interest rate. The problem arises where an individual applies for a loan and the lender, it is later contended, forced him to incorporate for the purpose of agreeing to pay the higher interest rate.

EXAMPLE: A, an individual, applies to *B* for a loan. *B* agrees to give A the loan, but later discovers that the interest rate is higher than the law allows. *B* directs A to form a corporation, and *B* makes the loan to the corporation. The corporation may be allowed to contend that the loan is usurious. *Feller* v. *Architect's Display Bldgs. Inc.*, 148 A2d 634 (N.J. 1959).

EXAMPLE: A applies to *B* for a loan and *B* directs him to form a corporation, which has a capital of $1,000. *B* loans the corporation $100,000, and the loan is guaranteed by A individually. Again the loan is usurious because it is clear that the loan is really being made to A, and the corporation is nothing but a sham. *Walnut Discount* Co. v. *Weiss,* 208 A2d 26 (Pa. 1965).

Where a loan is truly a corporate loan, as where the corporation has ample assets and applies for a corporate loan, the fact that payment of the note is, for additional security, guaranteed by individual shareholders, does not invalidate the loan and the individuals have no right to raise the defense of usury. 63 ALR2d 954.

It can be usurious to charge a borrower interest on the principal amount of the note, if the lender pays out only part of this amount.

EXAMPLE: A signs a note for $100,000, but *B*, the lender, pays him only $90,000 retaining $10,000, as a "commission." *B* charges interest on $100,000. If the charges (interest plus commission) exceed the lawful rate on a loan of $90,000, the loan is usurious. *Smith* v. *Parsons,* 57 NW 311 (Minn. 1893); *Garland* v. *Union Trust* Co., 165 Pac. 197 (Okla. 1917).

Brokers, in negotiating loans of other people's money, may charge the borrower a commission, even though the loan bears the highest rate of interest allowed by law. Such a commission is compensation to the broker for his services in obtaining the loan. But a commission charged *by the lender himself* in addition to the highest rate of interest renders the loan usurious. It is perfectly obvious that such a commission is merely a device employed to disguise a usurious transaction.

Lenders charge *points* because they want higher yields on their money than the stated interest rate in the mortgage.

EXAMPLE: A, a builder, is selling a home to *B*, and XYZ is giving *B* a mortgage of $10,000 for twenty years at 8 percent. *XYZ* demands two "points." This means he will either advance only $10,000 minus 2 percent thereof or *B* will have to pay *XYZ* $200 at closing. In either instance, the lender receives more than the maximum allowed by law.

If interest is charged on the full amount from the beginning, but only part of the loan is disbursed initially, the loan can be usurious.

EXAMPLE: A signs a note for $100,000 on a construction mortgage. *B,* the lender, charges interest on $100,000 from the start, but the loan is paid out only as construction goes forward. The loan is usurious. *Williamson* v. *Clark,* 120 So2d 637 (Fla. 1960).

A bona fide commitment fee, paid by the borrower to induce the lender to keep mortgage money available for a period of time if the borrower should need it, is not interest and has no effect on usury. *Paley* v. *Barton S. & L. Ass'n.,* 196 A2d 682 (N.J. 1964).

Notwithstanding the fact that the mortgage bears the highest rate of interest permitted, the mortgagee may charge the mortgagor with the expenses involved in making the loan, such as cost of title examination or cost of survey.

NEW DIRECTIONS: The entire subject of usury is immensely complicated. A great many statutes have been and are being enacted on this subject. The court decisions are numerous. Kratovil, *Modern Mortgage Law and Practice* (1972), Chapter 14.

§ 592. **Escrows.** An issue that is presently the subject of much litigation, legislation, and writing is the so called *mortgage escrow* or *impound* which lenders establish to insure payment of taxes and insurance. For many years, this device was an effective and virtually unchallenged tool which lenders used to insure that necessary payments were made. Of late, however, consumer groups have taken to the courtroom and statehouse to correct some alleged abuses that may have crept into the use of this form of escrow. The attack has been primarily aimed at attempting to force the lender to limit the size of or pay interest on the impounded amount. The judicial response has been almost universally that the lender does not have to pay interest absent a statute, regulation, or mortgage provision to the contrary. *Sears* v. *First Federal Sav. & L. Assn.,* 275 NE2d 300 (Ill. 1971); *Tierney* v. *Whitestone Savings & Loan Assn.,* 83 Misc.2d 855 (N.Y. 1974). Borrowers then addressed their pleas to legislatures and found that the response was more favorable to the borrowers' situation. Perhaps the most significant factor in the ability of the legislature to respond was the fact that, as opposed to the courts which were called upon to act in the face of a contract binding upon the mortgagor and mortgagee, the legislation enacted takes prospective effect only, operating on transactions entered into after its effective date.

NEW LAWS: The legislatures have responded by enacting various laws relating to such escrow accounts. Some laws require that lenders pay interest on the funds. See Cal. Civ. Code § 2943. Others limit the size of the impound, Neb. Leg. Bill 502, Laws of 1976, or provide that the borrower be allowed the option of pledging an interest bearing savings account in lieu of the monthly escrow payment. Ill. Rev. Stat. 1975 Ch. 95, § 101 *et. seq.* The Real Estate Settlement Procedures Act falls into the category of those laws which limit the size of accounts held by lenders in connection with federally related mortgage loans. 12 U.S.C.S. § 2609.

Some creditors of borrowers have attempted without success to garnishee monies paid into these funds by borrowers. Kratovil, Modern Mortgage Law and Practice, § 225 (1972).

§ 593. **Possession and rents.** The difference in viewpoint between title theory and lien theory states is of greatest importance with respect to the mortgagee's right to the possession and rents of the mortgaged property. To illustrate the significance of this statement, let us list, in chronological order, some important dates in a defaulted mortgage transaction: (1) the date when the mortgage is signed by the mortgagor; (2) the date when the mortgagor first defaults; (3) the date when the mortgagee files his foreclosure suit; (4) the date of the foreclosure sale; and (5) the date when the statutory redemption period expires and the mortgagee receives the deed under which he becomes the owner of the mortgaged property.

Let us first make our broad generalizations and thereafter list the particular points of difference that exist. In general, the title theory states regard the mortgage as retaining some of its early character; that is, they view it as a conveyance of the land, so that immediately on the signing of the mortgage, the mortgagee has the right to take possession of the property and collect the rents thereof. On the other hand, the lien theory states regard the mortgage as merely creating the right to acquire the land through foreclosure of the mortgage so that the mortgagor remains the full owner of the land with the right to possession and rents until the statutory redemption period has expired and the foreclosure deed has issued to the mortgagee. In other words, at its most extreme, this difference in point of view represents to the mortgagee the difference between dates (1) and (5) in the above list so far as the right to possession and rents is concerned. In title states, therefore, rents are an important part of the mortgagee's security. In lien states, this is not so. *Grether* v. *Nick,* 213 NW 304, 215 NW 571 (Wisc. 1927).

Now let us analyze the situation in somewhat greater detail, from the point of view just expressed:

1. In a number of title theory states, Alabama, Maryland, and Tennessee, for example, the mortgagee, immediately upon execution of the mortgage, has the right to take possession and collect the rents of the mortgaged property. *Darling Shop Inc.* v. *Nelson Realty Co.,* 79 So2d 793 (Ala. 1953). The right exists even though the mortgage is silent on this point. There are two exceptions: (1) in recent times laws have been passed in some title states giving the mortgagor the right of possession until default occurs—in effect, these laws convert such states into intermediate states; (2) many mortgage forms used in title states give the mortgagor the right of possession until default.

2. In intermediate theory states, Illinois, New Jersey, North Carolina, and Ohio, for example, the mortgagor has the right of possession until his first default, but after default the mortgagee has the right to take possession.

3. In lien theory states, in the absence of a contrary provision in the mortgage, the mortgagor is entitled to possession and rents at least until the foreclosure sale.

4. In some lien theory states, either by express provision in the mortgage or by a separate assignment of rents signed at the time that the mortgage is signed, the mortgagor may give the mortgagee the right to take possession and collect rents as soon as a default

occurs, and such provisions are valid. *Penn Mutual Life Ins. Co.* v. *Katz,* 297 NW 899 (Neb. 1941); *Kinnison* v. *Guaranty Liquidating Corp.,* 115 P2d 450 (Cal. 1941); *Dick & Reuteman Co.* v. *Jem Realty Co.,* 274 NW 416 (Wisc. 1937). However, some of these lien theory states make special rules as to owner-occupied homes. In New York, for example, a homeowner cannot be compelled to pay rent pending foreclosure. *Holmes* v. *Gravenhorst,* 188 NE 285 (NY 1933).

5. In other lien theory states, the provisions described in number 4 are considered void as against public policy. *Rives* v. *Mincks Hotel Co.,* 30 P2d 911 (Okla. 1934); *Hart* v. *Bingham,* 43 P2d 447 (Okla. 1932). In some states that formerly took this view (for example, Minnesota, Washington, Oregon), statutes have been enacted validating the assignment of rents.

6. In all states, if the mortgagor, after defaulting in his mortgage payments, voluntarily turns over possession to the mortgagee, the mortgagee has the legal right to remain in possession. Notice that in number 5 it is the provision binding the mortgagor to give up possession *at some future time* when default occurs that is held void. The same agreement made *after default* is valid. The mortgagee is then called a *mortgagee in possession.*

7. Whenever a mortgagee takes possession before he has acquired ownership of the property by foreclosure, the rents he collects must be applied in reduction of the mortgage debt. A mortgagee does not become the owner of the property by taking possession. Foreclosure is still necessary.

8. Whenever a mortgagee has the right to possession and fails to exercise that right, allowing the mortgagor to remain in possession and to collect rents, the rents so collected belong to the mortgagor.

9. In many states, there is a statutory period of redemption. No general rule can be laid down as to the right of possession during this period, for each state has its own rule.

§ 594. Practical aspects of the problem. A mortgage lender seeks a regular return on a safe investment and does not wish to assume the responsibilities of management. A lender is most unlikely to make a loan that will require him to go into immediate possession of the land, and this right is, therefore, seldom exercised. On the mortgagor's default, however, it is imperative that prompt action be taken to seize the rents so that they will not be diverted to the mortgagor's own personal use. An eviction suit to enforce the mortgagee's right to possession is often a long, drawn-out affair, especially when the mortgagor is interposing all the legal obstacles available to him. However, if the mortgagee files a foreclosure suit, he might be able to have a receiver appointed, and this is the course usually preferred. Other technical reasons exist for preferring the remedy of receivership.

Courts differ as to the grounds for appointment of a receiver. Some say it is enough that the property be inadequate security for the mortgage debt. Other courts require a showing that the security is inadequate and that the mortgagor is insolvent. Still others appoint a receiver only when the property is in danger of destruction. 26 ALR 33.

§ 595. Rent reductions, lease cancellations, and advance payments of rent. A problem of considerable importance is the extent to which a receiver or a mortgagee entering into possession is bound by rent reductions, prepayments of rents, and lease cancellations effected by the mortgagor for a cash consideration. Such agreements are standard devices by which hard-pressed mortgagors pocket the future earning capacity of the land and deliver to the mortgagee the empty shell of the mortgaged asset. Again, differences exist between title theory and lien theory states. The following are some of the applicable rules:

1. In title and intermediate theory states, when the lease is made subsequent to the mortgage, the mortgagee is not bound by advance rent payments made by the tenant to the mortgagor, and upon appointment of a receiver or the mortgagee's taking possession of the land, the tenant will nevertheless have to pay rent thereafter to such receiver or mortgagee, even though he has already paid his rent in advance to the mortgagor. *Rohrer* v. *Deatherage,* 168 NE 266 (Ill. 1929). This rule follows from the rule that recording of the mortgage gives all the world, including subsequent tenants, notice of the mortgagee's rights, and these rights include the right to take possession on default. This rule is of special importance to a tenant who pays a large sum of money for the privilege of receiving a lease, for example, a tenant in a co-operative apartment, a tenant of commercial space who pays a large "bonus" for receiving his lease, or a tenant who plans to make substantial investments in alterations in reliance on his lease.

2. In title and intermediate theory states, if the lease antedates the mortgage, recording of the mortgage does not give the tenant notice of the mortgagee's rights, for recording of the mortgage gives notice only to those persons who acquire rights in the property after recording of the document. The question therefore arises, if the tenant, acting in good faith and in ignorance of the mortgage, prepays his rent to the mortgagor, and the mortgagor thereafter defaults, is this prepayment binding on the mortgagee, or must the tenant pay his rent again to the mortgagee? Some cases hold for the mortgagee and some for the tenant. *Anno., 1916 D Ann. Cas.* 200; 55 L.R.A. (N.S.) 233; 2 Jones, *Mortgages* 362 (8th ed. 1928). The mortgagee can protect himself at the time the mortgage is signed, by procuring an assignment of all existing leases and giving tenants notice at that time of his rights under such assignment.

3. In many lien theory states, the mortgagee is bound by advance payments of rents made in good faith by the tenant to the mortgagor, and when the mortgagee's receiver takes possession, he will find himself unable to collect any rents from the tenant. *Smith* v. *Cushatt,* 202 NW 548 (Ia. 1925); *Ottman* v. *Cheney,* 234 NW 325 (Wisc. 1931).

4. But even in lien theory states following the rule stated in number 3, if, at the time the mortgage is made, the mortgagee obtains from the mortgagor an assignment of rents and leases and notifies the tenants thereof, the mortgagee will not be bound by any advance payments of rent made by the tenant to the mortgagor. Also, no rent reduction granted by the mortgagor after the tenant has notice of this assignment will be effective. *Franzen* v. *G. R. Kinney Co.,* 259 NW 850 (Wisc. 1935).

5. Where, at the time of making the mortgage, the mortgagor, by a separate instrument assigns an existing lease to the mortgagee, and the lessee is notified of the assignment, the tenant and mortgagor cannot thereafter cancel the lease or reduce the rent so far as the mortgagee is concerned. On the mortgagee's taking possession, or on the appointment of a receiver, the tenant can be held to his lease. *Darling Shop* v. *Nelson Realty Co.,* 79 So2d 739 (Ala. 1954); *Metropolitan Life Ins. Co.* v. *W. T. Grant Co.,* 53 NE2d 255 (Ill. 1944); *Mercantile & Theatres Properties* v. *Stanley Co.,* 30 A2d 1936 (Pa. 1943); *Franzen* v. *G. R. Kinney Co.,* 259 NW 850 (Wisc. 1935). If there is no assignment of rents, and the lease is prior to the mortgage, a cancellation of the lease made by the mortgagor and lessee may be valid. *Metropolitan Life Ins. Co.* v. *W. T. Grant Co.,* 53 NE2d 255 (Ill. 1944).

6. The courts are less likely to be sympathetic toward advance payments of rent

made pursuant to a conspiracy entered into between the mortgagor and the tenant in an effort to deprive the mortgagee of the rents. *Boteler* v. *Leber,* 164 A 572 (N.J. 1933).

7. The courts are also very unsympathetic toward last minute rent reductions granted by the mortgagor to the tenant on the eve of foreclosure. *First Nat. Bank* v. *Gordon,* 4 NE2d 504 (Ill. 1936).

§ 596. Assignment of leases and rents. At the time the mortgage is signed, the mortgagee should require the mortgagor to sign a separate assignment of leases and rents. This document assigns to the mortgagee the mortgagor's interest in all existing leases, all leases to be executed in the future, and all rents falling due after the date of the mortgage, as additional security for payment of the mortgage debt. Lawyers have found that there is magic in the argument that the mortgage creates a lien on the land and that the assignment creates a lien on the rents. *Franzen* v. *G. R. Kinney Co.,* 259 NW 850 (Wisc. 1935); Note. 50 *Harv. L. Rev.* 1322 (1937). All existing tenants are notified of the making of the assignment. The assignment is recorded. *Franzen* v. *G. R. Kinney Co.,* 259 NW 850 (Wisc. 1935); *Fidelity Bankers Life Ins. Co.* v. *Williams,* 506 F2d 1242 (1974); 75 ALR 268. The following rules are applicable:

1. In most lien theory states, an assignment of rents enables the mortgagee to reach the rents accruing prior to foreclosure sale and to treat them as part of the security for his debt. This gives the mortgagee in a lien theory state virtually as favorable a position with regard to rents as the mortgagee has in title and intermediate states. In one or two lien states, an assignment of rents, like the mortgage clause giving the right to take possession on default, is held invalid as being opposed to public policy. *Hart* v. *Bingham,* 43 P2d 477 (Okla. 1935). Also, in a few lien states, an assignment signed contemporaneously with the mortgage is given only limited recognition. In these states, after a default occurs and the assignment has been activated, rents collected by the mortgagee can be applied only to maintain the property or to pay taxes or insurance. They cannot be applied in reduction of the mortgage debt. In general, the lien states in recent times have enacted laws recognizing the assignment of leases and rents. This was not a matter of choice but of meeting competition. Large scale lenders want a valid assignment of rents.

2. Since the assignment does not contemplate that the mortgagee will begin collecting rents, immediately upon the signing of the assignment, but only after a default occurs, the assignment is inoperative until it is activated by some action of the mortgagee. 59 CJS 414, 422; 2 Glenn, Mortgages, 940 (1943).

Rent collected by the mortgagor before the assignment is activated belongs to the mortgagor. *Sullivan* v. *Rosson,* 119 NE 405 (N.Y. 1918). Or they may become the property of a junior mortgagee who exercises greater diligence. If *A* holds a first mortgage and *B* a second mortgage on the same property, and if default occurs and *B* activates his assignment but *A* does not, *B* gets the rents. *Stevens* v. *Blue,* 57 NE2d 451 (Ill. 1944). Even specific language that the assignment will operate automatically on default has been held insufficient to activate the assignment. *Dime Savings Bank* v. *Lubart,* 38 NYS2d 252 (1942).

3. Everywhere, the assignment is properly activated if, after default and pursuant to the assignment, the mortgagor consents to collection of the rents by, and the tenants begin paying rent to, the mortgagee.

4. In title and intermediate theory states, the assignment is activated on default by the mortgagee's serving notice on the tenants to pay rent to the mortgagee. The mort-

gagor's consent is unnecessary. *Grannis-Blair Audit Co.* v. *Maddux,* 69 SW2d 238 (Tenn. 1934). Frequently, however, the mortgagor and mortgagee making conflicting demands upon the tenants and the issue must be resolved by a court which may prefer to appoint a receiver. Lifton, *Real Estate in Trouble: Lender's Remedies Need an Overhaul,* 31 Bus. Lawyer 1927, 1932 (1976). Where the mortgagee is a substantial financial institution, it can usually overcome the tenant's fears about being liable for rent to his landlord, by offering the tenant an indemnity agreement.

5. In some lien theory states, the assignment can be activated in the same manner as in title theory states. *Kinnison* v. *Guaranty Liquidating Corp.,* 115 P2d 450 (Cal. 1941).

6. In other lien theory states, the assignment can be activated only by the mortgagee's filing a foreclosure suit and applying for the appointment of a receiver, *Dick & Reuteman Co.* v. *Jem Realty Co.,* 14 P2d 659 (Kan. 1932); *Hall* v. *Goldsworthy,* 274 NW 416 (Wisc. 1937); *State C. & Hall* v. *Goldsworthy,* 14 P2d 659 (Kan.) or obtaining possession of the property. *Lincoln Crest Realty, Inc.* v. *Standard Apartment Development,* 211 NW2d 501 (Wisc. 1973). Of course, these same steps will serve to activate an assignment in a title or intermediate state.

7. Rents collected by the mortgagee under an activated assignment must be applied to taxes, repairs, insurance, and, in most states, the mortgage debt.

8. Whenever a mortgagee acts under an activated assignment, he does not destroy existing leases, as sometimes occurs when a mortgagee takes possession under his mortgage. An assignment preserves valuable leases.

9. A mortgagee acting under an assignment is accountable to the mortgagor only for rents actually collected.

10. When a mortgagee who holds an assignment of rents sells and assigns his mortgage, he should also assign the assignment of rents to the assignee of the mortgage. *Koury* v. *Sood,* 62 A2d 649 (R.I. 1948).

With respect to the language of the assignment, some suggestions might be pertinent:

1. It should be a document separate from the mortgage. *Harris* v. *Lester,* 54 NYS 864 (1898); *Franzen* v. *G. R. Kinney Co.,* 259 NW 850 (Wisc. 1935); Note, 50 *Harv. L. Rev.* 1322 (1937). *Contra-Kinnison* v. *Guaranty Liquidating Corp.,* 115 P2d 450 (1941). It should assign the mortgagor's interest in all existing leases and the interest of the mortgagor, or his assignee, in leases that may be executed in the future by the mortgagor or his assigneees. Leases of any importance should be specifically set forth in the assignment. The assignment should merely give the mortgagor the privilege of collecting rent until default. Careful draftsmanship is very important. The courts make the distinction between a pledge of the rents as additional security and an absolute assignment effective in operation upon default. *In re Ventura-Louise Properties,* 490 F.2d 1141 (1974).

SUGGESTED CLAUSE: Notwithstanding that this instrument is a present assignment of said rents, it is understood and agreed that the undersigned has permission to collect the same and manage said real estate and improvements the same as if this assignment had not been given, if and so long as only the undersigned shall not be in any default whatever with respect to the payments of principal and/or interest due on said loan, or in the performance of any other obligation to be performed thereunder, but this permission terminates automatically on the occurrence of default or breach of covenant.

It should be recorded.

WARNING: In some states the courts have held, quite erroneously, that such an assignment is not entitled to be recorded. 75 ALR 261. In these states the mortgage should make specific reference to the accompanying assignment of rents and, for greater safety, state that all of the terms thereof are incorporated in the mortgage.

2. The mortgage should refer to the assignment of rents and the assignment of rents to the mortgage, so that the mortgagee can resort to one or the other as convenience dictates, and should permit entry under mortgage as to part of the premises and under assignment as to other parts of the premises.

EXAMPLE: As to one store in the building, a lease junior to the mortgage is so unfavorable that it should be terminated and the tenant ousted. Enter under the mortgage in title and intermediate states.

EXAMPLE: As to another store, a lease junior to the mortgage is very favorable. Enter under the assignment.

3. The right to cancel or alter leases should be included.

4. The assignment should include the right to use and possession of furniture, appliances, and so forth. While such a provision will be helpful, neither a rent assignment nor the appointment of a receiver is a substitute for a security agreement and financing statement under the Uniform Commercial Code. In other words, if there is valuable personal property on the mortgaged premises, for example, a hotel, the mortgagee may not have the legal right to the possession of such personal property unless he has legal chattel security. Note, 44 *Yale L.J.* 701 (1935).

5. The assignment should include the right to operate the business and to take possession of books and records, stationery, promotional material and so forth.

6. The assignment should confer the right to apply rents to the payments on furniture bought on credit, to insurance premiums on personal property, and so forth.

7. The assignee should be given the right to apply rents to the mortgage debt. Otherwise some states limit application of rents collected to taxes and maintenance. *Western Loan & Bldg. Co. v. Mifflin,* 297 Pac. 743 (Wash. 1931).

8. The document should provide that the assignee shall not be accountable for more monies than he actually receives from the mortgaged premises, nor shall he be liable for failure to collect rents.

9. The document should forbid any cancellation or modification of leases by the landowner and should also forbid any prepayment of rent except the normal prepayment of monthly rent on the first of the month.

10. Authority should be given the assignee to sign the name of the mortgagor on all papers and documents in connection with the operation and management of the premises.

11. The assignment should provide that any assignee of the assignment shall have all the powers of the original assignee.

12. It should contain a recital that (a) all rents due to date have been collected and no concessions granted and that (b) no rents have been collected in advance.

13. It should provide that the assignee may execute new leases, including leases that extend beyond the redemption period.

14. Compliance with the U.C.C. filing requirements is not necessary. *In re Bristol Associates Inc.,* 505 F.2d 1056 (1974).

Of course neither an assignment of rents nor any other device can make a good lease out of a bad one.

EXAMPLE: A shopping-center lease to a department store provides that if 5 percent or more of the parking lot is condemned, the tenant may terminate the lease. This is a key lease, providing revenue for retirement of the mortgage. It must be amended because if 5 percent or more of the parking lot is condemned, for example, for a street widening, and the tenant terminates the lease, the mortgage will go into default.

If the lease provides for a security deposit by the tenants with the landlord, an assignment of leases and rents standing alone gives the mortgagee no right to the security deposit. *Anuzis* v. *Gotowtt,* 248 Ill.App. 536 (1938); *Keusch* v. *Morrison,* 269 NYS 169 (1934), 52 CJS 473. Specific language should be included in the assignment transferring all rights in deposits.

§ 597. Active assignment of leases and rents. In recent times mortgage lenders have turned to a device that has certain advantages where a building is to be constructed with mortgage funds for a high-credit tenant. As soon as the lease is made, the landlord assigns his interest in the lease and all rents thereunder to the mortgage lender. The assignment calls for the mortgage lender to begin collecting rents *immediately* on completion of the building. The lease refers to the assignment, and it also is recorded, thus making certain that the mortgagee's rights are treated as recorded rights, good against the whole world. The lease is a "net" lease under which all taxes, insurance premiums, and so forth are borne by the lessee, and no burdens or payments are borne by the lessor or the mortgagee. The rent payments exactly equal the mortgage payments. A mortgage accompanies the transaction, but the main security is the assignment. The loan is for the full cost of construction of the building. With a high-credit tenant like Sears or Woolworth, a lender can lend with complete security on a transaction of this sort. The assignment is good against a subsequent bankruptcy of the lessor. It also prevails over subsequent federal liens, subsequent creditors of the mortgagor, subsequent attempts of the mortgagor to cancel the lease or obtain prepayment of the rent. In short virtually nothing can occur that will prevent full collection by the lender.

§ 598. Acceleration. The mortgage and mortgage note usually provide that in case of any default the entire principal sum shall become immediately due and payable. This clause is known as the *acceleration clause.* If it is not present, the mortgagee must file separate foreclosure suits as each installment of the mortgage debt falls due and is defaulted. Manifestly, the acceleration clause is one of the most important terms of the mortgage.

There are two kinds of acceleration clauses, automatic and optional. The theory of the automatic clause is that the happening of the event *ipso facto,* advances the maturity of the debt. The optional clause, as its name implies, merely gives rise to the ability of the lender to call the debt due. The latter form is preferable as it obviates those problems caused by accidental or minor defaults while it gives the lender the ability to protect its interest.

While we usually think of acceleration in terms of payment type defaults, mortgages usually are so drafted as to allow acceleration for nonmoney type defaults, and courts have allowed a mortgage to accelerate because of a mortgagor's failure to keep a building in repair, 69 ALR3d 773, or failure to keep insurance in force. 69 ALR3d 774.

The operation of the acceleration clause upon the borrower's default may bring about a harsh result. Some courts, even when confronted with minor deviations caused by the borrower's mistake or inadvertence, find themselves powerless to avoid the strict application of the mortgage language. Other courts, finding themselves not so hamstrung, have gotten around the language either by holding its operation to be unconscionable in the given instance or by deeming some act of the mortgagee to have negated the impact of the language. Rosenthal, The Role of Courts of Equity in Preventing Acceleration Predicated upon a Mortgagor's Inadvertent Default, 22 *Syr. L. Rev.* 897 (1971).

EXAMPLE: Where an acceleration is declared only because of the mortgagor's failure to pay real estate taxes, the courts will allow the mortgagor to cure this default before foreclosure is filed. *Kaminski* v. *Longon Pub Inc.,* 301 A2d 769 (N.J. 1973); 31 ALR 731.

EXAMPLE: Acceptance of past-due interest payments may operate as a waiver of the mortgagor's right to accelerate upon a prior default. 97 ALR2d 997. This result is especially a reality in view of today's stress upon not treating the mortgagor unconscionably.

It is clear that consumerist, proborrower judicial attitudes have no use for the older decisions.

NEW DIRECTIONS: Courts have begun to set accelerations aside on the ground of unconscionability. This is a new ball game. *Federal Home Loan Corp.* v. *Taylor,* 318 So2d 203 (Fla. 1976); *Miller* v. *Pac. First Fed. S. & L. Assn.,* 545 P2d 546 (Wash. 1976).

In other instances courts have refused to follow the letter of the acceleration clause.

EXAMPLE: A mortgage and note provided that in case of default the mortgagee could declare an acceleration "without notice to the mortgagor." The court set aside an acceleration declared without notice to the mortgagor. *White* v. *Turbidy,* 183 SE2d 363 (Ga. 1971). This is contrary to earlier decisions on this point. There is, however, a strong trend either by statute or case law to require such a notice. In effect, this gives the mortgagor an opportunity to cure defaults. A mortgagor must be given notice of an intended acceleration and a reasonable time to cure defaults. *Haase* v. *Blank,* 187 NW 669 (Wisc. 1922). Some states allow the foreclosure suit to stand as notice of the mortgagee's election to accelerate, *Home Federal Savings & Loan Assn.* v. *LaSalle National Bank,* 264 NE2d 704 (Ill. 1970), but better practice is to give formal notice, and such action is mandatory when foreclosure is by power of sale. *Crow* v. *Heath,* 516 SW2d 225 (Tex. 1974). *Contra, S & G Investment Inc.* v. *Home Federal Savings & Loan Assn.,* 505 F2d 370 (D.C. Cir. 1974).

EXAMPLE: A mortgagee had been in the habit of accepting tardy payments. The court held that he could not accelerate without giving the mortgagor a reasonable opportunity to pay. *Stinemeyer* v. *Wesco Farms, Inc.*, 487 P2d 65 (Ore. 1971).

EXAMPLE: Conscionable conduct is a prerequisite to the lender's ability to utilize the accelercition clause and courts are increasingly favorable to the borrower's point of view in making this crucial determination. *See FHLMC* v. *Taylor*, 318 So2d 203 (Fla. 1975).

NEW LAWS: Legislatures have passed laws which, within defined time limits, give the borrower the right to cure defaults by paying the sums necessary to make the mortgagee whole. See Ill. Rev. Stat. 1975, Ch 95 § 57; Col. Rev. Stat. Ann. § 38–39–118 discussed in Comment, 52 *Den. L. J.* 637 (1975). This right of the borrower to reinstate the mortgage will be found in the FNMA mortgage form.

§ 599. Acceleration upon the conveyance of mortgage land. A question which frequently arises relates to the validity of a clause in the mortgage (*due on sale clause*) permitting the mortgagee to declare an acceleration of the mortgage debt in the event of a sale of the property by the mortgagor where the buyer does not pay off the old mortgage. Typically, the mortgage calls for interest at a rate lower than the going rate at the time of conveyance. The mortgagee's ability to declare an acceleration forces a purchaser either to seek alternate financing or reach an agreement with the mortgagee on a higher interest rate in consideration for the mortgagee's agreement not to accelerate. In either event the mortgagee is able to increase the level of return on its portfolio of outstanding mortgages. More directly, other lenders use a clause which permits the increase of the rate of interest, instead of the acceleration of the maturity of the debt, upon the transfer of the property. This type of clause is subject to less criticism as it does not restrain the actual transfer of the property. *Miller* v. *Pacific First Federal Savings & Loan Assn.*, 545 P2d 546 (Wash. 1976).

Some courts almost automatically uphold the validity of the *due on sale* clause. *Gunther* v. *White*, 489 SW2d 529 (Tenn. 1973). Others find it to be a reasonable restraint upon sale protecting the security interest of the lender. *Baker* v. *Loves Park Savings and Loan Assn.*, 333 NE2d 1 (Ill. 1975). These courts allow the reasonable restriction upon the freedom to deal freely with the land and recognize the need of the lender to rely upon the personal integrity and credit worthiness of the borrower and not the vendee, whose personal and financial qualities are unknown to the lender.

On the other hand, there is authority for the proposition that the use of the clause will be found to be invalid where it is exercised in an unconscionable manner.

EXAMPLE: Courts may find the use of the clause to be unconscionable when it is used only to lever an excessively higher interest rate from the purchaser, was not revealed to the mortgagor, or where the clause is used solely to obtain an assumption fee from the buyer. Note, 27 *Stanf. L. Rev.*, 1109 (1975). But see *Crocket* v. *First Federal Savings and Loan Assn.*, 224 SE2d 580 (N.C. 1976).

The strong tendency of the courts in this area of the law seems to require that the lender show that the use of the clause is based upon reasonable grounds—*Baltimore Life Ins. Co.* v. *Harn,* 486 P2d 190 (Ariz. 1970); *Malouff* v. *Midland Federal Savings & Loan Assn.,* 509 P2d 1240 (Colo. 1973)—and indeed, where the mortgagee fails to show that the action triggering the clause will endanger the mortgage security, the court will set aside the acceleration. *Sanders* v. *Hicks,* 317 So2d 61 (Miss. 1975); *Tucker* v. *Pulaski Federal Savings and Loan Assn.,* 481 SW2d 725 (Ark. 1972).

EXAMPLE: The lender must show that the clause is invoked to preserve the security from waste or depreciation, or that there is a greater chance of default by the vendee rather than the mortgagor. The lender's interest in keeping its portfolio returning current interest rates will not suffice, *Tucker* v. *Lassen Savings and Loan Assn.,* 526 P2d 1169 (Cal. 1974). *Contra, Malouff* v. *Midland Fed. S. & L. Assn.,* 509 P2d 1240 (Colo. 1973).

The issue arises as to what action by the mortgagor will give rise to the acceleration. Initially, the examination must be made of the language contained in the mortgage. Once it is determined what events are specifically enumerated as giving rise to acceleration, the application of the language may be quite simple.

EXAMPLE: A clause which prohibited further "encumbrances," is trigged by suffering a junior mortgage to be placed against the land. *La Sala* v. *American Savings and Loan Assn.,* 489 P2d 1113 (Cal. 1971).

The problem of construing the language of the mortgage to determine its applicability to the event may not be so obvious.

EXAMPLE: The due on sale clause allowed acceleration if the mortgagor "sells, conveys or alienates" the mortgaged land. The mortgagor entered into an installment sales contract which was held to be sufficient to trigger the operation of the clause. *Tucker* v. *Lassen Savings and Loan Assn.,* 526 P2d 1169 (Cal. 1974). (Clause operates upon the execution of installment contract but justification for its use must be demonstrated.) Obviously, many questions remain to be answered in this regard. It is evident that the earliest "due on sale" clauses were poorly drafted. Now mortgagees have learned by experience to be explict about installment sales, junior mortgages, and so forth, as triggering the clause.

NEW LAWS: This area of the law includes not only judicial developments but also legislative developments. Counsel must be constantly aware of this. Colorado prohibits acceleration on account of transfer unless the lender reasonably determines that the buyer is financially unable to handle the debt. Col. Rev. Stat. Ann., Sec. 38–30–165. Virginia prohibits prepayment penalties where the prepayment results from the enforcement of the due on sale clause which must appear in conspicuous type. Va. Stats. (1975) Ch. 6.1-23 and 6.1-24. See also, Cal. Civ. Code Sec. 2924.6.

DRAFTING TIP: It would not seem prudent today to draft a clause which expressly prohibited the sale, conveycnce, lease, and so forth of the mortgage property. American courts dislike restraints on the sale of land. More properly the clause should be drafted to provide for optional acceleration upon the happening of specified events which would trigger the operation of the clause. The draftsman must, in light of the variations of local conveyancing practice, consider and specify which occurrences would trigger the operation of the acceleration clause including, for example, an installment contract. This question should not be left for the courts to decide. If all that is desired is the ability to increase the interest rate to current levels upon a conveyance, the escalator clause should be so written. See Kratovil, Modern Mortgage Law and Practice, Sec. 142 (1972).

REFERENCE: Comment, 20 *S.D. L. Rev.* 329 (1975); 69 ALR3d 713.

FEDERAL MORTGAGES: A federal savings and loan association may not exercise a due on sale clause upon: (1) the creation of any lien or other encumbrances inferior to the association's mortgage; (2) creation of a purchase money security interest for household appliances; (3) transfer by devise, descent, or by operation of law upon the death of a joint tenant; or (4) grant of a leasehold interest of three years or less not containing an option to purchase.

§ 600. Deed of mortgaged premises. Generally when mortgaged land is sold, the mortgage is paid and released during the process of sale for the reason that the existing mortgage usually does not meet the financing requirements of the buyer. For example, if land is sold for $15,000 and there is an existing mortgage of $13,000, which has been paid down to $6,000, the buyer will want a new mortgage of more than $6,000. Thus, it becomes necessary to retire the old mortgage in the process of closing the sale. However, it is perfectly possible to sell mortgaged land without providing for retirement of the old mortgage. For example, where *A* owns land worth $15,000 on which there is a mortgage securing a debt of $5,000, the arrangement between seller and buyer can be that there will be a payment to the seller of the sale price ($15,000) less the amount of the mortgage debt ($5,000), in this case, $10,000. Obviously, the understanding here is that the buyer will pay the balance of the mortgage debt. In this situation, where the buyer is to pay the mortgage debt when and as it matures, the deed from the seller to buyer may take one of the following forms:

1. The deed may provide that it is subject to the mortgage, which the purchaser assumes and agrees to pay. This is called an assumption clause.
2. The deed may merely recite that the property is subject to the mortgage.
3. The deed may be a quitclaim deed with no subject clause.

The following rules apply:

1. When the deed of the mortgaged premises recites that the grantee *assumes and agrees to pay* the mortgage or *assumes* the mortgage, it imposes on the grantee personal liability for the payment of the mortgage debt. Osborne, Handbook on the Law of Mortgages, §§ 253 *et. seq.* (2nd ed. 1972). The mortgagee when he forecloses may obtain a deficiency judgment or decree against such grantee when the sale price is less than the amount of the debt. In this way the mortgagee may obtain a personal judgment against such grantee for the difference between the amount of the foreclosure sale and the amount of the mortgage debt.

2. Where the deed merely recites that the land is taken "subject to" the mortgage, the grantee is usually not personally liable for the payment of the mortgage debt. *Pearce v. Desper*, 144 NE2d 617 (Ill. 1957).

3. Where the mortgagor enters into a contract to sell merely his equity over and above the mortgage and thereafter gives the buyer a quitclaim deed, the buyer does not become personally liable to the mortgagee.

§ 601. Assignment of mortgage. Often a mortgagee wishes to sell his mortgage. In fact, many mortgages are originated for prearranged purchasers. The manner in which the transfer may be accomplished depends upon whether the mortgage in question is a deed of trust or regular mortgage. A deed of trust is usually given to secure a negotiable note which passes from hand to hand, very much as money. Such a note may be payable to the bearer. In that case, merely handing the note to the purchaser will be sufficient to transfer title thereto. Endorsement is unnecessary. If the note is payable to the order of a named person, that person must endorse the note over to the purchaser. In the case of a deed of trust securing negotiable notes, a sale of the mortgage is affected by properly transferring the notes by delivery or endorsement, depending on the character of the note.

In the case of a regular mortgage, it is necessary to execute an assignment, which is a brief form reciting that the mortgagee, the assignor, transfers and assigns the mortgage and mortgage note to the purchaser thereof, the assignee. The mortgage is identified by a recital of the names of the parties thereto, its date, the recording date, the book and page where the mortgage is recorded, and so on. The assignment should be signed by the mortgagee, acknowledged, delivered to the assignee, and recorded. The mortgage note, too, should be endorsed or delivered to the assignee along with the original mortgage.

The mortgage cannot be assigned except in connection with a sale of the mortgage debt. The reason for this is that the mortgage is incidental to and exists only for the purpose of securing payment of the debt. A person who does not own the mortgage debt can have no reason for obtaining the mortgage and any attempt to assign the mortgage without a transfer of the debt is a nullity. *Commercial Products Corp.* v. *Briegel,* 242 NE2d 317 (Ill. 1968). The assignee of the mortgage must insist on receiving the mortgage note, since if the mortgagee has already transferred the mortgage note to someone else, he can no longer make a valid assignment of the mortgage.

On the other hand, whatever is sufficient to transfer the mortgage debt will transfer a mortgage given to secure it. This is because the debt secured by the mortgage is the principal thing and the mortgage is a mere security for its payment. Thus, if a regular mortgage secures a note, its transfer without an assignment of the mortgage will give the transferee the right to foreclose the mortgage. But as a practical matter, for the assignee's protection, it is necessary to obtain an assignment of the mortgage. The reason for this is that in the case of a deed of trust securing negotiable notes, everyone is supposed to know that it is likely that the notes will be sold. However, in the case of a regular mortgage securing a note payable to the mortgagee, unless an assignment of the mortgage is filed in the recorder's office, subsequent purchasers or mortgagees of the mortgaged premises are entitled to assume that the mortgagee continues to hold the mortgage note.

EXAMPLE: A executed a regular mortgage to *B* to secure a note payable to *B's* order. *B* endorsed the note to *C*, but no assignment of the mortgage was recorded. Thereafter, *A* sold the mortgaged land to *B*, and *B* entered a satisfaction of the mortgage on the public records. *B* then mortgaged the land to *D*. It was held that *D's* mortgage was a first mortgage on the land, since when *D* took his mortgage on the land, the earlier mortgage appeared from the public records to have been released by the apparent owner thereof. *Bowling* v. *Cook*, 39 Ia. 200.

When the mortgage secures a nonnegotiable note, a purchaser of the mortgage takes it subject to all defenses to which it was liable in the hands of the original mortgagee. *Holly Hill Acres Ltd.* v. *Charter Bank*, 314 So2d 209 (Fla. 1975). This means that if the original mortgagee has been guilty of fraud or some other conduct that would make it impossible for him to foreclose the mortgage, any person to whom he sells the mortgage will also be unable to foreclose.

EXAMPLE: A mortgages his land to *B* to secure a nonnegotiable note for $5000, but *B* never pays out the money to *A*. *B* sells the mortgage to *C*. *C* will be unable to foreclose the mortgage.

Shortly before the Civil War, in an effort to give the purchaser of a mortgage better protection than he had enjoyed in the past, American mortgage bankers began the experiment of having the mortgage secure a negotiable note. The experiment proved highly successful. In all states except Illinois, Minnesota, and Ohio, it is now the rule that *a holder in due course* of a negotiable note secured by a mortgage, that is, one who buys the note and mortgage in good faith before the debt is overdue and without knowledge of any infirmities, takes the mortgage as well as the note, free from defenses that would have been available to the mortgagor against the original mortgagee. The theory is that negotiable notes, like money, should pass freely from hand to hand, without the necessity of any inquiry by purchasers thereof as to the possible invalidity of the paper. And since the mortgage is a mere security for the note, it should enjoy the same protection that the law accords to the note.

EXAMPLE: A gave *B* a mortgage securing a negotiable note for $50,000, but never received any money from *B*. *B* sold the note and mortgage to *C* before the due date of the note. *C* can foreclose the mortgage even though *A* never received the mortgage money. As an innocent purchaser of a negotiable note, *C* is protected against any defenses that exist between *A* and *B*.

A purchaser of a mortgage can also be protected against unknown infirmities existing as between the mortgagor and the original mortgagee by insisting that he be furnished a statement signed by the mortgagor stating that he has no defenses to the enforcement of the mortgage. This document is variously called a *waiver of defenses, estoppel certificate, no set-off certificate,* or *declaration of no defenses*. Under standard mortgage practice, it is addressed to "all whom it may concern" and is signed by the mortgagor at the time the mortgage is signed.

The practical effect of a waiver of defenses is to give the assignee a legally enforceable mortgage even though the mortgage does not secure a negotiable note and the mortgagee could not have successfully foreclosed. For example, if the mortgagee had paid out no money or had received payment in full, he could not foreclose. But an assignee who receives a waiver of defenses can foreclose, since he received the mortgagor's written assurance that the mortgage is valid and enforceable. 59 CJS 531; 110 ALR 457.

EXAMPLE: A gave *B* a mortgage securing a note for $50,000, but never received any money from *B*. *B* sold the note and mortgage to C before the due date of the note. *B* also delivered to C a waiver of defenses signed by A. C can foreclose the mortgage even though *A* never received the mortgage money. As an innocent purchaser relying on a waiver of defenses, C is protected against any defenses that exist between *A* and *B*.

Before purchasing a mortgage, one should always check the public records for any prior recorded assignment of the mortgage, since in many states, where there are two or more assignments of the mortgage by the mortgagee, the first recorded assignment prevails.

The assignee should also obtain the mortgagee's evidence of title, assignment of chattel security agreements, if any, and other such papers.

The assignee of a mortgage may foreclose for the full amount due on the mortgage even though he purchased at a discount. 2 Jones, Mortgages § 997 (1928).

§ **602. Notice of assignment.** The purchaser of a note secured by either a regular mortgage or deed of trust should always give personal notice to the mortgagor that he has purchased such note. If he fails to do so, and the mortgagor afterward in good faith makes a payment to the original mortgagee, this payment will reduce the mortgage debt accordingly. This rule is generally followed where the mortgage note or bond is nonnegotiable.

Except in Illinois and Minnesota, it is the rule that the purchaser of a negotiable note need not notify the mortgagor of his purchase, and if the mortgagor continues to make payments to the original mortgagee, he cannot claim that the mortgage debt has been reduced thereby. This places the burden on the mortgagor of demanding production of the mortgage note and endorsement of each payment thereon.

In Illinois and Minnesota, even where the mortgage secures a negotiable note, the mortgagor may continue to make payments to the original lender until he receives notice of the assignment. *Napieralski* v. *Simon,* 64 NE 1042 (Ill. 1902). The Illinois-Minnesota rule is based on the inconvenience to the mortgagor of requiring production of the mortgage paper each time a payment is made on the mortgage debt.

Whenever notice of assignment is necessary, the notice should be given personally to the mortgagor. Merely recording an assignment of the mortgage ordinarily will not suffice. The mortgagor should not be subject to the burden of making constant searches of the records to see if the mortgage has been assigned, especially since it requires little effort for the assignee to serve a personal notice on the mortgagor. 89 ALR 196. However, any purchaser of the property from the mortgagor is usually required to take notice of such a recorded assignment. *Erickson* v. *Kendall,* 191 P 842 (Wash. 1920).

§ **603. Payment.** The mortgagor, to release himself from personal liability on his note, must see that he pays the money to the holder of the note. This is also true of any purchaser of the mortgaged premises. He is bound at his peril to pay the debt to the one entitled to receive payment. Upon paying the mortgage note, the party should demand that the canceled note be delivered to him. This prevents any further transfer or negotiation of the note and is of particular importance where payment is made prior to the maturity of the note.

Payment also has the effect of destroying the mortgage lien to the extent of such payment. When the mortgage is paid in full, the lien is ipso facto extinguished. *American National Insurance Co.* v. *Murray,* 383 F2d 81 (5 Cir. 1967). However, it is customary to record a release, satisfaction or discharge of the mortgage in order to clear the public records in the recorder's office.

§ **604. Payment to agent.** A mortgagor, before making payment to an agent of the mortgagee, should ascertain the agent's authority by inquiring of the mortgagee or by requiring the agent to produce a power of attorney from the mortgagee. *Coxe* v. *Kriebel,* 185 A 770 (Pa. 1936).

§ **605. Prepayment of mortgage debt.** In the absence of an agreement to the contrary, the mortgagee has a contractual right to have his money earning the stipulated interest for the agreed period. *Dugan* v. *Grzybowski,* 332 A2d 97 (Conn. 1973). The mortgagor has no right to insist upon making payment before maturity, even by offering to pay the principal and all interest to the maturity date. *Peter Fuller Enterprises Inc.* v. *Manchester Sav. Bank,* 152 A2d 179 (N.H. 1959). Accordingly, it is to the mortgagor's advantage to provide in the mortgage and the mortgage note that the debt is payable *on or before* the due date, *Fortson* v. *Burns,* 479 SW2d 722 (Tex. 1972), or that the debt is payable in monthly payments of a stated sum *or more,* or payments are to *not less than* a given amount. *Peters* v. *Fenner,* 199 NW2d 795 (Minn. 1972). Also, a specific clause may be inserted conferring upon the mortgagor the privilege of prepaying the mortgage debt. This is known as a *prepayment privilege.* In corporate trust deeds securing issues of bonds, the comparable provision is that providing for *redemption* of bonds prior to their stated maturity dates. Such provisions enable the mortgagor to refinance when money is cheaper or to retire the mortgage where he has entered into a contract of sale that requests him to deliver title free and clear of any mortgage.

Occasionally a mortgagor whose mortgage does not have a prepayment clause, defaults in his payments hoping to force the mortgagee to accelerate. Thereupon, he reasons, he can pay off the mortgage. The trouble is, it will not work. The mortgage usually has a clause in it stating that if the mortgagor defaults, the mortgage may foreclose as to the defaulted payments only, subject to the continuing lien of the mortgage as to the remainder of the debt. Thus, all the mortgagor succeeds in doing is to incur attorney's fees and foreclosure costs.

Where a mortgagor takes advantage of a mortgage provision which allows prepayments on any monthly payment date and suddenly becomes pinched for ready cash, he may contend that he has the right to skip payments until the prepaid amount is exhausted. This contention will not prevail. In effect the prepayments are applied against the last payments falling due. *Smith* v. *Renz,* 265 P2d 160 (Cal. 1954). Some recent cases hold that where the mortgagor has been making prepayments, he will not be in default until these prepayments have been exhausted by application to current payments. *Bradford* v. *Thompson,* 470 SW2d 633 (Tex. 1971).

NEW LAWS: Various forms of limitations on prepayment penalties have found their way into the fabric of mortgage law. In some states prepayment penalties may only be exacted during the initial years of the loan, Cal. Civ. Code. § 2954.9, or if the interest exceeds a certain rate, prepayment penalties are absolutely forbidden. Ill. Rev. Stat. 1975 Ch. 74 § 4.

FEDERAL MORTGAGES: HUD mortgages are usually required to carry a provision which permits the mortgagor to prepay and the imposition of a prepayment penalty is prohibited. *See e.g.* 24 CFR §§ 203.22(b) and 234.37(b). FHLBB regulations provide that borrowers may prepay their home mortgage loans without a penalty unless there is an express penalty provision in the loan contract. Even when the penalty provision is expressed, it cannot exceed six months advance interest. 12 CFR § 545.6–12(b).

Other typical approaches to the prepayment problem include:

1. Mortgage provisions that set out a sliding scale with either no prepayment allowed or a larger penalty imposed on prepayment during the early years of the mortgage and a decreasingly burdensome penalty as the mortgage matures.
2. The giving of a notice of intention to prepay prior to prepayment.
3. The allowance by some mortgagees of prepayment without penalty upon the sale of a house where the buyer finances his purchase through the same mortgagee, or where the mortgagor finances his new home through the same mortgagee.

§ 606. Limitations. In all states, a promissory note ceases to be enforceable after a certain time if no payments are made thereon. Such a note is said to be barred by limitations. The period varies from state to state. In most states, the fact that the mortgage note is barred by limitations only prevents the obtaining of a personal judgment on the note and does not prevent foreclosure of the mortgage. But in other states, the mortgage is automatically barred whenever the mortgage note is barred.

In many states, if a period of twenty years elapses after the maturity date of the mortgage note, the mortgage is presumed to be paid. The mortgagee, however, may overthrow this presumption by proving that the mortgage has not been paid, but has been kept alive by partial payments of principal or interest thereon. Since this rule makes it dangerous to disregard even an old recorded mortgage, some states go further and provide by law that after a stated period of time, the mortgage becomes void. The period varies from state to state. In Michigan it is thirty years; in Kentucky, fifteen years.

§ 607. **Extension agreements.** Where the mortgagor and mortgagee agree to extend the maturity date of the mortgage note, the priority of the mortgage over those who took their interest between the recordation of the mortgage and the execution of the extension agreement remains undisturbed. The same is true when the earlier mortgage or note is replaced by another bearing a later maturity date. A different result follows, however, where in addition to merely extending the maturity date, the extension works a prejudice against the interests of the intervening interest holders.

EXAMPLE: As a result of an economic downturn, mortgagor's business activity and profits are sharply reduced. To cope with this problem, mortgagor and mortgagee agree to alter the payoff schedule on the mortgage covering mortgagor's plant. It is agreed that principal payments would be deferred for eighteen months, mortgagee only being required to pay interest for that period. The ultimate maturity date is thereby extended eighteen months. Priority over junior mortgagees remains the same. This is a valid extension.

EXAMPLE: Mortgagor and mortgagee agree to extend the maturity date and increase the interest rate. This agreement results in a split priority for the mortgage over junior lienors. To the extent of the unpaid principal and original interest, the mortgage is senior; to the extent of the increased interest, the priority will date from the modification date. This agreement results in a highly unusual priority problem: (1) the original mortgage principal and interest will have a first lien; (2) the second mortgage will take second place, subject only to (1) above; (3) the increased interest will have a third lien on the property: *See, for example, Bowen* v. *American Arlington Bank,* 325 So2d 31 (Fla. 1975).

A question arises whether the first mortgagee can overcome this handicap by language inserted in the first mortgage. No case has been discovered indicating that this can be done. Probably it is impossible. The granting of the extension is like an "optional advance."

REFERENCE: Kratovil and Werner, Mortgage Extensions and Modifications, 8 *Creighton L. Rev.* 595 (1975).

HUD MORTGAGES: Where the mortgagor defaults because of circumstances beyond his control, he may enter into a forbearance agreement wherein mortgage payments may be altered or suspended for a specified period. 24 CFR § 203.340. Also, HUD may approve a modification of the amortization provisions by recasting the balance due over the original term of the mortgage or an extended term. 24 CFR § 203.342. Recent cases have held that the HUD insured mortgagees must seek to aid the distressed debtor and, absent such efforts, foreclosure is not allowed. *FNMA* v. *Ricks,* 83 Misc2d 814 (N.Y. 1975).

§ 608. **Release, satisfaction, or discharge of mortgage.** Although the payment of the mortgage debt discharges the mortgage, it nevertheless remains on the public records as a cloud upon the title until it has been released. The common method of releasing a mortgage or deed of trust is by execution, acknowledgment, delivery, and recording of a *release deed,* also variously called *satisfaction, discharge* or *deed of reconveyance,* executed under seal by the trustee or mortgagee.

These formalities are necessary even though full payment has the effect of extinguishing the lien of the mortgage. Payment is not revealed by the public records and without the recordation of a properly executed satisfaction or release deed, the mortgage remains a defect in title.

§ 609. **Partial release.** When a mortgage conveys several distinct tracts of land, it is often provided in such a mortgage that on payment of a certain specified portion of the debt the mortgagor shall be entitled to a release of the mortgage as to a certain tract of land. Such a release is known as a partial release. In the absence of such a provision, the mortgagor is not entitled to any release of the mortgage except upon full payment of the mortgage debt. When a blanket mortgage is placed on an entire subdivision, such a provision is indispensable, since otherwise the subdivider could not furnish lot purchasers with clear title to their lots.

Release schedule. Typically the release clause will contain a schedule showing what lots may be released and the amount of payment for the lot or lots released. This must be set forth in accurate detail. *White Point Co.* v. *Herrington,* 73 Cal Reptr 885 (1968).

Default. Unless the mortgage provides otherwise, the mortgagor can legally insist on a partial release even if he is in default in his mortgage payments. 115 ALR 1038; 59 CJS 759. Hence it is best for the mortgagee to insist on a clause preventing this result.

CLAUSE: No partial release will be issued if an uncured default in payment of principal or interest or breach of covenant exists hereunder.

§ 610. **Marshalling of assets.** There is danger to a first mortgagee who releases part of the land where junior liens may exist.

EXAMPLE: *R* mortgages Lots 1 and 2 to *E*. *R* thereafter mortgages Lot 1 to *E-2*. *E* knows about the mortgage to *E-2*. Despite this, on *R*'s request, *E* releases Lot 2 from *E*'s mortgage, thereby throwing all the burden of *E*'s mortgage on Lot 1. This may cause *E* to lose part or all his priority over *E-2* as to Lot 1. Kratovil, *Modern Mortgage Law and Practice* § 233 (1972). Hence every mortgage should contain a clause designed to prevent this result.

CLAUSE: The mortgagee reserves the right to release any part of the mortgaged premises from the lien of this mortgage or to release the personal liability of any person for the debt hereby secured without regard to the effect upon junior liens or encumbrances.

§ 611. **Deed by mortgagor to mortgagee.** Earlier the deed absolute problem was described. There is a second type of deed absolute problem. At times a mortgagor will find that he is unable to pay the mortgage debt. In this event, the mortgagee may, of course, foreclose the mortgage. Foreclosure, however, usually costs the mortgagee time and money. He may wish to make some arrangement with the mortgagor for acquiring ownership of the land without the necessity of foreclosure. This is accomplished by means of an agreement between mortgagor and mortgagee whereby the mortgagor agrees to sell the land to the mortgagee for a small sum of money, and the mortgagee, in return, agrees to cancel the mortgage debt. The mortgagor thereupon gives the mortgagee a deed, and the mortgagee cancels the notes and releases the mortgage. The courts are inclined to be suspicious of such transactions, since the mortgagee is in a position to exert pressure on the mortgagor. To give validity to such a sale by the mortgagor, it must appear that the conduct of the mortgagee was, in all things, fair and frank and that he paid for the property what it was worth, and that he did not coerce the mortgagor into signing the deed. In order to protect himself, a mortgagee entering into such a transaction should take the following precautions:

1. He should examine the title to the land to make sure that no other liens, such as judgments or junior mortgages, attach to the land after the date of the mortgage.

2. A written contract should be entered into between the mortgagor and mortgagee. This contract should show that it was the mortgagor, not the mortgagee, who proposed the transaction. This renders it difficult for any court to hold that the mortgagor was coerced, since the agreement itself shows that he took the initiative in the transaction. The contract should also provide that the deed is given in full satisfaction of the mortgage debt. *Rooker v. Fidelity Trust Co.*, 109 NE 766 (Ind. 1915). In some states the same result is accomplished by putting a clause in the deed or in a separate affidavit.

3. The mortgage should be released and the mortgage and mortgage note canceled. If the mortgage debt is not canceled, courts tend to regard the deed as merely additional security for the debt rather than an outright sale of the mortgagor's equity, 129 ALR 1495.

4. The mortgagee should not enter into any contract to resell or reconvey the land to the mortgagor, though he may safely give the mortgagor an option to repurchase the premises. 129 ALR 1473.

HUD MORTGAGES: A mortgagee in a HUD mortgage may acquire the security from a mortgagor by a deed in lieu transaction if the following conditions are met: (1) The mortgage must be in default at the time the deed in lieu is executed and delivered; (2) The credit instrument must be canceled or surrendered to the mortgagor and the mortgage must be satisfied of record; (3) The mortgagor must give a warranty deed and convey good marketable title. 24 CFR § 203.357.

As you can see, this section presents a problem much like that presented in § 571. The problem is one of determining whether the deed is actually given with the intention to transfer the absolute ownership of the land or was given primarily as additional security, without the intention of extinguishing the mortgage.

§ 612. Federal forms. Mortgage "law" cannot be discussed in light of cases and statutes alone. The mortgagor and mortgagee make the "law" applicable to their transaction by the execution of the documents in the mortgage package. As the Federal government has dominated the residential mortgage industry, so has it dominated the wording of the mortgage documents. This influence comes from both the standards imposed by statutes and regulations discussed in the earlier sections of this chapter, and from the promulgation of uniform instruments. FNMA and FHLMC have jointly drafted these documents with the aid and assistance of some of the nation's leading authorities on mortgage law and practice.

The documents contain provisions uniform throughout the country and also are individually tailored for use in the various states and include both a note and mortgage or deed of trust. Also available are riders for the mortgage documents where the mortgaged property is a unit in a condominium or planned unit development.

The substance of some of the uniform provisions of these forms follows:

1. Borrower is entitled to prepay the principal obligation in whole or in part.

2. Borrower must pay monthly payments to the lender for the establishment of escrow accounts for the payment of taxes. Unless the agreement between borrower and lender, or the applicable law requires, lender shall not be required to pay borrower interest on the funds so held.

3. Borrower must pay all taxes, assessments, liens, and so forth levied against the property and perform all of the obligations imposed by any declaration of covenants relating to a condominium or planned unit development.

4. Borrower must not commit waste or permit deterioration of the property.

5. Borrower must keep the property properly insured.

6. Borrower agrees in advance to extensions and modifications of the mortgage obligation granted to any successor in interest of the borrower.

7. Lender may waive the right to accelerate upon a sale of the property if the credit of the purchaser is satisfactory and the rate of interest to be paid by the purchaser to the lender is agreed upon. If such waiver is given and the buyer executes an assumption agreement which is accepted by the lender, the lender shall release the borrower from liability.

NOTE

US $. . . . ., Wisconsin
City

. . . ., 19. . . .

FOR VALUE RECEIVED, the undersigned ("Borrower") promise(s) to pay. . . . ., or order, the principal sum of . . . . .Dollars, with interest on the unpaid principal balance from the date of this Note, until paid, at the rate of. . . . . .percent per annum. Principal and interest shall be payable at. . . . ., or such other place as the Note holder may designate, in consecutive monthly installments of. . . . . .Dollars (US $. . . . .), on the. . . . . .day of each month beginning. . . . ., 19. . . . . Such monthly installments shall continue until the entire indebtedness evidenced by this Note is fully paid, except that any remaining indebtedness, if not sooner paid, shall be due and payable on. . . . .

If any monthly installment under this Note is not paid when due and remains unpaid after a date specified by a notice to Borrower, the entire principal amount outstanding and accrued interest thereon shall at once become due and payable at the option of the Note holder. The date specified shall not be less than thirty days from the date such notice is mailed. The Note holder may exercise this option to accelerate during any default by Borrower regardless of any prior forbearance. If suit is brought to collect this Note, the Note holder shall be entitled to collect all reasonable costs and expenses of suit, including, but not limited to, reasonable attorney's fees.

Borrower shall pay to the Note holder a late charge of. . . . . .percent of any monthly installment not received by the Note holder within. . . . . .days after the installment is due.

Borrower may prepay the principal amount outstanding in whole or in part. The Note holder may require that any partial prepayments (i) be made on the date monthly installments are due and (ii) be in the amount of that part of one or more monthly installments which would be applicable to principal. Any partial prepayment shall be applied against the principal amount outstanding and shall not postpone the due date of any subsequent monthly installments or change the amount of such installments, unless the Note holder shall otherwise agree in writing. If, within five years from the date of this Note, Borrower make(s) any prepayments in any twelve month period beginning with the date of this Note or anniversary dates thereof ("loan year") with money lent to Borrower by a lender other than the Note holder, Borrower shall pay the Note holder (a) during each of the first three loan years . . . . .percent of the amount by which the sum of prepayments made in any such loan year exceeds twenty percent of the original principal amount of this Note and (b) during the fourth and fifth loan years . . . . .percent of the amount by which the sum of prepayments made in any such loan year exceeds twenty percent of the original principal amount of this Note.

Presentment, notice of dishonor, and protest are hereby waived by all makers, sureties, guarantors and endorsers hereof. This Note shall be the joint and several obligation of all makers, sureties, guarantors and endorsers, and shall be binding upon them and their successors and assigns.

Any notice to Borrower provided for in this Note shall be given by mailing such notice by certified mail addressed to Borrower at the Property Address stated below, or to such other address as Borrower may designate by notice to the Note holder. Any notice to the Note holder shall be given by mailing such notice by certified mail, return receipt requested, to the Note holder at the address stated in the first paragraph of this Note, or at such other address as may have been designated by notice to Borrower.

The indebtedness evidenced by this Note is secured by a Mortgage, dated. . . . ., and reference is made to the Mortgage for rights as to acceleration of the indebtedness evidenced by this Note.

. . . .(Seal)

. . . .(Seal)

. . . .(Seal)

Property Address   *(Execute Original Only)*

WISCONSIN—1 to 4 Family—6/75—**FNMA/FHLMC UNIFORM INSTRUMENT**

MORTGAGE

THIS MORTGAGE is made this . day of . . . . ,
19 . . . . , between the Mortgagor
. . . . (herein "Borrower"), and the Mortgagee,
. . . . , a corporation organized and existing
under the laws of whose address is. . . . .
. . . . (herein "Lender").

WHEREAS, Borrower is indebted to Lender in the principal sum of. . . . . Dollars, which indebtedness is evidenced by Borrower's note dated . . . . (herein "Note"), providing for monthly installments of principal and interest, with the balance of the indebtedness, if not sooner paid, due and payable on. . . . . ;

TO SECURE to Lender (a) the repayment of the indebtedness evidenced by the Note, with interest thereon, the payment of all other sums, with interest thereon, advanced in accordance herewith to protect the security of this Mortgage, and the performance of the covenants and agreements of Borrower herein contained, and (b) the repayment of any future advances, with interest thereon, made to Borrower by Lender pursuant to paragraph 21 hereof (herein "Future Advances"), Borrower does hereby mortgage, grant and convey to Lender, with power of sale, the following described property located in the County of . . . . , State of Wisconsin:

which has the address of . . . .
(Street) (City)
. . . . (herein "Property Address");
[State and Zip Code]

TOGETHER with all the improvements now or hereafter erected on the property, and all easements, rights, appurtenances, rents, royalties, mineral, oil and gas rights and profits, water, water rights, and water stock, and all fixtures now or hereafter attached to the property, all of which, including replacements and additions thereto, shall be deemed to be and remain a part of the property covered by this Mortgage; and all of the foregoing, together with said property (or the leasehold estate if this Mortgage is on a leasehold) are herein referred to as the "Property"

Borrower covenants that Borrower is lawfully seised of the estate hereby conveyed and has the right to mortgage, grant and convey the Property, that the Property is unencumbered, and that Borrower will warrant and defend generally the title to the Property against all claims and demands, subject to any declarations, easements or restrictions listed in a schedule of exceptions to coverage in any title insurance policy insuring Lender's interest in the Property.

WISCONSIN—1 to 4 Family—7/76—**FNMA/FHLMC UNIFORM INSTRUMENT**

UNIFORM COVENANTS. Borrower and Lender covenant and agree as follows:

1. Payment of Principal and Interest. Borrower shall promptly pay when due the principal of and interest on the indebtedness evidenced by the Note, prepayment and late charges as provided in the Note, and the principal of and interest on any Future Advances secured by this Mortgage.

2. Funds for Taxes and Insurance. Subject to applicable law or to a written waiver by Lender, Borrower shall pay to Lender on the day monthly installments of principal and interest are payable under the Note, until the Note is paid in full, a sum (herein "Funds") equal to one-twelfth of the yearly taxes and assessments which may attain priority over this Mortgage, and ground rents on the Property, if any, plus one-twelfth of yearly premium installments for hazard insurance, plus one-twelfth of yearly premium installments for mortgage insurance, if any, all as reasonably estimated initially and from time to time by Lender on the basis of assessments and bills and reasonable estimates thereof.

The Funds shall be held in an institution the deposits or accounts of which are insured or guaranteed by a Federal or state agency (including Lender if Lender is such an institution). Lender shall apply the Funds to pay said taxes, assessments, insurance premiums and ground rents. Lender may not charge for so holding and applying the Funds, analyzing said account, or verifying and compiling said assessments and bills, unless Lender pays Borrower interest on the Funds and applicable law permits Lender to make such a charge. Borrower and Lender may agree in writing at the time of execution of this Mortgage that interest on the Funds shall be paid to Borrower, and unless such agreement is made or applicable law requires such interest to be paid, Lender shall not be required to pay Borrower any interest or earnings on the Funds. Lender shall give to Borrower, without charge, an annual accounting of the Funds showing credits and debits to the Funds and the purpose for which each debit to the Funds was made. The Funds are pledged as additional security for the sums secured by this Mortgage.

If the amount of the Funds held by Lender, together with the future monthly installments of Funds payable prior to the due dates of taxes, assessments, insurance premiums and ground rents, shall exceed the amount required to pay said taxes, assessments, insurance premiums and ground rents as they fall due, such excess shall be, at Borrower's option, either promptly repaid to Borrower or credited to Borrower on monthly installments of Funds. If the amount of the Funds held by Lender shall not be sufficient to pay taxes, assessments, insurance premiums and ground rents as they fall due. Borrower shall pay to Lender any amount necessary to make up the deficiency within 30 days from the date notice is mailed by Lender to Borrower requesting payment thereof.

Upon payment in full of all sums secured by this Mortgage, Lender shall promptly refund to Borrower any Funds held by Lender. If under paragraph 18 hereof the Property is sold or the Property is otherwise acquired by Lender, Lender shall apply, no later than immediately prior to the sale of the Property or its acquisition by Lender, any Funds held by Lender at the time of application as a credit against the sums secured by this Mortgage.

3. Application of Payments. Unless applicable law provides otherwise, all payments received by Lender under the Note and paragraphs 1 and 2 hereof shall be applied by Lender first in payment of amounts payable to Lender by Borrower under paragraph 2 hereof, then to interest payable on the Note, then to the principal of the Note, and then to interest and principal on any Future Advances.

4. Charges; Liens. Borrower shall pay all taxes, assessments and other charges, fines and impositions attributable to the Property which may attain a priority over this Mortgage, and leasehold payments or ground rents, if any, in the manner provided under paragraph 2 hereof or, if not paid in such manner, by Borrower making payment, when due, directly to the payee thereof. Borrower shall promptly furnish to Lender all notices of amounts due under this paragraph, and in the event Borrower shall make payment directly, Borrower shall promptly furnish to Lender receipts evidencing such payments. Borrower shall promptly discharge any lien which has priority over this Mortgage; provided, that Borrower shall not be required to discharge any such lien so long as Borrower shall agree in writing to the payment of the obligation secured by such lien in a manner acceptable to Lender, or shall in good faith contest such lien by, or defend enforcement of such lien in, legal proceedings which operate to prevent the enforcement of the lien or forfeiture of the Property or any part thereof.

5. Hazard Insurance. Borrower shall keep the improvements now existing or hereafter erected on the Property insured against loss by fire, hazards included within the term "extended coverage", and such other hazards as Lender may require and in such amounts and for such periods as Lender may require; provided, that Lender shall not require that the amount of such coverage exceed that amount of coverage required to pay the sums secured by this Mortgage.

The insurance carrier providing the insurance shall be chosen by Borrower subject to approval by Lender; provided, that such approval shall not be unreasonably withheld. All premiums on insurance policies shall be paid in the manner provided under paragraph 2 hereof or, if not paid in such manner, by Borrower making payment, when due, directly to the insurance carrier.

All insurance policies and renewals thereof shall be in form acceptable to Lender and shall include a standard mortgage clause in favor of and in form acceptable to Lender. Lender shall have the right to hold the policies and renewals thereof, and Borrower shall promptly furnish to Lender all renewal notices and all receipts of paid premiums. In the event of loss, Borrower shall give prompt notice to the insurance carrier and Lender. Lender may make proof of loss if not made promptly by Borrower.

Unless Lender and Borrower otherwise agree in writing, insurance proceeds shall be applied to restoration or repair of the Property damaged, provided such restoration or repair is economically feasible and the security of this Mortgage is not thereby impaired. If such restoration or repair is not economically feasible or if the security of this Mortgage would be impaired, the insurance proceeds shall be applied to the sums secured by this Mortgage, with the excess, if any, paid to Borrower. If the Property is abandoned by Borrower, or if Borrower fails to respond to Lender within 30 days from the date notice is mailed by Lender to Borrower that the insurance carrier offers to settle a claim for insurance benefits, Lender is authorized to collect and apply the insurance proceeds at Lender's option either to restoration or repair of the Property or to the sums secured by this Mortgage.

Unless Lender and Borrower otherwise agree in writing, any such application of proceeds to principal shall not extend or postpone the due date of the monthly installments referred to in paragraphs 1 and 2 hereof or change the amount of such installments. If under paragraph 18 hereof the Property is acquired by Lender, all right, title and interest of Borrower in and to any insurance policies and in and to the proceeds thereof resulting from damage to the Property prior to the sale or acquisition shall pass to Lender to the extent of the sums secured by this Mortgage immediately prior to such sale or acquisition.

6. Preservation and Maintenance of Property; Leaseholds; Condominiums; Planned Unit Developments. Borrower shall keep the Property in good repair and shall not commit waste or permit impairment or deterioration of the Property and shall comply with the provisions of any lease if this Mortgage is on a leasehold. If this Mortgage is on a unit in a condominium or a planned unit development, Borrower shall perform all of Borrower's obligations under the declaration or covenants creating or governing the condominium or planned unit development, the by-laws and regulations of the condominium or planned unit development, and constituent documents. If a condominium or planned unit development rider is executed by Borrower and recorded together with this Mortgage, the covenants and agreements of such rider shall be incorporated into and shall amend and supplement the covenants and agreements of this Mortgage as if the rider were a part hereof.

7. Protection of Lender's Security. If Borrower fails to perform the covenants and agreements contained in this Mortgage, or if any action or proceeding is commenced which materially affects Lender's interest in the Property, including, but not limited to, eminent domain, insolvency, code enforcement, or arrangements or proceedings involving a bankrupt or decedent, then Lender at Lender's option, upon notice to Borrower, may make such appearances, disburse such sums and take such action as is necessary to protect Lender's interest, including, but not limited to, disbursement of reasonable attorney's fees and entry upon the Property to make repairs. If Lender required mortgage insurance as a condition of making the loan secured by this Mortgage, Borrower shall pay the premiums required to maintain such insurance in effect until such time as the requirement for such insurance terminates in accordance with Borrower's and Lender's written agreement or applicable law. Borrower shall pay the amount of all mortgage insurance premiums in the manner provided under paragraph 2 hereof.

Any amounts disbursed by Lender pursuant to this paragraph 7, with interest thereon, shall become additional indebtedness of Borrower secured by this Mortgage. Unless Borrower and Lender agree to other terms of payment, such amounts shall be payable upon notice from Lender to Borrower requesting payment thereof, and shall bear interest from the date of disbursement at the rate payable from time to time on outstanding principal under the Note unless payment of interest at such rate would be contrary to applicable law, in which event such amounts shall bear interest at the highest rate permissible under applicable law. Nothing contained in this paragraph 7 shall require Lender to incur any expense or take any action hereunder.

8. Inspection. Lender may make or cause to be made reasonable entries upon and inspections of the Property, provided that Lender shall give Borrower notice prior to any such inspection specifying reasonable cause therefor related to Lender's interest in the Property.

9. Condemnation. The proceeds of any award or claim for damages, direct or consequential, in connection with any condemnation or other taking of the Property, or part thereof, or for conveyance in lieu of condemnation, are hereby assigned and shall be paid to Lender.

In the event of a total taking of the Property, the proceeds shall be applied to the sums secured by this Mortgage, with the excess, if any, paid to Borrower. In the even of a partial taking of the Property, unless Borrower and Lender otherwise agree in writing, there shall be applied to the sums secured by this Mortgage such proportion of the proceeds as is equal to that proportion which the amount of the sums secured by this Mortgage immediately prior to the date of taking bears to the fair market value of the Property immediately prior to the date of taking, with the balance of the proceeds paid to Borrower.

If the Property is abandoned by Borrower, or if, after notice by Lender to Borrower that the condemnor offers to make an award or settle a claim for damages, Borrower fails to respond to Lender within 30 days after the date such notice is mailed, Lender is authorized to collect and apply the proceeds, at Lender's option, either to restoration or repair of the Property or to the sums secured by this Mortgage.

Unless Lender and Borrower otherwise agree in writing, any such application of proceeds to principal shall not extend or postpone the due date of the monthly installments referred to in paragraphs 1 and 2 hereof or change the amount of such installments.

10. Borrower Not Released. Extension of the time for payment or modification of amortization of the sums secured by this Mortgage granted by Lender to any successor in interest of Borrower shall not operate to release, in any manner, the liability of the original Borrower and Borrower's successors in interest. Lender shall not be required to commence proceedings against such successor or refuse to extend time for payment or otherwise modify amortization of the sums secured by this Mortgage by reason of any demand made by the original Borrower and Borrower's successors in interest.

11. Forbearance by Lender Not a Waiver. Any forbearance by Lender in exercising any right or remedy hereunder, or otherwise afforded by applicable law, shall not be a waiver of or preclude the exercise of any such right or remedy. The procurement of insurance or the payment of taxes or other liens or charges by Lender shall not be a waiver of Lender's right to accelerate the maturity of the indebtedness secured by this Mortgage.

12. Remedies Cumulative. All remedies provided in this Mortgage are distinct and cumulative to any other right or remedy under this Mortgage or afforded by law or equity, and may be exercised concurrently, independently or successively.

13. Successors and Assigns Bound; Joint and Several Liability; Captions. The covenants and agreements herein contained shall bind, and the rights hereunder shall inure to, the respective successors and assigns of Lender and Borrower, subject to the provisions of paragraph 17 hereof. All covenants and agreements of Borrower shall be joint and several. The captions and headings of the paragraphs of this Mortgage are for convenience only and are not to be used to interpret or define the provisions hereof.

14. Notice. Except for any notice required under applicable law to be given in another manner, (a) any notice to Borrower provided for in this Mortgage shall be given by mailing such notice by certified mail addressed to Borrower at the Property Address or at such other address as Borrower may designate by notice to Lender as provided herein, and (b) any notice to Lender shall be given by certified mail, return receipt requested, to Lender's address stated herein or to such other address as Lender may designate by notice to Borrower as provided herein. Any notice provided for in this Mortgage shall be deemed to have been given to Borrower or Lender when given in the manner designated herein.

15. Uniform Mortgage; Governing Law; Severability. This form of mortgage combines uniform covenants for national use and non-uniform covenants with limited variations by jurisdiction to constitute a uniform security instrument covering real property. This Mortgage shall be governed by the law of the jurisdiction in which the Property is located. In the event that any provision or clause of this Mortgage or the Note conflicts with applicable law, such conflict shall not affect other provisions of this Mortgage or the Note which can be given effect without the conflicting provision, and to this end the provisions of the Mortgage and the Note are declared to be severable.

16. Borrower's Copy. Borrower shall be furnished a conformed copy of the Note and of this Mortgage at the time of execution or after recordation hereof.

17. Transfer of the Property; Assumption. If all or any part of the Property or an interest therein is sold or transferred by Borrower without Lender's prior written consent, excluding (a) the creation of a lien or encumbrance subordinate to this Mortgage, (b) the creation of a purchase money security interest for household appliances, (c) a transfer by devise, descent or by operation of law upon the death of a joint tenant or (d) the grant of any leasehold interest of three years or less not containing an option to purchase, Lender may, at Lender's option, declare all the sums secured by this Mortgage to be immediately due and payable. Lender shall have waived such option to accelerate if, prior to the sale or transfer. Lender and the person to whom the Property is to be sold or transferred reach agreement in writing that the credit of such person is satisfactory to lender and that the interest payable on the sums secured by this Mortgage shall be at such rate as Lender shall request. If Lender has waived the option to accelerate provided in this paragraph 17, and if Borrower's successor in interest has executed a written assumption agreement accepted in writing by Lender, Lender shall release Borrower from all obligations under this Mortgage and the Note.

If Lender exercises such option to accelerate, Lender shall mail Borrower notice of acceleration in accordance with paragraph 14 hereof. Such notice shall provide a period of not less than 30 days from the date the notice is mained within which Borrower may pay the sums declared due. If Borrower fails to pay such sums prior to the expiration of such period. Lender may, without further notice or demand on Borrower, invoke any remedies permitted by paragraph 18 hereof.

NON-UNIFORM COVENANTS. Borrower and Lender further covenant and agree as follows:

18. Acceleration; Remedies. Except as provided in paragraph 17 hereof, upon Borrower's breach of any covenant or agreement of Borrower in this Mortgage, including the covenants to pay when due any sums secured by this Mortgage, Lender prior to acceleration shall mail notice to Borrower as provided in paragraph 14 here of specifying: (1) the breach; (2) the action required to cure such breach; (3) a date, not less than 30 days from the date the notice is mailed to Borrower, by which such breach must be cured; and (4) that failure to cure such breach on or before the date specified in the notice may result in acceleration of the sums secured by this Mortgage and sale of the Property. The notice shall further inform Borrower of the right to reinstate after acceleration and the right to assert in the foreclosure proceeding the non-existence of a default or any other defense of Borrower to acceleration and sale. If the breach is not cured on or before the date specified in the notice, Lender at Lender's option may declare all of the sums secured by this Mortgage to be immediately due and payable without further demand and may invoke the power of sale and any other remedies permitted by applicable law. Lender shall be entitled to collect all reasonable costs and expenses incurred in pursuing the remedies provided in this paragraph 18, including, but not limited to, reasonable attorney's fees.

If Lender invokes the power of sale, Lender shall give notice of sale in the manner prescribed by applicable law to Borrower and to the other persons prescribed by applicable law. Lender shall publish the notice of sale and the Property shall be sold in the manner

prescribed by applicable law. Lender or Lender's designee may purchase the Property at any sale. The proceeds of the sale shall be applied in the following order: (a) to all reasonable costs and expenses of the sale, including, but not limited to, reasonable attorney's fees and costs of title evidence; (b) to all sums secured by this Mortgage; and (c) the excess, if any, to the clerk of the Circuit Court of the county in which the sale is held.

19. Borrower's Right to Reinstate. Notwithstanding Lender's acceleration of the sums secured by this Mortgage, Borrower shall have the right to have any proceedings begun by Lender to enforce this Mortgage discontinued at any time prior to the earlier to occur of (i) the fifth day before sale of the Property pursuant to the power of sale contained in this Mortgage or (ii) entry of a judgment enforcing this Mortgage if: (a) Borrower pays Lender all sums which would be then due under this Mortgage, the Note and notes securing Future Advances, if any, had no acceleration occurred; (b) Borrower cures all breaches of any other covenants or agreements of Borrower contained in this Mortgage; (c) Borrower pays all reasonable expenses incurred by Lender in enforcing the covenants and agreements of Borrower contained in this Mortgage and in enforcing Lender's remedies as provided in paragraph 18 hereof, including, but not limited to, reasonable attorney's fees; and (d) Borrower takes such action as Lender may reasonably require to assure that the lien of this Mortgage, Lender's interest in the Property and Borrower's obligation to pay the sums secured by this Mortgage shall continue unimpaired. Upon such payment and cure by Borrower, this Mortgage and the obligations secured hereby shall remain in full force and effect as if no acceleration had occurred.

20. Assignment of Rents; Appointment of Receiver. As additional security hereunder, Borrower hereby assigns to Lender the rents of the Property, provided that Borrower shall, prior to acceleration under paragraph 18 hereof or abandonment of the Property, have the right to collect and retain such rents as they become due and payable.

Upon acceleration under paragraph 18 hereof or abandonment of the Property, and at any time prior to the expiration of any period of redemption following sale of the Property, Lender shall be entitled to have a receiver appointed by a court to enter upon, take possession of and manage the Property and to collect the rents of the Property including those past due. All rents collected by the receiver shall be applied first to payment of the costs of management of the Property and collection of rents, including, but not limited to, receiver's fees, and then to the sums secured by this Mortgage. The receiver shall be liable to account only for those rents actually received.

21. Future Advances. Upon request of Borrower, Lender, at Lender's option prior to release of this Mortgage, may make Future Advances to Borrower. Such Future Advances, with interest thereon, shall be secured by this Mortgage when evidenced by promissory notes stating that said notes are secured hereby. At no time shall the principal amount of the indebtedness secured by this Mortgage, not including sums advanced in accordance herewith to protect the security of this Mortgage, exceed the original amount of the Note.

22. Release. Upon payment of all sums secured by this Mortgage, Lender shall release this Mortgage, without charge to Borrower. Borrower shall pay all costs of recordation, if any, unless applicable law provides otherwise.

23. Redemption. If the Property is three acres or less in size and Lender in an action to foreclose this Mortgage waives all right to a judgment for deficiency and consents to Borrower's remaining in possession of the Property (unless the Property has been abandoned), then the sale of the Property may be six months from the date the judgment is entered, as provided by Section 846.101 of the Wisconsin Statutes.

24. Attorney's Fees. If this Mortgage is subject to Chapter 428 of the Wisconsin Statutes, "reasonable attorney's fees" as used herein shall mean only those attorney's fees allowed by said Chapter.

IN WITNESS WHEREOF, Borrower has executed this Mortgage.

Signed, sealed and delivered in
the presence of:

.... (Seal)
—Borrower

.... (Seal)
—Borrower

STATE OF WISCONSIN, ... County ss:

The foregoing instrument was acknowledged before me this .... by ....
(date)

....
(person acknowledging)

My Commission expires:

....
Notary Public, State of Wisconsin

This instrument was prepared by ....

__________(Space Below This Line Reserved For Lender and Recorder)__________

20

Mortgages: Construction Loans

§ 613. **In general.** Construction lending encounters some rather technical rules of law and involves some rather complicated paper work. Nevertheless the need for it is great and growing. America's appetite for new construction is insatiable.

Building operations depend on mortgage credit. Before subcontractors (electrical contractors, plumbing contractors, and so forth) and building material suppliers put their labor and materials into a house, they want to know where their money is coming from. Since the builder lacks the capital to pay these people from his own funds, he must be able to show them that he has a dependable source of mortgage money. Even if a dependable source of mortgage money exists, subcontractors and materialmen want their money rather promptly. Materialmen may extend credit for thirty or forty days. Subcontractors often want payment when they complete their particular portion of the construction job, which means that some mortgage lender must be persuaded to advance the mortgage money as the building goes up. And the only assurance subcontractors and materialmen have faith in is a binding contract by the mortgage house to advance the mortgage money as construction goes forward. This contract arises when the builder, as prospective mortgagor, applies in writing to a mortgage lender for the required mortgage loan and the mortgage lender gives its written commitment to lend the money.

§ 614. **Interim and permanent loans—takeout commitments.** A construction loan requires considerable supervision on the part of the lender. This is for the business reason that the mortgage lender wants assurance that construction of the house actually will be completed; that the construction will not be faulty but be according to the construction plans and specifications approved by the lender; and that no mechanics' liens will arise in the process of construction. All mortgage lenders are willing to engage in construction lending, especially on large loans. Some want long-term permanent mortgages on completed buildings. On the other hand, mortgage lenders who do engage in construction lending (*interim lenders*) do not want their funds tied up over the long period of time, often fifteen years or longer, that it takes to pay off a mortgage. They want to turn their capital over constantly. Especially on large loans, their income is derived not from interest on mortgage loans, but from *commissions* which the builder pays in order to receive the mortgage loan and from *service charges.* This latter item requires a word of explanation. In order to keep its capital turning over, the interim lender expects to sell the mortgage loan, after completion of construction, to a bank, insurance company, or other investor that is willing to take the mortgage as a permanent investment. The sale is often to a *permanent lender* with whom the construction lender has some permanent working arrangement, that is, the construction lender may be a *loan correspondent* for the permanent lender. After completion of the building, the mortgage is sold and assigned to the *permanent lender,* and, after sale of the mortgage to the permanent lender, the loan correspondent looks after the payment of taxes and insurance renewals, collects the mortgage payments, and remits the payments to the permanent lender, making a charge, the *service charge,* for this service. Before he agrees to finance construction of the house, the interim lender insists on the issuance of a *takeout commitment* by the permanent lender, that is, an agreement by the permanent lender to buy the construction mortgage after the house has been completed free from mechanics' liens and after all risks of construction are over.

SUGGESTION TO CONSTRUCTION LENDER: Make the construction loan commitment subject to the same conditions as those contained in the takeout commitment. That is, if the permanent lender is making requirements, for example, as to chain store and other key leases that he wants signed, the construction loan commitment should be subject to the same requirements, so that when these are met, all you need do is see that the building is finished properly and on time, and you can then demand that the permanent lender take over. It is even a good idea to have all the documents required by the permanent lender prepared and approved as to form by the permanent lender before the construction loan agreement is signed. This will avoid the pitfall of having the construction loan commitment signed and then running into an insoluble difference with the permanent lender, thus forcing you to look elsewhere for a permanent lender.

As an alternative to this type of *takeout commitment*—an alternative made necessary because construction loans to builders are smaller in amount than loans on completed houses—the construction lender may be willing to finance construction if the builder or mortgagor can procure from some permanent lender a commitment to make a new mortgage loan when the building has been completed, the proceeds of the new mortgage loan to be used to pay off the construction mortgage. This is also called a *takeout commitment.*

When the loan arrangements contemplate that the construction mortgage will be released and a new mortgage given to a permanent lender, usually the first step is for the prospective mortgagor in the permanent mortgage to apply to the permanent lender for the permanent mortgage loan. The permanent lender then gives its commitment to this mortgagor, who then gives an assignment of the commitment to the construction lender.

As soon as the assignment has been given, the construction lender commits to make the construction loan and notifies the permanent lender of the assignment, so that no modifications or cancellations between the mortgagor and the permanent lender will be binding upon the construction lender. In other words, the assignment of commitment and notice thereof give the construction lender the legal right to enforce the commitment against the permanent lender. The construction lender often takes the permanent loan commitment and the assignment to his banker and borrows perhaps 90 percent of the construction money on the faith of these documents.

At times the permanent loan commitment is obtained at the outset, the thought being that construction cannot take place until the permanent financing is arranged.

§ **615. Construction loan agreement.** A construction loan is paid out in installments as construction goes forward. During the construction period, which may extend over a year on big jobs, other liens may come into being. It is important to preserve the priority of the construction mortgage over such liens.

EXAMPLE: *A* records a construction mortgage to *B* on February 1, 1978. On March 1, 1978, construction begins. On April 1, 1978, *B* makes his first disbursement of construction funds to the general contractor and subcontractors. On May 1, 1978, *A* records another mortgage to C to obtain funds for final completion of a building on another tract of land and receives this money in May 15, 1978. On June 1, 1978, *B* makes another disbursement on the construction mortgage. *B* will wish to be certain that this disbursement and all subsequent disbursements have priority over C's mortgage. C will argue that he comes ahead of all disbursements made after the recording of his mortgage. Hence it is important that *B* come under the protection of the *obligatory advances rule*. This means that before disbursement begins on the construction loan *A* and *B* should sign a construction loan agreement which obligates *B* to pay out the money as construction goes forward. Two problems arise in this connection:

1. It may be contended that the advances are, in fact, optional (rather than obligatory) if the construction loan agreement authorizes the mortgagee to stop making loan advances under certain circumstances, for example, when the construction fails to go forward according to the agreement. 80 ALR2d 201. The fact that the agreement gives the lender the privilege of discontinuing disbursement does not render subsequent advances optional. *Landers-Morrison-Christenson* Co. v. *Ambassador Holding* Co. (Minn.) 214 NW 503; *Hyman* v. *Hauff,* 138 N.Y. 48, 33 NE 735. But see 80 ALR2d 201 listing some cases holding to the contrary. In all contracts if one party stops performing the other party may also do so, but he need not do so. Third parties, such as junior lienors (second mortgages, etc.) cannot force the lender to decide the often extremely difficult question of whether the borrower is inexcusably in default. He may, if he wishes, continue to perform, and indeed the law encourages him to do so. Moreover, the construction lender has no real choice. A half-finished building, subject to vandalism and destruction by the elements, is no security at all, and all mortgagees have the right to protect their investment by advancing additional funds, such as taxes and construction funds, and such advances enjoy full priority over liens attaching after the recording of the mortgage. For full discussion of this problem, see Kratovil and Werner, Mortgages for Construction and the Lien Priorities Problem—the Unobligatory Advance, 41 *Tenn. L. Rev.* 311.

2. The provisions of the construction loan agreement tend to be rather general and vague, such as the requirement that insurance policies be "satisfactory to the lender." It

is sometimes argued that the agreement is void for uncertainty. For example, what kind of insurance was meant? Fire? Builder's risk? Liability? If the contract is void for uncertainty, all advances by the lender would be optional, and the lender's various advances might be subordinate to other liens, such as judgment liens attaching during the course of construction. As a matter of law, it is not necessary that all details be settled with precision. Reasonable satisfaction and reasonable certainty are adequate guidelines for judges and businessmen. *Collins* v. *Vickter Manor*, 47 Cal.2d 875, 306 P2d 783. Such contracts are not void.

A good part of the construction lender's requirements can be incorporated in the lender's *printed form* construction loan agreement. Any deviation from the form should be covered in advance in the loan commitment, for legally a lender cannot demand provisions in the construction loan agreement that are not in the loan commitment. The loan commitment should, of course, call for the borrower to sign the lender's standard form construction loan agreement as modified by the loan commitment. This enables the lender to omit from the commitment a mass of detail that might frighten away a timid borrower.

§ 616. Matters to be answered by construction lender before disbursement begins. In making a construction loan, the lender asks himself some questions an intending builder would ask, such as:

1. Will the building violate zoning laws either as to type of building or setback lines?
2. Will it violate recorded building restrictions?
3. Does the building have the legal right to connect to sewer and water?
4. Will the building interfere with existing drainage or utility lines?
5. What does the survey show as to the true boundaries and area of the property and encroachments by the building or by adjoining owners?

All mortgage houses also follow certain practical precautions in construction loans. Each subcontractor's bid is checked to see that there is no underbid or overbid. If he underbids, he may threaten to walk out on the job unless he gets more money. If he overbids, the value simply is not there for the work done. Mortgagees also check the financial rating of homeowner and builder to see that the job is within their financial capacity. They require the homeowner to put up his share of the construction cost with the mortgagee, and this money is the first money used as construction begins.

§ 617. Construction loan disbursement. Before any disbursement is made on bigger jobs, the lender will obtain a certificate from his architect that work is in place (according to the building contract, plans, and specifications in the lender's files) warranting the disbursement requested; he will have the owner's signed direction to make the disbursement; he will procure lien waivers as construction proceeds; he will have the architect certify that the balance of loan proceeds will suffice to complete the building; the lender will stop disbursement if unauthorized extras appear or liens appear or if loan proceeds appear inadequate to complete construction; at each disbursement, a date-down survey will be furnished showing that new construction is within lot lines and does not violate building lines or other regulations established by zoning ordinances, building codes, or private building restrictions.

Construction funds held by the lender cannot be garnisheed by other creditors. Kratovil, Modern Mortgage Law & Practice, § 224 (1972).

§ 618. Mechanic's lien protection. A mortgagee paying out a construction loan must protect both itself and the mortgagor against mechanics' liens. This is not an easy task. To accomplish this purpose some mortgage lenders arrange with a title insurance company to examine mechanic's lien waivers as construction goes forward. Under one such arrangement (*interim certification*), the owner, having funds for the first progress payments, pays his contractor, subcontractors and materialmen when the first payment falls due. He then is given lien waivers by each of the parties so paid, which he delivers to the title insurance company. The title insurance company examines them for sufficiency, also checking each waiver against the general contractor's affidavit which lists the persons who furnished work and material. When it is satisfied, it issues an endorsement to its policy insuring that, to the extent of the money thus paid out, the property is free and clear of mechanics' liens. In reliance on this endorsement, the mortgage lender pays to the owner money equal to the first such progress payment, and the process is repeated until the building is completed.

Alternatively, the title company is given the mortgage money in escrow, as progress payments are due, and pays to the persons who have furnished labor and material, using checks that contain a lien waiver, so that each mechanic cashing a check automatically, by endorsing it, waives his lien to the extent of the money so paid.

§ 619. Suggestions to the construction lender to protect against mechanics' liens. Whether the loan proceeds are paid by a title company or the mortgagee itself, certain precautions are necessary:

1. In a majority of the states (called *priority states*), if a mortgage is recorded and becomes a lien on the property *before any construction begins*, the mortgage will enjoy priority over any mechanic's lien arising out of such construction.

It is obvious that if visible construction actually begins before the mortgage is recorded or becomes a lien, some or probably all of the mechanics' liens will be prior and superior to the mortgage. It is therefore necessary for any construction mortgagee to know exactly when construction begins.

SUGGESTION: Immediately after recording of the mortgage, let the lender take affidavits from the builder and homeowner that construction has not begun or material been delivered to the site, and let him verify this by an actual inspection of the premises. The inspector should make a written report, with a photograph of the property, which report should be signed and dated and held in the mortgage file against the possibility of litigation.

In this connection, it is to be observed that staking off lots, cutting trees, and removing brush do not constitute the commencement of construction. They are merely preparatory to the commencement of construction. *Clark* v. *General Electric Co.*, 243 Ark. 399, 420 SW2d 830; *Reuben E. Johnson Co.* v. *Phelps*, 156 NW2d 247 (Minn.). For work to constitute the commencement of construction, within the meaning of the rule, it must be of such a substantial and conspicuous character as to make it reasonably apparent that building has actually begun. 1 ALR3d 822.

2. In any state where prior recording of the mortgage gives the mortgagee no protection, the mortgagee usually has no choice but to see that no mechanic's lien claims are filed. Keep in mind, also, that increasingly today courts require the construction lender to protect the mortgagor against mechanics' liens. The construction lender should therefore procure from the general contractor a sworn list of all the subcontractors he has hired, and as each disbursement is made, he procures a supplementary affidavit reflecting any changes. Each such affidavit shows how much work or materials each subcontractor has put in, and each subcontractor, on receiving payment of that amount, gives a *partial lien waiver* for all work and material furnished *to the date of the affidavit.* The general contractor also gives such waivers. Dollar amounts recited in the affidavits are checked against dollar amounts recited in the lien waivers. Any discrepancy is questioned, for it may reveal an unauthorized extra. As each subcontractor receives *final* payment for his work, he gives a *final waiver* for all work and materials *furnished or to be furnished* so that he can claim no lien for work needed to correct defective construction that shows up. Special state statutes should be followed. In Florida, the mortgagee should record the construction mortgage at least one day before notice of commencement of construction is recorded. In California, the mortgagee should record a notice of completion as soon as construction has been completed, for this starts the running of the period for the filing of mechanics' liens.

The *landowner* also gives the mortgagee an affidavit listing all persons furnishing work or materials *on his order,* for some owners let work out to parties other than the main contractor.

The mortgagee makes payouts as the building goes up, according to a schedule included in the construction loan agreement. He makes payouts directly to the subcontractors. The general contractor often brings in waivers signed by subcontractors, states that he has paid them in full, and asks that he be paid the amount represented by these waivers. To comply is risky. A dishonest builder will forge lien waivers. Such waivers are void. And even if the lien waivers are genuine, the builder may have paid the subcontractors with "rubber" checks, and when the checks "bounce," the subcontractors may file foreclosure suits despite the lien waivers. Probably they will not prevail in such suits, for the homeowner or mortgagee relied on the lien waivers in paying out, and the courts would say that the subcontractors are therefore barred or *estopped* from repudiating their lien waivers. *P. A. Lord Lumber Co.* v. *Callahan,* 181 Ill. App. 323; *McClelland* v. *Hamernick,* 264 Minn., 345, 118 NW2d 791. Check each lien waiver carefully. Most of them come from corporations, and if the corporate seal is attached and a certificate of acknowledgment appears thereon, you can depend on its regularity. Trouble arises with respect to the thousands of unincorporated enterprises. You may get a lien waiver by "Triangle Plumbers," whoever they are, signed by "Joseph Doakes," whoever he is. He might be the office boy, of course, and wholly unauthorized to sign anything. Verify these the best way you can. Often a phone call will suffice.

Before making payment to any subcontractor, the lender should require him to sign a verified statement as to all material put into the job and any sub-subcontractors he has hired. Just as in many states the law requires you to see that all the general contractor's subcontractors are fully paid, so it is required in many states that you see that each subcontractor's sub-contractors are fully paid. If any material used was procured on credit, you must make payment to, and get a waiver from, the materialman for he is also entitled to a lien.

3. The lender should hold back part of the final payment until the time for filing or serving lien claims has been passed. Check the records for lien claims before making this last payout.

4. The mortgagee may insist that the building contract contain a waiver of all me-

chanics' liens and be recorded in the recorder's office. In some states (Illinois and Indiana, for example) this wipes out all mechanics' liens. 76 ALR2d 1097. Its practical disadvantage is that subcontractors may refuse to work on such a job if they get wind of this blanket waiver.

§ 620. **Contractor's bonds.** On large construction projects surety company bonds are often employed to provide assurance that the building will be completed according to contract and free and clear of any mechanic's lien claims. Such bonds provide protection against events such as the following: (1) The general contractor goes bankrupt, and a new contractor demands a higher price to complete the building. (2) The general contractor finds that he has underbid the job and simply refuses to go forward with it. (3) The general contractor completes the job but fails to pay his subcontractors, who therefore file mechanic's lien claims against the property.

Since this area of law is extremely technical, some oversimplification becomes necessary. The owner gets his best protection when he receives two bonds from the surety company, both on forms approved by the American Institute of Architects (AIA). One bond, the *performance bond,* provides assurance that the building will be completed as per contract. If the general contractor fails to do so, the bonding company takes over and completes the job. The bonding company also gives the owner an AIA *payment bond* which assures the owner that material and labor furnished in construction of the building will be fully paid for, so that no mechanics' liens will be filed. These bonds contemplate that the owner will adhere to the construction contract. For example, contracts on big construction usually call for progress payments to be made at various phases of construction, and the general contractor is to be paid for a phase only when and if the owner's architect certifies that this phase has been properly completed and lien waivers have been produced by the general contractor showing that all subcontractors and materialmen have been paid for work and material on this phase. Such provisions protect the bonding company.

EXAMPLE: If the owner pays the general contractor in advance, before the phase is completed, or pays without requiring production of lien waivers as called for by the constuction contract, the owner will lose all his bond protection.

The *payment bond* protects the subcontractors and materialmen. Thus, if a subcontractor is not paid, he can take his claim directly to the bonding company. And even if the owner loses all his bond protection on the performance bond because of his failure to abide by the construction contract, the subcontractors and materialmen retain their protection under the payment bond. 77 ALR 62, 118 ALR 66.

When an owner hires a reliable contractor and obtains surety bonds, he has good protection. The general contractor knows that if he falls down on the job and the bonding company is compelled to step in, the word will get around, and the contractor will be unable to get a surety bond on his next job. In other words, the contractor must keep his credit good with the bonding companies or he is out of business.

The mortgage lender who is advancing the construction funds also wishes to be protected by the surety bonds. Bonding companies are usually willing to add the name of the mortgagee as a party protected by the surety bonds. However, the bonding company will then add a clause to the bonds that is commonly called the *Los Angeles clause*. In practical effect, this clause makes the mortgage lender's protection contingent upon the owner's performing his part of the bargain under the construction contract. The philosophy here is that the bonding company carefully checks the general contractor and is willing to guarantee that *he* will do his job, but is unwilling to insure that *the owner* will do his job. Thus, for example, if a construction job will cost $10,000,000, of which $8,000,000 will be supplied by the mortgage lender and $2,000,000 will be supplied by the owner, the mortgage lender is not protected if the owner fails to come up with his $2,000,000.

In certain situations the bonding company will be willing to give the construction lender a *completion bond*. This is a bond that assures the lender that the building will be completed according to contract and free and clear of mechanics' liens. Here the bonding company is assuring that both the contractor and the owner will perform properly. This would be in a situation, for example, where a bank is constructing a new bank building and is borrowing part of the construction money from an insurance company. The bonding company is willing to assure the insurance company that a top-notch contractor and a reliable bank working together will complete the building properly and free of all liens.

In some states, one wishing to free his land from filed mechanics' liens may procure and file in some public office a surety company bond protecting against such liens. *Jungbert* v. *Marrett,* 313 Ky. 338, 231 SW2d 84. Of course if such a bond is requested, the surety company will probably ask to have collateral put up, but the bond wipes out the liens and insures litigation at leisure with the mechanics' lien claimants if there is any contention that their work was done improperly. Almost everywhere, purchasers, mortgagees, and title companies will accept such surety bonds, even though there is no law that the bond wipes out the lien.

REFERENCE: 2 *Real Estate Review* 88.

§ 621. **Disbursement of construction mortgage funds.** The question of the consequences of improper disbursement of construction loan funds is one of extreme difficulty. There are situations of different sorts and even in identical situations the courts are often in disagreement. Let us consider the possibilities:

1. The mortgage lender pays out all the construction funds. He pays out the money before work is in place justifying the payment. As a result the mortgage funds are insufficient to complete the building. Often this is due to the fact that the general contractor has diverted the funds to other jobs. The mortgagor suffers, and subcontractors file liens and also suffer. The lender is liable to parties injured. *Nolan* v. *Colorado Mtg. Co.,* 137 Colo. 103, 322 P2d 98 (1958); *Robinson* v. *Keaton,* 239 Ark. 587, 393 SW2d 231 (1965);

Cook v. *Citizens S. & L. Ass'n,* 346 So2d 370 (Miss. 1977). If the construction mortgage recites that the money will be advanced for construction work on the mortgaged land, some courts hold that the lender is liable to mechanic's lien claimants if the money is diverted to other projects. *First Nat. Bank of Conway* v. *Conway Sheet Metal Co.,* 244 Ark. 963, 428 SW2d 293 (1968). *Contra: Coke Lumber & Mfg. Co.* v. *First Nat. Bank,* 529 SW2d 612 (Tex. 1975); *House* v. *Scott,* 429 SW2d 108 (Ark. 1968); *James* v. *First Fed. S. & L. Assn.,* 312 NE2d 605 (Ill. 1974).

2. In Louisiana the construction lender has no liability unless he has assumed actual supervision of the project. *Ross* v. *Continental Mtg. Investors,* 404 F.Supp. 922 (1975).

3. In Ohio a construction lender who disburses the funds to the mortgagor has no liability either to the mortgagor or subcontractors for diversion of funds by the general contractor. *Gardner Plumbing Inc.* v. *Cottrill,* 338 NE2d 757 (Ohio 1975), criticized in 45 *Cincinnati L. Rev.* 492.

4. In New York, if the construction loan agreement specifically authorizes the construction lender to make disbursements before work is in place, subcontractors cannot complain if the lender takes advantage of this provision. *Ulster Svgs. Bank* v. *Total Communities Inc.,* 372 NYS2d 793 (1975).

5. Where *X* has a lien prior to the lien of the construction mortgage, and he subordinates his lien to the construction mortgage, and the construction lender fails to police disbursement, so that part of the loan proceeds go to other projects, a problem of great difficulty is presented. *Fikes* v. *First Fed. S. & L. Assn.,* 539 P2d 251 (Alaska 1975); *Forest Inc. of Knoxville* v. *Guar. Mtg. Co.,* 534 SW2d 853 (Tenn.); Kratovil, Modern Mortgage Law & Practice, § 253 (1972).

6. Where the construction lender's inspections of the building are done negligently, the lender is liable to the mortgagor. *Equitable S. & L. Assn.* v. *Hewitt,* 67 Ore. 280, 135 P. 684 (1913). A *purchaser* from the mortgagor has no standing to complain of the defects. *Callaizakis* v. *Astor Dev. Co.,* 280 NE2d 512 (Ill. 1972).

7. In California, New Mexico, and Virginia, laws have been passed to the effect that the construction lender shall not be liable for the negligence of the *borrower* in constructing homes unless the loss is a result of the act of the lender. But the lender is still liable to the mortgagor if the lender is negligent in disbursing the loan funds. *Mendoza* v. *Commercial Standard Ins. Co.,* 129 Cal. Reptr. 91.

8. Where the lender pays out mortgage money, but fails to obtain lien waivers, so that mechanic's liens are filed against the property, the lender is liable to the mortgagor. *Speight* v. *Arkansas S. & L. Assn.,* 239 Ark. 587, 393 SW2d 228 (1966); *Hummell* v. *Wichita F. S. & L. Assn.,* 190 Kan. 43, 372 P2d 67 (1962); *M. S. M. Corp.* v. *Knutson Co.,* 167 NW2d 66 (Minn. 1969); *Arten* v. *Citizens Homestead Assn.,* 163 So2d 403 (La. 1964).

REFERENCES: 80 ALR2d 201; 39 ALR3d 247; 47 *N. Car. L. Rev.* 989; 54 *ibid* 952; 10 B. C. *Ind. & Comm. L. Rev.* 932; 49 *Neb. L. Rev.* 863; Kratovil, Modern Mortgage Law and Practice, Chapter 17 (1972) Construction Loans.

RESERVED: §§ 622–632.

21

Mortgage Foreclosures and Redemption

§ 633. **Necessity of foreclosure.** When a mortgage goes into default after all efforts to salvage the property for the mortgagor by sale, refinancing, and so forth have failed, the mortgagee must foreclose his mortgage, for it is only by foreclosure that he can acquire ownership of the property.

§ 634. **Types of foreclosures.** Methods of foreclosure vary from state to state. A common method involves a court proceeding filed by the mortgagee, called a foreclosure suit. In such suits the court orders a public auction sale of the property, and the sale is held by an officer of the court. Up to the time of the foreclosure sale, the mortgagor, his wife, any junior mortgagee, or even the mortgagor's tenant may come in, pay off the mortgage, and stop the foreclosure. This, you will remember, is the equitable right of redemption. In states that have statutory redemption, the highest bidder at the foreclosure sale usually receives a certificate of sale reciting that he will be entitled to a deed if no redemption is made. In states that do not have a statutory redemption period, the highest bidder receives a deed to the land, and this deed gives him ownership of the mortgaged land, free and clear of the rights of the mortgagor.

§ 635. **Statutory redemption.** The equitable right of redemption is cut off by a sale under a foreclosure judgment, or decree, since that was the object of the foreclosure suit. After the foreclosure sale, in many states, an entirely different right arises, called the statutory right of redemption. Laws providing for statutory redemption give the mortgagor and other persons interested in the land, or certain classes of such persons, the right to redeem from the sale within a certain period, usually one year, but varying in different states from two months to two years after the sale.

Most statutory redemption laws were passed in a time when America was predominantly agricultural. Most mortgagors were farmers. When the weather was bad, crops failed, and foreclosures followed. It seemed logical to suppose that next year might bring better weather and good crops. Hence laws created the statutory redemption period, usually one year, and usually the law was so worded that the mortgagor had the right to possession during that year.

At the expiration of the redemption period, if redemption has not been made, the purchaser at the foreclosure sale receives a deed from the officer who made the sale.

Statutory redemption is usually accomplished by payment to the officer who made the sale of the amount of the foreclosure sale plus interest. After redemption the mortgagor holds the land free and clear of the mortgage.

In a number of states there is no statutory redemption after sale. Immediately after the foreclosure sale a deed is given to the purchaser, and he thereupon acquires ownership of the land. In states that do not permit redemption after the foreclosure sale, provision is often made for postponing the sale in some way in order to permit the mortgagor to effect a redemption or discharge of the mortgage prior to the foreclosure sale.

§ 636. Deficiency judgment. A mortgage foreclosure sale is regarded as a payment of the mortgage debt in an amount equal to the sale price. If the foreclosure judgment, or decree, finds that there is $5000 due to the mortgagee on his mortgage, and the property is sold for $4500, the mortgage debt is thereby reduced by $4500, leaving a deficiency of $500 due the mortgagee. Since by virtue of the promissory note that usually accompanies a mortgage, the mortgagor becomes personally liable to the mortgagee for the mortgage debt, the mortgagee is entitled to a personal judgment against the mortgagor for the amount of the deficiency.

In many states, laws have been passed limiting the mortgagee's right to a deficiency decree.

§ 637. Foreclosure by exercise of power of sale. In many states, mortgages may be foreclosed by exercise of a power of sale without resort to any court proceedings. If the mortgage is, in form, a trust deed, a provision will be found therein conferring on the trustee the power to sell the land in the event of a default in the mortgage payments. If the instrument is a regular mortgage, the power of sale is conferred on the mortgagee. However, in Colorado, the power of sale must be exercised by an official known as the public trustee, and in Minnesota, the sale is made by the sheriff or his deputy.

In states where this method of foreclosure is employed, the mortgage or trust deed spells out the events of default that will give the trustee or mortgagee power to sell the premises, and it also sets forth the notice of sale that must be given and the other formalities that must be complied with in making the sale. The state law may also specify the notice of sale that is to be given. In some states, personal notice to the mortgagor is necessary, but in others, advertisement is sufficient. Some state laws provide that a notice of default must be recorded and a stated period of time must elapse thereafter before the sale is held. This gives the mortgagor a final opportunity to pay his debt.

A measure of uncertainty has crept into this area lately. Some courts have found that foreclosure by power of sale without giving the mortgagor or landowner personal service and an opportunity to be heard prior to the sale is an unconstitutional deprivation of property without due process of law. *Turner* v. *Blackburn,* 389 F.Supp. 1250 (1975). Other courts hold to the opposite view. *FNMA* v. *Howlett,* 521 SW2d 428 (Mo. 1975).

Unless the mortgage allows him to do so, the mortgagee cannot purchase the property at his own foreclosure sale, either in his own or his wife's name, or in the name of some third party, and if he does so, the sale may be set aside. *Mills* v. *Mutual B. & L. Assn.,* 6 SE2d 549 (N.C. 1940). The trustee in a deed of trust is likewise forbidden to purchase at his own foreclosure sale. However, the holder of the note secured by a deed of trust is permitted to purchase at the trustee's sale. Deed of trust forms usually expressly permit the trustee to bid at the foreclosure sale, and such provisions are valid. Experience indicates that there will be fewer lawsuits attacking a foreclosure sale if the sale is held by some impartial individual. A lender who uses some individual in his employment as trustee in his deeds of trust often finds it expedient to appoint some disinterested third party as trustee if foreclosure becomes necessary.

The sale is usually at public auction, and a deed is executed to the highest bidder. Whether or not redemption is allowed depends on the local law.

§ 638. **Foreclosure by other methods.** Other methods of foreclosure —strict foreclosure, foreclosure by entry and possession, and foreclosure by writ of entry—are allowed in a small number of states. These involve technical procedures that are only of local interest.

§ 639. **Foreclosure—conscionable conduct.** No matter what the method of foreclosure may be, lenders must always be mindful that today's courts protect consumers, and in the mortgage transaction the borrower is the consumer. Evidence of the protection given to borrowers may be found in recent cases requiring lenders to ascertain the reasons for default and make a concerted effort to avoid foreclosure by voluntary forbearance or recasting the mortgage. *FNMA* v. *Ricks,* 372 NYS 485 (NY 1975). While these cases may apply to a particular class of lenders (FHA and VA mortgagees) and have been undercut by subsequent proclamations by the Department of Housing and Urban Development, the decisions once again announce to lenders that conduct towards borrowers must be conscionable or foreclosure will not be allowed.

EXAMPLE: *B* lost his job and fell four payments in arrears on his mortgage. *L* began foreclosure proceedings whereupon *B,* once again employed, tendered the past due payments. *L* refused the tender because it did not include the attorney's fees incurred in beginning foreclosure. Foreclosure would not be allowed as *L*'s conduct was unconscionable. *Brown* v. *Lynn,* 385 F.Supp. 986 (1974).

REFERENCE: Comment, 53 *Chi-Kent L. Rev.* 703 (1976).

These decisions are reflections of not only the law but also the "fireside equity" practiced by many judges when they sit in foreclosure courts. Frequently, foreclosure will not be allowed unless the borrower is at least three or four payments behind and good faith settlement negotiations have produced no results.

§ 640. **Mortgagee as purchaser at foreclosure sale.** For several reasons, the mortgagee is often the only bidder at the foreclosure sale. The mortgagee is allowed to bid up to the amount of the mortgage debt without producing any cash. The reason is obvious. If he were to pay cash, the officer holding the sale would have to hand the cash back to him in payment of the mortgage debt, for after all, the sale is held to raise money to pay the mortgagee. Again, in states that have redemption laws the highest bidder will not get ownership of or possession of the property until the redemption period is over, and then only if no redemption is made. Land speculators, who are the chief bidders at public land sales, are unwilling to have their money tied up for long periods with such uncertainty as to ultimate ownership of the property.

§ 641. **Mortgagee as owner.** Whenever and however the mortgagee becomes the owner of the property (either by foreclosure or deed in lieu of foreclosure), he must take all the precautions that an owner takes.

Immediately after the foreclosure sale, existing insurance policies must be indorsed to give protection to the mortgagee as an owner, or new policies must be obtained. Reliance on the old policy may be misplaced, since satisfaction of the debt by purchaser at the foreclosure sale or in the deed in lieu transaction satisfies the mortgage debt and may simultaneously extinguish the lender's protection. *Whitestone Savings & Loan Assn.* v. *Allstate Ins. Co.,* 270 NE2d 694 (N.Y. 1971). The necessity of other insurance such as liability, workmen's compensation, dram shop, and so forth should be determined. Since foreclosure usually extinguishes any leases entered into after the mortgage, new arrangements should be entered into with the tenants. *Kage* v. *1795 Dunn Road, Inc.,* 428 SW2d 735 (Mo. 1968). A new owner's title insurance policy should be obtained, and the currency and amount of real estate taxes and assessment payments should be examined. Inquiry should be made of the desirability of retaining or releasing the building manager. The building itself should be inspected for conditions potentially dangerous to tenants, compliance with local, state and federal safety laws as they apply both to employees and others, and conditions that could damage the building or hinder its marketability.

§ 642. **Soldiers' and Sailors' Civil Relief Act.** The Soldiers' and Sailors' Civil Relief Act, passed by the Congress of the United States, affects mortgages in several ways.

1. The court in which proceedings to enforce the mortgage are brought is given power to stay or postpone the foreclosure proceedings.

2. If the landowner is in military service, the mortgage cannot be foreclosed by exercise of the power of sale contained in the mortgage unless the mortgagee first obtains a court order authorizing such foreclosure. If the mortgagee does not know whether or not the owner is in military service, he is gambling if he simply forecloses by exercise of the power of sale. If the owner is not in military service and has not been in military service within three months of the date of the sale, the sale is valid, while if the owner is in military service or was in military service at any time within three months of the date of the foreclosure sale, the foreclosure is void. For this reason, the mortgagee may prefer to foreclose his mortgage by foreclosure suit, even though the mortgage contains a power of sale, since he is thus assured of acquiring good title.

3. In states that have a redemption period following the foreclosure sale, it is now the law that the period of military service shall not be included in computing the redemption period. If a mortgage is foreclosed while the landowner is in military service, the redemption period may be indefinitely prolonged. *Ill. Nat. Bank* v. *Gwinn,* 61 NE2d 249 (Ill. 1945).

4. The holder of an obligation of a person in military service that bears interest at a rate in excess of 6 percent is allowed to collect only 6 percent interest during the period of military service if the mortgagor's ability to pay interest is affected by his military service.

A career soldier is not entitled to the benefit of this statute.

REFERENCE: Kratovil, Modern Mortgage Law and Practice, Ch. 36 (1972).

RESERVED: §§ 643–653.

22

Land Use Controls: Building Restrictions

§ **654. Private and public controls distinguished.** Use of land is controlled in two ways, namely, through *private* controls and through *public* controls.

EXAMPLE: A buys 100 acres of farmland and divides it into 100 residential lots by means of a recorded plat of subdivision which specifies that all lots must be used only for the construction of single-family dwellings. This is *private* control of use of land by means of building restrictions.

EXAMPLE: The City of X adopts a zoning ordinance by which part of the city is zoned for residential use, part for stores, and part for industry. This is *public* control of land use.

Private land use controls rest on the philosophy that where private ownership of land is recognized, as it is in America, ownership of land includes the right to sell it on such terms as please the landowner, including the right to restrict the future use of the land in some way that seems desirable *to the seller*.

There is a parallel, but quite different philosophy, namely, that use of land must be controlled, not in the interest of private individuals as such, but in the public interest. Both methods co-exist under our American law with some overlapping and some conflict.

Historically, private controls antedate public controls by many years. Hundreds of years ago in England, a landowner might have given away his land and included some whimsical or capricious requirements in his gift that, while legally enforceable, contributed nothing toward the practical control of land use.

EXAMPLE: Gifts on the following conditions were sustained by the courts: that the donor reside in the house on the land; that donee would lose the land if he were educated abroad; that donee must always write his name "T. Jackson Mason"; that the minister of donee's church always wear a black gown in the pulpit. *65 U. of Penna. L.R. 527.*

If you bought a home in those early days, there was nothing to prevent your neighbor from constructing a slaughter house, tannery, or other offensive use adjoining your dwelling. Thus matters continued until 1848, when the courts first evolved the idea that if a land developer deeds out all the lots in the subdivision with identical restrictions providing, for example, that only single-family dwellings are permitted in the subdivision, *any lot owner can obtain a court order preventing any other lot owner from violating this restriction.* This was one of the great milestones in the history of law.

While this innovation was truly of immense importance, and remains so, certain problems arose.

EXAMPLE: A plat of subdivision provides that only single-family residences shall be erected in the subdivision, and houses are built and sold in reliance on this restriction. X buys land across the street from the subdivision and erects a tannery thereon. There is nothing the homeowners can do.

For this reason, much later, and not really effectively until 1926 when the United States Supreme Court first sustained the validity of zoning ordinances, a new kind of land use control came into being, namely, a system of *public controls,* implemented by a *zoning ordinance* allocating permitted uses to the various areas of the city. This was and is a far more effective system of land use controls, one that controls the entire area of the city. In an area the city has zoned as residential only, which may and usually does embrace an area greatly exceeding in extent the area one private developer might acquire and restrict, all homeowners are protected against offensive uses.

This development, however, has not rendered private building restrictions obsolete.

EXAMPLE: A, a land developer, acquires 40 acres of land in an area zoned by the city for single-family residences. He records a plat of subdivision which contains restrictions that no residence shall be erected costing less than $75,000. This the city cannot do. Yet it definitely restricts the occupancy of the area in a way that seems desirable to the developer and his customers.

§ 655. Private restrictions in general. Private restrictions fall into five main categories:

1. Whimsical or capricious restrictions imposed by the seller because of some whim or prejudice, such as a restriction that neither tobacco nor liquor shall be used on the premises sold or that there shall be no card-playing on the premises.

2. Covenants for the benefits of land sold or land retained. These last are restrictions imposed by a landowner who owns two adjoining tracts of land and sells one of them.

EXAMPLE: A, owning Lots 1 and 2, with a house on Lot 1, sells vacant Lot 2 with a clause in the deed that no building shall be erected in the front thirty feet of the lot. This protects the view from the front of A's house. Or A could have sold the house lot, with a restriction that no buildings shall be erected on the front thirty feet of the lot retained.

3. Restrictions imposed by a subdivider or land developer with a view to making the subdivision attractive, such as a restriction that only single-family dwellings shall be erected in the subdivision. This is the most important category. These are the restrictions that create a *general plan.*

4. Affirmative covenants running with the land, discussed later herein.

5. Conditions. These are restrictions providing for a reverter of title if they are violated. They also are discussed later.

§ 656. Creation of general plan restrictions. In order to attract lot purchasers, a subdivider or land developer often evolves a building scheme or general plan for restricting the lots in the tract undergoing development to obtain substantial uniformity in building and use. For example, the plan often contemplates that only residences shall be erected, thus excluding stores and industrial uses. The effect is to create a restriction that any lot owner may enforce against any other lot owner. Restrictions upon the use of property, imposed as a part of general plan for the benefit of all lots, give to the purchaser of any lot a right to enforce such restrictions against the purchaser of any other lot. Such restrictions are enforced on the theory that each purchaser buying with knowledge or notice of the general plan impliedly agrees to abide by the plan. 26 CJS Deeds 167.

EXAMPLE: The map or plat of a certain subdivision provides that the subdivision lots shall be used for residence purposes only. A, one of the lot owners, seeks to open a store on his lot. Any lot owner can obtain an injunction preventing A from using his lot for store purposes.

General plan restrictions were originally created by incorporating identical restrictions in all deeds by the subdivider. *Field Ppties. Inc.* v. *Fritz,* 315 So2d 101 (Fla. 1976); 4 ALR2d 1364. This is not the usual practice today. The character that a particular development is to assume is planned at the same time that the acreage is first subdivided into building lots. The subdivider incorporates in the recorded plat or map of the subdivision itself uniform restrictions to which all lots are subject. Clearly the plan is general. *Case* v. *Morisette,* 475 F.2d 1300 (1973). It is best to have each deed state, "subject to restrictions in recorded plat." And since every lot purchaser must take notice of the recorded plat, he has constructive notice of the restriction. Therefore any lot owner may enforce the restriction against any other lot owner. Recently these building schemes have become so elaborate that there is not enough room for them on the plat or map. Hence the restrictions are set up in a recorded *declaration of restrictions* recorded simultaneously with the plat and referred to in the plat. Legally this is as though the restrictions had been set forth in the plat. Subsequently, as sales of the lots are made, the deeds contain clauses stating that the land is subject to such recorded restrictions.

Of course the privilege of creating restrictions is by no means confined to subdividers. Any landowner is at liberty to insert restrictions in his deed when he sells and conveys the land. An enforceable restriction may be inserted in a contract for the sale of land. The landowners in a particular area may enter into an agreement subjecting their land to restrictions.

§ 657. Enforcement of general plan restrictions. If a general plan restriction is violated, *the court will issue an order (injunction) forbidding the violation. Anyone who disobeys the order can be jailed. Structures erected in violation thereof can be ordered demolished. Stewart* v. *Finkelstone,* 206 Mass. 28, 92 NE 37 (1910). For a general plan restriction to be enforced, the one seeking enforcement need only show that the violator purchased his lot with notice of the restriction, either from a recorded document or from actual knowledge of the restriction. The question as to enforcement of a general plan type restriction, then, arises when one lot owner attempts to violate a restriction, and another lot owner seeks a court order prohibiting such attempted violation. The court will ask two questions: (1) Is there a general plan? (2) If there is, did the violator purchase his land with actual knowledge or with notice from the public records of the existence of the general plan? If the answer to these questions is in the affirmative, the restriction will be enforced, except in the situations hereafter discussed.

As to who may enforce a general plan restriction, any lot owner, or his tenant or mortgagee, or contract purchaser may do so. 51 ALR3d 556; 26 C.J.S. Deeds § 167. As long as the subdivider owns any lot in the subdivision he can enforce the restriction. However, when he has sold the last lot, he no longer has any economic interest to protect. Nearly all courts say that he thereupon loses his right to enforce. *Kent* v. *Koch,* 333 P2d 411 (Cal. 1958); *Canel Coal* v. *Indiana,* 78 Ind. App. 115, 134 NE 891 (1922).

The conscientious developer continues to want orderly development of his subdivision even after his last lot is sold. He will therefore create a home owner's association in the form of a nonprofit corporation at the time he creates his subdivision. The plat or declaration of restrictions confers on this association the right to enforce the general plan restrictions. As lots are sold, the lot owners become members of this association. They pay dues to the association, and a fund is thus formed to finance, among other things, a lawsuit if a violation of the restrictions is threatened. This device is valid. *Neponsit Property Owners Assn.* v. *Emigrant Industrial Svgs. Bank,* 278 N.Y. 248, 15 NE2d 793 (1938); *Merrionette Manor Homes Impt. Assn.* v. *Heda,* 11 Ill. App. 2d 186, 136 NE2d 556 (1956).

§ 658. Interpretation of general plan restrictions. The problem of framing restrictions that will carry out the intention of the subdivider is a difficult one. Much litigation has centered around this point. 20 Am.Jur.2d 752.

Location restrictions. When the plat or map of a subdivision shows a line designated as a building line extending across the front portion of the subdivision lots, this is sufficient to create a building line restriction. No substantial parts of buildings may then be erected beyond the building line. Building line restrictions may also be created by restrictions in the deed. The purpose of a building line is twofold: to insure a certain degree of uniformity in the appearance of the buildings and to create a right to unobstructed light, air, and vision. The fact that a small porch, awning, stoop, steps, or an overhanging bay window extends beyond the building line will not constitute a violation of the restriction.

In dealing with the interpretation of building restrictions, keep in mind that the courts are trying to discover and give effect to the intention of the subdivider. Where he leaves his intention in doubt, the court faces a difficult problem. It must be as practical as possible. Common sense must be applied. The literal language of the restriction must often be disregarded. Certainly common sense dictates that minor violations of restrictions must be disregarded. The problem concerns where to draw the line. What, for example, is a "small porch"? However, a so-called bay window that is really the front wall of the house is a violation of the restriction. 55 ALR 332, 172 ALR 1324. Likewise a carport is part of the house and is a violation. *Garden Oaks* v. *Gibbs,* 489 SW2d 133 (Tex. 1972).

Incidental use. A use purely incidental to a permitted use is permitted.

EXAMPLE: Shop in hotel. *Blakely* v. *Gorin,* 313 N.E.2d 903 (Mass. 1974).

CAUTION: When a restriction provides that no building shall be erected within a certain number of feet of the street line, it is the line where the lot meets the street that is meant. In other words, some plat of a subdivision shows this particular lot as fronting on some street. Where the lot ends, the street begins. Often enough, to be sure, the city paves only the middle part of the street strip, and laymen sometimes speak of this as the "street," which is erroneous. The street extends to the lot line and includes not only the roadway, but also the parkway or planted area, if any, sidewalks, if any, and so on. Building line restrictions are measured from the true street line, not from the curb line. *Trunck* v. *Hack's Point,* 204 Md. 193, 103 A2d 343 (1954).

Residence purposes. Many restrictions provide that "the land shall be used for residence purposes" or that "only residences shall be erected on this real estate." Under this type of restriction, any kind of building devoted exclusively to residence purposes may be erected, including a duplex house or an apartment building. 14 ALR2d 1376. If the restriction permits construction of only "private," "single," or "detached" residences, only single-family dwellings are permitted. *Flaks* v. *Wichman,* 128 Colo. 45, 260 P2d 737 (1953). And a prohibition of *apartments* prohibits a *condominium. Callahan* v. *Weilan,* 279 So2d 451 (Ala. 1973); 65 ALR3d 1212.

If the owner occupies his residence, he may take in lodgers. However, if the building is completely converted into a boarding house, the restriction is violated, for this is a business rather than a residential use. Use of the premises as a tourist home also violates a residential restriction. *Deitrick* v. *Leadbetter,* 175 Va. 170, 8 SE2d 276 (1940). If the restriction provides that the premises shall be used only as a residence for one private family, this will prevent the letting of rooms to lodgers. *Sayles* v. *Hall,* 210 Mass. 281, 96 NE 712 (1911). It will also prevent the doubling up of two or more families.

Where the premises are restricted to residence purposes, the erection of a private garage for the use of the occupants of the main dwelling is permitted.

A restriction limiting the use to residence purposes is deemed to prohibit churches. *Housing Authority* v. *Church of God,* 401 Ill. 100, 91 NE2d

500 (1948); *Hall* v. *Church,* 4 Wis. 2d 246, 89 NW2d 798 (1958); 13 ALR2d 1239. Likewise, schools, parking lots, filling stations, and rest homes would be prohibited. 43 ALR 1138, 124 ALR 1012. As to incidental uses, such as a doctor's seeing patients, see 21 ALR3d 641.

Dwelling. Restrictions sometimes limit use of the land to *dwelling purposes.* 38 ALR3d 1419. In Illinois, New Jersey, North Carolina, Ohio, and Pennsylvania, such restrictions do not prohibit the erection of apartment buildings since apartment buildings are "dwellings." *Leverich* v. *Roy,* 338 Ill. App. 248, 87 NE2d 226 (1949); 14 ALR2d 1376. However, in Massachusetts, Michigan, and New Hampshire, apartments are not considered to be *dwellings.* Townhouses are not "dwellings." *Shapiro* v. *Levin,* 223 Pa. Super. 536 (1973).

A good residential restriction might read as follows:

SUGGESTED FORM: Only one detached single-family dwelling and private attached garage appertaining thereto shall be erected on each lot. No use shall be made of said premises except such as is incidental to the occupation thereof for residence purposes by one private family residing in a detached, single-family dwelling.

This form has the following advantages: The phrase "single-family dwelling" keeps out apartments and other multiple dwellings. Single dwellings will not do the trick because in some states, a restriction against single dwellings does not prohibit a duplex or apartment.

Vocabulary is important. A *duplex* consists of two single-family dwellings, each on its own lot, but sharing a party wall that straddles the line between the lots. A *bi-level* is a two-story house designed for occupancy by one family. A *two-flat* is a building with two apartments, one above the other, designed for occupancy by two families. A two-flat is not a single-family dwelling. 14 ALR2d 1376. The use of the word "detached" keeps out duplexes or row houses. The stipulation as to occupation by one private family keeps out lodgers and prevents doubling up of families.

If a restriction merely specifies the type of building that can be built but is silent regarding the use of the building, an argument may be advanced that the building can be used for any purpose. As a rule, courts try to give effect to the obvious intention by holding that use of the structures must conform to the purposes for which it was erected. 155 ALR 1000.

EXAMPLE: A restriction provided that "no structure shall be built except for dwelling purposes." A dwelling was erected. Later, the owner of the dwelling attempted to use it as a beauty parlor. The court held that the building could be used only for dwelling purposes. *Holderness* v. *Central States Finance Corp.,* 241 Mich. 604, 217 NW 764 (1928). Obviously, the restriction was badly drafted. If it had been properly drafted, litigation could not have arisen.

The restriction should restrict the use of the *land* as well as use of the *building.* If the restriction deals only with use of the building, the argument may be advanced that any use of the land is permitted. *Albrecht* v. *State Highway Commission,* 363 SW2d 643 (Mo. 1963). Again, courts will usually come to the rescue by holding that the intention was to restrict use of both building and land.

EXAMPLE: A restriction provided that no building erected on the land should be used for any purpose other than as a private dwelling place. The landowner attempted to use the vacant land as a parking lot. He contended that the restriction applied only to the use of buildings and therefore did not apply to vacant land. The court held that it was the intention to restrict use of both building and land. *Hoover* v. *Waggoman,* 52 N.M. 371, 199 P2d 991 (1948); 155 ALR 528, 1007. It has even been held that a restriction calling for only one detached single-family dwelling per lot impliedly forbids occupancy by two families. *Freeman* v. *Gee,* 423 P2d 155 (Utah 1967).

Duplex. Often one will hear the argument that a duplex is really two single-family dwellings connected by a party wall. *Stephenson* v. *Perlitz,* 537 SW2d 287 (Tex. 1976); *Easterly* v. *Hall,* 182 SE2d 671 (S.C. 1971). To keep out duplexes, it is therefore advisable to have your restriction read that only *detached* single-family dwellings may be built. *Freeman* v. *Gee,* 423 P2d 155 (Utah 1967).

Business purposes. When the restriction forbids use of the premises for business purposes, the following are not permitted: gasoline filling stations, billboards, and parking for business purposes. Especially in older deeds, one is likely to find restrictions prohibiting use of the property for a "trade or business." Suppose a doctor uses a room of his home as an office for the practice of medicine. This would not violate such a restriction because the practice of medicine is not a *trade* or *business;* it is a *profession. Auerbacher* v. *Smith,* 19 N.J. Super. 191, 88 A2d 262 (1952); 21 ALR3d 641.

Fences. A restriction against "fences" does not bar hedges.

Brick construction. Brick veneer satisfies a requirement for brick construction. *Luciano* v. *Paratore,* 88 N.Y.S. 2d 715.

Structures. At times a restriction will prohibit the erection of a "structure" of a particular kind.

EXAMPLE: A restriction prohibited the erection of a structure detrimental to a high-class residential district.

At other times the restriction may prohibit erection of a "structure" on the front thirty feet of a lot.

In both cases the court must decide the meaning of the word "structure." 75 ALR3d 1095. It seems impossible to draw any conclusions. The cases are decided on the specific facts of each case. They involve fences, walls, driveways, walkways, mobile homes or house trailers, earth fills, air conditioners, sheds, tennis courts, and so on. 75 ALR3d 1095.

§ 659. **Senior citizens.** There are, of course, numerous subdivisions restricted to senior sitizens. This is accomplished by means of general plan type restrictions in a declaration of restrictions. They are entirely valid. 68 ALR3d 1239.

SUGGESTION TO DRAFTSMAN: Since the old law frowns on restrictions on the *sale* of land, frame your restrictions in terms of restrictions on *occupancy* since these present no legal problem.

§ **660. Defective restrictions.** Many restrictions are so poorly drafted that they fail to achieve their main purpose.

EXAMPLE: A restriction provided that "no flat roof dwelling house shall be erected." Since no other type of building was mentioned, a flat roof church could be erected. *Corbridge* v. *Westminster,* 18 Ill. App.2d 245, 151 NE2d 822 (1958).

You can see that many restrictions, particularly the older ones, are negative in form. They contain enumerations of prohibited uses, such as apartments and businesses. Such devices are doomed to failure. In the first place, nobody ever makes the list of excluded uses long enough, and nobody, of course, can cover the uses that do not even exist today but will crop up in the future. This is why, particularly for residential property, modern restriction plans simply specify the one type of permitted use that is, "Only detached single-family dwellings shall be constructed, and the premises shall be used only as a residence for one private family."

§ **661. Plans of buildings.** Often a scheme of restrictions provides that no building shall be erected until the plans and specifications therefor have been approved by the developer or subdivider. Such provisions are valid, but any refusal to approve plans will be set aside by the courts if such refusal is capricious, arbitrary, or unreasonable. *Hannula* v. *Hacienda Homes,* 34 Cal.App.2d 442, 211 P2d 302 (1949); 19 ALR2d 1268; 47 ALR3d 1232.

§ **662. Ingress and egress for a prohibited use.** Occasionally a lot in a restricted residential subdivision is acquired by one who seeks to use it for the benefit of nonresidential land outside the subdivision. This is not permitted.

EXAMPLE: A plat restriction permitted only residential use of the lots. X, who owned a restaurant across the street from the subdivision, bought 3 lots in the subdivision, meaning to use them for access to the restaurant and parking. The court prohibited this. *Bennett* v. *Consolidated Realty Co.,* 226 Ky. 747, 11 SW2d 910, 61 ALR 453 (1928); 25 ALR2d 904.

§ **663. Mobile homes.** Mobile homes present some interpretation problems.

EXAMPLE: A restriction prohibited "trailer homes." A mobile home 12 feet wide and 64 feet long, which was tied to the ground with cables and connected to septic tank, was brought into the subdivision. This is not a "trailer home." *Crawford* v. *Boyd,* 453 SW2d 232 (1970); *Hussey* v. *Ray,* 462 SW2d 45 (Tex. 1970).

EXAMPLE: A restriction prohibited "mobile homes." A typical mobile home was installed, placed on a cement foundation, and connected to utilities. The restriction was violated. The fact that, at the moment, the structure could not be moved, did not prevent its being a "mobile home." *Smith* v. *Bowers,* 463 SW2d 222 (Tex. 1971); *Brownfield* v. *McKee,* 334 NE2d 131 (Ill. 1974).

EXAMPLE: A restriction forbade any lot owner "to erect a dwelling having less than 1150 square feet of inside living area." A lot owner who put a mobile home on his lot did not violate this restriction. He did not "erect" anything. *Dotson* v. *Hannaford,* 177 SE2d 376 (Ga. 1970). *Contra: Timmerman* v. *Gabriel,* 470 P2d 528 (Mont. 1970).

EXAMPLE: A restriction prohibited metal or brick siding on any building. This would exclude a mobile home. *Lawrence* v. *Harding,* 225 Ga. 148, 166 SE2d 336.

§ 664. Modification, extension, and release of general plan restrictions. If the right to modify general plan is not reserved in the deeds, plat, or declaration, it takes a unanimous vote of all lot owners (probably also their mortgagees) to modify or release the restrictions. *Steve Vogli & Co.* v. *Lane,* 405 SW2d 885 (Mo. 1966); 4 ALR3d 570. This is rarely obtainable.

EXAMPLE: All owners but one signed a release of the restrictions. He was entitled to enforce the restrictions. *Evangelical Church* v. *Sahlem,* 254 N.Y. 161, 172 NE 455 (1930).

In recent restriction plans, subdividers have often included a clause giving themselves the right to waive or dispense with the restrictions as to some or all of the lots. This is dangerous. A number of courts have held that such a provision destroys the uniformity necessary to a general plan, and therefore the restrictions cannot be enforced by one lot owner against another. 19 ALR2d 1282.

When the right to modify the restrictions is reserved to the developer by the deeds, plat, or declaration, he may validly exercise this right. *McComb* v. *Harly,* 132 N.J.Eq. 182, 26 A2d 891; 4 ALR2d 570.

In providing for periodical extensions and modifications of the restrictions in the declaration, thought must be given to the voting arrangements.

EXAMPLE: There is a difference between "the owners of a majority of the lots" and "a majority of the lot owners."

Where the right to modify restrictions is reserved in the plat, declaration of restrictions or deeds, any modifications voted by the required majority must be general in their nature.

EXAMPLE: A majority of the landowners voted to take one lot out of the restrictions so that a filling station be erected on it. This was invalid. *Riley* v. *Boyle,* 434 P2d 525.

Any amendment must be reasonable and must leave the plan basically intact. *Flamingo Ranch Estates* v. *Sunshine Ranchers,* 303 So2d 665 (Fla. 1974).

§ 665. Mortgage foreclosure. One must exercise care concerning any mortgage that is recorded prior in time to the declaration of restrictions.

EXAMPLE: *R* records a construction mortgage on some vacant but subdivided land to *E*. Thereafter he records a declaration of restrictions. He sells a few lots, and deeds are recorded to the buyers. Then he defaults on his mortgage, which is foreclosed. The restrictions are wiped out by the foreclosure. *Boyd* v. *Park Realty Corp.,* 137 Md 36, 111 A 129 (1920).

The construction mortgage should have stated that it was subject to a declaration of restrictions to be recorded later, or simultaneously with the recording of the declaration of restrictions *E* could have recorded a subordination of his mortgage to the restrictions.

§ 666. Minor violations. Earlier it was stated that courts will not force removal of trivial encroachments. A court is a tribunal where revenge or punishment in the way of reprisal has no place. *Kajawski* v. *Null,* 177 A2d 101 (Pa. 1962). The courts will "balance the equities." *De Marco* v. *Palazzolo,* 209 NW2d 540 (Mich. 1973). If an unintentional minor violation of a restriction is involved, the courts will not compel its removal. This has been explained in connection with location restrictions. The same rule applies to other violations.

EXAMPLE: A restriction limited the height of buildings to twenty-five feet. By mistake a landowner erected a building that was twenty-six feet high. The court refused to compel him to remove the offending one foot.

And where the right to modify or release restrictions is reserved in the subdivider, only he can exercise the right, and when he conveys out all the lots, the right ends. *Pulver* v. *Mascolo,* 237 A2d 97 (1967); *Richmond* v. *Pennscott Builders, Inc.,* 251 N.Y.S.2d 845 (1964).

§ 667. Factors that render general plan restrictions unenforceable. In considering what factors render restrictions unenforceable, it is necessary, first of all, to distinguish between restrictions that do not provide for a reverter of title and those that do. We consider first the general plan type restrictions, which are traditionally enforced by means of an injunction, or court order, forbidding violation. Such orders are not granted lightly. Various circumstances are considered by the courts in determining whether such an order should be granted.

General principles. In determining the legal duration of a restriction, which is the subject matter of much of this section, keep in mind that courts are practical. Even if the restriction recites that it will exist "forever," courts are likely to terminate it when it has become useless. *Ferguson* v. *Zion Ev. Church,* 190 P2d 1019 (Okla. 1948).

Change in neighborhood. A court will not, as a rule, enforce a restriction by injunction when the neighborhood has so changed in character and environment as to make it unfit to continue the original use. 4 ALR2d 1111; 53 ALR3d 492; 26 CJS Deeds § 171.

EXAMPLE: A restriction provides that lots in the subdivision shall be used only for residence purposes. Gradually the neighborhood changes character, and stores and factories creep in. This often happens because no single homeowner wishes to incur the expense of hiring an attorney and litigating the right of his neighbors to violate the restrictions. When it becomes impossible to characterize the area as residential, courts will refuse to enforce the restriction on the ground that it is no longer possible to carry the original plan into effect. However, if the change in neighborhood affects only a part of the subdivision while the remainder is unchanged, the restrictions may be enforced in the area that remains unchanged. *O'Neill* v. *Wolf,* 338 Ill. 508, 170 NE 669. Suppose *A* owns a house in a restricted subdivision, but six blocks away, a number of violating structures are erected. *A*'s acquiescence in these violations will not bar him from stopping a violation next door to him or in the same block. In other words, these previous violations are so remote from him that they do not constitute a change in his immediate neighborhood, nor could A be charged with undue neglect in enforcing his rights. *Meek* v. *Yarowsky,* 236 Mich. 251, 210 NW 226.

A question on which the courts are not in agreement relates to changes that occur outside the subdivision.

EXAMPLE: A plat restriction limits the subdivision to residential uses. As the surrounding area changes, many stores are built across the street from the subdivision. Some courts insist that the front tier of lots in the subdivision must hold the line and the restrictions continue in force. *Oritz* v. *Jeter,* 479 SW2d 752; 2 Am.Law Ppty. § 9.39. Since it is not always easy to get people to buy homes across the street from the stores, other courts will allow changes of this nature to sway them in refusing enforcement of the restrictions. *Hecht* v. *Stephens,* 464 P2d 258 (Kan. 1970); *Exchange Nat. Bank* v. *City of Des Plains,* 336 NE2d 8 (Ill. 1975).

The effect of the enactment of a zoning ordinance that conflicts with the building restrictions is considered elsewhere.

Numerous violations. Even when the restricted neighborhood has not changed its general character, the right to enforce a particular restriction may be lost by abandonment. When the property owners in the subdivision have violated the restrictions and the violations have been so general as to indicate an abandonment of the original general plan, the restrictions will not be enforced. The reason for this is that the purpose of the restriction can no longer be carried out. It would be an injustice to a property owner to compel him to conform to a restriction that most of the other owners have violated when such enforcement would be of no benefit to the party seeking to enforce the restriction.

EXAMPLE: A building line was established across a block consisting of fifteen lots. On nine of the lots, buildings were erected that extended across the building line. The owner of a lot that had remained vacant began construction of a building that would also violate the building line. The owner of another vacant lot sought a court order to prevent this violation. The court order was refused. The value of the building line had been destroyed by the numerous violations. *Ewersten* v. *Gerstenberg,* 186 Ill. 344, 57 NE 1051 (1900).

Abandonment. Even in the absence of numerous violations a landowner's acquiescence in violations of restrictions may render restrictions unenforceable. Restatement, Property § 561; 26 CJS Deeds § 169.

EXAMPLE: A plat restricts all the lots to single-family dwellings. Without protest by others, *A* builds an apartment buiding on Lot 5 and *B* builds an apartment building on

Lot 7. *X* now seeks to build an apartment building on Lot 6, which is sandwiched between the existing apartments. He may do so.

And there may be a *partial abandonment*. This leaves the remainder of the restrictions enforceable. *Donahoe* v. *Marston,* 547 P2d 39 (Mont. 1976).

EXAMPLE: A plat restriction provided that all lots were to be used for residence purposes and only single-family dwellings could be erected. A number of two-flats were erected. Now one lot owner wishes to put in a store. He cannot do so. *Noyes* v. *McDonnell,* 398 P2d 838. Likewise minor violations of a building line furnish no excuse for major violations. *Carter* v. *Conroy,* 544 P2d 258 (Ariz. 1976).

Violations by party who seeks to enforce restriction. One who violates a nonreverter type restriction in some substantial degree or manner cannot procure a court injunction restraining the violation of the restriction by others. Restatement, Property § 560; 26 CJS Deeds, § 169, p. 1163; 4 ALR2d 1142.

EXAMPLE: A plat restriction permits only single-family dwellings to be erected. *A* constructs a two-flat. His neighbor, *B,* now seeks to erect a three-flat. *A* cannot prevent this.

Delay in enforcing restrictions. Where a nonreverter type restriction, as distinguished from a condition, is involved, a person wishing to prevent a violation must act promptly.

EXAMPLE: A subdivision plat contains a nonreverter type building restriction forbidding the construction of anything but single-family dwellings. *X,* who owns a house in this subdivision, observes that *Y,* another lot owner, is erecting a filling station. After construction of the station has been completed, *X* files a suit to have it demolished. The court will refuse to interfere. *X* has been guilty of undue delay. 12 ALR2d 394; 36 ALR2d 861, 870.

Restrictions about to expire by lapse of time. Many restrictions specifically state a time limit for their expiration. Suppose construction of a building that violates the restriction is begun a year or so before the restriction has expired by lapse of time. Here the courts may refuse to enforce the restriction for the simple, practical reason that to do so would be of little practical benefit.

Statutes of limitations. In some states laws have been enacted limiting the period of time for bringing a suit for *violation* of a building restriction.

EXAMPLE: In Missouri, such a suit must be brought within two years after the date the restriction was violated. Sec. 516.095 Mo. Stat. New York has a two-year limitation on building line violations and in Massachusetts, the period is six years. In Massachusetts, building restrictions unlimited in duration expire after 30 years. Basye, *Clearing Land Titles* (2d ed. 1970) § 143. In Colorado a suit to enforce a restriction must be brought within one year from the date of violation. *Wolf* v. *Hallenbeck,* 123 P2d 412 (1942).

State laws placing time limits on enforcement of restrictions. A number of states—Arizona, Georgia, Massachusetts, Michigan, Minnesota, Rhode Island, and Wisconsin, for example—have enacted laws providing that after the lapse of a stated number of years restrictions become unenforceable. Basye, Clearing Land Titles, § 143 (2d ed. 1970). And in all states having marketability of title laws, restrictions will expire after the permitted time unless kept alive by new recording as provided in the law. *Semachko* v. *Hopko,* 301 NE2d 560 (Ohio 1973).

Other factors. Courts are more merciful when the violation is not willful but is due to accident or mistake, as where my surveyor makes an error, and as a result my building extends over a building line. They are also more merciful toward minor violations than they are toward major violations. Of course if the party seeking to enforce the restriction has said or done something that would encourage me to go ahead with the violation, he will get no help from the courts.

§ **668. Conditions.** A condition is a restriction that is coupled with a *reverter clause.* This clause provides that if the restriction is violated, ownership reverts to the grantor in the deed.

EXAMPLE: A deeds a lot to *B* with a provision forbidding sale or use of intoxicating liquor on the lot and that in case of violation, ownership reverts to *A.* In time the premises are sold to *X,* who puts in a drugstore with a liquor department. *A* files a suit. The court will give the property back to *A.*

The outstanding characteristic of a condition is the fact that if it is violated, the grantor may get his land back by filing a suit to obtain possession. He need not pay any compensation for it. Any mortgages or other interests in the land created after the creation of the condition are extinguished if the condition is enforced, again without payment of compensation to the mortgagee. This rule operates so harshly that courts are reluctant to construe a provision as a condition. In nearly all states, if the restrictive provision is followed by a clause providing that in the event of a violation of the restrictions the title to land shall revert to the grantor in the deed, the restrictive provision is a condition. If the deed contains no reverter clause, that is, a clause providing for a reverter or forfeiture of title in the event of violation of the restrictions, the restrictive provision is usually a covenant. The nomenclature employed by the parties is by no means decisive as to the character of the restriction created.

EXAMPLE: A deed contained this clause: "These presents are upon the express condition that the said premises shall not be used or occupied as a tavern or public house." There was no reverter clause. It was held to be a covenant. *Koch* v. *Streuter,* 232 Ill. 594, 83 NE 1072 (1908). Violation would not cause a reverter.

Occasionally the condition is referred to herein as a *reverter type restriction.*

§ **669. Enforcement of conditions.** When a condition (that is, a reverter type of restriction) occurs in a deed but the condition forms no part of any general plan, enforcement is relatively simple. The condition can be enforced by the grantor in the deed, or, if he is dead, by his heirs. Other lot owners in the same subdivision cannot enforce the condition.

Suppose, however, that *X* subdivides a tract of land and in selling the lots includes in each deed an identical condition. Here the problem grows far more complex. One thing is clear. The same building restriction may be both a condition and a restriction. For example, if the restriction sets forth that it is a covenant and restriction on behalf of all lot owners in the subdivision and in addition, that the grantor may declare a reverter if the restriction is violated, then, of course, any lot owner can enforce the restriction by injunction, treating it as a nonreverter type general plan restriction, but the grantor may also enforce it by declaring a reverter of title. *O'Malley* v. *Central Church,* 67 Ariz. 254, 194 P2d 444 (1948). Suppose, however, that one can deduce the existence of a general plan only from the fact that the conditions in all deeds happen to be identical. There is no language indicating that the provision is also to be treated as a covenant in favor of other lot owners. Here some courts are willing to allow other lot owners to enforce the condition on the theory that a covenant in their behalf must have been intended. *Sayles* v. *Hall,* 210 Mass. 281, 96 NE 712 (1911); *Simon* v. *Henrichson,* 394 SW2d 249 (Tex. Civ. App. 1965); *Genske* v. *Jensen,* 188 Wis. 17, 205 NW 548 (1925). Other courts see only what is on the printed page. Since the provision reads like a simple condition, only the grantor or his heirs are permitted to enforce it. *Werner* v. *Graham,* 181 Cal. 174, 183 Pac. 945; *Whitton* v. *Clark,* 112 Conn. 28, 151 Atl. 305 (1930); *Finchum* v. *Vogel,* 194 So2d 49 (Fla. 1966); *Goodman v. Bingle,* 48 SW2d 432 (Tex. Civ. App. 1932).

A recorded condition can be enforced against any subsequent purchaser or mortgagee of the land. Enforcement of a condition by the grantor in the deed containing the condition, or by his heirs, if he is dead, extinguishes all subsequent titles and rights in the land.

EXAMPLE: A conveys a lot to *B* with a condition in the deed that the premises shall not be used for the sale of liquor. The deed provides that in the event of violation of this provision, title to the property shall revert to A. *B* sells and conveys the property to C, who places a mortgage thereon to *D*. Thereafter, C leases the building to *E*, and the latter uses the property for the sale of liquor. A brings suit to recover the land on the ground that the condition has been violated. A will be allowed to recover the land and all buildings erected on it without payment of any compensation, and he will have good title free and clear of the mortgage and lease.

For the above reason, mortgagees are often reluctant to loan money on land that is subject to a condition. In fact, many insurance companies, which are authorized by law to loan money on first mortgages only, cannot legally make a loan on land that is subject to a condition. The problem may be handled in a number of different ways.

1. The person who has the right to enforce a reverter (the grantor in the deed creating the condition, or his heirs) may always release the reverter outright to the landowner.
2. The person who has the right to enforce a reverter may *subordinate* this right to

a mortgage by a document stating that the reverter right is *subject to* the mortgage. If the subordination is unequivocal, the mortgagee, when he forecloses, completely extinguishes the condition.

3. Many subdividers who place conditions in their deeds also include provisions in their deeds stating that the reverter right is subordinate to all mortgages. These provisions are broad in their terms and protect any mortgagee who may take a mortgage on the land.

4. In some instances title companies will insure against loss caused by a reverter of title.

§ 670. Factors that render conditions unenforceable. In many states, especially where older court decisions are still followed, the factors discussed above that would prevent enforcement of a *nonreverter type* restriction have little application to conditions, that is, *reverter type restrictions.* For example, in nearly all states, the grantor in a deed containing a condition, or his heirs, if he is dead, has the right to enforce a condition even though the neighborhood has so changed that enforcement is of little practical utility. In one or two modern states, however, the change of neighborhood rule is now also applied to conditions, and conditions will not be enforced where the neighborhood has changed. *Letteau* v. *Ellis,* 122 Cal. App. 584, 10 P2d 496 (1932); *Cole* v. *Colorado Springs,* 381 P2d 13 (Colo. 1963); *Koehler* v. *Rowland,* 275 Mo. 573, 205 SW 217 (1917); *Townsend* v. *Allen,* 250 P2d 292 (Cal. 1953).

Again, in every state, laws exist allowing a certain time, often as long as twenty years, for the bringing of a suit to declare a reverter of title and to enforce a condition. This period of time runs not from the date of the deed containing the condition, but from the date the condition is violated. Often situations arise where, after the condition has been violated, no action has been taken to enforce the condition, and the landowner continues in possession, perhaps for several years. Mere delay in enforcing a condition, so long as the period allowed by law has not expired, does not, in most states, bar enforcement of a condition. But if the one who has a right to declare a reverter stands idly by, apparently acquiescing in the violation of the condition, sees valuable improvement being made by the landowner, and delays proceedings to enforce the condition until after the improvements have been completed, some modern courts feel that this conduct is so unfair to the landowner that they refuse to enforce the condition. 39 ALR2d 1111.

Reverter acts. In some states laws have been passed outlawing conditions after a certain specified period of time has elapsed from the date of their creation. *Trustees* v. *Batdorf,* 6 Ill.2d 486, 130 NE2d 111 (1955). But see *Bd. of Educ.* v. *Miles,* 15 N.Y.2d 364, 207 NE2d 181, criticized in 1965 *Law Forum* 941. Marketability of title laws also have this result.

Nominal conditions. A number of states have statutes that conditions may be disregarded when they become "merely nominal" or "without substantial benefit to the parties." Basye, Clearing Land Titles (2d ed. 1970) § 143.

EXAMPLE: A subdivider deeded out all lots with a reverter clause against trade or business. After he had deeded out all lots he could not enforce the conditions. They had only nominal value to him. He could not be hurt by violations. *Ingersoll Engineering Co. v. Crocker*, 228 Fed. 845 (Mich. 1915).

Acquiescence in violations. Sometimes a general plan is revealed by the existence of identical conditions in deeds. In such case, if the owner of the reverter right follows a course of conduct that results in numerous violations of the conditions, he will, in some states, be denied the right to enforce any of the conditions. 39 ALR2d 1133.

EXAMPLE: A, a subdivider, sold all the lots in the subdivision by deeds containing conditions against sale of intoxicating liquor. Later, he voluntarily released this clause as to a number of lots, and saloons were built on the released lots. He was refused the right to enforce any of the unreleased conditions. *Wedum-Aldahl Co. v. Miller*, 18 Cal. App.2d 745, 64 P2d 762 (1937).

It can be seen that while the older and stricter court decisions freely allow the enforcement of conditions, the modern decisions are beginning to apply to conditions the same rules that they apply to nonreverter type restrictions.

§ 671. Covenants running with the land. The topic covered in this section is best explained by an illustration.

EXAMPLE: A owns two adjoining lots, Lots 1 and 2. A sells Lot 1 to *B*, and in the deed he inserts a clause stating that *B* covenants to keep in repair the fence between the two lots. Lot 2 enjoys the *benefit* of this covenant. Lot 1 bears the *burden* of the covenant. Any subsequent owner of Lot 1 must comply with this covenant and will be liable to pay damages to the owner of Lot 2 if he fails to do so. Any subsequent owner of Lot 2 will be able to enforce this covenant. *Such an affirmative covenant runs with the land,* much in the same fashion as an appurtenant easement runs with the land, the *burden* of the covenant running with Lot 1 and the *benefit* running with Lot 2.

Courts are somewhat reluctant to see land burdened with covenants that impose *personal liability* on subsequent owners, for such covenants tend somewhat to restrict saleability of such land. These requirements are of diminishing importance today, for most covenants relating to land are *negative covenants,* that is, covenants *restricting the use of land, and these are enforced today by means of injunctions rather than damage suits.*

EXAMPLE: A, a subdivider, sells all lots in the subdivision by deeds providing that only single-family dwellings can be erected. *B* buys a lot and attempts to build a store. *C*, another lot owner, obtains a court order forbidding such construction.

In issuing such orders courts ignore all the technicalities that surround damage suits. As long as a property owner bought his land with notice, either actual or from the public record, that the land was bound by a covenant, he is subject to court injunctions compelling obedience. In modern times, in other words, the old-fashioned method of enforcing covenants by damage suits that may not be decided by a jury until years after the suit has been filed, and then may offer only a slim chance of persuading a jury or collecting the damages a jury may award, has given way to the new, effective method of enforcing a restrictive covenant by a judge's injunction order that may issue within a few days after suit is filed. *Affirmative covenants,* such as those requiring payment of assessments for maintenance of common grounds in a planned unit development, still pose the problems relating to covenants running with the land.

§ 672. **Racial restrictions.** Racial restrictions, that is, restrictions prohibiting use of occupancy by, or sale of, the land to persons other than members of the Caucasian race are discussed elsewhere.

§ 673. **Suggestions:**

If you are about to buy real estate, you are concerned with several questions about restrictions: (1) Do any restrictions exist that will hamper or prevent the use you intended to make of this land or prevent construction of the building you have in mind? (2) What does the contract of sale say about restrictions? (3) Assuming that you are buying improved real estate and therefore have no building problem, are there reverter clauses in the restriction under which you may lose your title or that may hamper your financing of the real estate? (4) If there are restrictions, and the restrictions are desirable from your point of view, do you get the right to enforce them against other property owners?

In answering Question 3 above, keep in mind that if there is a condition containing a reverter clause, and some prior owner violated the clause by constructing the wrong type of building or by committing some other violation, the grantor in the deed containing the condition has the right to take the property away from you.

In answering Question 4 above, keep in mind the rules stated in the text. Lot owners get the best protection when the restrictions are incorporated in the map or plat of the subdivision, since this leaves no room for doubt that there is a general plan. The lot owners get the least protection in cases where the restrictions are imposed by the subdivider, who includes conditions in his deed to the lot owners. Except in a few states, only the subdivider or his heirs can, as a rule, enforce such conditions, and the subdivider is likely to lose interest once he has sold all lots in the subdivision. Also, when the subdivider has created conditions, the lot owners must be prepared to go to him each time they mortgage their lands and buy from him a subordination of reverter. Mortgagees usually insist on this protection, and lot owners have no recourse but to pay for it.

If you are attempting to obtain the release of a restriction, you must keep in mind the rules regarding the persons who may enforce the restriction. For example, if you buy a lot in a subdivision and the plat or map of the subdivision contains a restriction that only single-family dwellings shall be constructed, it is a waste of time to obtain the consent of the owners of the two neighboring lots to the construction of a two-flat building, because any lot owner in the subdivision can block construction of such a building.

RESERVED: §§ 674–684.

23

Land Use Controls: Zoning and Building Ordinances

§ 685. **In general.** This is a very difficult subject to master for several reasons. Each tract of land is unique. My house or lot usually differs in some way from my neighbor's house or lot. As will be seen, the court tailors its decision to the particular tract of land. Again, most real estate law goes back hundreds of years, and much of it has remained relatively stable. The law of deeds and easements, for example, changes very little. But zoning really dates back only to 1926. Prior to that time it was considered illegal. In 1926 the United States Supreme Court held that zoning was valid. Since that time, moreover, the country has changed. The inner city is blighted, and is surrounded by suburbs determined to keep things as they are in their particular suburb. Some courts sustain the suburban officials in this effort.

EXAMPLE: A village "zoned out" apartments, limiting construction to single-family dwellings. The court sustained this zoning. This effectively limits occupancy to middle-class or well-to-do people, because poor people cannot afford to own homes erected on expensive suburban land. However, another court ruled that if there was enough vacant land for apartments, the village must zone some of it for apartments. The village cannot "zone out" the poor.

Remember that there are fifty states, and each is at liberty to adopt its own views because the United States Supreme Court has largely chosen to ignore zoning in recent years. The Supreme Court changes its mind frequently, and when this occurs, the "constitution" changes. This is also true of the state courts.

EXAMPLE: New Jersey court decisions were formerly quite favorable to the suburbs. Now they are leading the fight to open the suburbs to the poor.

Reading zoning decisions is a difficult task. The court must give a reason for its decision. But often the decision does not state the real reason.

At times one can glean from the language of the decision the feeling that the court suspected that the developer had improperly influenced the zoning officials to get a zoning change. Obviously, the court, in striking down the change, will state a "legal reason" for its decision, not the real reason. The financial rewards in zoning changes are very great and people succumb to temptation. A tract of land may increase its value twentyfold or more if the zoning is changed.

The decisions, it is evident then, are far from harmonious. Judges are people. By and large they are well-to-do. Many own their own homes. Many live in the suburbs. Unconsciously perhaps, this creeps into judicial thinking.

Nevertheless, there are some rules, and the areas of conflict can be explored.

Types of litigation situations. Although there are many variations on this theme, there are several *main* types of zoning litigation situations.

EXAMPLE: A developer buys land in a residential suburb and seeks a zoning change to permit construction of an apartment and store complex. The village refuses. The developer goes to court.

EXAMPLE: In the example given above, suppose the village chooses to change the zoning and permit the complex to be constructed. Now the neighbors go to court to block construction.

EXAMPLE: A developer wishes to develop an area in a village, and the village refuses rezoning because it is financially unable to supply needed expansion of schools, sewer, water, and so forth. The developer goes to court.

§ 686. History. The first zoning ordinance was adopted by New York City. Its purpose was to prevent the garment district from spilling over into the fashionable Fifth Avenue shopping area. But the real history of zoning began in 1926, when the Supreme Court held zoning valid. *Village* of *Euclid* v. *Ambler Realty Co.,* 272 U.S. 365, 47 Sup. Ct. 114, 71 L. Ed. 303 (1926). Historically, the Village of Euclid was founded by some land surveyors who liked the location they had surveyed and named the town after their favorite mathematician. Today, "cooky cutter" zoning that divides the municipality into rigid zones with rectangular lots in each zone, as was done in the Village of Euclid, is derisively referred to as "Euclidean zoning."

Early zoning ordinances generally divided the city into three zones: residential, commercial, and manufacturing. Only residences were permitted in residence districts. Both stores and residences were allowed in commercial zones. All types of uses were permitted in manufacturing zones. Attached to the ordinance was a map showing zone boundaries.

Since only residential uses were permitted in residential zones, residential use came to be known as a *preferred use*. All other zones were *cumulative zones* in that they permitted residences in commercial zones, for example, and stores and residences in industrial zones.

Modern zoning ordinances usually create a greater number of classifications. Residential districts may be divided into single-family districts and multiple-family districts. Multiple-family zones may be divided into *walk-ups* and *high-rise* (elevator building) zones. Commercial zones may be divided into retail and wholesale districts, industrial zones into heavy and light industry zones. Small stores may be permitted in apartment buildings and planned unit developments.

Originally all states enacted *zoning enabling acts* which granted zoning power to their cities and villages and laid down the ground rules. Today many cities have *home rule* powers and need not obey the state zoning enabling act.

§ **687. Noncumulative zoning.** Attempts are being made now to have zoning ordinances that do more than keep industries and stores out of residential zones. They are being used to exclude residences from commercial and industrial zones. Ordinances zoning certain areas exclusively for industrial purposes are fairly widespread and are valid. *Roney* v. *Board of Supervisors,* 138 Cal. App. 2d 740, 292 P2d 529 (1956); *People ex rel.* v. *Morton Grove,* 16 Ill.2d 183, 157 NE2d 33 (1959); *Lamb* v. *City of Monroe,* 358 Mich. 136, 99 NW2d 566 (1959). Obviously, it is just as injurious to the welfare of the community to permit residential development of land needed for industrial expansion as it is to permit industrial expansion in residential neighborhoods. We must remember that in our growing country the supply of usable land is limited, and zoning is the chief tool that communities utilize to insure wise use of our limited land areas.

Some early decisions held such noncumulative zoning invalid. It is unlikely that any of these rulings would stand today.

§ **688. Zoning—validity—in general.** Determining the validity of zoning is basically a state court function. The United States Supreme Court determined the *general validity* of zoning in *Village of Euclid* v. *Ambler Realty Co.,* 272 U.S. 365, 71 L. Ed. 303 (1926). It then decided that a state, acting under its police power, could compel a landowner to accept a substantial reduction in his land value as long as there was a corresponding benefit to the public. Thereafter, in *Nectow* v. *Cambridge,* 277 U.S. 183, 72 L. Ed. 842 (1928) the Supreme Court decided that while a zoning ordinance could be valid *in general* it might work such a hardship as to a particular tract of land that it would be held invalid *as applied to that tract of land.*

EXAMPLE: A zoning ordinance zoned a small tract of land for residential purposes. This tract of land was cut off from other residential lots by railroad tracks and by the intersection of diagonal streets was entirely surrounded by property zoned for industrial use; and was practically worthless as residence property. The *zoning map,* in other words, put the land in the wrong zone. It was held that the zoning ordinance was not valid *as applied* to this particular tract of land. Insofar as the zoning ordinance limits property to a use that cannot reasonably be made of it, it is invalid. *Tews* v. *Woolhiser,* 353 Ill. 212, 185 NE 827 (1933).

Having laid down some general principles, the Supreme Court thereafter refused to decide zoning cases, leaving the problem of deciding validity to the state courts. Thus, in discussing the validity of a zoning ordinance we are discussing its validity *as applied to a particular tract of land.* Each of the fifty states is pretty much at liberty to decide that issue under its own state constitution. The fact that most state constitutions are modeled after the federal constitution is no guaranty of uniformity. Far from it, for judges are people. The decisions exhibit a wild diversity, because judges entertain diverse views on what is proper zoning.

In the ordinary zoning case, we are dealing with a particular tract of land. In general, the landowner is trying to put in an apartment, a planned unit development, a mobile home court, an industrial plant, and opposition is encountered. There are some approaches to this problem that reveal a degree of uniformity. As can be seen, the validity of zoning in general is beyond question. Most of the litigation then, is over amendments or "rezoning" of a particular tract of land. Or else, a landowner attacks the zoning *map* that is attached to every zoning ordinance. He argues that his land is placed by the *map* in the wrong type of zone. Unsuitable zoning is illegal zoning.

As can be seen, there is an unspoken balancing process at work. The court considers the proposed rezoning. Is the new proposed use nuisancelike so that it is sure to be harmful to its neighbors? The odds are against it, if it is. Is it relatively benign, like a strictly residential planned unit development? Its chances are good. Does it fit well into the pattern of existing uses so that its neighbors will not suffer too much? Very likely it will prevail. And so on.

§ 689. Validity—factors to be considered. In dealing with zoning validity one is faced with a variety of situations, namely: (1) the attack may be leveled against the entire ordinance which is a rarity; (2) the attack may be leveled against the zoning ordinance *as applied* to a particular tract of land, as in *Tews* v. *Woolhiser;* (3) the attack may be leveled against the *granting or refusal* of: (a) an amendment to the ordinance (rezoning); (b) a variance; or (c) a special exception.

Passing for a moment item (1) above, the factors to be considered in all these situations are these:

1. The character of the neighborhood.

EXAMPLE: One who seeks to thrust an apartment, industrial plant, or mortuary in the midst of a neighborhood of single-family dwellings will not succeed. Conformity to surrounding uses is one of the objectives of sound zoning.

2. The extent to which property values are diminished by the particular zoning restriction and the extent to which the public is benefited.

EXAMPLE: An area is zoned single-family, but one vacant lot sits between two nonconforming apartments. No one thinking realistically would erect a house on this site. The owner must be permitted to erect an apartment. Under the concept of the police power a landowner cannot be compelled to accept a harmful and sharp reduction in land value unless there is some corresponding benefit to the public. Here it is obvious that the vacant lot has zero value if zoned single-family. No public purpose is served.

EXAMPLE: In the leading case of *Village of Euclid* v. *Ambler Realty Co.,* 272 U.S. 365 (1926), the village enacted a zoning ordinance under which Ambler's tract of sixty-eight acres fell into a single-family zone. This reduced its value from $10,000 per acre to $2500.00 per acre. Nevertheless, there were residences to the east and west of the property, so that the zoning did indeed benefit large segments of the public. A landowner can be compelled to accept a reduction in land value if the ordinance is *reasonable* and there is a *benefit to the public.*

Another way of stating this rule is that the ordinance must not be *confiscatory as applied to the land in question.* A zoning decision by the authorities will not be held confiscatory unless the land cannot yield a reasonable return if used only for the purposes permitted in the zone. If the land is in a residential zone, this requires proof that residential development is not feasible and that use of the property for any of the permitted purposes in the zone is likewise not feasible. *Wackerman* v. *Town of Penfield,* 366 N.Y.S.2d 718 (1975).

And if the use being made of the land approaches the nuisance type of use, the court will sanction substantial destruction of land value. The theory is that no one has a constitutional right to operate a nuisance.

EXAMPLE: Where the ordinance in effect stopped the operation of an existing brickyard, diminishing land value by over 90 percent, the ordinance was sustained. The brickyard was surrounded by residences. *Hadacheck* v. *Sebastian,* 239 U.S. 394 (1915).

3. The extent to which removal of the existing limitation would affect the value of other property in the area.

EXAMPLE: The general area in question was generally vacant and far removed from any residential area. The landowner must be given a permit to build an outdoor theater. The restriction in the ordinance against theaters had no *beneficial effect* whatsoever on the surrounding property. *People ex rel* v. *Village of Skokie,* 408 Ill. 397, 97 NE 310 (1951).

EXAMPLE: In an area zoned for heavy industry, it was irrational to single out the petroleum industry and exclude it. The area was already permeated with odors from existing, legal plants. *Tidewater Oil Co.* v. *Mayor & Council of Carteret,* 193 A2d 413 (N.J. 1963). Here we find no *benefit to the public.*

4. The suitability of the property for the zoned purpose.

EXAMPLE: The land was zoned single-family but was located in a district predominantly business and industrial and was worth ten times more for these purposes than as residential. The zoning is invalid as applied to this tract of land. Here the harm to the landowner is great, and there is no benefit to the public. *Galt* v. *County of Cook,* 405 Ill. 396, 91 NE2d 395 (1950).

5. The existing uses and zoning of nearby property.

EXAMPLE: *Tews* v. *Woolhiser, supra,* is a good illustration of this rule.

6. The length of time under the existing zoning that the property has remained unimproved considered in the context of land development in the area.

EXAMPLE: A tract of land was a vacant island surrounded by business buildings. It was zoned for parking. As such it remained in use as a parking lot for twenty-five years, although its value for office building use would be much greater. The ordinance was held invalid as applied to this land. *Vernon Park Realty* v. *City of Mount Vernon,* 307 N.Y. 493, 121 NE2d 517 (1954). As to this land the ordinance was *confiscatory.* Such well-located property would normally be developed in much less than twenty-five years. While a zoning ordinance need not zone property for its *highest and best use* (a phrase invented by land appraisers), this is a factor to be considered. Moreover an unspoken factor here is that cities often provide municipal parking lots and here, in effect, the city is forcing the landowner to furnish a public service. The land is reasonably adapted to office-building use. No reason can be given why it was not so zoned. Certainly its use for this purpose would be compatible with existing uses.

EXAMPLE: The land in question was zoned for residential use. For twenty years it remained vacant. During that period, development was totally stagnant. The only buildings in the area were a cow stable, a dairy farm, and a city incinerator. The property was worthless for residential purposes. The court held that the zoning was invalid as applied to the land. *Arverne Bay Cons. Co.* v. *Thatcher,* 278 N.Y. 222, 15 NE2d 587 (1938).

7. The relative gain to the public as compared to the hardship imposed on the landowner.

EXAMPLE: Some of the examples given above illustrate this principle aptly. Indeed, the example last given is an excellent illustration.

8. A city cannot validly zone private land for what are essentially public purposes.

EXAMPLE: City zoned land for school purposes. *City of Plainfield* v. *Borough of Middlesex,* 69 NJS 136, 173 A2d 785 (1961). City zoned land as a wildlife preserve. *Morris Co. Land Imp. Co.* v. *Parsippany-Troy Hills Twp.,* 40 N.J. 539, 193 A2d 232 (1963). Both ordinances are invalid as applied.

Where the zoning is invalid as applied to a particular tract of land, one of several things may happen: (1) The landowner may obtain a court judgment holding the zoning ordinance invalid as applied to the land, and the city then zones it properly; (2) the court may grant the landowner permission to erect an appropriate building. This is frowned upon. The opposing theory is that zoning is not a court function. But in practice this is often done, and it works; (3) the city, upon request of the landowner, may rezone the land properly because, after looking the situation over, it decides that it cannot win the lawsuit.

§ **690. Motives.** Often changes in legislation are motivated by considerations that are illegal—racial bias, for instance. No city, however, would be foolhardy enough to admit this fact. Indeed, it would be carefully concealed behind a thicket of legal verbiage. 71 ALR2d 568.

NEW DIRECTIONS: A school district conveyed its land to a Catholic diocese. After much maneuvering, the diocese requested rezoning to apartment use. Some 250 persons in the area, all white, signed a petition against the rezoning. The rezoning was denied by the city, and the court held that it must rezone. The court found the denial of rezoning was racially motivated. *Dailey* v. *City of Lawton,* 296 F.Supp. 266 (W.D. Okla. 1969), aff'd 425 F2d 1037 (10th Circ. 1970).

§ 691. **Reasonableness as a test.** In recent times, much of the technical verbiage of the older cases has disappeared. The real test of the validity of zoning is its *reasonableness.* Disregard "taking property," "confiscatory zoning," and instead ask the question: Is the zoning totally unreasonable? An ordinance requiring all building lots in Manhattan to be of a minimum size of one hundred acres would be totally unrealistic. Our forefathers gave our legislatures the police power, that is, the power to pass laws, but not to act indiscriminately. If the regulation is totally unreasonable as applied to particular land, it is invalid. *Fred F. French Inv. Co.* v. *City of N.Y.,* 39 N.Y.2d 587, 350 NE2d 381 (1976). Viewed in this light, the task of the courts becomes a good deal simpler and a good deal more sensible. When a court holds that a particular zoning decision is invalid *as applied* to a particular tract of land, it is holding that *in the circumstances* the zoning is unreasonable.

§ 692. **Change of neighborhood.** A change of neighborhood may invalidate existing zoning. *Manger* v. *City of Chicago,* 257 NE2d 473 (Ill. 1970).

EXAMPLE: In an area zoned single-family the authorities made no effort to enforce the zoning. Stores crept in everywhere so that the few remaining vacant lots were surrounded by stores and were totally unfit for residential use. The area had become a business area. The village must permit stores on the vacant lots. *Scott* v. *Springfield,* 83 Ill. App. 2d 31, 226 NE2d 57 (1967); *Vigilant Investors Corp.* v. *Hempstead,* 34 App. Div. 2d 990; 312 NYS2d 1022 (1970).

The same result occurs where the city affirmatively causes the situation.

EXAMPLE: The city fathers handed out variances so liberally that nonconforming stores in the area were allowed to expand all over the area. The few remaining lots cannot be held to single-family dwelling use. *Metrop. Bd. of Zoning Appeal* v. *Sheehan Const. Co.,* 313 NE2d 78 (Ind. 1974).

§ 693. **Zoning—validity—federal courts' role.** As has been stated, this country has a federal Constitution. In determining whether a zoning law or local activity violates the federal Constitution, the United States Supreme Court has the final word. However, even if that court should hold that the federal constitution has not been violated, that decision is of minor consequence in zoning law. Each state has its own constitution. What *that* constitution permits is determined by the *state courts.* Thus, an ordinance held "valid" by the Supreme Court is valid only so far as federal law is concerned. The State Supreme Court may hold the very same ordinance *invalid* as a violation of the *state constitution,* which becomes the final and binding decision. The federal court decisions get the headlines, but, in point of fact, they are of relatively minor importance. The United States Supreme Court has tended to ignore zoning altogether and when it chooses to decide a zoning case, it takes such a liberal view that land developers have little to fear from the federal courts. Thus, it has been said that, "the exercise of sound discretion does not, of course, always require a slavish adherence to federal constitutional minimums." *State* v. *Smith,* 347 A2d 816 (N.J.). The United States Supreme Court has, in fact, encouraged the state courts to exercise their independence. *Oregon* v. *Hass,* 420 U.S. 714, 719, 46 L. Ed. 2d 313 (1975).

§ **694. Rezoning—referendum—federal rights.** The Supreme Court has held that the federal Constitution is not violated by making rezoning subject to referendum approval by the people of the municipality. *City of Eastlake* v. *Forest City Enterprises, Inc.,* 416 U.S. 668, 96 S. Ct. 2358, 2361 (1976). This leaves the state courts free to deal with this problem as they choose. Some courts will follow the Supreme Court's view that this is simply returning power to the people. Other courts will hold the referendum device illegal.

§ **694a. Zoning exactions.** The subject of *forced dedication,* whereby the municipality approves a plat only if the developer agrees to exactions of some sort, donation of land to the public, for example, occurs in connection with plat approval. Some municipalities make the same kind of exactions a condition to granting rezoning or a zoning variance or special exception.

This, predictably, will receive a mixed response in the courts. Most decisions will be favorable if the exaction is reasonable in the circumstances. *Sommers* v. *City of Los Angeles,* 62 Cal. Reptr. 523 (1967); *Board of Education* v. *Surety Developer,* 63 Ill.2d 193, 347 NE2d 149 (1975). *Unreasonable* exactions are a sneaky way of blocking development. They are invalid. *James City & County* v. *Rowe,* 216 Va. 128, 216 SE2d 199 (1975).

§ **695. Senior citizens and children.** It has been held to be unlawful to zone out senior citizens. *Shepard* v. *Woodland Twp. Planning Bd.,* 128 N.J. Super. 379, 320 A2d 191 (1974). It has also been held invalid in some states to limit occupancy to senior citizens. A zoning ordinance designed to zone out children by limiting the number of bedrooms in an apartment building is illegal. *Molino* v. *Mayor and Council of Borough of Glassboro,* 281 A2d 401 (1971 N.J.).

NEW DIRECTIONS: **The better modern rule is that a municipality may limit a particular residential zone to senior citizens. Their needs, curb ramps for wheel chairs, for example, are largely peculiar to the elderly. They need a zone that caters to their needs. *Taxpayers Assn.* v. *Weymouth Tp.,* 71 N.J. 249, 364 A2d 1016 (1976); *Hinman* v. *Planning and Zoning Comm.,* 26 Conn. Supp. 125, 214 A2d 131 (1965); *Maldini* v. *Ambro,* 36 N.Y. 481, 33 NE2d 403 (1975).**

§ **696. Aesthetic considerations.** A number of court decisions now sustain zoning provisions that are based solely on aesthetic considerations. *Berman* v. *Parker,* 348 U.S. 26 (1965).

EXAMPLE: An ordinance required new buildings to conform to the architecture of existing buildings. It was held valid. *State* v. *Wieland,* 269 Wisc. 262, 69 NW2d 217 (1955).

§ 697. **Accessory uses.** Every zoning ordinance recognizes that certain uses different from, but incidental to, the main use prescribed in the zone are normal. Such uses are legalized under the name *accessory uses.* Many accessory uses are found in residential zones.

EXAMPLES: Coin-operated washing machines and dryers in apartment buildings also pay telephones, postage vending machines, swimming pools and skating rinks for which a charge is made, milk vending machines, etc., are accessory uses. *Newark* v. *Daly,* 85 N.J.S. 55, 205 A2d 459 (1964). Likewise, a food shop in a large apartment hotel is often permitted. A private garage on the rear of a residential lot is universally permitted. A doctor expects to see patients in his home even though he lives in a residential area.

§ 698. **Bulk zoning.** *Bulk zoning* is zoning that regulates the size and shape of the buildings to be erected and their location on the land. The purpose of this type of zoning is to control population density, open space, and access to daylight and air. The ordinance requires that any building erected must leave specified areas along the front, side, and rear of the lot which must not be built upon.

§ 699. **Churches.** It is well established that a zoning ordinance must not exclude churches or synagogues from residential districts. 74 ALR2d 377.

§ 700. **Schools.** *Public* schools, of course, are not subject to zoning ordinances. *Hall* v. *City of Taft,* 47 Cal.2d 177, 302 P2d 574 (1956). The only controversy, then, relates to *private* schools. The courts are not in agreement on this question. The more general view is that private schools, like churches, cannot be excluded from residential areas. *Roman Catholic Welfare Corp.* v. *City of Piedmont,* 45 Cal.2d 32, 289 P2d 438 (1955). 11 *Miami L.Q.* 68.

§ 701. **Pornographic zoning.** In recent times some municipalities have confined pornographic movies and bookstores and nude dancing establishments to a single "combat zone" or "mini zone." This keeps these undesirable uses out of other neighborhoods. It is a valid exercise of the police power under the federal constitution. *Young* v. *American Mini-Theaters,* 96 S. Ct. 2440 (1976). Of course, state courts remain at liberty to deal with this problem under the various state constitutions. The Supreme Court suggested in the *Young* case that these matters should be tried in the state courts.

§ 702. **Prohibitory zoning.** Two techniques are available when a village wishes to exclude unwanted uses, such as oil drilling. For example, the zoning ordinance may explicitly prohibit drilling for oil or extraction of minerals. 10 ALR3d 1241. Whether the exclusion will stand up depends on the circumstances surrounding the particular tract of land.

EXAMPLE: A landowner whose land adjoined the city dump applied for rezoning that would permit oil drilling. Refusal of rezoning was held invalid *as applied* to this land. How could oil drilling possibly debase an area next to the city dump? 10 ALR3d 1241.

EXAMPLE: A landowner applied for rezoning to permit oil drilling. His land was so close to the city water well that it created danger of contamination. Refusal of rezoning was sustained *as applied.* 10 ALR3d 1241.

As can be seen in both examples, the court considered the validity of the zoning *as applied* to the particular tract of land.

Another technique simply fails to provide a home in the ordinance for the unwanted uses. *Hohl* v. *Leadington,* 37 N.J.L. 271, 181 A2d 150 (1962); *Wiley* v. *County of Hanover,* 163 SE2d 160 (Va. 1968). The result is the same regardless of the technique involved.

A valid approach to this problem resorts to the *as applied* test.

EXAMPLE: In Skokie, a suburb of Chicago, in an area then far from any residences, the zoning ordinance was amended to exclude motion picture theaters. It was held to be invalid *as applied,* and an outdoor movie theater was permitted. *People ex rel.* v. *Village of Skokie,* 408 Ill. 397, 97 NE2d 310 (1951).

EXAMPLE: In another case involving a county zoning ordinance, the area in question was bounded by a railroad and a highway, and nearby uses consisted of a farm, a car dealership, industry, a par-three golf course and a quarry. Refusal of a special exception for a trailer park was reversed by the court. Such action was invalid *as applied* to this land. The court stated that denial of a special exception must bear some reasonable relationship to the public welfare, and that the gain to the public here would be small as balanced against the hardship to the landowner. *Pioneer T. and S. Bank* v. *McHenry County,* 41 Ill.2d 77, 241 NE2d 454 (1970).

EXAMPLE: The village totally excluded trailer parks. The court pointed out that such a blanket exclusion could not stand up because it disregarded the circumstances surrounding each tract of land in the village. The court pointed out that the facts might establish that a trailer park is a legitimate use somewhere in the village. The court observed that the total exclusion of a legitimate use carries with it the duty to provide a zoning board hearing in which a landowner could test the legitimacy of the exclusion, presumably via the special exception technique. Should the city fail to provide such a hearing then, the court held, the court must provide a judicial special exception technique to determine whether the use should be allowed. In such hearings it might be established that the exclusion *as applied* bore no substantial relation to the public health, morals and welfare. *High Meadows Park* v. *Aurora,* 112 Ill. App. 2d 220, 250 NE2d 517 (1967).

A balancing test has been suggested. Note: Legitimate Use Exclusions Through Zoning: Applying a Balancing Test, 57 *Cornell L. Rev.* 461 (1971). Under this test the court would consider the character of the community. For example, mobile homes are appropriate in rural areas. Also to be considered is the strain on utilities, transportation, and municipal services. The court should consider the availability of alternatives to exclusion, such as regulation. Hardship to the landowner is to be considered, particularly loss of profits. Also to be considered is the possibility of relocating the use elsewhere in the region. The standard test as to whether the prohibition bears a reasonable relation to public health, safety, welfare is applicable. The court should consider the present character of the community and its plans for the future.

§ 703. Development control zoning—sewer, water and school problems—downzoning. In many cases villages have refused to rezone single-family zones to apartments or other such uses and have given as a reason the shortage of sewer, water, or school facilities. Or the village may engage in *downzoning.*

EXAMPLE: The village rezoned A's land from multi-family dwelling to a single-family dwelling because it lacked sewer facilities. This was held invalid. *Westwood Estates v. Village of South Nyack,* 23 NY2d 424, 244 NE2d 700 (1969). To like effect is *Appeal of Gersh,* 437 Pa. 237, 263 A2d 395 (1970). This is *downzoning.*

EXAMPLE: The town increased minimum lot size from 35000 square feet to three acres and six acres because of lack of sewer facilities. The court upheld the ordinance but admonished the city that the change must be temporary only. *Steel Hill Development Inc. v. Town of Sanbornton,* 469 F2d 956 (1972). This is also *downzoning.*

It can be seen from the examples given that the efforts of some villages are bent toward holding the population stable, keeping things "as they are now," barring developers who bring in a new, unwanted population. And yet, at times, a genuine health problem or school problem exists. The cases, of course, are in utter confusion.

EXAMPLE: Downzoning by rezoning commercial to residential has been sustained. *Shelburne Inc. v. Conner,* 315 A2d 620 (Del. Ch. 1974). But rezoning of a single block to "zone out" apartments has been rejected as "spot zoning," *G. & D. Holland Const. Co. v. City of Maryville,* 12 Cal. App. 2d 989, 91 Cal. Rept. 227 (1970).

EXAMPLE: The desire of the villagers to keep the village rural does not justify increasing the minimum lot area from one to two acres and the minimum lot frontage from 100 to 200 feet. *Kavanesky v. Zoning Board,* 160 Conn. 397, 279 A2d 567 (1971); *Oakwood at Madison, Inc. v. Twp. of Madison,* 283 A2d 353 (N.J. 1971).

A village that stubbornly refuses to provide sewage disposal facilities for a developer may find itself held liable to the developer for the value of his lands.

EXAMPLE: A developer applied to the village for a permit to build, which could not be granted because the sewage disposal system was inadequate. For nine years the village dragged its feet, doing nothing to modify its sewage system. Since this made the developer's land valueless, the village was liable to him for the value of the land. *Charles v. Diamond,* 366 N.Y.S.2d 921 (App. Div. 1975). This lack of facilities is a gimmick that the courts see through and will no longer view patiently. This is no longer the rule in New York. Likely, it will not be followed at all. The financial burden on the village is too great.

The situation seems to break down into several sharply conflicting points of view, namely: (1) the village cannot use its shortage of facilities as an excuse for refusal to grant proper rezoning. *Appeal of Kit Mar Builders Inc.,* 439 Pa. 466, 268 A2d 765 (1970); (2) the shortage in facilities is one factor that may be considered in refusing rezoning to the developer. *Adams* v. *Reed,* 123 So2d 606 (Miss. 1960); (3) the village may impose a zoning freeze of *limited* duration so long as it has a program for correcting the problem.

As can be seen, blanket, haphazard, unplanned restrictions, especially those of indefinite duration, are likely to be held invalid. However, if the development control zoning is carefully planned and is limited in time, it will be sustained by the courts.

Phased development zoning.

NEW DIRECTIONS: The Town of X adopts a zoning amendment under which erection of homes by a merchant builder would require a special permit. The standards for the issuance of special permits are framed in terms of the availability to the proposed subdivision of five essential facilities or services, specifically: (1) public sanitary sewers or approved substitutes; (2) drainage facilities; (3) improved public parks or recreation facilities, including public schools; (4) state, county, or town roads (major, secondary or collector); and (5) firehouses. No special permit issues unless the proposed residential development has accumulated fifteen development points, to be computed on a sliding scale of values assigned to the specified improvements under the statute. Subdivision is thus a function of immediate availability to the proposed plat of certain municipal improvements, the avowed purpose of the amendments being to phase residential development to the town's ability to provide the above facilities or services. This was held valid. *Golden* v. *Planning Board of Town of Ramapo,* 30 N.Y.2d 359, 285 N.E.2d 291 (1972). This promises to become a celebrated case, and the technique is likely to be used in many areas. This is *phased development zoning.*

§ 704. **Single-family zones.** It is axiomatic that in single-family zones only one house per lot occupied by a single family will be permitted. But as times change, customs change. Many couples choose to live together today without marrying. So the zoning definition of a "single family" has tended to change.

A well-known case on family zoning is *Village of Belle Terre* v. *Boraas,* 416 U.S. 1, 39 L.Ed.2d 797 (1974). Here a zoning ordinance restricted residence in the entire community to single-family dwellings and prohibited occupancy by more than *two unrelated persons,* while permitting occupancy by any number of persons related by blood or marriage. The ordinance was sustained. The quietude of the single-family dwelling area and its benefits for the rearing of children were pointed out. The decision has been criticized. 1977 U. of Ill. L. Forum at 917.

The family is perhaps the most revered institution in American life. Hence, any ordinance that forbids members of the same family to live together is invalid.

EXAMPLE: A grandmother cannot be prohibited from living with her grandson. A brother and sister must be allowed to live together. Zoning cannot slice into the family itself. *Moore* v. *City of East Cleveland,* 97 S. Ct. 1932, 52 L.Ed.2d 531 (1977). As an example, when a family's breadwinner dies, the broader family comes together for mutual assistance. The law cannot forbid this. The law protects the "extended family."

Litigation involving single-family zoning ordinances is common. Although there appear to be almost endless differences in the language used in these ordinances, they contain three principal types of restrictions. First, they define the kind of structure that may be erected on vacant land. Second, they require that a single-family home be occupied only by a "single housekeeping unit." Third, they often require that the housekeeping unit be made up of persons related by blood, adoption, or marriage, with certain limited exceptions. Although the legitimacy of the first two types of restrictions is well settled, attempts to limit occupancy to related persons have not been successful. The state courts have recognized a valid community interest in preserving the stable character of residential neighborhoods that justifies a prohibition against transient occupancy. Nevertheless, in well-reasoned opinions, the courts of Illinois, New York, New Jersey, California, Connecticut, Wisconsin, and other jurisdictions have permitted unrelated persons to occupy single-family residences notwithstanding the existence of an ordinance prohibiting, either expressly or implicitly, such occupancy. *Moore* v. *City of East Cleveland,* 52 L.Ed.2d 531 (1977).

§ **705. Apartments.** The leading case on zoning held that apartments may be excluded from single-family dwelling zones. *Village of Euclid* v. *Ambler Realty Co.,* 272 U.S. 365 (1926). The state courts have followed a like rule.

EXCEPTION: A tract of land can be so located that *as applied* to that tract single-family zoning would be invalid, for example, a single lot located in a single-family zone between two large nonconforming use apartments.

EXCEPTION: Courts following the exclusionary zoning theory force the city to make room for apartments.

§ **706. Incentive zoning.** A rather recent development in zoning law is incentive zoning. This is a type of zoning calculated to induce the landowner to introduce amenities the city deems desirable. This type of zoning employs the Floor Area Ratio concept (F.A.R.).

EXAMPLE: The floor area ratio of a building is the ratio which the floor area within the building bears to the area of the lot occupied by the building. For example, a building occupying 40,000 square feet of lot area in a zone allowing an F.A.R. of 10:1 could have 400,000 square feet of total floor area in all the stories of the building. But if, for example, the building is located in San Francisco, an F.A.R. bonus is given if the building affords direct access to the rapid transit system, and in such case it would be allowed additional square feet of floor area. 21 Syracuse L. Rev. 895. In short, F.A.R. establishes a relationship between total land area and total floor space. Thus, under a F.A.R. regulation of 1:1, a developer could build a one-story structure covering the whole lot, a two-story structure covering half of the lot, or a four-story structure covering a quarter of the lot. Bartke & Lamb, Upzoning, 17 *William & Mary L. Rev.* 701, 705.

An extremely imaginative type of incentive zoning was developed in connection with the Lincoln Center for Performing Arts in New York City. The district zoning permitted developers 20 percent more floor space on provision of certain amenities, notably, pedestrian malls, galleries, covered plazas, and pedestrian-oriented circulation improvements. Elliott and Marcus, From Euclid to Ramapo: New Directions in Land Development Controls, 1 *Hofstra L. Rev.* 56.

§ **707. Historic areas and landmarks.** The literature on preservation of historic areas and landmarks through zoning is extensive. *See, e.g.,* Bibliography of Periodical Literature Relating to a Law of Historic Preservation, 36 *Law and Contemp. Prob.* 442 (1971); also, Symposium of Historic Preservation, 36 *Law and Contemp. Prob.* 309–444 (1971); Martha's Vineyard: The Development of a Legislative Strategy for Preservation, 3 *Environmental Affairs,* 396 (1974). Of recent interest is *Rebman* v. *City of Springfield,* 111 Ill.App.2d 430, 250 NE2d 282 (1969) (sustaining establishment of historical zone around the Abraham Lincoln home in Springfield and citing many cases holding that the preservation of historical areas is well within the concept of public welfare). To like effect are *M. and N. Enterprises Inc.* v. *City of Springfield,* 111 Ill.App.2d 444, 250 NE2d 389 (1969), and *Fitzpatrick* v. *City of Springfield,* 10 Ill.App.3d 317, 293 NE2d 712 (1973). Where the economy of the area depends on tourism engendered by the historic quaintness of the area, the zoning is likely to be sustained. 63 *Columb. L. Rev.* 708, 720. Historic zoning prevents changes in the historic nature of the area.

Landmarks consisting of isolated buildings present a different problem. Note: Landmark Preservation Laws: Compensation for Temporary Taking, 35 *U. of C. L. Rev.* 362 (1965).

EXAMPLE: In *Lutheran Church in America* v. *City of New York,* 345 NY2d 121, 304 NE2d 371 (1974). An attempt to freeze an individual landmark that was located in a high economic development area failed.

The constitutional issue can be avoided, of course, by payment of compensation. It has been argued that the city could condemn a development easement by paying an award equal to the difference between the fair market value of the land before taking (when the landowner would have the right to demolish and construct to the highest and best use) and the fair market value immediately after taking the development easement. Note: Landmark Preservation Law: Compensation for Temporary Taking, 35 *U. of Chicago L. Rev.* 362 (1965). Such a device is virtually certain to stand up if attacked in the courts.

Predictably, *area zoning* will fare better than the freezing of individual *landmarks. Fred F. French Inv. Co.* v. *City of New York,* 39 N.Y.S.2d 587, 350 NE2d 381 (1976); *People* v. *Ramsey,* 28 Ill.App.2d 252, 171 NE2d 246 (1960).

The New York courts appear to have introduced a new idea on the subject of landmark preservation.

EXAMPLE: The owners sought to construct an office building on the Grand Central Terminal, a landmark building. The courts sustained the city's refusal to grant a permit. The court took the position that Penn Central, the landowner, owned other real estate in the vicinity of the terminal that would lose value if the Terminal were not in operation. This is a new idea. You do not just look at the landmark property to see if it is operating at a loss. You look at the landowner's real estate in the vicinity to see how it would be affected by demolition of the landmark. *Penn Central Transp.* Co. v. *N. Y. City,* 46 L.W. 2035 (1977). The Supreme Court has affirmed this case.

§ **708. Airport zoning.** In airport zoning the height of structures within a stated radius of the airport is limited. One court has held such zoning valid. *LaSalle Nat. Bank* v. *County of Cook,* 340 NE2d 79 (Ill. 1975). Other courts hold to the contrary. *Roark* v. *City of Caldwell,* 394 P2d 641 (Ida. 1964); 13 Hastings L. Q. 397; 1972 *Urban L. Ann.* 69; 12 *UCLA L. Rev.* 1451.

§ **709. Nonconforming uses.** All zoning ordinances make some provision for continuation of nonconforming uses.

EXAMPLE: To invalidate an existing store use in a residential area would be unconstitutional deprivation of property. This is a simple proposition.

There is a second type of problem involved here.

EXAMPLE: An area is zoned for multifamily dwellings. A developer buys it and obtains a permit to construct an apartment. The neighbors become aware of the situation and persuade the village to rezone the area to single-family dwellings. *If construction has not yet begun,* there is, as yet, most courts say, no nonconforming use. Perhaps the developer can attack the new zoning on other grounds, but not on the ground that he has a nonconforming use.

Virtually all courts agree that *if construction has begun* under a valid permit nonconforming use status has been achieved and construction may be completed even though the zoning is amended after commencement of construction and forbids erection of such a structure. *Lutz* v. *New Albany City Plan Comm.,* 101 NE2d 187 (Ind. 1951). The construction must be done in good faith and not hastily, simply to obtain nonconforming use status. In New York the construction must be substantial. *Reichenbach* v. *Windward at Southhampton,* 364 N.Y.S.2d 283 (1975).

A generous court has accorded nonconforming use status after a permit has been issued, survey made, site cleared, and ground leveled. *Griffin* v. *Martin County,* 157 Cal. App.2d 507, 321 P2d 148 (1958). Some courts have held that nonconforming use status was not attained where permit was issued, building plans made, and construction mortgage signed. *Paramount Rock Co.* v. *County of San Diego,* 40 Cal. Rept. 74, 180 Cal.App.2d 217. *Contra: Hull* v. *Hunt,* 55 Wash.2d 492, 331 P2d 856 (1959).

Zoning ordinances, in permitting nonconforming uses, permit ordinary repairs to be made, but they sometimes forbid *structural alterations* of a nonconforming building. A structural alteration is such as would change the physical structure of the building or would change an old building in such a way as to convert it into a new or substantially different structure.

EXAMPLE: A operated a milk plant which was a nonconforming use in a residential zone. His attempt to replace decayed wooden walls with brick walls was a prohibited structural alteration. *Selligman* v. *Von Allmen Bros. Inc.*, 297 Ky. 121, 179 SW2d 207 (1944). 87 ALR2d 99.

Nonconforming uses, it is felt, should be gradually eliminated. *Cole* v. *City of Battle Creek,* 298 Mich. 98, 298 NW 466 (1941). The theory is that zoning seeks to safeguard the future in the expectation that time will repair the mistakes of the past. However, the treatment a particular nonconforming use will receive if it seeks to increase or change its use appears to vary considerably owing to differences in zoning ordinances. 87 ALR2d 4.

Once a nonconforming owner abandons the use of his property for a nonconforming purpose, he loses his right to make a nonconforming use of the property and must thereafter use it only in conformity with the uses allowed to other properties in the neighborhood. Were the law otherwise, an owner could keep his property in a nonconforming class forever.

EXAMPLE: The owner of a nonconforming slaughterhouse took down the smokestack and definitely discontinued the slaughterhouse business. He thereby lost his right to make a nonconforming use. *Beyer* v. *Mayor of Baltimore,* 182 Md. 444, 34 A2d 765 (1943). Also where an old nonconforming house trailer was sought to be replaced by a new one, the change was refused because the old use had been abandoned. *Town of Windham* v. *Sprague,* 219 A2d 548 (Me. 1966).

But a mere temporary discontinuance of the nonconforming use, as when a landowner is temporarily unable to procure a tenant, will not constitute an abandonment of the right to resume such use. *Landay* v. *MacWilliams,* 173 Md. 460, 196 Atl. 293 (1938). 114 ALR 993.

If a nonconforming building is either destroyed or partially destroyed by fire or other casualty, many ordinances forbid rebuilding.

Recently, ordinances have been passed that attempt to place a time limit on the right to continue a nonconforming use. To the extent that the *amortization ordinances* prohibit continuance of the nonconforming use after the useful economic life of the building has come to an end, most courts would consider them valid. 42 ALR2d 1146.

The rule of invalidity *as applied* is, as one might expect, applied to amortization of nonconforming uses. Thus, the court must consider: (1) the nature of the surrounding neighborhood to determine whether discontinuance of the use will have any beneficial impact and to determine if the nonconforming use, in fact, conforms to other nearby use; (2) the value and condition of the improvements on the premises to determine quantum of damage if use is discontinued; (3) the cost of relocation and all other costs of relocating the business; (4) whether the time allowed permits the landowner to make plans for the future of his business. *Harbison* v. *City of Buffalo,* 4 N.Y.2d 553, 152 NE2d 42, 176 N.Y.S.2d 598 (1958).

§ 710. Amendments and rezoning—spot zoning. Amendments to the zoning ordinance are constantly being sought by landowners whose land will thereby become more valuable. For example, land is more valuable for industrial or commercial purposes than it is for residential purposes, so rezoning of residential land for industrial purposes will greatly increase its value. Some of such rezoning is invalid. Particularly objectionable is *spot zoning,* where the city by amendment of its ordinances, singles out and reclassifies one piece of property in a particular zone without any apparent basis for such distinction. 51 ALR2d 267.

EXAMPLE: A zoning ordinance was amended to permit construction of a mortuary in a residential district. This was held invalid as spot zoning. *Mueller* v. *Hoffmeister Undertaking Co.,* 343 Mo. 430, 121 SW2d 775 (1938). 51 ALR2d 263.

Spot zoning rules. The following are some of the circumstances that will validate rezoning that, on the surface, appears to be "spot zoning."

EXAMPLE: A large area was rezoned for shopping center purposes because it was at the hub of a natural traffic concentration pattern. *Temmink* v. *Baltimore County,* 205 Md. 489, 109 A2d 85 (1954). Traffic is the key to this problem. The same approach is applicable to supermarkets. *State* v. *East Cleveland,* 169 Ohio St. 375, 160 NE2d 1 (1959).

EXAMPLE: Zoning of all four corner lots in a large residential district for commercial uses. Here the need for service business in a residential area is the key. *Marshall* v. *Salt Lake City,* 105 Utah 111, 141 P2d 704 (1943).

EXAMPLE: Rezoning to permit apartments in an area of older homes, thus increasing tax revenues of city. *Rodgers* v. *Village of Tarrytown,* 302 N.Y. 115 (1951).

EXAMPLE: Rezoning to get needed electrical substation in a residential area. *Holt* v. *City of Salem,* 192 Ore. 200, 234 P2d 564 (1951).

As can be seen, illegal spot zoning is basically a reclassification of a small area in such a manner as to disturb the surrounding neighborhood. It is a discordant and unneeded use. None of the examples fall in this category.

Where a real change in circumstances has taken place since the original ordinance was passed, an amendment that conforms the ordinance to the new circumstances will be valid.

EXAMPLE: At the time the original zoning ordinance was adopted, the only structure in an area zoned industrial was a factory. Thereafter, many single-family residences were built in the area, but no new factories. To protect the homeowners, the area was rezoned for residential purposes, the old factory remaining as a nonconforming use. This is valid rezoning. *Atlantic Coast Line R.R. Co.* v. *Jacksonville,* 68 So2d 570 (Fla. 1953).

EXAMPLE: Where an urban redevelopment displaced many families, creating a need for many units to house those displaced, a single-family dwelling zone could be revised to permit apartments. *Malafronte* v. *Planning Board,* 230 A2d 606 (Conn. 1967).

EXAMPLE: X owned an area that was zoned commercial. A large city park was opened across the street. The city rezoned the area for apartments. This change in circumstances makes the rezoning valid. *People ex rel* v. *City of Chicago,* 2 Ill.2d 350, 118 NE2d 20 (1954).

Or where the original zoning was a mistake the city can in most states correct the error.

EXAMPLE: A lot that was unsuitable, because of topography and soil conditions, for single-family dwellings was included in a single-family dwelling zone. To correct this error, the lot was rezoned for apartments. This is valid. *Eggebeen* v. *Sonnenburg,* 239 Wis. 213, 1 NW2d 84 (1941).

An amendment to the zoning ordinance will not be valid if it zones an area for a purpose for which it is in no way adapted so that the area becomes useless.

EXAMPLE: In an area almost completely industrial, the city rezoned a portion for apartment purposes, hoping thereby to keep the area vacant until funds could be raised to buy it for a city playground. The rezoning is invalid.

Where the amendment to the zoning ordinance is in the nature of a comprehensive revision of the earlier zoning ordinance, there is a strong presumption of its validity. The suspicion with which courts view amendments to a zoning ordinance is confined to individual piecemeal amendments. *City of Baltimore* v. *N.A.A.C.P.,* 221 Md. 329, 157 A2d 433 (1960).

The courts have been liberal in sustaining rezoning of portions of residential areas to permit shopping centers. 51 ALR2d 263; 76 ALR2d 1172.

§ 711. Amendments—after permit applied for. The city can, in some states, amend the zoning after a building permit has been applied for but before it has been granted.

EXAMPLE: After X had applied for a permit to build a building that complied with a zoning set-back line of 24 feet, the city passed an amendment changing the setback to 49 feet. The court sustained refusal of the permit. *Builders Const.* Co. v. *Daly,* 10 N.J. Misc. 861, 161 Atl. 189 (1932). Until construction begins, the property has not achieved status as a *non-conforming use.*

However, in other states courts will strike down an eleventh-hour attempt to block construction where a landowner has in good faith made plans and applied for a permit in reliance on an existing ordinance. These same courts, however, may sanction the refusal of a permit where the landowner is attempting to rush through a permit in the knowledge that the city is working on an amendment that would block the intended construction, *CT&TCo.* v. *Village of Palatine,* 22 Ill. App.2d 264, 160 NE2d 697 (1959). Note, Ex post facto zoning, 1971 *Urban Law Annual* 63.

§ 712. Amendments—after building permit issued. If a landowner receives a building permit and commences substantial construction in reliance thereon, the city cannot amend the ordinance so as to block the construction described in the permit. *Prescault* v. *Wheel,* 132 Vt. 247, 315 A2d 244 (1974). Basic fairness is becoming the test.

EXAMPLE: X applied for and received a permit to build an apartment. He graded, excavated, and put in a foundation. The city then attempted to rezone the area to exclude apartments. X can go forward with his building. *Deer Park Civic Assn.* v. *City of Chicago,* 347 Ill.App. 346, 106 NE2d 823 (1952).

§ **713. Amendment conditions.** A common complaint about zoning amendments is the fact that so far some courts have not permitted the amendment to contain conditions.

EXAMPLE: A developer seeks rezoning of his land from single-family to apartments. He exhibits beautiful artist sketches of the proposed building. He is granted the rezoning. He proceeds to erect a cheap, ugly building. He cannot be stopped.

§ **714. Planning.** City and regional planning figures prominently in the life of many communities today. State laws authorize the adoption by planning commissions of master plans. Such a commission plans for the systematic and orderly development of the community, with particular regard for the location of future major street systems, transportation systems, parks, recreation areas, industrial and commercial undertakings, and residential areas, the creation and preservation of civic beauty, and other kindred matters, all looking not only to the present, but with a view to the orderly development of the unbuilt, as well as the built-up areas.

Generally, at present, the formulation of a master plan is not a precondition to the enactment of a zoning ordinance. True, the zoning ordinance must be rational and bear within itself some evidence of logical planning, but if that is present, it suffices. *Angermeier* v. *Sea Girt,* 27 N.J. 298, 142 A2d 624 (1958).

NEW DIRECTIONS: Increasingly, the courts are looking for some comprehensive plan to guide them in their decision as to the validity of zoning. If there is a plan and the zoning or rezoning conforms to that plan, the courts are likely to sustain it. If the existing zoning is inappropriate when compared with an existing plan, the courts may strike it down. *Fasano* v. *Board of County Commrs.,* 264 Ore. 574, 507 P2d 23 (1973).

EXAMPLE: The plan showed the area was ideal for multifamily housing, but the ordinance zoned it as single-family. It must be rezoned multifamily. *City of Louisville* v. *Kavanagh,* 495 SW2d 502 (Ky. 1973).

NEW DIRECTIONS: If the municipality has no plan at all, the courts are likely to regard this as a good basis for striking down a zoning change. If the city has no plan, any change is, arguably, a planless change. *Forestville* v. *County of Cook,* 18 Ill.App.3d 230, 309 NE2d 763 (1974). Planless change creates a hodgepodge of incompatible uses. If the court is to decide the validity of a proposed zoning change, it is entitled to know the city's long range plans for the general area. *801 Avenue C, Inc.* v. *City of Bayonne,* 127 N. J. Super. 128, 316 A2d 694 (1974); *Hall* v. *City and County of Honolulu,* 530 P2d 737

(Hawaii, 1975). This is one of the battlegrounds that will surely be fought on, hammer and tongs. The city fathers prefer to keep their plans secret, meanwhile zoning much land for single-family dwellings or industrial use, always intending to rezone the land when the "right" developer comes along and they have had a look at him. If they must come out into the open, and show on their plans that the area has a long-range future for multi-family dwellings, they will have a hard time rejecting rezoning for this purpose. At the same time the courts want to see "in public" what the long range plans are so that they can make a rational decision on the score.

The articles are very numerous.

REFERENCES: 9 *Urban L. Ann.* 69 (1975); 7 *Urb. Law.* 731; 12 *Syracuse L. Rev.* 342; 35 *Temple L. Q.* 59; 116 *U. Pa. L. Rev.* 25; 29 *Fordham L. Rev.* 635, 20 *Law & Contemp. Problems* 351; 10 *Williamette L. J.* 358–393 (1974); 40 ALR3d 372; 43 *Geo. Wash. L. Rev.* 120.

§ **715. Amendments—rezoning.** When a municipality passes an ordinance of general application, such as a law fixing a maximum speed limit, ordinarily this does not require notice to anyone unless some state law requires it. However, where *rezoning* of a tract of land is involved, that is, amending the zoning ordinance or the zoning map, the latest court decisions regard this more in the nature of a lawsuit between the owner of the land and his neighbors. Of course, every lawsuit requires notice to the landowners affected and gives them an opportunity to be heard. Recently progressive courts have held that as a matter of constitutional law an ordinance rezoning land requires notice to the neighbors and an opportunity to state their objections. *Fasano* v. *Board of Commissioners,* 264 Ore. 575, 507 P2d 23 (1973); *Snyder* v. *City of Lakewood,* 592 P2d 371 (Colo. 1975); *Fleming* v. *City of Tacoma,* 81 Wash.2d 292, 502 P2d 331 (1972); *West* v. *City of Portage,* 221 NW2d 303 (Mich. 1974).

EXAMPLE: In an area zoned single-family and improved largely by residences, one landowner proposes that the city rezone his land to multi-family. His neighbors must be given notice, and a hearing must be held. Many ordinances routinely provide for such notice and hearing. And the notice given must be a reasonable notice.

EXAMPLE: A zoning ordinance provided that the zoning ordinance could be amended by publication of notice in a newspaper. This is invalid. Neighboring landowners can easily be found and given notice by name and by mailing. *American Oil Corp.* v. *City of Chicago,* 331 NE2d 67 (Ill. 1975). The rule that rational planning prior to zoning change also requires such planning to precede the granting of a special exception or variance. *Kristenson* v. *City of Eugene Planning Comm.,* 544 P2d 591 (Ore. 1976). Listening to the neighbors helps the authorities to make a rational decision.

§ **716. Variances.** Even the best ordinance may cause unintentional hardship to particular tracts of land. Some elasticity is needed if these hardship cases are to be dealt with. Most ordinances create a board, usually called the *board of adjustment* or *board of appeals,* which is given the power to authorize individual property owners to deviate from the terms of the ordinances where literal compliance would cause *undue hardship or prac-*

tical difficulties. This authorization is called a *variance.* The courts have worked out a number of requirements that must be met if a variance is to be granted.

1. The hardship must be special and peculiar to the particular property.

EXAMPLE: A lot is so irregular in shape that if all the front, rear, and side line restrictions were observed, no building at all could be built on the lot.

If the hardship complained of is a condition which affects all property in the district, the hardship is not special and peculiar to any lot in the area and no individual lot owner will be granted a variance.

EXAMPLE: Foul odors from a nearby industrial area exist in an area zoned as residential. No residential lot owner will be granted a variance to build a factory. A plea must be made to the authorities to amend the ordinance.

2. Hardship means that if the landowner complies with the provisions of the ordinance, he can secure no reasonable return from, or make no reasonable use of, his property. 29 *N.C.L Rev.* 250. With respect to income property, a party seeking a variance must prove that the land in question, if devoted to its existing or any permitted use, will not yield a reasonable return. This involves a detailed showing of the price paid for the property, the taxes assessed, expenses of operation, annual income, and so on. Then if the net income earned is not a reasonable return on the amount invested, hardship is shown. *Crossroads Recreation* v. *Broz,* 4 N.Y.2d 39, 149 NE2d 65 (1958). The landowner should also show that reasonable return cannot be anticipated from other permitted uses. *Forrest* v. *Evershed,* 7 N.Y.2d 256, 164 NE2d 841 (1959). The fact that a man could make more money by devoting his property to another purpose is not legal hardship. Everyone knows that land is worth more for commercial or industrial purposes than it is for residential, and yet most of our land must necessarily be zoned residential.

3. The hardship must not be self-created.

EXAMPLE: A departs from the plans attached to his application for a building permit and builds his home five feet closer to the side lines of his lot than the ordinance allows. When the building inspector stops him, *A* applies for a variance. He will not get it.

EXAMPLE: The city in question has an ordinance specifying a minimum lot area. A owns a building on a legal size lot. He then sells the building and enough of the land so that the building still occupies a legal building site. However, the portion of the lot left to A is now less than legal size. He will not be given a variance to permit him to build. *Board of Zoning Appeals* v. *Waskelo,* 240 Ind. 594, 168 NE2d 72 (1960).

4. The proposed new use must not change the essential character of the neighborhood. It must be consistent with the general plan of the ordinance.

EXAMPLE: A variance will not be granted to permit introduction of a cemetery into an area zoned residential.

Some courts are so strict on this point that they will not allow a variance that changes the *use* permitted by the ordinance. In other words, they will allow deviation only from the area, height, and location regulations of the ordinance.

EXAMPLE: Some courts will not permit a variance for an apartment house in a single-family area because this would be a *use* variance. *Lee* v. *Board of Adjustment,* 226 N.C. 107, 37 SE2d 128 (1946); 168 ALR 1.

However, most courts will permit a use variance where the hardship is great.

EXAMPLE: A owns a vacant lot in a single-family dwelling zone, and nonconforming apartment buildings are his neighbors on both sides, that is, these buildings were built before the ordinance was passed and are allowed to continue in operation. He will be given a variance for the erection of an apartment building. The sound reason for this variance is that no one can be induced to build a single-family dwelling on such a building site.

In granting a variance, the zoning board may impose conditions. *Vlahos* v. *Little Boar's Head District,* 101 N.H. 460, 146 A2d 257 (1958); *Zweifel Mfg. Co.* v. *Peoria,* 11 Ill.2d 489, 144 NE2d 593 (1957).

EXAMPLE: The board may put in a condition that the architecture of the permitted building conform to the architecture of neighboring structures, or that certain areas be left open and landscaped.

A variance may be limited in time.

EXAMPLE: A variance given for five years is valid. *Bringle* v. *Board of Supervisors,* 4 Cal. Reptr. 493, 351 P2d 765 (1960).

Questions may arise as to who may apply for a variance. Clearly the landowner may do so. A contract purchaser is also qualified. However, one who is merely negotiating for the purchase of the land cannot apply for a variance.

The larger the tract of land involved, the greater the likelihood a variance will be held invalid. *Topanga Assn.* v. *County of Los Angeles,* 113 Cal. Reptr. 836, 522 P2d 12 (1974). Large tracts should be dealt with by amendment.

§ 717. Special exceptions. A common provision in zoning ordinances authorizes the board of appeals to issue special permits for special purposes, such as public utility structures, churches, hospitals, private schools, clubs, or cemeteries. Obviously, institutions of this character must be located somewhere, but some control must be exercised by the zoning authorities over their location so that adverse effects on the other property owners will be held to a minimum. Typically, the ordinance may list a number of different uses that may be licensed "where public convenience and welfare will be substantially served." *Dunham* v. *Zoning Board,* 68 R.I. 88, 26 A2d 614 (1942). The distinction between special exceptions and variances is a technical one. In the case of variances, the board is given authority to authorize violations of the zoning ordinance in hardship cases. In the case of special exceptions, the ordinance itself lists certain cases in which certain special uses are to be permitted, and the board only determines whether facts exist to bring the particular case within the terms of the ordinance. *Stone* v. *Cray,* 89 N.H. 483, 200 Atl. 517 (1938). It is not necessary to show "practical difficulties or unnecessary hardship," as is true in variance cases. *Montgomery County* v. *Merlands Club,* 202 Md. 279, 96 A2d 261 (1953).

NEW DIRECTIONS: Looking toward the future, one might hazard the guess that increasing resort will be made to the special exception technique. In other words, variances will be hard to get, because by and large they will represent unwelcome deviations from the zoning ordinance. But the things the city really wants, such as garden apartments, shopping centers, and research laboratories will be readily procurable by means of an elastic special exceptions provision in the ordinances. *Cameo Park Homes, Inc.* v. *Planning Commission,* 150 Conn. 672, 192 A2d 886 (1963); *Ranney* v. *Istituto,* 20 N.J. 189, 119 A2d 142 (1955).

In some states, the special exception is referred to as a *special use. Tullo* v. *Township of Millburn,* 4 N.J.S. 509, 149 A2d 620 (1959). In others, it is called a *conditional use. Tustin Heights Assn.* v. *Board,* 170 Cal. App.2d 619, 339 P2d 914 (1959).

§ 718. The floating zone. A *floating zone* is a special use district. No specific location is assigned to it in the zoning ordinance. When the need for such a zone arises, the same public body that enacts the zoning ordinance enacts an amendment to the ordinance carving a new zone out of some existing zone. It differs from the special exception in that, at least in the earlier ordinances, a zoning amendment passed by the city council or board of trustees was needed to create a floating zone.

Also in this unique type of zoning amendment, the usual rules applicable to zoning amendments are not applied. For example, in some states, for a valid zoning amendment one must show that a mistake was made in the original zoning ordinance or that the conditions have changed, requiring rezoning. This rule is inapplicable to floating zones. *Haldemann* v. *Board of Commrs.,* 253 Md. 298, 252 A2d 792 (1969).

EXAMPLE: Cluster housing in a planned unit development is often allowed to float to any part of the village.

There are a number of decisions sustaining the validity of the floating zone. *Rodgers* v. *Village of Tarrytown,* 302 N.Y. 115, 96 NE2d 731 (1951); *Huff* v. *Board of Appeals,* 214 Md. 48, 133 A2d 82 (1957); *Cheney* v. *Village 2 at New Hope,* 429 Pa. 626, 241 A2d 81 (1968). There are a few cases to the contrary. *Rudderow* v. *Twp. Committee,* 114 N.J.S. 104, 274 A2d 854 (1971).

If one must hazard a guess as to the future of the floating zone, the conjecture must be that its prospects look bright. The initial hostility of planning officials has been converted to approbation. Mosher, The Floating

Zone: Legal Status and Application to Gasoline Stations, 1 *Tulsa L. J.* 149, 156, 166, 167 (1964). The criticism that zoning amendments lend themselves to political influence is not well taken. It is a well-known fact that zoning ordinances traditionally zone large areas for single-family dwellings in the full knowledge that developers will come forward requesting apartment or other zoning, thus giving the authorities an opportunity to "take a look" at the developer and development.

This argument would invalidate all rezoning. Moreover, the anti-rezoning view can easily be circumvented under modern ordinances by allowing desired uses, such as research laboratories, to "float" into any zone on issuance of a special exception permit. *Summ* v. *Zoning Comm. of the Town of Ridgefield,* 150 Conn. 79, 186 A2d 160 (1962). Indeed, it has been frankly acknowledged that the special exception technique lends itself to the introduction of desirable uses into residential and other districts. *Lazarus* v. *Village of Northbrook,* 31 Ill. 2d 146, 199 NE2d 797 (1964). Moreover, conditions may validly be attached to a special exception. *Houdaille Constr. Mats. Inc.* v. *Board of Adjustment,* 92 N.J. Super. 293, 223 A2d 210 (1967). In this manner the authorities can impose requirements that might be complied with prior to issuance of a building permit, such as greenbelt buffer areas. The proponents of floating zones, it appears, will surely carry the field.

§ 719. Planned unit developments—cluster housing. The planned unit development (hereafter referred to as PUD) is one of the novel ideas in housing. Such developments consist of town houses, homes, apartments (both garden and high-rise), or combinations of such buildings, all with common open areas and some with private recreation facilities. The advantages offered are:

1. lower priced homes achieved by cost savings through more efficient land use and planning
2. small, private yards with a minimum of maintenance chores and a maximum of time and energy for recreational activities in the common areas
3. common areas of green open space providing an attractive setting
4. in some cases, shared facilities for swimming, golf, fishing, and so forth, and a recreation center for crafts, meetings, and other group activities
5. maintenance furnished by homeowner's association

The phrase *cluster housing* means that the individual homes, usually party-wall row houses, or apartment buildings are grouped together on relatively small plots of land with large surrounding areas of land left open for common recreational use. The cluster form of development is economical because the clustering of houses with party walls reduces the cost of supplying utilities and roads. Often a PUD is placed in a floating zone.

The old-fashioned zoning ordinance, with its rigid allocation of specific uses to specific zones, its building lines, and its minimum-area requirements, does not lend itself to the PUD type of development. Cluster development calls for smaller homesites, the land subtracted from homesites being added to common areas. However, the PUD can be listed as a special exception in the zoning ordinance. Alternatively, the zoning ordinance may include a special section devoted to the PUD, calling it variously a *Community Unit Plan, Dwelling Groups, Group Housing, Planned Residential Development,* or *Planned Building Groups.* Because approving a development of this sort involves a considerable exercise of discretion, it seems wise to provide that final approval of a special exception for a developer's proposal to create a PUD zone should rest with the city council, just as if an amendment to the zoning ordinance were being considered, and some ordinances so provide. *Rodgers* v. *Village of Tarrytown,* 302 N.Y. 115, 96 NE2d 731 (1951); *La Rue* v. *East Brunswick,* 68 N.J. Super. 435, 172 A2d 691 (1961); *DeMeo* v. *Zoning Comm.,* 148 Conn. 68, 167 A2d 454 (1961). The applicant for such zoning may, under many ordinances, be a government agency, since urban redevelopment plans sometimes call for a PUD.

Where cluster housing occurs in a residential zone that permits the type of housing planned for the PUD, it is simply a form of density zoning and offers no legal problems.

§ 720. **Contract zoning.** An application by a landowner for rezoning often results in bargaining with the planning board or the city's governing body. At times a formal covenant is entered into by the landowner and the city contemporaneously with the rezoning.

EXAMPLE: In granting rezoning of land from residential to shopping center use, the city exacted a recorded covenant from the landowner that he would maintain a buffer area of landscaped land between the center and adjoining residential land. This was held valid. *Buchholz* v. *City of Omaha,* 174 Neb. 862, 120 NW2d 270 (1963).

Some courts disapprove of contract zoning. The arguments against contract zoning are:

(1) It is illegal to "bargain" for legislation. *Baylis* v. *City of Baltimore,* 219 Md. 164, 148 A2d 429 (1959). This argument is specious. Much of the legislation on our books was initiated and lobbied through by private interests. Moreover, the rezoning could have been enacted without any conditions. *Church* v. *Town of Islip,* 8 N.Y. 2d 254, 168 NE2d 681 (1960). Why, then, would the imposition of beneficial conditions invalidate it? Also, since rezoning deals, as it often must, with particular parcels of land, it is difficult to legislate sensibly without taking cognizance of the special conditions relating to that particular parcel. *Ibid.*

(2) The rezoning is not in accordance with the state zoning enabling act, which contemplates division of the city into zones plainly appearing on the zoning map. Contract zoning introduces a control of land use that appears in the recorder's office but does not appear on the city's legislative records. *Treadway* v. *City of Rockford,* 24 Ill.2d 188, 182 NE2d 219 (1962). Contra: *Goffinet* v. *Christian County,* 357 NE2d 442 (Ill. 1976).

It has been suggested that this sort of bargaining is commonplace and stands a good chance of acceptance if it is accomplished by means of "private restrictions" voluntarily created and recorded by the landowner. Hagman, *Wisconsin Zoning Practice,* 11 (1962). At least one court has accepted this suggestion.

EXAMPLE: The city of *X* suggests to *D*, a developer, that he record a declaration of restrictions restricting a specified area in his development for golf course purposes over a period of twenty-five years. He does this. In return the city rezones a part of the area from detached single-family dwellings to town houses. This arrangement is valid. *State ex rel Zupancic* v. *Schimenz,* 174 NW2d 533 (Wis. 1970).

At times a contract zoning ordinance provides that if the contract is breached, the zoning reverts back to the preexisting zoning. Such a provision is manifestly invalid. *Stiriz* v. *Stout,* 210 N.Y.S.2d 325 (Sup. Ct. 1960). Every legislative change of zoning requires a careful weighing of the need for such action in the light of the circumstances then prevailing. The automatic reverter provision is the antithesis of proper legislative consideration.

It remains impossible to make a definite statement of the law on this subject. Some courts reject contract zoning. Others permit it. Others permit a form of it. A leading authority states that the trend is in favor of permitting contract zoning. Hagman, *Urban Planning and Land Development Law,* 308.

REFERENCES: 12 *UCLA L. Rev.* 897; 24 *Maine L. Rev.* 263; 1972 *Urban L. Ann.* 219; 67 *Dick. L. Rev.* 109; 23 *Md. L. Rev.* 121; 23 *Hastings L. J.* 825; 51 *J. Urban L.* 94; 1974 Planning, Zoning and Em. Dom. Inst. (S.W. Legal Foundation) 121; 63 *Ill. B. J.* 132.

§ 721. Density—in general. Density zoning deals with a number of related items all designed to reduce density of residential occupancy, for example: (1) minimum lot size or area; (2) minimum frontage; (3) front, back and side yards; (4) maximum lot coverage (open space zoning); (5) minimum building size. The general purpose, to prevent overcrowding, is a valid one. *Town of Durham* v. *White Enterprises Inc.,* 348 A2d 70 (N.H. 1975).

In large scale residential developments, sophisticated density concepts are applied.

EXAMPLE: The ordinance may divide up the residential area of the city into districts of differing residential density. Thus, if our particular area permits single-family, duplexes, town houses, and apartments, the applicable zoning may permit a density of five dwelling units per acre. The developer, developing ten acres, let us say, can build fifty single-family units, or twenty-five duplexes, or five ten-unit buildings or one fifty-unit building. The usual lot size and building bulk restrictions apply unless combined with clustering.

As to zones other than residential, density is discussed under incentive zoning.

Front, back, and side yards require no discussion since they occasion no problems. Bulk variances deal adequately with the situation. For example, when sprawling ranch homes became popular after World War II, zoning boards handed out front and side line variances by the thousands.

§ 722. Density—minimum lot area. Many decisions sanction minimum area residential lot requirements. The theoretical legal basis for such zoning is that spacing buildings farther apart prevents the spread of fire and provides for ample light, air, and adequate sewage disposal. *Simon* v. *Town of Needham,* 311 Mass. 560, 42 NE2d 516 (1942); *Barnard* v. *Zoning Bd. of Town of Yarmouth,* 313 A2d 741 (Maine 1974). In a rural area, a minimum lot area of five acres has been sustained *as applied. Honeck* v. *County of Cook,* 12 Ill.2d 257, 146 NE2d 35 (1957). In connection with the validity of such zoning, courts consider the character of the area. A rural area *not in the path of development* is a favorable characteristic. Also favorable is the predominance of large tracts in single ownership, also the presence of historic sites. The presence of smaller lots in the neighborhood is unfavorable to the validity of the zoning. *Marquette Nat. Bank* v. *County of Cook,* 24 Ill.2d 497, 182 NE2d 147 (1962) (minimum area of 20,000 square feet held invalid where neighboring lots were 10,000 square feet in area); *Christine Bldg.* v. *City of Troy,* 367 Mich. 508, 116 NW2d 816 (1962) (requirement of 21,780 square feet held invalid where most lots were 15,000 square feet or less). Here the competitive disadvantage makes the larger lots virtually unsalable. Increase in minimum lot area is sometimes characterized as *upgrading.* Thus, an increase of minimum lot area from two acres to four acres has been sustained. *Senior* v. *Zoning Comm. of Town of New Canaan,* 153 A2d 415 (Conn. 1959). The courts have said that the maximum enrichment of developers is not a controlling purpose of zoning. *Ibid.*

In recent times environmental factors (water pollution, for example) have been cited in favor of such zoning. *Steel Hill Development Inc.* v. *Town of Sanborton,* 469 F2d 956 (1st Circ. 1973).

This type of zoning faces the problem of *substandard* lots, that is, smaller lots platted and sold before the *upgrading* by zoning amendment. In general, the courts have required the city to issue building permits or to have invalidated the zoning as to such substandard lots. *Harrington Glen Inc.* v. *Municipal Bd. of Adjustment,* 243 A2d 233 (N.J. 1968); *Fulling* v. *Palumbo,* 21 NY2d 30, 286 NY2d 249 (1967); *Grace Bldg. Co. Inc.* v. *Hatfield Twp.,* 329 A2d 925 (Pa. 1974) (holding that lot owner cannot be required to buy adjoining lot in order to come into compliance with the amendment). *Contra: Grobman* v. *City of Des Plaines,* 322 NE2d 443 (Ill. 1975) (denying relief to owners of substandard lot where they refused adjoining owner's offer to purchase).

An occasional decision refuses to protect the purchaser of a substandard lot on the ground that his purchase of the lot was a gamble. He bought the lot fully aware that it was substandard, probably at a bargain price. *Phoenix* v. *Beall,* 524 P2d 1314 (Ariz. 1974). This is akin to *self-created hardship,* which is a valid basis for refusing a variance.

§ 723. **Density—minimum frontage or lot size.** Minimum frontage requirements have been sustained. *Clemons* v. *City of Los Angeles,* 36 Cal. 2d 95, 222 P2d 439 (1950). With respect to such requirements, the problem of substandard lots has arisen quite frequently. Many ordinances exempt *previously platted lots* from this requirement. *Graves* v. *Bloomfield Planning Bd.,* 235 A2d 51 (N.J. 1967). In any case the courts have gone far in protecting substandard lots. *Milano* v. *Town of Patterson,* 93 NYS2d 419 (1947) (requirement of sixty foot frontage inapplicable to previously platted twenty-three foot lot). Courts have granted flexible relief. *Ziman* v. *Vill. of Glencoe,* 275 NE2d 168 (Ill. 1971) (court imposed three-foot side yard requirement). But a denial of a variance will be overthrown. A permit must be granted. *Jacquelin* v. *Horsham Twp.,* 312 A2d 124, 10 Pa. Comwlth 473 (Pa. 1973). As in the case of minimum area cases, occasionally relief is denied to a purchaser who buys *with knowledge* of the problem, *Klehr* v. *Zoning Bd.,* 320 NE2d 498 (1974 Ill. App.).

The owner of a substandard lot cannot be compelled to buy additional frontage. Nor can he be compelled to sell to a neighbor. *Smith* v. *Smith,* 53 N.J.S. 590, 140 A2d 58 (1958).

When an owner owns several contiguous substandard lots he must comply with the new frontage requirements. In effect, he must resubdivide the frontage into lots that comply with the new requirements. *Citizens Bank and Trust Co.* v. *City of Park Ridge,* 5 Ill.App.3d 77, 282 NE2d 751 (1972).

Checkerboarding is always struck down. This is a situation in which an owner of a number of contiguous platted lots conveys out alternate lots in order to qualify each substandard lot for a permit. Note, 16 *Syracuse L. Rev.* 612 (1965).

§ 724. **Density—minimum building area.** Prescribing a minimum building area compatible with health requirements is within the police power. *Lionshead Lake, Inc.* v. *Twp. of Wayne,* 10 N.J. 165, 89 A2d 693, appeal dismissed, 344 U.S. 919, 73 S.Ct. 386, 97 L.Ed. 708 (1953) (requirement of 768 square feet for one-story building sustained). The only substantial issue in this area is whether such a requirement can occur on a *graduated basis,* with differing minimum building areas in differing residential zones. One court has rejected this approach. *Medinger Appeal,* 377 Pa. 217, 104 A2d 118 (1954). The logic of *Medinger* is superficially attractive. If a building area of 1000 square feet suffices to protect public health, it is difficult to sustain a requirement of 1800 square feet in zone B. However, this approach overlooks the compatability argument. Houses of differing value do indeed occur in the various areas of the city, and to keep new houses compatible with existing houses is a legitimate objective of zoning. *Garelick* v. *Board of Appeals,* 350 Mass. 289, 214 NE2d 60 (1966). The cases have been collected elsewhere. 9 ALR2d 1374, 1409. In line with the compatability argument, a requirement of large houses in an area characterized by smaller homes could be invalid for that reason.

§ 725. **Density—minimum building area per dwelling unit.** Zoning ordinances often prescribe a minimum lot area per dwelling unit. It is obvious that this is another version of the minimum lot area requirement, and still another version of the minimum building area requirement. The ordinances discussed here do not limit lot size but prescribe a minimum lot area per dwelling unit. *First National Bank of Skokie* v. *City of Chicago,* 25 Ill.2d 366, 185 NE2d 181 (1963) (2500 square feet per dwelling unit sustained). Once again, the problem of graduated area requirements crops up.

EXAMPLE: An ordinance specified various building areas in different zones. In an R-3 district the minimum lot area per dwelling unit was 2500 square feet, while the minimum lot area in R-4 district was 9000 square feet per dwelling unit. Such an ordinance was held valid. *Cosmopolitan National Bank* v. *City of Chicago*, 22 Ill.2d 367, 176 NE2d 367 (1961).

§ 726. **Exclusionary zoning—large lot zoning—apartments.** One of the recent developments in zoning law is the appearance of the doctrine of *exclusionary zoning*. The attitude of the courts embracing this doctrine is, in large part, that the public welfare requirement of the police power does not stop at the city limits. Courts cannot think in terms of the welfare of the *municipality* and its present inhabitants in testing the zoning. In some states the *tight little island* concept of zoning is outmoded. Sager, Tight Little Islands: Exclusionary Zoning, Equal Protection and the Indigent, 21 *Stanf. L. Rev.* 767 (1969). The wants and needs of all the people living in the *region* must be considered. The poor people must not be zoned into the decaying central city and zoned out of suburbs. Some early decisions in this area struck down large lot zoning. *National Land and Investment Co.* v. *Kohn,* 215 A2d 597 (Pa. 1956); *Appeal of Kit-Mar Builders,* 439 Pa. 466, 268 A2d 765 (1970); *Board of County Supervisors of Fairfax County* v. *Carper,* 200 Va. 653, 107 SE2d 390 (1959). The inequitable aspect of such zoning, bearing heavily as it does on those who cannot afford to buy large lots, has long been the subject of discussion.

Now the battle is out in the open. The authorities, and they are numerous, are collected in *Township of Williston* v. *Chester Gale Farms, Inc.,* 300 A2d 107 (Pa. 1973). The Williston case also collects the authorities on exclusion of apartments from suburbia as a form of exclusionary zoning. Many poor people simply cannot afford to buy a house. However, the Supreme Court of Michigan has recently rejected the view that a village must provide for apartments. *Kropf* v. *City of Sterling Heights,* 391 Mich. 139, 215 NW2d 179 (1974).

The federal courts will shy away from this question. The "hot potato" will be tossed back to the state courts.

In the state courts the issue is left in doubt at this time.

§ 727. **Exclusionary zoning—mobile homes.** As one might expect, the decisions regarding attempted exclusion of mobile homes are sharply conflicting. 42 ALR3d 598 (1972). Perhaps the most celebrated decision is *Vickers* v. *Twp. Committee of Gloucester Twp.,* 37 N.J. 232, 181 A2d 129 (1962), *cert. den. and appeal dismissed,* 371 U.S. 233. This decision sanctioned total exclusion of mobile homes from the village, but the dissenting opinion became the landmark for striking down exclusionary zoning as a tool to "zone out" the poor and is now the law in New Jersey. There are many decisions. 42 ALR3d 598, 604. Directly contrary to *Vickers* are *Bristow* v. *City of Woodhaven,* 35 Mich. App. 205, 192 NW2d 322 (1971) and *Green* v. *Twp. of Lima,* 40 Mich. App. 655, 199 NW2d 243 (1972). Here the courts emphasized the right of citizens of the general community to decently placed, suitable housing within their means and that the strictly local interests of a municipality must yield to the overall state interests of the public at large.

NEW DIRECTIONS: With the price of conventional housing soaring into the strato-

sphere, it seems a reasonable guess that more and more courts will force suburbs that have ample open space to accept mobile homes.

§ **728. Exclusionary zoning—town houses.** Courts that compel a developing municipality to admit mobile homes will extend the same privilege to town houses. *Dublin Properties* v. *Bd. of Commrs.,* 342 A2d 821 (Pa. 1975).

§ **729. Exclusionary zoning—Mount Laurel.** The most important state court decision on zoning is *Southern Burlington County NAACP* v. *Twp. of Mount Laurel.* 67 N.J. 151, 336 A2d 713 (1975). Very often other courts have followed in the footsteps of the highly-respected New Jersey Supreme Court. Therefore its influence will be felt nationwide. Mount Laurel is a "developing municipality," that is, one with a good deal of vacant land left. Its zoning ordinance was a rather typical suburban ordinance. The residential zones permitted only single-family dwellings. Apartments and mobile homes were not permitted. Over 4100 acres were zoned exclusively for industry, even though only 100 acres were occupied by industry. These aspects tended to keep out the poor and were obviously so intended. The court held that virtually the *entire ordinance* was void because its entire scheme and plan were designed to keep out low- and moderate-income housing. This alone makes the case important. It holds, in effect, that *the typical suburban zoning ordinance is invalid.* The case holds, moreover, that the public benefit idea that sustains the validity of zoning ordinances in the first place is the public benefit of the *region. The zoning must benefit those who live outside the municipality, not simply the residents of the municipality. Outsiders have a right to travel into the municipality and then remain there. The municipality must accept a "fair share" of the disadvantaged.* It must adopt a new zoning map with smaller lots that the poor can afford. Space must be allocated, the court said, for apartments and mobile homes. Justice Hall, the best-informed state judge in zoning matters, wrote the opinion for a unanimous court. It surely will be followed in Pennsylvania. *Kaiserman* v. *Springfield Twp.,* 348 A2d 467 (Pa). New York will follow Mount Laurel. *Golden* v. *Planning Board of Town of Ramapo,* 30 NY2d 359, 285 NE2d 291 (1972). What other states will follow it is, of course, a matter for conjecture. To the extent that it is followed, it will render obsolete the various types of density provisions, such as large-lot zoning in areas similar to Mount Laurel. The court found that the actions of the municipality were "deliberate." Hitherto the courts, in deference to the legislative bodies whose actions they were examining, had always entertained the view that the legislation was motivated by pure motives. Mount Laurel suggests that courts will no longer close their eyes to the obvious. After all, the court said, the poor must live somewhere.

A warning note must be struck. The court made it plain that its decision has no application to the fully built-up suburbs with only a few vacant lots left. Only municipalities with substantial open space that lie in the path of inevitable future, residential, commercial and industrial demand and growth are affected.

The few vanguard decisions, like Mt. Laurel, are "mere harbingers of what looms as the major, domestic, social and political battle of the decade ahead, a battle whose outcome will be of enormous importance in determining the structure of United States society for many years to come." *Twp. of Williston* v. *Chesterdale Farms, Inc.,* 300 A2d 107 (Pa.). No references are given because this last case contains a sufficient number. Moreover, the "law" will come out of battles still to be fought. Note that the decision makes no mention of race. It establishes the principle that discrimination against low income groups is unlawful.

§ 730. **Exclusionary zoning—the United States Supreme Court.** In *Warth* v. *Seldin,* 422 U.S. 490 (1975), the United States Supreme Court was confronted with a zoning ordinance virtually identical with that in the *Mount Laurel* case. The Supreme Court, in effect, refused to hear the case at all. As repeatedly stated, the Supreme Court means to toss all the zoning "hot potatoes" to the state courts.

§ 731. **Exclusionary zoning—the integrated community.** In some states that hold exclusionary zoning invalid, the courts feel that the municipality, as a whole, must be an integrated whole. This provides a balanced mix of single-family, apartment, and commercial uses and in doing so, the municipality must consider regional needs, keeping in mind the effect of the ordinance on neighboring communities. *Berenson* v. *Town of New Castle,* 38 N.Y.2d 102, 341 NE2d 236 (1975).

EXAMPLE: The municipality cannot totally exclude multifamily dwellings. This would deny access to persons who cannot afford to own homes. The ordinance failed to take into account regional needs. As can be seen, the court was forced to take over the planning function because the municipalities failed and refused to engage in sensible planning. This again presents the argument in recent cases that rational planning must precede rational zoning.

§ 732. **Exclusionary zoning—commercial property.** In the states that reject exclusionary zoning as invalid, there is some law to the effect that this rule applies to exclusion of commercial uses.

EXAMPLE: A township adopted zoning that permitted commercial uses in only 47 out of its 11,200 acres. Also, the commercial area was zoned into 10 acre minimum lots, but in that area were a private school, a meeting house, a church, a firehouse, and six farmhouses. Evidently the township wished to confine commercial uses to a central business district. The court held that, in practical effect, commercial uses were excluded and that this was illegal. *Sullivan v. Board of Supervisors of Lower Wakefield Twp.,* 348 A2d 464 (Pa. 1975).

§ 733. **Inclusionary ordinances.** To insure that housing for lower income people will be built and widely dispersed, several communities (Fairfax County, Virginia; Montgomery County, Maryland; and Los Angeles, California) have adopted ordinances requiring developers to include a minimum amount of subsidized or low-cost housing in their projects. Kleven, Inclusionary Ordinances—Policy and Legal Issues in Requiring

Private Developers to Build Low Cost Housing, 21 *U.C.L.A. Rev.* 1432 (1974). One such ordinance was held invalid. *Board of Supervisors* v. *Carper,* 214 Va. 635, 198 SE2d 600 (1973).

§ **734. Effect of zoning ordinance on restrictions.** Restrictions contained in a deed, plat, or property owner's agreement are neither nullified nor superseded by the adoption of a zoning ordinance. *Chuba* v. *Glasgow,* 61 N.M. 302, 299 P2d 774 (1956); *Schwarzchild* v. *Wolborne,* 186 Va. 1052, 45 SE2d 152 (1947).

EXAMPLE: A deed provided that use of the land thereby conveyed was restricted to residence purposes. Thereafter, an ordinance was passed zoning this area for commercial purposes, and the owner attempted to construct a gasoline station thereon. It was held that the deed restriction would be enforced, and a court order was entered forbidding erection of the gasoline station. *Dolan* v. *Brown,* 338 Ill. 412, 170 NE 425 (1930).

However, a change of use in the zoning ordinance does help to show that a change in the neighborhood has taken place, and the court may well decline thereafter to enforce the building restrictions on the ground of change in neighborhood. *Goodwin Bros.* v. *Combs Lumber Co.,* 275 Ky. 114, 120 SW2d 1024 (1938); *Austin* v. *Van Horn,* 225 Mich. 117, 237 NW 550 (1931); 26 CJS Deeds § 171 (2).

NEW DIRECTIONS: The older zoning ordinances permitted residences to be erected in any zone (cumulative zoning). The newer ordinances, by and large, forbid residential uses in commercial and industrial zones. Where the earlier building restriction calls for residential use and later zoning ordinance forbids residential use, the zoning ordinance supersedes the restriction. *1.77 Acres of Land* v. *State,* 241 A2d 513 (1968); *Grubel* v. *MacLaughlin,* 286 Fed.Supp. 24 (1968); *Key* v. *McCabe,* 54 Cal. 2d 736, 356 P2d 169 (1960); *Blakely* v. *Gorin,* 313 NE2d 903 (Mass. 1974); Hagman, Urban Planning, 308.

§ **735. Mortgages.** Zoning laws are binding on mortgagees. When a mortgagee loaned money for construction of a building that violated a zoning ordinance, the court refused to protect him although he was ignorant of the fact that the ordinance was being violated, since in dealing with real estate, all who are interested are required to take notice of zoning laws. *Siegemund* v. *Building Commissioner,* 263 Mass. 212, 160 NE 795 (1928). Accordingly, a mortgagee making a construction loan should satisfy himself that the contemplated improvement complies with existing ordinances. Otherwise he may find construction of the building halted by a court order after part of his mortgage money has been paid out.

§ **736. Enforcement of zoning ordinance.** It is usually provided in the zoning ordinance that any property owner wishing to erect a building must first apply to the commissioner of buildings or other proper official for a building permit. Every such application must be accompanied by plans and specifications of the contemplated structure. The official inspects the plans and declines to issue the permit if a violation of the zoning ordinance is disclosed. If, despite the fact that the contemplated structure would violate the zoning ordinance, the building permit is nevertheless issued, any other property owner whose property would suffer special damage by erection of the proposed structure, for example, a neighbor, may, if he acts promptly, obtain a court order prohibiting the erection of the building. *Garner* v. *County of DuPage,* 8 Ill.2d 155, 133 NE2d 303 (1956). Although it is advisable to do so, the complaining property owner need not first request the public authorities to take action. *Fitzgerald* v. *Merard Holding Co.,* 106 Conn. 475, 138 Atl. 483 (1927). If the complaining owner acts promptly in asserting his rights, but construction of the building is nevertheless begun, the offending property owner may be ordered by the court to demolish the illegal portion of the structure.

EXAMPLE: Despite protests of an adjoining owner before the commissioner of buildings and the Zoning Board of Appeals, a permit was issued to a property owner to construct an apartment building that violated the zoning ordinance in that it did not have a one-foot setback for every nine feet or rise above a height of seventy-two feet. While litigation was pending to declare the permit invalid, the apartment building corporation proceeded with construction of the building. Eventually, the courts declared the permit invalid, and the adjoining owner filed suit to compel the corporation to reconstruct the building to conform to the zoning ordinance. It developed that such reconstruction could be accomplished only at a cost of $343,837.07 Nevertheless, the court ordered the building corporation to reconstruct the building to comply with the ordinance. *Welton* v. *40 East Oak St. Bldg. Corp.,* 70 F2d 377 (1934).

It is held in some states that if a permit is issued, and in reliance thereon erection of the building is begun, the city cannot thereafter enforce the zoning ordinance if it is discovered that the permit should not have been issued. *Shellburne Inc.* v. *Roberts,* 224 A2d 250 (Del. 1966). The law on this point is chaotic. 1971 *Urban Law Annual* 63.

§ 737. Enforcement of zoning ordinance—estoppel. Often the landowner contends that because of some action or inaction of a city official, the city is precluded (*estopped*) from enforcing the ordinance. Often the courts reject such contentions.

EXAMPLE: The city allowed an apartment building to stand for over 43 years although it violated the zoning ordinance. The city now seeks to fine the apartment owner. It can do so. The long delay does not bar city action. The philosophy here is that important public rights ought not be lost by inaction of public servants. *G & S Mtg. & Invest. Corp.* v. *City of Evanston,* 264 NE2d 740 (Ill. 1970).

§ 738. Recent developments. Perhaps the most interesting recent development in zoning is the appearance of an excellent article that contains an excellent analysis of recent developments. McKay, Preserving "The Blessings of Quiet Seclusion": The Eastlake Decision and a Community's Right to Control Growth, 1977 *U. of Ill. Law Forum* 895 (1977).* An effort will be made to summarize the observations this fine article contains:

1. Zoning decisions that force a suburb to provide apartment or other zones where poor people can live compel the more affluent residents to pay higher taxes to provide services that the less affluent receive but cannot pay for.

2. Zoning validity is basically a matter for state courts to decide under the state constitutions. It is to be expected that the various state courts will reach different conclusions on the same set of facts.

3. Various results have been reached in court decisions dealing with ordinances requiring an affirmative vote of residents in the *vicinity* for some land use decision, for example, to permit billboards. These decisions are inapplicable where a referendum of *all* the voters in the suburb is required. Failure of the voters to act wisely or unselfishly does not affect the validity of a referendum under the federal constitution.

4. State courts deciding the referendum question under state law have disagreed. In some states the courts have elected to treat zoning as a process that requires rational planning, which automatically rules out referendums. Referendums lead to planless decisions. *Kelley* v. *John,* 162 Neb. 319, 75 NW2d 713 (1956).

5. However, some states, about twenty-two in fact, have constitutions that specifically authorize referendums. These provisions sanction referendums regardless of what the zoning laws provide.

6. Some state courts have held that the constitutional provisions permitting referendums apply only to broad, general legislation, not to the relatively unimportant rezoning of a lot in a suburb. Rezoning a lot is not really legislation. There is disagreement in the state courts on this point.

7. The Supreme Court, by holding that the federal constitution allows a suburb to permit only single-family dwellings has thrown the entire problem of exclusionary zoning to the state courts. *Moore* v. *City of East Cleveland,* 97 S.Ct. 1932 (1977); *Village of Belle Terre* v. *Boraas,* 416 U.S. 1 (1974). This is fortified by the Supreme Court's view that the federal constitution does not prohibit wealth discrimination as found in exclusionary zoning ordinances. *Village of Arlington Heights* v. *Metropolitan Housing Development Corp.,* 97 S.Ct. 555 (1977).

8. However, the state courts have complete liberty to outlaw exclusionary zoning if such a decision is based on the state constitution.

§ 739. **Building codes.** Most cities have adopted building codes specifying in great detail various requirements as to the construction of buildings, including requirements as to fireproof construction, load and stress, size and location of rooms, means of exit, windows and ventilation, sanitary equipment, electrical installation, chimneys, heating plant, mechanical refrigeration, illumination of exits, and standpipes. Often these are divided into separate codes, such as the electrical code or plumbing code. Innumerable special provisions will be encountered relating to special types of structures, such as theaters, schools, hospitals, garages, amusement parks, billboards, canopies, marquees, illuminated roof signs, and grandstands. Hazardous use units, such as drycleaning establishments, grain elevators, or paint-spraying rooms, are also subject to special regulations.

The fact that a building was erected while an older, more lenient law was in effect does not insulate it from newer, more rigid requirements. As long as the new standards are reasonable, the old buildings must conform to them.

EXAMPLE: An ordinance required tenement houses to have a supply of water on each floor. All old buildings must comply with this ordinance. *Health Dept.* v. *Trinity Church,* 145 N.Y. 32, 39 NE 833 (1895).

EXAMPLE: An ordinance required all hotels for transients to provide automatic sprinklers. It was held valid. *City of Chicago* v. *National Management,* 22 Ill. App.2d 445, 161 NE2d 358 (1959).

A landowner who proposes to erect a building must establish not only that it will comply with the zoning ordinance, but that all requirements of the building code will be complied with. Hence an application for a building permit, with its accompanying plans and specifications, is examined not only for possible zoning ordinance violations, but also for possible violations of the building code. Thus the application may be handled by a number of different departments of the city, such as the fire department, board of health, or boiler inspection department, before the permit is finally issued.

Permits are required not only where new construction is contemplated, but also where enlargements, alterations, or substantial repairs of existing structures are to be made.

Many zoning and building ordinances provide that no newly constructed building may be occupied until inspected by a city official for violations of ordinances. If no violations exist, a *certificate of occupancy* is issued by the city. Obviously it is dangerous to buy and pay for a newly constructed building without determining that a certificate of occupancy has been issued.

Local ordinances often provide that the commissioner of buildings or other proper official shall make an annual inspection of certain types of buildings. If any violation of the building code is disclosed, the owner or occupant is required to make the necessary alterations to make the building comply with the code. It is customary in some localities for an intending purchaser to cause a search to be made in the various departments charged with enforcing the building ordinances, such as the tenement house department, the building department, the fire department, or the health department. If any record of an existing violation is thereby disclosed, the seller is required to cure the violation. In order to avoid delay in closing the deal, the seller may permit the buyer to retain a portion of the purchase price as security to insure the seller's subsequent removal of the violation.

To achieve uniformity, states are beginning to adopt state building codes, as in New Jersey.

A building that is dangerously unsafe is a public nuisance and may be demolished by the city authorities without payment of compensation to the owner. *City of Honolulu* v. *Cavness,* 45 Hawaii 232, 364 P2d 646 (1961). Quite commonly laws and ordinances covering this situation go on to provide that the city has a lien, quite like a mortgage, on the vacant land for the expenses of demolition. This is called a *demolition lien.* In some states this lien is given priority over existing liens, such as mortgages.

There is some degree of uniformity throughout the country in building codes. Building Officials and Code Administrators, International, Inc. (BOCA), publish the BOCA Code, used primarily in the Midwest and East. The Southern Building Code Congress publishes a code used in the South. The International Congress of Building Officials publishes the Uniform

Building Code, covering the West. Thus, to the lawyer, a court decision interpreting any of these Codes can be used in any city that has adopted the Code. The BOCA Code is amended every three years. The other Codes are also amended at times as technology changes.

Building code violations—liability of landlord for injuries. The matter of a landlord's liability for personal injuries where he violates *state* laws is being discussed elsewhere. See Ch. 37. The new cases are beginning to apply this idea to *city* code violations. *Whetzel* v. *Jess Fisher Management Co.,* 282 F2d 943 (1960). Some of the older cases do not go this far. Today there are hundreds of "home-rule" municipalities in this country. Each one of these is similar to a little state legislature for that particular city. If *L* violates a home-rule ordinance, he is likely to be liable in a good many cities.

EXAMPLE: The home-rule city of *X* passes an ordinance requiring all apartment stairways to be well-lighted twenty-four hours a day. *L* turns off the lights at 11:00 P.M. despite the protests of tenants. *T* is injured on a dark stairway. He can sue *L*. It is the same as if a state law had been violated. Some pro-landlord courts probably will continue to hold against the tenant.

RESERVED: §§ 740–750.

24

Land Development, Regulation, Subdivisions, and Dedication

§ 751. **Dedication.** Dedication involves the landowner's setting apart his land for some public use, followed by an acceptance of such donation by the public. Dedication is of two kinds—common law and statutory.

§ 752. **Common law dedication.** No particular form is required for a common law dedication. It is not necessary that there be any written instrument. There must be an intention on the part of the landowner to dedicate his land to the public. He must, either by his words or acts, offer the land for some public use, and the public authorities must accept the offer. On acceptance of the offer, the city acquires an easement in the land dedicated.

EXAMPLE: A owned a tract of land. He fenced off the tract, locating the fence approximately thirty-three feet north of the south line of his land. This thirty-three-foot strip was used by the public as a road and was later paved by the city. A's acts showed an intention to offer the strip as a street, and the city's acts showed an acceptance of that offer. The city acquired an easement in the land for street purposes. Ownership of the street remained in A.

Once an offer of dedication has been accepted by the city it is irrevocable. 86 ALR2d 877. Whether it can be revoked *before* acceptance depends on the state law. 86 ALR2d 860.

If the intention to dedicate is lacking, there is no dedication.

EXAMPLE: Suppose I own land abutting on a public street and have a store thereon located some five feet from the street line. To induce the public to look into my store windows, I pave the strip between the store and the street. This does not operate as a dedication of the strip as part of the street, for my intention here is simply to make a more profitable utilization of my private property, not to give it to the public. *Nickel* v. *City* (Mo.App.), 239 SW2d 519.

For the same reason, any sign placed on such a strip indicating that the same is private property will prevent the creation of a dedication, even though the public is permitted to use such strip. 18 CJS 91. Some owners of private streets or alleys periodically place chains across the street or alley or imbed markers in the pavement to show an absence of intention to dedicate.

It is often said that land can be dedicated only by the true owner thereof. *O'Rorke* v. *City of Homewood,* 237 So2d 487 (Ala. 1970). This is true. Nevertheless, dedications can be and are made by owners whose land is subject to easements or other rights. 69 ALR2d 1236.

EXAMPLE: *R* owned land over which *X*, a neighbor, had a recorded driveway easement. *R* filed a plat in which he included the driveway in a public street dedicated by the plat. This is valid. The city acquires its rights subject to the rights of *X* to continue to exercise his rights under the easement. This is simply an application of the rule that one acquiring an easement does not acquire the exclusive right to its use. (See § 80.)

§ 753. Subdivision plats. Successful subdivision planning involves far more than the mere drawing of street and lot lines on paper; it includes the planning of neighborhoods. This planning begins with the selection of the raw land, the economical planning of streets, lots, and utilities, and the control of house design. After a plan has been arrived at, the lots, parks, and streets into which the land is to be divided are staked out by a land surveyor, and permanent monuments are placed at the corners of the subdivision. After this has been done, the surveyor plots on paper the manner in which the land has been subdivided. This is called *platting the subdivision.*

The plat is signed and acknowledged by the owner. If the land is mortgaged, the mortgagee must join in the plat. 63 ALR2d 1160. Then it is necessary to obtain the written approval of various city and other authorities. This approval merely signifies that the plat conforms to local law. After all this has been done, the plat is recorded in the recorder's office. It then constitutes an offer of *ownership* of the public places shown on the plat.

§ 754. Dedicated areas. Plats often contain donations or dedications of areas for parks or schools. One common trouble with these dedications is their ambiguity.

SUGGESTIONS:

1. Do you want to create rights in the general public or only in the lot owners in the subdivision? For example, if you mark a tract of land on the plat as "beach" or "park," is it intended that the *general public* may use the area, or is it intended that only *lot owners* shall use the area? The decisions are conflicting. 11 ALR2d 562. Make your intention clear. Place a legend on the plat as follows: "A perpetual easement appurtenant to each lot in this subdivision is hereby created for use of the area marked 'beach' as a private bathing beach only for owners of lots in this subdivision, members of their family, and guests. This must not be construed as a dedication to the general public. Ownership of the area is reserved to the subdivider and does not pass by any deed or mortgage of a lot."

2. To what *specific use* is the dedicated area to be put? For example, what is meant by such a general, ambiguous phrase as "public square"? Is it something like a park? Could a courthouse be built on it? a school? a church? a swimming pool? an athletic stadium? Spell out the specific use you want.

3. Who is to be the *legal owner* of the dedicated area? The city? The subdivider?

The adjoining landowners? There is some advantage to putting ownership in the city. For example, it will usually rid the subdivider of the burden of paying taxes on the area and will relieve him of personal liability for accidents that may occur on the area. A plat of dedication may give only an easement. 11 ALR2d 549. Give the city a deed. Approval of a plat by a city is *not* an acceptance of ownership.

4. Is a *present gift* intended or merely some possible gift in the future? For example, what is meant by the phrase "reserved for park"? Or "proposed park?" *Anderson* v. *Tall Timbers Corp.*, 378 SW2d 16 (Tex. 1964). Does such a phrase create present rights in the lot owners or the city, so that the subdivider may not change his mind a year from now and build a house on the tract? Don't use ambiguous phrases.

5. Is the utility strip dedicated to the public? A plat often shows a strip across the rear of the lots marked *easement for public utilities.* Some courts feel that the use of the word *public* makes this a dedication to the public. *Nichol* v. *Village of Glen Ellyn,* 89 Ill. App.2d 467, 231 NE2d 462 (1967); but other courts disagree. *Island Homes* v. *City of Fairbanks,* 421 P2d 759 (Alaska 1966). This should not be left in doubt, for if the strip is not dedicated to the public, there is some control in the landowner over which companies come into that strip with their services.

SUGGESTION: Place a legend on the plat as follows: "A perpetual easement is hereby created over, in favor of all lot owners in this subdivision, under, and across the area marked *easement for public utilities* as an easement appurtenant to each lot in this subdivision for the installation, use, maintenance, repair, and replacement of public utilities, including sewer, water, gas, electricity, telephone and telegraph. Said areas are not dedicated to the public."

Even where the public authorities never accept a particular street, public park, or other public area so designated on a plat, any lot owner in the subdivision has a private right to have the area used as platted and may obtain a court order forbidding any other use. *Newton* v. *Batson,* 223 S.C. 545, 77 SE2d 212 (1953); *McCorquodale* v. *Keyton,* 63 So2d 906 (Fla. 1953).

Approval of the subdivision plat by the city or other public body is not an automatic *acceptance* of the streets, parks, and other public areas depicted on the plat. 26 CJS 479. *Acceptance* is shown by the city's paving the streets, putting in sewers, and so on. 52 ALR2d 263. Therefore, if you want the city to assume *immediate responsibility* for these areas, you had best get the city council to pass an ordinance accepting this dedication. And if you want the city to have complete ownership of a park, for example, it is best to give the city a deed to the area and have the city council pass an ordinance accepting it although in many states acceptance of a plat operates as a transfer of ownership to the city. Once an area has been dedicated, neither the subdivider nor the city can use the land for a purpose other than the dedicated purpose. *City of St. Louis* v. *Bedal,* 394 SW2d 391 (1965).

§ 755. Conditional dedications-reservations by dedicator. A landowner making a dedication has the right to impose conditions. 26 CJS *Dedication* § 30.

EXAMPLE: *R* dedicated land to *E City* as a highway subject to the condition that the city provide a frontage road giving him access to the highway. This the city failed to do. *R* can revoke the dedication. *People* v. *Lorenz,* 34 Ill.2d 445, 216 NE2d 123 (1966).

Likewise a dedicator may reserve a private easement over land he dedicates. 3 *Am. Law of Ppty.* § 12.132.

EXAMPLE: *R* dedicates a park to *E City,* reserving an easement of ingress and egress over a specified portion of the park.

§ **756. Subdivision regulation.** During the real estate boom of the 1920's countless subdivisions were laid out with no thought for potential need. Plats were recorded showing streets and parks that never materialized. Lots were sold to ignorant people who had no notion of their true value. When the crash of 1929 arrived, lot sales stopped. The market for vacant lots totally disappeared. Real estate taxes were not paid. These premature subdivisions became a disaster area. 36 *Mo. L. Rev.* 1. Hence laws were passed requiring a developer to submit his plat for approval before it is recorded. State and Federal laws require various disclosures to be made to lot purchasers. In general, the legal philosophy is that if a landowner chooses to subdivide his land and to record a plat for that purpose, the public can legitimately impose reasonable restrictions on his use of the public records to accomplish his objectives. Even more important, the community has a stake in avoiding the problems of unpaid taxes and unusable streets that premature platting creates and an even greater stake in preserving the health of the community through proper sewer and water installations.

Today subdivision of land is subject to strict controls. The governing body of the city or village or a planning board may retain in its own hands the power to approve or disapprove proposed subdivisions, or, where the state law permits, this power may be delegated to a planning commission. Control over land subdivision is exercised over the entire city and often a surrounding area of several miles. *Prudential Co-op Realty Co.* v. *City of Youngstown,* 118 Ohio St. 204, 160 NE 695 (1928); 11 ALR2d 524. However, this power to *approve* plats of land outside the city limits does not confer power to *zone* the area outside the city. *City of Carlsbad* v. *Caviness,* 66 N.M. 230, 346 P2d 310 (1959); *Village of Bensonville* v. *County of Du Page,* 30 Ill. App.2d 324, 174 NE2d 403 (1961). The city adopts regulations establishing standards of subdivision design, including regulations concerning utilities, streets, curbs, gutters, sidewalks, storm and sanitary sewers, fire hydrants, street lighting, street signs, and width, depth, and area of lots. No subdivision plat may be recorded unless it has been approved, and approval is withheld unless the plat complies with the regulations. In lieu of requiring installation of streets, utilities, and so on, before approval, the commission may accept a surety company bond guaranteeing that the installation will be made. It is impractical to install streets and then have them pounded to rubble as construction goes forward.

Like zoning, plat approval is a type of land use control. But it is different from zoning. There are two separate laws. They should not be confused.

NEW DIRECTIONS: There is some tendency today to combine the two in one law.

If a subdivider records his plat without the required approval, he runs the risk that the planning board or the city may procure a court order stopping all sales. Wrongful Subdivision Approval by the Plan Commission: Remedies of the Buyer and City. 29 *Ind. L. J.* 408 (1954). Moreover, in most states the law forbids the recording of a plat unless city approval is endorsed thereon. And in many states, selling land in an unapproved subdivision plat is subject to a fine. In some states, California, Michigan, and New Jersey, for example, the buyer of a lot in an unapproved subdivision may change his mind, abrogate the sale, and get his money back. Platting, Planning & Protection—A Summary of Subdivision Statutes, 36 *N.Y.U.L. Rev.* 1214 (1961). In other states—Idaho, Iowa, Massachusetts, Michigan, Nebraska, Rhode Island, and Wyoming, for example—the buyer of a lot in an unapproved subdivision may sue the seller for damages. Building permits are refused where the lots front on an unapproved street. Sometimes the subdivider divides up his area into building sites, but instead of recording a plat showing these building sites as lots on the plat, he sells off the sites by metes and bounds descriptions. No plat is recorded. Any such attempted evasion of the law is ineffective. Such conduct can be fined, and a court order can be issued forbidding such metes and bounds sales. In many states the recorder of deeds will refuse to accept for recording a deed in a metes and bounds subdivision. Also, building permits will be refused the lot owners.

Generally it is required that the plat and subdivision conform to regulations or plans set forth in a statute or ordinance. The city, in other words, cannot arbitrarily withhold its approval. Its disapproval must be based on failure of the plat to conform to some general set of rules applicable to all developers. *Beach* v. *Planning Comm.*, 141 Conn. 79, 103 A2d 814; *People* v. *Massieon,* 279 Ill. 312, 116 NE 639.

§ 757. Forced dedication. As the need for public control of platting gained acceptance, the pendulum began to swing steadily toward more rigorous controls. The cities, in addition to controlling the size and direction of streets, grading and paving, gutters and drainage, water and utility installation, etc., began to insist on dedication of land for schools and parks, and other contributions to the public. The requirements as to streets, sidewalks, sewer, and water have been upheld as valid. Yearwood, Accepted Controls of Land Subdivision; 45 *J. of Urban Law* 217 (1967). 36 *Mo. L. Rev.* 1. The other requirements have aroused controversy.

When it comes to city exactions of great magnitude, such as those requiring the developer to contribute parks, school areas, and sewage treatment plans, the problems become very difficult.

The city has two great powers, the police power and the power of eminent domain. The police power is the power to pass reasonable laws for the good of the public. The power of eminent domain is the power to acquire land for public purposes by paying for it. Where forced dedication is employed and sustained, the court is saying that this is an appropriate situation for exercising the police power. This does not require the payment of any compensation.

The following exactions were held valid without payment of compensation:

EXAMPLE: An ordinance requiring that the location, width, and alignment of platted streets conform to existing contiguous streets and to the city plan, and that abnormally steep grades, sharp curves, or dangerous intersections be avoided.

EXAMPLE: An ordinance requiring the subdivider to dedicate ample streets to the city. *Ayres* v. *City of Los Angeles,* 34 Cal.2d 31, 207 P2d 1 (1949).

EXAMPLE: An ordinance requiring the subdivider to pave streets and install utilities, gutters, and storm sewers. *Brous* v. *Smith,* 304 N.Y. 164, 106 NE2d 503 (1954); *Petterson* v. *Naperville,* 9 Ill.2d 233, 137 NE2d 371 (1956).

EXAMPLE: The city required 4 per cent of the platted area to be set apart for parks and playgrounds. This was held valid because the need for parks and playgrounds was created by the subdivider's activity. *Aunt Hack Ridge Estates Inc.* v. *Planning Comm.,* 160 Conn. 109, 230 A2d 45.

EXAMPLE: An ordinance requiring subdivider to dedicate land or pay a fee in lieu thereof for park purposes. *Assoc. Home Builders* v. *City of Walnut Creek,* 94 Cal. Reptr. 630, 484 P2d 606 (1971). This case contains a valuable review of the law on the subject.

Among regulations held invalid without payment of compensation are the following:

EXAMPLE: Ordinance increasing price of building permit, listing various charges, vastly in excess of the cost of processing the permit. *Merrelli* v. *St. Clair Shores,* 355 Mich. 575, 96 NW2d 144; *Daniels* v. *Point Pleasant,* 23 N.J. 357, 129 A2d 265.

EXAMPLE: Ordinance charging the subdivider $400 per acre to connect to city sewer system. *City of Los Angeles* v. *Offner,* 55 Cal.2d 103, 358 P2d 926 (1961).

EXAMPLE: Ordinances requiring subdivider to donate land for schools, parks, etc. *Pioneer Bank* v. *Mt. Prospect,* 22 Ill.2d 375, 176 NE2d 799; *Ridgemont Development Co.* v. *East Detroit,* 358 Mich. 387, 100 NW2d 301. Contrary decisions on this point are: *Jordan* v. *Menomonee Falls,* 28 Wis.2d 608, 137 NW2d 442; *Billings Properties Inc.* v. *Yellowstone County,* 144 Mont. 25, 394 P2d 182 (1964); *Jenad Inc.* v. *Scarsdale,* 18 N.Y.2d 78, 218 NE2d 673 (1966).

EXAMPLE: Ordinance requiring subdivider to contribute money for school or park. *West Park Ave. Inc.* v. *Ocean Twp.,* N.J., 244 A2d 1.

EXAMPLE: Ordinance limiting the number of permits a builder can receive at one time. *U.S. Home & Develop. Corp.* v. *LaMura,* 214 A2d 538 (N.J.).

EXAMPLE: Ordinance requiring subdivider to pay city 10 per cent of the value of the subdivision where the plat showed no open public spaces. *Coronado Develop. Co.* v. *McPherson,* 189 Kan. 174, 368 P2d 51 (1962).

EXAMPLE: Refusal to approve plat because of the added burdens new housing would impose on public facilities. *Beach* v. *Planning Comm.,* 141 Conn. 79, 103 A2d 814.

EXAMPLE: Ordinance requiring dedication of land for street 700 feet distant from the subdivision. *McKain* v. *Toledo City Plan Comm.,* 270 NE2d 370.

Some more recent cases offer additional illustrations:

EXAMPLE: A residential developer and school board entered into an agreement under which the developer agreed to contribute land and pay the board a sum of money for each home constructed. In return the developer received zoning special use permits. The court held the contract valid. *Board of Education* v. *Surety Dev. Inc.,* 321 NE2d 99 (Ill. 1975). The philosophy here, is that the developer may be properly required to bear burdens which are "specifically and uniquely attributable" to his development activities. *Dept. of Pub. Works* v. *Exchange Nat. Bank,* 334 NE2d 810 (Ill. 1975).

EXAMPLE: A developer was required to dedicate land for a school site. Held, valid. *Morris Community H. S. Dist.* v. *Morris Develop. Co.,* 320 NE2d 37 (Ill. 1974).

EXAMPLE: The developer was required to contribute $120,000 toward drainage facilities. The court sustained this because the needs created by the development can be charged against the development. *Divan Builders, Inc.* v. *Planning Board,* 334 A2d 30 (N.J. 1975). The court gave consideration to the fact that improvement of drainage was made necessary by the development.

EXAMPLE: However, the court held invalid a requirement by the County Planning Board that the developer dedicate a strip of land fronting on a county road where there was no perceivable connection between this requirement and the proposed development. *181 Inc.* v. *Salem County Planning Bd.,* 336 A2d 501 (N.J. 1975).

EXAMPLE: A requirement that the developer install water mains was held valid. *Deerfield Estates Inc.* v. *Twp. of East Brunswick,* 60 N.J. 115, 286 A2d 498 (1971).

EXAMPLE: The requirement of a deposit by the developer without specifying its use was illegal. *Broward County* v. *James Development Corp.,* 311 So2d 371 (Fla. 1975).

EXAMPLE: Substantial "tap in fees" (charges for connecting with the sewer system) have been sustained where the proceeds were to be used for improving the sewer system. *Home Builders Ass'n.* v. *Provo City,* 503 P2d 451 (Utah 1972).

EXAMPLE: The requirement was held valid that a developer pay for street grading, curbing, sidewalks, water mains, and sewers. *In re Spring Valley Development,* 300 A2d 736 (Me. 1973).

EXAMPLE: A city may require that a developer donate land for recreation purposes because the need was "specifically and uniquely attributable" to the development.

Frank Ansuini Inc. v. *City of Cranston,* 264 A2d 910 (R.I. 1970); *Dept. Pub. Works* v. *Exchange Nat. Bank,* 334 NE2d 810 (Ill. 1975).

NEW DIRECTIONS: As can be seen, there seems to be a strong current trend toward sustaining these exactions. In part, this new trend stems from the view that land developers buy land cheap because it is zoned agricultural or for single-families. This is done deliberately by the municipality because it wishes to consider the desirability of the developer who comes in for rezoning to multifamily or commercial. Once rezoning is granted the land value shoots up astronomically. There is a feeling that the developer should share part of this increment or windfall with the municipality that conferred it.

REFERENCES: 43 ALR3d 862; 45 *J. of Urban Law* 217.

The city's requirement that the developer give land for parks and schools must be reasonable. There is a very recent trend toward holding zoning ordinances invalid where they tend to keep the poor out of the suburbs. This idea has been applied to forced dedications.

EXAMPLE: The city of X adopts such extreme requirements for park and school dedications that the price of lots and homes is forced up, because the developer has less land to sell. The requirement may be held invalid. *Oakwood at Madison, Inc.* v. *Tp. of Madison,* 371 A2d 1192 (N.J. 1977).

License tax on the business of developing. In lieu of, or in addition to forced dedication contributions, some cities have imposed a license tax on the business of constructing dwellings.

EXAMPLE: Newark, California imposed a license tax on the business of constructing dwellings. The courts sustained this. *Assoc. Home Builders* v. *City of Newark,* 95 Cal. Reptr. 648 (1971). Nevada has a law of this sort.

NEW LAWS: Vermont has enacted a capital gains tax on real estate sales. It has been held valid. *Andrews* v. *Lathrop,* 132 Vt. 256, 315 A2d 860 (1974).

These devices are schemes for capturing for the public, part of the increase in value created by public approval of his project.

Housing grants—land use controls. The Housing and Community Development Act of 1974 (HUDA) provides for federal (HUD) grants to municipalities. This was once used to compel municipalities to accept low and moderate income housing.

EXAMPLE: The City of Hartford challenged in court HUD grants in seven suburban communities. The court invalidated the grants because HUD made them without first assessing the housing needs of low income persons. *Hartford* v. *Hills,* 408 F.Supp. 889 (D. Conn. 1976). This view has been rejected.

§ **758. Development rights.** Prof. John Costonis has pioneered the idea of transferring development rights.

NEW DIRECTIONS: A developer owns a landmark building, which he plans to demolish so that he can erect a modern office building. The city negotiates with him and he transfers to the city his "development rights" in the old building. The city in turn grants him additional development rights on other land he owns in the area, so that he can build a more extensive building than the law otherwise allows. This is a great oversimplification, but it conveys the idea. Development Rights Transfer and Landmark Preservation, 9 *Urban L. Ann.* 131 (1975). In New York it has been squarely held that a city has no power to substitute transferable development rights for cash compensation through eminent domain proceedings. *French Investing Co. v. City of N.Y.*, 385 NYS2d 5 (1976); *Marbro Corp. v. Rumsey*, 28 Ill.App.2d 252, 171 NE 246.

Note that there is no problem if the city *buys* or *condemns* the development rights of the landmark premises. That is as valid as the scenic easement discussed much earlier. Eckert, Acquisition of Development Rights: A Modern Land Use Tool, 23 *U. Miami L. R.* 349 (1968). But transfer of development rights, land use experts argue, is "confederate money," or "pie in the sky." The landowner is entitled to *cash* when the municipality locks him into a beautiful but uneconomic building, thus taking away his right to demolish and erect a larger building.

REFERENCE: Gerstell, Needed: A Landmark Decision, 8 Urban Law 213 (1976).

§ 759. Development rights—farm land. A special problem exists with respect to farm lands.

EXAMPLE: X owns a farm that has been in his family for many years. As the nearby suburbs expand, his land becomes valuable for a development, his real estate taxes soar. For example, his land might be worth $1500 per acre for farming, but $10,000 to $25,000 per acre for development. Under state law, all land must be taxed uniformly at its full market value. X's taxes will go up.

One solution to this problem is for the county to buy the farmer's development rights. He is paid the excess value above the $1500 per acre. He gives the county a release of his development rights. He and his successors may continue to farm the land. However, no one can use the land for development for housing or purposes other than farming. This reduces the land value back to $1500 per acre. This situation is currently happening in Suffolk County, on Long Island, and elsewhere.

This technique of purchasing development rights was first used to preserve scenic areas. It is now being used to preserve landmarks and farm lands.

Perhaps it will help you to understand this concept if you think of property ownership as a bundle of rights.

EXAMPLE: X owns land improved with a store building. X leases the building to Y for ten years. X has parted with his right to possession for ten years. In the same way X can sell to the county his right to develop the land.

§ 760. Interstate Land Sales Act. The Interstate Land Sales Act requires that certain disclosures be made *prior* to the selling of unimproved subdivision lots consisting of fifty or more parcels as part of a common promotional plan utilizing the means of interstate commerce or the mails. 15 U.S.C.A. § 1701 *et. seq*. Unimproved land is land on which no buildings have been constructed. Where condominium units are offered for sale prior to the construction of the building, the Act is applicable. Lehtonen, Interstate Land Sales Full Disclosure Act and Its Effect on Land Titles, 50 *Title News* 29 (Jan. 1971).

The Act requires the developer to submit a *statement of record* to HUD before any lots are sold. This statement must furnish comprehensive information concerning the history of the developer and its principals—bankruptcy, convictions, disbarment, and so forth; legal description, topography and climate; condition of title to the land; conditions of the offer to sell and range of selling prices; access; utilities; recreational facilities; taxes; and so forth.

Financial statements of the developer, together with copies of easements and building restrictions affecting the property and other informational documents must be filed with statement of record.

The *property report* is in question-and-answer form and is a condensed version of the information contained in the statement of record. It is submitted with the statement of record. The property report must also list special risk factors relating to potential appreciation, obligation to pay the entire outstanding balance to the lender notwithstanding the availability of defenses against developer, and so forth.

The statement becomes effective thirty days after filing if no objection is made to it. Until this thirty-day period has expired, any sale of lots is unlawful.

The property report must be furnished to each lot purchaser at least forty-eight hours before he signs the contract of purchase, unless the purchaser acknowledges in writing that he has received the report and made an inspection of the lot. If the property report is not furnished to the purchaser, he may, at any time, set the transaction aside and demand the return of his money. A willful violation of any of the provisions of the act or regulations may lead to criminal penalties. A purchaser may also sue the developer if the statement of record or property report contains an omission or an untrue statement of material fact.

The following transactions are exempt from the act:

1. The sale or lease of real estate not pursuant to a common promotional plan to offer to sell fifty or more lots in a subdivision.

2. The sale or lease of lots in a subdivision all of which are five acres or more in size.

3. The sale or lease of any lots on which there is a residential, commercial, or industrial building, or the sale or lease of land under a contract obligating the seller to erect such a building thereon within a period of two years.

4. The sale or lease of real estate under or pursuant to court order.

5. The sale of evidences of indebtedness secured by a mortgage or deed of trust on real estate.

6. The sale of securities issued by a real estate investment trust.

7. The sale or lease of real estate by any government or government agency.

8. The sale or lease of cemetery lots.

9. The sale or lease of lots to any person who acquires such lots for the purpose of engaging in the business of constructing residential, commercial, or industrial buildings or for the purpose of resale or lease of such lots to persons engaged in such business.

10. The sale or lease of real estate that is zoned for industrial or commercial development under certain circumstances.

11. The sale or lease of real estate free and clear of all liens, encumbrances, and adverse claims and which each and every purchaser or his or her spouse has inspected the real estate which he has purchased or leased prior to the signing of a contract to purchase or lease. (The presence of reservations and dedications for utilities, nondelinquent real estate taxes, and assessments and beneficial building restrictions does not disqualify the property for this exemption.) To obtain this exemption a formal filing with HUD is required.

12. The sale or lease of lots, each of which exceeds 10,000 square feet and each of which will be sold for less than $100, including closing costs.

13. The lease of lots for a term not to exceed five years, provided the terms of the lease do not obligate the lessee to renew.

Further, HUD may exempt other developments if it is determined: (1) the subdivision contains less than 300 lots; (2) the subdivision is entirely in one state; (3) solicitation is entirely or almost entirely limited to the state where the subdivision is located; (4) promotional efforts are confined to that state; and (5) no more than five percent of the sales in any year are made to residents of other states.

REFERENCES: Walsh, Consumer Protection in Land Development Sales, 44 *Conn. B. J.* 403 (1970); Kerr, Guide to the Interstate Land Sales Full Disclosure Act: A Checklist for Developers, 4 *RELJ* 416 (1976). Gose, Interstate Land Sales, 9 *RP, P&TJ* 7 (1974); Comment, 51 *Ore L. Rev.* 381 (1972); Comment, 1974 *Wisc. L. Rev.* 558; 24 CFR § 1700 et. seq.

§ 761. Local regulations. Regarding sales not covered by the Interstate Land Sales Act, most states have their local laws regulating lot sales. Comment, 21 *Rutgers L. Rev.* 720 (1967); Walter, The Law of the Land: Development Legislation in Maine and Vermont, 23 *Maine L. Rev.* 315 (1971).

§ 762. Regulation of land sales—FTC. Because the Interstate Land Sales Act has not been very effective, the Federal Trade Commission now regulates interstate land sales also, and to a considerable extent its regulations overlap the Interstate Land Sales regulations. Both regulations forbid deceptive advertising, unfair sales techniques, and unfair provisions in land sale contracts. The FTC feels that its ability to punish harshly developers who violate its regulations will deter fraud in the sale of vacant lots.

§ 763. Development regulation. An example of modern development regulation is the new law adopted in Vermont.

EXAMPLE: Vermont's new law provides for an Environmental Control Board and seven district environmental commissions. The latter agencies process permits which must be obtained for proposed developments of more than one acre in towns without duly adopted permanent zoning and subdivision regulations. In communities having these codes, permits are required for any development encompassing more than ten acres. Permits are awarded if the District Commission is satisfied that the proposed subdivision is found acceptable in four major aspects: that it will not unduly pollute air, land, or water; that it will pose no unreasonable burden on a community's capacity to deliver municipal services; that the application conforms to any duly adopted local, regional and state plan and that the project "will not have an undue adverse effect on the scenic or natural beauty of the area, aesthetics, historic sites, or rare and irreplacable natural areas."

Because of concern for the protection of the environment scores of new laws and court decisions are appearing.

NEW DIRECTIONS: Because of concern for the environment, the land developer is or will be required to submit his plans to some public body that will grant him approval to go ahead only if no appreciable adverse effect on the environment will occur. *Friends of Mammoth* v. *Mono City Board,* 104 Cal. Reptr. 16. This will be especially true in offshore areas, swamplands, and wetlands.

EXAMPLE: *ABC Village* enacts a zoning ordinance barring all high-rise apartments. This ordinance is invalid. Developers cannot be singled out to bear all the financial burdens of pollution. *Westwood Forest Estates, Inc.* v. *Village of South Nyack,* 23 N.Y.2d 424, 297 N.Y.S.2d 129 (1969); 1 *Urban Law,* 228.

EXAMPLE: A developer bought a wilderness area. The county refused a building permit because it wanted the land kept in its natural state. This action was held invalid. If the public wants wilderness areas preserved, it, the court thought it must condemn them. *Harbor Farms Inc.* v. *Nassau County Planning Comm.,* 334 N.Y.S.2d 412 (1972).

NEW DIRECTIONS: Among the recent developments in this area are statutes providing for *state* regulation of land use. Keep in mind that traditionally *cities* and *counties* regulated land use. Now the *state* is stepping in.

EXAMPLE: Hawaii has created a State Land Use Commission, which has divided the state into *urban, rural, agricultural* and *conservation* areas and land use in each area is limited to the uses permitted by state laws.

Some state laws are pretty drastic.

EXAMPLE: In Delaware heavy industry is forbidden in a strip of coast land one to five miles wide.

EXAMPLE: Maine divides the state into *protection districts, management districts, holding districts,* and *development districts.* In protection districts, where presently development is negligible, the state will endeavor to preserve the present status.

The large-scale development is particularly vulnerable to state regulation.

EXAMPLE: In Maine and Vermont all large-scale developments are subject to state regulation. *In re Spring Valley,* 300 A2d 736 (1973).

NEW DIRECTIONS: Florida has enacted the Environmental Land and Water Managment Act of 1972. Florida, of course, has vast expanses of marsh land, which developers can acquire cheaply. Such marsh land is essential to the health of the ecology. Florida divides the state into zones or areas. Thus, there are areas of "critical state concern."

EXAMPLE: Areas containing or having a significant impact upon environmental, historical, natural, or archaeological resources of *regional or statewide importance,* such as Big Cypress Swamp, the Florida Keys, or a jetport, or a new community. The Act sets forth principles for development of such areas. Municipalities must adopt development regulations that comply with these regulations or the state will impose regulations on the area.

Then there are areas involving development of regional impact (DRI).

EXAMPLE: A large hospital, a large shopping center, or a large housing development. These areas are not mapped by the state but are so designated when a developer proposes to build a project of the type listed in the state law as a DRI. The developer is required to fill out an enormously complex application, perhaps hundreds of pages in length. It is then considered by the municipality and a regional planning agency. As is evident, the Florida scheme focuses on relatively large developments.

NEW DIRECTIONS: By contrast, in Vermont state controls apply to residential developments with ten units or more, and in Maine the magic number is twenty acres. As can also be seen, regarding regulated projects, a developer must often obtain two approvals, one from the state or a regional commission and one from the municipality. This applies, for example, to California, Vermont, Maine, and the coastal zones of New Jersey and North Carolina. Also there is a third factor, environmental control, which brings in a third agency, such as the one established under the Federal Clean Air Act. This agency handles shopping centers and new towns, where the concentration of automobile traffic creates air pollution. At times the regulations will conflict with the Environmental Protection Agency (EPA) pushing for smaller parking areas (to restrict traffic) and the local agencies pushing for larger parking areas (to reduce traffic densities). Basically, this means that the expense of land development, including the cost of paying real estate taxes for as much as two years, goes up sharply.

NEW DIRECTIONS: Some developers now do not buy land. They simply buy an option or contingent contract, effective when all the legal hurdles have been surmounted. This also pushes up the cost of houses.

NEW DIRECTIONS: Some states (Colorado, for example) have taken over the regulation of prefabs. This is done because the villages have attempted to zone them out.

NEW DIRECTIONS: Prefabs are largely constructed at a factory, and therefore regular mortgage financing is not available. Construction is financed under the Uniform Commercial Code, just as the sales of chattels are financed.

NEW DIRECTIONS: A good discussion of the law relating to the new problems of land regulation will be found in Leahy, Environmental Issues in Local Land Use Regulation, 11 *RPP & TJ* 457 (1976).

§ 764. Phase development—moratoria. Some municipalities have provided for phased development.

EXAMPLE: In 1966, the Town of Ramapo, New York, adopted a master plan that had been two years in the making for the future development of the town. It also adopted a comprehensive zoning ordinance. Nine-tenths of the town's unincorporated area was zoned residential. To implement the plan, the town enacted a capital budget for the construction of streets, parks, sewers, and so forth. This plan called for installation over an eighteen-year period, with specific phases to be completed at the end of the sixth and twelfth years. In 1969 an amendement to the zoning ordinance was adopted. This amendment required that a special permit would be necessary in order to construct a residence. When a permit was applied for, the zoning board would consider the area to be built upon, including availability of sewers, parks, schools, roads, firehouses. Each item was assigned a point value. A minimum of fifteen points was required to qualify for a permit. If public facilities were lacking, the developer was at liberty to construct the needed facilities at his own expense. In this fashion, he could proceed with his development as soon as he acquired the required points. The town considered only its own needs. The area outside the town was ignored. A residential developer applied for plat approval. His plan did not conform to the permit requirements. He was turned down. The ordinance was held valid. *Golden* v. *Town of Ramapo,* 30 N.Y.2d 359, 285 NE2d 291, 334 N.Y.S.2d 185, App. dsd 409 U.S. 1003, commented on in *47 N.Y.U. L. Rev.* 723 (1972). The scheme is called *phased development*.

A water-short municipality, after imposing a *moratorium on development,* must make a good faith effort to augment its water supply in order to permit the landowner, particularly the land developer, to proceed with erection of buildings. It is only after such efforts have proved fruitless that the hookup moratorium may be continued and, of course, development must stop because the water supply is unable to support added population. Note, The Thirst For Population Control, 27 *Hastings L. J.* 753 (1976). In short, a municipality can reasonably be expected to exert reasonable efforts. It cannot be expected to perform miracles.

REFERENCES: Note, Phased zoning: Regulation of the Tempo and Sequence of Land Development, 26 *Stanf. L. Rev.* 585 (1974); Burke and Dienes, Creating a Community; Process of Land Development for Urban Growth, 9 *Houston L. Rev.* 189; Gibson and Simms, New Community Development, 11 *Wash. L. J.* 227 (1972).

NEW DIRECTIONS: "No growth" regulation. The Town of Petaluma adopted a housing and zoning plan that specified that only five hundred new home permits could be issued per year for five years. The federal courts sustained this. *Const. Ind. Assn. of Sonoma County* v. *City of Petaluma,* 522 F2d 897 (1975). The court held that the concept of public-welfare is sufficiently broad to uphold Petaluma's desire to preserve its small town character, its open spaces, and low density of population, and to grow at an orderly and deliberate pace. Obviously some state courts disagree violently with this point of view. *Harbor Farms Inc.* v. *Nassau Planning Comm.,* 40 App. Div. 2d 517, 334 N.Y.S.2d 412 (1972); *II Management & Control of Growth* (Urban Land Institute) 237. Stopping the growth of Petaluma does not stop the nation's population growth. It merely directs it somewhere else. It is disappointing to watch the federal courts dodging this issue. The *Petaluma* decision disregards the right of every citizen to travel everywhere and build a home when he finds a place he likes. Constitutional Law—Rights to Travel—Phased Development Plan Unconstitutionally Burdens the Right to Travel of Persons Excluded, 28 *Vand. L. Rev.* 987 (1975). As explained in the chapter on Land Use Controls-Zoning, federal court decisions get headlines, but the state courts are not bound to follow them.

§ 765. Moratoria—sewer and water problems. Some municipalities have resorted to the moratorium to stop unwanted construction.

EXAMPLE: Cities that lack adequate sewer or other facilities have imposed a moratorium on issuance of building permits. If the time period is reasonable and the city has a definite plan for solving the problem, the moratorium has been sustained by some courts. *Smoke Rise Inc.* v. *Washington Suburban San. Comm.,* 400 F.Supp. 1369 (1975) (sustaining five-year moratorium); II Management & Control of Growth (Urban Land Institute, 1200 18th St. N.W. Washington, D.C. 20036 (very valuable collection of articles). Fairfax County, Virginia, tried a "no growth" moratorium approach, but lost. The Virginia Supreme Court held that permits *must* be issued to land developers. *City of Richmond* v. *Randall,* 205 Va. 506, 211 SE2d 56 (1975).

One writer takes the following position on moratoria: (1) the moratorium is valid if an actual emergency exists and a law or ordinance authorizes the moratorium; (2) the moratorium must be limited in time; (3) the city must have a program to end the emergency; (4) it is up to the court, not the village, to determine if these requirements exist. The Thirst for Population Control, 27 *Hastings L. J.* 753.

EXAMPLE: In Colorado an interesting situation arose. The county in question required that the developer make arrangements for water and sewer service before receiving approval for his residential building plans. The city of Boulder was the only provider of sewer and water in the entire area, including land outside the city. The developer applied for such service and was refused, although it could readily be furnished. The court held that the city must furnish the sewer and water. The county and the city had contrived a situation between them under which the developer could not go ahead without sewer and water, but the city, the only provider, could refuse to furnish these services. Plainly this indefinite ban on development violates the developer's rights under the state constitution. *Robinson* v. *Boulder,* 547 P2d 228 (Colo. 1976), commented on in 5 Real Estate L. J. 170.

However, a moratorium on building permits for a reasonable time, while the city attempts to cope with the problem, is valid. If during that time it is established that there simply is no water available for further building, the city can make the moratorium permanent. "You cannot get blood out of a turnip, and you cannot get water out of a dry well."

§ 766. Moratoria—school problems. Where school facilities are overcrowded, the village can validly impose a temporary, reasonable moratorium designed to study and solve the problem. *Builders Assn.* v. *Superior Court,* 529 P2d 582 (1974).

§ 767. Revocation of permit—city liability.

NEW DIRECTIONS: In many cases developers proceeded in good faith to spend money for engineers, architects, and so forth, after receiving a building permit. Then the city, usually in response to pressure from neighbors, revoked the permit, finding some illegality on which to base its action. The courts have just begun to hold the city liable for reimbursement of the developer's expenses. *154 East Park Ave. Corp.* v. *City of Long Beach,* 171 *N.Y.L.J.* #2, p. 19 Col. 8 (Jan. 3, 1974). The courts are getting fed up with "dirty tricks."

§ 768. Revocation of permit—change in zoning.

NEW DIRECTIONS: A developer obtained rezoning. New officials were elected to the zoning board. They rezoned the land, offered to buy it, and engaged in other harassment of the developer. The Florida Supreme Court sustained an injunction against the city's "dirty tricks" and allowed the developer to proceed as originally planned. It said, "every citizen has the right to expect that he will be dealt fairly by his government." *Hollywood Beach Hotel* Co. v. *City of Hollywood,* 329 So2d 10 (1976).

§ 769. Failure to enforce drainage regulations.

NEW DIRECTIONS: A developer was given a permit on the condition that he provide proper drainage. He failed in this regard. An adjoining owner sued the city for failure to enforce its own drainage regulations. The city was held liable. *Breiner* v. *C. & P. Home Builders Inc.,* 398 F.Supp. 250 (1975).

§ 770. Resubdivision. A platted area is sometimes replatted *or resubdivided.* For example, if an ill-conceived subdivision, using the old-fashioned gridiron pattern, were to be acquired by a modern developer, he would go to the city and request that all streets and alleys be vacated, that is, officially abandoned by the city. Thereupon he would resubdivide the area into larger, irregular lots on curvilinear streets with utility easements over the rear substituted for outmoded alleys.

§ 771. Sewer, water, and other utilities. When a land developer installs sewer, water, and other utilities in the streets or alleys of the development, the developer has no right to remove the utilities that he has installed. These utilities, as well as the street, are dedicated to the use of the lot owners. *Stegall* v. *Jackson,* 244 Miss. 169, 141 So2d 236 (1962); *City of Snyder* v. *Bass,* 360 SW2d 426 (Tex. 1962); *Oden* v. *Seattle,* 432 P2d 642 (Wash. 1967). Suppose, however, that he buys ninety-five lots in an existing subdivision of one hundred lots. No utilities have been installed. Under the state law in this particular state, the city, not the lot owners, owns the street. He makes a contract with the city under which he is to install sewer and water pipes in the street but is to retain ownership thereof. This contract is duly recorded. Thereafter, the owners of the other five lots seek to connect to his sewer and water pipes. They have no right to do so. They did not buy their lots in reliance on any representation made by him and cannot connect with his pipes. *Atchison* v. *De Roo,* 332 Ill.App. 251, 75 NE2d 46 (1947). Of course the people who buy their lots from him and rely on his representations as to sewer and water are protected.

SUGGESTION: A subdivider who wishes to retain ownership of his sewer and water mains, so that he can charge for their use, should make and record in the recorder's office a conveyance of such mains to his own water company before he makes any deed of lots to purchasers. Once a deed is made to a lot purchaser, it is arguable that the water main in the street in front of his lot belongs to the lot purchaser or is dedicated to his use, and therefore the subdivider cannot charge the lot purchaser for its use, where no deed to a water company has been recorded.

NEW DIRECTIONS: Extension of utilities is a function of proper land development regulation. In the foregoing, the assumption was made that an abundance of water, sewer service, gas, and electricity exists and that all one needs is the legal right to tap into such service in order that development may proceed. In these times it has become evident that America suffers from an acute shortage of all of these heretofore abundant matters. Hence, extension of such a service has become a matter of proper land use and development regulation.

Subdividers often place dotted lines on their plats and mark the indicated areas "easement for public utilities." This phrase is too brief and general. What type of facilities are included in the phrase public utilities?

SUGGESTION: Place a legend on the plat as follows: "A perpetual easement is hereby created over, in favor of all lots owners in this subdivision, under, and across the area marked *easement for public utilities* as an easement appurtenant to each lot in this subdivision for the installation, use, maintenance, repair, and replacement of public utilities, including sewer, water, gas, electricity, telephone, and telegraph. Said areas are not dedicated to the public."

§ 772. **Mobile homes.** Under the Mobile Home Construction and Safety Standard Act passed by Congress in 1974, HUD is authorized to issue a national construction and safety code for mobile homes. That code, containing variations necessary to meet different climatic and geographic conditions, was issued in September of 1975.

This is an unusual program because the federal law states that all state and local laws that are not identical to the HUD code must fall. Therefore, if you have a state law, whether it is lower or higher, that is not identical to the standard, that portion of the local law that is not the same is preempted and is no longer enforceable.

In a sense, therefore, what this mobile home program represents is the first national building code. It is, of course, limited to the mobile home area.

§ 772a. **Energy crisis.** The Energy Conservation and Production Act passed in August 1976, was designed to encourage more efficient use of depletable energy resources and to help reduce utility costs to individual occupants of buildings.

The bill provides that any new building—commercial, residential or industrial—must comply with standards to be developed by HUD in cooperation with other agencies of the federal government, state government, and industry and consumer groups. The work, in terms of developing performance standards for energy, is to be completed within a three to three and one-half year period.

The standards are compulsory in that there is a heavy penalty if states or localities do not adopt the same standards, equivalent or higher standards.

Once the standards are set, should a state or a locality fail to adopt them or equivalent ones, all federal assistance for the construction of buildings, direct or indirect, other than a limited category such as that involving revenue-sharing funds, will be suspended until the locality either adopts those requirements or begins the process of adopting those requirements.

§ 773. Suggested steps prior to land acquisition or signing of contract to purchase:

1. The developer should check the land itself carefully, considering the following: (a) Existing drainage—for example, do neighbor's ditches and ditch easements cut across your building sites? (b) Future drainage problems—for example, if you increase flow of drainage water into ditches or streams, you may face lawsuits from downstream owners. (c) Sewage problems—for example, consider possible legal objections by neighbors to location of your proposed sewage treatment plant. (d) Power lines, especially underground, and sewers that may cut across your building sites. It is usually impossible to compel a utility to remove its wires even though it occupies the land unlawfully, for it can remain, on paying for the land it occupies. (e) Streams, which you will not be permitted to obstruct or pollute.

2. Soil tests should be made. Check for buried radioactive waste.

3. The developer should check local zoning and building ordinances to determine what type of structure the area is zoned for; what lot size and building area restrictions exist; what building ordinance setback lines exist on the front, rear, and side lines of the lots. Also, check your building code for its requirements as to building construction, septic tanks, and such. In many areas, for example, septic tanks are wholly illegal, and the city can legally require you to put in sewer connections. 64 CJS 267. If there is the slightest doubt as to your ability to get the area rezoned to permit the buildings you have in mind, plan to make your contract of purchase contingent on your ability to procure rezoning within a specified time. Keep in mind that even if existing zoning allows the type of dwelling you have in mind, it may forbid the shopping center, motel, cocktail lounge, swimming pool, or dining room you also have in mind. And if you have in mind installing your own sewage treatment plant, that may require rezoning a portion of the land.

If the development lies outside of a city, the developer will consider the desirability of entering into an annexation agreement, under which the development is brought within the city limits. This agreement brings up the question of the zoning the city will impose. The problems of contract zoning arises.

4. Especially in the case of farm land, the developer will find that he has a combined problem of rezoning and plat approval. Plat approval brings up the question of forced dedication. The obvious course is to work simultaneously on both problems. There is no point in spending time and money on rezoning, with its public hearings, only to find that the plat approval requirements are too burdensome.

5. The developer should check to see if he will have the right to hook up with city sewer and water. A city that operates a city water supply system must serve impartially and on like terms all who apply for service. *City of Danville* v. *Danville Water Co.,* 178 Ill. 299, 53 NE 118 (1899); 48 ALR2d 1225. Hence, as a rule, the city should not deny the request of a land developer to service his development, as long as he is prepared to comply with its reasonable regulations. *Reid Development Corp.* v. *Parsippany-Troy Hills Township,* 10 N.J. 229, 89 A2d 667 (1952). The city may, however, decline to extend its mains to an area not previously served where the cost of the extension would be grossly disproportionate to the individual needs presented. 48 ALR2d 1225. The demand for the extension of mains must be reasonable considering the need for it and the revenue obtainable. 94 CJS 58. This does not mean that the particular extension must pay for itself. Lack of profit on the extension is important only insofar as it affects the over-all return from the entire system. *In re Board of Fire Commissioners,* 27 N.J. 192; 142 A2d 85 (1958). Since real estate developers are a separate class of water users, the city may take the position

that if the developer wants an extension, he must pay for it, on the theory that the city ought not to be asked to participate in the risk of failure of the developer's enterprise. *Woodside Homes* v. *City of Morristown,* 26 N.J. 529, 141 A2d 8 (1958).

Generally, a city is under no obligation to furnish water outside the city limits. 48 ALR2d 1230. This being true, if the city is requested to extend its pipes outside its limits, it may demand that the entire cost be borne by the party desiring the extension. *Yardville Estates* v. *City of Trenton,* 66 N.J. Super. 51, 168 A2d 429 (1961). However, if the city is the sole supplier of water and sewer service in the area it must supply those who are beyond the city limits. *Robinson* v. *Boulder,* 547 P2d 228 (Colo. 1976).

In a few states, the city has the same duty to allow property owners to tie into its sewers as it has with respect to water pipes. *Knudson* v. *Neal,* 320 Ill. 136, 150 NE 626. But in most states, property owners are not allowed to tie into an adjoining sewer without the city's consent. 64 CJS 266. Of course to protect the health of its inhabitants a city may compel a property owner in the city to connect with its sewers at his own expense. 64 CJS 267.

If the development lies outside the city the developer will consider the advisability of having his land annexed to the city. Again, the problem of the annexation agreement arises. The city may exact conditions.

Alternatively, the developer may contract with the city for it to furnish sewer and water at an agreed price. Check the city's requirements in this regard. These may require incorporation of your development as a water and sanitary district. 94 CJS 60. If you plan to form a profit-making corporation to provide water or sanitation, you will probably have to get a certificate of convenience and necessity from some local commission. Be sure you can get it. For example, a water system based on deep wells may not be acceptable to the commission. Existing companies offering similar service may oppose you. Consider, also, that the rates you charge will be set by the commission. If you are in an arid state, check the law to see if existing water rights of the land can be converted to the new use that you have in mind, and remember that any increased use of water may bring objections from other users. If you are buying a water right, check it as carefully as you check title to the land you are buying. Plan to make your contract of purchase contingent on your ability to make satisfactory arrangements in all these regards within a specified time.

6. With respect to the services of a private utility company furnishing gas, electricity, and so on, a land developer can often reach an agreement by private negotiation for extension of service to his development. If, however, the company refuses to extend service, the question arises whether it can be compelled to make the extension.

In the first place, the company cannot be compelled to extend service into an area that it cannot legally serve. Usually the area in which the company can operate is defined by a certificate of public convenience and necessity issued by some utility commission. If the area is one in which the company can operate, the utility commission will nevertheless refuse to compel the company to extend its services into the area if the present demand is extremely low and the probability of an increased future demand is so low that the cost of extending service will be likely to far exceed any possible yield from the investment. However, if over the long run the extension can be expected to produce a profit, an extension will be ordered even though the cost of the newly extended service cannot be covered by reasonable charges for a considerable length of time. The company will be compelled to take a loss during the years of initial operation of the extension as long as it can continue to make a fair return on all of its property.

The design of utility easements for a land development presents special problems today because of the presence in modern developments of curvilinear streets, loop streets and cul-de-sacs. It is therefore best to consult the utility companies at some early stage. The wise counsel of the experienced utility company engineers will insure the developer that his utility plan will be approved by the Plan Commission. Especially for the lot purchaser who will build his own home it is a plus to be able to show him the precise location of essential utilities. And, of course, the preplanning enables the utility companies to extend their facilities without delay. Therefore, the developer should submit several copies of a preliminary plat to each utility involved and discuss the location of utility easements. In addition to location of utilities, the minimum width of the easement can be established in these conversations. The easements should be so established that there is no jog as the lines pass from one block to another. Irregular shaped lots will sometimes require poles and guys, and are therefore to be avoided. For lots facing on curvilinear streets, rear easements are run in a series of straight lines, with points of deflection kept to a minimum. The plat should require that no permanent structures be erected on or across utility easements and should give the utility company tree-trimming rights.

SUGGESTED FORM: An easement is hereby reserved for and granted to *ABC Company* and *XYZ Company* and their respective successors and assigns within the area as shown by dotted lines on the plat and marked "Easement," to install, lay, construct, renew, operate, and maintain conduits, cables, poles and wires, overhead and underground, with all necessary braces, guys, anchors, and other equipment for the purpose of serving the Subdivision and other property with telephone and electric service; also is hereby granted the right to use the streets for said purposes, the right to overhang all lots with aerial service wires to serve adjacent lots, the right to enter upon the lots at all times to install, lay, construct, renew, operate and maintain within said easement area said conduits, cables, poles, wires, braces, guys, anchors, and other equipment, and finally the right is hereby granted to cut down and remove or trim and keep trimmed any trees, shrubs, or saplings that interfere or threaten to interfere with any of the said public utility equipment. No permanent buildings or trees shall be placed on said easement, but same may be used for gardens, shrubs, landscaping, and other purposes that do not then or later interfere with the aforesaid uses or the rights herein granted.

7. Often land assemblies include old subdivisions platted with *paper streets,* these being streets shown on the subdivision plat, but which were never accepted or paved by the city. It is wise to touch base with the city authorities in advance to make sure that the city will be willing to pass a *vacation ordinance*. This formally abandons the public's claim to the streets. Incidental to this operation is the check, usually made by the city, to determine whether utilities were installed on the paper streets. If there were, the developer must negotiate with the utilities over the cost of relocation if he plans to build over the streets.

The developer may find his plans hampered by the official filing in some public office of maps of future streets. The idea here is that if the developer plans to erect buildings in the path of such projected streets, he must procure a permit to erect the building, or alternatively if a permit is not granted, the city may later condemn the land for a street without paying compensation for the building. 36 ALR3d 751, 794; 37 *id.* 127.

In this day of the limited access highway, the developer should check with the highway department before buying land fronting on a highway. He may be refused curb-cuts except on the side streets.

8. Check your local law to see if local regulations require you to have a contractor's license to build. If it does, and you lack a license, you probably will be unable to collect for work that you do, and mortgage lenders will refuse to extend you credit. *Checkering* v. *George R. Ognowski Co., Inc.,* 501 P2d 952 (Ariz. 1972).

9. Submit your project informally to your local Planning Commission. The Commission will give you informal suggestions. Adopt them, for without subsequent formal Commission approval, your program is blocked. Find out what streets, parks, and other public places you will be required to dedicate to the public in your plat; what requirements exist as to location and width of streets; what you will be required to install in the way of street grading and paving, curbs, gutters, sidewalks, water and other utilities, fire hydrants,

street lighting, and street signs. Many builders donate land requested by the village even where they consider this is illegal forced dedication, for they do not wish to engage in prolonged litigation or face harassment by village officials if the village loses the lawsuit.

10. Talk informally to your local FHA people, if FHA financing is contemplated. They will want much the same information as the Planning Commission and will also give you many helpful suggestions as to lot and utility layout and protective covenants. Adopt their suggestions.

11. Consult with your Real Estate Commissioner if your state has such an official. Get his suggestions.

12. Check with all environmental control regulatory bodies.

13. Check the effect of the Interstate Land Sales Act on your plans. Also check the local land sales regulations.

§ 774. Suggestions to developer concerning his contract to purchase:

1. Check every objection to title listed in the contract of sale as something you must take subject to. Easements, water rights, utility lines, or building restrictions must be set forth specifically, not generally. The document number and recorder's book and page of the easement or other instrument must be given, and your lawyer must read it and explain it to you before you sign the contract. Consider whether any listed objection interferes with your plans. If it will be necessary for the seller to join in the subdivision plat, the contract should require him to do this.

2. You will want the seller to warrant in the contract that he knows of no matters that would interfere with the development, including, for example public projects scheduled for the area, proposed changes in laws or ordinances, suits or proposed suits by neighboring landowners, earth slides on neighboring land, soil problems or other physical conditions of the land, adequacy of drainage, lack of access to existing streets.

3. The contract should give the purchaser full and free access to the property for all purposes incident to the development.

4. The contract should require the legal and physical status of the land to be the same at closing as at the date the contract is signed, for example, no new leases or no construction of any kind.

5. You may wish to make the contract contingent on your procuring within a specified time: (a) a written engineer's report covering soil conditions; (b) the city's agreement to let you tie into the city's water and sewer systems, indicating the cost and who bears the expense; (c) a utility company's agreement to extend service to the area.

6. Even where the seller will not allow the contract to be contingent on rezoning, you will need a clause requiring him to join in the application for rezoning, because he is after all, the landowner.

7. If the sale price is fixed on the basis of acreage, land that is not usable should not be included in the computation even though the seller's deed will include it. For example, a drainage ditch may make one acre or more unusable:

CLAUSE: "At a price of $________________ per usable acre, but if survey reveals acreage of less than ________________ usable acres, buyer shall have the right to rescind within ________________ days after delivery of copy of survey to buyer. Areas falling in (a) open or dedicated public streets or ways, (b) in private or public easements of ingress or drainage or (c) in areas fenced by adjoiners are not deemed usable acres. All other acres are deemed usable."

8. A good tax lawyer should be consulted as to the most advantageous way of setting up the payment of the purchase price.

9. The contract must not contain any restriction on the right of the buyer to assign the contract. In the first place, the developer may find an opportunity to re-sell at a profit, perhaps to persons seeking an income tax shelter. Then he can use the funds for other deals. Or he may wish to assign the contract to a mortgage house that will pay off the sale price and give the developer a leaseback. This last is not applicable, of course, where the development is a residential development.

§ 775. Suggestions to the developer as to steps subsequent to signing of contract.

1. Within the time allowed by the contract, attend to the matters to which the contract was made contingent, such as procuring: (a) rezoning, if needed; (b) annexation to a city, if needed; (c) formal Planning Commission approval of a preliminary plat of subdivision.

2. Make formal application to your mortgage man for a loan. With the application you will furnish plans and specifications of the houses that you plan to build, also a copy of the proposed subdivision plat showing the lots and blocks, location of proposed buildings, walks, driveways. These documents should reveal that your project will comply with: (a) local ordinances; (b) building restrictions in deeds and plats; (c) Planning Commission requirements.

3. The mortgagee now gives you its commitment to make the mortgage loans desired.

4. When all the contingencies provided for in your contract of sale have been taken care of, you are ready to close the deal, following usual closing procedures. Make sure that you are obtaining clear title to the entire subdivision tract. For complete protection in acquiring title, close the deal in escrow. See that the seller's deed and the title insurance policy contain no title objections that would hamper your construction, such as building restrictions, easements, drainage ditches, utility lines, roads, mineral rights, or oil leases. If you have been careful, these were not mentioned in the contract of sale and therefore do not belong in the deed. The deed should be recorded.

5. The subdivider now has his surveyor stake out the tract in accordance with the tentative plat. He also installs the required improvements, such as sewer, water, and paving, or gives a surety bond guaranteeing such installation. 46 *J. of Urban Law* 67. He then has his surveyor prepare the final plat and submits it to the Commission for final approval. In addition to the things already mentioned, this final plat will have a surveyor's certificate, certifying to the accuracy of the survey and plat; also the subdivider's certificate, certifying that he is the owner of the land, and his signature and notarial acknowledgement; a city engineer's certificate to the effect that all improvements—streets, sewers, and so on—have been properly installed or that a bond or certified check has been posted by the subdivider to insure their proper installation; building restrictions as required by the Commission, or an accompanying declaration of restrictions, which is referred to in the plat; certificate by the tax collector that all taxes are paid, and the approval of the Commission. The final plat is then recorded. Make no sales until your subdivision plat has been recorded. Any attempt to do so is a crime in many states; building permits will be refused the purchaser; and in any event a deed description that refers to an unrecorded plat is unacceptable to title companies.

6. Consult your local title insurance company and enter into a contract with it for the issuance of your title policies as houses are sold. Builders are given special, reduced rates by title companies.

7. Individual construction mortgages are recorded, and title is again examined to cover the recording of individual mortgages. A construction loan agreement is signed for each mortgage. Preconstruction affidavits are signed and a preconstruction inspection made. The mortgagee notifies the mortgagor to commence construction. Do not start construction until you receive this notice.

8. Get adequate insurance coverage before construction starts. Lawsuits for injuries to workmen or members of the public can ruin you. Get contractor's liability and workmen's compensation insurance. If you are building for a home buyer, he should be warned to procure his own liability insurance. Your insurance will not cover him. Fire and other insurance are indispensable. Get the builder's risk insurance policy.

9. Any change in plans—usually installation of additional items requested by home buyers who are now in the picture—must be cleared with the mortgagee. Increasing the recorded mortgage to take care of extras is impracticable. Therefore the mortgagee should demand a deposit of 100 per cent of the extra cash needed.

10. Consult FHA at every step if FHA financing will take place.

§ 776. Suggestions as to methods of financing acquisition of land for subdivision purposes.

There are several ways of financing the purchase of land for subdivision purposes.

1. The subdivider may pay cash, which poses no special legal problems. One advantage to the subdivider is that he plats the land as he pleases without any control exercised by the seller; such would not be true if the seller were to extend credit. The obvious disadvantage is that it strips the subdivider of needed cash.

2. The subdivider can contract with the seller for purchase of land with the price payable in installments, the seller to deed various specified parcels to the subdivider as specified amounts are paid. The number of parcels that should be released in this fashion each year is often dictated by income tax considerations. This means, of course, that the seller in the beginning retains title to the land. Therefore, if the entire area is to be subdivided at once, the seller must join in the plat of subdivision, for technically he is the owner of the property. Naturally the contract of sale must specify that the seller will cooperate in this fashion. The seller may not be eager to do this. Joining in the subdivision plat may technically make the seller a subdivider, and this will increase his income tax. In addition, the seller is likely to object to joining in any plat because he thereby becomes a developer subject to the penalties of the Interstate Land Sales Act and local similar regulations. There are other disadvantages to the seller. All land developments are speculative, and there is always the possibility that the subdivider will go broke. The seller may find his land cluttered with partially finished homes and burdened with mechanic's lien claims. Even taking into consideration the cushion provided by the developer's cash payments, sewer and street installations, and so forth, the seller may not find it easy to interest another, solvent subdivider in completing the project, and from a business point of view it cannot be allowed to remain partly finished. To raise money for the contract payments, the subdivider is almost certain to enter into contracts with home buyers for the sale of buildings, and when he goes broke, these contracts will most likely be recorded and create serious clouds on the title to the property. Anyone who extends credit to a subdivider faces these problems.

3. Often the developer signs an option to purchase the land from the seller. Under a typical option, the developer agrees to exercise the option at intervals over a period of time. Every three months or so, for example, the developer is required to buy and pay for a certain number of building sites. Failure to keep up with this purchase program results in

extinguishment of the option, which is known as a *rolling option* because the subdivider buys one piece, builds on it, then rolls on to the next piece. An advantage of this method is that the subdivider can quit at any time without incurring liability to the seller; this would not be true if a contract of sale were used.

4. If the seller of such a large tract is well-to-do, as he often is, he can usually be persuaded to extend credit to the developer by accepting a down payment, giving a deed to the developer, and taking back a blanket purchase money mortgage on the entire tract for the balance of the purchase price. As an individual lot is sold, the developer uses part of the sale price to make a payment on the blanket mortgage, whereupon he will request a release of the blanket mortgage as to that particular lot. It is of utmost importance that any such mortgage contain a partial release clause specifying that on the payment of a certain sum of money any individual lot will be released from the blanket mortgage. It is best to have this mortgage in the form of a trust deed to a trust company or bank, which is expressly given power to receive money and make partial releases. In this way delays are avoided when the seller-mortgage owner is out of town. When the developer plans to build the buildings with construction funds procured on mortgages signed by the developer rather than by the home buyer, it is of great importance that the purchase money mortgage contain either a partial release clause, as above stated, or alternatively a subordination clause obligating the mortgagee to execute subordination agreements, subordinating the purchase money mortgage to various construction mortgages as they are executed. Under the subordination method, as to individual buildings under construction, the construction mortgage becomes a first mortgage, and the earlier blanket purchase money mortgage becomes a second mortgage. This is necessary because the construction lender insists on having a first mortgage. The subordination method has only limited utility because the FHA and many mortgage houses object to the existence of any second mortgages. Under the partial release method, a builder operating, let us say, in a one-hundred-lot development selects ten lots, pays cash for partial releases, and now has clear title for his construction mortgage. As payments come in from buyers of these houses, he acquires funds for additional partial releases. Obviously, the developer should be sure that his purchase contract with the seller provides for partial releases or subordination agreements. It should also require the seller to join in the subdivision plat, for in many states the landowner and all mortgagees must join in any subdivision plat. Another advantage of the rolling option is that it eliminates the seller from the platting process. As each parcel is paid for, it is deeded to the subdivider, who subdivides and develops that parcel. Also this method conserves the developer's capital. He need not buy the entire area at one time. Moreover, where the land is farmland, the portion not under development will be taxed at the lower rates farmland traditionally is subject to. The objection to this means of subdividing is that it results in piecemeal platting and development, which are awkward, costly, and often objectionable to mortgage lenders.

5. In some states, the seller and subdivider have found it convenient to deed the land to a bank or trust company in trust. The purchase contract is made a part of the trust agreement. Individual mortgages are signed by the trustee as they are needed. All partial releases and subordinations are avoided, because the trustee has clear title to the land and its mortgages are all first mortgages. When a sale is made, the purchaser receives his deed from the trustee. Payments made by the subdivider on his contract or option are made to the trustee and forwarded by it to the seller. If the subdivider defaults, the trustee deeds all unsold lots back to the seller. There are some technical, legal traps in this type of transaction, and only very skilled attorneys should attempt it.

6. Where a purchase money mortgage is used, the developer should seek to obtain a clause giving him the right to forego mortgage payments during the first two years of the mortgage, when the developer will be paying money for improvements but receiving no income.

§ 777. **When construction can begin.** Obviously no work can begin on streets or sewers until: (1) the planning authorities have approved, at least, tentatively the subdivision plat; (2) the attorney for the developer is satisfied that the Interstate Land Sales Act and local statutes along this line can be complied with; (3) all environmental control regulations can be complied with; (4) firm deals have been made with the city or utility company on furnishing sewer, water, and utilities; (5) zoning and building code problems have been definitely settled and building permits will be forthcoming. In this connection, it may be possible to get the public officials to work with the developer simultaneously on plat approval requirements and rezoning matters, so that once the requirements of the public bodies have been agreed to by the developer, he is reasonably certain that no further exactions will be forthcoming.

RESERVED: §§ 778–788.

25

Wetlands, the Public Trust, Beaches and Navigable Waters

§ 789. **Definition of the problem.** There are two types of wetlands. *Inland wetlands* are marshes such as those found in every state of the union. *Coastal wetlands* are *estuarian* lands (salt marshes). An estuary occurs where an arm of the sea (salt water) extends inland to meet the mouth of a river (fresh water). The tides alternately flood and expose tidal marshes. Both types of wetlands are shallow. Land development is possible through "dredge and fill" operations. It is only recently that we have come to realize that our very national existence depends upon these wetlands and that these wetlands are disappearing as building construction goes forward. The reasons why these wetlands must be preserved are too numerous to mention, but a few will be listed:

1. Wetlands are nature's way of controlling floods. Wetlands act as giant sponges, absorbing vast amounts of water and releasing it gradually. If you pave the area, you have a flood problem. Estuarian lands, with their mixture of peat, bog, moss, and so forth, absorb incoming storms and are nature's way of preventing floods.
2. Inland wetlands maintain ground water at proper ground water levels. If you drain this ground water, a desert may result.
3. Estuarian lands are an important source of food supply. Carbohydrates and vitamins wash out to sea from the estuaries and greatly increase the number of fish and oysters that the ocean can produce. By far the greater quantity of ocean fish depends for survival on the estuaries. The deep sea, by and large, is empty of fish. A great many ocean fish can reproduce only in the estuaries. The classic illustration is that of the salmon that come back to the stream of their birth and go upstream to spawn. The fishermen, the fishing villages, and the tourist trade, therefore, depend upon the estuaries. Wild fowl, such as ducks and geese, cannot exist without the wetlands. They are necessary for reproduction, migration, and as winter feeding grounds. In these areas, hunters bring in substantial local revenue. Wild rice, turkey, deer, and so forth depend upon wetlands.
4. Wetlands absorb polluted air and water and make them clean and wholesome.

A recent court decision points up the legal problems that arise in the wetlands area.

EXAMPLE: Ronald and Kathryn Just, land developers, bought a large tract of land in Wisconsin. When their plans became public knowledge, Marinette County passed an ordinance making any reasonable use of wetlands land impossible. Cranberry picking and other low-or no-income activities were permitted. When the Justs went ahead in defiance of the law, they were stopped by the courts. The Wisconsin Supreme Court sustained the law. *Just* v. *Marinette County,* 56 Wisc.2d 7, 201 NW2d 761 (1972), *cert. den.* U. S. Sup. Ct. The land was thus rendered worthless. The court, in a ruling contrary to hundreds of previous decisions said that a landowner has no constitutional right to develop his land! The dilemma is plain. If all developers are allowed to develop wetlands, the landowners are protected from loss of their money, but in the meantime the surrounding country may perish.

The Marinette County case presents rather clearly a problem that exists in American constitutional law. Each governmental body, federal or state, has, among others, two problems that frequently come into conflict, the *police power* and the power of *eminent domain.*

EXAMPLE: X owns *Blackacre.* The city wants this land for a street. The city files a petition under its power of *eminent domain.* A jury fixes the value of the land, the city pays it, and the street is installed. This is an exercise of the power of eminent domain. No controversy exists.

Each significant public body also has *police power,* the power to govern. This is the great power of government, but it has its limits. The city, for example, can take *X*'s land in the preceding example for a street because *X* refuses to sell. But it must exercise the power of eminent domain to do so.

The situation is complex. The greater the need for preservation of the public safety in a given situation, or the closer the landowner's use approaches the nuisance level, the closer the courts come to permitting the city to destroy the landowner's land value without paying him compensation.

EXAMPLE: In the city of Los Angeles, a residential section expanded until it closely approached a brick works that gave off a foul odor. The city passed an ordinance making brick-making illegal in the city. The courts upheld the decision because, in balancing the harm to the public against the gain to the public, it was clear that the gain to the public outweighed the benefit to the brick-maker.

EXAMPLE: In the city of X a disastrous fire broke out. To save the balance of the city, the fire department dynamited a row of buildings to create a fire break. The city does this under the police power. It need not pay a penny of compensation. *Surrocco* v. *Geary,* 3 Cal. 70 (1853). The police power was properly exercised because of the great public danger.

Thus, the question arises: In any given situation, is the danger to the public so great that filling in the wetlands would cause a calamity? If so, arguably the city can exercise its police power, its power to regulate and pay no compensation. If the danger does not reach these proportions, it must compensate the landowner.

This is a very great simplification of the problem over which the courts and scholars have fought bitter battles in the last few years. There is an almost total lack of agreement, and here we can merely draw attention to a few of the conflicting points of view.

The decisions. The decisions, of course, are conflicting:

Pro-developer decisions: (1) *Morris County Land and Imp. Co.* v. *Twp. of Parsippany-Troy Hills,* 40 N.J. 539, 193 A2d 232 (1963). Here the township had amended its zoning ordinance to create a meadowlands zone designed to preserve the swampland for flood control purposes. Only minor uses were permitted, such as commercial greenhouses. The landowner wished to develop his land for intensive commercial development. The court held for the developer.

(2) *State* v. *Johnson,* 265 A2d 711 (Me. 1970). The state of Maine passed a wetlands law. The state court held that the preservation of wetlands was a laudable purpose but that the cost must be publicly borne. The landowner must be paid by the state if his development rights are to be taken away.

(3) *Mac Gibbon* v. *Board of Appeals,* 350 Mass. 635, 255 NE2d 347 (1970) is to the same effect as the above two cases.

Antideveloper cases. Sibson v. *State,* 336 A2d 239 (N.H. 1975) and other cases follow the lead of *Just* v. *Marinette County. Sibson* involved a denial of a building permit that was to cover four acres of salt marshland that was part of a one hundred acre tidal wetland. The court sustained this denial because of the harm to the public. See also *Brecciaroli* v. *Connecticut Commr. of Environmental Protection,* 36 *Conn. L. J.* No. 42, p. 4 (Sup. Ct. Jan. Term 1975); *Potomac Sand and Gravel Co.* v. *Governor,* 293 A2d 241 (Md. 1972); *S. Volpe & Co., Inc.* v. *Board of Appeals,* 348 NE2d 807 (Mass. App. 1976); *State* v. *Reed,* 78 Miss. 2d 1004 (N.Y.).

§ **790. Environmental factors.** A final obstacle to land development in marshes is the emergence of the concept that environmental factors must be considered before a "dredge and fill" permit is issued. *Zabel* v. *Taub,* 430 F2d 199 (5th Circ. 1970) *cert den.* 401 U.S. 910 (1971).

§ **791. Conclusions on wetlands.** It is difficult to extract rational rules out of all this, but certain things are plain with respect to *Just* v. *Marinette County.* The Wisconsin court's view that a landowner has no constitutional right to develop his land cannot possibly be correct. How would this country have reached its present state of development if this is the law? Who will buy vacant land if it can be taken from him without payment of a penny of compensation? Definitely it should not be the law. There is a vast body of law on purchase and condemnation of development rights. Ironically, Wisconsin has pioneered in the purchase of development rights and is still doing so in acquiring scenic easements. "Development rights" exist. Also, the court failed to require evidence of the facts demonstrating the impact that the proposed development would have on the area in question. How can a rational decision be made if the facts are not known? Obviously all these cases should be decided on their particular facts. Siegan, Other People's Property, 102 *et seq* (1976). This last is the approach in zoning law, where each case is tested by looking at the ordinance *as applied* to the particular tract of land.

The choice is a difficult one, and the solution to the problem is nowhere in sight. State courts will differ. The United States Supreme Court is unpredictable. If unlimited development is permitted, the fishing and resort industries will be destroyed without compensation. That seems unfair, yet the danger to the public is very great. If the owners of marshlands and estuarian lands are not permitted to develop their properties, the loss to them is also very great. Here is a choice between two very great evils. Some courts will pick one side, other courts will pick the other.

§ 792. **Compensable regulations.** One solution to the problem in which land developers are pitted against the public, and the evidence shows that proceeding with the development would cause great public harm, is to combine the two great powers of government, the police power and the power of eminent domain. Comment: Compensable Regulations: Outline of a New Land Use Planning, 10 *Williamette L. J.* 451 (1974). Rhode Island has already passed a law to compensate landowners for restrictions on the development of wetlands. *Ibid* p. 454. Under this system the landowner receives *some* compensation for the restrictions placed on his right of development, but not the full market value of the land. Of course, developers are unhappy with this solution. The environmental enthusiasts are also unhappy. But the fact of the matter is that the landowner is entitled to some payment, and tax money is nowhere in sight to buy all these lands at market value. In legal effect, this is quite similar to the *scenic easement* or *development rights easement* discussed earlier. The landowner retains ownership of the land, is entitled to make some use of the land, but is not entitled to develop it. Anything less than this offends our sense of what is fair and just.

§ 793. **The public trust doctrine.** Some states have used a different approach to avoid paying the landowner compensation.

EXAMPLE: In *International Paper Co.* v. *Mississippi State Highway Dep't.*, 271 So2d 395 (Miss. 1973), a landowner claimed ownership of an island in the Pascagoula River because a prior owner, from whom he had purchased the island, had received a grant from the state. The state of Mississippi argued, and its supreme court held that ownership of all tidelands, including the spaces between ordinary high and low water mark, the bed of a bay, and all bodies of land arising from the bay floor are forever held in a public trust by the state. Such land cannot be sold to private persons. Of course, since the state owns the land it can control whatever is built thereon. A number of states follow this public trust rule. Its application currently, is hard to predict.

EXAMPLE: Marks, the owner of land abutting on the ocean, sought to fill and develop the tidelands abutting his property. The court held the power of the state to control its navigable waters and the land beneath them was held in a public trust and was within the absolute control of the state. *Marks* v. *Whitney*, 6 Cal.3d 251, 491 P2d 374, 98 Cal. Reptr. 790 (1971).

§ 794. **Navigable waters.** Another approach to the problem rests upon the claims of the federal and state government to control of navigable waters. It is, of course, elementary that both governmental bodies have and exercise control over navigable waters. What is surprising is the position they maintain, sustained by the courts, that "once navigable, always navigable." *U.S.* v. *Stoeco Homes,* 359 F.Supp. 672 (D.N.J. 1973). Thus, even though land under navigable water was filled and built as long as one hundred years ago, it is still navigable, and either public body can compel removal of the improvements. Navigable water is subject to federal and state *servitudes.* It is elementary that either government can halt construction if it can show that the construction is on "navigable waters." In this context, water is "navigable" if it is, or once was navigable, or if it is, or once was part of the tidelands and marshlands of the aquatic ecosystem surrounding the navigable water. *Potomac Sand and Gravel Co.* v. *Governor,* 266 Md. 358, 293 A2d 241 (1972).

EXAMPLE: Landowner wanted to dredge in the navigable waters of Boca Ciega Bay in order to create a trailer park. The permit was denied by the United States because construction would have a destructive effect on wildlife. *Zabel* v. *Taub,* 430 F2d 199 (5th Circ. 1970).

EXAMPLE: Where the builder erected mobile homes on coastal marshland without a permit, he was compelled to remove them. *U.S.* v. *Moretti,* 478 F2d 418 (1973).

EXAMPLE: The court blocked construction of a housing development in Ocean City, New Jersey, because it fell within the limits of "navigable waters." *U.S.* v. *Stoeco Homes, Inc.,* 359 F.Supp. 672 (D.N.J. 1973).

§ **795. Beaches.** Since the history of this country began, it has been assumed that one who buys lands abutting on waters, navigable or non-navigable, has the right to enjoy the beach as his private domain. In lands abutting on tidal waters this right generally stops at the high-water mark. Landward of that line the public has no right to picnic or stroll. *In re Opinion of Justices,* 313 NE2d 561 (Mass. 1974). In recent times the courts have suddenly discovered that the public should be allowed to use and enjoy these beaches and have evolved a variety of theories that would enable the public to enjoy such rights, much to the disgust of riparian landowners who paid vast sums of money for their riparian rights and the right to enjoy these beaches in privacy. Some remarkable legal decisions have been handed down in order to enable the public to enjoy the beaches.

EXAMPLE: In California it has been held that where a riparian landowner over a five-year period made no objection to the use of his beach by the public, there exists an *implied dedication* to the public, and the landowner must allow public use. The reference here is to the beach area above high-water mark, where ordinarily the public has no rights. *County of Orange* v. *Chandler-Sherman Corp.,* 126 Cal. Reptr. 765, 5 *S.W.U.L. Rev.* 48 (1973); 11 *Santa Clara L. Rev.* 327.

EXAMPLE: In Oregon the courts have held that the public has a *customary right* to the use of the dry sand area. *State ex rel Thornton* v. *Hay,* 462 P2d 671 (Ore. 1969).

EXAMPLE: In New Jersey it has been held that land contiguous to a beach is unique and therefore subject to strict zoning. *Frankel* v. *Atlantic City,* 63 N.J. 333, 307 A2d 562

(1973). This makes sense. Any person buying beach property ought to recognize that the public will want it kept free from undesirable uses.

EXAMPLE: Under the "public trust" rule, Massachusetts holds that land *below* the high-water mark, even though sold by the state to a private landowner, remains subject to the public rights of fishing and navigation. *In re Opinion of the Justices,* 313 NE2d 561 (1974).

No doubt other states will reach out into the beaches under some theory or other to give the public rights therein. As can be seen, the California rule punishes the "nice guy." The Oregon rule, discovering a customary right after millions have been spent by purchasers of riparian land, seems unfair. The fact is, that private landowners are now being punished for years of public neglect.

REFERENCES: 4 *Seaton Hall L. Rev.* 662 (1972) and 86 *Harv. L. Rev.* 1582 (1972) discussing *Just* v. *Marinette County;* Large, This Land is Whose Land? Changing Concepts of Land as Property, 1973 *Wisc. L. Rev.* 1039 (especially valuable discussion); Note, State and Local Wetland Regulation: The Problem of Taking Without Just Compensation, 58 *Va. L. Rev.* 876 (1972) (valuable); Douglas P. Hill, Coastal Wetlands in New England, 52 *Boston U. L. Rev.* 724 (1972); Binder, Taking Versus Reasonable Regulation: A Reappraisal in Light of Regional Planning and Wetlands, 25 *U. of Fla. L. Rev.* 1, (1972) (valuable); Kramon, Section 10 of the Rivers and Harbors Act: The Emergence of a New Protection for Tidal Marshes, 33 *Md. L. Rev.* 229 (1973) (valuable); E. J. Morris, Federal Navigation Servitude; Impediment to the Development of the Waterfront, 45 *St. John's L. Rev.* 189 (1970); Note, The Public Right of Navigation and the Role of No Compensation, 44 *Notre Dame Lawyer* 236 (1968); Comment, State Navigation Servitude, 4 *Land & Water L. Rev.* 521 (1969); Bartke, The Navigational Servitude and Just Compensation—Struggle for a Doctrine, 48 *Ore. L. Rev.* 1 (1968).

RESERVED: §§ 796–806.

26

Environmental Law

§ **807. In general.** Environmental laws and the trend those laws represent have created what is sometimes a hostile and expensive atmosphere for any developer to operate within. Often both local citizens and governmental agencies involved with a project have almost a programmed animosity towards the developer's motives and what he is attempting to accomplish. Laws, ordinances, regulations, and agencies have created a maze of red tape that causes the developer added expense and delay. Nonetheless, the goal of these enactments and programs is vital to the continuing well-being of the nation. Balance is crucial and emphasis shifts as priorities change. The energy crisis may temper the literal thrust of environmental laws and regulations. For example, coal may once again achieve some of its former dominance as a fuel, as oil becomes increasingly scarce.

§ **808. NEPA.** The National Environmental Policy Act (NEPA), 42 USCS § 4321 et seq., among other things, requires that federal agencies prepare an environmental impact statement on major federal actions that significantly affect the quality of the human environment. These reports must detail: the environmental impact of the proposed action; adverse environmental effects, which cannot be avoided should the proposal be implemented; alternatives to the proposed action; the relationship between local short-term uses of man's environment and the maintenance and enhancement of long term productivity; and any irreversible and irretrievable commitments of resources that would be involved in the proposed action should it be implemented. 42 USCS § 4332(c). Once the statement is prepared and comments from other concerned federal agencies are obtained, the agency review process may go forward giving due consideration to environmental factors. *Environmental Defense Fund Inc.* v. *Corps of Engineers,* 470 F2d 289 (1972).

Though the act places the ultimate burden of statement preparation upon the federal agency, the developer will be involved in providing data. Indeed, it is in the developer's best interest to assist in the quick and efficient preparation of the report as even preliminary work cannot go forward without the statement.

EXAMPLE: Without the statement being prepared the developer may be enjoined from cutting trees on wooded tract prior to the construction of housing project. *Silva* v. *Romney*, 473 F2d 287 (1973).

This assistance may be through the developer's in house staff or through the efforts of a private concern that specializes in the preparation of these reports.

§ **809. Environmental control—air.** From a federal air pollution point of view (see 42 USCS 1857 et seq.), the developer must be concerned with whether or not the development is a stationary source of emission, produces hazardous materials, or creates an indirect source of pollution.

The federal law calls for the states to have authority and procedures to evaluate and prevent development where the emissions from the development itself, or those "mobile source activities" associated with it, interfere with the attainment or maintenance of air quality standards. 40 CFR § 51.18 (1975).

EXAMPLE: The shopping center developer must not only be concerned with the refuse of the exhaust systems and smokestacks of the structure; he must also design the facility so that traffic flow is such that exhaust fumes from cars attracted to the site do not foul the air.

As a point of interest, developers in areas where the air is relatively clean should not feel that, because the air is well within the relevant air quality standards, there is a margin for pollution. The concept of "non-degradation" is part of the Clean Air Act. *Sierra Club* v. *Ruckelshaus,* 344 F. Supp. 253 (1972) *aff'd.* 4 ERC 1815 (1972) *aff'd. sub. nom. Fri* v. *Sierra Club,* 412 US 541 (1973). Congress, by stating that the purpose of the Clean Air Act is "to protect and enhance" the quality of the nation's air resources, expresses its intent to improve the quality of the nation's air and to prevent deterioration of air quality. Thus, in areas where the air is pristine, the air quality standards adopted must provide, to the maximum extent practicable, for continued maintenance of air quality. This concept has special impact in the West, where the air is clean and the skies are clear.

§ **810. Environmental control—water.** Concern must also exist about any discharge of liquid effluent prohibited or regulated by the Federal Water Pollution laws. 33 USCS § 1151 *et seq.* These laws require that a permit be obtained by every facility discharging effluent into the navigable waters or those water bodies that flow into navigable waters. This includes nearly all water bodies in the country.

§ **811. State and local environmental legislation.** What may loosely be called state environmental control laws are also significant factors to be reckoned with. Not only do they partially implement the federal laws, but also they run the gamut from protecting the air and water to regulating wildlife and plant life. In some states, laws patterned after NEPA have been enacted that require the preparation of impact statements where major nonfederal actions have a significant effect upon the environment. See, for example, Calif. Pub. Res. Code § 21000 *et. seq*. In their extreme form, state environmental laws require impact statements to be filed for the granting of zoning variances and even for the approval of minor land subdivision.

EXAMPLE: A landowner applied to the local governing body for approval of a subdivision of a parcel of land. The governing body granted the approval without preparing an environmental impact report. This action was successfully challenged and the resolution approving the subdivision was rendered null and void. *Meyers* v. *Board of Supervisors,* 129 Cal. Reptr. 902 (1976).

Of invaluable assistance to the counsel confronted with the complexity of state environmental enactments are the handbooks published by the state and local bar associations and local institutes for continuing legal education.

EXAMPLE: Conn. Bar Assn., Environmental Legislation and Litigation and the Real Estate Lawyer.

Beyond state legislation, there has been a flurry of ordinances by counties and municipalities relating to control of the local environment.

§ **812. Private actions.** The various regulatory agencies are not the only sources of environmental law enforcement. Some statutes, 42 USCS § 1857 *et seq*. and Constitutional provisions, give individuals who are not directly injured the power to enforce a right to a clean environment. *Parsons* v. *Walker,* 328 NE2d 920 (Ill. 1975). Similarly, private parties may resort to the age-old concept of nuisance. 60 ALR3d 665.

RESERVED: §§ 813–823.

27

Homeowners' Association

§ 824. **The home association.** The homeowners' association is an interesting legal creature. It derived its early utility in connection with enforcement of general plan building restrictions in the old-fashioned subdivision of single-family dwellings.

EXAMPLE: *R* plats a subdivision of one hundred lots and in the accompanying declaration of restrictions creates a restriction that only single-family dwellings shall be erected and a fifteen-foot front building line shall be observed. The declaration also provides that *XYZ Corporation,* a nonprofit corporation whose members are the lot owners in the subdivision, shall be empowered to enforce the restrictions and shall collect an annual assessment from each lot owner. Ultimately *R* sells out all the lots. He now has lost interest in protecting the lot owners. *E,* a lot owner, begins construction of a store that will come all the way to the street line. Any one homeowner might be disinclined to hire a lawyer and engage in litigation. However, *XYZ Corporation* warns *E* to discontinue construction and to remove the foundations he has constructed. *E* knows this is no empty threat. He complies.

§ 825. **Legal form of association.** The home association has been called a private government. Gibson & Simms, New Community Development, 11 *Washburn L. J.* 227, 230 (1972). It is an incorporated, nonprofit corporation formed under the declaration of restrictions. *Merrionette Manor Homes Improvement Assn.* v. *Heda,* 136 NE2d 556 (Ill. 1956); *Garden Dist. Prop. Owners' Assn.* v. *New Orleans,* 98 So2d 922 (La. 1957); *Neponsit Property Owners' Assn.* v. *Emigrant Industrial Savings Bank,* 15 NE2d 793 (N.Y. 1938); *Rodruck* v. *Sand Point Maintenance Comm.,* 295 P2d 714 (Wash. 1956). Unincorporated associations must be avoided, for traditionally these have very little in the way of legal existence or status. *Moffat Tunnel League* v. *U.S.,* 289 U.S. 113 (1933); Note 40, *Ind. L. J.* 420 (1964). Moreover, in any unincorporated association, the members have the risk of unlimited liabilities, for example, for personal injuries. Likewise, an unincorporated association cannot hold ownership of land. *Delaware L. and Dev. Co.* v. *First Church,* 147 A 165 (Del. 1929); Ford, Dispositions of Property to Unincorporated Non-Profit Associations, 55 *Mich. L. Rev.* 67, 235 (1956).

There is something of a misnomer here. We constantly talk of the *home association.* But in truth, often there is no true legal association. The body selected to act as the home association is often a nonprofit *corporation.* For convenience we shall refer to the body as the *home association.*

The association is formed in accordance with the declaration. There are by-laws and a corporate charter. In the beginning the developer and his associates are the members of the corporation. A nonprofit corporation, be it noted, has no *shareholders.* It has *members.* As homes are sold, each homeowner automatically becomes a member of the corporation.

§ 826. **Association as a vehicle for enforcing restrictions, liens, and covenants.** In any land development where both a home association and a declaration exist, the right of enforcement of restrictions, liens, and covenants is transferred by the declaration to the home association. *Merrionette Manor Homes Improvement Assn.* v. *Heda,* 136 NE2d 556 (Ill. 1956); *Garden Dist. Prop. Owners' Assn.* v. *New Orleans,* 98 So2d 922 (La. 1957); *Neponsit Property Owners' Assn.* v. *Emigrant Industrial Savings Bank,* 15 NE2d 793 (N.Y. 1938); *Rodruck* v. *Sand Point Maintenance Comm.,* 295 P2d 714 (Wash. 1956). Subsequent owners of the land become burdened with the restrictions of these declarations and covenants and obtain the benefits of the association. *Lincolnshire Civic Association Inc.* v. *Beach,* 364 NYS2d 248 (1975).

At times, it is suggested that the association is acting as agent of the property owners. *Neponsit Ppty. Owners' Assn.* v. *Emigrant Ind. Sav. Bank,* 15 NE2d 793 (N.Y. 1938). At other times it is suggested that it is acting as a third-party beneficiary of the covenants in the declaration. *Anthony* v. *Brea Glenbrook Club,* 130 Cal. Reptr. 32 (1976). Note, 40 *Ind. L. J.* 420, 430 (1964). Or it is acting as the assignee of the developer. *Ibid.* Occasionally it is simply said that the association is a "covenient instrument by which the property owners may advance their common interests." *Neponsit Property Owners' Assn., Inc.* v. *Emigrant Ind. Sav. Bank,* 15 NE2d 293 (N.Y. 1938); Note, 24 *Cornell L. Q.* 133 (1939); *In re Public Beach, Borough of Queens,* 199 NE 5 (N.Y. 1935). It does no harm to combine all these thoughts into the declaration.

FORM: *XYZ Home Association,* as agent for the property owners under an irrevocable agency coupled with an interest, as beneficiary of all the covenants and provisions herein contained and as assignee of declarant, is vested with the right in its own behalf and in behalf of all owners and parties interested in the land described in this declaration to enforce all the covenants, liens, restrictions, and provisions herein contained.

§ 827. **Further uses and functions of the association.** The home association-corporation was the logical vehicle to carry out its subdivision type activities when condominiums came along. Every condominium has a corporation of this type in which all the apartment owners automatically become members.

In some states, the condominium form of ownership may be utilized for horizontal and vertical developments. For example, townhouses and cluster homes may be sold as condominiums, and the owners of those units become members of the condominium owners' association. In any case, the powers of the association are those established by the Declaration, Charter of Incorporation, and By-Laws. In many developments the powers and functions of the association are extensive and include the maintenance of the common elements such as stairwells, elevators, lobby, recreation building and green areas. The association in a PUD also maintains the parks, private streets, and other common areas. If a city is not providing such service, the association collects refuse, provides sewer and water and other services normally performed by a city. Commonly today it performs exterior maintenance on the buildings and maintains the green areas around the buildings.

This last function relieves the unit owners of tasks regarded as burdensome today and enables the unit owner to devote his leisure time to recreation. The association levies and collects assessments for the services it performs. It enforces the building restrictions set forth in the declaration and deeds.

SUGGESTED FHA FORM (FHA FORM 1400): In addition to maintenance upon the Common Area, the Association shall provide exterior maintenance upon each Lot which is subject to assessment hereunder, as follows: paint, repair, replace and care for roofs, gutters, downspouts, exterior building surfaces, trees, shrubs, grass, walks, and other exterior improvements. Such exterior maintenance shall not include glass surfaces.

In the event that the need for maintenance or repair is caused through the willful or negligent act of the Owner, his family, or guests, or invitees, the cost of such maintenance or repairs shall be added to and become a part of the assessment to which such lot is subject.

Industrial parks also have associations to carry out much of the same tasks as those of the homeowners' association. In a shopping center, the operative entity may be called a merchant's association.

§ 828. Mechanics of control. The mechanics by means of which the association exercises its control and powers are set forth in the declaration, the corporate charter, and the bylaws of the corporation. (See FHA Form 1400, VA Form 26-8200 for illustrations.)

§ 829. Stages in transfer of control of common areas. One can think of the transfer of control over the development as taking place in phases. First comes the phase of land acquisition and assembly. Next comes the rezoning and plat approval stage. Next comes the preparation, execution, and recording of the declaration. Up to this moment the declaration lacks legal efficacy, for the developer owns all the land. Easements, covenants, and restrictions require divided ownership, with one property owner enforcing his rights against others. Finally comes the phase when the developer makes deeds to lot purchasers, subjecting the lots sold and the lots retained by him to the scheme of restrictions, covenants and easements, and beginning the transfer of control to the homeowners.

Again, as the lot or homesite sales proceed, under the declaration and corporation documents, the developer's representation decreases, until ultimately the developer's rights are phased out. By establishing the association, the developer has absolute power in the beginning stages of growth of the development. By appointing the first board of directors he maintains effective control for the first several years of development. As development continues, however, the control of the board shifts to the owners through their ever-increasing vote.

§ 830. **Income tax problems.** In the past, tax problems existed for home associations. The danger existed that reserves accumulated for future repairs were subject to being taxed as income. Now the association may avoid that result if: (1) I.R.S. form 1120-H is filed electing the benefit of the new tax laws; (2) at least 60 percent of the association's income is derived from membership assessments; and (3) at least 90 percent of the association's expenditures is for maintenance and operation of the property.

Even the making of this election will not relieve the association of the obligation of paying taxes on earnings such as interest on reserves, profits on coin operated machines, rental income from the lease of commercial space, charges for nonmembers' use of amenities.

Whether the election is made or not, the association must file a federal income tax return.

§ 831. **Regulation.** As with condominiums, there are various forms of disclosures required of developers of projects where homeowners' association are involved. These regulations may be on the federal level, as required by the Interstate Land Sales Act, on the state level as required by state land sales acts or subdivision laws, or on the local level as required by county or municipal ordinance. In some instances there may even be regulation directed specifically at offerings of memberships in homeowners' associations. Parness, Homeowners' Associations: Consideration for the Practicing Attorney, 46 N.Y.S.B.J. 357, 360 (1974). The task for the developer and his attorney is to determine which regulations apply, and to comply with their requirements.

REFERENCE: *The Homes Association Handbook,* Technical Bulletin 50 (1964), and *Community Builders Handbook,* both published by Urban Land Institute, 1200 18th Street, N.W., Washington, D.C. 20036.

RESERVED: §§ 832–842.

28

The Declaration of Restrictions, Easements, Liens, and Covenants

§ **843. In general.** In today's land transactions property rights of considerable complexity are generated. This is true particularly of the condominium, the planned unit development (PUD), and the town house. Supplementing the local zoning ordinance in such development there will be found a scheme of private building covenants, easements, liens, and restrictions. The landowner in a condominium or PUD will covenant to do a number of things, for example, to pay maintenance assessments, which are foreclosable liens on the homesites or apartments. Each landowner in a condominium, PUD, or town house will enjoy a number of valuable easements over his neighbors' property, and his own property will be subject to easements in favor of his neighbors. There is general agreement among property lawyers that these detailed rights should be set forth in a *declaration of restrictions, easements, liens, and covenants,* and that only relatively brief reference should be made to them in the deeds of conveyance. *Leverton* v. *Laird,* 190 NW2d 427 (Ia).

The legality of this device rests upon the rule that if a recorded document, such as a deed, makes reference to another document recorded in the same office, the two are read together. Thus the provisions of the declaration are treated legally as "set out" in the deed. 82 ALR 412, 416.

§ **844. Declaration and other document provisions.** The home association declaration in a PUD is modeled in part after the condo declaration, which in turn is modeled after the declaration used to create building restrictions. Among other provisions, it will place some limit on a homeowner's right to make alterations in his unit.

In both the condo and the PUD, buyers like to see some limit on the increase in annual assessments, but there should be a provision that a stated percentage of unit owners can, at a regularly called meeting, authorize an expenditure that exceeds the maximum. If the roof leaks, for example, it must be fixed regardless of cost.

Many declarations contain a provision for fining a unit owner who violates building restrictions, altering his PUD unit without submitting plans to the plan committee, violating swimming pool rules, and so forth. Provision for such fines is included in the declaration, but details should be left to the by-laws. The by-laws should provide for notice to the offending unit owner and a hearing before the board. It is best that the findings and decision of the board be written up formally and placed in the association record book.

Every set of by-laws should state a percentage of the membership that will constitute a quorum. It is best to keep this percentage low. Members tend to shun these meetings. A member who monopolizes meeting time with irrelevant trivia can make meetings tiresome and boring.

The association should hold meetings in strict accordance with its by-laws and elect officers at the proper time. The elected secretary should keep careful custody of the association books and papers, insurance policies, and so forth. In a PUD the common area will be covered by title insurance in the name of the association. Of course, the association will take out liability insurance. It will take out hazard insurance on buildings owned by the association, for example, on recreation buildings. In a condo it will take out liability and hazard insurance.

If the local law requires the lien of an unpaid assessment to be recorded, the secretary attends to this and keeps the recorded notice of lien in his records. The by-laws will provide for interest on delinquent assessments.

Of course, assessments cannot be levied if the purpose is one not authorized by the documents. *Spitser* v. *Kentwood Home Guardians,* 24 Cal. App.3d 215 (1972).

Federal requirements exist as to FHA, VA, FNMA, and FHLMC loans.

§ **845. Restrictions.** Since all that is needed to create enforceable building restrictions or easements is a recorded document that gives public notice of such restrictions or easements, a recorded declaration will suffice for this purpose, when followed by deeds referring thereto. *Davis* v. *Huguenor,* 408 Ill. 468, 97 NE2d 295; *Kosel* v. *Stone,* 146 Mont. 218, 404 P2d 894; *Lawrence* v. *Brockelman,* 155 N.Y.S.2d 604.

There will be restrictions as to the homesites or apartments and restrictions as to the common areas. For obvious reasons, the developer must not retain the right to modify the restrictions. This may destroy the general plan and render the restrictions unenforceable. 19 ALR2d 1282. Also the declaration must be recorded before any deed or mortgage is recorded, for any deed recorded before the declaration will not be subject to the restrictions, easements, or other rights created by the declaration. All deeds are expressly made subject to the declaration.

For the protection of the developer in a PUD, a provision should be included making it clear that restrictions covering the present development do not "pour over" into his subsequent neighboring developments. *Craven County* v. *First-Citizens Bank and Trust Co.,* 237 N.C. 502, 75 SE2d 620; *Finucan* v. *Coronet Homes,* 191 SE2d 5 (S.C. 1972).

It is usual to provide that the restrictions will run till a stated date, and then continue for successive ten-year periods unless altered or abrogated by a vote of the lot or apartment owners. Care must be exercised in expressing the percentage vote. A *majority of the lot owners* is not the same as a vote of *the owners of a majority of the lots.* For example, a lot owner may die leaving fifteen heirs, and a question will arise whether they are entitled to one vote or fifteen votes. Probably one vote per homesite or per apartment is a workable rule, such vote to be cast only if a majority of the owners of that lot or apartment agree on their vote. The same observations are applicable to an amendment of the declaration in any other respect.

§ **846. Easements.** Since the law does not specify any particular form an easement must take, the creation of easements by means of a recorded declaration followed by a deed containing grants and reservations of the easements is universally recognized as a proper means of creating easements. The right to use the common areas must be accomplished by the creation of easements and covenants. It should not be done by *dedication.* A dedication is a giving of rights to the *public*. Hence, use of the word *dedication* is to be avoided for this word has no place in the creation of private, as distinguished from public, rights. *Drye* v. *Eagle Rock Ranch, Inc.,* 364 SW2d 196 (Tex. Civ. App.).

When a tall building is divided into office space (lower floors) and residential apartments (upper floors) the declaration of easements is quite complicated. It is accompanied by or incorporated into an operating agreement, which sets out the duties of the party who is to operate the elevators, repair water pipes and electrical systems, and so forth.

§ **847. Phased development.** It is quite possible to develop an area in several stages. This is a convenience to the developer. He can limit his investment to stage one, and, if it is not a success, he need not develop additional stages. The additional, undeveloped stages can be sold as raw land. It then becomes important to assure that the building restrictions on stage one do not "pour over" into the future undeveloped stages.

However, as to the common elements, for example, the swimming pool in stage one, the declaration should make clear whether or not the developer has the power to bring in several successive stages, all of which will share the use of the pool. Drafting can help.

CLAUSE: The developer reserves the right to add as an adjoining development a development no larger than the present development, containing a substantially identical number of substantially identical units, all of which will be subject to a declaration substantially identical with this declaration. In no event shall any land other than the present development be burdened by any restrictions, liens, covenant or easements affecting the present development in the absence of a provision to the contrary.

§ **848. Party walls.** Where party walls are involved, as in the town house, the declaration will contain a detailed provision regarding same, including a provision that the cost of reasonable repair and maintenance shall be shared by the owners who make use of the wall in proportion to such use.

§ **849. Lien of assessments.** Both in the condominium and the PUD, the home association will want a provision in the declaration giving it the right to levy assessments on the homeowner for maintenance of the common areas. Again, this can be done in the declaration, since the law requires no great formality for the creation of equitable or contractual liens. *Prudential Ins. Co.* v. *Wetzel,* 212 Wis. 100, 248 NW 791. Such assessment liens are enforceable by foreclosure, like a mortgage. *Rodruck* v. *Sand Point,* 48 Wash.2d 565, 295 P2d 714. The lien serves an important purpose. As the section on covenants shows, the declaration also gives the association the right to *sue* the homeowner for assessments, and to get a judgment against him. The covenants, in other words, create *personal liability*. But where the homeowner is financially irresponsible, or simply disappears, so that summons cannot be served upon him, the lien for his delinquent assessments can be foreclosed. Both methods of enforcement should be provided for. The declaration should state that any delinquent assessment bears interest at the highest legal rate and that attorney's fees are collectible as part of the assessment.

§ **850. Lien and assessment—priority thereof with respect to mortgages.** In both the condominium and the PUD there will usually be two liens, the lien of the mortgage on the home or apartment, and the lien of the assessments. Obviously a question will arise as to whether foreclosure of a mortgage will wipe out delinquent assessment liens or vice versa. A mortgage recorded subsequent to the recording of the deed and declaration creating the lien is subject and subordinate to such lien, even as to assessments accruing subsequent to the recording of the mortgage. *Prudential Ins. Co.* v. *Wetzel,* 212 Wis. 100, 248 NW 791. Foreclosure of the assessment lien wipes out the mortgage. Mortgages that antedate the effective date of the declaration or deeds will be prior and superior to the assessment liens (*Kennilwood Owners' Assn.* v. *Kennilwood,* 28 N.Y.S.2d 239), so that foreclosure of the mortgage will cut out all unpaid assessments and the future liability of the lot to pay assessments. This creates a potential conflict. Mortgagees, especially those who are required by law to loan only on first mortgages, will insist that the lien of all assessments, even those created by an earlier declaration, be subordinated to the lien of their mortgages. The wishes of the mortgagee must prevail, since otherwise financing cannot be obtained. However, once the mortgage is foreclosed and the mortgagee has become the owner of the lot, the lien of future assessments should be binding on the mortgagee, as they would be on any other homeowner. This can be accomplished by a clause in the declaration as follows:

SUGGESTED FORM: The lien of the assessment provided for herein shall be subordinate to the lien of any mortgage or mortgages now or hereafter placed upon the properties subject to assessments and running to a bank, savings and loan association, insurance company or other institutional lender; provided, however, such subordination shall apply only to the assessments which have become due and payable prior to a sale or transfer of such property pursuant to a decree of foreclosure, or any other proceeding in lieu of foreclosure. Such sale or transfer shall not relieve such property from liability for any assessments thereafter becoming due nor from the lien of any such subsequent assessment.

§ **851. Covenants.** The creation of covenants that will impose *personal liability* on future landowners, for example, to pay maintenance assessments, is a technical matter. Hence in this instance it seems desirable to refer to the declaration for the text of the covenants, but to spell out *in the deed* the language by which the grantor and grantee, and their successors in ownership, agree to perform their covenants. Likewise, a covenant binding on the association to maintain the common areas, collect assessments impartially, and the like seems desirable. Of course, where the plan is that the association will provide, at its expense, maintenance of the homesite and of the exterior of the home, that must be spelled out in detail in the declaration.

§ 852. **Association as a vehicle for enforcing restrictions, liens, and covenants.** The enforcement of *restrictions, liens,* and *covenants* can legally be transferred through the declaration to an association or corporation formed by the home or apartment owners. *Merrionette Manor Homes* v. *Heda,* 11 Ill.App.2d 186, 136 NE2d 556; *Neponsit Property Owners' Assn.* v. *Emigrant Industrial Savings Bank,* 278 N.Y. 248, 15 NE2d 793; *Rodruck* v. *Sand Point Maintenance Comm.,* 40 Wash.2d 565, 295 P2d 714. (*See* Chapter 27.)

§ 853. **Deed clauses to implement the declaration.** To fully implement the declaration it is necessary to insert a clause in the deed to the homebuyer or apartment buyer. Such a clause might be as follows:

SUGGESTED FORM: Subject to Declaration of Easements, Restrictions, Liens, and Covenants dated ________________ and recorded in the Office of the Recorder of Deeds of ________________ County, as Document No. __________ which is incorporated herein by reference thereto. Grantor grants to the Grantee, his heirs and assigns, as easements appurtenant to the premises hereby conveyed, the easements created by said Declaration for the benefit of the owners of the parcel of realty herein described. Grantor reserves to himself, his heirs and assigns, as easements appurtenant to the remaining parcels described in said Declaration, the easements thereby created for the benefit of said remaining parcels described in said Declaration, and this conveyance is subject to said easements and the right of the Grantor to grant said easements in the conveyances of said remaining parcels or any of them, and the parties hereto, for themselves, their heirs, personal representatives, and assigns, covenant to be bound by the covenants, restrictions, and agreements in said document set forth. Said covenants and restrictions are covenants running with the land both as to burden and benefits, and this conveyance is subject to all said covenants and restrictions as though set forth in full herein. The land hereby conveyed is also subject to the liens created by said Declaration, and same are binding on the grantees, their heirs, personal representatives, and assigns. All of the provisions of said Declaration are hereby incorporated herein as though set forth in full herein.

In some decisions it has been held that the filing of the declaration would suffice to create restrictions even though they were not mentioned in the subdivider's deeds. *Kosel* v. *Stone,* 146 Mont. 218, 404 P2d 894; *Steuart Transp. Co.* v. *Ashe,* 304 A2d 788 (Md. 1973). But in California precisely the opposite has been held. There the declaration is totally ineffective unless the deeds refer to it. *Smith* v. *Rasqui,* 1 Cal. Reptr. 478. However, it suffices to state in the deeds that the land is "subject to covenants, conditions, restrictions, and easements of record," *Seaton* v. *Clifford,* 100 Cal. Reptr. 779; *Davis* v. *Huguenor,* 408 Ill. 468, 97 NE2d 295. Obviously this is a poor practice. The full suggested form should be used.

Where the owner of a condominium apartment, PUD unit, or town house is placing a mortgage on his property, a clause is inserted in the mortgage along the following lines:

CLAUSE: Subject to Declaration of Easements, Restrictions, Liens, and Covenants dated ______________ and recorded in the Office of the Recorder of Deeds of __________ County in Book ________ page ________ as Document No. ___________, which is incorporated herein by reference thereto. Mortgagor grants to the mortgagee, its successors and assigns all rights of every description created by said Declaration for the benefit of the mortgaged premises, same to run with the mortgaged land. The provisions of said Declaration regarding liens of assessments are also incorporated herein by reference thereto.

§ 854. **Sale by homeowner.** The declaration should provide that upon sale of a home or apartment, the seller shall not be liable for assessments levied or covenants or restrictions breached thereafter. Unless this clause is included there is a legal possibility of continuing liability.

§ 855. **Membership corporation.** The declaration will set forth who the members are to be in the home association created for a PUD or for a condominium.

§ 856. **Marketable Title Acts.** Under the Marketable Title Acts, rights in land—including covenants, restrictions, private assessment liens, and, in some instances, easements also—terminate after a stated period of time unless fresh recordings are made to keep these interests alive.

REFERENCE: For sample declaration of restrictions for detached single-family dwellings see FHA Land Planning Bulletin No. 3—Protective Covenants Data Sheet 40, also Sample Form Protective Covenants, both set forth in the Appendix to Community Builders Handbook, published by Urban Land Institute, 1200 18th Street, N.W., Washington, D.C. 20036.

RESERVED: §§ 857–867.

29

Town Houses

§ 868. **In general.** In the present building boom, land costs and construction costs have risen sharply, and row houses—now called town houses —have penetrated many areas of our country. In former times, row houses were most often erected facing the street, so that in driving by a block of row houses you would see a solid wall of housefronts. Nowadays you are more likely to see the houses erected at right angles to the street line, as in Figure 3.

It is obvious that by laying out the houses at right angles to the street line, many more houses can be erected than would be possible if the houses were erected fronting on the street.

The town house is, historically, the first of the modern housing developments to make extensive use of the concept of shared common ground, though on a very small scale.

Like the more modern subdivisions of single-family dwellings it is invariably set up with a declaration of restrictions, to which is added a declaration of necessary easements.

It is a transition from the single-family detached home to the garden development, with town houses found in the planned unit development.

Commonly, town houses are built as individual units in a series of five to ten houses, with party walls and a side yard on the end units only.

Clearly this arrangement makes extensive use of easements. The walls, of course, are party walls, and easements must exist for this purpose. Also, all houses except those closest to the street need easements of ingress and egress over a central walk. Easements are also needed for common gutters and downspouts, common sewer and water lines, common electric light and telephone wires, and so forth. In many cases, builders of these projects have proceeded with complete indifference to the legal requirements of such a situation and have sold off such units without any mention of the easements required. Probably implied easements exist for all these necessary common uses. *Gilbert* v. *Chicago T. & T. Co.,* 7 Ill.2d 496, 131 NE2d 1 (1956). A better way of handling this is by use of a declaration of easements.

With increasing frequency townhouse developments are organized un-

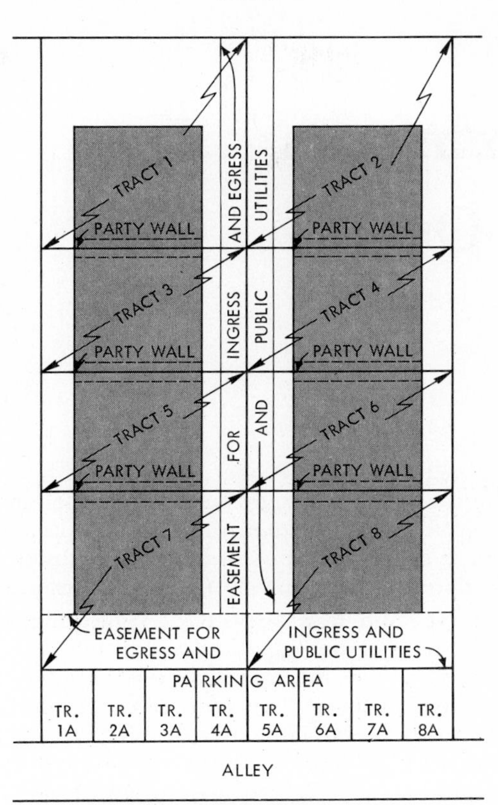

SOLID LINES ARE PROPERTY LINES.
SHADED AREAS DEPICT BUILDINGS.

FIGURE 3

der the condominium form of ownership and are therefore subject to the local condominium law.

In some states the town house development with its dwelling units and common areas is depicted on a recorded plat. In other instances the boundaries of the units and common areas are depicted on a map attached to the declaration.

If there are to be common areas owned by a home association, such a development is treated in this text as a *planned unit development,* and its legal aspects are discussed under that heading.

REFERENCE: *Organizing the Townhouse in Indiana,* 40 Ind. L. J. 419; Krasnowiecki, Condominiums Compared to Conventional, Subdivisions with Homes, 1 *RELJ* 323 (1972); Krasnowiecki, Townhouses with Home Associations: A New Perspective, 23 *Penn. L. Rev.* 711 (1975).

RESERVED: §§ 869–879.

30

Condominiums and Co-Ops

§ 880. **Introduction.** Today one can own an apartment in one of two ways, namely, either as a *cooperative apartment* (hereinafter, for brevity, referred to as a *co-op*) or as a *condominium*. To be sure, a condominium is a form of cooperative ownership, but since legal distinctions exist between the two types, a difference in nomenclature seems necessary.

§ 881. **Mechanics and legal aspects of traditional co-op ownership.** Cooperative apartments can be organized on either a trust or corporate basis, but the latter is by far the more popular. Under the corporate arrangement, a corporation is formed, and ownership of the land and building is acquired by the corporation. The corporation places a mortgage on the land for the purpose of buying, or, if the land is vacant, for the purpose of building. Since no mortgagee will lend up to the full value of the building, the balance of the necessary funds is raised by sale of stock to the prospective tenants. When he has purchased a specified number of shares, proportional to the value of the apartments, the prospective tenant receives a long-term lease of the apartment called a *proprietary lease,* from the corporation. The word *proprietary* means that it has the *attributes of ownership,* that it gives rights equivalent in *economic benefit* to outright ownership. Legally, however, a proprietary lease is a lease, and landlord and tenant law is applicable to it. This lease gives the tenant the right to possession of his apartment for the term specified in the lease, but requires the tenant to pay rent to the corporation, which rent payments consist of his pro rata share of the amounts needed to cover mortgage debt, taxes, and operating expenses. The annual cash requirements for the building are established by the board of directors of the corporation, and this sum is divided among the tenants in proportion to the number of shares allocated to each apartment, the bigger apartments having the larger shareholdings and assessments.

Restrictions are placed on the right of the lessee to assign or sublet. The common provision restricts the transfer of the stock and lease without the consent of the board of directors, thereby insuring some control over occupancy of the apartments. Of course, the consent cannot be arbitrarily withheld. *Sanders* v. *Tropicana,* 229 SE2d 304 (N.C. 1976). The lease provides that it is subject to any future mortgage placed on the building by the landlord corporation. A mortgage usually requires a two-thirds vote of the tenants. This clause facilitates refinancing of the existing mortgage.

It is significant that both a tenant's interest under a lease (his *leasehold*) and shares of stock are legally considered to be personal property. Thus, a sale of a co-op apartment is a sale of personalty.

EXAMPLE: *R* entered into a contract to sell his co-op apartment to *E*. *E* made an earnest money deposit as is common in sales of land. *E* failed to go through with the deal. *R* declared the earnest money forfeited. *E* sued *R*, and the court held that since a sale of personalty was involved, damages must be determined under the Uniform Commercial Code, which confine the seller's damages to loss on re-sale to another party and incidental expenses. *Silverman* v. *Alcoa Plaza Associates*, 323 N.Y.S.2d 39 (1971); Note, 21 *Buff. L. Rev.* 555 (1972); Comment, 29 *Wash. & Lee L. Rev.* 189 (1972).

There are, of course, many other legal consequences of this rule. For example, on the death of an apartment owner, his leasehold and shares pass to his administrator or executor, rather than to his heirs. As a result, a simple, informal sale by the executor or administrator is possible without the difficulties attendant upon sale of land owned by a deceased person.

§ 882. Sale of co-op apartment. The following suggestions may be appropriate for sellers and purchasers of existing co-op apartments:

1. You cannot afford to have the title to the entire building brought down to date. What you can do is have your lawyer check the existing title insurance policy, abstract, and opinion to see that the building corporation has good title to the property (subject only to the mortgage and the proprietary leases). This title evidence may be several years old. Supplement this by getting an affidavit from the secretary of the corporation to the effect that the condition of title remains today as it was on the date of the title evidence which your lawyer examined and that no lawsuits are presently pending against the corporation. Some states, Illinois and New York, for example, have laws which allow the title companies to insure individual cooperative owners' interests.

2. Since you are buying the lease and stock of the present tenant, get the secretary of the building corporation to sign an affidavit stating: (a) that the stock is in fact owned by your seller and is fully paid for; (b) that the lease is owned by your seller, free of any subleases; (c) that the stock and lease are free from any assessments other than the current ones shown on the financial statement submitted to you by the corporation; (d) that the stock is free of restrictions on its transfer or those restrictions have been satisfied. 99 ALR2d 236; (e) that no defaults have occurred in the building's mortgage payments; (f) that none of the other tenants is currently behind in his payments; (g) that no proposal to remodel the building or increase assessments has come before the directors within the past year, for this may be why your seller is moving out; (h) how much space is rented to persons other than tenant-stockholders, for if this figure gets too high, you lose your income tax benefits; and (i) what insurance is carried presently. Get a certified copy of the co-op charter and bylaws and the directors' resolution authorizing your seller to sell you his lease and stock, for all co-ops restrict the right of the tenants to transfer their rights. Have your lawyer check the lease that you are about to buy and explain to you the restrictions (on remodeling of apartments, for example, or the right to sell, sublease, or operate a business in the apartment) and liabilities (special assessments, for example) that it creates. Have him explain what maintenance costs you must pay yourself, such as decorating.

3. It is quite important that an apartment seller who lists his apartment with a real estate broker for sale insert the *no deal, no commission clause* in the listing. This is important because if the co-op board turns down the purchaser, the seller does not want to be liable for a commission.

4. It is important that the contract of sale specify what appliances and other articles go with the sale of the apartment. The sale does not include these articles unless so specified, and normally they do not belong to the building corporation. The contract should also contain various warranties by the seller, such as a warranty that he owns the shares and lease and will so continue at closing, free of any liens or adverse interests, including mechanic's liens, that the shares are fully paid for, that no lease defaults will exist at closing, that the seller has no knowledge of building code violations, if any, or proposals to increase apartment assessments. For the seller's protection the contract states that it is subject to approval by the co-op board, and that if the approval is refused, the buyer obtains return of his deposit. The contract clause as to closing costs requires some special attention. The seller normally agrees to pay the corporation's charges for transfer of the shares and lease.

If the buyers are husband and wife who wish to own the apartment in joint tenancy, the contract of sale should so state, and special language may be needed because of the personal property nature of the lease and shares.

EXAMPLE: In Illinois a deed of land to A and B "in joint tenancy" creates a joint tenancy. But to create a joint tenancy in shares and a leasehold probably requires the phrase "as joint tenants with the right of survivorship and not as tenants in common."

5. In states where a judgment against the owner of a leasehold creates a lien thereon, it probably will be necessary to have a title company make a search for such judgments.

6. If valuable furniture and appliances are being transferred, the buyer's lawyer may wish to make a search for Uniform Commercial Code financing statements against the seller.

§ 883. Co-op on leasehold. Where a co-op is to be erected on a leasehold created by a ground lease, it will be necessary to include rather complex provisions in the ground lease for the protection of the leasehold mortgagee. For the protection of the tenants, a complex clause will be needed requiring the lessor (or any subsequent ground owner) to join in any necessary refinancing mortgage. This is needed because as the leasehold mortgage is reduced by payments, the apartment equity grows correspondingly in value. At some point, the apartment value will be such that a buyer who can pay cash for it may be hard to find. At that point it may be desirable to refinance with a larger mortgage, thus reducing the value of the apartment equities.

§ 884. Co-ops—securities problem. In the cooperative apartment complex that is purchased for residential purposes, there appears to be no problem with entanglements caused by the Federal Securities law.

EXAMPLE: In a large New York cooperative, prospective purchasers made a recoverable deposit on their apartments by buying shares of stock in the nonprofit housing corporation which held title to the property. The shares of stock were allocated to purchasers on the basis of the number of rooms in their apartment. When the tenant wanted to move out, he had to offer his stock back to the corporation at the initial selling price.

The court found that the mere description of the certificates as "stock" did not render it a security subject to the Federal Securities law. Noting that the purchasers intended merely to acquire a residential apartment for personal use rather than an investment for profit to be derived from the managerial efforts of others, the court found no security present. *United Housing Foundation, Inc. v. Forman,* 421 US 837 (1975).

§ 885. **Condominiums—in general.** In a condominium apartment, the purchaser of an apartment or unit receives a deed that gives him absolute ownership of the apartment that he has purchased and ownership of an undivided interest or share in the common elements.

EXAMPLE: *ABC Corporation* acquires a tract of vacant land. It obtains a construction mortgage loan from *XYZ Bank* and erects a building containing fifty apartments. *E* wishes to buy one of these apartments, Apartment #1. *ABC Corporation* sells *E* a deed that conveys to him (1) Apartment #1, and (2) a 2 percent interest in the ownership of the *common elements.* The common elements include the land itself including all the ground area and air space above it and around it except the apartments; the outside walls of the building; the foundation; the roof; the basement; the stairs; halls; foyers; elevators; swimming pool; janitor's apartment; water tanks; fire escapes; exits; heating plant; central air conditioning; incinerator; pumps; ducts; machinery; and so on. Thus, *E* winds up owning his own apartment just as if it were a separate house, and a 2 percent interest in the common elements. As to the common elements *E* becomes a tenant in common with the other apartment owners, just as if a deed of the common elements had been made to *E* and his forty-nine neighbors as tenants in common. The construction mortgage, which covered all the land and the entire building, is released as to the two items conveyed to *E,* namely, his apartment and his share of the common elements. To finance his purchase, *E* borrows $15,000, which he obtains by giving to *DEF Corporation* a mortgage on Apartment #1 and his 2 percent interest in the common elements. *E* now owns, as an absolute owner, his apartment and his 2 percent interest in the common elements, subject only to his own mortgage to *DEF Corporation.* In becoming the owner of an apartment the condominium owner technically becomes the owner of the *space* bounded by the inner surfaces of the apartment walls. Under the condominium laws such ownership of space is perfectly legal. Indeed, that such space is part of the land and can be separately owned and conveyed has long been taken for granted. 4 Powell, Real Property, 721.

§ 886. **Common elements—limited common elements.** Some state laws permit a class of common elements known as *limited common elements.* These are common elements shared by less than all unit owners, such as special corridors or stairways, common to certain apartments or a particular floor. These are collectively owned by the unit owners whose apartments they serve. Even though these areas are not for the use of all unit owners, they are subject to strict controls.

EXAMPLE: An owner of limited common elements that were originally built as screened enclosures remodeled the area by installing jalousie windows in lieu of the screens. The jalousies had to be removed or proper consents obtained. *Sterling Village Condominium, Inc. v. Breitenbach,* 251 So2d 685 (Fla. 1971).

§ 887. **Leasehold condominiums.** Under the original condominium laws of most states, a condominium could not be created on land in which the developer has only a long-term ground lease. Statutory revisions have accommodated this gap. See e.g. Cal. Civ. Code, § 783; Fla. Stat. Ann. § 711.08; Va. Code Ann. § 55-79.54. Where leasehold condominiums are allowed, certain precautions should be exercised:

1. Be sure that proper care is taken to insure that the individual unit owners can protect their interests by making their separate payments of the lease rentals. This may be accomplished by a lease clause limiting forfeiture to be lodged only against those unit owners in arrears in lease payments. State law may also afford some protection. Va. Code Ann. §§ 55–79.54.

2. Check the duration of the underlying ground lease. The documentation is apt to be pretty complicated. Sakai & Reskin, Leasehold Condominiums, 2 *Conn. L. Rev.* 37 (1969).

§ 888. Condominiums—the declaration. Before any of the apartments are sold, the owner-developer makes, signs, and records a declaration that should contain:

1. A description of the land and the building.

2. A description of each of the apartments, giving the number of each unit and all other data necessary for its identification.

3. A description of the common elements.

4. A statement of the share of each apartment owner in the common elements. This share should be expressed as a percentage rather than a fraction.

5. A provision that ownership of an apartment and of the owner's share of the common elements shall not be severed or separated and that any conveyance or mortgage of the one without the other is prohibited; also, that any partition suit with respect to the common elements is forbidden.

6. A grant of easements to each apartment owner giving him rights of ingress and egress and other easement rights. As time goes by, buildings often settle. Thus, the condo unit sinks slightly into a part of the common elements (the interior of walls that separate units) not assigned to the unit by the surveys, and common elements encroach into the units. To dispose of this problem, the condo declaration provides that as the building settles, the unit owner enjoys an easement to occupy the area not assigned to him by the surveys. Comment, 50 *Calif. L. Rev.* 299, 303 (1962). In tall buildings, the upper floors sway a good deal in a high wind. This is readily perceived when the water in the wash bowl sloshes around and chandeliers hung on chains sway perceptibly. Obviously, a unit in this area trespasses into the air space (common element) surrounding the building. It is probably a good idea to include a "sway easement" in the declaration. Incidentally, people who suffer from giddiness should give this matter thought before purchasing a unit in an upper story.

NEW LAWS: Encroachment easements exist by virtue of statute in some states thereby allowing an easement for encroachment where the encroachment is the result of a deviation from the plat and plans of construction, repair, renovation, restoration, or settling or shifting. This statutory easement will not protect unit owners in the event of their wilful or intentional misconduct, or exculpate the contractor from liability for reason of failure to comply with the plans. *Code. Va.* §§ 55–79.60.

7. Building restrictions setting out the permitted use of the apartment.

8. Provisions relative to the administration of the property by an association of the condominium owners. This contemplates the creation of an association or nonprofit corporation consisting of all the co-owners and the drawing up of rules and regulations governing administration of the property. While details of operating rules may go into the by-laws of the corporation, the declaration should provide for creation of a basic central authority to manage the building, to adopt rules and by-laws, to see that all occupants obey the rules and pay their assessments, and to keep the common elements in repair.

9. A provision giving the condominium association the right to levy assessments on the apartment owners for maintenance, and so forth, and creating personal liability on the unit owner plus a foreclosable lien on each apartment for any delinquency in paying the assessments applicable to each apartment unit, and stating the maximum assessment permitted.

Alternatives to foreclosure or eviction for nonpayment of assessments exist.

EXAMPLE: The association may post a list of delinquent owners in the recreation area or may deny the delinquent owner the use of the recreation facilities. To be safe, the declaration must provide for this latter remedy. Lowell, Prahl, Alessio and Cazares, Land Use and Operational Controls in the Planned Development, 9 *San Diego L. Rev.* 28, 60 (1971).

Major buildings and projects present unforeseen engineering and legal problems that cause extraordinary expenses which the association must face.

EXAMPLE: Some cities have required installation of sprinkler systems in high-rise buildings. This can result in a big special assessment. Problems may also exist with elevator cables in high-rise buildings. Replacement could result in heavy assessments. These problems show the need to maintain adequate reserve levels to be built up over the expected useful life of the major replacement items such as roofs, carpeting in common areas, heating and cooling plant, and so forth.

10. A provision that in the case of an apartment owner choosing to sell his apartment, the condominium association shall have the right of first refusal, that is, the right to buy the apartment at the same price the apartment owner's buyer is willing to pay. This device must not be used as a means of racial discrimination. Comment, 50 *Calif. L. Rev.* 299, 317 (1962). Rather, this is a tool to insure compatibility and financial responsibility of the members of the venture. A provision that the unit shall not be occupied until the family has been approved by the board is valid. Ross, Condominiums and Preemptive Options: The Right of First Refusal, 18 *Hastings L. J.* 585 (1967). The declaration should provide that the right of first refusal does not apply to a sale made by a mortgagee who has acquired an apartment by foreclosure. A provision which limits the ability of a unit owner to lease his apartment is allowable. *Seagate Condominium Assn., Inc.* v. *Duffy,* 330 So2d 484 (Fla. 1976); *Kroop* v. *Caravelle Condo., Inc.,* 323 So2d 307 (Fla. 1975) (allows one lease per period of ownership); *Holiday Out in America* v. *Bowes,* 285 So2d 63 (Fla. 1973) (declaration granted developer the exclusive right to rent units). The approval of a sale of a unit cannot be conditioned upon the purchaser's acceptance of a management contract in favor of the developer or a corporation he controls. This violates the *antitrust* laws. *Miller* v. *Granados,* 529 P2d 393 (1976).

11. Provision that in the event of total or substantial destruction of the building by fire or other hazard, or where the property reaches obsolescence, a stated percentage of co-owners' votes shall determine whether to rebuild or sell the property. A number of states have laws on this point.

12. A provision that each condominium owner is to keep his apartment in repair at

his own expense but is not to interfere with the exterior of the building or any of the common elements.

13. A provision is needed stating that all easements, covenants, and agreements in the declaration run with the land. Some statement is also needed that the benefit and burden of these covenants run with each unit. A provision should be included that when any apartment owner sells, his personal liability for future breaches of these covenants ends with the sale.

14. A provision should be included giving a majority of the apartment owners the right to amend the declaration and providing that such amendment shall be binding on all present and future landowners. The provision giving the right to amend gives the developer pretty broad power while he still controls a majority of the units. Hence, it should be restricted to give the unit owners protection against unfair amendments.

15. Most declarations have a clause obligating each unit owner to abide by all the rules or by-laws promulgated by the home association. Needed flexibility is obtained in this way since new and necessary rules can be enacted through the simple majority vote of a quorum, instead of a majority of the apartment owners. It is important that a method of enforcement exists for these rules. The declaration should allow the association to obtain injunctive relief. In this way the association may, in a serious case, have the court order the violation to cease.

16. Resort type condominiums present special problems. Suppose you put a clause in the declaration that rentals shall be for a minimum of two weeks. This type of restriction eliminates the danger of a motel type operation. But, if the restrictions on renting get too strict there is the danger that more and more units will be sold to permanent residents, who may amend the declaration to eliminate renting altogether. This, of course, is bad for those who bought the units basically for investment purposes, hoping to profit through renting the unit most of the year.

17. Reasonable restrictions against pets or children under a specified age will probably be upheld. *Coquina Club, Inc.* v. *Mantz,* 342 So2d 112 (Fla. 1977). They should go into the rules or by-laws of the association, since views on this subject may change from time to time, and it is easier to amend the rules than the declaration.

18. If the developer plans to generate income for himself from coin operated laundry machines or from a TV antenna, he will want a provision in the declaration giving him this right and forbidding any amendment or by-law that terminates this right.

19. If there is a construction mortgage on the property, the mortgagee should join in the declaration.

Obviously, since each state has its own condo law, it will be necessary to check that law and comply with it. Also, there have been numerous articles written by fine lawyers, well versed in the provisions of local law, i.e. Merrill, An Overview of California Condominium Law, 6 *SW. U. L. Rev.* 487 (1974).

§ 889. Common law condominiums. If a condominium does not substantially comply with the state law, it probably is a common law condominium. *Thisted* v. *County Club Tower Corp.,* 405 P2d 432 (Mont. 1965). Doubts on this score seem not well-founded. It is well known that a subdivision plat that does not comply with the law is a common law plat. *Sundstrom* v. *Village of Oak Park,* 30 NE2d 58 (Ill. 1940). The analogy seems persuasive except where the state law expressly states that *all* condominiums *must* conform to the statute. But the disadvantages of failure to comply with statutes are great. They include the following: (1) the assessor is not obliged to make a separate assessment on the unit and its common elements; (2) a mechanic's lien for work ordered by one tenant might attach to the whole building; (3) the restriction on partition of the common elements might be valid for only twenty-one years.

§ 890. **Phased construction.** Good business sense and financing requirements frequently require that an entire project be constructed in phases with new buildings started only as sales justify.

EXAMPLE: A builder is constructing four buildings with sixty units in each. To begin construction on all buildings would be foolhardy except in the very best of market conditions. If a lender had a 50 percent presale requirement, the builder would have to sell 120 units before the first sale could be closed. This may well discourage sales. All units may have to be constructed before the survey could be made, a prerequisite for a declaration in many states. These are only some of the problems that can be avoided by the phased development. Geis, Representing the Condominium Developer: Tending the Paper Jungle, 10 *R.P.P.&T.J.* 471 (1975). Obviously, this problem does not exist in the high-rise condominium.

On the other hand, phasing creates some administrative problems for the ultimate unit owners.

EXAMPLE: In the above example, each phase would have its own association, and there would be an umbrella association to manage the recreational and other facilities that serve the entire complex. This is the *umbrella association.*

Many of the problems of the phased condominium are discussed in Kratovil, Modern Real Estate Documentation, § 809 *et seq.* (1975).

§ 891. **Land descriptions in the declaration.** The declaration should be executed by the landowner, acknowledged and witnessed in accordance with the local requirements for recording, and should be recorded in the recorder's office.

It should describe the following elements: (1) the land comprising the entire project area, for which a traditional legal description can be used, but which should be given a distinctive designation, for example, *the project parcel;* (2) each apartment, by whatever method is employed, giving it in addition a distinctive number, as *Apartment Parcel 1;* (3) the land and space that are to be owned in common by the apartment owners, for which one shortcut would be a description such as *the project parcel excepting Apartment Parcels 1 to 100, both inclusive, all herein above described,* and which can also be given a designation, for example, *the co-ownership parcel.*

The Condominium Survey is a three-dimensional marvel of greater sophistication than the normal two-dimensional version. Before progressing too far, it is best for the developer to submit the survey of even an experienced condominium surveyor to the title company for approval.

§ 892. **Description of apartments.** Notwithstanding the fact that condominium units may be cubes of air, it is as necessary that this "real property" be described with the same exactness used in describing any other piece of real estate. There are three methods by which a unit of air space can be described:

1. *The subdivision plat method.* You record a plat of subdivision of air space and the air lots representing the individual units by means of a drawing. This will permit conveyance of a particular unit by its number, as shown on the plat.

2. *The land and apartment survey.* A survey is first made of the land, showing the location of the building. Space surveys of each unit on each floor are then made showing the elevation of the floor and ceiling surfaces, the dimensions of the inside surfaces of the walls of each unit, and their location with reference to the boundaries of the land projected vertically upward.

3. *Floor plan method.* In lieu of individual apartment surveys, make a survey of the land showing the location of the building and attach to it floor plans showing each unit's location, dimensions, and elevation from the ground floor surface, with a certification by the architect that the building was built substantially in accordance with the plans.

One difficulty with these methods is that the typical condominium unit is an apartment in a multilevel building.

PROBLEM: How does one describe the perimeters of an apartment located, let us say, on the twentieth floor of an apartment building? How does one describe with legal accuracy the exact height above ground level of the floor and ceiling of the apartment? Remember that a condo unit is basically a cube of space. Space is considered to be land that can be deeded and mortgaged. But it is harder to describe than a simple two-dimensional tract of land, such as a lot on which a house has been erected. As regards the house lot, the surveyor can go on the tract of land and place monuments or markers at the lot corners. But one cannot plant markers in the sky. Hence, the problem.

One part of the problem is simple. The surveyor can depict on the ground the proposed perimeters of the apartment unit and then state that such perimeters extended upward indefinitely. To grasp this idea, imagine a rectangular lot, with stakes at all four lot corners. Then imagine the lot lines thus created as extending up to the sky. Now you have the perimeters of the lot, however high you go, since surveyors, given the outlines of a tract of land at ground level, can, by use of instruments, extend the lot lines upward to the heavens. No problem.

The other problem is more difficult. Legally, one cannot measure the height of the floor and ceiling from "the ground." The "ground" is not a stable and definite legal marker. Indeed, in the process of erecting a building, the construction crew invariably levels and changes the grade of the ground. Many condo apartments are contracted for sale before construction begins. Hence, the problem.

Engineers have solved this problem.

EXAMPLE: In Chicago, for example, the city, by ordinance, has established an artificial horizontal plane beneath the surface of the entire city. This plane is uniform throughout the city. At many places throughout the city, concrete markers are placed extending about six feet downward from the sidewalk. The sidewalk is used because its grade is rarely altered. Each such monument contains a legend, stating, for example, "twenty feet above Chicago City Datum." The *Datum* is the artificial legal subsurface that extends at the same level throughout the entire city. The markers are called *Bench Marks*. There are hundreds scattered throughout the city, each identified by location and number. Now a surveyor, plotting a condominium unit on the twentieth floor, can show on his survey that the floor of the apartment is located ____ feet above Chicago City Datum as established by Bench Mark ____. The same is done with the ceiling. With this system, establishing vertical boundaries is a simple task for the surveyor.

The U.S. Geodetic Survey has established its own *datum* and *bench marks*. Some surveyors prefer to use these because they are considered more accurate than city datum and city bench marks.

§ 893. **Provisions of the deed.** The individual deed of a unit need not necessarily be a complex document insofar as its legal description is concerned. The basis for such description will already have been provided by: (1) recording of the subdivision plat; (2) recording of the declaration to which were appended the land and apartment surveys containing legal descriptions of the various apartments; or (3) recording of the declaration to which were appended the land survey and building floor plans, in which case the legal descriptions of the apartments will have been set forth in the declaration.

Thus, in the deed, the legal description of the individual apartment could be as follows:

PARCEL I

The absolute and indefeasible fee simple title to the parcel of land, property, and space designated as Apartment Parcel 100 in the plat of subdivision recorded in the Recorder's Office of __________ County, __________ on November 1, 19____ as Document No. 123456 (or: "in the Declaration recorded, etc." as the case may be).

The description of the common elements could be as follows:

PARCEL II

The absolute and indefeasible fee simple title to an undivided ____ percent interest in the land, property, and space known as Lot 1 in Block 1 in Jones Subdivision, in Section ____, Township ____, North, Range ____ East of the ________ Principal Meridian, excepting from said Lot 1 all the land, property, and space designated as Apartment Parcels 1 to 100, both inclusive, in the plat of subdivision recorded in the Recorder's Office of ________ County, ________ on November 1, 19____ as Document No. 123456 (or: "in the Declaration recorded, etc." as the case may be).

The apartments excepted in Parcel II should, of course, consist of all the family units in the building. Should there be any units that are intended to be rented for commercial facilities, they should not be included among the apartments excepted, since they would be classed as part of the common elements.

An additional paragraph could be included in the developer's deed to the first purchaser of an apartment, conveying all the rights, benefits, easements, privileges, options, and covenants created by the declaration. It will do no harm to repeat in this clause the statement that these run with the land, for it is this document that gives life to the covenants.

Because of a dearth of modern cases touching on the specific question of whether ownership of the space occupied by an apartment or upper floor in a building would survive destruction of the building, it would be advisable to include in the deed a provision that it is the intention of the parties thereto that the ownership rights thereby conveyed shall so survive.

§ **894. Conversion.** Rather than construct a condominium project from the ground up, some developers have used the approach of converting an existing apartment house into a condominium. The prime consideration for the developer in this regard is to be certain that he has an underlying mortgage that accommodates the sell-off.

EXAMPLE: O, an owner of an apartment building, wants to convert it to condominiums. The building is encumbered with an existing mortgage that permits no prepayment. Conversion is effectively blocked until the lender can be persuaded to accept a prepayment, for which he may well extract a prepayment charge.

Typically, the existing financing is not adequate, for financing of conversion costs, such as attorney's fees, title costs, engineering work, refurbishment, and marketing expenses must be obtained. The developer will obtain financing that will pay off the existing mortgage and provide the funds for conversion expenses.

Some states have reacted to the storm of protests launched by tenants who have been ousted as a result of apartment houses being transformed into condominiums. The resulting legislation has been primarily aimed at protection of the tenants.

EXAMPLE: Maryland law now provides that the conversion cannot be carried out unless the tenants are notified 180 days in advance. Anno. Code Md. RP § 11–102.1. This insures that the tenant has adequate time to find a new rental unit elsewhere. Virginia has enacted a statute setting forth certain requirements which a condominium converter must adhere to. These requirements include statements from the converter of any fees due from the purchasers on or before closing, a statement of expenditures made on repairs, maintenance, operation, or upkeep of the buildings within the last three years, the proposed budget of the condominium prorating the budget expenses on a per unit basis, a statement of provisions for reserves for capital expenditures, a statement of the present condition of all structural components and major utility installations in the structure, and a provision for notice to existing tenants. Code Va. § 55–79.94.

Municipalities have recognized the need for available rental units and the depletion of this inventory by conversion. They have responded to tenants' needs by adopting ordinances relating to conversion.

EXAMPLE: A suburb of Chicago has enacted a conversion ordinance which requires an elaborate inspection to determine compliance with codes in effect both at the time of original construction and at the time of conversion and notification to tenants.

There have been some attempts to "zone out" condominium conversions. In this way a municipality attempts to enforce a zoning ordinance to block a condominium conversion where the former structure was in compliance with the zoning ordinance. Some states have outlawed such ordinances.

NEW LAWS: Some states now provide that condominium conversions or condominiums in general must not be treated differently by any zoning or land use ordinance that would permit a physically identical project or development under a different form of ownership. Code Va. §§ 55–79.43. Thus, zoning which allows only multifamily or apartment structures may not be utilized to prevent the conversion of the apartment building to units of individual ownership. Conversions which do not conform to current land use and site plan regulations may be required to obtain special use permits or variances prior to becoming a condominium. Where the current zoning would require 1.5 parking spaces for every living unit if the condominium were to be newly constructed, the converter may be required to obtain a special use permit or variance.

§ 895. Suggestions in purchasing a new condominium:

1. It is necessary to determine that the condominium documents conform to the state law. If not, dangerous consequences ensue. For example, the tax assessor may refuse to give your apartment a separate tax assessment. Title companies insure compliance with local law.

2. Be sure that the structure conforms to local zoning ordinances and does not violate private restrictions such as those in a recorded plat or deed restrictions.

3. Determine whether the contract provisions giving the developer the right to cancel out if a stated percentage of apartments are not sold are likely to be invoked considering, in this case, the percentage already sold.

4. Check whether the burden of assessments for maintenance, and so forth, falls entirely on the apartments sold or is shared by the developer in proportion to the apartments remaining unsold and still owned by the development. In general, of course, the entire subject of assessments and the factors that make up the assessment level—maintenance costs, payroll expenses, cost of keeping up the recreational facilities, reserves, and so forth should be studied.

5. Check whether the voting rights of the sold apartments give the apartment purchasers at least a minority representation in the homeowners' association. For example, if a majority vote of the apartments in the building can elect a home association board of directors, the developer will have absolute control until a majority of the apartments are sold.

6. Check whether the documents require all purchasers to get their financing from a specified mortgage lender and, if so, what the lender's terms are likely to be.

7. Consider whether the prospective occupancy is such that the membership is likely to vote future assessments for maintenance and renovation in excess of your financial abilities as a purchaser.

8. The early contracts of sale for a condominium apartment will permit the developer to amend or modify the declaration but should not permit him to increase the buyer's assessments, or to increase the apartment cost, or to reduce the seller's obligation to pay the expenses on unsold apartments.

9. The contract of sale may state that the purchaser's rights are subordinate to the construction mortgage. This is necessary for the mortgagee's protection. *State Savings and Loan Association* v. *Kauaian Develop. Co.,* 445 P2d 108 (Ha. 1968).

10. Determine what is done with your deposit or earnest money. The most conservative approach is to require that it be held in escrow. Many buyers who did not protect themselves had their deposits lost when the developer got into financial difficulty. Recent legislation in some states requires the deposit of these funds into a separate escrow account. See Fla. Stat. Ann. § 711.25(1); Va. Code Ann. § 55-79.95.

11. What is the reputation of the management firm?

12. Determine the duration of the management contract (keeping in mind that long-term contracts may lock you into inefficient management).

13. How much authority is delegated to the manager by the association? Too much authority strips the unit owner of a voice in the running of the project.

14. Who does the hiring and firing of employees? If the board interferes, favoritism can creep in and efficient management becomes difficult.

15. Pay scales of employees should track with pay scales generally.

16. Has the board met regularly and have there been genuinely democratic elections so that no clique runs the operation? In this connection, check the by-laws for duration of the term of board members.

17. Check the present composition of the board, if possible. Lawyers and accountants, for example, are likely to do a better job in running the building than nonprofessionals.

18. Look at the physical attributes of the apartment. Do carpeting, draperies, furniture and other furnishings in the model go with the unit? Is the unit located near the noisy parts of the building, lobby, elevators, trash chute, and so forth?

19. What parking and storage space is allocated to the particular unit?

20. Determine whether the common elements include the recreation areas (swimming pool, tennis courts, and so forth) or whether they are excluded from the condominium, retained by the developer, and then leased to the association on a long-term basis.

REFERENCE: © Baird & Warner, What You Should Know About Condominium Ownership. Portions of check list reprinted by permission.

Unit purchasers should keep in mind that under modern law the seller of a new building warrants by implication the fitness of the building and that this rule applies to condominiums. *Gable* v. *Silver,* 258 So2d 11 (Fla. 1972).

§ 896. Assessments. As has been stated, the condo declaration creates personal liability on the unit owner plus a foreclosable lien for delinquent assessments. Both devices require court action and are clumsy and time-consuming. In some states, Illinois, for example, a unit owner can now be evicted like a delinquent tenant if he fails to pay his assessments.

§ 897. Liability for injuries—liability insurance. The condo owners are owners and occupants of the common elements. As such owners and occupants, they become liable for injuries sustained by third parties to the same extent as any other owner. This liability corresponds to the liability of a landlord for proper maintenance of facilities enjoyed in common by the tenants, such as common stairways. It is this rule that makes it important for the condo to have adequate and comprehensive liability insurance. Workmen's compensation, elevator liability insurance, and the like are also needed. Knight, Incorporation of Condominium Common Areas? An Alternative, 50 *N.C.L. Rev.* 1, 6 (1971). A closer question relates to the possible liability of the apartment association to a condo owner.

EXAMPLE: A, a condo owner, sustains injuries because of a negligently maintained common stairway. He sues the apartment association. By the modern rule, he will be allowed to recover his damages. *White* v. *Cox,* 95 Cal. Rptr. 265 (1971); Note, 25 *Vand. L. Rev.* 271 (1972). The theoretical legal problems are: (1) As a condo owner, A is, in effect, suing himself. (2) There are technical problems in suing an unincorporated association. In some states one or the other of these obstacles may prevent lawsuits of this nature.

§ 898. Condominium insurance. Insurance of the condominium is a problem that can be solved through coordination of efforts.

Each unit owner can obtain fire and other hazard insurances on his apartment and its share of the common elements. Note the problem in insuring a condo unit, which is a cube of air space. Should a loss occur, the damage to the common elements must be repaired as a single enterprise for the benefit of all owners. The *master policy* covers the common elements. The laws of some states require that the condominium board obtain insurance on both the common elements and the units. See *Ill. Rev. Stat.* ch. 30, § 312. It is extremely important that a dovetailing of coverage exist between the unit and master policies so that as far as any unit owners are concerned, the entire structure and range of risks are covered. This proper match of policies avoids a conflict or gap in coverage for such items as partitions, floor coverings, wall coverings, furniture, and fixtures. This problem can be avoided if the new standard form policies are used, and the association and unit owners purchase a package of coverage from the same broker who then tailors the unit owners' policies to meet individual needs.

The standardized master policies (MLB-29 through MLB-29D) provide coverage for the common elements, which, when properly used together with the unit owners' policy (HO-6), constitute the basis for a well-rounded insurance program. The HO-6 covers the amount of the interior of the unit not covered by the master policy, and personal liability coverage. Rohan, Reskin & Sanchisico, Recent Development in the Field of Insurance of Condominiums Project, 48 *St. John's L. Rev.* 1084 (1974). These master policies waive the subrogation rights of the insurer as against any unit owner.

EXAMPLE: A, the owner of unit 12, falls asleep while smoking. The resultant fire causes smoke and water damage to the hallways. The master policy insurer could pay the loss to the association and by virtue of subrogation rights proceed to recover for the loss as against A. The waiver of the subrogation right prevents this from happening. The loss is paid by the insurance company and the matter is over.

Many lawyers feel that losses to the common elements should be paid to the insurance trustee named in the condominium declaration. The trustee is then authorized by the declaration to *adjust* the loss, that is, to agree with the insurance company as to the amount of loss and be exclusively entitled to hire contractors to rebuild the common elements.

The HO-6 policy provides coverage for $1000 of unscheduled personal property, and $1000 of unit owner's additions and alterations (fixtures, installations, or additions comprising the part of the building within the unfinished interior surfaces of the perimeter walls, floors, and ceilings of the units). The coverages may be increased by a special endorsement which can be tailored to meet the individual needs of the unit owners.

EXAMPLE: One special endorsement will provide coverage of property (other than the unit) owned solely by the insured and located on the premises, for example, a cabana.

Obviously the developer, the association, and the unit owners are in need of the services of an insurance consultant experienced in insuring condominiums.

§ 899. Condominium—termination due to destruction of building. The situation where the building is destroyed by fire or other casualty varies from state to state. Where rebuilding takes place with adequate insurance funds, the problems are not excessively complex. Where, however, a percentage of the owners have the right to vote to sell the property and divide the proceeds, problems exist unless the state law spells out a program. This has been done in some states, for example, New York, Hawaii, Mississippi, Nevada, Illinois, and Missouri.

§ 900. Operational aspects—new condominiums. A number of steps must be taken to put a new condominium in operation. Among them are: (1) the election, in accordance with the by-laws, of a governing board by the unit owners; this usually takes place when about 75 percent of the units have been sold and occupied; (2) election of officers; (3) appointment of committees; (4) transfer of control from the developer to the newly elected board; (5) hiring of a new building manager, if it is desired to replace the developer's manager who has functioned from the date of first occupancy to the date the first board was organized; (6) review of insurance placed by developer; (7) review by the board of the completion of the building in accordance with plans and specifications; (8) adoption of rules governing swimming pools, pets, parking, and so forth. Hennessey, Practical Problems of Residential Condominium Operation, 2 *Conn.B.J.* 12 (1969).

After the completion of the building, normal operations include preparation of budgets by the Budget Committee, setting of assessments by the board, annual audits, approval of sales by unit owners, repair of building, etc. 2 *Conn. L. Rev.* 12. The common elements are operated and controlled by the board and the manager hired by the unit owners in accordance with the rules adopted by the unit owners. As a rule, no unit owner will be permitted to tinker with the common elements. *Sterling Village Condominium, Inc.* v. *Breitenbach,* 251 So2d 685 (Fla. 1971).

§ 901. Operational aspects—by-laws. The rules and regulations adopted by the association must be reasonable and related to the health, happiness, and enjoyment of the unit owners.

EXAMPLE: Each unit of a project had its own washing machine. The use of these machines in the various apartments caused water to back up into other apartments. The noise and vibrations from the use of the appliances annoyed other tenants. A rule prohibiting the use of the apartment machines was held valid. *Forest Park Cooperative, Inc.* v. *Hellman,* 152 NYS2d 685 (1956). A rule was also upheld that prohibited alcoholic beverages in clubhouse facilities. *Hidden Harbour Estates, Inc.* v. *Norman,* 309 So2d 180 (Fla. 1975). The Florida courts also upheld a rule that prohibited the leasing of an apartment unit more than once during a period of ownership. *Kroop* v. *Caravelle Condominium, Inc.,* 323 So2d 307 (Fla. 1975).

§ 902. **Operational aspects—management contracts.** It is essential to the success of a condominium and the happiness of its residents that the complex be properly managed. This is easier said than done. Unit owners themselves are generally incapable of managing a large complex. Capable managers are at a premium. Some developers have, while they retained control of the association and board of directors, entered into long-term management contracts with entities that they control, at terms very favorable to the management firm. These contracts are hard to break. 73 ALR3d 613.

NEW LAWS: Some states now limit the duration of condominium management contracts or allow the unit owners to review and ratify or cancel the contract if they find it oppressive. Fla. Stat. Ann. § 711.13(4).

These contracts may also run afoul of antitrust laws. *Miller* v. *Prandos,* 529 F.2d 393 (1976). The condominium declaration on a newly constructed building should provide that the management contract between the developer and the management firm will be assigned by the developer to the association at some point in time, usually when 75 percent of the units are sold.

The manager exercises important functions. He collects the monthly assessments of unit owners and payments due from concessions, such as for laundry services. He is the condominium bookkeeper and makes periodic reports to the board on receipts and expenditures. He does the ordinary work of a building manager, such as contracting for decorating, maintenance, water and utilities, hiring, firing, and paying building employees. He reports the income tax, pays the building's real estate taxes, maintains the building's bank account, and so forth. The manager also takes the "heat" when tough decisions must be made.

§ 903. **Title insurance requirements—purchase of old or new condominium covering the apartment and its share of the common elements.** A prudent purchaser of a condo apartment will demand a title insurance policy. Preferably it will contain specific coverage against mechanics' liens. It should also contain assurance that there are no delinquent condominium assessments, for such condominium assessments are, by law, a foreclosable lien on the apartment. In this connection, the management group furnishes the title company a certificate that all assessments have been paid, and the title company takes the risk of any inaccuracy in this certificate. The title company, in addition to making its usual search of the public records, also searches for assessment liens filed by the management group, for in some states these must be recorded. The title company also satisfies itself that the right of first refusal has been properly eliminated, and its policy insures the purchaser on this score. To supplement this coverage, the purchaser should demand a letter from the secretary of the condominium's board of directors that no unusual special assessments are in contemplation, for an apartment may go on the market because its owner wishes to avoid payment of a large assessment, for example, for automatic elevators.

In some areas it is commonly required by purchasers and mortgagees of condo units that the title company insure that the condominium complies with the local statute. By special request this assurance is procurable everywhere.

§ **904. Mortgages.** The condominium mortgage should provide that it is subject to the declaration; that the mortgagor's breach of any of the covenants of the declaration, or the failure to pay assessments as they come due are defaults under the mortgage giving rise to the mortgagees' right to accelerate; that the mortgagee may pay delinquent assessments, and add those sums to the mortgage debt; and that the mortgagor will not vote to amend the declaration without the mortgagee's consent.

FNMA, FHLMC, and FHA, covering, in effect, all first mortgages, require that the declaration provide for notice to the mortgagee of any defaults, to enable the agency to cure defaults and prevent foreclosure. The declaration must allow the mortgagee who acquires a unit by foreclosure to sell free from the right of first refusal and free from any assessments except those accruing after the mortgagee has taken possession. The declaration forbids, as to any mortgagee, any change in the shares of assessments, any change in common elements allocated to the mortgaged unit, or any partition or physical change in the unit or common elements.

When the FNMA/FHLMC uniform instrument is used in conjunction with the financing of a condominium unit, the Condominium Rider set out in the Appendix to this chapter is used. The Appendix also contains a rather well-drafted form of condominium mortgage.

§ **905. Sale of condominiums—mortgage aspects.** The sale of an existing condo unit is similar to the sale of a house, as far as mortgage financing is concerned. The contract of sale will be contingent on the buyer's ability to get mortgage financing, and describing it. When the mortgage financing has been procured, the title search is made; the deal is closed; the new mortgage is recorded; the old mortgage is paid off and released.

§ **906. Condominiums—regulation.** In some states the condominium declaration may constitute a subdivision, requiring approval of public authorities, as in the case of plat of subdivision. Condominiums and their marketing are now under close scrutiny at the local level. States, municipalities, and counties are adopting condominium laws and ordinances under their police powers to protect the health, safety, and well-being of local residents. Disclosure requirements are frequently a part of those laws. Comment, 123 *U. Penna. L. Rev.* 639 (1975).

EXAMPLE: A condominium development could be subject to disclosure type requirements of securities laws, Interstate Land Sales Act, state land sales laws, and local condominium ordinances. While some of these may be inapplicable where another law has substantially similar requirements, the paperwork can be an immense task.

§ **907. Securities law problems.** Many condominium developments are leisure-oriented projects in vacation areas. The unit purchaser intends to live in the unit for part of the year and hold the unit available for rent for the rest of the year. A managing agent is hired to rent out the various units. Taxpayers in high income brackets are attracted by the tax deductions for taxes, mortgage interest, maintenance charges, insurance, and depreciation. This form of operation, however, raises the specter that the development may be subject to both federal and state securities laws.

The Securities Exchange Commission has taken the position that the offering of a condominium must be in compliance with the registration and prospectus delivery requirements of the securities laws if any one of the following criteria are met:

1. The condominiums, with any rental arrangements or other similar service, are offered and sold with emphasis on the economic benefits to the purchaser to be derived from the managerial efforts of the promoter, or of a third party designated or arranged for by the promoter, from rental of the units.

2. The offering of participation in a rental pool arrangement. In a rental pool all rentals are collected by the manager and divided equally among owners of identical units.

3. The offering of a rental or similar arrangement whereby the purchaser must hold his unit available for rental for any part of the year, must use an exclusive rental agent, or is otherwise materially restricted in his occupancy or rental of his unit. Securities Act Release No. 5347 *CCH Fed. Sec. L. Rept.* Par. 79,163 (1973).

Registration requirements may also be mandated by state securities or *Blue-Sky* laws.

EXAMPLE: An agreement for the sale of one of six units in a condominium project requires that the buyer enter into an exclusive management and rental agreement. Personal use of the unit was limited, in that the time for use had to be reserved far in advance; the owner had to maintain his unit in a rentable condition and had to pay a flat monthly fee for promotional activities to stimulate rentals. Promotional materials emphasized the investment rather than the residential aspects of ownership. The court relied upon the authorities based upon the federal securities law to find a violation of state law. *Lowery* v. *Ford Hill Investment Co.*, 556 P2d 1201 (Col. 1976).

Not all rental arrangements fall under the securities laws, such as when the units are not sold with an emphasis on the economic benefits befalling the purchaser from the managerial efforts of others. A unit buyer may enter into a *nonpool* rental arrangement with an agent who is not designated or required to be used as a condition of purchase. This result follows whether or not the rental agent is affiliated with the developer.

EXAMPLE: *D*, a developer, offers condominium units in an ocean-front high-rise building. The sales emphasis is on the resort aspects of the development, and not on appreciation and return on investment caused by the developer's affiliate real estate management company's activity. In fact, no rental pool agreement is part of the package. *D* does, however, have a local real estate corporation which will, if asked, attempt to rent individual units for periods specified by the owners. No rental pool arrangement is available. No securities law registration is required. *See generally, Joyce* v. *Richie Tower Properties*, 417 Fed. Supp. 53 (1976).

REFERENCE: Burnman and Stone, Federal Securities Law and the Sale of Condominiums, Homes and Homesites, 30 *Business Lawyer*, 411 (1975); Rohan and Reskin, Condominium Law and Practice, Chapter 18.

§ 908. **Time-sharing condominiums.** In a recreational setting, the use of condominiums is not generally year-round. Equating the need for part-time use with a purchaser's desire to spend less but at the same time get the benefits of present condominium ownership is the time-sharing condominium concept. This device enables the buyer to use "his" unit for a given segment of the year with other owners having the use of the unit for other year segments.

EXAMPLE: Mid-rise and high-rise buildings are constructed at a seaside golf and tennis resort. The units are submitted to the condominium form of ownership. The units as a whole are not marketed but rather one twenty-sixth ownership interests in the units are sold to many buyers, entitling the buyers to use the property for a specified portion of the year.

There are three basic forms of this type of ownership. In a *Tenancy in Common* format, purchasers are granted an undivided interest in the unit, the interest reflecting the percentage of the year that the owner anticipates using the property. The purchasers also agree to use specific time periods. In an *Interval Ownership* situation, purchasers are granted an estate for years for the agreed time period of each year. Upon the termination of this revolving estate for years (a period that corresponds with the expected useful life of the project), all the owners become tenants in common of the whole. Thirdly, under a *Vacation License,* the developer retains ownership and agrees to allow the "buyers" to use the premises for a stated period each year for a given number of years.

§ 909. **Time-sharing condominiums—declaration.** The declaration for the time-sharing condominiums must address itself to the following special matters:

1. Use and service periods with relevant undivided interests in the common elements.
2. Exclusive right to use, and occupancy of each of the time-sharing owners for their relevant periods.
3. Collection and payment of costs such as telephone charges, firewood, repairs attributable to any owner's use, and common costs.
4. Waiver of right to partition.

REFERENCE: Merritt & Cowan, Time-Sharing Ownership of Vacation Residences, 1 #4 *ALI-ABA Course Materials J.* 89 (1977).

§ 910. **Advantages and disadvantages of condominium ownership.** The advantages of the condo as compared with the co-op are these:

1. The condo owner has his own mortgage covering only his apartment and his share of the common elements. The advantage to him, as against co-op ownership, is very great. Under the co-op form, if any substantial number of tenants get into financial difficulty, as happens during an economic depression, the blanket mortgage covering the entire building could go into default, and the resulting foreclosure would wipe out all the tenants.

2. The advantages the condo enjoys with respect to mortgage financing should make the condo easier to sell or resell than a co-op, since it enlarges the number of potential buyers.

EXAMPLE: *A* owns a condo apartment which he can sell to *B* for $30,000. *B* can obtain a mortgage loan of approximately $24,000, so that he needs only $6,000. *A*'s existing mortgage, whatever its amount, would be paid off in the process, just as if *A* were selling a house. If *A* were selling a co-op in a comparable building on which the building mortgage had been paid down to 50 percent of the property value, *A* would be selling his apartment equity for $15,000 subject to the building mortgage, and he would have to find a buyer who has $15,000 in cash, for lenders do not lend on co-ops.

3. Again, if a person desires a debt-free shelter, as many senior citizens do, a condo purchaser can pay cash for his apartment, as many purchasers do. A co-op purchaser has no choice but to accept his apartment subject to the mortgage on the building.

4. Co-op leases provide that the lease may be terminated for failure to meet a monthly assessment or because the apartment owner has become bankrupt or been guilty of objectionable conduct. The condo owner is more secure in this regard.

5. Like the mortgage, the tax assessment is an individual assessment on the unit and its share of the common elements. As long as this tax is paid, failure of some of the other unit owners to pay their taxes does not affect a unit that is not delinquent.

6. In a co-op, work and materials ordered by one tenant can result in a mechanic's lien against the entire building. In a condo, the lien is confined to the apartment where the work was done.

The advantages a co-op enjoys over a condo are these:

1. In a co-op, the apartment owner has the right to leave. If he has bad luck and cannot keep up his monthly payments, he can sublease his apartment, sell it, or at the worst, give it back to the landlord corporation. The modern co-op lease gives the lessee the right to cancel the lease after a specified number of years by surrendering his stock and his lease to the landlord corporation. In the condominium the owner, having signed a note and mortgage, has no right simply to "walk away." In case of default and foreclosure, there is always the possibility of a deficiency judgment.

2. Another advantage that the co-op possesses is the ease with which one can control the type of neighbors one will have in the building. In the co-op, the lease provides that it cannot be assigned or subleased except with the written consent of the landlord corporation. The stock certificate provides that it can be transferred only in connection with an authorized transfer of the lease. This method has the advantage of simplicity and unquestioned legality. *68 Beacon St.* v. *Sohier,* 194 NE 303 (Mass. 1935); *Weisner* v. *791 Park Ave. Corp.,* 160 NE2d 720 (N.Y. 1959). Probably these restrictions must be exercised "reasonably." For example, a refusal of consent based solely on racial grounds would not stand up in court. In the condominium method, the situation is more complicated. Typically, each owner of a condominium apartment holds his apartment subject to a right of first refusal should he desire to sell. Such a right of first refusal is probably valid. *Gale* v. *York Center Community Co-operative, Inc.,* 171 NE2d 30 (Ill. 1961). However, the method is clumsy. Also, since it calls for the apartment owners to buy the apartment at the price the selling apartment owner can obtain from an outsider, it requires a special assessment on the apartment owners.

3. Getting rid of a co-op owner who defaults in his monthly payments or fails to abide by the by-laws is easier in the co-op than in the condo. Just as an ordinary lease

can be terminated for default in rent or breach of covenant, so also a co-op lease can be terminated for like grounds and the co-op lessee evicted by quick and inexpensive forcible detainer proceedings. *Green v. Greenbelt Homes, Inc.*, 194 A2d 273 (Md. 1963). In a condo, if a particular apartment owner fails to pay his monthly assessments, a lien on his apartment can be foreclosed, just as a mortgage is foreclosed, but the proceeding is costly and time-consuming. Making the condo owner behave, when his conduct becomes objectionable, is difficult.

4. The condo, since it is owned by many people, not by a single corporation as in the case of the co-op, has no feasible way of putting a mortgage on the building in its later years when remodeling or repairs are needed. A few states have laws covering this point.

5. Where for one reason or another it becomes advisable to sell the building and the tenants wish to do so, this can be accomplished in co-ops by a vote of a percentage of the shareholders (who, of course, are the tenants). A two-thirds vote usually suffices. In the case of a condo, sale of the building is apt to require a unanimous vote, except in certain special situations, as where the building is destroyed by fire.

In both co-ops and condominiums the apartment owner enjoys the benefits of ownership. As the value of the building goes up and the mortgage is reduced by payment, his equity increases.

Both the condo owner and the co-op owner have the right to defer payment of income tax on a capital gain where the apartment is sold at a profit. Both have the same right to deduct from income for income tax purposes all payments made on mortgage interest and real estate taxes.

Both the co-op and the condo are entitled to FHA insurance. Both types of apartments are usually run by a manager selected by the co-op or condo board.

RESERVED: §§ 911–921.

CONDOMINIUM RIDER

THIS CONDOMINIUM RIDER is made this .... day of ...., 19...., and is incorporated into and shall be deemed to amend and supplement a Mortgage, Deed of Trust or Deed to Secure Debt (herein "security instrument") dated of even date herewith, given by the undersigned (herein "Borrower") to secure Borrower's Note to ....
.... (herein "Lender") and covering the Property described in the security instrument and located at ....
(Property Address)

The Property comprises a unit in, together with an undivided interest in the common elements of, a condominium project known as ....
(Name of Condominium Project)
.... (herein "Condominium Project").

CONDOMINIUM COVENANTS. In addition to the covenants and agreements made in the security instrument, Borrower and Lender further covenant and agree as follows:

A. Assessments. Borrower shall promptly pay, when due, all assessments imposed by the Owners Association or other governing body of the Condominium Project (herein "Owners Association") pursuant to the provisions of the declaration, by-laws, code of regulations or other constituent document of the Condominium Project.

B. Hazard Insurance. So long as the Owners Association maintains a "master" or "blanket" policy on the Condominium Project which provides insurance coverage against fire, hazards included within the term "extended coverage," and such other hazards as Lender may require, and in such amounts and for such periods as Lender may require, then:

(i) Lender waives the provision in Uniform Covenant 2 for the monthly payment to Lender of one-twelfth of the premium installments for hazard insurance on the Property;

(ii) Borrower's obligation under Uniform Covenant 5 to maintain hazard insurance coverage on the Property is deemed satisfied; and

(iii) the provisions in Uniform Covenant 5 regarding application of hazard insurance proceeds shall be superseded by any provisions of the declaration, by-laws, code of regulations or other constituent document of the Condominium Project or of applicable law to the extent necessary to avoid a conflict between such provisions and the provisions of Uniform Covenant 5. For any period of time during which such hazard insurance coverage is not maintained, the immediately preceding sentence shall be deemed to have no force or effect. Borrower shall give Lender prompt notice of any lapse in such hazard insurance coverage.

In the event of a distribution of hazard insurance proceeds in lieu of restoration or repair following a loss to the Property, whether to the unit or to common elements, any such proceeds payable to Borrower are hereby assigned and shall be paid to Lender for application to the sums secured by the security instrument, with the excess, if any, paid to Borrower.

C. Lender's Prior Consent. Borrower shall not, except after notice to Lender and with Lender's prior written consent, partition or subdivide the Property or consent to:

(i) the abandonment or termination of the Condominium Project, except for abandonment or termination provided by law in the case of substantial destruction by fire or other casualty or in the case of a taking by condemnation or eminent domain;

(ii) any material amendment to the declaration, by-laws or code of regulations of the Owners Association, or equivalent constituent document of the Condominium Project, including, but not limited to, any amendment which would change the percentage interests of the unit owners in the Condominium Project; or

(iii) the effectuation of any decision by the Owners Association to terminate professional management and assume self-management of the Condominium Project.

D. Remedies. If Borrower breaches Borrower's covenants and agreements hereunder, including the covenant to pay when due condominium assessments, then Lender may invoke any remedies provided under the security instrument, including, but not limited to, those provided under Uniform Covenant 7.

IN WITNESS WHEREOF, Borrower has executed this Condominium Rider.

________________________________ —Borrower

________________________________ —Borrower

CONDOMINIUM RIDER—1 to 4 Family—6/75—FNMA/FHLMC UNIFORM INSTRUMENT

CONDOMINIUM DEED OF TRUST
WITH ASSIGNMENT OF RENTS

This Deed of Trust, made this .... day of ....
19......................., between ....
....
hereinafter referred to as, the Trustor, ...
....
hereinafter referred to as, the Trustee, and THE EQUITABLE LIFE ASSURANCE SOCIETY OF THE UNITED STATES, a corporation duly organized and existing under the laws of the State of New York, having its principal office at 1285 Avenue of the Americas, New York, N.Y. 10019, hereinafter referred to as, the Beneficiary,

WITNESSETH: That the Trustor grants, transfers and assigns to the Trustee in trust, with power of sale, that real property in City of .... County of .... and State of .... (said State being hereinafter referred to as, the "State") described as follows:

which described real property does not exceed 3 acres.

AND ALSO, all the estate and interest, homestead or other claim, as well in law as in equity, which the Trustor now has or may hereafter acquire in and to the real property, including but not by way of limitation, the percentage of common elements constituting a part thereof, together with all easements and rights of way used in connection therewith or as a means of access thereto; and all and singular the tenements, hereditaments and appurtenances thereof, including all fixtures and articles of personal property now or at any time hereafter attached to or used in any way in connection with the use, operation and occupation of the real property, and any and all buildings and improvements now or hereafter erected thereon, all of which collectively hereinafter shall be referred to as, the premises. The fixtures and articles of personal property shall include but without being limited to, all window shades, inlaid floor coverings, wall beds, washing machines, dryers, dishwashers, disposals, stoves, ranges, ovens, refrigerators, radiators, and all heating, lighting, plumbing, gas, electric, ventilating, refrigerating, air-conditioning and incinerating fixtures and equipment of whatsoever kind and nature, except household furniture not specifically enumerated herein, and are hereby declared and shall be deemed to be fixtures and accessory to the freehold and a part of the premises as between the parties hereto, their heirs, legatees, devisees, executors, administrators, successors and assigns, and all persons claiming by, through or under them.

AND ALSO, all of the rents, issues and profits of the premises, SUBJECT, HOWEVER, to the right, power and authority hereinafter given to and conferred upon the Beneficiary to collect and apply such rents, issues, and profits.

FOR THE PURPOSE OF SECURING:

ONE: The payment of an indebtedness in the principal sum of ....
.... Dollars ($.........................) with interest thereon according to the terms of a certain Note of even date hereinafter referred to as, the Note, which by reference is hereby made a part hereof, executed by the Trustor, delivered to the Beneficiary and payable to its order, and any and all extensions or renewals thereof.

TWO: The payment of all other sums with interest thereon becoming due or payable under the provisions hereof to either the Trustee or the Beneficiary.

THREE: The performance and discharge of each and every obligation, covenant and agreement of the Trustor herein contained.

To HAVE AND TO HOLD the premises upon the following express trusts, to wit:

A. TO PROTECT THE SECURITY OF THIS DEED OF TRUST THE TRUSTOR AGREES:

1. To keep the premises in good condition and repair; not to remove or demolish any building or improvement erected thereon; to complete or restore promptly and in good and workmanlike manner any building or improvement which may be constructed, damaged or destroyed thereon, and to pay when due all claims for labor performed and materials furnished therefor; not to suffer any lien of mechanics or material men to attach to the premises; to comply with all laws affecting the premises or requiring any alterations or improvements to be made thereon; not to commit, suffer or permit waste thereof, or any act upon the premises in violation of law or of any covenants, conditions or restrictions affecting the premises; to cultivate, irrigate, fertilize, fumigate, prune and do all other acts which from the character or use of the premises may be reasonably necessary, the specific enumerations herein not excluding the general.

2. To promptly, upon receipt thereof, deliver to the Beneficiary a true copy of every notice of default received by the Trustor with regard to any obligation of the Trustor under the provisions of the Condominium Act of the State, (the "Condominium Act"); the Declaration of Condominium (the "Declaration"); the Rules and Regulations (the "Rules and Regulations"); or the By-Laws (the "By-Laws") adopted by any organization or corporation created to facilitate the administration and operation of the Condominium of which the premises form a part (the "Association").

3. To keep and perform all covenants, agreements and provisions in the Declaration, By-Laws and Rules and Regulations on the part of the Trustor to be kept and performed, and failure of the Trustor so to do within a period of thirty (30) days after notice from the Association or from the Trustee or Beneficiary, or in the case of such default which cannot with due diligence be cured or remedied within such thirty (30) day period, if Trustor fails to proceed promptly after such notice to cure and remedy the same with due diligence, such failure shall constitute a default hereunder.

4. That if any action or proceeding be commenced either at law or in equity purporting to affect the security hereof (except an action to foreclose this Deed of Trust or to collect the debt secured thereby), to which action or proceeding the Beneficiary of this Deed of Trust is made a party, or in which it becomes necessary to defend or uphold the lien of this Deed of Trust, or in which it may be necessary or proper to prove the amount of the indebtedness, the Beneficiary may appear in or defend any such action or proceeding; and in any such event, the Beneficiary may be allowed and pair; and the Trustor hereby agrees to pay all costs, charges, disbursements and fees, including the cost of evidence of title, as well as reasonable attorneys' fees, incurred in any such action or proceeding in which the Beneficiary may appear; and all such sums and the interest thereon, at the highest rate permitted by applicable law, shall be a lien on the premises, prior to any right or title to, interest in or claim upon the premises, attaching or accruing subsequent to the lien of this Deed of Trust, and shall be deemed to be secured by this Deed of Trust and by the Note which it secures. In any action or proceeding to foreclose this Deed of Trust, or to recover or collect the debt secured thereby, the provisions of law respecting the recovery of costs, disbursements and allowances shall prevail unaffected by this covenant.

5. To pay as the same become due and payable; All taxes and assessments affecting the premises, including assessments to appurtenant water stock; all taxes upon the debt secured hereby; all incumbrances, charges and liens, with interest, on the premises or any part thereof, which appear to be prior or superior hereto, and all costs, fees and expenses of this Trust, and to deposit with the Beneficiary, all receipts or other satisfactory evidence of the payment of taxes, assessments, charges, claims and liens of every nature affecting or which may affect the premises or any part thereof; also for any statement regarding the indebtedness secured hereby, any amount demanded by the Beneficiary not to exceed the maximum allowed by law at the time such request is made.

6. That should the Trustor fail to make any payment or to do any act as herein, or in the Declaration or By-Laws, provided, then the Beneficiary or the Trustee, but without obligation to do so and without notice to or demand upon the Trustor and without releasing the Trustor from any obligations hereof, may: Make or do the same in such manner and to such extent as either may deem necessary to protect the security hereof, including specifically, without limiting their general powers, the right to pay any and all rents, taxes and assessments affecting the premises, including, but not by way of limitation, all payments to the maintenance and reserve funds and all assessments as required by the Declaration or By-Laws or any resolution adopted by the Association pursuant to either thereof and including assessments on appurtenant water stock and taxes upon the debt secured hereby, as the same become due and payable, and, also, the right to make additions, alterations, repairs and improvements to the premises which they or either of them may consider necessary or proper to keep the premises in good condition and repair, the Beneficiary or the Trustee being authorized to enter the premises for such purposes; pay, purchase, contest or compromise any encumbrance, charge or lien which in the judgment of either appears to be prior or superior hereto; and, in exercising any such powers, pay, necessary expenses, employ counsel and pay his reasonable fees.

7. The Trustor shall not, except with the prior written constent of the Beneficiary: (a) institute any action or proceeding for partition of the property of which the premises are a part; (b) vote for or consent to any modification of, amendment to or relaxation in the enforcement of any provision of the Declaration or By-Laws; and (c) in the event of damage to or destruction of the property of which the premises are a part, vote in opposition to a motion to repair, restore or rebuild.

8. To pay immediately and without demand all sums so expended by the Beneficiary or the Trustee, pursuant to Clause A.6. above, with interest from date of expenditure at the highest rate permitted by applicable law.

B. IT IS MUTUALLY AGREED THAT:

1. The Association will at all times, while any of the indebtedness secured hereby remains unpaid, keep or cause to be kept insured the units (including the premises) and the common elements, now or hereafter constituting the condominium project, of which the premises form a part, against such hazards and in such amounts, in such form or forms of policies and with such endorsements thereon, all as specified in the Declaration and By-Laws, and in companies selected by the Association, authorized to do business in the State, and will pay or cause to be paid the premiums thereon at the time and place the same are payable, and, at the option of the Beneficiary, will deposit true copies of such policies and renewals thereof with the Beneficiary. In the event the Association or the Trustor fails or refuses to provide the said insurance coverage, and the evidence thereof, as above required, the Beneficiary or the Trustee, but with obligation to do so, and at the expense of the Trustor, may take out fire insurance with extended coverage, vandalism and malicious mischief endorsements, covering the premises for its benefit as Beneficiary, and may add the premium therefor to the unpaid balance of the indebtedness secured hereby. All casualty insurance policies shall have a Standard Mortgage Clause attached, modified to provide that the insurance proceeds shall be payable to the Association or to an Insurance Trustee, as provided by the Declaration, and such insurance policies shall provide that they shall not be cancelled without at least 10 days prior written notice to the Beneficiary. In the event of loss or damage to the units or the common elements or any part thereof, the

Trustor will give immediate written notice to the Beneficiary, who may make proof of loss if not made promptly by the Association. The proceeds of any such insurance shall be applied, subject to and in pursuance of the provisions of the Declaration and By-Laws, on account of the cost of rebuilding or repairing the units and common elements damaged or destroyed, provided the proceeds of insurance collectible by the Association or the Insurance Trustee are sufficient to pay for such rebuilding or repairing, or, if insufficient, the deficiency is furnished by the unit owners, otherwise, or in the event the unit owners elect not to restore the damaged property, such insurance proceeds, to the extent payable to the Beneficiary and the Trustor, shall be applied to the indebtedness secured hereby. If the Trustor shall procure any other insurance of the kind herein described, the same, even though not required hereunder to be carried by the Trustor, shall be made payable to and claimable only by the Beneficiary and, whether so made payable or not, may be recovered by the Beneficiary in any appropriate proceedings and shall be similarly applied. In the event of foreclosure of this Trust Deed or other transfer of title to the premises in extinguishment of the debt secured hereby, all right, title and interest of the Trustor in and to any insurance policies then in force shall pass to the purchaser or assignee. The Trustor or the Association is free to procure the required insurance from any insurance company authorized to do business in the State.

2. Any award for damages now or hereafter made in connection with any condemnation of the units (including the premises) or the common elements or any part thereof now or hereafter constituting the Condominium project, of which the premises form a part, for public use and any award or damages arising from any cause of action for injury or damages to the said units or the common elements, whether or not the Trustor shall be in default hereunder, is hereby assigned and shall be paid to the Beneficiary and applied by the Beneficiary upon any indebtedness secured hereby in such order as Beneficiary may determine, subject, however, to the prior right of the Association or the Insurance Trustee to receive and use such award for the restoration of the said units or the common elements pursuant to the Declaration and By-Laws. The Trustor agrees to execute such further assignments of any such awards or damages as the Beneficiary may require.

3. By accepting payment of any sums secured hereby after its due date, the Beneficiary does not waive its right either to require prompt payment, when due, of all other sums so secured or to declare default for failure so to pay.

4. Without affecting the liability of any person, including the Trustor, for the payment of any indebtedness secured hereby or the lien of this Deed of Trust upon the premises for the full amount of the indebtedness then remaining unpaid (other than any person or property specifically released by the Beneficiary), the Beneficiary may, at any time, or from time to time and without notice do any one or more of the following: Release any person now or hereafter liable for payment of such indebtedness or any part thereof; extend the time or otherwise alter the terms of payment of any indebtedness; accept additional security therefor of any kind; or substitute or release any property securing such indebtedness.

5. At any time or from time to time, without liability therefor and without notice, upon written request of the Beneficiary and presentation of this Deed of Trust and the Note for endorsement, and without affecting the personal liability of any person for payment of the indebtedness secured hereby, the Trustee may: Reconvey any part of the premises; consent to the making of any map or plat thereof; join in granting any easement thereon; or join in any extension agreement or any agreement subordinating the lien or charge hereof.

6. Upon written request of the Beneficiary stating that all sums secured hereby have been paid, and upon surrender of this Deed of Trust and the Note to the Trustee for cancellation and retention and upon payment of its fees, the Trustee shall reconvey, without warranty, the premises then held hereunder. The recitals in such reconveyance of any matters or facts shall be conclusive proof of the truthfulness thereof. The grantee in such reconveyance may be described as "the person or persons legally entitled thereto."

7. As additional security for the indebtedness secured hereby and for the performance of all other obligations of the Trustor hereunder, the Trustor hereby gives to and confers upon the Beneficiary the right, power and authority, during the continuance of these Trusts, to collect the rents, issues and profits of and otherwise deal with the premises, as hereinafter in this paragraph provided, reserving to the Trustor the right, prior to any default by the Trustor in the payment of any indebtedness secured hereby or in the performance of any agreement hereunder, to collect and retain such rents, issues and profits as they become due and payable. Upon or at any time after any default, the Beneficiary, at its option, without notice, and irrespective of whether Declaration of Default has been delivered to the Trustee and without regard to the adequacy of security for the indebtedness hereby secured, either in person or by agent with or without bringing any action or proceeding, or by a receiver to be appointed by a court, may enter upon, take possession of, manage and operate the premises, or any part thereof; make, cancel, enforce or modify leases; obtain and evict tenants, and fix or modify rents and do any acts which the Beneficiary deems proper to protect the security hereof, and either with or without taking possession of the premises, in its own name, sue for or otherwise collect and receive such rents, issues and profits, including those past due and unpaid, and apply the same, less costs and expenses of operations and collection, including reasonable attorney's fees, upon any indebtedness secured hereby, and in such order as the Beneficiary may determine. The entering upon and taking possession of the premises, the collection of such rents, issues and profits and the application thereof as aforesaid, shall not cure or waive any default or notice of default hereunder or invalidate any act done pursuant to such notice.

8. In the event of the passage, after the date of this Deed of Trust, of any laws of the State, deducting from the value of the premises for the purpose of taxation any lien or charge thereon, or changing in any way the laws for the taxation of deeds of trust, or debts secured by deeds of trust, for state or local purposes, or the manner of the collection of any such taxes, so as to affect this Deed of Trust, the Beneficiary at its option may, at any time after the expiration of 30 days from and after the effective date of any such law, declare all sums secured hereby immediately due and payable by the execution and delivery to the Trustee of a written declaration of default and demand for sale, whereupon all sums secured hereby shall become and be immediately due and payable.

9. Upon default by the Trustor in the payment of any indebtedness secured hereby or in the performance of any agreement hereunder, or upon failure of the Association to maintain fire and extended coverage insurance as above required, or upon failure of the Association to keep the common elements in good condition and repair, the Beneficiary may declare all sums secured hereby immediately due and payable by delivery to the Trustee of a written declaration of default and demand for sale, and the Trustee or the Beneficiary shall thereafter file or cause to be filed for record a notice of such default and of election to cause the premises to be sold. The Beneficiary also shall deposit with the Trustee this Deed of Trust, the Note and all documents evidencing expenditure secured hereby.

Notice of sale having been given as then required by law and 3 months having elapsed after recordation of such notice of default, the Trustee, without demand on the Trustor, shall sell the premises at the time and place of sale fixed by it in the notice of sale, either as a whole or in separate parcels and in such order as it may determine, at public auction to the highest bidder for each in lawful money of the United States, payable at the time of sale. The Trustee may postpone the sale of the premises by public announcement at such time and place of sale, and from time to time thereafter may postpone such sale by public announcement at the time fixed by the preceding postponement. The Trustee shall deliver to such purchaser its Deed conveying the premises so sold, but without any covenant or warranty, express or implied. The recitals in such Deed of any matters or facts shall be conclusive proof of the truthfulness thereof. Any person, including the Trustor, the Trustee or the Beneficiary as hereinafter defined, may purchase the premises at such sale.

After deducting all costs, fees and expenses of the Trustee and of this Deed of Trust, including the the cost of evidence of title in connection with the sale, the Trustee shall apply the proceeds of the sale to the payment of: All sums expended under the terms hereof, not then repaid, with accrued interest at the highest rate permitted by applicable law; all other sums then secured hereby, and the remainder, if any, to the person or persons legally entitled thereto.

10. In the event of any default hereunder, the provisions contained in the foregoing subparagraph B.7. and B.9. shall not be construed to preclude the Trustee or the Beneficiary from enforcing any appropriate remedy against the Trustor, or from proceeding by suit to foreclose, or by suits at law or in equity to enforce payment of all sums secured hereby as the Beneficiary may elect or as the Trustee may be advised.

11. The Beneficiary may at any time or from time to time substitute in such manner as may be provided by law a successor or successors to any Trustee named herein or acting hereunder, which successor-Trustee shall thereupon succeed, without conveyance from the Trustee-predecessor, to all of its powers, duties, authority and title; or in the event of the absence of any such law providing for the substitution of trustees in deeds of trust, the Beneficiary may, with like effect, make such substitution from time to time by instrument in writing executed and acknowledged by the Beneficiary and recorded in the office of the Recorder of the county or counties in which the premises are situated. Said instrument shall contain the date of the execution of this Deed of Trust, the name of the original Trustor, the Trustee and the Beneficiary, the book and page where this Deed of Trust is recorded, and the name of the new Trustee.

12. Except insofar as now or hereafter prohibited by law the right to plead, use, or assert any statute of limitations as a plea of defense or bar of any kind, or for any purpose, to any debt, demand, or obligation secured or to be secured hereby, or to any complaint or other pleading or proceeding filed, instituted, or maintained for the purpose of enforcing this Deed of Trust, or any rights thereunder, is hereby waived.

13. The invalidity of any one or more covenants, phrases, clauses, sentences or paragraphs of this Deed of Trust shall not affect the remaining portions or any part thereof, and this Deed of Trust shall be construed as if such invalid covenants, phrases, clauses, sentences or paragraphs, if any, had not been inserted herein.

14. The trusts hereby created shall be irrevocable by the Trustor.

15. This Deed of Trust applies to, innures to the benefit of, and binds all parties hereto, their heirs, legatees, devisees, executors, administrators, successors and assigns. The term, Beneficiary, means the original Beneficiary hereunder or any future owner and holder, including pledges, of the Note secured hereby. In this Deed of Trust, whenever the context so requires, the masculine gender includes the feminine and or neuter, and the singular number includes the plural. All obligations of each Trustor hereunder are joint and several.

16. If the State is a "community property" state and if this Deed of Trust and the Note are executed by a married woman, and if such Deed of Trust describes any community property of such married woman and her husband, and if all sums secured by this Deed of Trust are not paid in full out of the proceeds of the Trustee's sale, or otherwise, such undersigned married woman hereby assents to the liability of her separate property for any unpaid balance of all sums secured by this Deed of Trust, subject, however, to any limitation or restriction now provided by law upon the recovery of a deficiency judgment following a sale under a purchase money deed of trust, and upon the further express condition that such assent shall not be deemed to create a present or any lien, charge, or obligation upon such separate property, and that such property can be resorted to in satisfaction of such unpaid balance only by attachment, execution or other legal process.

17. The Trustee accepts this Deed of Trust, duly executed and acknowledged, when it is made a public record as provided by law. The Trustee is not obligated to notify any party hereto of pending sale under any other deed of trust or of any action or proceeding in which the Trustor, the Beneficiary or the Trustee shall be a party unless brought by the Trustee.

18. The Beneficiary may release for such consideration, or none, as it may require, any portion of the premises without, as to the remainder of the security, in anywise impairing or affecting the lien and priorities herein provided for the Beneficiary or improving the position of any subordinate lienholder.

19. Provided, however, that upon the payment of the indebtedness secured hereby and the performance of all the covenants and conditions contained herein and in the Note, the Beneficiary will execute and deliver to the Trustor a request to the Trustee to reconvey the premises to the Trustor. It is understood, however, that all recording and other expenses incurred in effecting such reconveyance shall be borne by the Trustor.

C. THE INSERTION BY THE TRUSTOR of his mailing address opposite his signature hereto shall be deemed to be a request by the Trustor that a copy of any notice of default and of any notice of sale hereunder be mailed to him at such address as provided by law.

MAILING ADDRESS FOR NOTICES			SIGNATURE OF TRUSTOR
Street and Number	City	State	
....	....	....	....
....	....	....	....
....	....	....	....
....	....	....	....

31

Planned Unit Developments

§ 922. **The planned unit idea.** The *planned unit development* (hereafter referred to as PUD) is one of the newer ideas in housing. Such developments consist of town houses, homes, apartments (both garden and high-rise), or combinations of such buildings, all with common open areas and some with private recreation facilities. The advantages offered are:

1. Lower priced homes achieved by cost savings through more efficient land use and planning.
2. Small, private yards with a minimum of maintenance chores and a maximum of time and energy for recreational activities in the common areas.
3. Common areas of green open space providing an attractive setting.
4. In some cases, shared facilities for swimming, golf, fishing, etc., and a recreation center for crafts, meetings, and other group activities.
5. Maintenance furnished by homeowners' association.

§ 923. **Cluster housing.** The phrase *cluster housing* means that the individual homes, row houses, or apartment buildings are grouped together on relatively small plots of land with large surrounding areas of land left open for common recreational and park developments. The cluster form of development is economical because the clustering of houses reduces the cost of supplying utilities and roads.

§ 924. **Home association described.** An important feature of most planned unit developments is the home association, which is vested with control of the common areas.

A home association is a nonprofit corporation operating under documents through which (1) each homeowner is automatically a member, with voting rights usually allocated at one vote per family unit, and (2) each homesite is automatically subject to a charge for a proportionate share of the expenses for the home association's activities, such as common property maintenance. Outdoor lighting, street maintenance, furnishing water, landscape maintenance, garbage and trash collection, security services, and exterior maintenance of individual home properties are among the services a home association may undertake.

§ 925. Outline of legal steps to take in creating a PUD. The PUD documents should:

1. Legally create an automatic-membership, nonprofit corporation with voting rights in each family unit.
2. Include a contract by the developer to convey ownership of the common areas to the home association within a reasonable, definite time.
3. Appropriately restrict the uses of the home lots and common areas.
4. Grant each lot owner easements for the use and enjoyment of the common property.
5. Create a lien on each home lot for assessments which will (a) assure sufficient funds for maintenance of the common areas but (b) provide adequate safeguards for the lot owners against undesirably high charges.
6. Include covenants by the home association to operate and maintain the common areas.

Before the first lot is sold, the land developer incorporates the nonprofit home association, and records the land subdivision plat and declaration of covenants and easements for all of the land in the planned unit. His plat identifies (1) property to be transferred to public agencies, such as any proposed public streets, (2) the individual homesites, (3) the common areas to be transferred by the developer to the home association, and (4) any other parcels, such as a church site or shopping center, to be kept by the developer or transferred to others.

Recorded contemporaneously with the plat is a *declaration of easements, covenants, restrictions, and liens.* It is hereafter referred to as the *declaration.*

§ 926. Common areas—plat provisions. Since it is imperative that the common areas be kept in the ownership of the home association and not dedicated to the public, the recorded plat must bear on its face a legend relative to all the common areas indicating that the area is *not* dedicated to the public and that its ownership is reserved to the developer (who later will deed it to the association). If such a legend is lacking, courts may hold that any area having the appearance of common ground is, by implication, dedicated to the public. However, since the home buyers will want the developer to deed the land to the home association, an agreement to do so should be contained in the plat or in the accompanying declaration or in a separate contract. Also, appropriate language must be incorporated in the text of the plat to indicate that the individual homeowners take easements in the common properties but no ownership therein. This means that the legend on the plat should be quite comprehensive, as:

Full ownership of the tracts marked *park, playground, private lake, golf course* (describe all other such areas) is retained in *ABC* (the developer) for ultimate conveyance to *XYZ,* a nonprofit corporation whose membership will be composed of homeowners in this development, all according to the provisions of the declaration of restrictions, easements, liens, and covenants filed contemporaneously herewith, and hereby made a part of this plat. Conveyances of lots in this subdivision shall not be deemed to convey title to any part of the retained areas. Said areas are not dedicated to the public. With respect to the total area embraced in this plat, and all parts thereof, easements, covenants, liens, and restrictions are created in and by the declaration aforesaid.

§ 927. Common areas—agreement of developer to convey to home association. The declaration will contain an agreement that not later than a set date the developer will convey the common areas to the home association. The declaration should be signed as *accepted* by the home association so that it can enforce this agreement.

§ 928. Common areas—easements—paramount rights of home association. The declaration should create easements in favor of all of the homeowners in the development for access over the private walks and streets, for utilities, water, sewers and other services, and for use of the common areas, etc., but it should make such easement grant expressly subject and inferior to certain rights of the home association. These rights should include the right of the association to exercise, free and clear of all private rights created in the homeowners, the following rights: (1) the right of the association to suspend the enjoyment of the common areas by any homeowner and the furnishing of services by home association (garbage removal, furnishing water, and so forth) to the delinquent homeowner while his maintenance assessments remain unpaid; (2) the right to manage, maintain, and control the common areas for the benefit of the homeowners, and to promulgate reasonable rules toward this end; (3) the right to dedicate part or all of the common properties to the public for public use; (4) the right of the home association to charge reasonable admission and other fees for the use of the common areas.

§ 929. Common areas—public or private ownership—right to dedicate. The right to dedicate part or all of the common properties to the public is also important. Since many planned unit developments seek out less expensive land beyond the boundaries of existing villages or cities, the home association, on occasion, is set up initially to furnish urban services to the community. As soon as a village is formed and is prepared to furnish urban services (streets, sewer, water, and the like), the home association may choose to transfer these systems to the village. Provision for such ultimate transfer must be made in the declaration. It is true that public ownership of the other common areas (swimming pools, etc.) would eliminate the burden of paying real estate taxes thereon and the cost of maintaining the common areas, but such public ownership, especially of recreational common areas, would encourage public use, which would adversely affect the residents of the subdivision; hence it is to be avoided. An alternative is the creation of a public district with the same boundaries as the development. This public body can levy assessments for maintenance but is responsive to the wishes of the voters who are homeowners in the development.

§ 930. Common areas—artificial lakes. In some planned developments, an artificially created lake is one of the attractive common facilities. It is quite clear that neither the public nor any public body has any rights whatever in lakes so created. The developer has the legal right to reserve to himself the right to dictate who may use the lake, or he may grant this right to the homeowners. *Mayer* v. *Grueber,* 138 NW2d 197 (Wisc. 1965); *Thompson* v. *Enz,* 154 NW2d 473 (Mich. 1967).

§ **931. The declaration—building restrictions.** The declaration will establish a comprehensive general plan of restrictions governing minutely the structures and uses permitted in the development, both on the homesites and on the common areas. The plat or declaration should also vest in the home association the right to pass upon the plans of any structure to be erected by any home buyer. 40 ALR3d 864.

§ **932. The declaration—covenants.** The declaration will contain covenants binding on each homeowner to pay the assessments levied on his lot for maintenance charges, which covenants create a *personal liability* on which a personal judgment can be obtained by the association against a defaulting homeowner. It will also contain covenants by the home association to (1) maintain and operate the common property; (2) administer architectural controls; (3) enforce other covenants; and in some cases (4) maintain all or part of the exterior of individual homes. The covenants provide for amendments, but any amendment requires a vote of the homeowners.

§ **933. The declaration—lien for maintenance.** The declaration provides for the imposition of a maintenance assessment, usually annually, on each lot in the development. Home associations tend to operate somewhat informally. The danger here is that if procedures grow too lax (meetings held on days other than those set in by-laws, notice of meeting lacking or defective, etc.), the assessments made by the association may be declared invalid. *Noremac, Inc.* v. *Centre Hill Court, Inc.,* 178 SE 877 (Va. 1935).

§ **934. The declaration—restraints on sales.** Any provision in the declaration or deeds that a homeowner cannot sell his lot except by consent of a majority vote of the association is invalid. Such a clause is an illegal restraint on alienation (sale). *Mountain Springs Assn* v. *Wilson,* 196 A2d 270 (N.J. 1963). Also invalid is any clause where only a member of the home association can purchase a homesite. *Ibid.* Nor can the declaration or by-laws of the association provide that sales by a homeowner to a future purchaser can only be made to a purchaser approved by the association. *Tuckerton Beach Club* v. *Bender,* 219 A2d 528 (N.J. 1966). No refusal to sell can be racially motivated. *Sullivan* v. *Little Huntington Park,* 396 U.S. 229 (1969). It is safe to provide that any homesite purchaser automatically acquires membership in the home association as a normal incident of home ownership. Other acceptable provisions are discussed in the condominium chapter.

§ **935. Mortgage problems.** A mortgage on a PUD homesite should contain a covenant of the mortgagor to pay all assessments and a covenant not to vote to amend the declaration without the mortgagee's written consent.

It is a good idea for the declaration to provide that mortgages of PUD units shall require the mortgagor to remit to the mortgagee as part of his monthly payment his monthly PUD assessment. This insures prompt collection of this assessment. The rider to be affixed to any FNMA/FHLMC Uniform instrument covering a mortgage on a unit in a PUD is attached as an Appendix to this chapter.

Under FHA and VA rules it is necessary that all common areas be owned by the home association free of any mortgage. Thus, if the seller to the developer takes back a purchase money mortgage, it should contain a provision for release of the common areas from the mortgage on payment of a nominal sum.

§ 936. **Taxes on common areas.** The common areas have no sales value to a third party. They are encumbered with easements that render them valueless to any purchaser. The value of the common areas is reflected in the increased value they contribute to the residential areas. Hence, the tax assessor should not assess the common areas at the value they would have if unencumbered by easements. *People* v. *O'Donnel,* 139 App. Div. 83, 124 N.Y.S. 36 (1910); *Matter of Crane-Berkely Corp.* v. *Lavis,* 238 App. Div. 124, 263 N.Y.S. 556 (1935).

There is no guarantee of this result until the matter has been worked out with the local assessor. Assessors tend to be rather independent individuals. Basically, the problem is one of persuasion.

§ 937. **Regulation.** Just as in the condominium situation, state and local governments have reacted to developer abuses by enacting consumer legislation relating to assessments, management contracts, recreation area leases, and so on.

§ 938. **Condominium compared.** Although there is nothing in the concept of the condominium which would prevent its use as a PUD, basically there is no need to create a condominium. A PUD home has its own mortgage as does a condominium apartment. Furthermore, it is not necessary to distribute the ownership of the common properties among the lot owners as in condominiums. The PUD makes a different but satisfactory provision for the common areas.

Planned residential development. Presently peculiar to California is the *planned residential development* (PRD), under which the developer and zoning authority establish a plan for the development. The lots are substandard, and there are common areas as in the PUD, but each homeowner acquires an undivided interest in the common area, as in the condominium. Lowell, Land Use and Operational Contracts in the Planned Development, 9 *San Diego L. Rev.* 29, 36 (1971).

§ 939. **Zoning.** The old-fashioned zoning ordinance, with its rigid allocation of specific uses to specific zones, its building lines, and its minimum-area requirements, does not lend itself to the PUD type of development. Cluster development calls for smaller homesites, the land subtracted from homesites being added to common areas. However, the PUD can, it seems, be listed as a special exception in the zoning ordinances. Goldston & Schever, Zoning of Planned Residential Developments, 73 *Harv. L. Rev.* 241, 251 (1959). Alternatively, the zoning ordinance may include a special section devoted to the PUD, calling it variously a Community Unit Plan, Dwelling Groups, Group Housing Planned Residential Development, or

Planned Building Groups. Goldston & Schever, Zoning of Planned Residential Developments, 73 *Harv L. Rev.* 241, 253 (1959). Because approving a development of this sort involves a considerable exercise of discretion, it is wise to provide that final approval of a developer's proposal to create a PUD zone should rest with the city council, just as if an amendment to the zoning ordinance was being considered, and some ordinances so provide. *Rodgers* v. *Village of Tarrytown,* 96 NE2d 731 (N.Y. 1951); *LaRue* v. *East Brunswick,* 172 A2d 691 (N.J. 1961); *DeMeo* v. *Zoning Comm.,* 167 A2d 454 (Conn. 1961); Goldston & Schever, Zoning of Planned Residential Developments, 73 *Harv. L. Rev.* 241, 255 (1959). The applicant for such zoning may, under many ordinances, be a government agency, since urban redevelopment plans sometimes call for a PUD.

The village cannot thrust PUD zoning on the landowner if the land is not suited to that purpose.

As can be seen, the PUD zone is a sort of floating zone. (See § 718.) And the modern courts that sustain floating zones will sustain PUD zoning.

EXAMPLE: X owned a 187-acre tract located in an area zoned for single-family residences. He sought to have it rezoned to planned unit development with cluster residential areas. This was done and upheld. *Orinda Homeowners Committee* v. *Board of Supervisors,* 90 Cal. Reptr. 88 (1970).

On the whole, the modern decisions are likely to sustain the validity of PUD zoning even though it is a far cry from "cooky-cutter," single-family dwelling zoning, 43 ALR3d 888, and even though the density requirements are different from those applicable to conventional subdivisions. *Peabody* v. *Phoenix,* 485 P2d 565 (Ariz. 1971).

EXAMPLE: PUD zoning was sustained against attack on the ground that PUD zoning departed from the uniformity one finds in old-fashioned zoning. The court pointed out that in a PUD zone true uniformity is achieved in that the cluster housing, typical of the PUD, is found in each PUD zone. *Orinda Homeowners Committee* v. *Board of Supervisors,* 90 Cal. Rptr. 88 (1970); *Prince George's County* v. *M. & B. Const. Corp.,* 297 A2d 683 (Md. 1972). *Contra: Nopro Co.* v. *Town of Cherry Hills,* 504 P2d 344 (Colo. 1972).

Zoning law does not require that each zone have only one permitted use. *Cheney* v. *Village 2 at New Hope,* 241 A2d 81 (Pa. 1968).

Obviously the PUD brings into play the concept of exclusionary zoning which is discussed in the chapter on zoning.

REFERENCE: Committee Report, 7 ABA Real Property, Probate & Trust Journal 61 (1972): cites cases pro and con on the validity of PUD zoning; Sternlieb, Buschell, & Hughes, Planned Unit Development: Environmental Suboptimization, 1 Environmental Affairs 694 (1972).

RESERVED: §§ 940–950.

PLANNED UNIT DEVELOPMENT RIDER

THIS PLANNED UNIT DEVELOPMENT ("PUD") RIDER is made this .... day of ...., 19...., and is incorporated into and shall be deemed to amend and supplement a Mortgage, Deed of Trust or Deed to Secure Debt (herein "security instrument") dated of even date herewith, given by the undersigned (herein "Borrower") to secure Borrower's Note to ....(herein "Lender") and covering the Property described in the security instrument and located at..

(Property Address)

.... The Property comprises a parcel of land improved with a dwelling, which, together with other such parcels and certain common areas and facilities, all as described in ....
....
....
(herein "Declaration"), forms a planned unit development known as ....
....

(Name of Planned Unit Development)

(herein "PUD")

PLANNED UNIT DEVELOPMENT COVENANTS. In addition to the covenants and agreements made in the security instrument, Borrower and Lender further covenant and agree as follows:

A. PUD Obligations. Borrower shall perform all of Borrower's obligations under the: (i) Declaration; (ii) articles of incorporation, trust instrument or any equivalent document required to establish the homeowners association or equivalent entity managing the common areas and facilities of the PUD (herein "Owners Association"); and (iii) by-laws, if any, or other rules or regulations of the Owners Association. Borrower shall promptly pay, when due, all assessments imposed by the Owners Association.

B. Hazard Insurance. In the event of a distribution of hazard insurance proceeds in lieu of restoration or repair following a loss to the common areas and facilities of the PUD, any such proceeds payable to Borrower are hereby assigned and shall be paid to Lender for application to the sums secured by the security instrument, with the excess, if any, paid to Borrower.

C. Condemnation. The proceeds of any award or claim for damages, direct or consequential, payable to Borrower in connection with any condemnation or other taking of all or any part of the common areas and facilities of the PUD, or for any conveyance in lieu of condemnation, are hereby assigned and shall be paid to Lender. Such proceeds shall be applied by Lender to the sums secured by the security instrument in the manner provided under Uniform Covenant 9.

D. Lender's Prior Consent. Borrower shall not, except after notice to Lender and with Lender's prior written consent, consent to:

(i) the abandonment or termination of the PUD;

(ii) any material amendment to the Declaration, trust instrument, articles of incorporation, by-laws of the Owners Association, or any equivalent constituent document of the PUD, including, but not limited to, any amendment which would change the percentage interests of the unit owners in the common areas and facilities of the PUD;

(iii) the effectuation of any decision by the Owners Association to terminate professional management and assume self-management of the PUD; or

(iv) the transfer, release, encumbrance, partition or subdivision of all or any part of the PUD's common areas and facilities, except as to the Owners Association's right to grant easements for utilities and similar or related purposes.

E. Remedies. If Borrower breaches Borrower's covenants and agreements hereunder, including the covenant to pay when due planned unit development assessments, then Lender may invoke any remedies provided under the security instrument, including, but not limited to, those provided under Uniform Covenant 7.

IN WITNESS WHEREOF, Borrower has executed this PUD Rider.

______________________________ —Borrower

______________________________ —Borrower

PLANNED UNIT DEVELOPMENT RIDER — 1 to 4 Family—6/75— **FNMA/FHLMC UNIFORM INSTRUMENT**

32

Land Use Controls: Private Controls Over Common Areas

§ 951. **In general.** In the chapters on the co-op, the condominium, the town house, the planned unit development, the industrial park, and the shopping center, there is one common thread—the presence of areas enjoyed in common by home or apartment owners or business enterprises. This chapter serves mainly as an invitation to observe the similarities and differences in the legal devices employed with respect to the common areas.

EXAMPLE: In the planned unit development the home association owns the common areas. The developer deeds the common areas to the home association corporation. The homeowners acquire easements for the enjoyment of the common areas. In some planned unit developments the common areas are later deeded to the village in which the land lies.

EXAMPLE: In the condominium, each apartment owner owns a percentage of the common areas and the rights of unit owners in the common areas are defined in the declaration described in a charter of rights, duties, and prohibitions regarding use of the common areas.

EXAMPLE: With the town house each lot owner owns a physical portion of the common areas and the rights of unit owners in the common areas are defined in the declaration. A home association sometimes exists and sometimes not. Where it does not, each unit owner does his own enforcing.

EXAMPLE: In the old-fashioned subdivision consisting of privately owned dwellings, home associations exist and enforce restrictions and liens.

EXAMPLE: In the shopping center the common areas are owned by the developer. A large department store may own its site in the center and enjoy easement rights in the common areas as set forth in a declaration. The tenants have their easement rights in the common areas as defined in their lease. The merchants' association plays a role in control of the common areas.

EXAMPLE: In the industrial park, various legal devices are employed.

RESERVED: §§ 952–962.

33

Land Acquisition and Assembly

§ 963. **In general.** One intending to build upon or develop vacant land must acquire it. The suggestions made in the chapters on contracts of sale and land development are, of course, applicable to the process of land acquisition. The mechanics of land acquisition and assembly call for special expertise.

§ 964. **Precautions prior to undertaking assembly.** Before undertaking a land assembly, the developer routinely visits with the title company and gets an idea of the ownerships involved. Obviously, it is easier to assemble three or four ownerships than thirty or forty ownerships. He also can get some idea as to the existence of building restrictions or easements that might thwart his building plans.

§ 965. **Gaps and gores.** It is often necessary to acquire and assemble the lands of several adjoining landowners, for example, for a subdivision, or a factory site. Here the danger is that the descriptions used may leave small gaps between the parcels.

EXAMPLE: *A* proposes to acquire the Northwest Quarter of Section 10 in a government township. He assumes that it contains exactly 160 acres, which it theoretically should contain. Actually, of course, owing to inaccuracies in surveying there is no such thing as a perfect quarter section, and it happens that this quarter section contains 161 acres. Suppose, then, that *A* acquires from *B* the "east eighty acres" of the quarter section and gets a deed from C to the "west eighty acres" of the quarter section. This leaves a one-acre strip between the two eighty-acre tracts. *A* thus does not acquire title to this strip.

These small strips between parcels are called *gores.*

This suggests the need for a *boundary survey* to be made by a surveyor before the contract is signed, so that the buyer's earnest money is not tied up until it can be seen that there are no gaps or gores.

Where one seller owns all the parcels being acquired, the surveyor can be asked to furnish a *perimeter description.* This is a description that describes the entire tract being acquired by metes and bounds. (See § 97.) Then the survey will be made while the title is being examined, and if gaps or gores are revealed, the buyer can report the title as unmarketable. Alternatively, the buyer can insist that the title company insuring the title furnish a special endorsement insuring *contiguity* of all the several parcels, in which case the buyer again can back out of the deal if the title company refuses to insure contiguity.

§ **966. Nominees.** Land is often acquired in the name of a nominee, often a skilled negotiator from a local real estate firm. This is done because asking prices soar when it becomes known that some well-known company is acquiring land in the area. The nominee need not disclose that he is acting for an undisclosed principal. Comment 32 *Ia. L. Rev.* 790 (1947). But if the seller inquires, the nominee must not misrepresent the identity of the purchaser, for if he does, the seller has the right to terminate the contract because a material misrepresentation has been made. Friedman, Contracts and Conveyances of Real Property (3d ed. 1975) § 2.2; 121 ALR 1162; 35 ALR3d 1374. Indeed, if such misrepresentation is made, the seller can have his deed set aside even after the deal has been closed, so long as he acts promptly on learning of the misrepresentation. The nominee must refrain from misrepresenting the use to which the property will be put. 35 ALR3d 1369.

EXAMPLE: *N* went to *R* and persuaded *R* to sell a vacant lot adjoining *R*'s home. He stated that he planned to build a house. When it later developed that *N* was buying on behalf of a church, the deed was set aside. *Keyerleber* v. *Euclid Congregation,* 143 NE2d 313 (Ohio 1957); 6 ALR2d 812.

This rule has special force where the seller retains some land and the buyer intends to devote the land to some offensive use, such as a junk yard, cemetery, or bar. 35 ALR3d 1370.

If the seller has turned down an offer made by the developer, use of a nominee thereafter is precluded. 6 ALR2d 812.

EXAMPLE: *D* offered to buy *R*'s lot. *R* refused to deal. *D* hired *N*, a nominee, to buy the lot. *R* can have his deed to *N* set aside. *Gloede* v. *Socha,* 199 Wis. 503, 226 NW 950.

If bad blood or previous dealings lead a buyer to believe that the seller will not sell to him, it is useless to hire a nominee. The seller can have the deal set aside. 6 ALR2d 814; 35 ALR2d 1374.

There seems to be some advantage in having the developer form a straw corporation with some bland name to acquire the land. This would be a wholly-owned subsidiary of the developer. The subsidiary could then hire the nominee, who if asked, or even if not asked, could truthfully state: "I'm working for *Real Estate Associates, Inc.*"

Where it is decided to attempt a secret assembly, some developers use a different nominee, lawyer, and real estate broker for each acquisition.

Obviously a nominee who has no judgments or other liens against him should be used. Often a bachelor is employed, for then no spouse's rights questions arise.

At times the nominee will request that his employer sign an indemnity agreement protecting the nominee against liability by reason of his ownership of the land.

§ 967. **Written authority.** Because an agent's authority to buy land must be in writing in some states, there should be a written contract of employment.

§ 968. **Trust declaration by nominees.** The nominee routinely signs a brief trust agreement reciting that he is acquiring the land and will hold it in trust for ______________________________ (the developer). This is acknowledged, just as a deed is acknowledged, but it is not recorded. This is an indispensable document, for example, if the nominee dies while the ownership of the land stands in his name. It is especially important in land assemblies that may take a long period of time. Some developers also require the nominee to sign an unrecorded quitclaim deed as soon as he acquires ownership of a parcel.

§ 969. **Escrows.** A seller who senses that he is not dealing with the real purchaser may become uneasy.

To quiet his fears the deal should be closed in escrow.

EXAMPLE: *N*, the nominee, tenders a contract of sale to *S*, the seller, with a provision therein that the entire purchase price will be held by *ABC Bank* under an escrow agreement providing that *S* either gets the entire purchase price or gets ownership of his land back just as it was before the contract was signed.

§ 970. **Subdivision trusts.** In Arizona extensive use is made of the *subdivision* trust.

EXAMPLE: *S* enters into a contract to sell vacant land to *P* for $100,000. *P* pays $20,000 down. *S* now makes a deed of the land to *ABC Title Company* in trust. *S* is the first beneficiary of the trust and *P* is the second beneficiary. The trustee files a plat of subdivision. *P* engages in sales of lots. Lot buyers make their payments to *ABC Title Company* which remits to *S* and *P*, according to a schedule with a minimum amount due periodically. The lot buyers receive their deeds from *ABC Title Company*. Ultimately *S* is paid the balance of the purchase price. If sales collapse and *P* cannot meet the schedule of payments, *S* can declare a forfeiture of *P*'s interest. Thereupon *ABC Title Company* deeds the unsold lots to *S*. Carlock, The Subdivision Trust—A Useful Device. 5 *Ariz. L. Rev.* 2 (1963).

§ 971. **Land trusts.** The land trust is an ideal vehicle for land assemblies. It enables the developer to acquire the individual parcels in the name of a trust company.

§ 972. **Holding agreements.** In California and Nevada a device somewhat similar to the land trust is used, but it is called a *holding agreement.*

§ 973. **Purchase money mortgage.** Often a developer buying a farm will be able to persuade the farmer to take back a purchase money mortgage for a good part of the purchase price. In such case the contract of sale must contain two clauses.

CLAUSE: This clause requires the farmer to join in the plat of subdivision. All plat statutes require all mortgagees to join in the subdivision plat. Otherwise, foreclosure of the mortgage would wipe out the streets dedicated by the plat.

CLAUSE: This clause requires partial release of the mortgage as a lot is sold to a home buyer. This is necessary because the home buyer also needs to get a mortgage, and his lender will want his mortgage to be a first mortgage.

Of course, the contract must be quite detailed as to the terms of the mortgage.

If the developer plans to put construction mortgages on the property, a further clause is needed.

CLAUSE: This clause subordinates the purchase money mortgage to any construction mortgage put on by the developer. This is done because the construction lender will want a first mortgage on the property. Caution is needed in drafting this clause. If it does not give enough standards or terms of the construction mortgage, it will be unenforceable. See Kratovil, Modern Mortgage Law and Practice, Chapter 21.

If there are barns or other buildings on the land sold, the contract and mortgage should give the developer the right to demolish them. A mortgagee can block demolition of buildings on mortgaged land unless the mortgage provides to the contrary.

§ 974. Options. Options are often used in land acquisitions.

EXAMPLE: X, an industry, plans a site that requires assembly of ten separately owned tracts of land. X hires agents who procure options on all ten tracts of land. If X is unable to obtain options on all ten tracts, X allows all options to lapse. If all ten options are procured, X exercises all options.

§ 975. Taxes. Assessors usually assess farmland considerably lower than subdivided land. This suggests that the development proceed in stages, if this is possible. Leave as much as you can in farmland until you are ready to go forward with subdivision and sale. And if you plan a commercial area, postpone platting this until you are ready to build, for the tax assessor will assess commercial land higher than residential land or farmland.

§ 976. Leasehold acquisitions. Obviously acquisition of a leasehold presents problems different from those involved in acquisition of outright ownership.

EXAMPLE: X, a condominium developer, acquires a leasehold. He then discovers that local law does not permit condominium developments on leaseholds.

EXAMPLE: X, a co-op developer, acquires a leasehold and erects a high-class apartment building. He encounters sales resistance. Prospective tenants point out that as the mortgage on the leasehold is reduced by payment, the equity of the apartment owner becomes so substantial that it becomes difficult to sell the apartment for cash and mortgage financing on a co-op is virtually unobtainable. This makes it almost necessary for the ground lease to contain some provision for the landlord joining in the ground lessee's financing. Obviously, there is a problem here.

RESERVED: §§ 977–987.

34

Building Construction

§ 988. **In general.** This chapter deals mainly with new home construction, with occasional mention of significant aspects of large-scale construction.

§ 989. **Construction contracts.** There are different types of construction contracts:

1. I own a lot and hire you to build a house according to certain plans and specifications prepared by my architect. This is a construction contract only.

2. You are a subdivider and builder. I pick out a site in your subdivision, and you contract to build a house (like one of your model homes, perhaps) and deliver the house and lot at a specified price. This is a contract for the sale of land and for the construction of a house. Both the law of sale contracts and the law of construction contracts are applicable to this situation.

3. You are a subdivider and builder, and I decide to buy a house that I find under construction in your subdivision. This is essentially the same as (2) above.

In situations 2 and 3 above you have the sell-and-build type of contract. The contract is one for the *sale of land* and also for the *construction of a home. Dieckman* v. *Walser,* 144 N.J.Eq. 382, 168 Atl. 582 (1933). It must comply with the requirements of law as to both types of contracts.

EXAMPLE: *R* contracted to sell *E* a lot and build a home thereon. The contract of sale portion was complete, but there were no plans or specifications giving the details of the building. The contract was invalid. *Griesenhauer* v. *Bellea Lake Development Co.,* 421 SW2d 785 (1967).

EXAMPLE: The contract called for sale of a lot and construction of a home, payment when home was ready for occupancy. The seller could not obtain a certificate of occupancy. (See § 739.) Since the seller could not perform the building part of the contract, he could not enforce the sale part. *Sloan* v. *Pinafore Homes, Inc.,* 310 N.Y.S.2d 731 (1970).

§ 990. **Types of sell-and-build contracts.** There are several types of sell-and-build contracts.

EXAMPLE: *V* contracts to sell a lot to *P*. The contract requires that *P* apply for a mortgage loan of $15,000, and is contingent on the procuring of this loan. When the loan is obtained, the deal is to be closed, deed and mortgage recorded, and thereafter *V* is to construct the building, using the mortgage money for this purpose. After the closing of the deal, the contract between the parties is simply a construction contract.

EXAMPLE: *V* contracts to sell a lot to *P*, to erect a house thereon, and when the house has been completed, to deed the completed house and lot to *P*. Here *V* will get his own construction loan, build the building with his own construction loan proceeds, and deliver the completed package to *P*. This has some advantages to *V*. The handling of the construction disbursements does not involve *P*, whereas in the previous example *V* must go to *P* for documents every time a construction disbursement is to be made. After all, in the previous example it is *P*'s money, loaned to him by the mortgagee, that is being used for construction.

EXAMPLE: *R* contracts to build a home for *E* and to deed the completed house and lot to *E*. *R* applies to *XYZ Savings and Loan Association* for a mortgage loan. A long-term mortgage in the sum of $20,000 is placed on the property by *R*, but XYZ loans only $18,000 to *R*. When the building is completed, *R* deeds to *E*, who assumes the mortgage and receives the additional $2,000, to enable him to pay *R*.

SUGGESTION TO HOME BUYER: When you buy from a professional subdivider and builder, you are often dealing with a man who does not yet own the land that he is selling you. He may have only an option or contract to buy the land. If the builder runs into financial difficulties, he may never be able to pay up his option or contract or be able to transfer ownership to you. Moreover, as financial troubles develop, mechanics' liens are filed and mortgage foreclosures instituted. In such case, you will find that the possibility of obtaining ownership or getting your money back is nil. Therefore, it is best for you to get a deed to the property as early as possible, before you have put too much money into the house.

§ 991. Sell-and-build contracts—signatures. Some sell-and-build contracts contain a clause that the seller is not bound unless an officer of the seller corporation signs for the corporation. Obviously, the buyer should not accept a contract signed only by a salesman. Indeed, it is always advisable to insist on an officer's signature.

§ 992. Sell-and-build contracts—mortgage clauses. Every sell-and-build contract has a clause requiring the buyer to apply for a mortgage loan. The deal will go one of two ways.

EXAMPLE: *R*, the builder, will convey the land to *E*. *E* puts on a mortgage, and *R* uses the proceeds of the loan to build the home.

EXAMPLE: *R* has *E* apply for a mortgage loan. As soon as the lender has approved *E* for the loan, *R* puts a construction mortgage on the lot and uses the proceeds of this loan to build the home. When the home is completed, *E* signs the permanent mortgage, the proceeds of which are used to pay off both *R* and the construction loan.

But in either case the buyer must qualify for a mortgage loan, so the contract calls for him to apply for a mortgage loan; the deal is off if he fails to qualify.

§ 993. **Delay in completion.** A prospective buyer should read the contract before signing it. The time set for completion is an important matter to a buyer who is planning to sell his present home. Carefully read the clause that gives the builder additional time to complete. It may be so broad that the completion date is virtually meaningless.

§ 994. **Sell-and-build contracts—subordination of contract to construction loan.** Many sell-and-build contracts contain a clause subordinating the contract to any construction mortgage put on the property by the builder.

EXAMPLE: *R*, a builder, sells a lot to *E* under a contract by which *R* will build a home for *E* like a model home he has displayed to *E*. *R* will now put a construction loan mortgage on the lot to *E-1*. Probably *E-1* will want to see the contract to make certain that the land is under contract and also to see the sale price. Having actual notice of the contract, *E-1*'s rights would be subordinate to *E*'s rights, and a deed from *R* to *E* could wipe out *E-1*'s mortgage. Therefore the contract will state that *E*'s rights are subordinate to *E-1*'s lien.

§ 995. **Sell-and-build contracts—builder liability.** Obviously the seller-builder in a sell-and-build contract has all the liabilities of a building contractor set forth in this chapter. *Jones* v. *Galewood,* 381 P2d 158 (Okla. 1963).

§ 996. **Suggestions to home buyer planning to have home constructed.** There are precautions a prospective home buyer should consider if a home is to be built for him:

SUGGESTION TO HOME BUYER: In any event, before you trust a builder who is unwilling or unable to give you a deed at the beginning, get a credit report on the builder. Such a report can be procured at small cost from a credit rating firm and will give you a good line on the reliability of your builder. Look up "Credit Rating and Reporting Agencies" in your telephone book. The material houses with whom the contractor has been dealing are usually excellent sources not only of credit references but also of information as to the contractor's ability to do the job. The home buyer should also request the contractor to give him the addresses of other buildings that he has built in the past. This will give the home buyer an opportunity to inspect the finished work of the contractor and to contact the owners for a recommendation. The finance houses with whom the contractor has done business in the past are also excellent sources of reference.

Obviously, any contract to build a house should contain a description of the house to be built. In this respect, most building contracts leave much to be desired. A few points are deserving of consideration. In the first place, many builders erect a model house that is shown to prospective purchasers. If the buyer likes the model, he may sign a contract to buy a lot and to have the builder construct a house like the model house, to which reference is made in the contract. This is an adequate description. A contract to build a house *like* another existing house is a contract to build an exact counterpart or copy of the existing house, in plan, kind, and quality of material. *Whaley* v. *Milton Const. Co.,* 241 SW2d 23 (Mo. App. 1951). Obviously, if the buyer wants certain variations from the model, these should be spelled out in writing in detail in the contract.

Other builders may have a number of different building plans to show prospects. Each of the plans has a supporting set of detailed specifications. Once the buyer has selected his particular plan, he signs a contract to have a house built *according to Ace Construction Company Plan No. 5 and specifications bearing the same number*. Again, such a description is adequate. *Hannan* v. *Handy,* 104 Conn. 653, 134 Atl. 71 (1926).

Then there is the home buyer who wants a house built according to his own particular ideas. Here detailed plans and specifications are of the utmost importance. In this area, experience reveals the pitiful ignorance of the average home buyer. Innumerable important items can be omitted from the specifications, and the home buyer will fail to detect the omission. Then as construction goes forward, various things come to light, and the home buyer finds that he must pay for "extras."

SUGGESTION TO HOME BUYER: **When you contract to buy a house "like" a certain model house, you are contracting to accept all the shortcomings of the model. Many such homes are sold on the basis of "glamor" items, such as kitchens. You had better have an experienced person look the house over to see to the adequacy of the heating plant, drainage system, foundation and footings, and other important things about which you know little. It is best to procure the plans and specifications of the model house and have them checked by an architect or builder, for there is much in a house that can be wrong and yet not meet the eye.**

§ **997. Extras.** Extras are probably the largest factor creating disputes between owners and contractors. There is a propensity on the part of some contractors to bid low in order to get the job and then try to bail their way out of a losing job by claiming extras. Also, an owner is frequently "inspired" during the course of construction and orders changes or extra work and materials indiscriminately without a definite understanding as to the cost. A contractor who is providing extras does not have to make a competitive bid in order to obtain the work. There is therefore a tendency on the part of some contractors to charge more money for extras than the ordinary markup used in bidding for work. The contract should therefore specifically require that all extra charges must be reduced to a written instrument, signed by the owner, describing the work to be performed and the amount to be paid. Such a provision is valid. 2 ALR3d 631. In the interest of both the contractor and the owner, this procedure should be religiously followed. The owner's architect has no power to waive this provision of the contract. He cannot order extras verbally. 2 ALR3d 686. However, if the owner himself verbally orders the extra work, he is liable. 2 ALR3d 658. By ordering the extras verbally, the owner has waived the provision requiring a change order to be in writing. Also, the contract should require the owner to deposit additional funds with the mortgage lender in order to assure the contractor and the mortgage lender that there will be adequate funds to complete the building when extra work or materials are ordered.

In addition to disputes with respect to the cost of extras, disputes often arise as to whether or not a given item is an extra or is included under the original contract. If the plans and specifications made a part of the contract are sufficiently detailed, the possibility of a dispute over whether a particular item is an extra can be minimized.

§ 998. **Progress payments.** If I hire you to erect a building on my land, the contract will almost certainly fix a total price for the entire job. However, your subcontractors will not wait for their money until the building is finished. Therefore the contract will call for *progress payments* to the general contractor and the subcontractors as the building goes up. A widely used formula provides for a payment of 35 percent of the proceeds to the contractor when the house is under roof, 30 percent of the contract price when the house is plastered, and the balance of 35 percent when the building is completed and accepted by the owner. However, the contract often provides that only 85 percent of the full amount of a progress payment due the *general contractor* is payable when the progress payment falls due. The owner holds back 15 percent of each payment due the general contractor (often called a *retention*) until the building has been completed and accepted by the owner with all lien waivers produced. On big jobs, the contract will call for retentions on work done by the bigger subcontractors. After all, you cannot tell whether heating or air conditioning will work until you try it, and if it doesn't, the retention is an effective inducement to get the necessary repairs done.

As a progress payment is demanded, the contract often calls for an inspection to be made by the owner's architect, who certifies that the work and material for which payment is claimed are in place and in accordance with the contract. If the owner has no architect, this inspection should be made by the mortgage lending institution. On FHA loans, an inspection will also be made by the FHA.

A question often arising is whether a contract that calls for progress payments is a total contract for a total job at a total price or can be broken up into as many parts as there are progress payments. In other words, is the contract divisible?

EXAMPLE: A contract to build a schoolhouse for a price of $2610 provided that $300 was to be paid when first floor joists were in, $300 when second floor joists were in, $1000 when the building was enclosed, $400 when the plastering was done, and the balance when the building was completed. After the plastering was completed and all payments made up to and including the payment due at that time, a windstorm destroyed the building. The court held: (1) A builder is not excused from completing the building by the fact that the building, while under construction, is destroyed or damaged by fire, storms, or sinking of the soil; he must rebuild and complete the job without a penny of additional compensation. (2) A building contract is entire; it is not divisible. A contractor who abandons the job, as this contractor did when the windstorm destroyed the building, has not earned a penny. Therefore he must refund to the owner all progress payments already made. *Superintendent of Schools* v. *Bennett,* 27 NJL 513. On both points, the court was correct. 22 ALR2d 1345.

However, if the contract is not to *build,* but to *repair* or remodel an existing building, the contractor is relieved of liability for further performance if the building is destroyed by fire or other casualty and the destruction is not due to the contractor's negligence. *Matthews Const. Co.* v. *Brady,* 104 N.J.L. 438, 140 A 433 (1928). Moreover, the contractor can recover for the value of labor and materials furnished up to the time of the destruction.

Failure of the landowner to make a progress payment is a material breach of the contract. It entitles the contractor to suspend work until payment has been made. *Watson* v. *Auburn Iron Works, Inc.,* 318 NE2d 508 (Ill. 1974).

§ **999. Mortgage money.** Any builder who builds on contract for a landowner should insist that the landowner have a definite commitment for a satisfactory construction mortgage loan before construction begins, and the construction contract should be made subject to this condition.

SUGGESTION TO BUILDER: Require the landowner to furnish you a photostatic copy of the lender's commitment to make the mortgage loan.

§ **1000. Cash down payments from home buyers.** Builders usually insist that the home buyer make a cash down payment. What to do with it is the question. Home buyers are often reluctant to pay a builder a large sum of money before construction has begun. And builders are often reluctant to start construction when they have no assurance that the home buyer will be able to come up with the money. One solution is to have the home buyer deposit his money with the mortgage house that is financing construction. This is acceptable to the mortgage house, for under the typical construction loan agreement, this deposit is used for the initial stages of construction, and the mortgagee's loan money is not used until later stages of construction have been reached. Another idea is to deposit the buyer's money with some bank as escrowee, with directions to turn the money over to the builder as specified stages of construction are reached. Another idea is to deposit the buyer's money with some bank as escrowee, with directions to turn the money over to the builder as specified stages of construction are reached.

NEW LAWS: In some states (New York, for example), new laws require the builder to keep the buyer's deposit in an escrow. In other states a builder who diverts the deposit to another job is guilty of a crime. *State of Washington* v. *Thomas William McDonald,* 463 P2d 174 (Wash. 1969). In still other states, laws making a builder criminally liable for diverting deposits to other jobs are invalid on the ground that imprisonment for debt is no longer legal. *State* v. *Janing,* 182 Neb. 539, 156 NW2d 9 (1968). Obviously this is a problem without a solution.

§ **1001. Architects.** A home buyer may hire an architect only to draw plans and specifications for his home or to draw plans and then to supervise the construction of the home. Since supervision requires time and attention, it entails greater cost. Usually it is best to pay the extra money and get the supervision. A house is built by a general contractor and numerous subcontractors. One or more of these may accidentally or intentionally try to use inferior work or materials. Only a supervising architect can prevent this. Some home buyers depend on the mortgage house or FHA inspectors to see that there is no cheating. Remember that inspections by mortgage men and the FHA cannot possibly be as thorough as those of your own architect.

Many building contracts provide that before the builder is entitled to receive any payment under the contract, the owner's architect must certify that the work has been properly done in accordance with the contract up to that point and that the builder is entitled to his payment. Usually the contract provides that the architect's certificate shall be conclusive on this question, which is a valid provision. If the architect disapproves the work, the builder will not receive the payment. 110 ALR 137. However, the builder will collect without the architect's certificate if the architect is guilty of bad faith or gross error.

EXAMPLE: The owner persuaded the architect to refuse a certificate, although neither had any complaint about the work or materials furnished. This action is tantamount to fraud, and the builder will collect without the certificate. *Cerny Pickas & Co.* v. *Dallach,* 249 Ill. App. 424 (1928).

The builder will not be entitled to payment if the architect in bad faith issues a certificate when actually the certificate should have been refused.

EXAMPLE: The architect knowingly accepted badly defective building material and certified that the builder was entitled to payment. The owner, through his own inspection, discovered the fraud and refused to pay. He was within his legal rights.

There are other pertinent rules regarding architects:

1. An architect has only those powers and authorities that his employer sees fit to give him; in general, an architect has no power to order changes in a building contract signed by his employer or to order extra work unless the owner has specifically given him this authority, and all persons dealing with an architect are on notice of this limitation on his powers. If the architect, though having no authority to do so, repeatedly orders extra work and materials and the owner pays for them knowingly and without protest, as where the extra work shows as such in monthly payout orders signed by the owner, the architect by this course of conduct becomes authorized to order extras. Because controversies often arise as to the extent of the architect's authority, it is best that the contract between the landowner and the architect for the architect's services and the building contract between the landowner and the contractor both specify what authority the architect has to give orders to the builder, how such orders are to be given (whether verbally or in writing), and so forth.

2. A supervising architect has authority to order the contractor to correct work that has not been performed in a proper manner or according to the contract or the plans.

3. The architect is duty bound to use ordinary skill and reasonable care and is liable for loss caused by his *negligence.* For example, if the architect is negligent and produces faulty plans, as a result of which damage ensues (walls crack, foundation gives way, and so forth) the architect is liable to his employer. 25 ALR2d 1085. Likewise if the architect negligently certifies that the builder is entitled to payments, whereas the work done is deficient in some respect and does not warrant payment, the architect is liable. 43 ALR2d 1229. Moreover, he forfeits all compensation in such case.

4. Like other agents, the architect must be loyal to his employer. If he fraudulently and in collusion with the contractor certifies that work has been done properly, when, in fact, the contrary is true, the architect is liable and forfeits his compensation. The same is true if the architect has secret agreements with building suppliers under which the architect is given a rake-off or payment for supplies ordered from them.

5. Unless it has been otherwise agreed, all plans and specifications prepared by the architect become the property of his employer. However, the American Institute of Architects contract form specifies that these documents are the property of the architect.

6. Young and inexperienced architects often agree to produce plans to the owner's "satisfaction" or "approval." Here the architect will receive no payment whatever if the owner disapproves of the result.

7. As a rule, the architect cannot recover if his plans call for a building that will violate local building ordinances.

8. Assuming that the architect exercises ordinary skill and care, he is not liable if the contractor is guilty of negligence and damage ensues, as where the contractor fails to protect the building from the elements. The difficulty here is that in some cases (settling of foundations, for example) it is hard to determine whether the loss was due to faulty plans and specifications prepared by the architect, faulty supervision by the architect, or faulty performance by the contractor despite the architect's care. Here the courts are quite likely to say that such things cannot happen where the architect is alert.

9. Home builders often press an architect for some categorical or flat commitment as to the maximum cost of construction. Here there is danger that a statement by the architect will be interpreted as a guarantee that the building will not exceed such cost, and he will be liable if such cost is exceeded and will forfeit all compensation.

Finally, you must remember that an architect may be hired only to draw plans and specifications, or he may also be hired to draw plans and supervise construction of the building. Obviously an architect hired only to draw plans has no liability for carelessness in the process of construction. He would be liable only if defective plans caused damage in the process of construction.

§ **1002. Substantial performance.** If a building contractor finishes the building in strict accordance with the plans and specifications and in a good and workmanlike manner, he is, of course, entitled to collect the full contract price. However, it is virtually impossible to complete a building contract in strict compliance with every tiny requirement of the plans and specifications. If the builder performs substantially according to the contract, he is entitled to collect the contract price, less a deduction that will compensate the owner for the builder's deviations from the contract. Substantial performance is hard to define. If the owner gets substantially the building that he contracted for, and the deviations are trifling and unintentional, there is substantial performance. For example, if I hire you to build a house according to my plans at a price of $12,000, and you fulfill your contract except that two rooms have the wrong wallpaper, which it would cost $100 to remedy, clearly there is substantial performance, and you are entitled to collect $11,900. The following are illustrations of cases where substantial performance was found lacking.

EXAMPLES: (1) The footings were inadequate for wet ground, so that the foundations sank and the floors sagged. *White* v. *Mitchell,* 123 Wash. 630, 213 Pac. 10 (1923); (2) the contract called for a six-room house, and the builder erected a five-room house; (3) the foundations and walls of the house cracked immediately after completion of construction due to a soil condition that the builder did not properly correct. *Newcomb* v. *Schaeffler,* 131 Colo. 56, 279 P2d 409 (1955); (4) in New York, it is generally held that if the deviations amount to more than 10 percent of the contract price, substantial performance is lacking. *Rochkind* v. *Jacobson,* 110 N.Y.S. 583.

If you contract to erect a building for me, and your performance is less than substantial, one of several consequences is possible:

1. If I am in a generous frame of mind, then even though the building is not the kind that you agreed to build, I may accept the building as a complete and satisfactory substitute for the building contracted for. Here I must pay the full contract price. No deductions are allowed because of the defects. *Zambakian* v. *Leson,* 77 Colo. 183, 234 Pac. 1065 (1925).

EXAMPLE: As the building went up, the owner inspected it and noticed the deviations from the contract. But he moved in, telling the builder that the building was satisfactory and that the contract price would be paid. This is full acceptance. All deviations were waived. *Hooper* v. *Cuneo,* 227 Mass. 37, 116 NE 237 (1917).

Often in these cases, you will find that the owner has with full knowledge of the defects paid the entire contract price. Since this is full acceptance, he cannot therefore sue the builder for damages because of defects he knew about when he paid his money. *Houlette & Miller* v. *Arntz,* 148 La. 407, 126 NW 796 (1910). And there are always words, acts, or both on the landowner's part indicating full acceptance of the building. *Aarnes* v. *Windham,* 137 Ala. 513, 34 So 816 (1903). Often the builder has a printed form that he asks the landowner to sign. This form recites that the building has been constructed in complete conformity with the contract.

2. I may accept the building as substantial performance but reserve the right to deductions because of the deviations.

EXAMPLE: The owner discovers defects as the building goes up, protests the defects, but continues to proceed with the builder on the basis and assumption that their contract is still in force. *Otto Misch Co.* v. *E. E. Davis Co.,* 241 Mich. 285, 217 NW 38 (1928). The builder gets the contract price, less a deduction to compensate for the deviations. *Gray* v. *Wood,* 220 Ala. 587, 127 So 148 (1930); 17 CJS 1101, 1105.

3. I simply move into the building because it is on my land and I cannot avoid it. My attitude at all times after discovering the defects is that the builder has breached his contract and ought not be paid anything. Most courts will nevertheless award the builder the value of the building, on the theory that it must be worth something to the landowner and that to give the builder nothing would be unduly harsh. Other courts, however, are less merciful with the builder. They say that I have a right to use my own land and the buildings on it, and since the builder's performance fell short of substantial performance, he is entitled to nothing. 5 Corbin, *Contracts* 551; 107 ALR 1411.

4. If I demolish the structure, or refuse to make any use of it, in most states the builder will be unable to collect a penny. 3 Corbin, *Contracts* 790.

§ 1003. Liability of seller-builder for defects in land or building. The subject of liability of the seller-builder for defects in land or building has grown tremendously in recent years.

In reading this material, one must be constantly aware of the fact that much of this material is new law, made *by the courts,* in very recent times. Some courts currently lag behind the times.

Also, one must be aware of the *remedies* that the courts afford. A court that is quite content to give a buyer his money back if the house that he buys turns out to be a lemon might not permit him to sue the seller-builder for damages. Or, a court that is quite content to allow the *first purchaser* to use a seller-builder for defects in the house might not allow a second purchaser of the now used house to sue the seller-builder.

The obligations of the seller of a *new* house under the old law differ from those of the seller of an *old* house. The obligations of the seller of a *completed* house differ from those of the seller of a house yet to be constructed. One who sells a house *to be constructed* has builder liability. One who sells a *completed* house does not, at least under some older cases. Suppose you, as a builder, have a house in the process of construction. *X* sees it and signs a contract to buy it. You have *builder liability* to *X*. As long as the seller has workmen on the job, the house is not fully completed, and therefore when the house is sold, the contract is treated as though it were a contract (1) to sell the land and (2) to finish the house. In short, it is a sell-and-build contract. Builder liability means that the courts hold the builder on two counts: (1) *he must build in a good and workmanlike manner;* (2) *the structure when completed must be reasonably fit for its intended purpose. Markman* v. *Hoefer,* 252 Ia. 118, 106 NW2d 59 (1960); *Jones* v. *Gatewood,* 381 P2d 158 (Okla. 1963); *Fain* v. *Nelson,* 56 Wash. 2d 217, 356 P2d 302 (1960). These are called *implied warranties.*

EXAMPLE: Exterior stucco peeled off soon after the house was completed. The builder is liable. He has failed to build in a good and workmanlike manner. The same would be true if the concrete footings were faulty and the building settled, causing cracked plaster and ill-fitting doors. 4 *Western Reserve L. Rev.* 361.

EXAMPLE: *X* builds a barn for *Y*, but the hayloft collapses when filled with hay. *X* is liable. The structure is not fit for its intended purpose.

In addition to liability on the two implied warranties, a builder is liable for failure to use ordinary care and skill. This is called *negligence liability*. For example, a builder must use ordinary care in the selecting of building materials, and if he should carelessly select beams of inadequate strength, he would be liable for injuries resulting from collapse of the house. However, if a builder uses ordinary care in the selection of building material, he is not liable for injuries caused by hidden defects in the materials.

EXAMPLE: You, as a builder, buy steel rods for roof trusses from a reputable dealer and, owing to hidden defects in the steel, the roof collapses. You are not liable, because you were not negligent.

There is an obvious defect in the law as stated above. Under the old law, the seller of a completed house has no builder liability.

EXAMPLE: A builder has fully completed a house at the time he sells it to you, and thereafter defects in construction come to light, such as inadequate waterproofing of basement walls, leaky roofs, faulty foundation, and so forth. The builder has no liability, because the implied warranties exist only where some construction remains to be done at the time the house is sold. Newer decisions reject this view.

The buyer of a newly completed house is at a disadvantage, because in an older house time brings to light the defects in construction and the buyer can see the defects for himself. To cure this situation, efforts are being made to get builders to give express warranties. If I buy a newly completed house from you, I could insist that you sign a document requiring you to make good any defects in construction that come to light within a year of the date of your deed conveying the property to me.

There is a historical reason for the distinction between sales of completed houses and houses not yet completed. The old law, which is today undergoing much change, but which still holds true in a few states, tells us that *when we buy a thing,* the rule is *caveat emptor.* We buy at our own risk unless we specifically demand and receive warranties of quality. This is the old law applied to sales of completed houses. The old law states that when you hire a man *to do a job,* he has a legal obligation to do the work correctly, which is the law that we apply to sales of houses to be constructed or completed.

NEW DIRECTIONS: Beginning in 1964 the courts began to throw the old rules overboard. They began to hold that in every sale of a *completed residence* by a *builder-seller* there is an implied warranty that the home was built in a workmanlike manner and is fit for habitation. *Carpenter* v. *Donohoe,* 154 Colo. 78, 388 P2d 399, 402 (1964); *Bethlahmy* v. *Bechtel,* 415 P2d 698 (Ida. 1966); *Waggoner* v. *Midwestern Develop., Inc.,* 154 NW2d 803 (S.D. 1967); *Moore* v. *Werner,* 418 SW2d 918 (Tex. Civ. App. 1967); *Humber* v. *Morton,* 426 SW2d 554 (Tex. 1968); *Theis* v. *Heuer,* 280 NE2d 300 (Ind. 1972) citing many articles; also *Tavaros* v. *Horstman,* 542 P2d 1275 (1976). The philosophy here is that the average buyer of a new home is ill-equipped to detect the defects and shortcomings of jerry-built construction. It is likely that all states will come to this point of view in time. 25 ALR3d 383. At this writing the new rule has been adopted in about half the states.

Most courts still limit the implied warranty of the building to a sale by a *builder-seller. H. B. Bolas Enterprises, Inc.* v. *Zarlings,* 156 Colo. 530, 400 P2d 447 (1965).

EXAMPLE: *V,* a builder-seller, sold a lot to *P* and constructed a home thereon for *P. P* lived there for a year and sold the house to *X.* There are no implied warranties by *P.*

The liability of the builder-seller extends only to the first purchaser.

EXAMPLE: *V,* a builder-seller, built a house. After completion of construction he sold it to *P-1. P-1* later sold it to *P-2.* The house developed cracks because of defective foundations. *P-2* repaired the cracks. He cannot sue *V.* Implied warranty liability, so far, has been applied only to sales of new houses. *Gallegos* v. *Graff,* 508 P2d 798 (Colo. 1973).

The idea of *products liability* arose in the sale of chattels.

EXAMPLE: Buick Motor Company manufactured a defective automobile. This was sold to its dealer, who sold it to *X. X* suffered injuries owing to the defects and recovered damages from Buick. *MacPherson* v. *Buick Motor Co.,* 217 N.Y. 382, 111 NE 1050 (1916).

Prior to this time, a person could sue only the person who sold him a defective product, for example, the car dealer. Now it is possible to sue the manufacturer. In its modern version as expressed in some decisions, products liability does not require the injured party to prove carelessness in manufacture. All that is needed is to show that the product was defective and that *bodily injury* resulted. The philosophy is that the manufacturer is better able to stand the loss than the injured party. He can raise his prices or take out insurance against such risks. *Greenman* v. *Yuba Power Products Inc.*, 59 Cal. 2d 57, 377 P2d 897 (1963); 76 *Yale L. J.* 887.

This view is beginning to appear in real estate law.

EXAMPLE: *XYZ Company*, a large national builder, erected a home that had a defective hot water system. The home was sold to *L*, who rented it to *T*. *T*'s son was scalded. *XYZ Company* was held liable. *Schipper* v. *Levitt & Sons, Inc.*, 44 N.J. 70, 207 A2d 314 (1965), noted in 51 *Cornell L. Q.* 389; 19 *Okla. L. Rev.* 417; 41 *Wash. L. Rev.* 166.

The liability extends only to those "in the business" of building. It would not apply to a homeowner selling his own home. 21 *Hastings L. J.* 483.

One important aspect of products liability is that it extends beyond the *first purchaser* of the house. *Cooper* v. *Cordova Sand & Gravel Co., Inc.*, 485 SW2d 261 (Tenn. 1972).

EXAMPLE: *V*, a merchant builder, built a house and sold it to *P-1*. *P-1* later sold it to *P-2*. *P-2*'s infant son was injured because of defective construction. *V* is liable. *Wright* v. *Creative Corp.*, 498 P2d 1179 (Colo. 1972).

In all of the following cases, a seller-builder was held liable to *his* purchaser for defects in construction on the theory of *implied warranty:*

EXAMPLES: Leaking roof.
Water seepage through foundation walls.
Well water polluted.
Abnormal settling of concrete slab foundation.
Sewer pipes not connected to city sewer.
Fire damage because chimney flue of fireplace not sealed with mortar.

Where new residential construction is approved for HUD mortgage insurance prior to the beginning of construction, the builder is required to deliver to the purchaser a warranty that construction was carried out in accordance with the plans and specifications. 12 USC 1701j-1. While technically this is not the same as the responsibility the courts have placed upon builder-sellers, many defects occur because of the builder's noncompliance with the plans and specifications.

EXAMPLE: A foundation may crack because it was installed over ground that did not meet the compaction requirements of the specifications or because concrete of a lesser grade than required in the specifications was used. Furthermore, specifications usually require that work be done in a workmanlike manner.

Where builder liability exists, the general contractor is liable even when the faulty work was done by a subcontractor. *Elliott Consol. School Dist.* v. *Basboom,* 227 F.Supp. 858 (1964).

When the completed work is reasonably certain to endanger third persons *if negligently constructed,* the contractor is liable for injuries to third parties.

EXAMPLE: The builder-seller sold to *A,* who sold to *B. B's* young son ran through an unmarked plate glass door. The builder should have used tempered safety glass instead of plate glass or placed a conspicuous red strip across the glass. *Wright* v. *Creative Corp.,* 498 P2d 1179 (Colo. 1972). The builder-seller must use due care.

EXAMPLE: The builder-seller constructed a home equipped with heavy cement planters. A little girl went with her parents to visit the occupants of the house. The planters fell on the girl, killing her. Builder-seller held liable. He has a duty to see that the residence is so constructed as to be reasonably free from dangerous hidden defects that will cause harm to those coming on the premises after the building has been completed and resold. *Calvera* v. *Green Springs, Inc.,* 220 So2d 414 (Fla. 1969). He is liable if he has been *negligent. Green Springs, Inc.* v. *Calvera,* 239 So2d 264 (Fla. 1970).

§ 1004. Warranties and insurance—new homes. The National Association of Home Builders has created a corporation known as Home Owners Warranty Corporation, located at National Housing Center, 15th and M Streets, N.W., Washington, D.C. 20005, to administer a program of quality protection for buyers of new homes. The program applies only to new homes and is offered only by builders who have been checked for the quality of construction they offer, and financial soundness. The coverage is transferable when you sell the house. In brief, it operates as follows:

Written warranty from the builder. At the time of closing or when the buyer moves in, both the builder and the buyer sign the HOW Home Warranty Agreement which explains the rights and obligations of both during the first two years of the program.

1st Year. The builder warrants against defects caused by faulty workmanship or materials due to noncompliance with HOW's Approved Standards for the first year of the Program.

2nd Year. The builder's warranty continues for the second year to protect against defects in the wiring, piping, and ductwork in the home's electrical, plumbing, heating, and cooling systems and against major structural defects.

Warranty insurance. American Bankers Insurance Company of Florida, which underwrites the HOW Program, backs the builder's written warranty for the first two years. If the builder cannot or will not perform his HOW warranty obligations, American Bankers Insurance assumes the responsibility.

Extended major structural insurance.

3rd–10th Year. A national insurance plan, also underwritten by American Bankers Insurance Company, directly insures the home buyer against major structural defects during the last eight years of the Program.

HOW home buyers receive several documents which detail the plan's coverage, itemize the reasonable exclusions, and describe the procedures for conciliation and arbitration of disagreements over defects. They receive a signed copy of the Home Warranty Agreement, insurance papers confirming that their home is enrolled in the HOW National Insurance Program, and a copy of the Approved Standards.

Obviously a buyer would be well advised to buy from a builder who offers this coverage. The one-time fee is $2.00 per $1,000 of the sales price of the home, which is inexpensive, and is paid by the builder.

If the builder goes broke, his warranty obligations will be fulfilled by HOW's underwriter, American Bankers Insurance Company of Florida. It insures the owner against defects in the home, but it does not insure against mechanics' liens, completion of the home, or other contractual issues between the builder and the owner.

REFERENCE: © Copyright National Assn. of Home Builders & Home Owners Warranty Corp. Reprinted by permission.

§ 1005. **Warranties of used homes.** The National Association of Realtors has a nationwide program of warranties issued in connection with the sale of used homes. Other organizations also offer warranties. Cost of the coverage, usually borne by the seller, ranges from $65 to $450. Most plans call for an inspection by the warrantor. Items covered usually include central heating and cooling systems, interior plumbing, electrical systems, roof, walls, ceilings, water heaters and softeners, and built-in appliances. Obviously a buyer who wants such a warranty should require the contract of sale to specify it.

VA warranties. The VA has requirements for warranties of good construction if it is to insure the mortgage loan. These requirements are:

1. An insurance-backed warranty for one year against defects caused by poor materials or workmanship.
2. A similar warranty for the first two years against faulty electrical, plumbing, and heating and cooling systems.
3. Direct insurance coverage for years three through ten against structural defects.
4. A system for handling disputes with builders and, if necessary, arbitration arranged by the American Arbitration Association or a similar group.
5. The VA requirements are strikingly similar to those of the Home Owners Warranty Corp. (HOW) plan.

§ 1006. **Consumer product warranties.** Typically, a builder incorporates into his structure various items that fall under "consumer products" as defined by the Magnuson-Moss Warranty Act. 15 USC § 2301 *et seq*. Because of this new law, he must, prior to the sale of any consumer product that is covered by a warranty, fully, conspicuously, and understandably disclose the terms of the warranty and whether it is "full" or "limited" in terms of its duration. 15 USC §§ 2302, 2303. The Federal Trade Commission has taken the position that the act applies to separate items of equipment attached to real property whether or not they are fixtures under state law. The key to understanding the separateness test lies in the distinction between the physical separateness of an item and the separate function of that item.

EXAMPLE: A furnace has a mechanical, thermal, or electrical function apart from the realty, whereas roofing shingles have no function apart from the realty. When sold by a builder to a home buyer as part of the home, the furnace is covered by the act and the shingles are not.

Using this test the FTC has decided that the following consumer products are covered by the act when they are sold as part of a home: boiler, heat pump, electronic air cleaner, exhaust fan, thermostat, space heater, furnace, air-conditioning system, humidifier, central vacuum system, smoke detector, fire alarms, fire extinguisher, garage door opener, chimes, water pump, intercom, burglar alarm, electric meter, water meter, gas meter, gas or electric barbecue grill, whirlpool bath, garbage disposal, water heater, water softener, sump pump, refrigerator, freezer, trash compactor, range, oven, dishwasher, oven hood, clothes washer, clothes dryer, ice maker.

Using the same test, the FTC has found that the following are not consumer products when sold as part of a home: radiator, convector, register, duct, cabinet, door, shelving, windows, floor covering, walls or wall covering, ceiling, vanity, gutter, shingles, chimney and fireplace, fencing, garage door, electrical switch and outlet, light fixture, electric panel box, fuse, circuit breaker, wiring, sprinkler head, water closet, bidet, lavatory, bathtub, laundry tray, sink, shower stall, plumbing fittings, medicine cabinet.

A last category or group contains separate items or equipment, which are consumer products under the act when sold as part of a condominium, co-operative, or multiple family dwelling because they are not normally used for personal family or household purposes within the meaning of the act: fusible fire door closer, TV security monitor, emergency backup generator, master TV antenna, elevator, institutional trash compactor.

REFERENCE: FTC advisory opinion 12/17/76, CCH *Trade Regulation Reports* Par. 21245.

Even though the builder does not make these pieces of equipment himself, he is nonetheless bound by the disclosure sections of the act because he is a "supplier" under the terms of the act. 15 USC § 2301(4).

The builder can comply with the terms of the law by clearly and conspicuously displaying the text or a quote of the text of the written warranty covering the consumer product in close conjunction to each warranted product; or by maintaining in each of the seller's locations an indexed binder containing copies of all warranties on consumer products; or, if the warranty text is printed on the product box, by displaying the package.

EXAMPLE: When the builder incorporates into his structure dishwashers, disposals, ranges, refrigerators, and range hoods he should either display next to, or taped onto the appliances, copies of the warranties given by the manufacturer of those appliances or keep in his model office a binder which contains those warranties. This binder should be displayed in a conspicuous place and potential buyers should be afforded the opportunity to review its contents prior to the sale. The builder should make similar disclosure of his own warranty if that warranty covers the consumer products.

REFERENCE: Peters, How the Magnuson-Moss Warranty Act Affects the Builders/Seller of New Housing, 5 *R.E.L.J.* 338 (1977).

§ **1007. Mobile homes.** In lieu of building a home, some couples, especially those of retirement age, buy a mobile home. This is hauled to a mobile home court, owned by the operator. There are *open* and *closed* courts. In a closed court the couple must buy their mobile home from the operator of the court. In an open court, the couple may buy their mobile home elsewhere. In any case, the couple rents the space occupied by their mobile home. The arrangement may be a month-to-month tenancy. It also may be a lease for a year or so, with rules incorporated therein concerning the use of the court. The great disadvantage is that the landlord has the usual rights of a landlord. If he ousts the couple at the end of their lease, they must haul their mobile home to another court. This can be expensive.

Some retirement courts forbid occupancy by children. The building code governing mobile homes is a federal code. The states have no control. Economically, it is argued that a mobile home depreciates in value like a car. A residence appreciates in value. Socially, mobile court living appeals to gregarious people.

§ **1008. Code violations.** In every contract to build, it is implied that the building will be constructed in conformity with all laws and ordinances. It is rather universally required that a building permit be issued by the city before construction is begun, and before such a permit is issued, the plans and specifications will be examined by the city to see if the building planned complies with all ordinances. However, after the permit is issued, the builder may nevertheless (either willfully in order to cut costs, or through ignorance or negligence) violate ordinances in the process of erecting the building. If the building as constructed violates laws or ordinances, the builder will be compelled to allow his buyer as an abatement or deduction from the contract price a sum adequate to remedy the defects. *Schiro* v. *W. E. Gould & Co.,* 18 Ill.2d 538, 165 NE2d 286, 49 Ill. B.J. 209 (1960). Or if the buyer discovers the ordinance violations after he has paid the entire contract price, he may sue the builder for damages. *Gutowski* v. *Crystal Homes, Inc.,* 26 Ill.App.2d 269, 167 NE2d 422 (1960); *Brunke* v. *Pharo,* 3 Wis.2d 628, 89 NW2d 221 (1958). Ordinance violations may also render title unmarketable. Advertising for sale a building that contains ordinance violations may constitute a fraud upon the buyer.

All of these legal remedies may be rather poor comfort to the landowner. If the building contains serious violations of ordinances, the city may refuse to permit the owner to occupy his building. It may compel demolition of the building. It may fine the landowner, and the fine may be very substantial, for each day of violation is often considered a separate criminal offense.

§ 1009. Suggestions:

1. Before starting construction, the builder should give thought to the mechanic's lien problem. Before he can collect any money on his contract, he will often be called upon to furnish a sworn statement showing all subcontractors and their contract prices. As he hires his subcontractors, he should make memoranda from which this affidavit can later be prepared.

2. The builder should also make arrangements to prove what work and materials are going into the building. If the builder is not paid and must establish a mechanic's lien claim against the premises, he must be able to prove in court (perhaps a year or so later) by truck drivers' tickets or other direct evidence of some witness present at the time, what materials were delivered to the building site and incorporated in the building.

3. Before starting construction, the builder should provide himself with all necessary insurance as to fire, casualty, and liability.

4. Before starting, the builder should also take whatever steps are necessary to shore up his neighbor's building or to notify the neighbor to attend to this. My neighbor has the right to have my land support his *land* in its natural condition, so that if both tracts are vacant, if I excavate near the line, and his soil falls into the excavation, I become liable to him for damages. However, if he erects buildings on his land, he has no right to have my soil support his *buildings.* But if I propose to excavate, I should notify my neighbor of my plans in good time, so that *he* may shore up and take other precautions to protect *his building.* Then if I proceed to excavate with due care, I will not be liable if his building tilts or collapses into my excavation if such fall is due to the weight and pressure of the building. Although I am not obligated, in the absence of a city ordinance, to support my neighbor's building, I may be liable to him for damage caused to his building by my excavation if the excavating is done without proper care. Failure to exercise proper care exists in the following situations: (a) where I fail to notify my neighbor of my intention to excavate, thus giving him no opportunity to protect his property; (b) where I notify my neighbor of my intention to excavate, but my excavation is deeper than, or different from, the excavation described in my notice; (c) where I leave my excavation open for a long period of time; (d) where I open the entire excavation at one time when it would have been possible and safer to dig in sections, as where the soil consists of sand, gravel, or loam; (e) where I allow water to collect in my excavation, and seepage of the water causes my neighbor's building to fall (*Horowitz* v. *Blay,* 193 Mich. 493, 160 NW 438); (f) where I allow water and silt from my neighbor's land to collect in my excavation, thereby withdrawing support from his buildings, which then fall (*New York Central* v. *Marinucci Bros.,* 337 Mass. 469, 149 NE2d 680; 50 ALR 486). In many cities, ordinances have been passed that impose on an excavator a qualified duty to support adjoining buildings. A specified notice (ten days is common) of any intended excavation must be given the adjoining owner, and he is given a right of access to the excavation for the purpose of protecting his building. If the excavation is less than a specified depth (nine, ten, and twelve feet are common) and it becomes necessary for the adjoining owner to extend his foundation downward, he must do so at his own expense. But the cost of extending the foundation below the specified depth is borne by the excavator. Ordinances of this type are common throughout the South and on the Pacific Coast. All code requirements for the construction of protective coverings over sidewalks, for fences surrounding the excavation, for shoring up sidewalks and streets, and so on should be complied with.

5. Before starting on construction, the builder should procure a survey showing the exact boundaries of the premises with the corners plainly marked. He should thereupon

recheck the applicable set-back ordinances and the provisions of all plat and deed restrictions. The building must comply with both public and private restrictions. He should especially watch for building line violations.

A building contract may contain the following provisions designed to protect the landowner against mechanics' liens:

1. A requirement that the building be completed free and clear of all mechanics' and materialmen's liens.

2. A clause waiving all mechanics' and materialmen's liens, both of the general contractor and all subcontractors and materialmen. If the state law requires a contract such as this to be recorded, the contract should be duly acknowledged (in order to qualify it for recording) and recorded.

3. A requirement that the contractor hold the landowner harmless against all mechanics' liens and mechanic's lien litigation.

4. A requirement that the landowner, his architect, and mortgage lender be furnished all contractors' statements, subcontractors' statements, partial waivers, and waivers of lien as construction goes forward according to the progress payments schedule.

5. A provision that subcontractors will be paid directly by the landowner or his mortgage lender, not by the general contractor.

6. A provision for a holdback of a percentage of all payments to the general contractor until a specified period of time has elapsed after completion of the building. This gives the landowner leverage to compel the general contractor to correct defective work without asserting any lien claim.

7. A provision that progress payments will be made only as a specified architect certifies that the work is in place and is satisfactory. The timing of the progress payments should coincide with the timing in the construction loan agreement.

With respect to the construction contract the following observations are pertinent:

1. Let the construction contract specifically provide at what stages payments are to be made, in what amounts, and how much is to be held back from each payment by the owner to insure correction of faulty work.

2. For the protection of all parties, let the construction contract provide what supervision the architect will provide, which should dovetail into the architect's contract with the owner; what drawings the architect will provide the builder; what authority the architect has to give orders to the builder; how such orders are to be given (whether verbally or in writing), and so on.

3. Where there is a supervising architect, be sure that the construction contract provides that no payments will be made except on the production of architect's certificates that the builder is entitled to receive payment and that the work done qualifies for payment both as to quality and quantity.

4. The contract should specify that the supervising architect has authority to order the contractor to correct work that was not performed in a proper manner according to the plans.

5. To prevent controversy, let the construction contract provide that final payment and acceptance by the owner will not bar any claims for latent defects.

6. Many construction contracts provide that the building is to be completed in a specified time and that the builder shall pay specified sums for delay beyond the specified

completion time, except where such delays are caused by strikes, bad weather, and so forth.

7. Building contracts should provide that the builder be obligated to protect the landowner against liability to adjoining owners, members of the public, and employees and subcontractors, and also to take out insurance policies to protect against such liabilities.

RESERVED: §§ 1010–1020.

35

Shopping Centers

§ 1021. **Types of shopping centers.** There are three kinds of shopping centers. They are the small *neighborhood center,* the larger *community* or *suburban center,* and the mammoth *regional center.* Certain legal problems are common to all centers.

§ 1022. **Zoning problems.** If the area in question falls outside the limits of any city or village, it may be subject to a county zoning ordinance. If it lies within a city or village, it will be subject to the local zoning ordinance. In either case, the zoning may prohibit business. The problem then becomes one of securing an amendment to the zoning ordinance or a special use permit.

After the local authority has been persuaded to amend the zoning ordinance or to grant a special use permit, the amendment must pass the test of the courts, for someone, possibly a businessman who will be adversely affected by the shopping center, may attack the rezoning. If the shopping center developer can demonstrate that the old zoning will work an unreasonable financial hardship on him without any benefit to the public, the amendments will be sustained. 51 ALR2d 263; 76 ALR2d 1172; 35 *Notre Dame Lawyer* 197. This is not considered illegal spot zoning. A shopping island in the middle of an area planned to be residential may be a benefit to the residential community. The shopping convenience of the adjoining residents is definitely a factor that the courts will consider in determining the validity of the rezoning. *Eicher* v. *Board of Zoning Appeals,* 209 Md. 432, 121 A2d 249. In this connection, the larger the area rezoned, the less likely it is that the action will be condemned as illegal spot zoning. *In re Lieb's Appeal,* 179 Pa. Super. 318, 116 A2d 860. Again, there is a benefit to the public in these outlying shopping centers in that business decentralization diminishes traffic congestion within the city. *Bartram* v. *Zoning Commission,* 136 Conn. 89, 68 A2d 308. This is especially true where downtown stores do not provide off-street parking. *Skinner* v. *Reed* (Tex. Civ. App.), 265 SW2d 850. Moreover, the shopping center increases the wealth of the city by attracting new business. *City of Waxahachie* v. *Watkins,* 154 Tex. 206, 275 SW2d 477. Thus it also creates additional tax revenues.

If, however, the authorities refuse to change the zoning to permit the center, it is difficult to persuade the courts to overthrow their decision.

§ 1023. **Vacation of streets.** If the shopping center promoter finds that the land he proposes to acquire has been subdivided into lots, he faces the problem of *vacating* the streets and alleys depicted on the plat of the subdivision, for his buildings will no doubt stand in the path of such streets. This means, first of all, persuading the governing body of the city or village to pass an ordinance vacating such streets and alleys. By *vacation,* the city relinquishes all public rights in the streets and permits the streets to be closed.

EXAMPLE: An old recorded plat of subdivision depicts streets. Actually the land is raw land. The streets have never been opened. Such streets are called *paper streets.* They exist only on paper. Nevertheless the municipality must enact an ordinance *vacating* such streets in order to show that it has relinquished its interest in them.

Downtown businessmen are often members of such governing bodies. They may view the prospect of a competing shopping area with hostility and vote against the vacation of streets.

All that part of the subdivision in which the vacated streets and alleys lie must be acquired by the promoter, because any lot owner whose land abuts on a street to be vacated can object to, and often block, a vacation. On the other hand, lot owners in the subdivision whose lots are remotely situated from the streets to be vacated have no standing to complain of the vacation.

In some states, when a street is vacated, title reverts to the orginal subdivider and it will therefore be necessary to procure a deed from him.

§ 1024. **Site planning.** In the early development of the proposed shopping center layout, the location of the building area and parking facilities must be established. Tentative locations must be assigned to the key tenants and then adjacent parking allocated. In addition to preparing the initial shopping center layout to be used in connection with obtaining your first tenants, it is also necessary to have your architect prepare a front elevation of the project in order to establish the character of the architecture.

After leasing to the first two or three tenants of the project, the shopping center layout and the location of the buildings and parking lot may be stabilized.

In the large, regional center, the major tenants (department stores) have a very considerable say in the layout of the center.

§ 1025. **Leases—shopping center problems in general—lease clauses—mortgage financing.**

The mortgage lender looks to lease revenue to furnish the cash flow for debt service. The terms of the lease, in consequence, have become a matter of grave concern to the lender.

In general the lender wants some clauses in the lease that differ from the clauses the owner wants. The lender wants assured income to retire the mortgage, which means the unconditional liability of triple-A tenants. He wants protection against the landowner's acts or defaults that might destroy the leases.

Interim and permanent lender. As between lenders, the interim lender who finances the construction of the center is concerned with construction and completion of improvements and compliance with tenant's requirements in this regard. But the takeout lender (see § 614) steps in after the tenants have accepted their leases and premises in writing, and has little interest in construction problems. On the other hand, the interim lender has no interest in rental income because he steps out of the picture as the tenants step in.

As for the landlord, he must satisfy the interim lender, the permanent lender, and the triple-A tenant if he is to get his financing, so he must defer to these parties to a great extent so far as lease clauses are concerned. Parenthetically, to the extent that the permanent lender is looking for a good *landlord's lease* because he may one day be landlord, he is also protecting the present landlord.

A young lawyer representing a landlord or his mortgagee should not feel that the standard, printed form of lease produced by a chainstore tenant is immutable. The chains are accustomed to negotiating changes in their printed forms. Hence the printed form must be read carefully and necessary changes made.

Clause specifying date of commencement of tenant's occupancy. The tenant will wish to defer his occupancy and commencement of rent payment until construction of the center has been completed and the other tenants are prepared to commence their occupancy. The landlord, however, will wish the tenant to begin his occupancy as soon as *his store* is completed. A compromise may require the tenant to occupy before the center is completed, but to pay only a percentage rent during that period. The lease may define the commencement of its term as the date construction of the shopping center is completed. *Wong* v. *D. Grazia* (Cal.) 386 P2d 817; 1964 *Duke L. J.* 645. 16 *Hastings L. J.* 470; 24 *Md. L. Rev.* 356; 12 *U.C.L.A. Rev.* 246; 66 ALR2d 733, 735. This is dangerous because of the rule against perpetuities, for completion is technically an indefinite date in the future, and the rule against perpetuities makes such indefinite documents void. This threat is met by providing that the commencement of lease and completion of center shall be not more than five years from date of lease, otherwise the lease to be void.

Duration of leases. The key leases must continue in force as long as the mortgage debt remains unpaid so that the mortgage debt dwindles to nothing by the time the lease has run out. Small tenants can have shorter leases so that, if the key tenants wish to expand, space will be available for them to do so.

Amount of minimum guaranteed rent. Percentage leases all provide for a minimum rent to be paid. This minimum rent must be adequate to pay taxes, insurance, maintenance, and still leave enough to retire the mortgage debt.

Exclusives. Commonly, certain tenants are given the exclusive right to operate a certain type of business in the center. The fact that the tenant is given an exclusive imposes a restraint on the activities permitted other tenants. Hence it is important that the lease be recorded so that all other tenants are given notice of this restraint, and it is better for the exclusive clause to describe the center accurately, so that subsequent lessees are put on notice of the extent of the restricted area. 51(C) CJS 625.

An exclusive should be carefully drafted or litigation will result. 97 ALR2d 4.

EXAMPLE: A lease to a delicatessen forbids "other delicatessen shops" in the center. Would this bar a supermarket from handling delicatessen items? One court has said "Yes." *Parker* v. *Levin,* 285 Mass. 125, 188 NE2d 502. Another court has said "No." *Mook* v. *Weaver Bros.,* 59 F2d 1028.

In general, where they are asked to enforce an exclusive, courts look for substantial overlapping of products and substantial competition. 97 ALR2d 46.

EXAMPLE: A junior department store that operates a variety department violates, to that extent, an earlier exclusive given to a variety store. *Variety, Inc.* v. *Hustad Corp.,* 145 Mont. 358, 400 P2d 408; 51(C) CJS 635.

An exclusive should be broad enough to protect the tenant but not so broad as to hamper other and different enterprises that make only incidental sales of competing items.

EXAMPLE: A lease to a supermarket stipulates that no other store in the center should sell food for consumption off the premises. This would keep out a bakery that could well be a distinct asset to the center. An exclusive given a candy store obviously should permit a drug store to sell boxed candies.

Obviously, a lease given in 1967 cannot restrict the operations of a tenant who holds a lease given in 1966 or earlier.

A landlord's violation of an exclusive may entail drastic consequences.

EXAMPLE: The developer gave *A* an exclusive for a variety store and later leased another site in the center to *B* for a variety store. When *A* stopped *B*'s operations, *B* successfully contended that there was a constructive eviction. This released *B* of all liability on his lease. *Variety, Inc.* v. *Hustad Corp.,* 145 Mont. 358, 400 P2d 408.

Where the lease gives the tenant an "exclusive," the lender will want the lease to provide that this can only be enforced by an injunction suit restraining another tenant from using the premises for the purpose in question. In other words, the lender will not want the tenant to have the right to terminate the lease for violation of the "exclusives" clause. It is not sufficient that the lease does not specifically give the tenant the right to terminate the lease for violation of the exclusive clause. Some courts have allowed the tenant to terminate his lease where the exclusive clause is violated on the ground that this was a "constructive eviction" of the tenant.

An exclusive may apply to additions to the shopping center as well as to the original center. 51(C) CJS 623.

Covenant as to use of premises. The lease should state the use which the tenant is to make of the premises and contain a covenant not to use the premises for other purposes. Both provisions are necessary. If this protection is lacking, a tenant who would like to "jump his lease" simply puts the premises to a use offensive to the other tenants and the landlord will be compelled to agree to a cancellation of the lease. Or, just as bad, the tenant may use the premises for a use for which another tenant has an "exclusive." Surprisingly, leases have been encountered which gave the tenant an "exclusive" but did not forbid him to use the premises for other purposes! Obviously the use must be one which is not forbidden by local zoning.

Radius clause. Objection can be raised to a clause which forbids the landlord to rent premises within a specified *radius* of the shopping center for a purpose that competes with the tenant's business. The shopping center promoter might sell the center and set up a competing use outside the center, and the lender would be powerless to prevent a cancellation of the lease by the tenant for this breach of the landlord's covenant. Perhaps the lender can get the tenant to sign a side agreement that he will not cancel the lease for such cause as long as the mortgage remains unpaid and that the clause is extinguished if the mortgagee acquires the center by foreclosure or deed in satisfaction of the mortgage debt.

In another form of the radius clause, the lease may forbid the tenant to open another store within three to five miles of the outer boundaries of the center.

Any radius clause must be drafted with strong protection against indirect violations, such as through the use of corporate affiliates, subsidiaries, members of the family, etc.

Restraint of trade. In the earlier days of shopping centers, exclusives and the radius clause were drafted without regard to their possible invalidity as violations of federal antitrust laws. Recently the Federal Trade Commission has banned some of these practices on the ground that they violate the federal antitrust laws. Kratovil, Modern Real Estate Documentation, § 599 (Prentice-Hall 1975).

REFERENCES: Halper, The Antitrust Laws Visit Shopping Center "Use Restrictions," 4 *Real Estate L. J.* 3 (1975) (very valuable); Eagle, Shopping Center Control: The Developer Beseiged, 51 *J. of Urban Law* 585 (1974); Note, The Antitrust Implications of Restrictive Covenants in Shopping Center Leases, 86 *Harv. L. Rev.* 1201 (1973).

NEW DIRECTIONS: In the large regional shopping centers it was the custom to exercise control over the tenant mix. At times this control was exercised by the *anchor tenant,* often a large department store like Gimbels. At times the control was exercised by a powerful developer, like Sears. Often discount houses were banned. Specialty shops were regulated by lease provisions, so that an appropriate mix of price ranges was achieved. The FTC has ruled that this is illegal price fixing. The courts have not as yet passed on it, but the developers have not resisted FTC action. This poses a serious problem to the large centers and their mortgage lenders.

NEW DIRECTIONS: The National Labor Relations Board has ruled that a shopping center developer has no legal right to forbid picketing by striking employees of a tenant.

Construction of center by developer. The lease will contain a covenant by the developer to build the center in accordance with the site plan, subject to such changes as the lease specifically permits. The lease will require the landlord to construct any building that the tenant is to occupy.

Since the project may have reached only the stage of general overall design, final working drawings of the tenant's store will not be available at the time the lease is executed. A workable way to handle the situation is to attach to the lease a synopsis setting forth the construction to be performed. The tenant must covenant to furnish the landlord a store and fixture layout in sufficient detail so that the landlord can prepare drawings and specifications for the construction work. The landlord should covenant to furnish, when construction is completed, an architect's certificate that the premises have been completed according to the synopsis.

The lease should require the tenant to give the landlord an *acceptance letter* when the landlord has completed all required construction work on the leased premises. The permanent mortgage lender will insist on seeing such acceptances, for he counts on revenue from the tenants to pay off the mortgage and wants to know that the tenants have no excuse for seeking to be relieved of their leases. The landlord will find that if he allows the tenant to take possession before the acceptance is given, the tenant, knowing that the landlord must furnish the mortgage lender these acceptances, may demand additional work he is not entitled to under the lease.

Shell and allowance. In smaller centers the landlord builds and finishes the stores, exterior and interior. A lease of a store in this situation is called a *turnkey lease.* In regional centers, the landlord may construct only a shell for the big tenant and bring the utilities to the perimeter of the store. The big tenant may build his own storefront, walls, floors, and ceilings. The landlord then gives the tenant an allowance against his rent of part of the money so expended by the tenant. Here the lease should: (1) furnish at least some sort of *outline specifications* if final plans and specifications are unavailable, for the tenant cannot intelligently decide how much rent to pay unless he knows what the construction work will cost him; (2) require the tenant to protect the landlord against mechanics' liens by furnishing a deposit, surety bond, etc., though a lease covenant by a triple-A tenant to pay all mechanics' liens may be sufficient; (3) require the tenant to carry builder's risk, workmen's compensation, and other insurance during construction; (4) require the tenant to hire labor that will not cause controversies with the developer's construction crew.

Projections beyond the front building line. Commonly the sketch attached to a lease will depict the proposed buildings, invariably establishing a common line for all the buildings. This, of itself, might establish a right in any tenant to object to any other building extending beyond this building line. 16 *Baylor L. Rev.* 11. It is best, of course, to spell this out in the lease.

Store hours, continuing operation, and inventory. The lease will specify the hours the store will remain open, as many hours as possible from the landlord's viewpoint. The tenant will be required to carry a full inventory for display and sale and full staff of employees, and to keep his store illuminated until a specified hour after closing.

A vital clause in the lease from the landlord's viewpoint is the clause requiring the tenant to remain in possession, to keep open, and to continuously operate his business during the term of the lease. A tenant who vacates the store, simply paying his minimum rent, creates a disaster area.

Tax escalation. Commonly the lease requires the tenant to pay a pro rata share of any increase in real estate taxes after the first year's assessment. Otherwise the developer's income could be watered down to the point where he could not keep up his mortgage payments.

Fixturing. The landlord does not usually install tenant's store fixtures today, but in those cases where he does so, the lease will require the tenant to pay an additional rent until this amount has been repaid to the landlord. The expenditure is a loan rather than a gift by the landlord.

Charges for and maintenance of common areas. The lease assesses the tenant for the maintenance of all common areas but requires the landlord to maintain them.

Repairs and maintenance. The lease usually requires the landlord to perform all structural maintenance and all outside repairs, including repairs of outside walls, roof, sidewalks, canopies, malls, and parking lots. Tenants are required to do maintenance inside their stores.

Percentage leases. For the landlord's convenience, it is desirable that all percentage leases be uniform with respect to the time of month when monthly statements of gross sales are to be furnished by the tenant.

Cancellation clauses. The lease should give either party the right to cancel if certain stages of the construction work has not been started by a specified date.

Key tenants. The smaller tenant will want the landlord to covenant: (1) that there are leases with stated key tenants; (2) that the leases are not cancellable; and (3) that the leases run for a specified period of time and prohibit these tenants from discontinuing business. Such leases may further provide that if a named key tenant discontinues operations, the small tenant may cancel his lease. This is sometimes called the *follow-the-leader clause*. It is dangerous, for if a key tenant moves, the shopping center may collapse. Alternatively, it may provide that the small tenant pays a lower rent until operations are resumed by a major tenant of caliber equal to that of the tenant who moved out.

Parking area and malls—easements and covenants. The lease should contain a covenant by the landlord to furnish a parking area with a basic minimum of parking area. The minimum is so calculated that even if the center is expanded, the parking ratio does not fall below a specified ratio. The lease grants the tenant an easement to use the parking lot, as it does with respect to use of malls, drives, walks, tunnels, and other facilities to be used in common by the tenants. *Gray Drug Stores v. Foto Fair, Inc.,* 288 NE2d 401 (Ohio 1971). Of course, it is probable that implied easements would arise for this purpose even if the easement clause was omitted but leaving the matter to chance would be poor draftsmanship from the tenant's point of view. Care must be exercised to make this an easement and not a license. It is customary to include a provision barring a tenant's employees from certain choice areas of the lot. Employees arrive early in the day, before shoppers arrive and are in a position to usurp preferred parking places unless the lease forbids this. The landlord customarily covenants to pave, light, and stripe the parking area; to police it; to keep it lighted, in repair, and free of ice and snow. Parking is only one of many easements that are important to the high-credit tenant. Ingress and egress over the drives, walks, and malls, for example, are others. Indeed, the tenant's right to enjoyment of all the common areas should be set out in some detail. This prevents the landlord from curtailing improvidently the basic rights of the high-credit tenant so important to the successful operation of the tenant's business. Once an easement has been granted, it cannot be removed without the tenant's consent. To maintain a degree of flexibility, it is well to reserve to the landlord (and this right will accrue to the lender in the event of foreclosure, if the clause so states) the right to make reasonable changes in the location of the easements without curtailing their area or availability to the lease. Many leases forbid the erection of buildings or structures in the parking lot. *Gray v. Foto Fair,* 288 NE2d 341 (Ohio 1971).

Facilities serving other premises. The landlord will routinely reserve in the lease the right and easement to run and maintain through the leased premises conduits, pipes, etc. needed to serve other areas of the center.

Evidence of title. The lease should require the landlord to furnish the tenant evidence of good title to the leased premises, preferably a leasehold title insurance policy. The tenant should check this policy to make sure there are no building restrictions forbidding the use he plans to make of the premises. In addition, the landlord should covenant that he has good title to the remainder of the center and should afford the tenant's lawyer an opportunity to check the landlord's title policy.

Subordination clause. There are legal advantages to a lender in having key leases prior and therefore superior to the mortgage. For one thing, in some states foreclosure of a senior mortgage automatically terminates a junior lease, and the lender is powerless to prevent this. For a like reason the lender objects to a lease clause subordinating the lease "to all institutional mortgages now or hereafter on said premises." An affirmative covenant by the tenant to *attorn* to the purchaser at the foreclosure sale might cure this problem. This is coupled with a *non-disturbance clause* under which it is agreed that the tenant's possession will not be disturbed as long as he is not in default under his lease. The net legal effect is that the purchaser at the foreclosure sale (normally the mortgagee) becomes the tenant's landlord after foreclosure. Also the lease should prohibit any subordination by the tenant to a junior mortgage, since foreclosure of the junior mortgage might then wipe out the lease. The problem of the subordinate lease is a thorny problem for mortgage lenders and there are no really 100 percent satisfactory solutions. Kratovil, Modern Mortgage Law and Practice (1972) §§ 250, 344.

Restrictions on assignment of lease. The perfect commercial lease from the landlord's point of view contains an absolute prohibition against an assignment or sublease of the demised premises by the tenant, since this assures the landlord (and, incidentally, the mortgage lender) that the original triple-A tenant will remain in possession. But the tenant who wants to move will try to contrive subterfuges to get around the prohibition. Accordingly, assignment clauses are written to prevent subterfuges. The clause should forbid the tenant to assign, mortgage, encumber, or sublet without the lessor's consent. A prohibition should also be included against permitting the demised premises to be used by others through concessions or even through occupation by others. In the event the tenant is a corporation, it should be spelled out that any transfer, sale, pledge, or other disposition of the corporate stock or voting securities shall be deemed a prohibited assignment, though such a provision is obviously impossible in the case of corporations having numerous stockholders. A lease to a chain store may, at the chain's request, permit assignment to a subsidiary of the chain so long as the chain is willing to sign a guarantee of payment of rent and so long as the operation will continue in substantially the same fashion and without changes of signs or other physical features that "pull" shoppers to the area.

Before consenting to an assignment, the landlord and his mortgagee must determine that the assignee's operation will not violate an "exclusive." If the lease is a percentage lease, he should not consent to an assignment to a tenant whose gross volume of business is substantially smaller than that of the present tenant, for percentage rents are based on gross receipts, not net receipts.

Covenants in general. Every shopping center lease contains covenants on the part of the landlord and covenants on the part of the tenant. Among the provisions the lender hopes and expects to find are the following tenant's covenants: to operate his business continuously; to remain open a certain number of hours per day; to keep his quarters illuminated until some specified hour each night; to pay a proportionate share of maintaining, policing, lighting, and insuring the parking area and other common areas; to pay for central services such as air conditioning, heat, water, janitorial service, and utilities, if landlord is to furnish same; to pay a share of any increase in real estate taxes over the amount levied when the center becomes operational; to repair and maintain the store *interior* including doors and windows and be responsible for glass breakage; to avoid trash accumulation; to submit proposed signs and awnings for landlord's approval (which chain stores will resist); and to maintain membership in a merchants' association.

Among the common covenants, also, are those forbidding signs, displays, vending machines, or other unsightly objects on the mall in front of the store. Use of loudspeaker advertising or garish sales ("going-out-of-business sales") is also forbidden.

Ordinarily the parties contemplate that any party who succeeds to the landlord's ownership or the tenant's leasehold will enjoy the benefit of and be bound by the covenants. It is best to spell this out in the lease. This insures the right of the lender to enforce these covenants against the tenant in the event he acquires ownership through foreclosure. By the same token, the tenant will have the right to enforce covenants on the part of the lessor. Hence the lender must analyze the lease covenants that place duties on the landlord to determine whether they are unduly burdensome, such as covenants to rebuild or repair, regardless of cost. It may be possible to negotiate a side-agreement with the tenant that specific burdensome covenants will not be enforceable against the lender.

The covenants on the landlord's part should be covenants that the lender is able to perform, if necessary, so that if the landlord defaults, the lender can step in and perform and thus prevent termination of the leases by the tenant.

EXAMPLE: A landlord who happens to own a nearby "Kiddieland" can covenant to furnish complimentary tickets to a tenant who sells children's shoes. A lender succeeding to ownership of the center could not perform this covenant, and so it must not be included in the "covenants that run with the land."

EXAMPLE: A mortgage covers *part* of a shopping center. A lease to a tenant in this part of the center requires the landlord to restore or replace *any building in the center* damaged by fire, etc. If the mortgagee forecloses, he cannot restore any building in the other portion of the center and yet, as the new landlord, if he fails to do so, he will be in default under the lease.

Cancellation clauses. Any clause giving the tenant a right to cancel out because of events other than the landlord's breach of covenant is disturbing to a lender. For example, the value of the lease is affected by any clause giving the right to cancel if *any* part of the parking lot is condemned, for example, for road widening or if the tenant's sales do not average a specified dollar amount (the *kickout clause*).

If the lease provides for cancellation in the event the landlord fails to pay "any" mortgage, this might include the lender's own mortgage and would pull the rug from under him when he needs protection most. If possible, the lease should provide that any lender will receive notice from the tenant of the landlord's breach of covenant and be given an opportunity to cure it before the tenant cancels the lease. There should be no objection to this if the notice is required only if the lender first informs the lessee in writing of his name and address. This is analogous to the situation in a leasehold mortgage where the landlord agrees to notify the lender of a tenant's default and to give the lender the right to cure it before the landlord declares a forfeiture of the lease. Alternatively, the lender may be able to procure a side-agreement with the tenant under which the tenant waives, as to the lender, the right to cancel the lease because of landlord's breaches of covenant, either altogether or until the lender has acquired ownership by foreclosure and can then control the situation. In one way or another, in other words, the lender should endeavor to insulate himself against the tenant's wriggling out of the lease because of the landlord's defaults, as the tenant will try to do if the lease proves economically disadvantageous.

Abatement of rent. The lease may give the lessee the right to an abatement of rent because of the landlord's breach of covenant. This is objectionable to the lender. The tenant conceivably can advance large sums of money to build an addition the landlord is obligated to build, and when the lender takes over the property by foreclosure he may be unable to collect rent until the tenant has recouped his expenditures. A good lender's lease states that rent is payable without set-off or deduction. *Orlowsky* v. *East House Enterprises,* 228 N.Y.S.2d 19 (1961).

Security deposits—prepayment of rent. The lease should authorize the landlord to transfer to any institutional lender securities deposited by the tenant to insure payment of rent and should permit the lender to retain the securities until the tenant is entitled to their return. If a tenant has prepaid rent for the last part of the term, obviously this is rent the lender will not be able to collect if he becomes the owner by foreclosure, and this should be weighed in determining the value of the lease.

Option to purchase. A lease clause giving a prior lessee an option to purchase the premises is a troublesome clause to the lender. In the first place, some fine lawyers believe such an option to be a prior "encumbrance" that makes the mortgage an illegal investment for an institutional lender. In the second place, no one can be certain of the consequences where there is an exercise of the option, with payment of the purchase price to the lessor. In many cases the courts have said that exercise of the option *relates back* to the date of the option. If exercise of the option *relates back,* it might wipe out the mortgage. *Kansas State Bank* v. *Bourgeois,* 14 Utah 2d 188, 380 P2d 931. At best, exercise of the option results in prepayment of the mortgage with no prepayment premium. And if the option is in the form of a "pre-emption right" to purchase the property at a price the mortgagor is willing to accept from a third party, some court decisions hold that this gives the tenant the right to buy from the lender at a price equal to the foreclosure sale price if the mortgage is foreclosed. Finally, it certainly is objectionable to take subject to an option where the option price is or could be less than the mortgage debt. The option to purchase, therefore, should be subordinated to the mortgage. It is perfectly possible to subordinate the option without subordinating the *lease*. In the document subordinating the option to the mortgage it should also be provided that if the tenant exercises his option and thus becomes the owner of the property, the lease shall nevertheless remain in existence for the benefit of the lender, so that he can collect rent thereunder if default occurs under the mortgage.

Options to renew. Of course, tenants will ask for renewal options. The developer will insist on a clause that there can be no exercise of such an option if the tenant is in default. He will try for a clause permitting exercise of the option only if the tenant has reached a specified level of sales performance.

Tenant's lien. The tenant may have a lien on the land for some purpose, as for example, to insure return of a security deposit or because the tenant made some repairs or performed some other act that was legally the obligation of the landlord. This lien, in the case of a prior lease, may be prior and superior to the lien of the mortgage, and may possibly make the investment illegal in some states. This lien and, indeed, any other lien the tenant may have by virtue of his status as a tenant, should be subordinated to the lien of the mortgage, or the lease should contain a general clause making all the tenant's liens subordinate to any mortgage thereafter placed on the property to an institutional lender.

Assignment of rents. The mortgage should be accompanied by a strong, detailed, recorded assignment of leases and rents, notice of which is sent to all existing tenants.

§ 1026. Fee parcels within center—easements and covenants. In recent times "anchor tenants," department stores mainly, in large shopping centers have not been content to be true tenants. Such a "tenant" has insisted on receiving a *deed* from the developer conveying to it the *fee simple title* to the premises to be occupied by the store. Thus, we find the department store area is an island of fee simple title in the midst of land owned by the developer and rented to tenants. This poses no great problem except additional paperwork. The architects and engineers for the developer, department store, and mortgage lender must get together and evolve a scheme of easements that will be needed by the store, and this can be incorporated in a declaration of easements. Of course, the deed conveying the land to the store must contain a clause referring to the declaration of easements. Likewise there will be reciprocal covenants as to the respective obligations of the store and developer. One of the parties must undertake to furnish heat and air conditioning. Exterior and interior maintenance must be agreed upon, and so on. These covenants can conveniently be included in the declaration. There will be restrictions, spelling out the uses to which the store premises can be devoted. Again, these can be included in the declaration.

It is impossible to keep this document brief. Easements for ingress and egress over the malls and walks are simple enough as long as they reach the public street. But the store's footings, foundations, walls, and roofs may extend into the malls, and easements may be created for this purpose. Easements for truck access to loading docks and for parking while loading and unloading must be included since these are not included in the normal parking easements each tenant receives as part of his lease. Easements for utilities, light, gas, water, telephone, sewage, and security systems are needed. Temporary easements are needed for storage of materials during the construction period.

Of course, the store will need parking easements. The question arises as to division of expenses for maintenance of malls, parking areas, and so forth. All this must be covered in the declaration. Likewise division of taxes, insurance, and management fees (if shopping center is to be managed by an agent) must be agreed upon and included in the declaration. Provision must be made for rebuilding if the store is damaged or destroyed by fire, and for construction free of mechanics' liens.

Major covenants are those binding the developer to construct his portion of the center and those binding the store to construct its building or buildings. Since these are formidable documents, they can be referred to in the declaration and appropriately identified so that they need not be recorded. The plans, specifications, working drawings, and so forth would swamp the recorder.

All of this, of course, must be submitted to and approved by the construction lender and takeout lender.

If any lease has previously been given a tenant, his easements to use the malls and parking areas are nonexclusive. Moreover, the plat plan made a part of the lease indicates the location, ownership, and identity of the store tenant. Hence the lease should present no problem.

Of course, a careful title search is made to ascertain that no prior mortgage exists, the foreclosure of which could extinguish the easements. The form of easement declaration is checked as it is drafted with the title company, so that the completed easement can be insured by the title company as an incident to the store property, for both the store owner and its mortgage lenders.

As is evident, the easements must be reciprocal in their nature, some running in favor of the department store and some running in favor of the developer, for example, so that the developer can run water lines or other shared facilities through the department store walls to service sprinkler systems in the adjoining buildings. Especially in the fully enclosed center, there are numerous party walls, which must be dealt with. Basically this is a problem for the engineers and architects. They tell the lawyers what is needed, and the lawyers reduce it to writing in proper form.

There will also be numerous covenants running with the land, outlining who bears what expense of repair, maintenance, and rebuilding in case of windstorm or fire. The mortgage lender will want to see the certificate of insurance regularly. Ordinarily the party carrying the insurance does the rebuilding.

It was stated that the developer gives the department store a deed to the fee title of the store area. In actuality, the situation is more complex. The developer will strive to exclude from his deed the land below the store structure, for this gives him, as owner, unlimited right to install pipes, conduits, sewers, and other facilities needed for other tenants. The developer may also attempt to exclude the roof and air space above the store structure. However, the store will insist on covenants limiting the use that can be made of the air space.

EXAMPLE: To take an extreme example, a large sign advertising the other department store would certainly be unwelcome.

Of course, the declaration of easements gives the store easements in the soil beneath the structure for pipes and so forth and also contains covenants concerning replacement of pipes.

§ 1027. Mortgagee as party. The mortgage lender will be a party to the agreement or the agreement will provide that it inures to any mortgagee if, for example, the developer has only a standby commitment on the permanent financing.

§ 1028. Taxes. As is true in all easement problems, other questions are present. See § 1189.

§ 1029. **The shopping center as public property.** A lot of dissension has developed over the issue of whether a shopping center is public property to the extent that pamphleteers or labor organizers can legally be excluded from its malls and shopping center. The "current" federal rule is that a shopping center is private property and that federal law does not require admission of pamphleteers or union organizers. *Lloyd Corp.* v. *Tanner,* 407 U.S. 551 (1972). The word "current" is used advisedly because the Supreme Court held exactly the contrary just four years earlier. *Amalgamated Food Employees Union* v. *Logan Valley Plaza,* 391 U.S. 308 (1968). The only difference between the two cases is that a change of two judges took place meanwhile. The courts seem to permit peaceful picketing on the malls if related to a strike against a shopping center tenant. *Hudgens* v. *N.L.R.B.,* 501 F2d 161 (5th Circ. 1974).

The importance of these federal decisions, as has been pointed out, has been inflated by the press out of proportion to its real significance. The most important decisions are those handed down by the state courts. Thus, in New Jersey, the courts continue to adhere to the *Logan Valley* rule and legally they may do so. *State* v. *Shack,* 58 N.J. 297, 277 A2d 374 (1971); *Diamond* v. *Bland,* 477 P2d 733 (Cal. 1971); *Sutherland* v. *Southeast Shopping Center, Inc.,* 478 P2d 792 (Wash. 1970).

The theory is that the public has a constitutional "free speech" right to enjoy on "public property." The issue on which the courts are divided is whether the shopping center is public property.

A related question is whether the malls of the center may become public ways by dedication. This can be prevented by sprinkling the malls liberally with bronze disks set in the malls and occasional discreet signs stating unequivocally that the entire area is private property and there is no intention to dedicate. *See* Ill. Rev. Stat., Ch. 83, § 12a. The theory, of course, is that there is no dedication if there is no *intention* to dedicate. *City of Greenville* v. *File,* 265 NE2d 518 (Ill. 1971).

RESERVED: §§ 1030–1040.

36

Industrial Parks

§ **1041. History and purpose of the industrial park.** The history of industrial parks is largely modern history. To be sure, there are older industrial parks, such as the Central Manufacturing District and Clearing Industrial District in Chicago. But as the surge to the suburbs took place after World War II, the industrial developer appeared on the scene. He took over important functions.

EXAMPLE: *R,* a developer, assembles tracts of acreage zoned for farm and residential purposes. He persuades the city to rezone for industrial purposes. He has thus performed the function of land assembly and rezoning. *R* then brings in sewer, water, and utilities. The soil has already been checked, also transportation facilities. *R* records a declaration of restrictions that calls for a property owners' association. As *R* sells or leases tracts for industry he can assure each industry that all legal and economic problems and headaches have all been solved. All the industry needs to do is build or lease its plant and begin operations. The disadvantages are really disguised advantages. The plant is required to observe setback lines, to landscape its facilities, and to screen off its trash removal facilities or truck docks. This costs money but enhances the value of its site. Moreover, the industry knows its neighbors will also be kept in line.

§ **1042. Advantages of industrial parks.** Industrial parks offer many advantages to small industry. (1) No time is lost in site preparation on land assembly. The site is there with streets, sewers, and utilities available. The site is in one ownership. (2) The zoning problems are minimal. The site, obviously, is zoned for industry. Of course the zoning and building code must be checked to see if there are restrictions on the type of use contemplated, particularly with an industry that causes pollution of some sort, but usually zoning is no problem. (3) There are no title problems. The developer has a clear title policy with no building restrictions or easements to complicate the industry's life. (4) There are operating economies. For example, there is a common sewerage plant, and the cost is shared by all the industries. There may also be a shared security force and shared eating facilities. (5) The park is usually protected by building restrictions established by the developer. For example, the developer establishes building lines, so that there is ample space around each plant, and reserves the right to pass on building plans, so that an aesthetically pleasing development is assured. The industry can therefore also omit the precaution of buying excess land to insulate itself from undesirable neighbors. (6) The industry can keep its working capital intact by accepting a build-and-lease arrangement with the developer.

§ 1043. Continuing management responsibility. Industries insist upon a continuing responsibility for the enforcement of the site restrictions. This is accomplished in one of two ways.

EXAMPLE: *R*, the developer, sells and leases sites to industries and incorporates building restrictions in the deeds and leases. Since *R* will require perhaps twenty years to dispose of all sites, and *R* enjoys a good reputation based on prior developments, *R* will own land during the entire development period that will provide a legal basis for enforcing the restrictions. Industries are quite content to rely on *R*.

EXAMPLE: *R*, the developer, causes a property owners' association to be formed, similar to the typical home association. This association has the legal right to enforce the restrictions set forth in the declaration of restrictions.

§ 1044. Types of deals—legal aspects. Typically the industrial developer offers the industry one of two types of deals. (1) The industry buys a site in the park, and, subject to the building restrictions set by the developer, constructs its own plant. (2) The developer sells a site to the industry, contracts to erect a building to the industry's specifications and leases the site and building to the industry. The legal aspects in all cases are mainly those discussed in various portions of this text, for example:

1. The zoning must be checked to be sure that it will accommodate a wide variety of industrial users.
2. A declaration of restrictions will be filed with the plat. Only industrial uses will be permitted.
3. An association of property owners will be formed to enforce the restrictions.
4. The subdivision plat will be submitted to all public officials concerned with land developments, and official approvals will be obtained. The plat will be recorded before any lots are sold.
5. Arrangements will be made to bring in utilities.

When a lot is sold, the developer may wish to reserve an option to repurchase the land within five years at the price for which it was sold if the land remains vacant. This is done to discourage purchase of such lots by speculators.

§ 1045. Public assistance. The need for industry, particularly in producing taxes and employment opportunities, has led to legislation which provides assistance to industry.

EXAMPLE: In Wisconsin a city may purchase land, install all improvements, such as roads, sewer, and water, and then sell or lease the land to industry, but may not build or own plants. 1961 *Wisc. L. Rev.* 378.

EXAMPLE: In many states laws have been enacted under which a municipal body of some sort buys or condemns vacant land, then leases it to an industry, issuing bonds to recapture its investment, the bonds payable from lease rentals. Commonly the lease gives the industry an option to buy the land. A reduced tax assessment or a tax freeze may also be given. In most states the validity of such laws has been sustained, but in a few states it has been held invalid as a use of public funds for private purposes. *Mitchell* v. *North Carolina Indus. Develop. Fin. Auth.,* 159 SE2d 745 (N.C. 1968). (Decision discusses the various state holdings.)

RESERVED: §§ 1046–1047.

37

Landlord and Tenant

§ **1048. In general.** In the centuries following the Battle of Hastings (1066), when William the Conqueror crushed the English armies and became King of England, the feudal system of real estate law that prevailed in a large part of continental Europe became part of the English way of life. Its intricacies are a twice-told tale and need not be repeated here. We must, however, look at the bottom rung of the social and economic ladder. Here we find the landlord renting a small farm to a tenant. Rent was often paid in the form of a share of the crops. Indeed, sharecropping still exists, though on a small scale. The house in which the tenant lived was a primitive structure. The tenant worked with primitive tools. He was a jack-of-all-trades and could repair almost any defect in house or tools. In 1588 England defeated the Spanish Armada; its ships began their long rule of the oceans of the world, and England became a trading nation. The formation of modern trading law (contract law) began. But in the meantime, the law of landlord and tenant had been formed. Basically it was pro-landlord law. The tenant took the premises as he found them, and the landlord had no obligation of repair.

Then, as time moved on, the Industrial Revolution changed the face of England. Many men worked in factories. Such a worker was not a jack-of-all-trades. Tenement buildings, the predecessor of the modern apartment, began to appear as cities grew up around the factories. Still, the courts applied the old agricultural landlord and tenant law to the new state of affairs. Beginning about 1970 the courts began to re-examine their thinking. *Javins* v. *First National Realty Corp.,* 428 F2d 1071 *cert. den.* 400 U.S. 925 (1970). Several things became evident. The tenant, since he was not a jack-of-all-trades, lacked the skill to make repairs. Repairs, by and large, were beyond the means of the low-income tenant. Obviously no bank would loan the low-income tenant money to make repairs. The defect might spring up in a portion of the apartment to which the tenant had no access.

Modern courts, recently made a 180-degree turn in their thinking on the law applicable to residential renting. They began to regard the renting of an apartment basically as a contract for the furnishing of services, including the service of maintaining the structure in a habitable condition, free from building code violations. This development made all of the flexibility that is characteristic of modern contract law available to the courts. This change of thought is surely the law of most states even though some state courts have not had the opportunity to so hold. See § 1095 *et seq*.

Meanwhile, the law relating to stores, industrial plants, and commercial leasing remained as it had been. Tenants of these structures had the sophistication to protect themselves. And much of the noncontroversial law relating to residential leasing also remained unchanged.

§ **1049. Leases and periodic tenancies.** The relationship of landlord and tenant may exist by virtue of a formal, written *lease* or of a periodic tenancy, such as a *tenancy from month to month*.

EXAMPLE: A sees an "apartment for rent" sign on a building, goes in, makes a verbal arrangement with the owner for the rental of an apartment, pays his first month's rent, and later moves in. He is a *tenant from month to month*.

EXAMPLE: Facts as above, but the landlord and tenant, instead of agreeing verbally, sign a lease for one year. A is a tenant under a lease.

One important difference between leases and periodic tenancies relates to the rights and liabilities of the parties during the existence of the landlord-tenant relation. When the relation of landlord and tenant exists without a written lease, the law implies certain rights and liabilities on the part of both. In a *month-to-month tenancy,* for example, the tenant is entitled to the exclusive possession of the rented premises, and the landlord has no right to enter thereon for the purpose of making repairs. But in many leases, the parties expressly agree that the landlord shall have this right. In other words, a lease is a contract, and most of the rights and duties of the parties are governed by rules of law.

Another difference between a lease and a periodic tenancy relates to the termination of the tenant's right of occupancy. In the case of a lease, at the expiration date fixed in the lease, the tenant need not give notice to the landlord before moving out, nor is any notice needed by the landlord to the tenant. In the case of periodic tenancies, certain notices must be given in order to terminate the tenancy.

§ **1050. Tenancy from month to month.** The tenancy from month to month is generally created when no definite term of letting is specified by the parties and the rent is payable monthly. This kind of tenancy is very common. A tenant who pays rent monthly and has no lease is a tenant from month to month.

A tenancy from month to month cannot be terminated except by giving notice. That is, the landlord cannot evict the tenant unless he first gives the tenant the notice required by law, and the tenant continues liable for rent unless he gives the landlord the required notice. In many states, a month's or thirty days' notice is required, but the period varies from state to state.

The notice to terminate a month-to-month tenancy must state a proper termination date, and must give the tenant the full number of days' notice to which he is entitled.

EXAMPLE: A rents an apartment to *B* on a month-to-month tenancy beginning as of the first of the next month. In the state in question a landlord must serve a thirty days' notice to terminate such a tenancy. After some months, *A* serves a notice on November 1st terminating *B*'s tenancy as of November 30th. The notice is void. It gives *B* less than thirty days' notice. *A* will lose the eviction suit and must serve a new and proper notice.

§ 1051. Tenancy from year to year. A *tenancy from year to year* is one that continues for a year and then is automatically renewed for another year and from year to year thereafter unless due notice of termination of the tenancy is given at the time and in the manner required by law for the termination of the tenancy.

While a year-to-year tenancy can be created in other ways, it most commonly is created when a lease for a year or more has expired and the tenant continues in possession paying rent, which the landlord accepts, and the parties have made no other agreement as to the character of the tenant's occupancy.

When a tenant has a lease for a year or longer, and after the lease has expired the tenant remains in possession of the premises, it is said that the tenant *holds over.* The landlord may, if he wishes, hold the tenant as a tenant from year to year. Observe that it is the landlord who may hold the tenant. The tenant cannot, by holding over, compel the landlord to extend the tenancy. The landlord may evict the tenant if he wishes to do so. But if the tenant holds over, even for one day, he becomes liable for another year's rent should the landlord wish to hold him. *Clinton Wire Cloth Co.* v. *Gardner,* 99 Ill. 151. Once the landlord accepts the rent, he also is bound to the tenancy. And once the tenancy is established neither party can terminate it in the middle of the year. And if either party wishes to end the tenancy *at the end of a yearly period,* proper notice must be served for this purpose.

In certain situations, a tenant who holds over after his lease has expired will not become a tenant from year to year.

1. Before the lease expires, the landlord notifies the tenant that if he remains in possession he will do so as a tenant from month to month. Or the landlord and tenant may specifically agree that the tenant remains as a month-to-month tenant. In either case, the new tenancy is a month-to-month tenancy.

2. The lease contains a clause that if the tenant holds over without any new agreement being reached, he does so as a month-to-month tenant. Other leases say that the lease is renewed for one year. The clause is valid.

3. Before the lease ends, the landlord and tenant negotiate for a new lease, and the negotiations are in progress when the lease ends. After the lease ends, the tenant remains in possession, paying a monthly rent. He is a month-to-month tenant. 49 Am. Jur2d § 1120. Be careful, however, for if negotiations have ceased before the lease ends, a tenant holding over will be held as a tenant from year to year.

4. Suppose that when the lease ends the tenant is so ill that his doctor forbids him

to move. In some states, this will nevertheless result in the creation of a year-to-year tenancy; in other states, a year-to-year will not be created. 49 Am. Jur.2d § 1117.

The rule that if a tenant holds over even one day after the expiration of his lease he becomes liable for another year's rent as a tenant from year to year is harsh, and many states have abolished or restricted it.

§ **1052. Tenancy at will.** A tenancy at will may be terminated by either party whenever he wishes to do so.

EXAMPLE: A tenancy at will arises under an agreement that the tenant may occupy until the premises are sold or rented to a third person, until the landlord is ready to construct new buildings, until the land is required by the landlord for his own use, or whenever the letting is for an indefinite term.

§ **1053. Lease defined.** A lease is both a contract and a conveyance. It is a conveyance by the landlord to the tenant of the right to occupy the land for the term specified in the lease. It contains a contract by the tenant to pay rent to the landlord and usually contains numerous other promises and undertakings by both landlord and tenant. The legal interest of the tenant in the land is called a *leasehold estate* or a *term for years.* It is legally considered to be personal property.

§ **1054. Necessity of writing.** In all but a few states, a lease for less than one year may be verbal, but a lease for a period longer than one year must be in writing.

§ **1055. Requirements of lease—in general.** Since in many states, laws require a written lease to comply with requirements applicable to deeds, a lease in writing should comply with such requirements. In a written lease, the landlord is referred to as *lessor* and the tenant as *lessee.*

§ **1056. The lessor.** The landowner and his or her spouse should be designated as lessors. The same reasons that make it necessary for the wife or husband of a landowner to join in a deed requires the spouse to join in a lease. *Fargo* v. *Bennett,* 35 Ida. 359, 206 Pac. 692; *Benson* v. *Dritch,* 244 SW2d 339 (Tex. 1951). As a matter of business practice, short leases such as one-year apartment leases are often made by the owner without his wife's signature, for in such situations, trouble is extremely improbable. A lessor should be of age and of sound mind. When the lease is executed by an executor or trustee, the will or other trust instrument must be examined to determine if he has power to make the lease in question. If the lessor is a corporation, the lease must be authorized by the directors or stockholders, as required by the local law.

§ **1057. The lessee.** The lessee should be of age and of sound mind. If the lessee is a trustee or executor, the will or other trust instrument must authorize him to enter into leases such as the one in question.

§ **1058. Description of the premises.** The lease must describe the leased premises with certainty. There is a tendency in short-term leases to designate the leased premises inadequately. Of course if it is an entire building that is being rented, it is sufficient to describe it by street number, city, and state.

§ 1059. **Duration or term of lease.** Leases are sometimes classified as *short-term* or *long-term* leases. This has no great legal significance. With the exception of the rule that leases for more than one year must be in writing, the rules governing short-term and long-term leases are generally the same. Long-term leases often run for ninety-nine years. In some states laws have been passed limiting the duration of leases. The lease should fix the date on which the term of the lease begins and the duration of the lease. In fixing the term of the lease, it is better to avoid a description of the term as running *from* a particular day *to* another day, since a question may arise as to whether or not a lease from or to a particular day includes or excludes such day. It is better to describe the term as *commencing on* a certain day and *ending on* a certain other day.

§ 1060. **Signature of lessor and lessee.** The signature of the lessor is necessary to give effect to a lease. It is the universal practice to obtain the lessee's signature also, though it is not essential that the lease be signed by the lessee if the lessee accepts the lease and takes possession of the leased premises. *Bakker* v. *Fellows,* 153 Mich. 428, 117 NW 52 (1908). It is customary to execute leases in duplicate. If the lessor signs one duplicate and hands this to the lessee, and the lessee signs the other duplicate and hands this to the lessor, the effect is the same as if both signatures had been placed on each duplicate. *Fields* v. *Brown,* 188 Ill. 111, 64 NE 1033.

§ 1061. **Seal.** In a number of states, written leases must be executed with the same formality as deeds. In these states, a lease should be under seal.

§ 1062. **Witnesses.** A few states require a lease that exceeds a certain specified duration to be witnessed.

§ 1063. **Acknowledgment.** Some states require leases that exceed a specified term to be acknowledged. In any case, if the lease is to be recorded, it should be acknowledged.

§ 1064. **Recording.** Even though a lease is not recorded, the tenant's possession will normally give the whole world constructive notice of his rights. However, this rule has been abolished in a number of states as to leases exceeding a specified duration—namely, one year in California, Florida, Georgia, Hawaii, Idaho, Mississippi, Montana, Oklahoma, Rhode Island and three years in Indiana, Minnesota, New Mexico, North Carolina, Ohio, Tennessee, Wisconsin, Wyoming. A few states specify longer durations.

In some states (New York, Pennsylvania, and Ohio, for example) the law permits the recording of a brief *memorandum of lease* instead of the original lease. This enables the parties to keep secret the rent specified in the lease.

§ 1065. **Rent.** Unless there is an agreement providing otherwise, rent is not due until the end of the rental period.

EXAMPLE: A agreed to rent certain premises to *B* as a tenant from month to month.

Rent was fixed at eighty dollars per month, but nothing was said as to time for payment of rent. The rent is not due until the end of each month.

Most leases, however, provide that rental is payable in advance on the first of each month.

Because of the embarrassment caused a landlord by his inability to put a new tenant in possession, and because of the difficulty attendant upon renting premises out of the normal season, a number of states require a tenant who remains in possession after the termination of his lease to pay double rent for the period intervening between the expiration of the lease and his eviction. And many leases provide that a holdover tenant shall pay double rent if he remains in possession after the lease has expired. The lease may provide for additional amounts other than double rent.

§ 1066. Rent—net lease and gross lease. There are various types of *net leases,* but, in general, such a lease requires the tenant to pay real estate taxes, special assessments, insurance premiums, and other charges normally borne by the landowner. The tenant assumes the risk that taxes may increase, special assessments may be levied, and that the building may be destroyed by fire. In a fully net lease the tenant must rebuild a destroyed building, paying rent meanwhile. In a gross lease the tenant pays only his rent, and the landlord bears taxes and other burdens normally borne by a landowner.

§ 1067. Rent—percentage leases. Leases of retail locations often provide for a *percentage rent.* Such a lease usually provides a minimum fixed rent. Over and above this minimum, the rental is fixed at a percentage of the tenant's gross sales. The percentage of gross income that is to be charged usually presents no great problem, for commonly accepted percentages for each type of retail establishment are published periodically by the National Association of Realtors. However, it is obvious that if such a lease is prepared for a department store in a shopping center, it will be necessary to fix different percentages for different departments within the single store. Deductions from gross sales are usually allowed for sales and luxury taxes and merchandise returned by the shopper. Care should be exercised to include in gross sales all income from vending machines, telephone booths, pay toilets, lockers, weighing machines, stamp machines, and so on; and also services rendered on the premises, hairdressing and the like. Services rendered at cost, clothing alterations and employees' cafeteria, for example, are usually excluded. Income from subtenants and concessionaires is included. The lease should state whether *gross income* includes sales made by mail and sales to employees. The lease should require the tenant to conduct business throughout the year, for obviously, if the store is closed, the percentage rent stops or drops. Further, the lease should fix the hours and days on which the store is to be open. A provision should also be included forbidding the establishment of a competing store within a specified radius. Since the landlord is depending on the particular tenant's ability to run a profitable business, the lease should forbid any assignment or sublease or even the occupancy of the premises by anyone other than the tenant, unless the landlord consents. The lease should require "continous operation" by the tenant and define what hours and days are meant by this phrase.

§ **1068. Rent—office leases.** In office leases, rent is often charged by the square foot. Hence it is important to know how many *usable* square feet the tenant is getting. The lease may define the square footage as including space occupied by pillars and so forth, which may be useless to the tenant.

§ **1069. Rent—escalation.** Because of the push of inflation, most commercial or industrial leases today contain a rent escalation clause. It must be carefully drafted. Of course, increase in taxes is a sound basis for escalation. 48 ALR3d 287. The trick in a new building is to find some three- or four-year period that will average out as the basis on which the step-up in rent will be predicated. This is necessary because the tax assessor sometimes gives the building assessment a "tax break" in the early years. *Rodolitz* v. *Neptune Paper Products Co.,* 22 N.Y.2d 383, 283 NE2d 682 (1976). Increases in building maintenance wages are one valid source of escalation. *Simons* v. *Federal Bar Bldg. Corp.,* 275 A2d 545 (D.C. 1971). Energy costs are sometimes included as a separate escalator. The newer leases permit the landlord to estimate the escalation and charge each month or quarter the amount of his estimated escalation. Thus, he is using the tenant's money to meet escalations. At the end of the year he settles up.

Another type of escalator ties the increase to increased real estate taxes and *operating costs.* This last poses some problems. Obviously it requires the landlord to furnish audited statements of increased operating costs and taxes. Also, some language is needed to limit the landlord's right to polish the brass doorknobs twice a week, so to speak, or to hire his brother at a fancy salary.

§ **1070. Ground leases and commercial leases distinguished—legal and financial aspects—mortgages of the leasehold.** There is no legal distinction between commercial leases and ground leases. Nevertheless, there are economic differences between them that have legal implications. A *commercial lease* is a lease of a building or part of a building such as a store to a tenant. If the tenant agrees in his lease to make improvements, as a rule they are limited in scope. In a *ground lease,* the landowner leases the vacant ground to a tenant who covenants in the lease to erect a building on the premises. The true ground lease is a *net lease* under which the tenant pays all expenses including taxes, insurance, and repairs. The landlord in a commercial lease and his mortgagee are concerned with the tenant's credit standing, since this is their assurance that the rent will be paid. This is the reason, for example, why you will find a shopping center promoter looking for national chain stores as tenants. And because the landlord and his mortgagee depend on the cash flow from triple-A tenants, the lease will forbid any assignment or sublease without the landlord's consent. In a ground lease, on the other hand, (1) the landlord looks for his security to the fact that the tenant will erect a valuable building on the property and will have to keep up his rent in order to prevent loss of his investment in the building by the landlord's forfeiting the lease for nonpayment of rent; and (2) the tenant expects to borrow money to erect the building. This makes it necessary to draft the lease in such a fashion that the lessee's rights under the lease (the "leasehold estate") can be mortgaged without the landlord's permission and the lease should so state. And since the mortgagee who forecloses will want the unhampered right to sell to anyone, the ground lease should not limit the lessee's right to assign without the landlord's consent. Also, the term of the lease should be long enough to make the mortgage on the leasehold a legal investment for banks, insurance companies, and other institutional investors. For example, a state law may provide that a mortgage on a leasehold is not a legal investment for banks or insurance companies unless the unexpired term of the lease exceeds twenty-one years. Some states have a fifty-year minimum.

To better enable the lessee to borrow money for the erection of the building, a ground lease may provide that the landlord will join in the mortgage, without, however incurring any personal liability by signing the mortgage note. Or the lease may provide that the landlord's title will become subordinate to the mortgage on the leasehold. The landlord who signs such a lease must understand that this weakens his legal position, since foreclosure of the mortgage will extinguish his ownership. On the other hand, if the construction mortgage is only on the leasehold estate, foreclosure of the mortgage simply results in transfer of the leasehold to the mortgage lender, who then becomes the tenant paying rent to the landlord.

When the construction mortgage mortgages only the leasehold, provision should be included in the lease for special notice to the mortgagee of the leasehold in case of default in payment of rent, so that the mortgage lender can step in and cure the defaults, thereby preventing a forfeiture of the lease, which would cancel his mortgage.

§ **1071. Use of the premises.** Unless the terms of the lease prevent it, the tenant may use the premises in lawful ways that were not discussed during the lease negotiations. This use by the tenant is often a point of controversy. Many leases state that the premises are leased *for the business of selling cigars,* or *to be used as a real estate office.* Oddly enough, courts seem to feel that such language does not limit the tenant to the stated use. Unless the lease states that the property is to be used *only* for a particular purpose, he may make any use of the property he wants to, so long as such use is not materially different from that to which the rented premises were customarily put. *Lyon* v. *Bethlehem Engineering Corp.,* 253 N.Y. 111, 170 NE 512 (1930); 51 CJS 1017.

SUGGESTION TO LANDLORD: Include a clause under which the tenant covenants to use the property only for a specific purpose. Include at the end of the tenant's covenants a clause giving the landlord the right to terminate the lease if the tenant violates any of his covenants. Be sure you state clearly what the permitted use includes. For example, if you specify that the tenant is to operate a drugstore, does this permit a lunch counter?

When the lease definitely restricts the use that the tenant may make of the premises and the tenant branches out into some unauthorized business, the landlord need not terminate the lease, even if the lease gives him power to do so. He may, instead, procure a court order forbidding the tenant to engage in the unauthorized business. This is desirable when the tenant is a highly solvent one, such as a chain store, and the rent is favorable to the landlord. It also protects the landlord in those cases where he has agreed with other tenants not to allow competing businesses in the same building.

A lease of business property automatically gives the tenant the right to advertise his business on the leased property if the lease does not forbid this use.

EXAMPLE: In the case of a lease of an entire building, it would give the tenant the exclusive right to place advertising signs on the walls and roofs of the building, for example, to maintain window signs and to have his name on a lobby directory board. In the case of a lease of a portion of a building, the lessee, not the landlord, would have the right to place advertising signs on the exterior walls of the portion leased to the tenant. 6 *De Paul L. Rev.* 63; 51 CJS. 1020; 20 ALR2d 941.

Usually, however, where various floors are leased to different tenants, the landlord is considered as retaining exclusive possession of the roof. And obviously, if *L* leases the second floor to *A* and the third floor to *B*, *A*'s signs must not extend above the dividing line between the second and third floors.

§ 1072. Incidental rights of lessee or tenant—services and easements. Among the incidental rights a tenant enjoys, though not mentioned in his lease, are:

1. The right of tenant, his guests, business visitors, deliverymen, etc., to use the means of access the building provides, namely, front and rear entrances, arcade entrances, lobbies, corridors, stairs, escalators, and elevators, suite entrances from reception rooms or private offices (though the landlord, through reasonable regulations, may require delivery to be made at a trademan's entrance, require freight to use freight elevators, etc.), also the right to use common toilets, common laundry facilities, etc., and the right to have electric wires and conduits, also water and steam and gas pipes, cross the landlord's part of the property to service tenant's quarters. This is an aspect of the law of implied easements, 24 ALR2d 123.

The landlord should try to get a provision giving him the right to make reasonable changes in these facilities. To accommodate a new tenant, for example, the landlord may wish to move the washroom to another floor.

2. The right to have heat, hot water, etc. furnished where the only means of obtaining them consists of facilities controlled by the landlord for the benefit of all tenants.

§ 1073. Liability of landlord. Until recent times the rule of *caveat emptor* (let the buyer beware) applied to the landlord and tenant relationship. Unless the lease provided otherwise the landlord had no duty to the tenant to put the rented premises in a habitable condition or to make any repairs whatever. Even if the building at the time it was rented was in a dangerous or ruinous condition or even wholly unfit for occupancy or use, or if it became so after it had been rented, the tenant had to pay the stipulated rent for the entire term of the lease. This, of course, placed the burden on a prospective tenant of making a careful inspection of the premises before signing a lease and of insisting that the lease contain covenants to keep the premises in repair if that was the tenant's wish and the landlord was willing to agree.

Since the landlord had no duty as to the condition of the premises, he was not liable to the tenant or his family for injuries or property damage suffered because of defects in the premises at the time of renting or occurring thereafter.

EXAMPLE: *L* rented an apartment to *T*. The flooring was obviously decayed and dangerous. It collapsed and *T* was injured. He had no right to sue *L*.

There were and are some exceptions to these rules:

1. When the landlord lets for a short term of a few days, weeks, or months a fully furnished house supposedly equipped for immediate occupancy as a dwelling, the landlord impliedly represents, in many states, that the premises are safe and habitable. If the premises are not habitable, as when they are infested with vermin, the tenant has the right to move out, and his liability for rent ceases. *Young* v. *Povich,* 121 Me. 141, 116 Atl. 26 (1922); 28 ALR 48. Also, the landlord is liable to the tenant and his family for injuries sustained from defects in the rented premises or the furnishings thereof. *Hacker* v. *Netschke,* 310 Mass. 754, 39 NE2d 644 (1942); *Mease* v. *Fox,* 200 NW2d 791 (Ia. 1972).

2. Where there are concealed defects that would make the premises dangerous to a tenant and that the tenant could not discover on an inspection of the premises, but that are known to the landlord, the landlord must inform the tenant of the existence of such defects. If he fails to do so, and as a consequence an injury is suffered by the tenant, his family, or his customers or guests, the landlord is liable for such injuries. *Mease* v. *Fox,* 200 NW2d 791 (Ia. 1972). Lawyers call this *fraud* liability.

EXAMPLE: Premises were leased as a barber shop and residence. Sewer gas often escaped into the premises which fact was known to the landlord. He did not disclose this fact to the tenant, and the tenant and his family became seriously ill from sewer gas. The landlord was liable for the injuries.

3. The landlord normally retains control over parts of the building used in common by the tenants, such as halls, stairs, elevators, and sidewalks leading from the building to the public street or sidewalk. With respect to such common facilities, the landlord must exercise due care to correct any dangerous conditions that develop. If he fails to do so, he is liable for injuries suffered by the tenant, his family, his customers or other persons lawfully on the premises, such as delivery men.

EXAMPLE: *L* leased a flat in his apartment building to *T*. The stairways were used in common by the tenants. A stair became defective, and this condition was brought to the attention of *L*, but he failed to correct it. *T* slipped on the stair and was injured. *L* was liable.

The duty of the landlord to use care to keep facilities used in common by the tenants in repair extends to appliances furnished by the landlord for the tenants' common use, such as laundry appliances, common toilets, playground equipment, and dumbwaiters. It also extends to the roof, chimneys, eaves, flues, outside walls, and swimming pools. 39 ALR3d 824. This duty extends also to the malls, walks, parking areas, etc., of a shopping center. 95 ALR2d 1344.

4. Where the landlord, even though not legally obligated to do so, makes repairs, but is negligent in so doing, he is liable for any resulting injuries.

EXAMPLE: *L,* though not obligated to do so, repaired a floor in an apartment that he rented to *T*. The work was carelessly done, and *T* was injured. *L* is liable. 78 ALR2d 1258.

§ 1074. Liability of landlord for injuries to third person. As a rule, whenever a landlord would be liable to a tenant, as, for example, when the landlord is careless with respect to care of common stairways, he will be liable to others who stand in the tenant's shoes, such as members of his family, guests, employees, and business visitors and delivery boys.

There are other situations where a landlord is liable to a third person.

1. When the landlord rents the premises for a purpose that involves the admission of large groups of the public as patrons of the tenant (amusement park, theater, etc.) and at the time the lease, or any renewal lease, is signed, the premises are in a dangerous condition (dangerous doorways, steps, floors), the landlord is liable to the tenant's patrons for any injuries that they may suffer. *Webel* v. *Yale University,* 125 Conn. 515, 7 A2d 215 (1939); 17 ALR3rd 422, 873.

EXAMPLE: *L* leased premises to *T* as a tavern, dance hall, and restaurant and *P,* a patron, was injured while dancing when her heel caught in a floor register. *L* is liable. *Torwick* v. *Lisle,* 268 Minn. 197, 128 NW2d 330 (1964).

2. With respect to pedestrians on public walks or streets adjoining the rented premises, there is an additional rule imposing liability on the landlord, namely: When the premises at the time of the renting are in a dangerous and defective condition, the landlord is liable to strangers for injuries resulting therefrom. 52 CJS 105; 31 ALR2d 1334.

EXAMPLE: At the time the premises were leased to the tenant, a hole in the sidewalk leading to a coal bin was in a defective condition, and a pedestrian was thereafter injured as a result. The landlord was held liable. *Great Atlantic & Pacific Tea Co.* v. *Traylor,* 239 Ala. 497, 195 So 724 (1940). The reason for this rule is that a dangerous condition of premises constitutes a *nuisance,* and the liability of the landlord results from his leasing premises on which a *nuisance* exists. *Morgan* v. *Sheppard,* 156 Ala. 403, 47 So 147. The liability exists even though the defect is not concealed. And if the premises were safe when originally leased but are defective when the lease is renewed, the landlord is liable for injuries sustained by strangers after the date of the renewal. Of course the tenant would also be liable for such injuries.

NEW LAWS: There are a number of state laws making landowners liable for deaths or injuries in private swimming pools. *Raponotti* v. *Burnt-Mil Arms, Inc.,* 273 A2d 372 (N.J. 1971).

In recent times court decisions and state law have in some states completely transformed the law of the liability of landlord to his tenant where residential premises are involved. *Jack Spring, Inc.* v. *Little,* 50 Ill.2d 531, 280 NE2d 208 (1972); *Mease* v. *Fox,* 200 NW2d 791 (Ia. 1972). Thus, the rules stated in this section and in the following four sections are still applicable to renting of commercial and industrial buildings and to the extent that they give rights to residential tenants are also still applicable, but the rights of the tenant as to residential premises have been greatly expanded in a number of states. This parallels the amazing spread of the new rules creating an implied warranty of habitability in the sale of new homes by professional builders.

NEW DIRECTIONS: It seems inevitable that the new rules in landlord and tenant law will spread as rapidly as those relating to sales of new homes. It is equally clear that these new rules will be resisted in some states, so that the law will run an uneven course.

REFERENCES ON LANDLORD'S LIABILITY: 68 ALR3d 382; 67 *id.* 490; 67 *id.* 587; 66 *id.* 202.

§ 1075. Lease obligating landlord to repair. If the lease requires the landlord to make repairs, and the landlord violates this obligation, the tenant may pursue one of the following courses:

1. He may abandon the premises if they become untenantable.
2. He may make the repairs himself and deduct the reasonable expense or cost thereof from the rent.
3. He may occupy the premises without repair and deduct from the rent the decrease in rental value occasioned by the landlord's failure to repair. Here, however, the tenant runs the risk of having his lease forfeited for nonpayment of rent if he appraises the situation incorrectly.
4. He may pay full rent and sue the landlord for the decrease in rental value occasioned by the landlord's failure to repair.

When the lease obligates the landlord to repair, and he fails to do so, and the tenant suffers an injury as a result, some courts hold the landlord liable; others do not. The view that the landlord should be held liable is growing in favor. 78 ALR2d 1252. Accompanying every contract is an unspoken duty to perform with skill and care and to be liable for negligent performance. 17A CJS *Contracts* § 494(1). In any event, the landlord has no duty to inspect the rented premises he has agreed to keep in repair, for normally the landlord has no right to enter on the rented premises without the tenant's consent. It is the tenant's duty to notify the landlord of any condition requiring repair, and no liability on the landlord's part arises until this has been done and the landlord has failed to make repairs as agreed. 163 ALR 314.

§ 1076. Statutes imposing duty to repair. The old rules relieving the landlord of the duty to keep rented premises in repair were evolved before the emergence of large cities, with the attendant problems of urban life. Obviously workers of low income living in tenements in large urban centers cannot afford to keep their premises in repair. If the landlord fails to make needed repairs, they simply are not made. In many states laws have been passed imposing on landlords the duty to keep rented housing accommodations in repair. 45 *Ill. L. Rev.* 205; 93 ALR 778; 17 ALR2d 704. In California, Montana, North Dakota, and Oklahoma, the tenant is given the right to move out if needed repairs are not made, but if the tenant is injured because of the landlord's failure to make repairs, the landlord is not liable. In some states, Michigan, New Jersey, and New York, for example, the landlord is liable if the tenant suffers injuries as a result of the landlord's negligent failure to make repairs. *Altz* v. *Lieberson,* 233 N.Y. 16, 134 NE 703 (1922); 17 ALR2d 708.

EXAMPLES: In states following the New York rule, landlords were held liable for the following injuries: tenant injured by fall of ceiling; tenant injured as result of landlord's failure to repair hole in bathroom floor; and tenant's child injured when defective radiator valves blew off.

In many cities, especially home rule cities, ordinances exist making the landlord liable for failure to repair or for violation of building codes. *Bell* v. *Willoughby Tower,* 46 Ill. App.2d 45, 196 NE2d 487 (1965).

§ **1077. State laws permitting tenant to make repairs.** A few states have laws permitting the tenant to make minor repairs where the landlord refuses to do so, typically limited to an amount not exceeding one month's rent, and to deduct this amount from the rent. 37 *Brooklyn L. Rev.* 396.

§ **1078. Repairs—office leases.** Most office leases require the tenant to surrender the premises at the end of the lease in their original condition, *ordinary wear and tear excepted.* This last clause is given its normal meaning.

EXAMPLE: When *T* surrendered the premises there were patches in the carpeting, a damaged air conditioner that ran all night because *L* had installed no thermostat, and scratches in office panels. This is ordinary wear and tear. *Urban Management Corp.* v. *Ford Motor Credit* Co., 263 So2d 404 (La. App. 1972).

§ **1079. Lease of building to be constructed by landlord.** Where a building or part thereof is leased to a tenant while it is in the process of construction, there is an implied warranty that the building is suitable for the tenant's purposes.

EXAMPLE: *L* leased a building under construction to *T* as a furniture store. The roof leaked and furniture was damaged. *L* is liable. *J. D. Young Corp.* v. *McClintic,* 26 SW2d 460 (Tex. 1930); 11 *B.U.L. L. Rev.* 119.

§ **1080. Eviction by title paramount.** If the tenant is evicted from the premises by a stranger having a paramount or better title than his landlord, the tenant is not liable to his landlord for rent accruing after such eviction.

EXAMPLE: *L* mortgaged his land to *M*. Thereafter, *L* leased the mortgaged land to *T*. *L* defaulted in his payments on the mortgage, and *M* took possession of the premises, as he had the right to do under his mortgage, evicting *T*. *T* is not liable for rents accruing after the eviction, since *M* is coming in under a paramount title.

§ **1081. Liability of tenant for injuries to third person.** When a stranger is injured by reason of a defective condition of the premises, it is often difficult to determine whether the landlord or tenant is liable. If the landlord has made no agreement to repair and the premises were in a safe condition when rented, and if the defective portion is in the exclusive possession of the tenant, the tenant is liable but the landlord is not, since the landlord has no control over such premises and is in no position to prevent the dangerous condition.

EXAMPLE: A stranger slipped and fell into a coal hole that was defectively covered but was in a safe condition when the premises were rented. The basement into which the hole opened was used by the first-floor tenant. He alone had a key to this basement, and the landlord had no access thereto. The tenant alone was liable. *West Chicago Masonic Assn.* v. *Cohn,* 192 Ill. 210, 61 NE 439 (1901).

Or suppose the tenant of an upper floor goes out, leaving the water running, and the water runs over and drips through the ceiling and ruins plaster and rugs in the apartment beneath. The landlord is not liable since the tenant is in exclusive possession of his apartment, but the tenant is liable both to his landlord and to the tenant below, because the damage resulted from his carelessness.

§ **1082. Insurance.** The prudent property owner should protect himself against liability claims by taking out Owners', Landlords', and Tenants' Public Liability Insurance, commonly referred to as O.L.&T. insurance, which provides coverage against legal liability for accidents resulting in bodily injuries or death arising out of ownership, occupation, or use of the premises. Liability for injuries sustained by employees is not covered by this policy, but they should be covered by workmen's compensation or employer's liability insurance. Insurance should be obtained protecting the landlord against liability for property damage. If there is an elevator on the premises, insurance will be needed to protect against injuries arising through operation of the elevator. Special "dram shop" insurance should be purchased if alcoholic beverages are sold on the premises.

§ **1083. Repairs and alterations by tenants—liability of tenant to landlord.** When the lease does not provide otherwise, the tenant has no duty to the landlord to make any substantial, extraordinary, or general repairs, such as the replacing of a worn-out furnace or water heater. But it is the tenant's duty to repair broken windows or leaking roofs and to take such other steps as are needed to prevent damage from the elements. If he fails to do so, he is liable to landlord for any resulting damage. *Suydam* v. *Jackson,* 54 N.Y. 450.

The tenant must not make any material change in the nature and character of the building leased, as by removing walls, cutting new doorways, and the like, even though such alterations increase the value of the property. The theory is that when the tenant vacates the building, the landlord should find it in much the same condition as it was when the tenant took possession. *F. W. Woolworth Co.* v. *Nelson,* 204 Ala. 172, 85 So 449 (1920).

When the lease obligates the tenant *to make repairs or to keep the premises in repair,* some courts say that the tenant must repair or rebuild if the building is damaged or destroyed by fire, flood, lightning, rain, accident, or other causes beyond the tenant's control. 45 ALR 12, 106 ALR 1358. Other courts today refuse to impose such a heavy burden on the tenant. *Seevers* v. *Gabel,* 94 Ia. 75, 62 NW 669. Under the modern law of unconscionability, it is unlikely that any court would force the tenant to rebuild. It is not a risk he consciously assumed. A lease provision for repairs may require the tenant to replace rotten floors, a worn-out furnace, and the like. The tenant is liable to his landlord for damage occasioned by carelessness, as where damage results from the tenant's negligence in permitting a bathtub to overflow. 10 ALR2d 1012.

§ 1084. Damage to or destruction of the leased premises. Unless the lease provides otherwise, the rule is that when *land and building* are rented, the tenant is not excused from paying rent if *building* is destroyed by fire, flood, or wind.

EXAMPLE: A lease was made of the premises at 143 and 145 Lake Street, Chicago, Illinois. The buildings were destroyed by fire, but the liability for rent continued. A lease containing a description by street number leases the land as well as the building.

Quite a number of states—Alaska, Arizona, California, Connecticut, Kentucky, Maryland, Michigan, Minnesota, Mississippi, Montana, New Jersey, New York, North Carolina, North Dakota, Ohio, South Carolina, West Virginia, and Wisconsin, for example—have abolished this harsh rule. In these states, it is the rule that if a building is destroyed or rendered untenantable, the tenant is relieved of further liability for rent. 35 *B. Y. U. L. Rev.* 1284. Many lease forms provide that if the building is destroyed by fire, the lease ends automatically. Predictably, many more modern courts will take this approach even where the lease is silent.

The rule that liability for rent continues when the building is destroyed does not apply to a lease of an apartment, flat, office, or floor of a building. Such a lease is not a lease of land.

When the building is not destroyed, but the apartment is rendered *untenantable* by fire, leases usually provide that the landlord has a certain time in which to make the necessary repairs, and in the meantime, the tenant is not liable for rent. Under this clause, if the landlord fails to make repairs during the specified period, the lease ends automatically.

The "untenantability" clause is poorly drawn at times. A fire may leave an office suite untouched but may destroy the elevators. Greater detail is needed than is found in many leases.

If the lease requires the landlord to *repair* the building, this may be interpreted as requiring him to *rebuild* it if it is destroyed by fire or other casualty. 38 ALR2d 685.

§ 1085. Damage or destruction of the leased premises *before* tenant

takes possession. If the rented premises are damaged by fire or other cause or otherwise rendered unsuitable for the use contemplated by the parties, and this occurs *before* *T* takes possession, *T* may terminate the lease without liability to *L*.

EXAMPLE: The building was destroyed by fire before *T* took possession. He could cancel the lease. Restatement, Property 2d § 5.2 (Tentative Draft). The theory is that *T* has no way of protecting the property before the possession date.

§ **1086. Taxes.** In the absence of a provision in the lease to that effect, the tenant is not obliged to pay real estate taxes on the leased land.

§ **1087. Fixtures.** The respective rights of landlord and tenant in and to fixtures installed by the tenant are discussed in Chapter 3.

Trade fixtures not removed by the tenant before he moves out become the property of the landlord. The fact that such items are attached to the landlord's building seems to make this result natural and acceptable to the courts. However, as to the tenant's ordinary personal property that is not in any way attached to the building, for example, furniture or stock in trade, this does not become the landlord's property simply because the tenant has moved out or been evicted. The landlord must keep or store these articles for the tenant. Some state laws cover this point.

§ **1088. Cancellation clause.** Leases may contain a clause conferring on the landlord the privilege of canceling the lease in the event of a sale of the property and upon giving a certain specified notice to the tenant. This clause is of value when the landlord sells the premises to a buyer who desires more or less immediate occupancy. Great care must be exercised in serving the notice of cancellation. For example, if the lease says that the *landlord* may cancel the lease in case of a sale, a notice served by his *purchaser* may be void. 163 ALR 1019. Notice of cancellation should be served personally unless the lease specifically allows notice by mail. Each tenant is entitled to his own copy of the notice.

§ **1089. Assignments and subleases.** Unless the lease provides otherwise, a lessee may assign his lease or sublet the premises. Whether a particular instrument is an assignment or sublease does not depend upon the name given the instrument by the parties. An assignment simply transfers the leasehold estate to a new owner, the assignee. A sublease creates a new and distinct leasehold estate in the sublessee. If the lessee transfers the *entire unexpired remainder* of the term created by the lease, the instrument is an assignment. If the lessee retains *part of the term, however small the part may be,* or transfers only part of the leased premises, the instrument is a sublease.

EXAMPLE: *L* leases certain premises to *T* for a term beginning on May 1, 1950, and expiring on April 30, 1952, at a rent of $100 per month. On July 1, 1950, *T* executes to *X* a "sublease" for a term beginning on July 1, 1950, and expiring April 30, 1952, at a rent of $150 per month. The instrument is an assignment.

EXAMPLE: *L* leases to *T* certain premises for a term beginning on May 1, 1950, and expiring on April 30, 1952. On July 1, 1950, *T* executes to *X* an "assignment" of said lease except the last day of the term. The instrument is a sublease.

The difference between assignment and sublease is important, since an assignee becomes liable to the original lessor for rent, whereas a sublessee is liable only to the sublessor, who, of course, is the lessee under the original lease. Of course the lessee in the original lease continues liable for rent to the original lessor, notwithstanding the assignment or sublease.

If the lease forbids an assignment without the lessor's consent, it does not necessarily prevent a sublease. If the lease forbids a sublease, it does not necessarily prohibit an assignment. As a rule, a commercial lease prohibits both assignments and subleases without the lessor's consent.

Suppose *L* makes a lease to *T Corporation,* and *X,* the holder of all the stock in *T Corporation,* sells all his stock to *Y*. This is not a violation of covenant not to make an assignment or sublease without the landlord's consent. The lease remains in *T Corporation*. Only the stock has been transferred. *Alabama Vermiculite Corp.* v. *Patterson,* 124 F.Supp. 441. Many leases forbid such a transfer of stock.

An assignment or sublease made without the lessor's consent, in defiance of the provisions of the lease, is not wholly void. If, after learning of the assignment or sublease, the lessor accepts rent from the assignee or sublessee, he waives his right to object to that particular assignment or sublease.

The spouse of the assignor need not join in assignment of the lease. A leasehold estate is personal property and there are no dower rights in personal property.

§ 1090. Mortgages of the leasehold. If the lease contains no provision that would prohibit a mortgage of the leasehold, the tenant may place a mortgage on the leasehold estate created by the lease. In such a mortgage, the description of the mortgaged premises should read somewhat as follows:

Leasehold estate created by lease dated May 1, 19_____ and recorded in the Recorder's Office of _________________ County, _________________, on May 2, 19_____, as Document 1,000,000, from John Smith, as Lessor, to Henry Brown, as Lessee, demising for a term of years commencing on May 1, 19_____, and ending on April 30, 19_____, the premises described as follows, to wit: (here insert description of leased premises).

One difficulty with such a mortgage is the fact that the tenant may default in his rent payments, and if he does, the landlord may declare the lease forfeited. Of course if default and forfeiture occur, the mortgage is thereby extinguished. A side agreement between the landlord and mortgagee may provide that before forfeiting the lease the landlord will give notice of the default to the mortgagee and a stated time to make good the defaults. It may also provide that if the lease is terminated, the mortgagee will be entitled to receive a new lease for the balance of the term on the same rent and terms as the old lease.

Another question that arises is with respect to the liability of the mortgagee for payment of rent. In title and intermediate states, which regard a leasehold mortgage as an assignment of the leasehold, the mortgagee becomes personally liable to the landlord for rent, under the rule stated in the preceding section that an assignee becomes liable to the original lessor for rent. *Williams* v. *Safe Deposit Co.,* 167 Md. 499, 175 Atl. 331 (1934). For this reason, it is a common practice in leasehold mortgages to omit the last day of the term, so that the mortgage mortgages the leasehold *except the last day thereof.* By excepting the last day of the term, the mortgage becomes a sublease rather than an assignment, and the mortgagee does not become personally liable to the landlord for rent due under the lease. Mortgages are treated as assignments or subleases depending on whether they cover all or less than all the unexpired term of the lease. In states that follow the lien theory of mortgages, a mere mortgage of the leasehold does not make the mortgagee liable for rent. Kratovil, Modern Mortgage Law and Practice, § 345.

§ 1091. Deed of rented premises. A landlord may, of course, sell his real estate, and the buyer will take it subject to existing leases and periodic tenancies. The deed alone confers on the buyer the right to collect rent falling due after the sale and the right to declare leases forfeited for nonpayment of rent if that right is reserved in the lease. *Lipschultz* v. *Robertson,* 407 Ill. 470, 95 NE2d 357 (1950). So far as the collection of future rent is concerned, it is unnecessary that the lessor execute to his purchaser an assignment of his rights under existing leases.

A tenant has the right to continue making rent payments to his original landlord until he is notified of a sale of the property. Therefore, one who buys rented property should promptly notify all tenants that all future rent must be paid to him.

A serious question arises when the tenant prepays the rent called for by the lease and the property is thereafter sold. The buyer of the property no doubt assumes that he will be entitled to collect the future rents called for by the lease and is then confronted by a tenant armed with rent receipts for such rent. In some states, the tenant must pay such rent over again to his new landlord, whereas in other states, the rent payments are good as against the new landlord. 49 Am. Jur.2d § 554.

§ 1092. Abandonment of the premises. Leases usually provide that if the lessee abandons the premises before the expiration of the lease, he shall nevertheless continue liable for rent until the expiration of the lease, and any reletting by the landlord shall not relieve the tenant of further liability.

However, upon abandonment of the premises by the lessee, it is the duty of the landlord in most states to mitigate damages, that is, to take charge of the property, and, if possible, relet or rerent it and thus reduce the amount for which the lessee remains liable. 40 ALR 190, 126 ALR 1219. The lessor may deduct the expenses of such reletting, including commissions and decorating, from the rent collected on such reletting, and he may apply the balance on the original tenant's liability.

EXAMPLE: A leased premises to *B* for one year at $50 per month. After six months, *B* abandoned the premises. The premises were vacant one month and were then relet to C

for $40 per month, the expenses of reletting, including commissions and decorating, being $50. The landlord thus realized on the reletting $200 minus $50, or $150. *B*'s liability is $300 minus $150, or $150.

The courts are not in agreement as to the extent of *L*'s duty where *T* abandons the premises. Some courts put the landlord under an obligation to seek another tenant so that the damages caused by *T*'s abandonment can be reduced. *Scheinfeld* v. *Muntz TV, Inc.,* 67 Ill. App.2d 28, 214 NE2d 506 (1966). Other courts require no affirmative action by *L*. But they do compel him to accept a suitable subtenant found by the abandoning tenant. *Reget* v. *Dempsey-Tegeler Co.,* 96 Ill. App.2d 278, 238 NE2d 418 (1968). 48 *Ill. B. J.* 546. Often the lease spells out the landlord's duties.

It is usual to insert a provision in the lease to the effect that the lessor shall not be under any obligation to relet and that he may permit the premises to remain vacant and sue the lessee for the full amount of the rent. This was the law in most states even in the absence of such a provision in the lease. 40 ALR 190, 126 ALR 1219. Under today's law there is a serious question whether the courts will compel the landlord to relet no matter what the lease says. Ordinarily the landlord will relet the premises rather than permit them to remain vacant, for rent collections from an existing tenant are money in the landlord's hands, whereas the liability of the previous tenant is at best a doubtful asset.

If the landlord relets after abandonment of the premises by the tenant, there is danger that this may amount to a surrender or termination of the lease, thus releasing the tenant from further liability for rent. In some states, a reletting automatically releases the liability of the tenant who has abandoned the premises, whereas in other states, the tenant is released *unless* the landlord gives him notice of his intention to hold him liable despite the reletting. 110 ALR 368. In the great majority of states, the question is regarded as one of intention. If the landlord's acts indicate an acceptance of the tenant's abandonment and an intention to regard the lease as terminated, the tenant's liability for future rent is terminated. 110 ALR 368. In effect, there is a *surrender*. As above suggested, the notice given by the landlord is employed to show that he does not intend to treat the lease as terminated by the abandonment. Suppose, however, that the landlord relets to a new tenant for a new term longer than the term of the original lease. In some states, this is viewed as being inconsistent with the continued existence of the earlier lease, and the earlier lease is therby terminated. *Ralph* v. *Deiley,* 293 Pa. 90, 141 Atl. 640 (1928); 61 ALR 773. Therefore the lease provisions covering this point (*the abandonment clause*) should include clauses giving the landlord the right to relet for a term longer than the original lease without in any way releasing the tenant's liability.

§ **1093. Surrender.** A *surrender* is an agreement by landlord and tenant to terminate the tenant's lease or tenancy, followed by a delivery of possession of the premises to the landlord. A surrender releases the tenant from liability for rent thereafter accruing.

EXAMPLE: **Premises were leased by *A* to *B* for the term from April 1, 1903, to**

April 1, 1906. On March 31, 1904, *B* told A that he wished to give up his lease, and A accepted this offer, telling *B* to allow a new tenant, C, to move in and to turn the keys over to him, C. This procedure was a surrender, and *B* was not liable for rent accruing thereafter.

Observe that it is the agreement between landlord and tenant that distinguishes a surrender from an abandonment by the tenant.

If the landlord, with the tenant's consent, gives a new lease to a stranger during the existence of the tenant's lease, this is a surrender.

EXAMPLE: A leased a store to *B*, who sold the business to C. A then gave C a new lease. This is a surrender of the old lease.

The making of a new lease between landlord and tenant operates as a surrender of a prior inconsistent lease. If the tenant merely abandons the premises, the fact that the landlord accepts the keys does not constitute a surrender.

§ 1094. Termination of tenancy for nonpayment of rent. Virtually all leases provide that the lease may be forfeited and the tenant evicted for nonpayment of rent or for violation of the terms of the lease.

Although the lease contains a clause permitting the landlord to declare the lease forfeited for nonpayment of rent, the landlord must not suddenly declare a forfeiture if he has been in the habit of accepting tardy rent payments. He must first notify the tenant to pay his rent by a specified reasonable time, and if the tenant fails to pay within the time specified, then and only then may the landlord declare a forfeiture. *Cottrell* v. *Gerson,* 371 Ill. 174, 20 NE2d 74 (1939).

Year-to-year and month-to-month tenancies likewise may be terminated on the giving of a short notice specified by law if the tenant defaults in his rent payments.

When the landlord evicts the tenant because of the tenant's defaults, the tenant's liability for future rent is ended unless the lease contains a clause, called the *survival clause,* to the effect that the tenant's liability shall survive such eviction. Such lease clauses are now commonplace.

§ 1095. Warranty of habitability. Perhaps the most meaningful new rule that has gained the widest acceptance is the rule that rented residential multifamily premises must be habitable and kept this way during the rental period. *Old Town Development Co.* v. *Langford,* 349 NE2d 744 (*Ind. App.* 1976), citing many cases and articles. This is an "implied warranty." Consult § 1048 for the origins of this rule.

What, precisely, is included in this warranty is something which the courts have not yet decided. At a minimum, the landlord warrants that the premises are free from substantial building code violations and will remain so during the rental period. Other courts go further, and it seems probable that most courts will expand the warranty beyond freedom from building code violations. Most courts, it is plain, will hold the landlord liable if the premises become unsafe or unsanitary, and thus unfit to live in. *Kline* v.

Burns, 276 A2d 248 (N.H. 1971); *Boston Housing Authy.* v. *Heminway,* 293 NE2d 831 (Mass. 1973); 40 ALR3d 73.

REFERENCES: 56 *B.U. L. Rev.* 1; 62 *Calif. L. Rev.* 1444; 25 *Case Western L. Rev.* 371; 56 *Cornell L. Rev.* 489; 77 *Dick. L. Rev.* 77; 1975 *Duke L. J.* 999; 40 *Fordham L. Rev.* 123; 58 *Ia. L. Rev.* 656; 39 *Mo. L. Rev.* 56; 16 *Vill. L. Rev.* 395.

Many reasons have been marshalled for finding that the landlord warrants the habitability of rented apartments. Tenants do not have the skills to keep apartments in repair and do not even have access to many plumbing, heating, and electrical facilities that fall into disrepair. *Javins* v. *First Nat. Realty Corp.,* 428 F2d 1071; *DePaul* v. *Kauffman,* 272 A2d 500 (Pa. 1971); *Mease* v. *Fox,* 200 NW2d 791 (Ia. 1972); 40 ALR3d 646.

REFERENCE OF GREAT VALUE: 1 *Real Estate Law Journal* 5 (1972).

References on implied warranty of habitability and freedom from code violations. 22 *Case Western Reserve L. Rev.* 739; 47 *Chicago-Kent L. Rev.* 1; 20 *Cleve. St. L. Rev.* 169; 2 *Conn. L. J.* 61; 56 *Cornell L. Rev.* 489; 20 *DePaul L. Rev.* 955; 1970 *Duke L. J.* 1040; 40 *Fordham L. Rev.* 123; 2 *Rutgers-Camden L. J.* 120; 23 *U. Fla. L. Rev.* 785; 31 *U. Pitt. L. Rev.* 138; 6 *U. of San Francisco L. Rev.* 147; 16 *Vill. L. Rev.* 383, 395.

Knowledge of tenant. The tenant's knowledge of building code violations when he rents the premises does not deprive him of his remedies. In all run-down buildings the code violations are clearly visible. *Foisy* v. *Wyman,* 111 Cal. Reptr. 7, 515 P2d 160 (1974). The implied warranty is to the effect that the premises will be *maintained* in habitable condition.

Two flats. The warranties rule applies to two flats. *South Austin Realty Assn.* v. *Sombright,* 361 NE2d 795 (1977).

Business properties. Presently, the courts have not applied the warranty of habitability to business properties. *Yuan Kane, Inc.* v. *Wm. Levy,* 26 Ill. App.3d 889, 326 NE2d 51 (1975); *Service Oil Co., Inc.* v. *White,* 542 P2d 652 (Kan. 1976); *Van Ness Indust., Inc.* v. *Claremont Paint Co.,* 324 A2d 102 (N.J. 1976); *Coulston* v. *Telescope Prod. Ltd.,* 378 N.Y.S.2d 553.

§ 1096. Reduction of rent. Some courts have awarded *T* a reduction in rent proportionate to the loss of habitability. *McKenna* v. *Begin,* 325 NE2d 587 (Mass. 1975); *Javins* v. *First Nat. Realty Corp.,* 428 F2d 1071 (1970); *Hinson* v. *Deli,* 26 Cal. App.3d 62; 102 Cal. Reptr. 66 (1972); *Academy Spires, Inc.* v. *Brown,* 111 N.J.S. 477, 268 A2d 556 (1970). They have even extended this remedy to public housing. *Housing Authority of City of Newark* v. *Scott,* 348 A2d 195 (N.J. 1976).

NEW LAWS: Some states (Hawaii, Louisiana, Maine, Massachusetts, Virginia, Washington, West Virginia, and Wisconsin) have passed laws providing for rent reduction.

NEW DIRECTIONS: Where the building is in violation of the implied warranty of habitability but the tenant pays full rent, the new decisions say that the landlord is liable to repay the excess rent to the tenant. It has been held that he can sue the landlord to get back part of the rent paid. *Berzito* v. *Gambino,* 114 N.J.S. 124, 274 A2d 865 (1970). He can also sue the landlord for damages. *Marini* v. *Ireland,* 56 N.J. 130, 265 A2d 526 (1970); *Winn* v. *Sampson Co.,* 398 P2d 272 (1965).

NEW LAWS: Maine has a new law to this effect.

§ 1097. Void lease because of building code violations. The presence of building code violations when the lease is signed may affect the validity of the lease.

NEW DIRECTIONS: Courts have held that the presence of building code violations when a lease of the apartment was signed rendered the lease void. *Glyco* v. *Schultz,* 289 NE2d 919 (Ohio 1972); *King* v. *Moorhead,* 495 SW2d 65 (Mo. 1973); 66 *Mich L. Rev.* 1953. This rule deprives the landlord of the benefit of all "fine print" in the lease. *Saunders* v. *First Nat. Realty Corp.,* 245 A2d 836 (1968); *Longnecker* v. *Hardin,* 130 Ill. App.2d 468, 264 NE2d 878 (1970); 21 *Vand. L. Rev.* 1117; *Robinson* v. *Diamond Housing Corp.,* 463 F2d 853 (1972). Or the tenant may choose to declare the lease void. *Mease* v. *Fox,* 200 NW2d 791 (Ia. 1972). If the code violations were not in existence *when the lease was made* it is not void. *Hinson* v. *Deli,* 102 Cal. Reptr. 661.

§ 1097a. Rent withholding.

Up to present times, if a tenant failed to pay rent, the landlord could have him evicted. Today the courts that recognize an implied warranty of habitability and freedom from building code violations have begun to devise additional remedies for the tenant if the premises are in disrepair. One of these is rent withholding, under which the tenant keeps the rent or part of it if the building or apartment becomes untenantable or substantial building code violations occur. The other is the rent escrow, under which the tenant pays the rent to the court or to a third party. Some cities and states have enacted laws along this line. *Clore* v. *Fredman,* 59 Ill.2d 20, 319 NE2d 18 (1975); *Mease* v. *Fox,* 200 NW2d 791 (Ia. 1972), 40 ALR3d 821. As a rule, when the building code violations have been corrected, the rent deposited in the escrow (or a part thereof) is released to the landlord. *Klein* v. *Allegheny County,* 269 A2d 647 (1972); *Bell* v. *Tsintolas Realty Co.,* 430 F2d 474 (1970); 29 *Md. L. Rev.* 202; 40 ALR3d 821; 46 *L.A.B. Bull.* 161. Of course, eviction is postponed as long as the rent is being paid into the escrow. *Kipsborough Realty Corp.* v. *Goldbetter,* 367 N.Y.S.2d 916 (1975); *Sabul* v. *Lipscomb,* 310 A2d 890 (Del. 1973).

References on rent withholding because of breach of implied warranty of habitability or presence of building code violations: 21 *Baylor L. Rev.* 372; 53 *Calif. L. Rev.* 304; 5 *Duquesne L. Rev.* 413; 56 *Geo. L. J.* 920; 39 *Geo. Wash. L. Rev.* 152; 57 *Ill. B. J.* 920; 2 *Loyola U. L. Rev.* (La.) 105; 55 *Minn. L. Rev.* 82; 66 *Mich. L. Rev.* 1753; 30 *U. Pitt. L. Rev.* 148; 66 *N.W.U. L. Rev.* 790.

NEW DIRECTIONS: Courts have begun to evolve additional new remedies for tenants where building code violations exist. First, the court finds that there is an implied covenant or obligation on the landlord's part to keep the premises free from major building code violations. Then, if the landlord fails to perform this duty, the court finds the tenant is entitled to a rent reduction. *Jack Spring Inc.* v. *Little,* 50 Ill.2d 351, 266 NE2d 338 (1972). Or the tenant can make the repairs and deduct the cost from future rents. *Marini* v. *Ireland,* 56 N.J. 130, 265 A2d 526 (1970); *Mease* v. *Fox,* 200 NW2d 791 (Ia. 1972).

§ 1097b. Retaliatory evictions. As the renters have grown more militant in reporting building code violations to the city authorities, landlords have retaliated by refusing to renew the leases of the militants. Up to recent times, the landlord would have been within his rights.

NEW DIRECTIONS: Today many courts would not permit the landlord to evict a tenant where his sole reason for doing so is a desire to retaliate for the reporting of building code violations. 40 ALR3d 753; 18 *Will. L. Rev.* 1119 (1973).

EXAMPLE: *T*, a tenant in an apartment, complained repeatedly to the landlord about building code violations. Receiving no satisfaction, *T* complained to the building department, which ordered *L* to cure the defects. When *T*'s lease expired, *L* filed an eviction suit. The court refused to evict *T*, because *L* was retaliating against *T*. The court allowed *T* to remain in possession until the code violations were eliminated and *T* could find another place to live. *Markese* v. *Cooper*, 333 N.Y.S.2d 63.

There are a number of cases holding that the entire doctrine of retaliatory eviction is inapplicable where the landlord simply seeks to oust the tenant so that he can remove a crumbling building from the housing market altogether. *Robinson* v. *Diamond Housing Corp.*, 463 F2d 853 (1972). This appears to make sense. If the landlord simply cannot keep the building in good shape, he should be permitted to demolish it. 51 *N.C. L. Rev.* 162 (1972).

But if the landlord raises the rent outrageously to get rid of a tenant who complains about building code violations, the tenant can move out and sue the landlord for damages, including damages for mental distress and punitive damages, that is, damages in an amount sufficient to constitute a punishment for the landlord's wrongdoing. *Aweeka* v. *Bonds*, 97 Cal. Reptr. 650 (1971).

Where the landlord's motives are to retaliate against a tenant who has complained of building code violations, he cannot evict the tenant *even after the tenant's lease has expired. Markess* v. *Cooper*, 333 N.Y.S.2d 63 (1972). As to landlord's motives, see Player, Motive and Retaliatory Eviction of Tenants, 1974 *U. of Ill. L.F.* 610.

So far the doctrine of retaliatory evictions has been applied only to residential properties. *Commercial Area Development* v. *Goodie Brand Packing*, 372 N.Y.S.2d 324 (1975).

NEW LAWS: Many states have enacted laws forbidding retaliatory eviction, for example, Massachusetts and New Hampshire. However, most of the law is judge-made law.

Motive—retaliatory eviction. To retaliate is to "get even" with someone for something he has done. This requires an *intention* to get even.

EXAMPLE (1): *T* complains to the city about building code violations in the building. Immediately *L* serves notice on *T* that his month-to-month tenancy is terminated. There is an intention to retaliate.

EXAMPLE (2): Facts as in the example given above, but *L* does not act until three years after *T*'s complaint.

Establishing intention to get even is simple in Example (1). It is next to impossible in Example (2).

Retaliatory eviction—the time factor. Many statutes have passed laws that fix a time that determines motivation.

EXAMPLE: In California, if *L* acts against *T* within sixty days after *T* has complained, it is assumed he is trying to "get even." Other states have other limits. Player, *supra*, p. 615.

Retaliatory eviction—landlord's protected activities. The landlord is not trying to "get even" if *T* complains, and *L* raises rents generally and evenly so that he can pay for the repairs. *L* must spread the cost over the anticipated life of the repairs. Player, *supra,* p. 623.

A landlord may take the entire building off the rental market if he feels the cost of needed repairs would be beyond his means, but he must not single out the tenant who complained and evict only him.

Retaliatory eviction—the philosophy underpinning the new rule. The philosophy that sustains and supports the new rule was expounded in *Edwards* v. *Habib,* 397 F2d 687 (D.C. Circ. 1968). The court reasoned: (1) building codes cannot be enforced unless tenants can report violations without fear of *L*'s vengeance; (2) use of the state courts to evict complaining tenants would be action by the state taken to punish *T* for exercising his constitutional right of *free speech.* Player, Motive and Retaliatory Eviction, 1974 *U. of Ill. Law Forum* 610 (excellent reference).

Retaliatory eviction—protected activities. Tenant activities against which *L* must not retaliate include: (1) tenants' meetings; (2) complaints to the building code department; (3) forming a tenants' union; and (4) lawful rent withholding. Player, *supra,* p. 614.

§ **1098. Limitations on the landlord's right to select tenants, renew leases and tenancies, and to evict tenants.** Under the old law, which is still true except regarding residential units, the landlord could rent to whomever he pleased, refuse to rent, refuse to renew leases, and evict any tenant whose lease or tenancy has been terminated. Now the court decisions and statutes are beginning to impose limits in all these regards:

NEW DIRECTIONS: *Public housing.* Where any public body is the landlord, the tenant's tenancy cannot be terminated without a hearing and inquiry into the reasonableness of the termination. *Thorpe* v. *Housing Authority,* 393 U.S. 268 (1968). Thus, in the case of such a landlord there are strict limits on the landlord's right to evict. *CHA* v. *Harris,* 275 NE2d 353 (Ill. 1976).

The quasi-public landlord. It certainly seems logical to hold that where a public body, such as a city or a housing authority, is the landlord, the tenant will have constitutional rights that tenants of private landlords do not have. But in recent times the notion has gained currency that private landlords who receive governmental assistance in some form are *quasi-public landlords,* and their tenants have at least some of the rights of tenants in public projects.

EXAMPLE: *L*, a landlord whose building was erected by FHA financing and who received a real estate tax exemption, could not refuse to accept *T* as a tenant because *T* was a welfare recipient. *Colon* v. *Tompkins Square Neighbors*, 294 F.Supp. 134 (1968). *L* cannot accept benefits from the government and turn his back on the wards of the government.

EXAMPLE: *L*, a landlord, in the identical situation of the landlord in the preceding example, refused to renew *T*'s lease. *T* had been an outspoken advocate of tenants' rights and had organized demonstrations against *L*. The court held that *L* could not evict *T* without giving him notice and a hearing to show that *L* was acting with good cause. *McQueen* v. *Drucker*, 317 F.Supp. 1122 (1970). *T* had the right to free speech.

EXAMPLE: Some courts require such landlords to give the tenants notice and to hold a hearing when the former wants to increase rents. 28 ALR Fed. 839.

This court-made law has now been formalized in HUD rules. 8 *Urb. Law*. 605 (1976).

§ **1099. Deposits in court.** Where a dispute exists between *L* and *T*, the eviction court has power to order the rent deposited in court until the dispute is resolved. *McNeal* v. *Habib*, 346 A2d 508 (D.C. 1975).

§ **1100. Landlord's duty to protect against criminal acts.** Traditionally, the landlord has been regarded as having no duty to protect his tenants against criminal acts of third parties. 59 *Georgetown L. J.* 1163.

NEW DIRECTIONS: However, under the new notion that the lease is a contract for services, the courts are beginning to place upon the landlord the duty to protect the tenant against criminal acts of third persons which he should have foreseen might occur. *Kline* v. *1500 Mass. Ave. Apt. Corp.*, 439 F2d 477. This would be especially true if the landlord's advertisements make mention of security protection or where the building is in a high-crime area or where the building has a record of criminal activity. 59 *Georgetown L. J.* 1185. There will be a tendency toward the application of a "higher-the-amount-of-rent, the-greater-the-duty-of-care" principle applied in the case of hotel guests. 59 *Georgetown L. J.* 1189.

EXAMPLE: *T*, an elderly tenant, was assaulted and robbed as he entered his apartment. The apartment was in a high-crime area. *T* sued his landlord, *L*, contending *L* was negligent in failing to provide adequate lighting and door locks. The Michigan Supreme Court held *L* was liable. *Johnston* v. *Harris*, 198 NW2d 409 (Mich. 1972); 43 ALR3d 331.

References on landlord's liability for failure to protect tenant against criminal acts: 74 *Dick L. Rev.* 543; 1970 *Duke L. J.* 1153; 5 *U. of San Francisco L. Rev.* 378.

EXAMPLE: *L* held liable to *T* because *L* failed to furnish adequate locks. *Braitman* v. *Erie Inv. Co.*, 350 A2d 268 (N.J. 1976).

EXAMPLE: *L* held liable where an intruder set fire to the building, causing damage to *T*'s property. *Warner* v. *Arnold*, 210 SE2d 350 (1974).

EXAMPLE: If a *second* burglary occurs, *L* is clearly liable. The facts show that burglary was foreseeable. *Stribling* v. *CHA*, 34 Ill. App.3d 551; 346 NE2d 47 (1975).

§ **1101. Single-family dwellings.** It has been held that the implied warranty does not pertain to single-family dwellings. *Vemba Dapkunas* v. *Bonnie Cagle,* 42 Ill. App.3d 644, 365 NE2d 575 (1976).

§ **1102. Welfare tenants.** Rent escrows are generally permitted where building code violations exist and welfare tenants are involved. Public funds must not be used to encourage violations of the law. 40 ALR3d 844.

§ **1103. Tenant unions.** Because one tenant has little bargaining power as against a landlord, tenant unions have been formed. 59 *Ill. B. J.* 732; 23 *U. Fla. L. Rev.* 79. These unions engage in collective bargaining with landlords. Tenant organizations which have recognized the need for more tenant control have developed a variety of goals. The most frequently sought goals include: (1) negotiation of a new lease for use between individual tenants and the landlord; (2) development of a grievance procedure and/or plan for arbitration of disputes; (3) recognition of the tenant organization as the exclusive representative of the landlord's tenants; (4) formulation of a satisfactory way to handle tenant needs and to bring the buildings into compliance with the building code; (5) participation of the tenant organization in decisions about rent increases; and (7) provision of adequate security for the dwelling units. 46 *L.A.B. Bull.* 163. Some tenant unions have engaged in rent strikes. 3 *Columbia J. Law & Social Problems* 1 (1967). By legal maneuvers some unions have been able to stall evictions for as long as nine months. 46 *L.A.B. Bull.* 162.

A landlord must not refuse to renew a tenant's lease simply because the tenant has been active in a tenants' union. *Engler* v. *Capital Management Corp.,* 271 A2d 615 (N.J. 1970).

§ **1104. Eviction—partial eviction—constructive eviction—partial constructive eviction.** A landlord who evicts his tenant wrongfully obviously can no longer collect rent. Indeed, even if the eviction is only from part of the premises, the same result follows.

EXAMPLE: *L* leased Lot 1 to *T*. The lot was improved with a house and garage. *L* wrongfully took possession of the garage. *T* is not liable for rent, even though he continues to occupy the house. *Tuchin* v. *Chambers,* 439 SW2d 849 (Tex. 1969).

If the landlord's conduct makes the premises untenantable, or if the stairways, walks, or elevators become unusable, a *constructive eviction* occurs, and if the tenant moves out as a result, he is no longer liable for rent. *Mease* v. *Fox,* 200 NW2d 791 (Ia. 1972).

EXAMPLE: *L* fails to supply heat in the wintertime to an apartment rented to *T*. *T* moves out. He is no longer liable for rent.

EXAMPLE: Infestation of apartment with vermin is a constructive eviction. This is a matter under control of landlord. 27 ALR3d 924.

EXAMPLE: Foregoing is especially true where caused by landlord's acts, as by his failure to pick up garbage. 27 ALR3d 935.

EXAMPLE: Infestation of a *house* presents a harder problem because the tenant has some measure of control here. Nevertheless, infestation of a house with rats is a constructive eviction, since this may be beyond tenant's control. *Lemle* v. *Breeden,* 51 Hawaii 426, 462 P2d 470 (1969). Of course, this would be a constructive eviction in an apartment.

EXAMPLE: Water leaking through a roof or into a basement is a constructive eviction. 33 ALR3d 1356.

Matters wholly beyond the control of the landlord are not a constructive eviction.

EXAMPLE: An adjoining tenant had noisy machinery that prevented tenant from holding seminars. There is no constructive eviction. *Finkelstein* v. *Levinson,* 343 N.Y.S.2d 849 (1973).

NEW DIRECTIONS: Changes are taking place in the old law of constructive eviction. The right to move out is worthless when there is an acute shortage of rental apartments. Thus, the line between actual eviction and constructive eviction has become blurred, and the courts are introducing new ideas that are designed to achieve justice and to place little emphasis on labels.

EXAMPLE: *L* leased a restaurant to *T. T* took possession, not knowing that part of the leased premises was not available for occupancy. The court held this was "actual partial eviction" and that *T* could occupy the occupiable part without paying rent. *Metzenbaum* v. *Crepes D'Asic, Inc.,* 367 N.Y.S.2d 645.

EXAMPLE: *L* leased *T* an apartment. *T* was forced to discontinue use of the terrace because of water dripping from the building's air conditioner. The court permitted *T* to remain in occupancy and to discontinue paying rent. The court held this was "partial constructive eviction." *East Haven Assoc., Inc.* v. *Gurian,* 313 N.Y.S.2d 927 (1970).

EXAMPLE: *T,* an orthodontist, resisted eviction because *L* was not furnishing proper heating and air conditioning. The court held that because of this breach on *L*'s part, *T* was not required to pay the rent and could not be evicted. *Demirci* v. *Burns,* 124 N.J.S. 274, 306 A2d 468 (1973).

EXAMPLE: *L* leased a store building to *T,* with a covenant to repair. Part of the building was destroyed by fire. The court allowed *T* to occupy the remainder of the building with a reduction of rent. *Coppola* v. *Tidewater Oil Co.,* 244 N.Y.S.2d 898 (1963).

NEW LAWS: Statutes are being enacted on the subject of rent withholding and the other new rules. *De Paul* v. *Kauffman,* 441 Pa. 386, 272 A2d 500 (1971). The New Jersey Statute even includes mobile homes in its retaliatory eviction statute. In Maryland *T* may repudiate the lease within thirty days of occupancy if the warranty of habitability has been breached.

§ 1105. Options to renew. Many leases contain an option or privilege of some sort to renew or extend the lease for an additional period, and such provisions have evoked considerable controversy. The following are some points to consider:

1. When the lease gives the tenant the "first right" or "first privilege" of receiving a new or extended lease, this simply gives the existing tenant a prior right if the landlord decides to continue renting the property. The tenant has no rights if the landlord decides to take the property off the rental market. 6 ALR2d 820.

2. When the lease contains a true option to renew, but says nothing about the tenant giving his landlord notice of his exercise of this option, it is sufficient in most states if the tenant simply remains in occupancy after the lease has expired. His remaining adequately exercises the renewel option, but it is a poor practice. *Basler* v. *Warren,* 159 F2d 41. To avoid controversy, well in advance of the expiration of the lease the tenant should give the landlord written notice of his exercise of the renewal option, and in a few states such notice is legally necessary. Nowadays most leases specifically require that notice be given the landlord a certain number of days before the end of lease that the tenant is exercising his renewal option. Naturally such provision must be strictly complied with.

3. Unless the lease specifically authorizes the notice of exercise of option to be given by mail, it should be personally served upon the landlord.

4. It is best that the notice be signed by the tenant personally. If the notice is signed by an agent for the tenant, some states require that the agent have written authority to bind the tenant.

5. Since the notice is technically an acceptance of an offer, you must keep in mind the rule of contract law that when you accept an offer you must not add to, subtract from, or in any way change the terms of the offer. About all you can safely say is "I hereby notify you that I hereby exercise the renewal option set forth in Paragraph 20 of our lease."

6. Where the lease runs to two or more tenants, all must join in the notice of exercise. *Kleros Building* v. *Battaglia,* 348 Ill. App. 445, 109 NE2d 221 (1952).

7. An option to renew does not continue into the renewal period. Successive renewals are not permitted unless the lease specifically provides for them. Were the rule otherwise, the tenant could renew the lease forever. *Hindu Incense Mfg. Co.* v. *MacKenzie,* 403 Ill. 390, 86 NE2d 214.

§ 1106. Options to purchase. Many leases, particularly those involving commercial or industrial property, give the tenant the option to buy the leased land. Concerning such options one would make the following observations:

1. When the tenant gives the landlord proper notice of the tenant's exercise of the option, a binding contract for the sale of the land results. Such an option should contain all the detailed provisions customary in a contract of sale, such as provisions regarding the kind of title to be given, the duty to furnish an abstract or other evidence of title, the type of deed to be given, and what items are to be prorated. Most options that one finds in leases are much too skimpy.

2. Many lease options give the tenant the first privilege to buy, "the first right to buy," or "the first refusal of the property." These are sometimes called *refusal form* or *first refusal options*. Often such options have been held by the courts to be conditional on the landlord's wish to sell. In other words, if the landlord decides to keep the property and does not place it on the market at all, the tenant cannot compel a sale of the property to himself. It is only where the landlord decides to sell the property while the lease is in effect that the tenant must be given the first right to buy. 34 ALR2d 1158.

3. Where the lease runs in favor of two or more tenants, all must join in the exercise of the option.

4. It is best that the tenant himself sign the notice of exercise of the option. In

some states, a notice signed by the tenant's agent is not valid unless the agent has written authority to sign. *Welsh* v. *Jakstas,* 401 Ill. 288, 82 NE2d 253 (1949).

5. Notice of exercise of the option is an acceptance of an offer. In contract law, the rule is that when one accepts an offer, one must not deviate from the terms of the offer even slightly. Thus, if the tenant writes that he exercises the option, "the deal to be closed at my office ten days from this date," he is, in legal effect, changing the contract, and the notice is void. *Morris* v. *Goldthorp,* 390 Ill. 186, 60 NE2d 857 (1945); *Standard Reliance Ins.* Co. v. *Schoenthal,* 171 Neb. 490, 106 NW2d 704 (1945).

6. The option cannot be exercised after the lease has been terminated for default in payment of rent. *Sandra Frocks, Inc.* v. *Ziff,* 397 Ill. 497, 74 NE2d 669 (1947); *Atlantic Richfield* Co. v. *Couture,* 344 NE2d 917 (Mass. 1976). However, if the notice is given after default in payment of rent, but before the landlord has decided to terminate the lease because of such default, the option is validly exercised. *Jader* v. *Costello,* 405 Ill. 181, 90 NE2d 778; 10 ALR2d 884. Contra: *Helbig* v. *Bonsness,* 227 Wis. 52, 277 NW 634; *Derman Rug Co., Inc.* v. *Ruderman,* 350 NE2d 727 (Mass. 1976). See 53 ALR3d 435.

7. A difficult question arises where a lease contains an option to purchase the property and also contains an option to extend the term or renew for an additional period. The various states are not in agreement as to the proper rule to be followed. In some states, the option to purchase the property continues during the extended or renewal period. *Emmett S. Hickman* Co. v. *American Realty, Inc.,* 227 A2d 688 (Del. 1971); *Atlantic Richfield* Co. v. *Couture,* 344 NE2d 917 (Mass. 1976); *Wanous* v. *Balaco,* 412 Ill. 545, 107 NE2d 791 (1952); *Hindu Incense Mfg.* Co. v. *MacKenzie,* 403 Ill. 390, 86 NE2d 214 (1949); *Didriksen* v. *Havens,* 136 Conn. 41, 68 A2d 163 (1963). However, in Maryland, Pennsylvania, and some other states, the option to purchase ends with the original term of the lease and does not continue into the renewal period. 37 ALR 1245; 163 ALR 711.

8. Where a lease contains an option to purchase, and at the expiration of the lease the tenant holds over and the landlord accepts rent, so that a tenancy from year to year is created, the authorities are once more divided as to whether the option continues into the tenancy from year to year. In some states, it is held that the option to purchase ends with the lease. *Wanous* v. *Balaco,* 412 Ill. 545, 107 NE2d 791 (1952). However, in Colorado, Indiana, New Jersey, and perhaps other states, the option to purchase continues into the tenancy from year to year. *Straley* v. *Osborne,* 278 A2d 64 (Md. 1971).

9. Once a lessee who has an option to purchase exercises his option, the lease comes to an end, and thereafter the relation between the parties is that of seller and buyer, not landlord and tenant. *Cities Service Oil* Co. v. *Viering,* 404 Ill. 538, 89 N.E.2d 392 (1950). For example, rent is no longer due, and the landlord cannot declare the lessee's rights terminated for nonpayment of rent. *Crowell* v. *Brady,* 169 Cal. App.2d 352, 337 P2d 211 (1959).

10. If a lease is assigned by the lessee, the option to purchase is assigned as part of the lease and may be exercised by the assignee, but if the lease is not assignable, then the option likewise is not assignable.

§ **1107. Unconscionability.** The notion that the court can strike down an unconscionable lease or any unconscionable provision thereof has become part of the law of landlord and tenant. Restatement Property, 2d § 5.5; Berger, Hard Leases Make Bad Law, 74 *Columb. L. Rev.* 791; 24 *Baylor L. Rev.* 443, 498.

EXAMPLE: An apartment lease obligated *T* to pay *L* as additional rent in attorney's fees upon commencement of any proceeding by *L* as a result of *T*'s default. The clause was held void. *Weidmen* v. *Tomaselli,* 365 N.Y.S.2d 681.

EXAMPLE: *L,* an oil company, leased a filling station to *T* under a lease with a clause stating that *L* would not be liable for loss or damage resulting from the negligence of *L*'s employees and that *T* would pay for any such loss. One of *L*'s employees sprayed gasoline over *T,* and severe burns resulted. The court held the clause void and awarded damages to *T. Weaver* v. *American Oil Co.,* 276 NE2d 144 (Ind. 1971).

The courts have even held that *L* must renew a lease if refusal to do so would be unconscionable.

EXAMPLE: *L,* an oil company, had leased the filling station to *T* for many years. *T* had spent a great deal of money in improving the station and building up a business. The court compelled *L* to renew the lease. *Shell Oil Co.* v. *Marinello,* 294 A2d 253 (N.J.).

§ 1108. Fair dealing. Some courts will strike down any provision of a lease if enforcement would not be considered "fair dealing." Berger, Hard Leases Make Bad Law, 74 *Columb. L. Rev.* 791, 805.

EXAMPLE: *L* leased commercial premises to *T* with an option to renew. *T* failed to exercise the option within the time allowed, but *L,* after such expiration, notified *T* that his lease would soon end. *T* then tendered to *L* the money needed to renew the lease, but *L* refused. The court held that *L* was not injured by the technical defect and compelled *L* to renew the lease. *George W. Miller & Co.* v. *Wolf Sales & Service Co.,* 318 N.Y.S.2d 24 (1971); 74 *Columb. L. Rev.* 791, 805. It will probably be a long time before other courts decide to be as liberal as this.

NEW LAWS: In New York, the legislature has enacted a law giving the courts the power to declare parts of leases unconscionable. The law is sound, but it only spells out a power the courts have always had. Again, the important idea here is that the boilerplate lawyers put in leases is really of little significance today. The courts will look at it. If they don't like it, they will knock it out. Until recent years, a lease between an oil company and a dealer was construed to create a simple landlord-tenant relationship that ended when the lease expired. But since the disruption of gasoline supplies during the 1973–74 Arab oil embargo, legislatures have increasingly regarded oil companies as something like public utilities and have been willing to pass laws chipping away at their freedom of action.

These laws restrict the right of oil company landlords to refuse to renew the tenant-operator's lease. It seems likely that a number of states will enact such laws. The first was enacted in California in 1975.

RESERVED: §§ 1109–1128.

38

Racial Integration in Real Estate

§ 1129. **Federal legislation—the 1968 law.** A federal "open occupancy" law was enacted in 1968. 42 U.S.C.A. § 3601 (Title VII).

The law covers dwellings, including homes and multifamily residences (two-flats, duplexes, apartments), and also vacant land acquired for construction for such purposes. No doubt acquisition of vacant land zoned for residential purposes will be regarded as subject to the law. Probably condominiums and co-ops will be regarded also as coming under the law. The law applies to sales, leases, and all types of rental arrangements. It does not include properties used *exclusively* for commercial or industrial purposes. But if *part* of the building is used for residential purposes, the building is subject to the law.

The law creates new and important rights. Some are spelled out fairly clearly. Others will come into sharper focus only after the Supreme Court has interpreted the law. Some observations can be made. Where *bias* against a person is based on race, color, religion, or national origin, the following are unlawful:

1. To refuse to sell or lease or negotiate for sale or lease because of such bias, or to discriminate in the furnishing of services or facilities.

EXAMPLE: A landlord cannot furnish maid service to white tenants and refuse this service to Blacks.

2. To discriminate in exacting terms of the sale or lease, for example by asking a higher price because of the race of the buyer.

3. To advertise in the newspapers or post notices on the building that particular races will not be welcomed as buyers or tenants.

4. To state that a dwelling is not available, where such statement is made because of the race of the party seeking to buy or rent.

5. For a lender to refuse a party a loan or to insist on higher interest rates or harsher loan terms because of racial reasons.

6. For real estate brokers to refuse membership in their organizations or multiple-listing services because of racial reasons.

7. To induce a person to sell by creating fears of racial change in the neighborhood.

Sale or rental of a single-family house is exempted if the house is sold or rented without the use in any manner of the facilities of a real estate broker or salesman and without the publication or posting of an advertisement indicating bias against non-Caucasians. The purpose here is to avoid (1) any inference that state-licensed machinery (brokers) can be employed to achieve discrimination and (2) the public humiliation to prospective purchasers or tenants occasioned in publication or posting of a notice that they are unacceptable as tenants or buyers.

But even if sold through the owner's efforts, the sale is not exempt if the seller owns more than three houses at any one time. Probably this exclusion for an owner of three houses is intended to benefit the person who owns a home and a summer or winter home.

As to this special exempt category (the seller who owns three houses or fewer), the exemption is limited in a highly technical way. The exemption applies only to a house in which the owner *resides* at the time of the sale or to an unoccupied house of which he was the most recent resident. Where this residence requirement is not complied with, the exemption applies only to one sale every two years. In other words, if I own three houses, live in one, and rent out the others, I am exempt from the law for each of the rented houses only for sales two or more years apart. One receives the impression that Congress was willing to exempt from the law a bona fide owner of three homes who seeks to sell them, as his circumstances dictate, without the aid of a broker. But Congress wanted no subterfuges which would permit a professional builder of residences to escape from provisions of the law. The law also exempts sale or rental of a dwelling meant for occupancy by no more than four families living independently of each other if the owner lives in one apartment.

Enforcement of the law is complex. In general, the Secretary of the Department of Housing and Urban Development (HUD) is entrusted with the machinery of enforcement. The following procedures are available, namely:

1. If there is a substantially equivalent remedy under a state law or ordinance, HUD notifies the appropriate state officials.

2. If within thirty days no action is taken by state officials, the party discriminated against may file suit in a federal court or in a state court.

3. The court may award damages, issue injunctions restraining violations of the law, and set aside deeds or leases, except that no deed or lease shall be set aside if entered into before a court order has issued and the grantee or lessee had no actual knowledge of the proceedings. One is left with the inference that a court that sets aside a deed to a white person can order a sale thereof to a Black who made an earlier comparable offer and was rejected because of racial bias. The court may also award damages to a party who proves he has been unlawfully discriminated against.

4. The United States Attorney General may obtain injunctions restraining violations of the law.

5. In certain instances the law provides for fines against, or imprisonment of, persons using force or threat of force to bring about racial discrimination in housing.

§ 1130. Federal legislation—the 1866 law. In a law passed by Congress in 1866 it is provided, in part, that American citizens of every race and color shall have *the same right* throughout the country to purchase, lease, sell, hold, and convey real and personal property as is enjoyed by white persons. Laying stress on the phrase "the same right," the Supreme Court has held that this law prohibits all racial discrimination, private and public, in the sale and rental of property. Thus, every "racially motivated refusal to sell or rent" is prohibited. *Jones* v. *Alfred H. Mayer Co.,* 392 U.S. 409 (1968). This law to some extent overlaps the Civil Rights Act of 1968, to some extent goes beyond it, and to some extent omits protection afforded by the 1968 law. 42 USCA § 1981 *et seq.*

EXAMPLE: A owns his home which he occupies with his family. This is the only land he owns. He offers it for sale without employing a broker, but declines to sell to *B,* a Black. His refusal is motivated by *B*'s race. This refusal is wrongful. Observe that such a situation is expressly omitted from the coverage of the 1968 law under which a person owning only one home and selling it without a broker is not forbidden to discriminate.

EXAMPLE: In the example given above, *B* seeks the aid of the Attorney General of the United States. He will not succeed. The 1866 law makes no provision for furnishing such aid.

EXAMPLE: A refuses to sell his *store* to *B,* a Black, his refusal being racially motivated. This refusal is prohibited by the 1866 law, but does not come under the 1968 law.

EXAMPLE: A owns a large apartment building. For racial reasons he refuses to rent an apartment to *B,* a Black. Both laws forbid this type of discrimination.

As the Supreme Court has pointed out, the law of 1866 does NOT do the following:

1. It does not forbid discrimination on grounds of *religion* or *national origin:*

EXAMPLE: *A,* a member of *XYZ Church,* owns only one home. He offers his home for sale without the aid of a real estate broker. As purchasers appear, he states verbally that he will sell only to members of *XYZ Church*. The 1866 law does not forbid such action.

2. It does not deal specifically with discrimination in the provision of services or facilities in connection with the sale or rental of a dwelling, for example, furnishing maid service to apartment tenants.

3. It does not prohibit advertising or other representations that indicate discriminatory preferences.

4. It does not refer explicitly to discrimination in financing arrangements or in the provision of real estate brokerage services.

5. It does not enable a rejected purchaser or tenant to call upon the Attorney General or any other federal officer for aid.

6. It makes no *express* provision for the bringing of damage suits by rejected purchasers or tenants, but the court has indicated it has kept an open mind on the question of whether a right to damages could be implied or inferred from the language and purpose of the law.

To the extent that such omissions are set forth in the 1968 law, probably they lack practical significance so far as dwellings are concerned. 22 ALR Fed. 359.

And, to repeat, while the 1968 law does not apply to stores, factories, or structures other than dwellings, these are covered by the 1866 law; though, again, while the 1866 law covers all buildings it is less comprehensive in the details of enforcement.

Problems arise here because Congress in enacting the 1968 law had assumed the 1866 law was more or less a dead letter as earlier court decisions had indicated, but after the 1968 law was enacted, the Supreme Court breathed life into the 1866 law, and we are now faced with two somewhat inconsistent laws relating to the same subject.

The Supreme Court has indicated that some rather effective remedies are available for enforcement of the 1866 law.

EXAMPLE: In 1965 *A*, a Black, sought to purchase a home from *B*, a professional builder, in a subdivision owned by *B*. *B* rejected *A*, his rejection being racially motivated. *A* filed an injunction suit against *B* to prohibit *B* from so discriminating. In 1968 the court entered a judgment ordering *B* to sell to A at the price prevailing at the time of the wrongful refusal in 1965, which is substantially less than the current market of such a home. *B* must absorb this loss. This example is the precise, factual situation in *Jones* v. *Alfred H. Mayer Co.*, 392 U.S. 409.

§ **1131. Court decisions—departmental rulings.** The first significant decision in the area of racial discrimination in housing was *Shelley* v. *Kraemer*, 334 U.S. 1, 3 ALR2d 441 (1948). This decision struck down as contrary to the Constitution of the United States a state court decision enforcing by injunction an agreement by property owners not to sell or lease to a Black. Our Constitution, the court stated, forbids any state action, including state court action, that tends to create discriminaion. Later the Supreme Court held that no party to such an agreement could sue for damages any other party who violated it by selling or leasing to a Black. *Barrows* v. *Jackson*, 346 U.S. 249 (1953). The thing forbidden by these decisions is state action, such as the issuance of court orders attempting to enforce racial covenants. These decisions did not state that racial covenants are void. They simply prohibited court action to enforce them.

As a result of the federal legislation heretofore discussed, these decisions are no longer significant. Racial covenants are totally invalid now. *Mayers* v. *Ridley*, 465 F2d 630.

Other federal court decisions make it clear that the courts mean to enforce the new federal law.

EXAMPLE: The courts have held that the recorder of deeds cannot record a racial covenant. *Mayers* v. *Ridley*, 465 F2d 630.

EXAMPLE: A landlord was forbidden to state that no Jews or Blacks had ever lived on the premises.

EXAMPLE: A newspaper can be enjoined from publishing discriminatory advertising. *U.S.* v. *Hunter*, 324 F.Supp. 529.

EXAMPLE: A city approved subdivisions in predominantly white areas while refusing approval of subdivisions in black areas, giving overloaded sewers as a reason. The court ordered the city to approve a subdivision in the black area and to permit hookup to city sewers. *L'Enfant Plaza North, Inc.* v. *D. C. Redevelopment Land Agency,* 437 F2d 698 (CA D.C. 1971).

EXAMPLE: Offer by seller-realtor to build identical houses for black customers in "another part of town" and threaten to force litigation before selling houses desired by customers violates the law. *U.S.* v. *Pelzer,* 484 F2d 438 (1973).

EXAMPLE: Violation of law is established by evidence that a Black plaintiff and his wife visited a real estate office seeking a new bilevel home in three suburban communities that had few black residents and that they were told by a salesman that no such properties were available, although another salesman offered listings for bilevel homes in those communities to two white couples shortly before and after plaintiffs' visit. *Johnson* v. *Jerry Pals Real Estate,* 485 F2d 528 (1973, CA 7 Ill.).

EXAMPLE: Evidence held sufficient to sustain a finding that a real estate broker, manager, and one salesman refused to negotiate for sale of a dwelling in a predominantly white area of Chicago because of racial prejudice against black couple seeking to purchase a home. The court concluded that when the salesman was ultimately induced to show property to the black couple, he did so in a grudging, uncooperative, and deliberately discouraging manner, and that the house was eventually sold to whites for substantially less than the figure quoted to the black couple by the salesman. *Seaton* v. *Sky Realty* Co., 491 F2d 634 (1971, CA 7 Ill.).

EXAMPLE: Exclusive rental agents found to have refused to rent to plaintiffs on the basis of their race are liable under the law for their unlawful conduct even where the management agreement stated that leases and tenants shall be approved by owner and where their actions are at behest of their principal. *Jeanty* v. *McKey & Pogue, Inc.,* 496 F2d 1119 (1974, CA 7 Ill.).

EXAMPLE: The court stopped realtors from placing "Sold" signs in front of houses in a white neighborhood in order to discourage blacks. *U.S.* v. *Pelzer Realty* Co., *Inc.,* 484 F2d 438 (1973).

EXAMPLE: *L* is not guilty of racial discrimination, however, if he rejects a tenant who does not meet *L*'s normal credit requirements. *Boyd* v. *Lefrak* Org., 509 F2d 1110 (1975).

Also, the Department of Justice has made some strong rulings in this area.

EXAMPLE: The Department has ruled that an appraisal report must not refer to population changes as affecting the value of the property.

EXAMPLE: The Department has ruled that title insurance policies must not show recorded racial restrictions.

EXAMPLE: The Department has ruled that an abstract of title must now show a recorded racial restriction unless it also states that same is invalid.

§ 1131a. **Permitted discriminations.** The federal law does not prohibit an owner from considering any factors other than race which he feels are relevant in determining whether to rent to one individual or another. Such factors, which an owner might consider, include the *credit standing of the applicant, his assets, his financial stability, his reputation in the community, his age, the size of his family, the ages of his children, his past experience as a lessee or tenant, the length of time he plans to occupy the premises, and whether he is or is not a transient.*

The owner may also consider more subjective factors in determining whether he will rent to one individual or another. Thus, he may consider the applicant's appearance, his demeanor, the owner's estimate of his trustworthiness or truthfulness or other subjective factors. Indeed, businessmen utilize such conclusions and opinions in their daily affairs.

Although such factors are subjective, they may be considered. Nonetheless, the owner may later be called upon to demonstrate in court that these and not racial motivations were responsible for his decision in refusing to rent or sell to a black. Subjective factors are by their nature difficult to prove and often have little more than the credibility of the individual witness behind them.

An owner may even refuse to rent to an individual simply because he does not like him. No one is required to rent or sell to an individual he doesn't like. As in other cases, however, the owner may later be called upon to demonstrate in court that his personal dislike of an individual, rather than the individual's race, was responsible for his decision to refuse him as a tenant.

The owner may consider such factors as those set out above in determining whether to rent or sell to *any* individual. He is not precluded by any federal statute from considering such factors. Indeed, *any* factor, other than race, which is relevant to a decision whether to rent or sell to an individual may be considered, and the list of factors set forth above is not intended to be, and could not constitute, an exclusive list. *Bush* v. *Kaim,* 297 F.Supp. 151 (1969), 7 *Seton Hall L. Rev.* 168 (1975).

§ 1132. **State constitutions, state laws, court decisions, ordinances, commission rulings and orders.** An increasing number of states and cities have enacted laws and ordinances forbidding racial discrimination in housing. Such laws set up commissions to hear complaints of racial discrimination. The following are illustrations of state commission orders and court decisions enforcing local open-housing laws.

EXAMPLE: An apartment owner discriminated against a Black by refusing to rent him an apartment. The Black filed a complaint with the state commission. An order was entered requiring the owner to rent an apartment to the Black at the regular prevailing rental and to desist from acts of discrimination in rental practices against the Black or any other persons because of race, religion, or national origin. *In re Ruth,* 12 *Race Relations Rep.* 1703 (Calif.).

EXAMPLE: A commission ordered the landlord to rent to a Black who had been refused occupancy for racial reasons. White tenants who later moved in with knowledge of the problem were required to vacate. *City of N.Y.* v. *Camp Const. Co.,* 11 *Race Relations Rep.* 1949 (N.Y.).

EXAMPLE: A white subdivision was subject to a recorded declaration giving the homeowners' association a pre-emption option, that is, the right to buy any homesite at the same price another party would offer. A homeowner entered into a contract to sell to a black. The contract was specifically made subject to the recorded declaration. The association then gave notice of exercise of its pre-emption privilege. The court held that exercise of such a privilege would be illegal under the state fair housing law if done solely because of racial bias. *Vaught* v. *Village Creek, 7 Race Relations Rep.* 849.

EXAMPLE: The court sustained a commission order ousting a white tenant because he was not a bona fide tenant ignorant of the landlord's earlier attempt to discriminate against a Black seeking to rent the same apartment. *Feigenblum* v. *Comm.,* 278 N.Y.S.2d 652.

EXAMPLE: The landlord accepted a Black tenant and then resorted to incredibly evasive tactics to discourage the tenant. He was held liable for damages. *Jackson* v. *Concord Co.,* 253 A2d 793.

EXAMPLE: The landlord refused to rent a house to a black, and a relative of the landlord agreed to cover up for the landlord by buying the house. Both were held liable. *Rody* v. *Hollis,* 500 P2d 97 (Wash. 1972). The damage awarded can be great ($20,000). *Parker* v. *Shonfeld,* 409 F.Supp. 896 (1976).

EXAMPLE: Midland, the owner of an apartment complex, restricted blacks to buildings 65 and 66, and there were only two black families in the remainder of the complex. Racial discrimination is established. *Midland Homes* v. *Penn. Hum. Rel. Comm.,* 333 A2d 516 (Pa. 1975).

EXAMPLE: The commission found the landlord guilty of discrimination in rejecting a Black tenant but refused to oust a white tenant to whom the landlord later rented the apartment. The white tenant was an innocent party unaware of the discrimination. The court sustained this ruling. *Comm.* v. *City Builders, Inc.,* 277 N.Y.S.2d 434.

EXAMPLE: A Black bought a vacant lot adjoining the seller's home, using a white nominee to accomplish the purchase. When the seller discovered the identity of the real purchaser he brought suit. The court refused to set aside the transaction. *Hirsch* v. *Silberstein* (Pa.), 227 A2d 638.

EXAMPLE: A landlord had no right to evict a tenant because the tenant married a Black. *Prendergast* v. *Snyder,* 50 Cal. Reptr. 903, 413 P2d 847.

EXAMPLE: Land developers have been ordered to sell houses to and build houses for Blacks. *Stanton Land Co.* v. *Pittsburgh,* 32 *Law Week* 2314; *Don Wilson Builders* v. *Superior Ct.,* 33 Cal. Reptr. 621; *Marano Const. Co.* v. *State Comm.,* 259 N.Y.S.2d 4.

EXAMPLE: The location of public housing (with multiracial occupancy) in a white neighborhood is not discriminatory or capricious for that reason. *Philbrook* v. *Chapel Hill* (N.C.), 153 SE2d 153.

EXAMPLE: An ordinance was held invalid where it created a "buffer zone" between Black and white residential areas and required deeper wells and larger septic fields in this area. *Anderson* v. *Forest Park,* 239 Fed.Supp. 576.

Quite a number of city ordinances forbidding discrimination—for example, by real estate brokers—have been upheld as valid. *Chicago Real Estate Board v. Chicago,* 36 Ill.2d 530, 224 NE2d 793.

§ **1133. Private parks.** Even private parks are subject to the federal laws against racial discrimination.

EXAMPLE: Little Huntington Park is a private park owned by a nonprofit corporation. *A,* who owned an adjacent house and stock in the corporation, leased his house to *B,* a black, and assigned his membership stock to *B.* The club cancelled *A*'s membership. The club's membership was open to every white person. The court thought this was comparable to a racially restrictive covenant. It held that *A* and *B* could recover damages against the corporation. *Sullivan* v. *Little Huntington Park, Inc.,* 396 U.S. 229 (1969).

If it is clear that the creator of the trust was determined to exclude blacks, the courts must let the land revert to the heirs of the creator of the trust. *Evans* v. *Abney,* 396 U.S. 435, 42 L. Ed.2d 930, 90 Sup. Ct. 628 (1970). This decision has been criticized. The court chose to permit a park to revert to private ownership rather than let blacks in.

REFERENCES: *69 Columb. L. Rev.* 1478; 2 *Loyola U. L. J.* (Chicago) 390; 5 *Val. U. L. Rev.* 172; 49 *N. C. L. Rev.* 148; 30 *Md. L. Rev.* 226; 21 *Syracuse L. Rev.* 1313; 35 *Notre D. Law* 277; 36 *id* 74; 45 *Ia. L. Rev.* 954.

§ **1134. Charitable trusts.** In former times quite a number of charitable trusts were set up for white persons only. These trusts can no longer be operated for the sole benefit of whites. 25 ALR3d 736.

EXAMPLE: A trust was established for "poor white male orphan children." The court held that exclusion of blacks violated the law, removed the old trustees, and appointed new trustees with directions to admit blacks. *Pennsylvania* v. *Brown,* 392 F2d 120 (3d Circ. 1968). A similar result was reached in *Dunbar* v. *Board of Trustees,* 461 P2d 28 (Colo. 1969), and *Bank of Delaware* v. *Buckson,* 255 A2d 710 (Del. 1969).

§ **1135. Public accommodations.** Under federal law, discrimination in the furnishing of public accommodations is forbidden.

EXAMPLE: A motel in Atlanta restricted its clientele to white persons. The court held that it could not refuse to admit blacks. *Heart of Atlanta Hotel, Inc.* v. *U.S.,* 379 U.S. 241 (1964).

EXAMPLE: Along the lines of the Little Huntington Park case is one in which a privately owned recreational area, which included a snack bar and facilities for dancing, swimming, picnicking, and miniature golf, was "a place of public accommodation" that had to be opened to all races. *Daniel* v. *Paul, Jr.,* 395 U.S. 298. Of much the same effect is *Tillman* v. *Wheaton-Haven Recreation Assn., Inc.,* 93 S. Ct. 1090 (1973), which involved a community swimming pool.

§ **1136. Housing projects.** Many local housing authorities and HUD have been instructed by the courts to develop housing projects in predominantly white areas. They must not be confined to the ghetto areas of the inner city. *Hills* v. *Grautreaux,* 96 S. Ct. 1538, 47 L. Ed.2d 792 (1976); Ackerman, Integration for Subsidizing Housing, 26 *Stanf. L. Rev.* 245 (1974); 47 *Chi-Kent L. Rev.* 253 (1970); 22 *Syracuse L. Rev.* 1139; 5 *Ga. L. Rev.* 603 (1971); 83 *Harv. L. Rev.* 1441; 64 *N.W.U. L. Rev.* 720.

A housing authority cannot discriminate in favor of a minority.

EXAMPLE: A housing authority gave preference to members of the Jewish faith because of the proximity of a synagogue to the housing project. This violated federal law. *Otero* v. *N.Y. City Housing Authority,* 314 F.Supp. 737 (1972).

§ **1137. City services.** The city must not discriminate racially in its provisions of municipal services.

EXAMPLE: In one town in question, 97 percent of the homes that fronted on unpaved streets and were not served by sewers were occupied by blacks; all street lights were installed in white sections; surface water drainage, traffic control signs, and so forth were all in white sections. This was invalid. *Hawkins* v. *Town of Shaw,* 437 F2d 1286 (5th Circ. 1971).

§ **1138. Oral contracts.** Oral contracts to sell land to blacks come under the federal law.

EXAMPLE: *V*, a vendor, entered into an oral contract to sell to *P*, a black. *V*, thereafter, tried to back out of the deal. The court held that it would enforce an oral contract where *V* was motivated by a desire to avoid selling to a black. *State* v. *Bergeron,* 187 NW2d 680 (Minn. 1971).

§ **1139. Contract buyers.** Where it can be shown that builders charge blacks higher prices for their homes, the builders are liable for racial discrimination. *Clark* v. *Universal Builders,* 501 F2d 224 (1974), 7 *Urb. Law* #3 (1975). The price differential can be excused only if the builder can show a reasonable excuse, such as a difference in credit rating.

§ **1140. Zoning.** There are many cases holding that zoning action can be unlawful racial discrimination.

EXAMPLE: The city of Black Jack hastily passed a zoning ordinance prohibiting new multiple-family dwellings when it became known that there were plans to build a low-and-moderate-income housing project within the city. The court held that as long as it was evident that the city's action actually produced racial discrimination it was not necessary to prove that the city officials were, in fact, racially biased. This was obvious since the effect of the ordinance was to prevent 85 percent of the blacks in the area from living in Black Jack. *U.S.* v. *Black Jack,* 508 F2d 1179 (8th Circ. 1974) cert den 43 U.S.L.W. 3674.

The courts, whether or not they approve of the law, are growing tired of pretending that the city fathers are not biased when, on some occasions, it is evident that they are.

In general, where the public authorities are taking action that will concentrate location of low-income housing in racially segregated areas, most courts will endeavor to block this move. 52 *J. of Urb. L.* 897.

EXAMPLE: A developer wanted to build a multifamily residential housing project and sought rezoning for that purpose. It was refused. However, the courts found that the refusal to rezone was due to the opposition of the white residents. The court ordered rezoning. *Dailey* v. *City of Lawton*, 425 F2d 1037 (1970), 5 *J. of Law Reforms* 357 (1972).

Apparently it is still necessary that an *intention* to discriminate be proved.

EXAMPLE: The Village of Arlington Heights is a suburb of Chicago. A developer wished to construct a low-income apartment complex. He therefore petitioned the village to rezone a parcel of land from single-family to multiple-family zoning. The village thought such rezoning unsuitable because of the presence of many single-family residences in the area. The Supreme Court held that no provision of the federal constitution had been violated because it had not been proved that the village was motivated by an *intention* to discriminate against *low-income* occupants. *Village of Arlington Heights* v. *Metropolitan Housing Development Corp.*, 97 S. Ct. 955, 50 L. Ed.2d 450 (1977). The court discussed only the federal constitutional issue. It then sent the case back to have the lower courts consider the possible violation of federal legislation against *racial discrimination*. The Federal Court of Appeals seems to hold that some such violation could be proved. *Metrop. Housing Develop. Corp.* v. *Village of Arlington Heights,* 558 F2d 1283 (1977). It is difficult to understand this decision. The federal law also requires proof of an *intention to discriminate*. This could not be proved.

§ 1141. Terms of sale or lease where the court orders sale or lease to a black. In analyzing the commission orders and court decisions sustaining them, one is struck by the fact that the courts have evolved something quite novel in real estate law. They have ordered the creation of contractual arrangements against the wishes of one party to the contract. They have ordered a landowner to lease to, to sell to, or to build, for a black who has been discriminated against because of racial bias. 16 *Stanford L. Rev.* 849. What remains unanswered is what the courts will do with the innumerable technical details of real estate transactions; namely, the permitted objections to title, the type of title evidence to be furnished the buyer, what prorations are to be made, what surveys and chattel searches are to be required of the seller, and so on. It is one thing to require a seller to sell to a particular buyer. It is quite another thing to spell out the terms of the transaction on the basis of which the deal is to be closed. No doubt, regulations, court decisions, and commission orders will clarify this situation in due time.

§ 1142. Proof of discrimination. Basically, what current legislation forbids is *discrimination*. *Discrimination* is not merely a state of mind. *Prejudice* is a state of mind, but *discrimination* is prejudice coupled with action or inaction motivated by that prejudice.

Discrimination can be shown by *express* proof of *intention. Hawkins* v. *Town of Shaw,* 461 F2d 1171 (5th Circ. 1972).

EXAMPLE: A builder stated that "no one is going to force me to sell a house in this development to a Black." This proves discrimination if followed by sales only to white persons. *Jones* v. *The Haridor Realty Corp.,* 37 N.J. 384, 181 A2d 481.

Or it may be established by circumstantial evidence.

EXAMPLE: *A* offered a house for sale for $35,000 on terms set forth in a broker's listing. Promptly *B,* a Black, tendered an offer at the price and terms stated. *A*'s refusal of *B*'s offer would be evidence of discrimination, especially if *A* sold later to a white person at the same price, thereby showing that his refusal of *B* was not motivated by a desire to withdraw the house from sale.

EXAMPLE: The fact that there are no Black tenants in an apartment building will weigh against the owner, and the refusal of even one financially qualified Black applicant for an apartment may be sufficient proof of discrimination. *U.S.* v. *Real Estate Development Corp.,* 347 Fed.Supp. 776.

EXAMPLE: A homeowner stated before witnesses that he would not sell to Jews. He therefore refused to sell to the complaining party, a Jewish person, and later entered into a contract to sell to a Gentile. The commission ordered the owner to sell to the Jew at the same price the Gentile offered. Observe the quandary of the seller here, who may find he has a legal liability to the Gentile. *Tisman* v. *Burda,* 12 *Race Relations Rep.* 1966 (N.Y.).

§ 1143. Blockbusting. Federal and state legislation and local ordinances forbidding "blockbusting" by real estate brokers are valid. 34 ALR3d 1432.

EXAMPLE: A broker is forbidden to tell property owners that the neighborhood is "going colored." This is true even if the prospective buyer asks this question. *Brown* v. *State Realty Co.,* 304 F.Supp. 1236.

EXAMPLE: The rule against blockbusting applies even to statements like "This is a changing neighborhood." *U.S.* v. *Mintzes,* 304 F.Supp. 1305.

§ 1144. Low-income housing. A new federal quota requires that 20 percent of all federally funded suburban family housing approved within the past year be reserved for low-income residents.

The regulations, issued by the United States Department of Housing and Urban Development, have raised an uproar among suburban officials.

The regulations were issued as part of an effort to implement a Supreme Court decision that upheld the power of HUD and the Chicago Housing Authority to provide low-income housing *in the suburbs* to relieve inner-city racial integration.

REFERENCES: 66 *Mich. L. Rev.* 1753; 4 *U. of Ill. L. Forum* 502 (1975); 21 *Vand. L. Rev.* 1117; 13 ALR Fed. 285; 24 L. Ed.2d 889.

RESERVED: §§ 1145–1155.

39

Taxes, Special Assessments, and Federal Income Tax

§ 1156. In general. General taxes are levied by various taxing bodies, such as states, cities, villages, counties, or school districts, to raise revenue needed for the performance of various public functions, such as maintaining roads, schools, parks, police departments, fire departments, county hospitals, and mental institutions. One of the most important sources of revenue is the tax on real estate. Although this tax is encountered in most, if not all, states, laws regarding levy, assessment, and collection of the tax vary considerably, so that few general statements can be made that will be universally true.

§ 1157. Constitutional aspects. One aspect of taxation has recently attracted much attention. Since schools are typically financed through local property taxes, the so-called "property-rich" areas provide more funds for education than the "property-poor" areas. The mathematics of this method of taxation results in better educational opportunities for some because more money is spent on facilities, while others from the "property-poor areas" receive what is thought to be an inferior education. The United States Supreme Court has determined that this is a matter for the states to regulate. *San Antonio Independent School District* v. *Rodiguez,* 411 U.S. 1 (1973). Some states have addressed this issue and found that this method for financing education violates constitutional principals. *Serrano* v. *Priest,* 487 P2d 1241 (Cal. 1971).

§ 1158. Steps in taxation. The nine principal steps in real estate taxation are: budgeting, appropriation, levy, assessment, review of the assessment, equalization, computation, collection of the tax through voluntary payment by the taxpayer, and collection of the tax through compulsory methods, such as tax sale.

§ 1159. Budgeting. Budgeting involves an annual determination of how much money is to be spent by each taxing body and for what purposes. Keep in mind that in each state there are numerous bodies—cities, villages, counties, school boards, and sanitary districts—that have the power to levy taxes, and each body must prepare its annual budget and make its annual appropriation and tax levy.

§ **1160. Appropriation.** Appropriation is the step whereby the taxing body formally enacts into law its decision to spend the money, with a specification of the particular purpose for which the money is to be spent, the amount to be spent for each purpose, and the source from which the funds are to be derived.

§ **1161. Levy.** The appropriation usually provides that part of the money to be spent is to be raised by property taxation. It thereupon becomes necessary to levy a tax for this purpose. When the legislative body of some taxing unit, such as the village board of a village or the school board of a school district, votes to impose a tax of a specified amount on persons or property, this action is known as the levy of a tax. The levy is an indispensable step in arriving at a valid tax.

It is the levy that provides a field day for tax lawyers. Various technical defects will invalidate part or all of the tax levy, and attorneys for railroads and other big taxpayers are most astute in discovering these technical defects. As a rule, only those taxpayers who file proper objections may take advantage of these technical defects. Taxpayers who pay their money without formal objection cannot get their money back if the tax is later held invalid.

§ **1162. Tax rate limitations.** In levying taxes, taxing bodies must see to it that they do not spend more than the law allows. Tax rate limitations will be found both in state constitutions and state laws.

§ **1163. Assessment.** Assessment of real estate for taxation involves determining the value of each parcel of land to be taxed. In assessing real estate, a book or list is first prepared by the proper officer, containing a description of all the taxable real estate in his town, county, or district and the names of the owners thereof. This book is turned over to the tax assessor, who proceeds to place a valuation on each parcel of land and enters such valuation in the book. This book is called the *tax list* or *assessment roll.*

In assessing land, the assessor should consider various factors, such as market price of similar land, income, depreciation, obsolescence, and reproduction cost of buildings. Actual methods vary widely. Farmland is still usually taxed at its market value, but urban land is often assessed differently. In assessing urban land, assessors often place a value on the land as though it were vacant and then value the building at what it would cost to build today, deducting from this figure an allowance for depreciation. The two valuations are then added together to fix the total assessment. Luce, Assessment of Real Property for Taxation, 35 *Mich. L. Rev.* 1217, 1229 (1937). Assessors may employ experts and use experts' scientific procedures as a basis for their valuations. But any wholesale turning over of valuation to experts would be illegal, for it is the assessor's judgment, based perhaps on expert advice, that the law requires.

In some states, it is the practice to assess property at a certain percentage of its true value. This is not objectionable as long as the assessor assesses all property at the same proportion of its true value. Likewise, if all the property is uniformly overvalued, the courts will not intervene. The main thing is uniformity. If a taxpayer can show that his property is assessed at its full value, whereas the rest of the property in the district is uniformly assessed at less than its full value, the court will lower the assessment complained of to the general level.

§ **1164. Uniformity.** Under various constitutional provisions it is required that the taxation of property be equal and uniform, so that taxpayers owning tracts of substantially equal value will pay substantially the same amount of taxes. This is an ideal difficult, if not impossible, to attain, and courts are aware of that fact. Hence if the assessor has made an honest mistake in assessing a particular tract of land, the courts as a rule will not intervene. Courts do not sit to correct mere errors in an assessment. The error can be corrected only by an appeal to the board of review or other body designated to review and correct the assessor's valuations.

§ **1165. Exemptions.** Each state grants various exemptions from taxation. The nature and form of these exemptions vary from state to state. Common exemptions are those extended to public property, charitable organizations, schools, religious institutions, and cemeteries. There are also some states that extend partial exemptions to senior citizens.

§ **1166. Review of assessment.** All states provide some method by which the taxpayer can have the assessor's valuation reviewed and corrected by some higher authority. The procedures vary widely. In New England, the reviewing board is often a town tribunal, such as the selectmen. In other areas, the reviewing officials may be called a *board of equalization* or a *board of review*. In some states, a further appeal is provided to a higher board of review. In other states, the decision of the first board of review can be appealed directly to some court. Culp, Administrative Remedies in the Assessment and Enforcement of State Taxes, 17 *N.C. L. Rev.* 118 (1939). As a rule, the taxpayer cannot appeal to the courts unless he has first appeared before the board of review or other initial reviewing body. *First Nat. Bank* v. *Weld County,* 264 U.S. 450 (1924).

§ **1167. Equalization.** Equalization is the raising or lowering of assessed values in a particular county or taxing district in order to equalize them with the total assessments in other counties or taxing districts.

EXAMPLE: The board of equalization deducts a certain percentage from all assessments made in a certain township because the township assessor valued the property on a higher level than did the assessors of other townships.

This function is usually performed by a board known as the *board of equalization*. The board of equalization does not handle complaints of individual taxpayers, but raises or lowers the assessment of each county or taxing district as a whole in order to bring the assessment into line with assessments in other counties or taxing districts.

§ **1168. Computation of tax.** The amount of the tax that a particular tract of land must pay is computed by multiplying the assessed value of the tract by the tax rate applicable to the land in that particular taxing district. The tax is then entered on the tax books.

§ **1169. Lien.** Tax laws usually provide that real estate taxes are a lien on the land. Often it is provided that such a lien is prior and superior to all other liens, both those that antedate and those that come after the date on which the tax lien attaches to the land.

§ **1170. Payment.** Payment to the proper official at the proper time discharges the lien of the tax.

When the *tax records* show a tax as paid, a purchaser or mortgagee who relies on such records is protected against enforcement of the tax should it later develop that the tax actually remains unpaid. *Jackson Park Hospital* v. *Courtney,* 4 NE2d 864 (Ill. 1936). A number of states make provision for the issuance of a certificate by some tax official showing all unpaid taxes on the property. Purchasers who rely on such certificates are generally protected against errors in the certificate. *Burton* v. *City of Denver,* 61 P2d 856 (Colo. 1936); *Amerada Petroleum Corp.* v. *1010.61 Acres of Land,* 146 F2d 99 (1944); 21 ALR2d 1273. When a landowner redeems from a tax sale and the certificate of redemption shows that all delinquent taxes have been thereby redeemed, a purchaser or mortgagee who relies on such a certificate will be protected if it later develops that some delinquent taxes in fact remain. *Jones* v. *Sturzenberg,* 210 Pac. 835 (Cal. 1922).

A purchaser or mortgagee is not ordinarily protected in relying on a *tax receipt* showing full payment of the taxes. Despite issuance of the receipt, the tax collector is allowed to show that a part of the tax remains unpaid. However, South Dakota has a law making a tax receipt conclusive evidence that all prior taxes have been paid.

§ **1171. Proceedings to enforce payment of taxes.** Various special remedies are provided by local law for the collection of unpaid real estate taxes.

Tax sale is a common method. It is usually preceded by the giving of notice, often by publication, to the delinquent taxpayer. Unless the taxpayer appears and defends, which he may do if the tax is illegal or if he has some other defense, a judgment will be rendered for the amount of the tax and penalty due. This judgment orders the land to be sold. Thereafter, notice of the coming sale is published, and on the date fixed for sale the land is sold at public sale. Usually a certificate of sale is issued to the purchaser, stating that he will be entitled to a deed at the expiration of the redemption period if no redemption is made. In some states, the state, county, or city is permitted to bid at the tax sale.

The landowner or other persons interested, such as mortgagees, may redeem the land from the tax within the period specified by the local law. If redemption is not made, a tax deed is issued to the purchaser.

Although state laws vary as to the validity of tax titles, a tax title acquired through normal tax sale usually constitutes the flimsiest sort of title, since deviation from the technical requirements of the law will invalidate the title. In some states, however, a tax deed is regarded as a conveyance of good title to the land. *Thomas* v. *Kolker,* 73 A2d 886 (Md. 1950); *Shapiro* v. *Hruby,* 172 NE2d 775 (Ill. 1961).

An alternative method of enforcement of the tax lien is by foreclosure, the procedure being similar to that employed in mortgage foreclosure. In some states, a good title can be acquired through tax foreclosure.

§ 1172. Effect of tax sale on junior interests. When real estate taxes obtain priority over junior interests either because they become a lien prior to the creation of the junior interests or by force of law, the law of many states results in a purchaser at a tax sale taking a title that is free of encumbrances such as mortgages, liens, and so forth.

EXAMPLE: O purchased property giving a purchase money mortgage to *M*. O failed to pay the real estate taxes levied against the property. The land was sold to *P* at a tax sale. *P* took the land free of *M*'s mortgage. Most lenders handle this problem by adopting some means, such as a mortgage escrow account, to insure that the taxes are paid.

Of course, the owner cannot, for his own benefit, use this theory to rid his property of liens to which it would otherwise be subject.

EXAMPLE: O owns property subject to a purchase money mortgage that he placed against the property. O allows the taxes to go into default and be sold. O then purchases at the tax sale. O holds the property subject to the mortgage. 134 ALR 289. The result would be opposite if *T*, a bona fide disinterested third-party purchaser, bought at the tax sale.

§ 1173. Termination of easement by tax sale. An almost insoluble problem exists with respect to the effect of a tax sale of the servient tenement. The owner of the easement, of course, receives his tax bill on the dominant tenement. He does not even receive the tax bill on the servient tenement.

EXAMPLE: A owns lot 1 and *B* owns lot 2. A grants to *B* an easement for ingress and egress for driveway purposes over the southern twenty feet of lot 1. A fails to pay his taxes and all of lot 1 is sold to *X* at a tax sale. Under the law in this state, a tax sale wipes out all prior easements. Obviously *B* must arrange to keep a check on the taxes on A's lot 1 and pay them, if necessary, to prevent loss of his easement. He can include a provision in the easement grant requiring A annually to furnish *B* a paid tax bill, and also a provision that any taxes advanced by *B*, or his successors, will be a foreclosable lien on lot 1.

The law on this subject has been in some confusion. In some states a tax sale does *not* destroy easements. *Northwestern Imp. Co.* v. *Lowry,* 66 P2d 792 (Mont. 1937); *Ariz. R.C.I.A. Lands, Inc.* v. *Ainsworth,* 515 P2d 335 (Ariz. 1973); *Clippinger* v. *Birge,* 547 P2d 871 (Wash. 1975); Restatement, Property § 509(2)(e). One basis of this rule is the thought that the land was assessed based upon its *value*. That value was determined by taking the easement into consideration.

EXAMPLE: Tract A is valued at $10,000 without being encumbered by an easement. Assessment is based upon this value. If the property were encumbered by an easement, its value would be $9,000. The assessment in the later case would be based upon $9,000.

By this same theory, the holder of the dominant estate is protected in that the easement will continue for the benefit of his land irrespective of the failure of the owner of the servient estate to pay taxes. The result is justified by the theory that the easement enhances the value of the dominant estate, and assessment is based upon this enhanced value. Comment, 20 *U. Chi. L. Rev.* 262, 264 (1953). In almost all states, laws have been passed to conform to the above. Ill. Rev. Stat. Ch. 120 § 7476. The minority view is discussed elsewhere. Note, 51 *Harv. L. Rev.* 361 (1937); See Powell on Real Property, Par. 686.

In a similar view, a tax sale will generally not extinguish a restrictive covenant to which the land is subject. 168 ALR 529, 536.

§ 1174. Soldiers' and Sailors' Civil Relief Act. The Soldiers' and Sailors' Civil Relief Act provides that when real estate is owned and occupied for dwelling, professional, business, or agricultural purposes by a person in military service or his dependents at the commencement of his period of military service and is still so occupied by his dependents or employees, such land cannot be sold for nonpayment of taxes or assessments except by permission of the court. The court will postpone the sale until after termination of the military service unless the ability of the person to pay such taxes or assessments has not been materially affected by reason of such military service. When the court does permit a sale or forfeiture of the property, the time allowed to redeem from such sale or forfeiture is extended so that redemption can be made at any time within six months after the termination of the military service. Also, the amount of interest or penalty that can be charged in case of any delinquent tax or assessment on such lands must not exceed 6 percent per annum.

§ 1175. Special assessments. There is a distinction between public improvements, which benefit the entire community, and local improvements, which benefit particular real estate or limited areas of land. The latter improvements are usually financed by means of special, or local, assessments. These assessments are, in a certain sense, taxes. But an assessment differs from a general tax in that an assessment is levied only on property in the immediate vicinity of some local municipal improvement and is valid only where the property assessed receives some special benefit differing from the benefit that the general public enjoys. *Production Tool Supply Co.* v. *City of Roseville,* 253 NW2d 350 (Mich. 1977). In fact if the primary purpose of an improvement is to benefit the public generally, as with, for example, the erection of a county courthouse, it cannot be financed by special assessments even though it may incidentally benefit property in the particular locality.

Special assessments are often imposed for opening, paving, grading, and guttering streets, construction of sidewalks and sewers, installation of street lighting, and so on.

§ 1176. Federal income tax. The law of federal income taxation is vast and complex, but there are some aspects of that law that are particularly relevant to even the most common real estate transactions. These rudimentary rules are best explained by example:

Mr. and Mrs. Homebuyer purchased their home for $62,500. They paid $12,500 down and took a mortgage for $50,000. The mortgage lender required the following: 1½ percent paid as "points" or loan origination fees, a $35 credit check fee, and a $40 appraisal fee. The real estate taxes on the house were $1200 per year payable December 31 of each year. The closing occurred April 1, 1971. The Homebuyers paid $200 in attorney's fees, $150 for title insurance, and $20 in recording fees. Shortly after purchasing the house, Homebuyers added a family room at a cost of $10,000.

The basis of the Homeowner's house is $62,500. That basis is adjusted by the following additions:

		$62,500
Attorney's fees on purchase	$ 200	
Title insurance	150	
Recording fees for deed	10	
Room addition [1]	10,000	
Total additions to basis		$10,360
Adjusted basis		$72,860

Mr. and Mrs. Homebuyer's tax deductions for the first year would include:

Points [2]	$ 750
Monthly interest payments	4,560
Real estate taxes [3]	900

Mr. and Mrs. Homebuyer's tax deductions for subsequent years would include:

Interest on mortgage	$4,420
Real estate taxes	1,200

Mr. Homebuyer uses part of his home for business purposes. The new rules covering deduction for "home office" expenses are very strict.

1. The deduction is only allowed if a portion of the residence is used *exclusively* and on a *regular basis* either as the taxpayer's principal place of business or as a place of business used by patients, clients, or customers in meeting or dealing with the taxpayer in the named cause of his trade or business. The exclusive use test is strict. Any dual personal and business use will disallow the deduction.

2. The deduction may not exceed the gross income derived from the use of the home office during the taxable year.

3. Only the portion of household expenses attributable to the "home office" are deductible and no "home office" deductions is allowed when the taxpayer has a primary place of business elsewhere and uses his "home office" only incidentally.

The Homebuyers sold their house on June 1, 1971, for $95,000. To ready the property for sale, they spent $200 to paint some hallways. The house was sold by a Realtor who earned a commission of $6,650.

The Homebuyers' itemized deductions in the year of sale of the old residence and purchase of the new included:

Penalty for prepayment of mortgage	$ 300
Interest on mortgage on old house	1,750
Real estate taxes on old house	540

[1] The costs of improvements, such as air conditioning, landscaping, garages, and even special assessments, may be added to the basis, but ordinary repairs may not.

[2] Points paid to acquire a home mortgage loan guaranteed by the VA or FHA are not deductible as interest.

[3] Note that amounts paid into a mortgage escrow for real estate taxes are not deductible until taxes are actually paid.

Tax may be payable on the "gain" from the sale of the residence. The gain would be calculated on I.R.S. Form 2119 as follows:

Selling price of residence		$95,000
Less commissions and expenses of sale:		
Realtor's commission	$6,650	
Attorney's fees	250	
Seller's title charges	200	
		$ 7,100
Amount realized		$87,900
Less adjusted basis of residence sold		72,860
Gain in sale		$15,040

The adjusted sales price ($87,700) is determined by subtracting the fixing-up expenses ($200) from the amount realized ($87,900). (The fix-up work must be paid within ninety days of the contract to sell.) If the Homebuyers do not buy a replacement residence they would calculate their long-term capital gain (the sale of this asset would receive long-term capital gains treatment since the residence was held for longer than one year) in the following fashion.

Gain taxable this year	$15,040
Less 50 percent	7,520
Net gain from sale of residence	$ 7,520

This $7,520 would then be added to the taxpayers' income for tax calculations.

Let us assume that rather than merely selling their old home, the Homebuyers purchased a new home within eighteen months before or after the sale. The purchaser price of that new home was $103,000. They paid 30 percent down, financing $72,100 through a 9 percent mortgage. The costs of closing included loan origination fees of 1 percent or $721, a service fee of $50, title insurance fees of $300, and attorney's fees of $300. The Internal Revenue Service says the Homebuyers *must* not recognize the gain on the sale of the old *principal* residence. Thus, they would not pay tax on the $7,520 as outlined above. The calculation follows:

Since the cost of the new residence ($103,000) is more than the adjusted sales price ($87,700) there is no taxable gain from that transaction. The $15,040 gain would be deferred and the adjusted basis of the new house would be:

Cost of new residence	$103,000
Less: gain on which tax is deferred	15,040
	$ 87,960

Attorney's fees on purchase	$ 300
Title insurance	300
Recording fee for deed	10
Adjusted basis of new residence	$ 88,570

If the Homebuyers purchased a new residence that cost $83,500, less than the selling price of the old, the calculations would be as follows:

Adjusted sales price	$ 87,700
Less: cost of new residence	83,500
Gain taxable this year	$ 4,200
Gain on sale	$ 15,040
Less: gain taxable this year	4,200
Gain on which tax is deferred	$ 10,840
Cost of new residence	$ 83,500
Less: gain on which tax is deferred	10,840
	$ 72,660
Attorney's fees on purchase	$ 300
Title insurance	300
Recording fee for deed	10
Adjusted basis of new residence	$ 73,270

If either of the Homebuyers were sixty-five years of age at the date of sale, they could utilize their *one-time* privilege to exclude part or all of the gain that would otherwise be taxed if they have used the property as their residence for five of the eight years preceding the sale. The election to so proceed is made by the completion of an additional part of I.R.S. form 2119. If the adjusted sales price is $35,000 or less, the entire gain on sale is excludable. If the adjusted sales price is in excess of $35,000, a portion of the gain is excludable. Let us return to the example in which the Homebuyers did not repurchase and assume that Mr. Homebuyer was sixty-six at the date of sale, and they elected to exclude the gain to the extent possible.

Divide the adjusted sales ($87,700) price into $35,000 to give the factor 0.399.

Gain on sale	$15,040
Multiplied by	0.399
Excludable portion of gain	$ 6,001
Gain on sale	$15,040
Less excludable portion of gain	6,001
Nonexcludable portion of gain	$ 9,039

This $9,039 would be reported as a capital gain, given the 50 percent treatment explained above and $4,519.50 reported as income.

If the Homebuyers had purchased an $83,500 condominium in the "sunbelt" the calculations would continue:

Adjusted sales price		$87,700
Less: excludable portion of gain	$ 6,001	
Cost of new residence	83,500	
		$89,501 [1]
Gain taxable this year		$ 0
Nonexcludable portion of gain		$ 9,039
Less: gain taxable this year		0
Gain on which tax is deferred		$ 9,039
Cost of new residence		$87,700
Less: gain on which tax is deferred		9,039
		$78,661
Attorney's fee on purchase		$ 300
Title insurance		300
Recording fees for deed		10
Adjusted basis of new residence		$79,271

If the condominium had cost more than $87,700, there would be no gain taxable this year, the entire gain would be deferred, and there would be no need to utilize the over sixty-five exclusion.

In buying and selling business property, several considerations should be kept in mind.

If possible, you should take gains and losses on sales of business property in separate years.

EXAMPLE: You sell Building A at a gain of $10,000 and Building B at a loss of $3,000. This loss of $3,000 reduces your capital gain to $7,000. But if you had waited until the following year to sell Building B, the loss of $3,000 could be used as a deduction from your ordinary income for that year. In the meantime, your capital gain of $10,000 in the previous year would still be taxable only at the low capital gains rate. In other words, you are better off using losses to reduce ordinary income, which pays a high tax, than to reduce capital gains, which pay a lower tax.

It is often advantageous to sell real estate on an installment basis rather than for cash. For example, if you sell Building A for cash, you must pay a tax on the entire profit thus made. But if you sell the building on an installment contract, with a down payment of 30 percent or less, you can spread this gain over the entire term of the contract. This installment-sale method can also be used to reduce taxes on the sale of a residence.

[1] Since this figure is greater than the adjusted sales price there is no gain taxable this year. If this figure were less than $87,700, the adjusted sales price, there would be a gain taxable this year, which would of course receive capital gain treatment.

Index

NOTE—References are to section numbers

NOTE—References are to section numbers

NOTE—References are to section numbers

NOTE—References are to section numbers

NOTE—References are to section numbers

NOTE—References are to section numbers

NOTE—References are to section numbers